Educational Psychology

SECOND EDITION

Educational Psychology

Focus on the Learner

LITA LINZER SCHWARTZ
Pennsylvania State University
Ogontz Campus

Holbrook Press, Inc.
Boston

Photo Credits

Tania D'Avignon, p. 2; The Bettmann Archive, p. 11; Elizabeth Resnick, p. 22; H. Armstrong Roberts, pp. 46, 50; Elizabeth Resnick, p. 61; Stock, Boston: Peter Vandermark, p. 85; Courtesy of the Children's Television Workshop, p. 89; Stock, Boston: Elizabeth Hamlin, p. 101; Bohdan Hrynewych, p. 130; Argonaut Photos, p. 136; Courtesy of Dr. David Wechsler, p. 143; Stock, Boston: Ellis Herwig, pp. 178, 202; Bohdan Hrynewych, p. 223; The Bettmann Archive, p. 242; Bohdan Hrynewych, p. 316; Stock, Boston: Elizabeth Hamlin, p. 333; Courtesy of The National Easter Seal Society for Crippled Children & Adults, Inc., p. 365; Imago: Christopher G. Knight, p. 371.

Cover Photo: Bohdan Hrynewych

© Copyright 1977 by Holbrook Press, Inc.

© Copyright 1972 by Holbrook Press, Inc.
470 Atlantic Avenue, Boston.

All rights reserved. Printed in the United States of America. No part of the material protected by this copyright notice may be reproduced or utilized in any form or by any means, electronic or mechanical, including photocopying, recording, or by any informational storage and retrieval system, without written permission of the copyright owner.

Library of Congress Cataloging in Publication Data

Schwartz, Lita Linzer.
  Educational psychology.

  Bibliography: p.
  Includes index.
  1. Educational psychology.   I. Title
LB1051.S385   1977   370.15   76-51456
ISBN 0-205-05745-4

To My Students

from whom I learn so much

The dedicated teacher affects all eternity; his influence never stops.

                    Henry Brooke Adams

Contents

Preface to the Second Edition   xi
Preface to the First Edition   xv

One   The World of Educational Psychology   1

   1   *Educational Psychology: Its Identity*   5

      OBJECTIVES OF EDUCATIONAL PSYCHOLOGY — THE "RELATIONS" OF EDUCATIONAL PSYCHOLOGY — A MODERN DISCIPLINE — SPECIFIC OBJECTIVES — SUMMARY

Two   Person, Environment, and Learning   21

   2   *Growth, Development, and the Learner*   25

      PRENATAL TO POSTNATAL INFLUENCES — SEX DIFFERENCES — MOTOR, PERCEPTUAL, AND LANGUAGE DEVELOPMENT — SUMMARY

   3   *The Environment and the Learner*   55

      INTRODUCTION — WITHIN THE FAMILY — SOCIAL CLASS DIFFERENCES — ETHNIC DIFFERENCES — PEER GROUP INFLUENCE — EFFECTS OF TV WATCHING — SUMMARY

   4   *Psychological Factors and the Learner*   93

      INTRODUCTION — THE SELF-CONCEPT — MOTIVATION — ANXIETY — ACHIEVERS — UNDER-ACHIEVERS — SUMMARY

Three   Intelligence and Evaluation   129

5 Intelligence: Theories and Tests 133

INTRODUCTION — WHAT IS INTELLIGENCE? — TESTS OF INTELLIGENCE — A CONTEMPORARY LOOK — SUMMARY

6 Mental Growth and Individual Differences 171

INTRODUCTION — THE CURVE OF MENTAL GROWTH — CLASSIFICATION OF INTELLIGENCE — HANDLING INDIVIDUAL DIFFERENCES — SUMMARY

7 Assessment and Evaluation 197

INTRODUCTION — EDUCATIONAL ASSESSMENT — EDUCATIONAL EVALUATION — GUIDANCE AND COUNSELING — SUMMARY

Four Learning About Learning 223

8 Learning: Theories and Variables 227

INTRODUCTION — WHAT IS LEARNING? — THEORIES OF LEARNING: THE ASSOCIATIONISTS — THEORIES OF LEARNING: THE COGNITIVE THEORISTS — THEORIES OF LEARNING: TWO TAXONOMIES — SUMMARY OF LEARNING THEORIES — VARIABLES AFFECTING LEARNING — CLASSROOM APPLICATIONS — SUMMARY

9 Concepts, Thinking, and Language 267

INTRODUCTION — CONCEPT FORMATION — THINKING — LANGUAGE DEVELOPMENT — SUMMARY

10 Creativity and Problem-Solving 293

INTRODUCTION — PROBLEM-SOLVING — CREATIVITY — SUMMARY

Five Learning and Teachers 315

11 Innovative Teaching for Learning 319

INTRODUCTION — DEVELOPMENT OF BEHAVIORAL OBJECTIVES — AUDIO-VISUAL TECHNIQUES — PROGRAMMED INSTRUCTION — "NEW" METHODS — SCHOOL-WIDE MODIFICATIONS — RESPONSE OF THE LEARNER TO INNOVATIONS — SUMMARY

12   *Learners Who Challenge Teachers*   *353*

INTRODUCTION: AN OVERVIEW OF EXCEPTIONAL CHILDREN — MAINSTREAMING — EMOTIONAL AND SOCIAL MALADJUSTMENT — THE PHYSICALLY DIFFERENT — THE CULTURALLY DIFFERENT — THE INTELLECTUALLY DIFFERENT — SUMMARY

13   *Teacher-Pupil Relations*   *389*

THE "CLIMATE" OF LEARNING — CHARACTERISTICS OF TEACHERS — TEACHER ATTITUDES AND LEARNING — TEACHER EFFECTIVENESS — SUMMARY

14   *The Teacher as Learner*   *419*

THE DESIRE TO TEACH — TEACHER EDUCATION

Epilogue   439
Glossary   443
Statistical Appendix   449
References   459
Index   487

Preface to the Second Edition

"Practice makes perfect" is an old adage. "Practice," in the form of widespread use of a text, helps an author move toward perfection when the time comes to revise that text. As a result of experience or practice, one tries to fill gaps, reduce inadvertent errors, and increase the usefulness of the text to both learners and teachers. Although the text's primary audience is the prospective teacher, the principles and practices presented are applicable as well to learners with career goals other than teaching and to settings other than the classroom.

The new edition of *Educational Psychology: Focus on the Learner* retains much of the format of the first edition. The chapters, and the sections into which they are grouped, are each introduced by a preview of their content. Furthermore, each chapter has an outline and ample subheadings. As needed, summaries are provided for sections within chapters as well as the usual one for an entire chapter. These organizational aids help maintain a sense of direction. The "Focus" units of the first edition have been retained. In addition, new content and needed clarification can be found in every chapter. Some of the specific changes are:

- Regrouping of chapters to increase comprehension
- Effects of television viewing
- Information on the Wechsler Intelligence Scale for Children—Revised
- Life-long learning and adult learners
- Problem-solving and creativity in a separate chapter
- Expanded discussion of behavioral objectives
- Introduction of new topics such as "mainstreaming" and pupil control ideology
- New approaches to teacher education.

At the same time, there has been a de-emphasis in areas that are not as critical in educational psychology as they were a few years ago.

Although a great deal of recent research has been added to this edition, it is impossible simply to discard any source published before a certain year. Many references of the 1950s (e.g., Erikson) and 1960s (e.g., Jensen; Rosenthal and Jacobson) are classics basic to later work in the 1970s. Other pre-1970 references make a specific point that may not have been repeated in a more recent study. Even so, more than half of the references cited are dated 1970 or later, reflecting current thought and practice as much as possible.

Experience and contemporary realities together renew the convictions that the teacher at any level needs to have as full a repertoire as possible of instructional techniques, that an eclectic approach to teaching is the most realistic one in view of the uniqueness of learners, and that adaptability is a valuable, virtually essential, characteristic of an effective teacher. Each point of view has something to contribute to the teacher and the learner. Learners have different learning styles and different experiential backgrounds, as teachers do, which mandate the use of different approaches to learning. This does not deny the need of the learner to work, to adjust, and to be flexible in relation to his studies and his teachers. The teaching-learning process requires "give and take" on the part of each participant, and a recognition that each is subject to human frailties. In focusing on the learner in this text, there is an assumption that we *all* are learning continually—some to be better teachers, some to be better learners, all to appreciate more fully what is involved in being a learner and an individual. Ultimately, the work of educational psychologists and teachers is to assist each individual along the road to self-motivation and self-actualization.

ACKNOWLEDGMENTS

In addition to those named below, there are many people who have, often unknowingly, contributed to this edition. First and foremost, there have been my own students who commented on strengths and weaknesses of the original text. Then there were the leaders of symposia, workshops, and conference sessions who communicated and shared their experiences. And third, there were colleagues and friends who, in informal ways, provided examples and felicitous phrases that fit a particular passage. Among the latter, my appreciation goes particularly to Jeanne Smith and Sunnie Spiegel, colleagues who have used the book and based their feedback on this. Much gratitude is due to Lu Woodman who labored diligently over the Statistical Appendix and served as a critical but friendly reader of many chapters. She and Betsy Olsen shared the responsibility and effort of typing the manuscript, for which I thank them both. Finally, the aid of the librarians at the Ogontz Campus is acknowledged with gratitude.

Suggestions from a number of reviewers have aided me in the task of revision, although we didn't always agree. My thanks for their efforts to: Arthur W. Combs of the University of Florida; Stephen B. Hillman of Wayne State University; Mary T Littlejohn of Winthrop College; Jay R. McDanel of Tarleton State University; Richard F. Purnell of the University of Rhode Island; William E. Roweton of Madison College; Robert Van Dyke Small of Mercer County College; and Joanne Rand Whitmore of George Peabody College.

At Holbrook Press, Paul Conway has been a most helpful Editor, and it has been a pleasure to work with him. Paula Carroll, Production Editor, has also smoothed the way for this edition.

The men in my life—Melvin, Arthur, Joshua, and Frederic—remain my greatest sources of inspiration and strength. I thank them for their continuing patience with stacks of books and papers, and with me.

Lita Linzer Schwartz
Abington, Pa.

Preface to the First Edition

With so many texts already published for the educational psychology course, why write another? Like many of my colleagues, I found good points in almost all of the available texts, but not exactly what I wanted in any single book. The solution? Write!

What are the "missing links" in educational psychology that I feel are so important? For one thing, a contemporary text should focus on the learner—who he is, what underlies his behavior in learning situations, how we can help him learn. Awareness that there are very few "average" learners in the classroom has been overlooked in traditional educational psychology courses, and yet all prospective teachers should know this. For this reason, one chapter focuses on the exceptional child in the school. Innovations are introduced almost daily, it seems, into the classroom, yet few texts look beyond programmed instruction and a rather limited use of audiovisual aids. Therefore, another chapter is devoted solely to innovations in the teaching-learning process. Few prospective teachers recognize that their personalities and attitudes largely determine the learning atmosphere and learners' attitudes in the classroom, or that they themselves need to continue learning throughout their professional lives. A chapter is devoted to each of these ideas. The details of case studies are often difficult to reproduce for students. Using "Focus" segments, this type of material is included throughout the book. The "Focus" segments also serve to highlight statements through discussion and comment on a single research study.

Although much of the content is traditional for a book of this nature, several features make the content less formidable. Reviewers have said that the material is high in readability, always an asset to a text. Chapters have been grouped into sections which have a unifying and meaningful theme. Each section, and each chapter, has an introduction, previewing the ideas to be met. Chapter outlines and ample use of subheadings in the text help the student to know where he is going in the chapter as he reads. The glossary and bibliography at the end of a chapter make reference to these study aids easier.

What I've really tried to do is to bring relevant and timely information to students in a course that is often stagnant. Even the introductory pages, which show historical antecedents of this modern field, are relevant to the student's greater awareness that much is to be learned from the past which can help in the future.

Most of all, as a mother as well as an educator, I am deeply concerned about the quality of future teachers. Teachers must be committed to being *good* teachers for their learners. I hope that by bringing ideas important to the teaching-learning process to the student in educational psychology, those who see teaching as "just a job" will be "turned off" and away from the teaching profession. Education is not the place for mediocrity.

ACKNOWLEDGMENTS

The critical comments, both positive and negative, of Ronald E. Johnson of Purdue University, Ebert L. Miller of Ball State University, Charles K. West of the University of Illinois, Warren R. Baller of the United States International University, Martin R. Wong of the University of South Florida, and E. Paul Torrance of the University of Georgia, have been of tremendous help in making this a better book than it might have been. They have helped to reduce errors in content, and contributed their special knowledge wherever appropriate. The deficiencies are mine, of course, not theirs.

John DeRemigis, Manager of Holbrook Press, and Barry Fetterolf, former Education Series Editor, have been patient and persevering during the book's lengthy preparation. The efforts of the Production Editor, Elydia P. Siegel, are also much appreciated. That deadlines were ever met at all is due to the excellent cooperation and typing skill of Mrs. Jean Hart, for which I thank her.

Finally, great gratitude goes to the men in my life—my husband, Melvin, who listened patiently and helpfully as I worked; and our sons, Arthur, Joshua, and Frederic, who made it so important to try to influence future teachers to be the best possible teachers for all learners.

Lita Linzer Schwartz

Educational Psychology

Part One

The World of Educational Psychology

To appreciate properly any new area of experience, it helps to know something of its history, objectives, and techniques. In the field of music, for example, there can be increased pleasure in listening to a Mozart or Brahms or Shostakovich symphony if you know something about the composer and the world in which he lived, as well as the structure of a symphony and the art or gift of making a combination of notes and instruments convey an image and a message.

In Part One, therefore, we will first look at educational psychology as a discipline related to other academic disciplines and to the teachers and learners who are most affected by its principles and practices. We will draw on some of the wisdom of the ages to provide historical perspective for teachers and learners alike. A discussion of the objectives of educational psychology and the research techniques used in this field will also help introduce you to this new area of experiences.

Preview

INTRODUCTION

OBJECTIVES OF EDUCATIONAL PSYCHOLOGY
    CONTENT
    ATTITUDES
    PRACTICE

THE "RELATIONS" OF EDUCATIONAL PSYCHOLOGY
    TO OTHER FIELDS OF STUDY
        Psychology
        Child Development
        Anthropology
        Sociology
        Philosophy
        Education
    TO THE TEACHER
    TO THE LEARNER

A MODERN DISCIPLINE
    RESEARCH
        Research Concepts:
            Idiographic and Nomothetic Studies
            Longitudinal and Cross-Sectional Studies
            Sampling Populations
            Independent and Dependent Variables
        Research Design
    TESTING
    PROFESSION

SPECIFIC OBJECTIVES

SUMMARY

1

Educational Psychology: Its Identity

INTRODUCTION

People as learners are at the heart of this book. We will focus on how the differences among people affect the ways in which they learn and also on the differences in approach that affect them as learners. These topics are basic to educational psychology as a course of study. Before turning to the learner and learning, however, let us look at the larger field in which they are studied.

What are the identifying marks of educational psychology? For one, this is a specialized field within the broad subject called psychology. It draws upon knowledge in many related fields, also. The principles of psychology and information drawn from other social and biological sciences are combined in many ways as they are applied to learners and learning. This emphasis on learners and learning is a key to the identity of the field.

In this chapter, we will examine the general objectives of educational psychology and the relationship of this field to other fields of study. We will also see how educational psychology in practice affects both learners and teachers. Some of the research methods used by educational psychologists will be discussed, since research is the basis for much of the material to be presented in this book. Finally, the specific objectives of this text will be stated.

OBJECTIVES OF EDUCATIONAL PSYCHOLOGY

There are general objectives in educational psychology, and there are specific objectives for this text. Looking first at the general picture, the objectives of educational psychology may be related to content, attitudes, and practice.

As in any field of study, there is content or information to be transmitted to the newcomer. Because new theories are developed and new applications of

Content

information are made, the content of educational psychology is ever-expanding. The content categories, however, do not change very much.

One category is child development, studied as it relates to learners and the learning process. Heredity, growth and maturation, environmental influences, language and thinking, the development of intelligence, and the process of socialization are all considered in relation to their effect on the child as a learner.

Another area of content is learning and the educative process. Here we examine not only the several theories of learning, but also the techniques of learning skills and problem-solving. We ask, and try to answer, questions such as: Why can one child learn a given skill and another not learn it? Is large- or small-group instruction more desirable in a given subject or at a given age level? Why is one "better" than the other? How can learners move most effectively from the elementary level to the secondary level? What is the best way to teach foreign languages? "It is obvious," according to Anastasi (1964, p. 488), "that the effective management of learning is the central problem of education." And it is a central problem in educational psychology.

The effective management of learning involves both input, the teaching process, and output, or measuring what the learner has learned. The questions asked above are on the input side. They lead to research, one of the functions of educational psychologists. Attempts to measure pupil learning lead to the development of tests and other methods of evaluation, another area of concern to educational psychologists. Evaluation inevitably leads to some form of grading or report, with which educational psychologists also are concerned. The effects of evaluation, after all, are seen later in the learner's motivation and learning performance. Motivation and achievement are two key concepts in this field. Similarly, methods of research design and the study of evaluation techniques are part of the content of educational psychology.

Within the broad category of content, still another area of real importance to the educational psychologist is the quality and quantity of teacher-pupil interaction. The effects of such interaction on learning are generally well recognized and are more frequently included in research today than was true several years ago. Although the teacher is not primarily a counselor, he or she does often function in that role. Even when youths complain about the "generation gap," they look to some teachers for guidance or as confidants. Why some teachers and not others? Study of the teacher-learner relationship and the search for means of improving teacher effectiveness in this area are continuing efforts. In fact, much of the educational psychologist's work is aimed at teaching teachers how best to help their pupils learn more effectively, both in and out of class.

Attitudes   The development of positive attitudes toward learning is another aspect of educational psychology. Closely allied to this goal is the fostering of the spirit of inquiry, and even skepticism. This is not an easy task.

In our discussion later on, several examples will show how positive attitudes can be encouraged through reinforcement and other techniques. It is also true, however, that the teacher is a model, a person with whom the learner can identify. If teachers exhibit in their own behavior a positive attitude toward learning and teaching, then this behavior will occur more frequently in their students.

Question

In what ways might the teacher show positive attitudes toward learning?

You might have included in your list the teacher's self-confidence that stems from his own competence in, combined with enthusiasm for, his subject matter. Another way is for him to show his willingness to look for answers or to help his students to do so. If the teacher will not ask questions or answer them, the subject matter appears to be closed. If it is closed—not open to inquiry—less interest, and therefore a less positive attitude is created in the learners. On the other hand, an open field for questions, like the open arms of a parent, appears warm and welcoming. Therefore, not only should the teacher welcome and stimulate questions, but also he should ask of himself: "What is important about this subject matter today?" "What research is being conducted in this field now?" "How can we apply what is being learned?" "In what ways can this information be taught most effectively?" In our study of educational psychology, we will try to demonstrate and communicate these vital attitudes.

Practice

How is educational psychology *practiced?* The first idea to come to mind, perhaps, is that educational psychologists teach others about their field of study. This is done in the classroom and through textbooks and constitutes the academic practice of educational psychology. Since this is a key subject in the professional education curriculum, the teaching of it is obviously a function of major importance. The educational psychology professor has the opportunity to influence thousands of prospective teachers during his career. He also has the responsibility to perform this function well.

Many educational psychologists, whether or not they teach, do research in the field. Their results, published or not, frequently lead to further research by themselves or by their colleagues or students. Knowledge in this field continues to develop from this practice of research.

The third major area of practice is the application of research findings in the learning situation. Often the practitioner is a school psychologist (whose training differs from that of an educational psychologist), a guidance counselor, an administrator, an educational consultant, or a classroom teacher. Since the teacher is a key figure, obviously it is important for the prospective teacher to become familiar with the principles and practices of educational psychology. Anyone working in the schools practices educational psychology in some way and has the responsibility of applying its principles and findings in ways most helpful to learners.

THE "RELATIONS" OF EDUCATIONAL PSYCHOLOGY

Psychology

To other fields of study Educational psychology is a special field in itself, although it is related to and bridges many disciplines, as seen in Figure 1.1. Its basic principles are those found in psychology. Its focus, however, is on the application of those principles to one specific role of the organism—as a learner. Much of what is included in an educational psychology course or text is unique in its approach because of this focus.

In his talks to teachers in 1892, William James (1892/1962) quite frankly admitted that psychology cannot provide all the answers for teachers. However, he pointed out that a knowledge of psychology can save teachers from error while at the same time enlightening them in their purposes and methods.

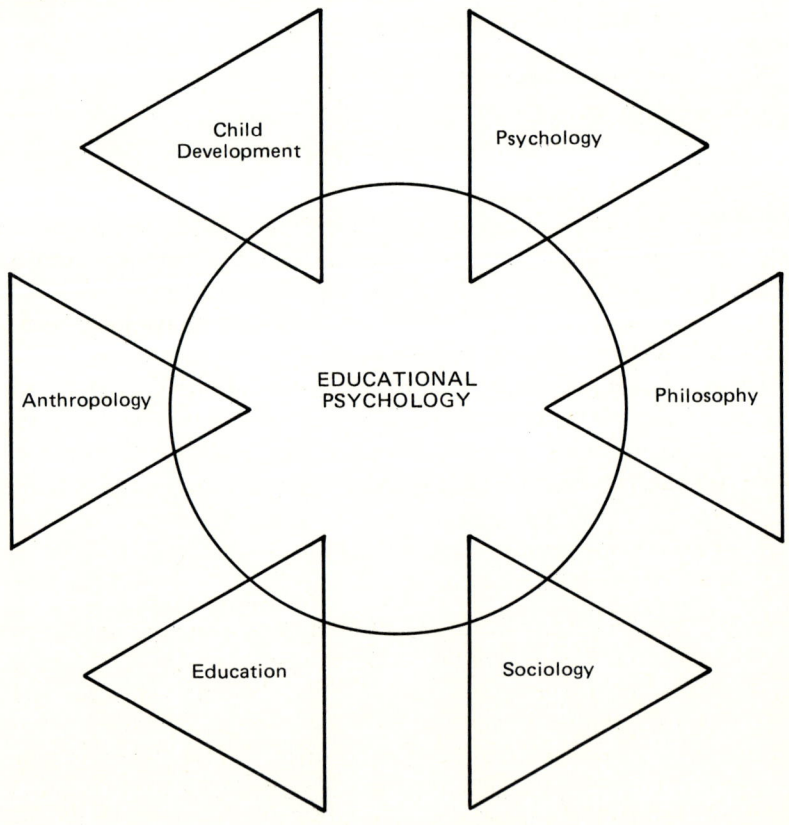

Figure 1.1 *The relationship of educational psychology to other fields of study.*

Child Development

In addition to psychology, there are ties to the field of child development (also called child or developmental psychology). The educational psychologist must be aware of the importance of changes in development which are a function of age and maturity. In educational psychology, the facts of child development are refocused so that their relation to the child as a learner can be seen. An understanding of the concepts of maturation, readiness, language development, motor coordination, and so forth, is vital to viewing the child's functioning in this role. If we are aware of what the child can do and comprehend, it is easier to devise methods of teaching him. A knowledge of child development principles also helps to determine what to teach him and when.

Can you find out how much a six-year-old understands about geography or history as compared with a sixteen-year-old? **Question**

Anthropology

There is increasing recognition that anthropology contributes an added dimension to educational psychology. The perspective it brings is particularly important as we attend to the differing value systems and modes of child-rearing among various cultural groups. Anthropologists have long been interested in cross-cultural studies, and their findings are now being applied increasingly in American classrooms. Greater mobility of people within this country and from other countries means that we have a greater variety of cultural groups in many schools. Respect for their heritage means that teachers must understand that heritage, its attitudes, values, and customs.

Sociology

Sociology has also contributed to educational psychology. Current concerns about sociocultural influences on the learner require that the educational psychologist understand sociological and social-psychological theories and concepts. The structure of the family and its value systems, attitudes, day-to-day functioning, and so on, are taught in both sociology and social psychology courses. Similarly, the effects of socioeconomic level, ethnic background, and peer group influence are important in shaping the individual as a learner.

Philosophy

Educational psychology is, of course, affected by philosophy, especially the philosophy of education. The ideas of whom should be educated and in what areas of study affect the "how" of teaching and the teaching situation. These in turn often affect what the educational psychologist studies and teaches. For example, humanistic philosophy is very popular today. Therefore, more studies focus on the person and his or her needs than on subject matter or teaching methods alone.

Education

The prospective teacher will also find that the professional courses, such as methods courses and student teaching, rest firmly on the ideas and principles communicated in educational psychology. The sequence of courses in the usual teacher-education curriculum points up the fact that students in an educational psychology course are at a crossroad: they can look backward to their general or basic courses and forward to the particular special professional courses as they examine the closely related fields of psychology and education.

To the teacher   A major task of educational psychology is to give the teacher a sense of direction in his work. It helps him to relate more effectively to the learner. One course or text cannot provide the answer to every question, however, or the solution to every problem. What can be done is to present the principles from which application to a specific situation can be deduced. Anastasi (1964, p. 487) has stated this clearly.

> Courses in educational psychology are designed to augment the teacher's understanding of human behavior, rather than to provide specific "rules" for effective teaching. . . . As in other fields of application, psychological training should provide the teacher with a point of view toward human behavior and a method for solving interpersonal problems as they arise. It should help him to decide what to look for and questions to ask in trying to understand situations encountered in the classroom.

Suggestions of resources and examples of particular problems, frequently based on research, are part of the course content. The teacher, prospective or in-service, must evaluate this information with care and not jump to conclusions about it with more enthusiasm than judgment. Innovation and analytic reports found in professional literature are to be studied carefully as to their applicability to the teacher's own situation.

Focus 1–1   Wisdom from the past for teachers:
". . . enforced learning will not stay in the mind. So avoid compulsion and let your children's lessons take the form of play." (Plato, in Beck, 1964, p. 217)
A child's instruction should ". . . be an amusement to him; let him be questioned and praised, let him never feel pleased that he does not know a

thing; and sometimes, if he is unwilling to learn, let another be taught before him, of whom he may be envious." (Quintilian, in Murphy, 1965, p. 15)

These two quotations support the approach of today's open education and child-centered classrooms, although they were written more than 2000 years ago.

A medieval Islamic thinker, Ibn Khaldoun, was one of the first to discuss the effects of cultural background on intelligence and learning. He compared the learning abilities of city dwellers and desert inhabitants, pointing out that the lives of the two were very different, and therefore one should not feel inferior to the other. In particular, he stressed the fact that they had not had the same types of experiences, which led to differences in the nature of intelligence between the two groups. (In Ulich, 1963, p. 201) This piece of wisdom from the past has meaning for us in two ways. First, our continu-

Elements of Plato's philosophy underlie much of today's educational practice.

> ing search for ways to assess validly the intelligence of today's culturally different, and for means to teach them effectively, reflects the same kind of problem. Second, we need to find ways to use their unique experiences in preparing them for life in the larger society.
>
> Awareness that today's educational challenges are similar to those faced by teachers centuries ago may be reassuring to students or teachers overwhelmed by daily classroom problems or differences in research reports.

Although the principles of one or another psychological school of thought may seem to rule the educational scene at a given point in time, it is suggested that the teacher be an *eclectic*. That is, it seems wiser for the teacher to draw upon those principles appropriate to his or her students than to try to fit the learners into the mold of a single psychological approach. To do this, the teacher must be acquainted with both new and traditional approaches in the field. In other words, the teacher should not jump on a bandwagon just because an idea or technique is new and/or popular.

Ultimately, each teacher must develop his or her own resources, personal and professional, in order to do the best possible job. Specific examples of how educational psychology can help the teacher to be increasingly effective will be apparent throughout this text.

To the learner And now the learner. How is educational psychology related to him? From one point of view, it affects what, when, where, and how he is taught. Through research in educational psychology, we:

1. learn which are the most effective ways to teach specific material to different children;
2. try to place the learner in the best possible learning situation—independent study, large or small group instruction, with one or several teachers for a given course;
3. estimate the optimal level or age at which subject matter should be presented;
4. determine what course material is appropriate to the needs, characteristics, and goals of each learner.

Learning affects the learner in several ways. It provides knowledge for everyday use as well as for future occupational tasks. It also often causes the individual to alter his ideas and behavior. Therefore, the contributions of research to educational practice have the greatest importance to the learner, although he may not be aware of them.

Educational psychologists are also concerned with how learners are affected in their learning by various characteristics. Research studies on the effects of sex and age (chronological, mental, and/or socioemotional) on learning in different fields are common. The attitudes, interests, and motivation of students are likewise frequently used variables in research on learning. Also studied are the effects of interference with the basic needs of hunger and sleep on learning. Other research centers on the effects of emotions on learning. How does anxiety affect learning? What does the pupil's attitude toward authority figures do to his learning ability? Still another area for research is that of physical and intellectual deviations and their effect on what and how the student learns. Truly, learners present educational psychologists with a rich array of challenging educational research questions. Throughout this book, appropriate examples of the resulting studies will be cited as they apply to the learner or the learning situation.

Focus 1–2

Wisdom of the ages regarding learners:

Maimonides, a 12th-century philosopher, stressed the learner's active participation in the learning process. He wrote that "Whoever studies audibly retains his learning, but one who reads silently forgets speedily." (Maimonides, in Birnbaum, 1967, p. 26)

Similarly, a 16th-century humanist, Vives, throughout his discussion of educational methods, ". . . constantly emphasizes the importance of involving the pupil, of making him practice himself instead of merely listening and memorizing." (Simon, 1967, p. 114)

Contemporary educators and psychologists, too, recognize that what the person learns for and by himself is better retained than what he is told by someone else. Such active participation in the learning process is a key principle of modern behaviorist theory.

Awareness of individual differences in the ability to learn was also recognized in ancient times. Confucius cautioned teachers about four defects that they might find in their pupils: "Some err in the multitude of their studies; some, in the fewness; some, in the feeling of ease with which they proceed; and some, in the readiness with which they stop. These four defects arise from the differences of their minds. . . . Teaching should be directed to develop that in which the pupil excels, and correct the defects to which he is prone." (Confucius, in Ulich, *op. cit.*, p. 22) Other ancients described students as those who learned readily but forgot readily; those who were slow to learn and slow to forget; others who could comprehend quickly and forget slowly (most desirable, of course); and a final group who learned slowly and forgot quickly.

Such individual differences among learners are seen today in most classrooms. The teacher needs to recognize and understand them in order to help all learners to progress.

A MODERN DISCIPLINE

As a modern discipline, educational psychology continues to study the psychological aspects of educational processes and problems. Learning and the learner are studied under a variety of conditions. The problems and processes examined are much the same basically as those that have been of concern for centuries—motivation, teacher-pupil relationships, learner differences, teaching techniques, and so on.

Research

In all fairness to today's teachers, it should be noted that research creates as well as solves problems. Many studies seem to be inconclusive. However, these may stimulate further studies that lead to solutions. Many studies are so complex and/or statistically sophisticated that they are not widely distributed. Hundreds of studies appear only in mimeographed form or in obscure monographs. It is impossible for one person to be aware of all research efforts. Moreover, the sheer quantity of research being conducted today makes it very difficult to be able to say, "Here is a solution!"

However, with all the faults that research may have, it is a major source of educational practice—the ways in which we try to teach the learner. For this reason, a brief review of research concepts and design is in order.

Research Concepts

Idiographic and nomothetic studies. Do you have a "baby biography" at home? That is, a book which tells when you first sat and walked, said a word, cut a tooth, and had a friend? If so, you have an example of an *idiographic* study. Idiographic studies deal with individuals rather than groups. School records for each student are another example of idiographic studies. Studies of groups, on the other hand, are called *nomothetic*. These include observations of classes as a whole or experimental studies such as of varying methods to teach eight-year-olds physical education. Most of the research reports included in this book are based on nomothetic studies.

Longitudinal and cross-sectional studies. There are also longitudinal and cross-sectional studies. *Longitudinal* studies, as the name implies, continue for extended periods of time, usually several years. We can learn a great deal about the continuing development of the individual or of groups of subjects from such a procedure.

The most famous longitudinal study is probably Terman's "Genetic Studies of Genius," begun with 1000 "geniuses" (IQs of 140+) in the 1920s, and continued today by other researchers. This group has been studied with regard to school achievement, length of schooling, adult occupations, health, personal adjustment, and a host of other variables. Over the fifty-year span of the study, some subjects have died, as has Terman himself. The loss of subjects and/or the investigator is a major hazard in longitudinal studies. Today, with people moving frequently, it is extremely difficult to keep a study group intact, even by mail. Families move from one neighborhood or city to another, children change schools, and the group of subjects shrinks. It is also difficult to control *independent variables,* such as parental occupation, teaching techniques, and teacher characteristics, over an extended period of time. For these reasons, many researchers prefer to use cross-sectional study techniques.

In *cross-sectional* studies, different groups of subjects are used for each grade or age level needed in the study. That is, rather than watching today's seventh-graders for six years until their high school graduation, we deal with comparable classes of seventh- through twelfth-graders in a single year. The advantages of concurrent or cross-sectional observation on experimentation are obvious:

1. the saving in years of study
2. less risk of losing subjects
3. more control over both research personnel and teaching personnel, and
4. fewer changes in background characteristics of the subjects.

Sample populations. What do we mean by sample population? There are more than 220,000,000 people in the United States. Obviously, we cannot test them all even with respect to a single variable. Nor would we want to test all of them, for children differ from adults, males from females, college freshmen from high school freshmen, and so on. Even trying to test all of the people of a given category would be impractical. We therefore take bits or samples of the population, study them, and draw conclusions from the results. Now, given a group of 200 tenth-graders in a suburban Chicago high school, what larger group do they represent? Are they a sample of all tenth-graders in the nation, or of their specific high school population, or of 15- and 16-year-olds in suburbia? If the same sized sample were drawn from a tenth grade in rural Arkansas, would the same results be obtained?

Clearly, it is necessary to define the population of which a particular sample is supposed to be representative. It is further necessary to define whether the sample is random, stratified, or biased.

A *random sample* is one in which each individual in a population has as much chance as any other in the population of being part of the research sample. For instance, if our study is to be concerned with a sample of tenth-grade math students in three city high schools, then Mort Perez in School A should have as much chance as Dot Chung in School B or Lee Brown in School C of being included in the final sample.

In what ways could you try to be sure that each had an equal chance of being picked?   **Question**

If there are 2000 students in the tenth-grade population of math students in the three high schools, and a sample of 300 is wanted, you could:

1. write each name on a slip of paper, place the slips in a barrel, shake it well, and then handpick the needed number;
2. choose every sixth student from an alphabetized list of the 2000 until you have 300 names;

3. use a table of random numbers (published in many statistics and psychology texts) to help make your selections. Researchers usually use the second or third method.

On the other hand, it may be important to the study to include subjects from all socioeconomic groups. Then you need a stratified sample.

A *stratified sample* contains subjects from various subgroups in proportion to their numbers in the general population. For example, if you are studying achievement levels, you should be concerned about the proportion of lower, middle, and upper socioeconomic groups in the total population, because it has been shown that this factor influences achievement. If 10 percent of the total population is considered to be upper-middle class, then 10 percent of the individuals in the sample should be from this group. Proportions of a wide variety of subgroups in the population can be obtained from U.S. Census data and similar sources.

The use of a stratified sample is often advisable if for no other reason than to avoid criticism of its absence. Stratified and random samples can be and are usually used together. To do this, an investigator determines the subgroups of the population to be included in his study, and then applies random sampling techniques within each subgroup.

A *biased sample*, that is, one which has not been randomly selected, provides misleading results. If only bright students volunteer to take a certain test, the findings will be quite different from those where the sample is composed of slow, average, and rapid learners. Although the results of testing with a biased sample may be statistically significant, they are really worth little because of the sampling error.

Independent and dependent variables. Independent variables are those factors that the researcher controls. That is, she selects subjects of certain ages, sex, grade levels, IQ scores, or socioeconomic background. She also decides which techniques or tests are to be studied. For example, the study may ask the question: "Do third-graders learn better in an open classroom or in a more traditional classroom?" The major independent variables here would be the grade level and the type of classroom setting.

Dependent variables are the outcomes of the study, often expressed as test scores. In the preceding example, the dependent variables would be the scores of the third-graders on various achievement or skills tests. The scores of third-graders in an open classroom setting would then be compared with the scores of those in a traditional classroom to answer the original question.

Research Design

Basically, research is problem-solving. That is, a question is asked: If A is true, what effect does this have on B? The first problem in research is to decide what gaps in knowledge exist and are important enough to be investigated. Obviously, there are many significant gaps in our knowledge about learners and learning. The would-be researcher must decide which ones interest her; what competencies she can bring to a study of them; and what practical considerations of time, techniques, and funding are involved. After making these decisions, she is ready to begin.

Step one in research is a review or survey of the literature related to the problem, using, for example, reports in professional journals. Depending on whether the study is to be published as an article or a book, the review of the literature is brief or detailed.

Step two is a statement of the problem and *hypothesis*. The problem may be simple or complex. It may have one independent variable and one dependent variable, or it may involve several variables. The researcher makes the decision on which variables to study. She then states what relationships she thinks exists or will result from her study.

Focus 1–3

A few sample problems in educational psychology are:

1. A comparison of attitudes toward grading by sex and grade level.
2. The relationship between anxiety and achievement.
3. Relations among physical skills, personality, and social adjustment in adolescent boys.
4. Teacher attitudes and pupil achievement.
5. The effects of individual instruction on motivation.

In each case, the researcher states her research question or hypothesis, followed by the associated *null hypothesis* of no difference. For two of the five problems, these might be stated as follows:

1. *Research:* Subjects differ in their attitudes toward grading by both sex and grade level.
   Null Hypothesis: There is no difference in attitudes toward grading in subjects of different sexes and grade levels, except by chance.

2. *Research:* High-anxiety subjects have lower levels of achievement than matched low-anxiety subjects. (Or, anxiety and achievement are negatively correlated.)
   Null Hypothesis: There is no difference in level of achievement between high-anxiety and low-anxiety subjects, except by chance.

Questions

Can you develop statements of hypotheses for the other problems?
Can you decide which would be independent variables and which dependent for each of these problems?

The third step in research is to develop methods and procedures. First, a decision must be made as to the population to be studied (fifth-graders, adolescent girls, introductory psychology students). An appropriate sample is then selected. In writing up the research, a brief description of the sample is given. Second, the researcher must choose her methods. What tests should be used to measure the variables? What, if anything, is the researcher going to do to her subjects that might affect her results?

After carrying out the procedures, the researcher states the results of her work. These may be presented as statistical tables or graphic illustrations, as well as in words in the report. (Several of the more frequently used statistical techniques are described in this book's Appendix.)

In step five, the results are discussed. That is, the researcher attempts to explain why the results were obtained. She might suggest what unforeseen (therefore uncontrolled) variables could have changed or contaminated the results and what possible implications of the results she sees. She might also compare her results with those of other investigators she cited earlier and explain why they confirm or conflict with earlier studies.

Finally, on the basis of the results obtained, the researcher states her conclusions. She may say simply that "The hypothesis that there is no difference between A and B is accepted (or rejected)," or she may restate the results as supporting or denying the hypothesis, depending on how the hypothesis was worded originally.

Usually, a brief summary of the problem, methods and procedures, results, and conclusions is included in a research paper. References used or cited are also included in a research report, much like the bibliography in a text.

Research studies are usually reported in a professional journal, such as the *Journal of Educational Psychology*, *Journal of Creative Behavior*, or *Developmental Psychology*, to name a few. They are also the basis for classroom practices and for further research. Understanding how research is done, then, helps the learner to evaluate its results.

Suggested Activity

To get the "feel" of research, you might look at copies of *Education Digest*, *American Education*, *Psychology Today*, or *Human Behavior*, in which research studies are summarized in nontechnical language. For each study read, find the statement of the problem, the hypothesis, methods/procedures, sample population, and results. Try to summarize the study in your own words.

Testing

The area of effort for which educational psychologists are perhaps best known is testing. Although the testing movement was originally focused on the measurement of intelligence (defined then as learning potential), today its horizons appear to be almost limitless. Psychological tests attempt to measure not only intelligence, but also motivation, attitudes toward learning, attitudes of pupils toward teachers and teachers toward pupils, creativity, the effects of changes in the classroom on the learner and his learning, and countless other variables. Through testing, educational psychology tries to provide information about educational problems and possible solutions to them.

Educational psychologists also develop means of evaluating learner ability and performance other than through written tests. In some cases, progress from one level of performance to another is used as a measure. In other instances, problem-solving situations are the basis for evaluation.

Profession

Approximately 10 percent of the total membership of the American Psychological Association also belongs to the APAs Division 15, the division for Educational Psychology. Many educational psychologists also belong to the American Educational Research Association, reflecting their interest in that field.

Educational psychologists are most often found as teachers in higher education institutions. They may or may not also be doing research. Many educational psychologists work within school systems as examiners, administrators, or consultants. All of them, however, are actively concerned with learners and learning in some way.

SPECIFIC OBJECTIVES

According to John Flanagan, President of APAs Division 15 in 1970, "Educational psychologists can function in two principal ways. First, as scientists to improve the understanding of how an individual obtains an education; and second, as applied technologists to improve current educational programs." (1970, p. 1) A major goal of this text, and of this chapter as a preliminary view of it, is to present many of the ways in which these efforts help you as a learner and as a prospective teacher. Any text, however, can offer only general guidelines, not guaranteed solutions to problems. It is up to you to apply the guidelines to aid learners as they learn.

A commonly accepted set of cognitive objectives includes knowledge, comprehension, application, analysis, synthesis, and evaluation. (Bloom, 1956) This text will provide the basis for knowledge of facts and theories in educational psychology. In the specific objectives to follow, you will be able to work on the five higher levels. After acquiring the knowledge basic to a concept, you should be able to:

1. Explain the relationship of educational psychology to other courses in your professional program.

2. Understand and evaluate the contribution of given research studies to the teaching-learning process.

3. Illustrate by example the influences of growth, development, sociocultural, and psychological factors on learning and the learner.

4. Discuss motivation as it relates to learning ability.

5. Understand the relationship of intelligence to learning ability, in terms of its different theories, aspects, and measures.

6. Understand the concept of individual differences and how these differences affect learning.

7. Distinguish among the major theories of learning and illustrate how each affects classroom practices.

8. Demonstrate the effect of classroom climate on learners.

9. Discuss the teacher's role in the learning process and its effects on learners.

10. Understand the importance of continued learning by teachers.

SUMMARY

The chapter opened with a presentation of the general objectives of educational psychology in the areas of content, attitude, and practice. This discussion was essentially a preview of the concepts with which this text is concerned.

This introduction to the field of educational psychology has already helped you to achieve the first of the specific objectives above. It has provided knowledge of the relationships among educational psychology and other fields such as psychology, child development, anthropology, sociology, philosophy, and education. The relationships of educational psychology to the teacher and to the learner were also discussed.

Next, we examined this modern discipline in relation to two of its major functions, research and testing. Educational psychology as a profession was also discussed. In conclusion, it can be seen that the unique identity of educational psychology lies in its application of the principles developed in a variety of fields, its narrowed focus on learners and learning, and its potential for growth through continued research.

Part Two

Person, Environment, and Learning

What makes a "learner?" One might as well ask what makes a strawberry shortcake delicious. We can itemize the ingredients and the order in which they are used in a recipe, but the way in which they blend together determines the final taste. Similarly, we can examine many of the factors which purportedly affect the ability to learn, but their unique interaction in each individual determines who is a "learner" and how much he can and does learn. There is no "cookbook" approach to describing a learner, or a nonlearner. As the Gestalt psychologists have stated, "The whole is greater than the sum of its parts."

In this section, we begin the study of the many factors which contribute to the development of the learner. In the next few chapters, we will be primarily concerned with nonintellectual factors affecting learning. Our first emphasis is on the psychological growth and development of the learner. Heredity is, of course, a basic factor here. There are other factors, however, less readily considered by those not working closely with education or psychology or sociology. Our second area of study, then, is the environment in which the learner develops. For example, birth order in the family has been reported to have some relationship both to the learner's motivation and his achievement. The ethnic group of which he is a part has attitudes toward education and achievement which subtly affect the learner even before he enters school. Finally, the individual feels and displays emotions in all of his behavior. Two emotional factors that are particularly relevant to his functioning as a learner are motivation and anxiety.

Generally speaking, then, we might say that Part Two is focused on the growth and development of the learner, environmental influences on him, and the critical interaction of his emotions and learning. These are the principal nonintellectual factors affecting the individual as a learner.

Preview

PRENATAL TO POSTNATAL INFLUENCES
    PRENATAL INFLUENCES
        Heredity
        Nature-Nurture
        Educational Implications
        Twin Studies
        Racial Differences (?)
        Other Prenatal Factors
    PERINATAL FACTORS
    POSTNATAL FACTORS

SEX DIFFERENCES
        Intellectual Achievement
        Creativity
        As Learners
        Sex-Segregated Classes
        Interests
        Summary

MOTOR, PERCEPTUAL, AND LANGUAGE DEVELOPMENT
    MOTOR DEVELOPMENT
    PERCEPTUAL DEVELOPMENT
    LANGUAGE DEVELOPMENT

SUMMARY

2

Growth, Development, and the Learner

PRENATAL TO POSTNATAL INFLUENCES

An egg is fertilized. Nine months later, a baby is born. In six more years, a child enters school, and after roughly twelve years of exposure to books and teachers, leaves the classroom for college, marriage, and/or the world of work. The child is "educated." From that first moment of fertilization, physiological processes and events modifying them have affected his ability to learn and to become "educated."

In this chapter, we will consider a number of such processes, beginning with heredity, which are related to the learner's physiological growth and development. Some affect particularly infancy and early childhood, others the later school years, but all are related to how the learner learns and what he learns. We will discuss first some prenatal influences, including heredity, prenatal maternal diet, prenatal and *perinatal* complications, and sex differences. Then we will consider postnatal influences such as general health level, nutrition, illness, and sleep. Finally, we will focus on motor, perceptual, and language development, which are so vital to the mastery of intellectual tasks in the classroom.

This is not an attempt to teach child development in one easy chapter. Rather, it is the application of material from that field to our study of the learner. A large body of evidence supports this emphasis on the role of preschool development and experiences as being crucial in later learning.

Heredity

Let us briefly review heredity theory as learned in biology and some psychology courses. Such theory is largely the work of Gregor Mendel in the nineteenth century, with amplification and refinement by mid-20th-century geneticists. Basically, each organism receives genetic material from each parent at the moment of conception. Some genes are dominant and some recessive. Generally, the organism displays the characteristic of the dominant gene

Prenatal influences

(e.g., for brown eyes) whether or not he has received a recessive gene (e.g., for blue eyes). If he has received *two* recessive genes, he displays the recessive characteristic. A basic design for the probability of inheriting different genetic combinations is shown in Figure 2.1. Such a simple example presupposes that

	Brown	**blue**
Brown	**Brown** **Brown** (brown eyes)	blue **Brown** (brown eyes)
blue	**Brown** blue (brown eyes)	blue blue (blue eyes)

Figure 2.1   *Probability of genetic combinations.*

we are "starting from scratch." Actually, with the exception of people exhibiting recessive traits (e.g., blue eyes), we rarely know an individual's genetic make-up (*genotype*) for certain because of the possibility of his carrying recessive genes transmitted and latent through several generations (i.e., always overcome by dominant genes). Thus, the sudden appearance of a redheaded child (*phenotype*) may occur in a family of brunettes. The varying possibilities of hereditary combinations are demonstrated in Figure 2.2.

You might notice in Figure 2.2, on both sides of the family, that blue eyes appear in the third and fourth generations. Only one paternal great-grandparent and one maternal great-grandparent had blue eyes. By the laws of heredity, at least one other great-grandparent (in this case, a parent of a grandfather) on each side had to have a recessive gene for blue eyes in order for this to happen. Similarly, the blonde-haired maternal uncle (third generation) must have received recessive genes from one of his darker-haired ancestors.

Suggested Activity   Trace an observable trait, such as eye color, or over-sized ring finger, in your own family.

Nature-Nurture

What has this to do with the learner? For decades, psychologists and others debated whether heredity or environment had the greater influence on what a person was like (particularly with reference to the level of intelligence), even to the point where they theorized about the percentage that each contributed. By the 1940s, however, the debate had largely ended with fairly

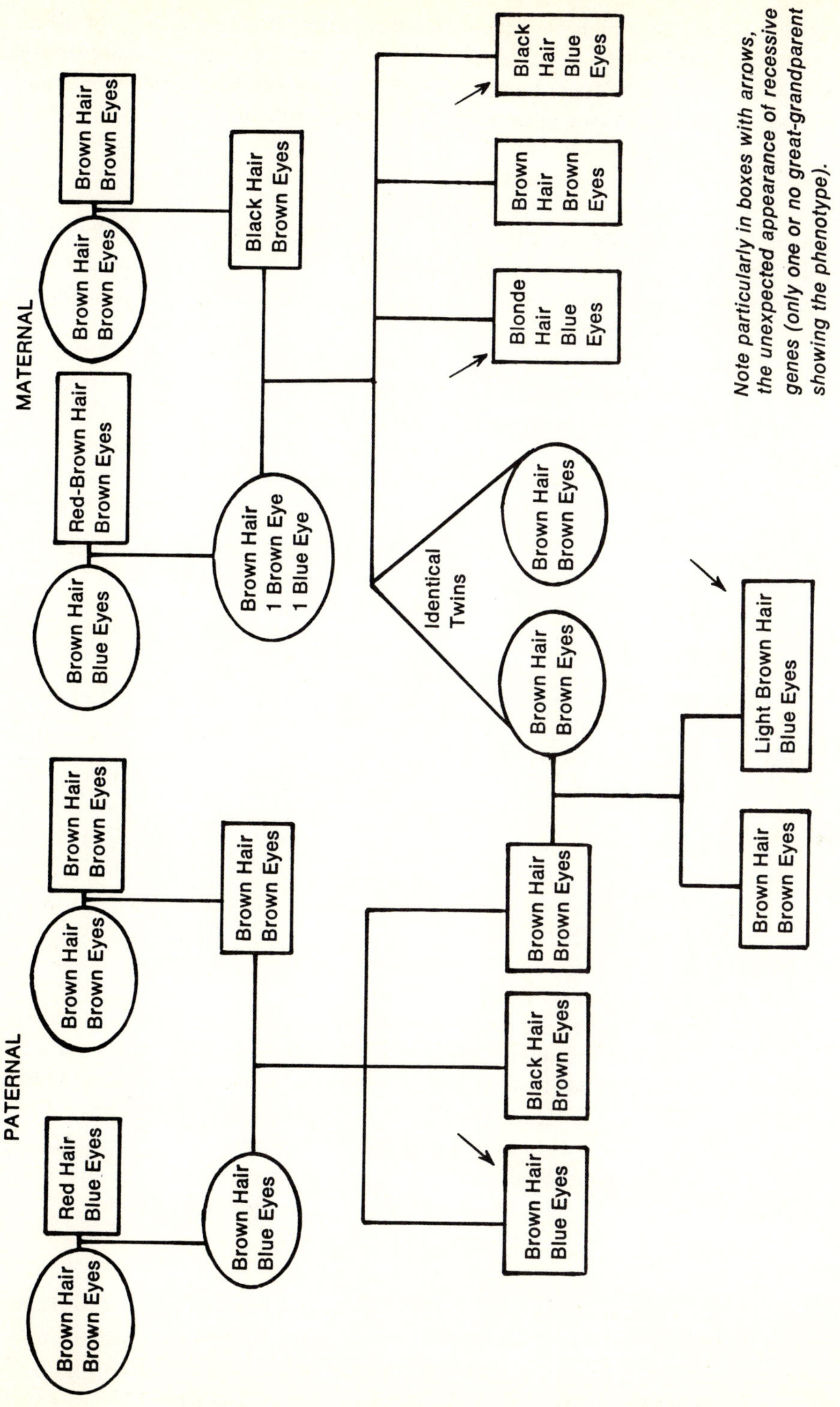

GROWTH, DEVELOPMENT, AND THE LEARNER 27

Patterns of heredity. **Figure 2.2**

general agreement that heredity and environment interact with each other, the relative contribution of each depending on the trait under consideration.

The position accepted by most psychologists (extreme geneticists and extreme environmentalists excepted) is well stated by Ausubel (1968, p. 243): "*Heredity* imposes *absolute* limits on level of cognitive attainment in the individual, influences the rate and patterning of his intellectual growth, and affects the differentiation of his intellectual abilities." *Environment,* on the other hand, ". . . determines the extent to which existing genetic endowment can be converted into overt functional capacity, and helps determine which *particular* components will be selectively emphasized as the latter capacity undergoes differentiation with advancing age."

In 1969, the ashes of the controversy were stirred by the publication of a lengthy article by Arthur Jensen, and the debate flamed anew. Jensen, a noted educational psychologist, asserted that intelligence (and therefore learning ability) was largely determined by heredity and that present efforts at compensatory education were futile since black children, at whom most of these efforts were aimed, had a poorer genetic pool on which to draw in terms of intelligence than whites. He believed, therefore, that they were less likely to profit from preschool education as currently structured. Jensen wrote that ". . . there are racial and social-class differences in *patterns* of abilities and that there are probably genetic as well as environmental factors involved in these differences." (1969b, p. 452) The revival of the old "nature-nurture" argument in relation to intelligence not only came to the forefront of psychological interest again, but also came to the attention of the public as Jensen's arguments were discussed in the public press.

William Shockley, a Nobel prize winning physicist, has been an active supporter of Jensen's point of view. Just as people can use statistics to support their point of view, he claimed, a criticism of Jensen's work that had been based on a computer simulation of a mathematical model had similarly used statistics in a biased way (1971). Shockley claimed that the simulation was so programmed that it explained any mean IQ differences between two groups in terms of environment, even when the difference could be shown to be primarily of genetic origin.

Where Jensen argues about inherited racial differences, Richard Herrnstein (1973) contends that compensatory education is useless because intelligence (mental ability) and *social status* are largely inherited. (Social status is underlined because of Herrnstein's claim that his arguments have been misinterpreted as being also tied to racial differences.) He argues that attempts to equalize educational and other opportunities will simply make the genetic factor more apparent, rather than less. Herrnstein avers that,

1. If differences in mental abilities are inherited, and
2. If success requires those abilities, and
3. If earnings and prestige depend on success,
4. Then social standing (which reflects earnings and prestige) will be based to some extent on inherited differences among people. (pp. 197–98)

Note that Herrnstein stresses social class differences rather than racial differences in this argument. However, much of what he says rests on the same assortment of studies as Jensen's work does.

Educational Implications

In rebuttal to Jensen's original article, Cronbach, also an eminent educational psychologist, wrote that Jensen ". . . does not see that, in writing for educators, it is pointless to stress heredity. The educator's job is to work on the environment; teaching him about heredity can do no more than warn him not to expect easy victories. Heritability of individual differences is not his concern." (1969, p. 345)

Further, Rohwer (1971) suggests that many of the differences in learning ability between the races are due to differences in having or not having the skills needed for early school success. He urges that disadvantaged children be helped to master these skills through specific school programs designed to promote successful learning among children from all backgrounds.

Jensen himself also later wrote on behalf of diverse instructional aims in order to provide for the differences among the majority of white and black children. (1972a, pp. 65–66)

> Educational pluralism of some sort, encompassing a variety of very different educational curricula and goals, will I think, be the inevitable outcome of the growing realization that the schools are not going to eliminate human differences. . . .
>
> . . . On the other hand, educational pluralism runs the risk that social, economic, ethnic background or geographical origin, rather than each child's own characteristics, might determine the educational paths available to him. . . . Academic aptitudes and special talents should be cultivated wherever they are found, and a wise society will take all possible measures to insure this to the greatest possible extent. At the same time, those who are poor in the traditional academic aptitudes cannot be left by the wayside.

Environmentalists are critical of the geneticists' basis for condemning compensatory education partly because of the arousal of the issue of racial differences. However, they are also critical of the sample populations with which genetic studies have been done. A further reason for criticism is the fact that the studies cited by Herrnstein, Jensen, and Shockley have been done over a 50-year period in which there have been great changes in values, attitudes, and social and economic policies—all of which affect education. In addition, it is unclear whether researchers on these studies have allowed for changes within families over time or the influence of siblings on each other, matters that will be discussed in the next chapter. The early and current research on genetic factors affecting intelligence does have value, but it can also have negative effects in the classroom.

Twin Studies

In the light of the continuing controversy about heredity and environment, it is wise to have some understanding of the bases for the arguments. All points of view can be substantiated by some research studies. The bulk of evidence for any viewpoint comes from studies of identical twins raised together and apart; fraternal or *dizygotic* twins; foster children; and correlations of abilities within families. Since identical twins have the same genetic constitution by virtue of being the product of a single fertilized egg that divided after conception (*monozygotes*), they are considered to be excellent subjects for studies of the nature-nurture problem.

Focus 2–1

> One example of research on twins is the Louisville Twin Study. The sample includes 142 pairs of white twins who have been part of this longitudinal study since birth. A recent report (Wilson, 1975a) compared the patterns of cognitive development for monozygotic and dizygotic twins on the Wechsler Preschool and Primary Scale of Intelligence at ages four, five, and six. "The results show that the monozygotic correlations started at a relatively high level and increased somewhat with age, as the measures of IQ stabilized." (p. 128) On the other hand, dizygotic twins' IQs had moderate agreement, with greater differences on subtest scores. Wilson concluded that the genotype had "a significant influence on cognitive patterning and development." (p. 132) Furthermore, he said that "Each home environment adds its own distinctive impress to the child's cognitive functions, but these influences act as modulators rather than primary determinants." (p. 132)
>
> In other words, Wilson found that the genetic component in intelligence is stronger than the environmental influence. This conclusion is supported by many earlier studies.
>
> For further information on the Louisville Twin Study, you are referred to Matheny (1975) and Wilson (1974).

In an earlier study by Vandenberg and Stafford (1967), the Minnesota Vocational Interest Inventory was administered to 53 fraternal twin pairs and 71 identical twin pairs. The results obtained were "interpreted as evidence for a hereditary component in interests in occupations requiring no scientific ability. The hereditary influence operates probably through personality variables." (p. 17)

Environmentalists would question such a strong statement, basing their criticism on similarities of interests generated in a household, or the influence of a parent on one or both of the twins. They might, for example, counter the genetic argument with the results shown in Table 2.1. Clearly, the test scores of identical twins reared apart resemble more closely those of fraternal twins than they do those of identical twins reared together.

Johnson (1963) summarized several studies by various investigators of 23 pairs of separated identical twins and arrived at a somewhat interesting conclusion. He had hypothesized that

If early environmental stimulation or deprivation has a significant effect on the measured intellectual ability of humans, then individuals who are genetically identical and who are exposed to a common early environment and thus have also shared the amount of stimulation that this environment offered, should resemble one another more closely in tested IQ than individuals who are genetically identical but who have not shared a common environment for any appreciable period of time. (p. 746)

Intra-pair correlations of identical twins reared together and apart, and of fraternal twins, on two intelligence and one achievement tests*

Table 2.1

	Monozygotic		Dizygotic
	Together	Apart	
Stanford-Binet	.910	.670	.640
Otis	.922	.727	.621
Stanford achievement	.955	.507	.883

*Newman, Freeman, and Holzinger, 1937.

Table 2.2 shows the reported differences in IQ between separated identical twin pairs and the age of separation. Note that the differences of 1–24 points found among twins separated at ages one to six years clearly contradict the hypothesis.

IQ differences between separated identical twins and the age of their separation*

Table 2.2

Early separation		Later separation	
Age of separation	IQ difference	Age of separation	IQ difference
9 days	1	1 year	19
½ month	1	1 year	5
1 month	4	1 year	1
1 month	3	14 months	4
1 month	1	18 months	12
1 month	6	18 months	12
1 month	1	18 months	24
2 months	2	18 months	7
3 months	15	2 years	10
5 months	17	2½ years	2
6 months	1	3 years	8
		6 years	9

*Johnson, 1963, p. 746.
The inverse relationship between IQ and amount of time spent in a common environment is significant ($p < .04$). (p. 746)

Question *Although this study appears to weaken the geneticists' argument, does it raise any questions in your mind concerning sample size, age of testing, and/or test used?*

Other criticisms of the geneticists' approach come from studies on (non-twin) children in varying environments, such as reports on foster children. Skodak and Skeels studied 25 foundling children, all of whom had been considered retarded in childhood. (1949) Some of the children were moved from the state institution for foundlings to one for the mentally retarded; others remained in the original institution. The former group received a great deal of tender loving care from the older residents in the institution. A follow-up study many years later (Skodak and Skeels, 1966) revealed that those who had been moved were leading more normal and productive lives, and had an average higher IQ, than the other group. Geneticists would suggest that the "normal" group had inherited more potential intelligence than the "retarded" group. Environmentalists would retort that the greater stimulation and attention paid the "normal" group by their institutionalized retarded attendants helped them to approach their intellectual potential to a greater extent, whereas the "retarded" foundlings were in a less stimulating environment with adverse results.

The Skodak and Skeels study has been widely cited as evidence for the influence of environment on intelligence. Jensen (1973) has criticized the study, asserting that its data have been misinterpreted. As in many other studies, the data *are* open to varying interpretation, depending on one's point of view.

Racial Differences (?)

Attention has also been paid to family and social factors in determining intelligence. In discussing the interaction of heredity and environment, Jensen says that

> Children with better than average genetic endowment for intelligence have a greater than chance likelihood of having parents of better than average intelligence who are capable of providing environmental advantages that foster intellectual development. Even among children within the same family, parents and teachers will often give special attention and opportunities to the child who displays exceptional abilities. . . . A bright child may also create a more intellectually stimulating environment for himself in terms of the kinds of activities that engage his interest and energy. And the social rewards that come to the individual who excels in some activity reinforce its further development. Thus the covariance term for any given trait will be affected to a significant degree by the kinds of behavioral propensities the culture rewards or punishes, encourages or discourages. (1969a, p. 38)

This statement reads much like the generally accepted interaction theory cited earlier, but rests on Jensen's explanation of the genetic viewpoint which includes additive genetic effects, *selective mating*, and the probabilities of genetic combinations as reviewed early in this chapter. Furthermore, using this emphasis, Jensen has postulated an inborn difference in intelligence between races that contradicts other evidence that finds no basis for a genetic interpretation of ethnic/racial differences in intelligence.

As Klineberg reported in 1935 and iterated in 1963, intelligence test scores of southern black children "improved in proportion to their length of residence in New York City." (1963, p. 200) However, he also reported that their scores were still below those of white children of similar socioeconomic level because of discrimination, variations in home atmosphere, quality of instruction in "ghetto" schools, and so forth. Klineberg also cited several studies in his 1963 paper in which he cautioned his readers to keep in mind the *range* of scores as well as averages when comparing population groups. He concluded that ". . . there is no scientifically acceptable evidence for the view that ethnic groups differ in innate abilities. . . . We can point to the improvement in achievement when conditions of life improve. We can emphasize the tremendous variations within each ethnic group, much greater than the differences between groups even under discrepant environmental stimulation." (p. 202)

Nonpsychologists, of course, develop their viewpoint from far less "evidence," statistical or theoretical, than has been presented here. And remember, too, that all of this controversy has grown around an event that is literally momentary in terms of time. The moment of conception establishes the individual's genetic components for her development from that instant on. Assuming that she has inherited normal genes, the organism henceforth is modified by environmental factors: prenatal, perinatal, and postnatal.

Other Prenatal Factors

One of the prenatal factors that has been seriously investigated in connection with the later development of the child is the mother's diet during pregnancy. For example, Harrell, *et al.* (1955), demonstrated that prenatal diet can affect the offspring's IQ by providing a dietary supplement to one group of low-income, pregnant women and *placebos* to a matched control group. The offspring were tested at ages three and four years, with children from the experimental group showing a significantly higher IQ than the children from the control group. Pasamanick, Knobloch, and Lilienfeld (1956) found that a relationship existed among socioeconomic levels, medical problems of pregnancy and birth, and psychological problems in the children. Some of these difficulties were attributed to deficiencies of the maternal diet during pregnancy. The psychological problems, too, of course, could affect the child as a learner. Other related research evidence has led to increased efforts to provide more prenatal care and more adequate prenatal diets for the poor of all races.

Several studies have shown also that *toxins* (poisons) in the blood supply (toxemia of pregnancy) may cause brain damage prior to or about the time of birth. Other prenatal conditions related to brain damage include bleeding during pregnancy and anoxia (undersupply of oxygen). As Jersild points out, "The effects of such brain damage may be apparent at birth or may not be particularly noticeable until later when a child begins to have difficulty at school." (1968, p. 52) We will have an opportunity to explore some of the effects of such damage in chapter 12, when we discuss children with learning disabilities.

If the mother has German measles (rubella) in the first trimester of pregnancy, or takes one of a long list of medications or drugs (the most infamous is thalidomide) during critical periods of prenatal development, physical changes frequently occur in the fetus. These ultimately have a direct or indirect effect on the individual's functioning as a learner. Birth injuries would have similar results.

Perinatal factors

Low birth weight and/or prematurity are also found to be related to intellectual development. In a study of 241 infants from birth through age seven, a significantly greater percentage of low birth-weight children, whether premature or full-term, were retained in grade, placed in special classes, or given special school services. (Rubin, Rosenblatt, and Balow, 1973). The low birth-weight children scored lower than the full birth-weight subjects on all measures of intellectual development, language development, school readiness, and academic achievement. Earlier studies by Gray and Miller (1967) and Drillien (1964) also showed that low birth weight and/or prematurity created children "at risk" psychologically and educationally. The high frequency of such births in the lower socioeconomic class, seen in several research studies, is related to poor maternal diet during pregnancy, which provides too few proteins and too many starches and carbohydrates; inadequate medical care despite the expansion of low-fee clinic services; pregnancies too close together; and pregnancies too early and too late in a woman's reproductive life.

Of interest, too, is a continuing study that focuses on the problems of babies who are "oversized" at birth. While confirming other research that indicates that low birth-weight babies are almost twice as likely to be mentally subnormal as are newborns of average weight, Babson and colleagues (1969, pp. 267–68) have found that oversized newborns have a similar problem. Tested at age four, the oversized newborns were found to be more than twice as likely to be mentally subnormal as their age-peers who were of average weight at birth (see Table 2.3). These were all white children from lower socioeconomic class homes. Their mothers had had an average of 10.8 years of schooling. The children were tested with the Stanford-Binet intelligence test, Form L-M, at the age of four years. Again, the findings are related to socioeconomic level and possibly prenatal diet and care, but the educational level of these mothers is much higher than is generally true in the populations cited by Jensen and other geneticists. For this reason, the heredity factor seems to be less important than the environmental factor here.

Table 2.3 *Comparisons of intelligence test scores**

Item	Low birth weight	Standard	Oversized
N	88	1126	74
Mean IQ	92.6	96.8	93.3
Total subnormal	16	119	17
Percentage subnormal	18.2	10.6	23.0

*Abridged from Table 2 (Babson, et al., 1969).

Postnatal factors

Assuming that an infant is born without prenatal or perinatal problems, there are still factors that can affect him as a learner by virtue of their effects on his body. It goes without saying that each individual has his own level of energy output, resistance to illness, nutritional needs, and patterns of physical development.

For example, a child with a low energy output may not really be "dull" or "lazy"; she may simply have less energy to use than most people. She may have dysfunctions in the thyroid gland (which are frequently correctable) or some other physical defect that reduces her effectiveness. Such an unrecognized malfunction may cause slowness in learning. (Dildine, 1964, pp. 130–31) If corrected, and *if* the child's self-image changes to conform to renewed physical health, the child *may* become a more normal learner. On the other hand, as with children who suffer chronic illnesses, the child may see herself as too weak to expend effort on learning. As Anastasi has pointed out, this attitude can be modified, by parents or others in the environment, with the result that the child becomes a learner, and perhaps even a scholar. (1958) the outstanding example of such a change must be Anne Sullivan's work with Helen Keller. Miss Sullivan has justly been called a "miracle worker," though Miss Keller's own persistence and courage in the face of her multiple handicaps is also amazing.

Focus 2–2

Relevant to the concept of low-energy output is the question of fatigue. There are several types of fatigue, among them physical and mental, that affect the learner. Mental fatigue more often results from boredom than "overwork," for interest in what one is doing can keep a person at work for many hours without interruption or rest. Boredom or lack of interest causes one to feel sleepy or restless, sometimes within minutes of undertaking a task. Physical fatigue, on the other hand, caused by physical effort beyond the body's strength to continue, or because of inadequate sleep or rest, often conflicts with the motivation to learn. A poignant illustration of the latter situation can be seen in the film "Children Without," where the young "heroine" falls asleep at her school desk day after day despite her anxiety to learn.

> (NEA, n.d.) Due to the conditions in her home, located in a lower-class Detroit neighborhood, she has too little sleep for her physical needs at night and therefore too little energy to function adequately during the day.

Tests on volunteer subjects have shown that "If a person is drowsy and near to sleep, he will be unlikely to show anything near maximum performance on any skill that he has already learned. . . . When drowsy, he may be quite incapable of performing many thinking skills and problem-solving skills which are performed with great facility when he is wide awake." (Travers, 1963, pp. 266–67) This is the reason, for example, that drivers are warned to pull off the road and take a nap when they become drowsy, before continuing their journey. This is also the reason why most students are better off getting a good night's sleep before taking tests rather than staying up most of the night to "cram."

Nutrition plays a role, too, in the postnatal activity of the learner, just as it had its effects in the prenatal period. Absence of food, like the absence of sleep, inhibits learning and performance. If you are disturbed by pangs of hunger, you can hardly concentrate on the words of a teacher or book. Too many children *do* come to school chronically hungry and become non-learners. Through federal and local programs, efforts are being made across the country to combat this problem.

Poverty, famine, and ignorance are all causes of poor diet, during both the prenatal and postnatal periods. In the emerging nations of Africa, for example, where today's children are needed for tomorrow's leaders, famine has robbed a whole generation of the opportunity to develop their mental capacity as fully as possible. (Rosenfeld, 1974) In the United States, too many children are similarly doomed because of improper and/or inadequate nutrition. (R. Lewin, 1975)

Inadequate diet, inadequate sleep, and inadequate energy all obviously detract from the individual's ability to focus on learning. Temporary setbacks in intellectual functioning may also occur as a result of headaches, stomach upsets, and the like. Vision and hearing defects tend to be more chronic and more damaging with respect to learning. Children should have both eyes and ears examined before entering school to minimize the effects of any previously undiscovered dysfunctions of these senses. Some conditions will not be remediable at a later age, for example, amblyopia or "lazy eye," and may affect the child's personality as well as his learning throughout the school years if not discovered and treated in the preschool years.

Teachers need to be alert to physical disabilities in their pupils, as well as to apparent changes in normally healthy children. There is no need to stress illnesses or handicaps, but adjustments made by teachers to aid students—temporary or for long periods of time—can be made subtly and without disturbance to other students.

SEX DIFFERENCES

A physiological factor that is rarely considered as such when discussing learners is sex differences. Because of this factor, the psychological make-up of the child differs. As will be shown in the next few pages, boys and girls are raised differently, and this must affect their performance as learners. Sex-role differentiation begins with toys purchased by parents and is reinforced as children begin to express their interests.

> Even more strongly, parents *"discourage* their children—particularly their sons—from engaging in activities they consider appropriate only for the opposite sex. . . . Although the dynamics underlying this parental reaction are not clear, it would appear that feminine behavior in a boy is likely to be interpreted as a sign of possible homosexual tendencies, and, as such, it is a danger signal to parents and triggers powerful anxieties in them—perhaps especially in fathers." (Maccoby and Jacklin, 1974, p. 339)

Was this early differentiation apparent in your own childhood? Do you see it happening in families today? **Question**

After the influence of the home, children's sex-role behavior is affected by their teachers' attitudes and practices. Grambs and Waetjen, in a forthright and explicit statement, clearly assert that at the elementary school level particularly,

> . . . the school appears neutral and strives to eliminate any idea of gender from the tasks set before students, but there is operative *in effect* a requirement that students conform to female definitions of learning tasks and school behavior. . . . The conformity demanded is that which is defined by women; inevitably boys will suffer to the extent that they do not or cannot learn the way women teachers say they should. Similarly, girls who express interests which appear more like boys', or talents which are in "boy" labeled activities are apt to be discouraged or ignored or otherwise made to feel their non-conformity. (1966, p. 63)

Is this point of view justified? Let us examine some of the large body of research that has been done in this area as we consider some general statements.

> It should be pointed out that factors such as sex, race, or sociometric status are not in any *direct* sense *causes* of high or low achievement. . . . both our schools and our society set subtly different social

and intellectual environments for girls and for boys. Boys are expected to be independent, somewhat aggressive, interested in things mechanical and scientific; girls are expected (even today, we suspect) to be "sweet," docile, somewhat domestic, and interested in things verbal and artistic. (Thorndike, 1963, p. 19)

Further support for this idea is seen in a study of the responses of 40 female first- and second-grade teachers to sex-typed behaviors in male and female children. (Levitin and Chananie, 1972) Although the teachers liked boys and girls equally well overall, the achieving girl was liked significantly more than the achieving boy, and the dependent girl was liked significantly more than the aggressive girl. The teachers also saw the aggressive boy and the dependent girl as more sex-typical than the reverse.

In discussing studies of sex differences in psychological differentiation, Witkin, *et al.*, suggest as one source of such differences our cultural emphasis on greater psychological differentiation for boys and limited psychological differentiation for girls. (1962)

Maccoby and Jacklin have commented that boys experience more intensive socialization experiences than girls. They suggest that "Adults respond as if they find boys more interesting, and more attention-provoking, than girls." (1974), p. 348)

Whatever the reason for this, children are aware, by three years of age, of their own sex, another person's sex, and cultural sex-typing. (Thompson, 1975, p. 344) This sex-typing seems to affect achievement throughout the school years, especially for boys. Dwyer found, for example, that "IQ was a better predictor of girls' reading achievement than their arithmetic achievement (and the reverse for boys), and it is assumed that social (sex role standards) factors accounted for part of this difference." (1974, p. 814)

In a longitudinal study, Bayley found that

> . . . the boys' scores, of both behaviors and intelligence, correlated throughout the 18-year span with maternal behaviors in the first 3 years. The girls' scores, on the other hand, showed persistent correlations primarily with indicators of parental *ability*. These sex differences in patterns of correlations led us to the suggestion that there are genetically determined sex differences in the extent to which the effects of early experiences (such as maternal love and hostility) persist. (1968, pp. 14–15)

Intellectual Achievement

Ausubel, on the other hand, cites a wide variety of studies which indicate that: 1) except for verbal fluency, sex differences in cognitive activities are not apparent at the preschool level and are therefore culturally determined and 2) girls show a slight superiority to boys in general intelligence during early adolescence with the differences particularly evident in verbal abilities for girls and spatial-mechanical abilities for boys. (1968, pp. 242–43)

In their survey of studies on sex differences, Maccoby and Jacklin found that the verbal superiority of girls becomes apparent at about age 11, and that the visual-spatial and mathematic superiority of boys similarly becomes clear in early adolescence. (1974, pp. 351–52) The sexes are about equal earlier in childhood. To these authors, it appears that differentiation is the result of the interaction of children's spontaneous learning, genetic factors, and socialization (cultural) pressures. (p. 360) That such differentiation occurs should be no surprise. After all, how many parents buy dump trucks, astronaut-type models, and construction sets for their little daughters?

Creativity

In two areas of research that are not strictly intellectual achievement, the emphasis on sex differences is borne out in interesting and related ways. Torrance and Aliotti used the Torrance Tests of Creative Thinking with 118 rural fifth-graders and found that "Girls perform at a consistently higher level than the boys on all of the verbal tasks. This is consistent with the greater emphasis in the United States on the verbal development of girls than boys. Most of the masculinity-femininity measures developed in the United States are heavily loaded with verbal factors. (1969, p. 55)

Ogletree (1971) found a similar superiority on the verbal Torrance Tests in 8—11-year-old English, Scottish, and German girls. Even on the figural battery, the English and German girls scored better than the boys. However, no sex differences among 12-year-old West Australian children on the same tests were obtained. (Dewing, 1970) These findings may reflect subtle cultural differences or other factors not identified.

The verbal productivity and uniqueness of girls would seem to contradict those who speak of low creative ability in females. What is fact is that females have generally not had the opportunity or the need to develop their creative talents. As Maccoby and Jacklin point out, "... until some of the situational factors that have hindered women's nondomestic achievements come to bear more equally upon the two sexes, it is impossible to know whether the initial potential for creative genius is equal in the two sexes or not." (1974, p. 163)

As open-school environments, programs directed toward individual growth potential, and expansion of opportunities for females increase in practice, some of these findings may change.

These ideas bring us full circle to the concept of expectations expressed by Grambs and Waetjen. Although variations have been found between the sexes in verbal ability, curiosity, creativity, and so forth, do they also affect children as learners?

As Learners

Let's begin at the beginning—the age of beginning school, that is. There are many psychologists who urge that boys be admitted to school six months to one year after girls of the same chronological age to permit compensation for the slower maturation rate of boys. This would mean that boys would enter the first grade at age six and a half to seven years, while girls would continue to enter at age six. Considerable overlap exists, however, in the range of maturity for each sex, with the result that some boys who were ready to learn would not be admitted to school, while younger, and possibly less mature, girls would be admitted. As Clark and others have stated, there would be ". . . as much injustice done as benefits gained." (Clark, 1959)

In a comparative study of children in grades three, five, and eight, Clark found no bias in favor of either sex on the California Test of Mental Maturity (a group intelligence test), but did find girls to be superior to boys in basic language skills on the California Achievement Tests ". . . even after differences that can be attributed to chronological age and mental age are worked out of the data." (1959, p. 76) Tyler, too, found that girls tend to do better than boys in the language area, while boys scored higher in arithmetic reasoning and science, but that the distributions of scores by sex overlapped considerably. (1960, p. 685) He also found that girls were assigned higher grades by their teachers and were more often accelerated in grade. Boys more often were retained in grade, especially at the primary level (p. 685), which tended to support the argument that they should be admitted to school later. The effect of pupils' sex on their relationships with teachers is a question to which we will return later, for there is considerable evidence of teacher bias in this area.

> *Comment:* Rather than set an arbitrary rule for admission, a reasonable solution would be to test *all* children with a test such as the Metropolitan Reading Readiness Test and perhaps a Vineland Social Maturity Scale. The admission decision would then be based on an objective evaluation of the individual child.

Sex-Segregated Classes

It has been suggested that perhaps children should be taught in sex-segregated classes. In an experimental program, this was done at the first- and second-grade level. The control groups were sex-integrated or sex-heterogeneous classes. On the basis of his findings, Tagatz concluded that despite sex differences in behavior, the experimental homogeneous grouping had no significant advantages at this level. (1966, pp. 415–18) One reason why there may have been no significant difference was that male teachers were not introduced into the experiment. Elsewhere, when a male teacher has led even a kindergarten class composed of all boys, such a group has learned more satisfactorily than other classes (all-boy classes with a female teacher, or heterogeneous classes with male or female teacher) in the same school. The influx of young men into elementary education in the late 1960s may have a similar long-range effect.

Grambs and Waetjen stated firmly that ". . . *it makes a significant difference whether the person we are teaching is a boy pupil or a girl pupil and that instructional provisions should be made accordingly.*" (italics theirs) (1966, pp. 59–60) They further asserted that at the elementary level, particularly, teacher-made tests tend to favor the "feminine" approach to thinking with the result that boys fared more poorly on these tests and suffered repeated blows to their self-esteem. Finally, at this level, they urge the inclusion of more male faculty members as coprincipals, counselors, and psychologists, teacher aides, tutors, teacher-researchers, and so forth, for "No matter how much we wish to deny it, *teachers behave according to what they believe is sex appropriate role behavior....*" (p. 66)

>*Comment:* This is a rather idealistic point of view. Traditionally, it has been believed that young children need a substitute mother-figure in the classroom at the elementary level. As a result, very few young men have been employed in primary classrooms. Those who did teach the younger children frequently moved quickly into administration as principals or into the superintendent's office where the job was considered more sex-appropriate and the salary was better.

In a study of eighth-grade English students, 199 boys and girls were divided into four sex-homogeneous and two sex-heterogeneous classes (the latter were control groups), with mixed teacher teams. That is, a male teacher taught an all-boy, an all-girl, and a mixed class, and a female teacher was assigned a parallel distribution of students. The teachers did not change their methods according to the sex composition of the classes. No conclusive evidence was found to favor the segregated classes in English achievement. However, "Some boys and girls in the experimental groups had a significantly better view of themselves as problem solvers as contrasted with their control groups, than they did at the beginning of the experiment." (Fisher and Waetjen, 1966, p. 412)

It seems appropriate to mention that girls, at the secondary and college levels, often welcome attendance at an all-female school. Those who are academically capable do not feel either that they must repress their abilities because of the social implications or that the boys threaten their academic standing. On the other hand, coeducation is seen as a more realistic situation in terms of the adult world, and even traditionally female or male colleges are moving in that direction. Certain secondary schools, particularly those in the church-related systems, however, remain largely sex-homogeneous institutions.

The question of sex-segregated classes has been a thorny one at all levels of education. On the one hand, segregation of any kind usually puts someone at a disadvantage. On the other hand, there is for girls, particularly, the release from pressure for sex-typed behavior previously noted. The whole question becomes moot, however, as Federal legislation makes it illegal to have sex-segregated classes or activities (Equal Rights Amendment; Higher Education Act of 1972, Title IX; and other laws related to basic education). (Scott, 1974) Girls and boys have equal rights to participate in sports, home economics and shop courses, and extracurricular activities. It is a long way, however, from the legislature to the classroom, and complete compliance with the spirit as well as the letter of the law may take some time, and presumably many court suits.

Interests

Another interesting investigation focused on the reading interests of ninth-grade black and white students in integrated schools in the southeastern part of the United States. The researchers found more difference in interests by sex than by race! They recommended that "on the basis of the results of this study those concerned with curriculum planning should consider the desirability of making provisions for the differences in interests and reading ability between the racial groups, as well as the sex differences in reading interests within the two groups." (Olson and Rosen, 1966/67, p. 325)

It is difficult, indeed, though perhaps desirable, to select literature assignments that appeal to adolescents of both sexes. Not only are parallel reading lists difficult to compile, but the teacher's preparation is doubled. In addition, there is again overlap of reading interests between the sexes. On the other hand, there are arguments in favor of ignoring the difference in reading interests by sex for this very reason: some girls really enjoy reading about international intrigue, battles, and similar "masculine" topics; some boys enjoy romantic and other "feminine" themes. The reading material provided even at the primary level may have little intrinsic interest for youngsters of either sex, but especially for boys. Much of it revolves around family life, and little boys of seven and eight are already breaking away from this theme as they become involved in team sports and other activities.

Suggested Activities

1. In this era of affirmative action, much to-do is being made about sex roles in textbooks. Obtain a sample of readers for several elementary school grades, and critically analyze their portrayal of sex roles, story themes, and overall interest content for boys and girls. A good basic reference is Austin, Clark, and Fitchett (1971).
2. Survey students at several grade levels to determine their reading interests and preferences. What conclusions can you draw?

Summary

To summarize, several investigators have found that boys and girls differ in their approaches to learning, their achievement in various subject matter areas, and their interests in subject content. This is variously attributed to genetic and cultural influences. Several of the authors cited commented strongly and critically about the apparent nonrecognition of such differences by school personnel, or at least self-deception in practice. They particularly stress the need for a greater masculine influence in the lower grades to offset the conformity to feminine expectations of behavior and the resulting assaults on boys' self-esteem. Boys tend to need more physical activity than girls, and teachers who ignore or resist this simple fact then tend to behave more negatively toward boys. If criticized for normal, boy-like behavior often enough, the boys develop negative feelings toward themselves (for being "bad"), toward the teacher, and toward learning. The girls, on the other hand, may also develop distorted attitudes toward themselves and toward learning because of the conflict aroused by sex-role expectations.

Much of the current concern about sexism in the schools is an outcome of the many years of psychological research in this area. It is also the result of the civil rights, humanistic and affirmative action programs. Continuing research is needed to assess the effects of the changes made in schools in response to these movements.

Question   *What effects would you predict?*

MOTOR, PERCEPTUAL, AND LANGUAGE DEVELOPMENT

Since the individual functions initially in the motor and perceptual areas, there have been attempts to discover whether there is a relationship between activities in these realms and later intellectual functioning. Obviously, the bulk of such research uses very young children as subjects, but occasional longitudinal studies are carried into the school years. Because of our interest in the individual as a learner, anything which affects him or her as a learner is relevant to our studies.

Motor skills are needed for the basic classroom activities of writing, drawing, doing tasks in sequence, and many other functions. Perceptual development is important for reading readiness, following directions, playing an instrument, and a wide variety of activities that involve the senses. Language development is a forerunner of all verbal learning. The data presented here will be referred to in greater detail in later chapters as appropriate.

All humans tend to follow a similar sequence of development, with similar abilities and functions emerging at rather predictable ages. There are, however, individual differences in the rate of development and level of activity within this pattern. There is no evidence to support the frequently expressed idea that if a child is above average in one area, then he will be below average in another. It is possible, though, that over-emphasis on a "strong" talent area may lead to lowered ability in another because of the lack of opportunity to learn or practice the latter.

On the other hand, there is evidence that indicates that children who are above average in different areas of development as infants are likely to continue to be superior in those areas as they grow older. In fact, in a study of fetal activity in the last trimester of pregnancy compared with infant activity at postnatal ages 12, 24, and 36 weeks, it was found that there was significant correlation between the total fetal activity reported by the mothers and later scores on the Gesell Developmental Schedules. Fetal activity and later motor activity were significantly related at all three infant ages, ". . . and at the 36-week test all correlations between fetal activity and postnatal development were significant, with motor, language, and total Gesell scores showing the highest relations." (Walters, 1965, p. 801) (Note: On the Gesell Schedules, scores can be obtained in the areas of language, adaptive, motor, and personal-social development.)

As in the study just mentioned, the majority of research studies indicate that activity level and intelligence are positively related. However, it is possible to examine this relationship from another angle. Maccoby, *et al.*, hypothesized that the ability to inhibit motor activity could be distinguished from a generalized low activity level and that such controlled lack of activity was *inversely* related to level of intelligence. In testing 41 children with an average age of four to five years and an average IQ of 136 (range 95–154), the investigators observed the nursery-schoolers in both free-play and directed-activities situations. They predicted that the most intelligent children would be those ". . . with the greatest discrepancies between their free-play activity scores (which will be high) and their inhibition test scores (where their amount of movement will be low)." (Maccoby, *et al.*, 1965, p. 764) The prediction was borne out in free-play activity, but was not supported entirely in inhibited motor activity. Since motor control becomes more specific at an older age, it is quite possible that the hypothesis would be fully confirmed with older children. There frequently appears to be less restlessness among those committed to intellectual activity at a high level than among those less intellectually involved.

There are problems in trying to predict later IQ from infancy tests. Tests like the Gesell Schedules, for example, focus on sensorimotor development in the early months of life. As the child reaches one year of age, test tasks begin to shift to verbal skills (understanding directions, repeating words). The verbal emphasis increases as the child grows older. Since tests of intelligence for preschoolers and older children tend to stress verbal learning, prediction is more accurate as the child is asked more to do verbal tasks (i.e., as he gets older).

In testing motor development, one must also realize that the examiner is a stranger to the infant. Some of the infant's performance will therefore depend on how he responds to strangers.

A third factor to consider is whether the infant has had practice in imitative games with the mother. Many of the tasks on infant IQ tests require the child to imitate something the examiner does. Obviously, the infant who has had practice in this activity has an advantage. (McCall, Hogarty, and Hurlburt, 1972)

It is possible, of course, that the more physically active infant evokes greater attention from the parents than a more passive one. This attention, in the form of handling, games, songs, reading, and so forth, in turn stimulates the infant by positively reinforcing his behavior. Such a cycle of mutual reinforcement can move from the motor activity sphere to more "intellectual" activities. This may happen also in the case of perceptual development.

Piaget's first stage of intellectual development lies in the exercise of innate sensorimotor mechanisms. The infant perceives strong stimuli and attempts to respond to them. The next two stages in Piaget's theory are labeled, appropriately, "primary" and "secondary" circular reactions. These tend to occur in the period from one to eight months of age. Here the infant begins to respond to objects with some discrimination. (Piaget, 1952) It has been suggested that

Motor development

Perceptual development

children who are deprived of perceptual stimulation opportunities, even at this early age, suffer some degree of intellectual retardation. This occurs particularly in the cases of institutionally reared or socially isolated children, but also within more normal family settings.

Figure 2.3   *Infants perceive and respond to stimuli.*

Research on both animal and human subjects suggests that there may be periods, especially in the perceptual and intellectual spheres, that are critical for development. If the organism by-passes these sensitive periods, for whatever reason, its future development may be impaired permanently. Infants need to have opportunities to perceive different kinds of objects, for example, if they are to learn to discriminate one from another. We expect the three-year-old nursery-schooler to be able to perceive color differences, or to be able to distinguish a square from a circle (although not necessarily by name). She should be able to perceive differences in common sounds and words. There are optimal times in the infant's life when her experiences will have the greatest effect on this later learning. These are the critical or sensitive periods. (Connolly, 1972)

Much of the *compensatory education* effort is directed toward helping children to gain motor, perceptual, and language experiences that should have occurred during sensitive periods, but did not. The results of a variety of intervention programs indicate ". . . that great expenditures of time and effort have not yet succeeded in permanently elevating IQs of disadvantaged children much." (Stanley, 1973b, pp. 7–8) Long-term intervention efforts by

Heber and his associates at the University of Wisconsin-Milwaukee, however, appear to be enabling children of retarded mothers to enter school with average or above-average intellectual functioning. (Strickland, 1971) This project was strongly criticized by Page, however, as being deficient in three ways: "biased selection of treatment groups, contamination of criterion tests; and failure to specify the treatments." (1972, p. 16) A response to these criticisms of the Milwaukee Project was slow in coming.

Until 1975, little had been published on the Milwaukee Project, so evaluation of it was indeed difficult. At that time, however, Heber and Garber (1975) presented a cautious paper on the results of their intervention work with children from early infancy to first grade. The children were black, born to mothers who scored lower than 75 IQ on the Wechsler Adult Intelligence Scale. As part of the intervention program, the 20 mothers in the experimental group were given training in basic literacy and arithmetic skills, vocational skills, family management, and their role in child development. The infants in the experimental group had learning experiences in the perceptual-motor, cognitive-language, and social-emotional areas of development five days a week, year-round from the time they were three-to-six months old until age six.

The objective of the family intervention program "was to provide the kind of learning opportunities that facilitate the acquisition of cognitive skills." (p. 406) By the time that the children were ready to enter first grade, measures of language development, problem-solving, and intelligence suggested that this objective was being approached. In addition, positive changes were observed in the interaction between experimental mothers and children. Children in the control group, who were tested regularly but who did not participate in the learning activities, appeared to decline in development over the same period of years. According to Heber and Garber,

> The failure of many children to learn seems to be due, at least in part, to restricted learning environments created for them in early life by mothers who are incapable of providing better ones. Children who have such developmental histories may develop behavior systems that are antagonistic to the learning they must do for successful school performance. (p. 432)

In other words, Heber and Garber believe that early intervention with retarded mothers and their children can prevent retardation in the children.

Other studies suggest that, even on a temporary basis, deprivation of sensory stimulation can cause emotional and intellectual problems. In a study with college students, for instance, the subjects were in a test state of sensory deprivation for 24 hours. Hallucinations and other unpleasant reactions resulted. Indeed, some of the subjects were so disturbed by these effects that they asked to be removed from the experiment. (Bexton, Heron, and Scott, 1954)

On the other hand, infants who do have opportunities for perceptual stimulation are more likely to develop normally in their intellectual functioning. The sales of colorful mobiles to be hung over cribs attest to parental acceptance of this finding.

There are children who are over-stimulated by their perceptions to the point where this excessive arousal has a negative effect on their intellectual performance. These children frequently suffer from a mild to severe cerebral dysfunction (organic brain damage) but are intellectually "normal" or bright otherwise. They are too easily stimulated by the multitude of stimuli that bombard human beings constantly and are unable to screen out the irrelevant stimuli. For them, reduction of sensory stimulation is a necessity for more adequate performance. Bare-walled classrooms, individual study carrels, and desks empty of all but the task at hand are some of the methods used to reduce stimulation.

Sometimes the child cannot sort out one sound or sight from the many, so he ignores them all. Imagine a similar situation with the sense of taste. If you were given a platter of food that combined many unharmonized spices, you would probably push it away as being unpleasant. On the other hand, if there were a purpose to tasting the dish—perhaps to identify the various seasonings—you would be more tempted to persist in trying to isolate each stimulus. It may be that the individual functioning at a high level of effort, intellectual or other, may similarly be able to screen out distracting and extraneous perceptual stimuli. This would enable him to focus attention exclusively on his intellectual or other tasks with higher achievement as a result.

Language development

The ability to speak is yet another example of physiological development related to intellectual functioning. The speech organs mature sufficiently in the first year of life to permit infants to make all of the sounds basic to any language. Through learning, these infants select sounds to reproduce and begin to "talk" at about age 15 months, with a range of 8–24 months. The age at which children start to talk is often seen as a clue to their future mental development and performance. The relationship between language development and intellectual functioning is positive, but the *correlation coefficient* is nowhere near perfect. In some cases, this is because parents anticipate and gratify their children's needs when the child signals them by nonverbal cues, thus reducing the need for use of language. It would seem the use of language begins when the child finds that his nonverbal behavior is inadequate.

Question

Under what conditions might nonverbal behavior be useless?

In Blank's analysis of the early cognitive functions of language, it is suggested that there are several reasons why the preschooler needs to develop language. These include: to communicate with those older than himself, to aid in problem-solving, to develop an understanding of natural environmental phenomena, to express emotions, to help auditory discrimination, and to recall missing objects or persons. (Blank, 1974)

Assuming that a child has adequate auditory and speech organs, he needs to experience sound early in life in order to learn language sufficiently well to function effectively by the time he enters school. He also needs to hear and speak clearly for effective listening and communication.

In a review of studies of language articulation and intelligence, Winitz found that the two were positively related, but concluded that no "functional" relationship existed. Instead, "With regard to children of normal intelligence, it is entirely possible that children who are above average in intelligence may, for the most part, come from families of high socioeconomic status, where language stimulation and reinforcement would be expected to be greater than for families of low socioeconomic status." (Winitz, 1964, p. 295) There might be not only greater stimulation and reinforcement, but also better clarity. Moreover, as was true for visual stimulation, it seems that deprivation of auditory stimulation may similarly be involved with critical periods.

Focus 2–3

> In some families, children are spoken to only when necessary, and even among the parents there is very little conversation. Preschoolers from such environments tend to have restricted vocabularies, relatively poor articulation, and poor listening discrimination abilities. This combination of language difficulties can handicap the child severely in his school learning for an extended period of time. If he cannot understand the teacher's words because of his inadequate listening abilities or his poor articulation, he falls behind and/or loses interest in the task of learning. Eisenberg, *et al.*, compared 160 black and white school children of low and middle socioeconomic class backgrounds who listened to female black and white speakers read lists of monosyllables. Some speakers from each race were educated, and others were not.
>
> Negro children showed generally poorer listening scores than whites, and Negro speakers generated slightly poorer intelligibility scores than whites, independent of the race and class of the listeners with one exception: uneducated speakers were understood better by members of their own race.
>
> A second experiment showed a small but significant relation between the listening scores the children obtained and their ability to rearticulate the lists to 40 teachers. Great variability within subjects probably overcame the effects of class. (Eisenberg, *et al.*, 1968. p. 1077)
>
> Such speech patterns, both in listening and articulation, are learned. We hear what we expect to hear and are accustomed to hearing. If someone from a different background, socioeconomic or geographic, speaks, we often strain to understand his words and may fail to understand him.

It is also true, as Hunt has pointed out, that a child accustomed to hearing many loud and meaningless vocalizations becomes so used to them that he "tunes them out." If this occurs, Hunt concluded, "then it's hard to make voice sounds serve as cues in learning." (Pine, 1968, p. 16) Elsewhere, Hunt asserted that children raised in environments of economic and cultural deprivation are seldom ". . . invited to note what is going on around them or to formulate their observations in their own language. These children are especially unlikely to learn the syntactical rules of the standard language." (Hunt, 1969, p. 19) The inability to speak, and later write, the language correctly is obviously also a handicap in the educational setting.

Words are learned, too, in terms of their utility in the child's life, frequency of use, and, depending on the circumstances, concreteness or abstractness. For example, "bed" is learned before "furniture" (specific before general), but "car" is learned before "Chevrolet" (abstract before concrete).

Figure 2.4 *Learning experiences for preschoolers and beginners. Not all learning takes place in the classroom or from books. Some of the learning experiences occur through fun and games, using the child's imagination and encouraging him to discover relationships. Many such materials can be improvised at home to reduce expenses.*

Words that are not important to the child, although they may be important in terms of intellectual evaluations, simply may not be learned at all. It is interesting to note that the vocabularies of children have changed over the years, partly because some words have become both more important and more familiar to them while others have almost faded out of the language. Palermo and Jenkins gave the Kent-Rosanoff word association test to 500 children each in grades 4–8, 10, and 12 and to 1000 college students. They found, contrary to studies done in 1910, that abstract responses increased to grade six and then declined and also that males gave more abstract responses than females. The authors attributed the greater use of abstract words by fourth- and fifth-graders at least in part to increased language stimulation in the 1960s (radio, television, audiovisual instruction, etc.). (Palermo and Jenkins, 1963) One need only listen to six-year-olds to become aware of the impact of the communications media. The youngsters are as familiar as some adults, when exposed to such language stimulation, with terms referring to space technology, environmental planning and problems, espionage, and so forth. Awareness of these changes in vocabulary is reflected in the word list of the new Vocabulary sub-test of the Wechsler Intelligence Scale for Children—Revised (Wechsler, 1974). A more extensive discussion of language development, in its relationship to thinking, will be presented in chapter nine.

SUMMARY

We have discovered and discussed in this chapter many influences on the learner that are primarily biological. The first factor was heredity. We dealt extensively with the re-awakened controversy about its role in the intellectual functioning of the individual. Jensen's genetic arguments were presented, followed by the opinions of several other psychologists. Since studies of twins were used to support arguments on both sides of the nature-nurture debate, and since they are interesting in themselves, they were included and discussed at some length. Depending on how the statistical results were interpreted, they supported either view.

Next, primarily physiological factors such as prenatal diet and health, perinatal weight and injuries, and postnatal conditions were introduced as they related to later learning ability of the child. The satisfaction of basic needs for food and rest were also included here. Considerable attention was given, also, to sex differences in learning and behavior, for, as several investigators have shown, there are real differences between boys and girls in the quality and quantity of their intellectual functioning and development. The effect of sex-role expectations as seen in the schools was an integral part of this discussion.

Finally, we briefly investigated the areas of motor, perceptual, and language development as they are related to intellectual development and later learning. Although patterns of development are similar for all children in these three functions, individual children follow their own timetable. In addition to the individual sequences, however, we pointed out the need for stimulation of the child, particularly in the perceptual and language areas, if the child is to develop normally. Sensory deprivation, that is, lack of adequate experience, from infancy through the preschool years has been shown to be harmful to appropriate intellectual functioning in middle childhood and later years.

For a further look at nonintellectual influences on the learner, we will go on to examine the situation of the learner in the family and larger environment in chapter three.

Preview

INTRODUCTION

WITHIN THE FAMILY
    BIRTH ORDER
        First-Borns
    SIBLING INTERACTION
    FOSTER CHILDREN
    MATERNAL EMPLOYMENT
    PATERNAL ABSENCE
    PARENTAL ATTITUDES

SOCIAL-CLASS DIFFERENCES
    INTELLIGENCE
    TEST PERFORMANCE
    CHILD-REARING PRACTICES
    ENRICHMENT

ETHNIC DIFFERENCES
    FOUR ETHNIC GROUPS COMPARED
    BLACK AMERICANS
    PUERTO RICANS
    MEXICAN AMERICANS
    AMERICAN INDIANS
    ASIAN AMERICANS
    JEWISH AMERICANS
    SUMMARY

PEER GROUP INFLUENCES

EFFECTS OF TV WATCHING

SUMMARY

3

The Environment of the Learner

INTRODUCTION

Every person is born into and grows up in some environment. Generally, he lives with his family, which may consist of parents and siblings, or possibly parents only, or perhaps with grandparents or other relatives in the home as well. There is evidence that shows his position in the family tends to have some effect on his functioning as a learner. Other studies indicate the importance to his performance of parental attitudes toward him and toward education. These attitudes are shaped in turn by the social-class milieu in which the family lives, and to some extent by religious and racial group affiliations. Apart from the family, the learner is influenced also by his peers and their attitudes toward him and toward education. Finally, the presence of television in the home, and what he watches on it, has some effect on his learning ability and performance. The focus in this chapter is on the learner in the midst of this multifaceted environment, and how its different aspects help or hinder him as he develops.

WITHIN THE FAMILY

To some, heredity and socioeconomic level are the major influences on intellectual functioning. Other investigators in the past century, however, have been fascinated with the role played by size of family and individual position in the family. Certainly becoming a family, as distinguished from being a married couple, brings changes to relationships between husband and wife—changes that inevitably are reflected in their behavior as parents.

When the wife finds out she is pregnant, attitudes and expectations toward impending parenthood are revealed by both of the prospective parents. If the child's arrival is anticipated happily and he or she then meets the expectations of the parents in appearance, abilities, personality, and behavior, a healthier and happier childhood can be predicted. However, if a child is not wanted or does not meet parental expectations, there may be an equally negative effect on development. Senn and Hartford, for example, found, in a small, longitudinal study, that "Mothers who are the most reluctant and negative about the approach of maternity continue to find the most disruption and dissatisfaction in life with the child." (1968, p. 519) In addition to the parental attitudes, one must consider the effect of the attitudes of grandparents with whom the young family may live or be in frequent contact, the sociocultural traditions of child-rearing practices that a particular set of parents has learned, and the status of the marriage itself on the early development of the child. These factors, plus the lack of experience of being a parent when the first child arrives, inevitably have a long-range influence, especially on the first-born.

Birth order

Sir Francis Galton, a noted British student of genetics, found that there were more only sons and first-born sons in his *English Men of Science* (1874) than statistical probability would warrant. In Terman's *Genetic Studies of Genius* (1925), there was again a disproportionate number of oldest children included in the population sample. Several other studies similarly suggest that first-born or only children appear to be favored intellectually. Is this due to a genetic factor or environmental factors?

Geneticists might say that the first-born child inherits the best genes from his parents and that later children receive genes from a less rich genetic pool. It would be very difficult to determine this with any degree of certainty. Environmentalists, on the other hand, would counter with the argument that the first-born has the benefit of being the sole object of parental attention for the crucial first years of childhood. This would mean that he is handled more often, read to more often, and so on, than his younger siblings. These positive aspects may be reduced somewhat by the already mentioned inexperience of the new parents. It should be remembered, too, that family circumstances change from the time the first child is born until all the later ones have arrived. With the first child, the parents may stay home because they can't afford to go out; later, the oldest child may "sit" or a paid sitter may care for the younger child.

Some of the differences between first-born and later-born children may reflect socioeconomic background. For example, the family housing may change over a period of years, resulting in more or less crowding in the home. Differences in verbal intelligence and educational aspiration have also been attributed to differences in the amount of time parents spend with first-born and later-born children and to the amount of time children spend with siblings. Glass, *et al.*, for example, found that third-born children scored significantly lower on these variables than first-born or only children. (Glass, Neulinger, and Brim, 1974, p. 810) From these and other examples, it is easy to see that there can be real differences in environment for children raised in the same household.

First-Borns

Altus studied several reports in the professional literature and found substantial evidence for the theory that the first-born is favored in intelligence and achievement, just as he has been in the inheritance of more material things (the laws of primogeniture in the aristocracy of England is a prime example). For instance, Altus quoted one investigator's conclusion which showed that nearly 60 percent of National Merit Scholarship finalists ". . . who came from families of two, three, four, and five children were first-born." (Altus, 1966, p. 45) In other studies, it was found that more first-borns were enrolled at high-prestige universities than would be expected by chance, for example, 61 percent at Yale and 66 percent at Reed College. (Altus, 1966, p. 46) Drawing on these and other research studies and observations, Altus concluded that the first-born child may do better than younger siblings in school because

> His curiosity, dependence upon adults, and greater conscience development doubtless makes him respond more affirmatively to the teacher and to the school. He should thus more frequently win the teacher's approval, which is expected of a student. If this inference is correct, it is easy to understand why the colleges attract such a high proportion of the first-born. (Altus, 1966, p. 48)

Several other investigators provide supporting evidence for this conclusion. In a study of entering college freshmen, first-borns were over-represented. In addition, female first-borns in this study were found to score significantly higher on the SAT (Scholastic Aptitude Tests) than later-born females. The tendency for first-born males was in the same direction for verbal SAT scores, although the difference in scores between first-born and later-born males was not statistically significant. (Walker and Tahmisian, 1967, p. 219)

For a younger age group, teacher grades and achievement test scores were compared for 129 pairs of first- and second-born siblings at the upper-elementary- and junior-high-school levels. "Differences between siblings on grades and test scores significantly favored the first-borns. The data also indicated that first-born superiority may be more pronounced for siblings close in age and for first-born girls." (Chittenden, Foan, Zweil, and Smith, 1968, p. 1223)

Focus 3–1

Bradley and Sanborn did a longitudinal study of over 1500 ninth-grade students, seeking "guidelines" for the selection of superior students. The guidelines included such criteria as size of vocabulary, effectiveness in communication, self-motivation, either a wide range of interests or a very strongly focused single interest, levels of creativity and curiosity, impatience with routine (often a characteristic of the highly creative), and ease of recognizing relationships. First-borns were consistently selected by teachers, year after year, as meeting these and other criteria of superiority to a greater extent than later-born students. They did not score significantly higher on intelligence tests, but apparently did have different opportunities and more favorable experiences that contributed to their higher achievement in later life. (Bradley and Sanborn, 1969, pp. 41–45) This is consistent with the statements earlier in this chapter that refer to the opportunities open to the first-born child during his tenure as an only child.

In *The Promised Seed* (1964), Harris reported that the differences between first-born and later-born sons appeared to be more a question of quality than quantity, particularly in terms of creativity. The first-borns tended to produce work that was more abstract and verbal; the later-born sons tended to give more practical and more perception-bound productions.

There is evidence, too, that under certain conditions, first-borns tend to be more dependent, which can affect learning. You may recall that Altus mentioned this in his conclusion. On the basis of a rather small study ($N = 40$), Gilmore and Zigler (1964) found that first-borns had less need for social reinforcers than did later-born children when such reinforcers were easily available. However, *under stress*, the first-borns appear in their study to be *more* dependent on social reinforcers. That is, under stress, they need more approval and/or acceptance by other people in order to function effectively.

The research data are not all consistent, however. Some investigators have found that birth order makes little or no difference in intelligence and/or achievement. This may occur because of a different emphasis in the research design. Other investigators, for example, might emphasize family size, family density, and sex of siblings, or other variables.

Schacter has demonstrated, for instance, that there is no birth-order effect operating in a general population sample or a high school sample, but there is clearly a birth-order effect at the college and graduate school levels. In studies in Minnesota, he reported that ". . . some 35.2 percent of high school students are first-born compared with 50.2 percent of college students and 57.8 percent of graduate students." (Schacter, 1963, p. 764) There is obviously some selection factor at work here, but why or what? Schacter explored possible economic factors, intelligence level, achievement, and motivation as tentative answers to this question. He did find a tendency for first-borns to earn higher average grades than their later-born classmates, but could not clearly attribute this finding to either ability or motivation. Schacter further reported that studies of intelligence did not agree that first-borns had consistently higher IQs than later-born children. (pp. 706–707) It would appear, however, from this and other studies, that first-borns do have a higher level of motivation to achieve than do later-born students.

Let's explore this idea for a moment. Why should there be a difference in motivation related to birth order? Just within the family unit, parents often put more pressure on the oldest child to do well for a variety of reasons. One reason is that the parents may see their children as "extensions" of themselves and may therefore involve their own egos in the success or failure of their children. The oldest, particularly, may be seen as the first to reflect credit or shame on them in the outside world. Secondly, the oldest child is frequently expected to serve as a model of desirable behavior for younger siblings. He must, therefore, achieve success to show these siblings that "it can be done." A third reason is tied to the second. That is, in the event of parental inability to support the younger children, the oldest may have to take on the role of the parents and needs maximum opportunity to succeed to achieve this. It is quite probable that the first-born child assimilates these responsibilities and becomes strongly self-motivated. Thus the resolution of the conflicts in research results might depend more on the personality characteristics of the first-borns than on their intellectual prowess.

What effects do siblings have on achievement motivation? Let's consider, first, the case where the oldest child is an academic achiever. Although he may be a model for his younger siblings, he may also be so accomplished and competent as to make his siblings give up trying to achieve because they feel they cannot succeed in competition with him. Contrariwise, some younger siblings may welcome the unstated competition and seek to surpass the first-born. In the second instance, the younger child is the achiever. Does the older sibling keep on trying? Does he feel so threatened by the younger one's accomplishments that he withdraws and becomes an underachiever? Does he seek another avenue to parental approval and attention?

Sibling interaction

A study of how second-born children view sibling roles, based on the responses of 578 white, middle-class children aged 5.5 to 13.5 years, adds some interesting sidelights to the family interaction picture. Bigner's data show that second-borns do indeed look up to the older sibling as a model. Some differences are seen due to the age of the child, his sex, the sibling's sex, and the age difference between the two children. Where the second-borns do "... look to their older siblings for social guidance or modeling, perhaps it is because they have learned to recognize and acknowledge the older child's social power and ability to provide certain functions in their relationship." (Bigner, 1974, p. 572) Certainly, the oldest child has led the parents through the joys and jolts of childhood once, so that it is easier for them to be aware of the younger child's needs when they arise. Frequently, the oldest can act as mediator between the parents and a younger sibling.

One must conclude that the interaction between or among siblings is so complex that it is difficult, if not impossible, to predict with any certainty the behavior as a learner of any child solely on the basis of birth order or family size and density.

If you have siblings, how do you see the role of the first-born and later-born children in your family?

Question

Interview all of the children in several families to ascertain their views on sibling roles and interaction. You might consider in your survey the effect of these variables:

Suggested Activity

1. sex differences among respondents (M v. F)
2. sex differences among siblings (is the oldest M or F?)
3. age differences among siblings (1 or 2 years v. 4 or more years)

4. generation differences among respondents (Do people in their 30s and 40s have a different view than children and adolescents?)

Foster children   While discussing family interaction and its effects on the learner, it seems appropriate to consider the influence of parent-surrogates on orphaned and adopted children in the same light. Until comparatively recent years, foster-home placement on a permanent or long-term basis did not occur until a child was six months of age or older. Until this late placement occurred, the infant was kept in an institution or in one or more short-term foster homes. This did not encourage the development of strong supportive family ties. Research, moreover, indicated that this practice led to emotional and/or stimulus deprivation, which in turn led to emotional and learning problems as the child grew older. According to a report by one psychiatrist, Dr. David Offord, "Even a delay of only a few months in adopting the baby may determine whether he aggressively will strike out against his parents, school and community in later life. . . ." (Drake, 1969, p. 32) Evidence supportive of this statement has led to a revision in placement practices, with happier results for the child as a person and as a prospective learner. Infants are now more often placed with their new families by the time they are two or three months old. (Note: There are exceptions. Asian children, for example, have usually spent a few years at home and/or in an orphanage before being placed with their adopting families in other countries. They then have cultural barriers to overcome as well as emotional reactions, all of which can affect them as learners.)

Maternal employment   Apart from birth order and family size, each family has its own "atmosphere." To begin with, what effect does maternal employment have on the child's behavior (emotional and cognitive)? It has generally been assumed that maternal employment results in child neglect and lowered motivation. Care must be taken, however, in discussing this assumption not to confuse the effects of maternal employment with the absence of mothering, such as is true for many institutionalized children. As Wallston (1973) suggests, studies of preschool children of working mothers in the United States, and of similar children in Israel and Russia, show that there are no harmful effects of maternal employment *if* there is adequate care by a substitute. It appears to be better for everyone concerned to have a satisfied working mother rather than a dissatisfied nonworking one.

Question   *If a nonworking mother is away from home much of the day, at social functions or doing volunteer work, does this affect her child?*

In a study of 400 cases in Los Angeles County where approximately one-fourth of the mothers were employed full-time, it was found that many of their children did not present problems in school. As the investigator concluded, "This would indicate that as long as the child is made to feel secure and happy the mother's full-time employment away from home does not become a serious problem." (Rouman, 1962, p. 114) Some special consideration is needed, however, in the care of younger and only children.

If the child is secure and happy, as Rouman suggests, this is one less obstacle to his effectiveness as a learner. A review of literature on the question indicates that the working mother provides a positive role model, in fact, for her daughters and encourages their independence, with these factors contributing to the daughters' higher achievement. (Hoffman, 1974, p. 224) Among school-age children in general, there is little evidence that maternal employment results in maternal deprivation. (Hoffman, 1974, p. 219)

Less often investigated is the effect of the father's absence on the learner. In a study of 100 nineteen-year-old college girls, it was suggested that ". . . the

Paternal absence

Fathers, as well as mothers, influence the development of children.

years from 1 to 9 compose a critical period for the development of quantitative skills in girls . . ." and that a negative correlation exists related to father absence on night-shift work during this period. (Landy, Rosenberg, and Sutton-Smith, 1969, p. 944) The finding with regard to quantitative skill development has been supported in other studies. The suggestion has been made in this regard that women are generally disinterested in mathematics and therefore cannot make up for the absent father who presumably is more interested in this field.

The father's absence is more common in lower-class than middle-class families. It is also becoming more common across class lines as divorces increase, unwed mothers choose to raise their children alone, and fathers' jobs require extensive traveling. The absence of a father poses difficulties for both boys and girls in understanding masculine roles. There are negative consequences also in achievement, particularly, as noted, in mathematical and analytical skills. In general

> The research on the relationship between father absence and the general level of the child's adjustment reveals that the loss of father for any reason is associated with poor adjustment, but that absence because of separation, divorce, or desertion may have especially adverse effects. The consequences may be more pronounced in general for boys than for girls. However, father loss seems especially detrimental to the adolescent girl's ability to interact appropriately with males. The younger the child when father absence occurs and the longer the extent of his absence, the greater may be the resultant disturbance. (Lynn, 1974, p. 279)

Parental attitudes

The determination of whether a child becomes a learner rests somewhat more solidly on parental attitudes and practices toward academic achievement. We have already discussed the importance of stimulation by the parents from infancy through the preschool years. A special parental responsibility is the encouragement of a positive self-concept in children, since this contributes mightily toward later achievement. (The role of the self-concept will be discussed in greater detail in chapter four.) The child who believes that his parents accept him as a capable and competent individual is more likely to maintain his efforts than one who lacks such a feeling. Two specific ways in which parents can direct their children toward educational achievement are 1) encouraging verbalization through frequent verbal communication and exposure to the uses of language and 2) helping them to learn to perform tasks well and independently. In the school situation, after all, the learner finds himself highly dependent on verbal skills and his own independent effort.

Interestingly enough, motivation toward achievement as related to parental efforts in these areas tends to depend to some extent on socioeconomic status and the sex of the child. For some people, even today, education is seen as rather unimportant for girls. An example of the relationship of socioeconomic status and the child's sex is seen in Callard's (1968) study. A sample of 80 four-year-olds was tested on "The relationship between achievement motive, as measured by tendency to resume a challenging task, and maternal expectancies regarding achievement. . . ." In the lower class, children of both sexes, ". . . tended to exhibit higher achievement motive when mothers indicated moderate, rather than extreme, expectancies. In the upper class, girls had higher achievement motive when mothers believed in early training for achievement and expressed controlling attitudes, while higher achievement motives in boys were associated with late ages for achievement-inducing." (Callard, 1968, p. 14) This finding has been supported by the results of other studies that used somewhat older sample populations.

If parents want their children to achieve in school, it is also important that they support the teacher's efforts by encouraging curiosity in their children, providing them with the opportunity and emotional support for study, teaching them respect for the role of the teacher, and explaining clearly their own values with respect to education and the reasoning behind those values.

The nature of parental attitudes toward learning and learners is shaped by the parents' own experiences as they grew up, and to some extent by their socioeconomic status and ethnic subcultural memberships. It is to the latter factors that we now turn.

SOCIAL-CLASS DIFFERENCES

Intelligence

There is no unanimity of opinion concerning the causal relationship between socioeconomic status and intelligence or achievement, although most educational psychologists and other professionals tend to view socioeconomic status as an important factor in educational performance. Some might even agree with Jensen that socioeconomic status in itself is not an environmental variable that is a primary cause of IQ differences.

At the opposite end of a continuum regarding the relationship between social class and intelligence, Havighurst assumed that mental superiority is largely a product of social environment. If this were true, then the intellectual level of the population would be raised greatly if all children had the advantages of an upper-middle-class environment. However, a high level of ability is found in some lower-class children. This occurs, according to Havighurst, because of unusual characteristics within the family such as high achievement motivation, thrift, interest or talent in the arts, and so forth. (Havighurst, 1964, pp. 211–12) This assertion is based on Havighurst's study of *Growing Up in River City*, where he found that the upper- and upper-middle classes produced almost twice as many mentally superior children and less than half as many children in the lowest quartile of intelligence as might be expected on the basis of random distribution of intelligence. Table 3.1

. . . shows the relation between social class and intelligence at the sixth-grade level. The middle social classes have far more than half of their members above average in intelligence, whereas the lower classes have more than half of their members below average. This relation is expressed by correlation coefficients of .34 and .28 between socioeconomic status and intelligence for sixth grade boys and girls respectively. (Havighurst, 1962, pp. 22–23)

Similarly, an analysis of school progress as related to social class indicates a strong correlation between these two variables. Four-fifths of the upper- and upper-middle class subjects ". . . went to college, while only one in twenty dropped out of high school. In the lowest social class, only two in fifty-seven boys went to college, and none of the girls did so." (Havighurst, 1962, p. 52) Doubtless, many of the lower-class students who drop out of school do so because of economic pressures within their families, but Havighurst also believes that their social environment does not provide stimulation or models conducive to learning.

Table 3.1 Social class and intelligence.

Intelligence quartile	Percent of each social class in each quartile			
	Male			
	Upper and Upper-Middle	Lower-Middle	Upper-Lower	Lower-Lower
IV (High)	33%	26%	16%	11%
III	48	27	28	16
II	19	31	26	32
I	0	16	30	41
Number ($N = 237$)	22	62	91	62
	Female			
	Upper and Upper-Middle	Lower-Middle	Upper-Lower	Lower-Lower
IV	62%	44%	19%	7%
III	14	25	28	20
II	5	20	30	40
I	19	11	23	33
Number ($N = 237$)	21	64	94	58

*Adapted from Havighurst (1962), p. 22.

Sociologists have also suggested that differences in learning orientation stem from different social-class outlooks. The middle class tends to be career- and achievement-oriented, while the lower class is understandably more security-oriented. The self-image of the latter group tends to be one of failure, inability to control the environment or their destiny, impotence, and incompetence. This concept is demonstrated in Gottlieb and Ramsey's summary of the 1960 Census Reports, in which they found that school progress was related to the socioeconomic status of the parents. (1967, p. 11) They pointed out, however, that low socioeconomic status *per se* does not imply lack of interest in education, but rather that the negative self-image described above contributes to the negative learning orientation of the children:

> Poor people fail to help their children not only by avoiding formal organizations and programs set up by the middle-class community but also by failing to assist their children informally at home. Having had a poor education themselves and lacking the skills of reading, language, and mathematics, they can hardly provide much in the way of meaningful help to their children. They are even incapable of directing them to professional help, for they know little of libraries (or even the process of obtaining a library card) and little about any other institutional aids and services. (Gottlieb and Ramsey, 1967, pp. 36–37)

Several years later, these findings have not changed significantly. Despite the awakening of racial awareness, women's assertiveness movements, and the efforts of social action groups to stir lower-class families toward learning, relatively little progress has been made. Education remains, apparently, fairly low on a priority list headed by hunger and housing.

Focus 3–2

Let's narrow the discussion somewhat. If, in a study of a representative sample of over 1400 infants, aged 1 to 15 months, no differences in test scores of mental and motor functioning are found on the basis of sex, birth order, parental education or residence, or race, but differences are found 3 years later which are related to socioeconomic variables, something is happening beyond heredity.

> Evidently, the period between 1 and 4 years of age is an important one in the development of mental and motor functions. This age period should be studied closely in an effort to seek out those environmental factors which are relevant to the development of intellect and those behaviors that appear to be resistant to environmental impacts and also in an effort to identify the behaviors and the specific age periods for which correlation between test scores and socio-economic ratings first occur. (Bayley, 1965, pp. 409–10)

In another investigation, one in which race was not a factor, Hess found these social-class differences among black mothers: 1) unrealistic levels of aspiration among working-class mothers, 2) ambivalence by working-class mothers toward community agencies, 3) a working-class emphasis on the teacher's *authority* while middle-class mothers emphasized learning in introducing their children to school, and 4) less guidance in problem-solving by working-class mothers. On the basis of these findings, Hess, too, asked "... what facilitating experiences are present in middle-class homes that typically do not occur in the working-class homes?" (1965, p. 18)

Several other research findings indicate substantially the same thing: there are social-class differences that affect the individual as a learner, and these differences are most frequently conveyed by the mother. Kandel and Lesser (1969), for example, found that middle-class mothers encouraged their children to continue their education more than lower-class mothers did. However,

> When the mother's educational plans and strength of encouragement are controlled simultaneously, the social class effects on the child's own plans disappear almost completely. . . . These parental attitudes and plans, in turn, are associated with social-class position. But for the child, the parent is clearly the link between social-class position and future life goals. (Kandel and Lesser, 1969, p. 220)

This strong maternal influence is one reason that many compensatory education programs emphasize direct work with the mother as well as the child.

Test performance Another aspect of the problem of social class and learning ability is that most verbal intelligence tests include items more familiar to middle-class children than to lower-class children. It is for this reason that psychologists are trying to develop "culture-free" or "culture-fair" tests. Performance, or nonverbal tests, tend to have less middle-class bias than verbal tests, which does help the lower-class child. Socially disadvantaged children usually score low on group intelligence tests, but they tend to score slightly higher on performance subtests than on verbal subtests. Cohen reported that such children

> . . . tend to earn lower Information and Vocabulary than Comprehension scores. This appears to be a persistent pattern differentiating socially disadvantaged from more advantaged children. In fact many middle and upper middle class children tend to have the reverse pattern. It appears that children from the "wrong" side of the tracks lack information about the world perceived by middle class children in making their way in the practicalities of everyday life. (Cohen, 1967, p. 39)

It is quite possible that children considered socially and academically disadvantaged in urban, middle-class schools could function adequately and independently in a less demanding and less technological setting. Although reading is essential today in almost any field of endeavor, practical knowledge is often equally important in most aspects of everyday life and in many occupations. According to Ausubel, the development of such practical skills may be at the expense of verbal skills due to inadequate stimulation of potentialities for verbal intelligence in early and middle childhood. He suggests that once this differentiated commitment of abilities is made, the child may be unable to respond satisfactorily to an enriched verbal environment, such as the school. To Ausubel, it is evident that the older such a child becomes, the more verbally retarded he will be. (1968, p. 190)

Some of the advantages enjoyed by the upper- and middle-class students on current intelligence tests can be attributed very simply to differences in opportunities available to them and not to lower-class children. The middle- or upper-class child is more likely to have better-educated parents who have better vocabularies, who own and read more books and magazines, and who expose their children to more "cultural" activities, than does his lower-class peer. Just these experiences would give the child an advantage on tests of information, abstract verbal relationships, and vocabulary. Studies of the use of language by lower-class children indicate, for example, that they have more limited vocabularies with which to express concepts and to communicate. They are then effectively cut off from understanding verbal interchanges in the larger society and remain "prisoners" fenced in by their subcultural group's language. (Gray and Miller, 1967, p. 484)

There are also social-class differences in child-rearing practices that appear to affect attitudes toward and behavior in the educative process. Elder and Bowerman (1963) studied 1261 Protestant seventh-graders and found that

Child-rearing practices

> Practices that encourage the child to understand and adopt rules of conduct and to develop the ability to govern himself accordingly are more commonly used by middle-class parents. Methods such as physical punishment, which inhibit self-reliance and which curtail disapproved behavior without facilitating the learning of parental values and norms, tend to be favored more by parents of lower-class status. (Elder and Bowerman, 1963, p. 904)

The trait of self-reliance is valued in the academic setting, and those who exhibit it are more likely to be acceptable to their teachers. This acceptance, in turn, leads to a positive attitude toward learning. Lower-class children do learn to be self-reliant, but this is more often in a "survival" sense than in an achievement orientation. Such a pattern tends to parallel the higher score on performance than verbal tests achieved by these children.

Self-reliance and achievement motivation are somewhat related to what has been called *locus of control*. This phrase refers to the belief a person has about who controls what happens to him. When the individual ". . . thinks that he can determine the way things turn out by the way he acts, we say he is internally controlled. When he believes that the things that happen to him are the results of the behavior of others (or of the stars, or the fates, or luck), he is externally controlled." (McCandless and Evans, 1973, p. 379) There is some indication in research that the feeling of powerlessness that exists often in the lower-class family is conveyed to the child, and leads to an external locus of control. Similarly, delay of gratification, or deferring of immediate rewards, is not stressed in the lower-class family. It is in middle-class families. Studies have shown that there is a relationship between the ability to delay gratification and the locus of control. The lack of ability for delay is associated with external locus of control and lower socioeconomic status. (Zytkoskee, Strickland, and Watson, 1971) From this and other evidence, one can say that different child-rearing practices among social classes affect the way in which the learner perceives himself and behaves.

Enrichment   Let us take for granted that there are social class differences in learning and intelligence. Despite Ausubel's pessimistic view, is there anything that can be done to reduce the learning gaps of lower-class children? Can the rate of measured retardation be *de*celerated? In other words, can the effects of social class be remediated or minimized? Apart from preschool programs and extensive tutoring, there are several programs in current use in secondary schools that attempt to bring an affirmative reply to that last question.

These programs have several goals: enriched educational experience, remediation of academic inadequacies, expansion of personal horizons, movement toward self-actualization, and reduction of the dropout rate. The programs demand much personal as well as professional effort on the part of their staffs. In addition, cooperation with many agencies in the supporting communities is necessary. Not every youth attains success, but enough do to make continuation of such special programs worthwhile.

ETHNIC DIFFERENCES

Minority groups in our population seek to maintain their cultural identity while simultaneously becoming assimilated into the larger society in terms of equal opportunity for individual self-development. In this section, we will explore particularly the nature and effect of ethnic differences and the conflict with respect to learning in several subcultural groups: blacks, Puerto Ricans, Mexican Americans, American Indians, Asian Americans, and American Jews. An understanding of ethnic differences is important if we are trying to help *all* students to become learners and all learners to find self-fulfillment.

Although not all of these groups are considered to be socially or educationally disadvantaged as a whole, they do differ sufficiently in attitudes to create disadvantages for some of their members in the classroom and subsequent adult life. There are several variables that affect younger minority-group members as learners, such as integration of the subculture in the schools, general group attitudes toward education, relevance of educational programs, and teacher behavior toward them. Several studies in recent years have indicated that what the child learns at home, in terms of attitudes and values, is more important to his progress as a learner than the methods or materials used to teach him. If the ethnic group's attitude toward the larger group is hostile because it sees little hope for opportunity to get ahead, then the child will be poorly motivated to become involved in a situation such as learning that can only lead to frustration. On the other hand, if learning is seen as the key to opportunity, the child is more likely to strive for academic achievement.

Perhaps social-class differences *do* produce significant differences in test scores, yet at the same time operate in parallel to ethnically related differences in ability patterns. That is, we need to consider whether there is an ethnic group emphasis on certain kinds of abilities more than on an overall achievement level. One of the more comprehensive, and classical, studies in this area is the research of Lesser, Fifer, and Clark (1965) with first-grade children representing middle- and lower-class membership in four minority groups. Their subjects came from Chinese, Jewish, black, and Puerto Rican backgrounds. As in other studies mentioned earlier, the middle-class children tended to have scores superior to those of the lower-class children and resembled each other more than they did lower-class subjects of their same ethnic groups. In addition, boys and girls demonstrated ability differences. More importantly, it was found that social-class and ethnic-group membership together affected IQ scores, but did not interact to affect patterns of mental ability. (Lesser, *et al.*, 1965, p. 102) This can be illustrated, perhaps, by showing relative ethnic-group standing in different abilities.

Four ethnic groups compared

Rank of ethnic groups on different ability tests (after Lesser, Fifer, and Clark). **Table 3.2**

Ability group	Verbal abilities	Reasoning	Numerical abilities	Space relations
Chinese	3	1	2	1
Jewish	1	2	1	2
Black	2	3	4	4
Puerto Rican	4	4	3	3

The authors concluded that ethnic group membership does modify mental ability patterns to an extent sufficient to warrant measuring these patterns in the light of such membership.

Focus 3–3

A similar study that used twelfth-graders as subjects ". . . revealed that for a given ethnic group males and females tended to exhibit patterns of mental abilities characteristic of their sex; these patterns were only slightly modified by ethnic background." (Backman, 1972, p. 9) Socioeconomic status had little effect on mental abilities, but its range was limited in this sample. No Puerto Ricans were specified in the Backman study, but about 35 percent were labeled "non-Jewish white." Using the other three groups studied by Lesser, *et al.*, Table 3.3 attempts to offer a parallel to Table 3.2. Two things should be noted here: 1) VKN, or Verbal Knowledges, is a measure of general information, and 2) the lower-middle and upper-middle class groups are combined for the sake of simplicity.

Table 3.3 *Rank of ethnic groups on different ability tests, by sex (after Backman).*

Ability group	VKN		Mathematics		Visual reasoning	
	M	F	M	F	M	F
Oriental	2	2	2	1	1	1
Jewish	1	1	1	2	2	2
Negro	3	3	3	3	3	3

There are some differences in patterns from the earlier study. Some of these may be due to the different age groups used. As Backman herself indicates, students who continue to twelfth grade tend to bias the results toward higher mental ability scores. With first-graders, there is a wider range of abilities. Nevertheless, some consistency is seen in the patterns.

Black Americans

The most prominent of our minority groups, in terms of population alone, is the black subculture. In chapter two, we discussed some of the arguments about the black person's ability to learn, innate or acquired. Jensen cited several studies which indicated to him that ". . . on the average, Negroes test about one standard deviation (15 IQ points) below the average of the white population in IQ . . ." and ". . . perform somewhat more poorly on those subtests which tap abstract abilities." (Jensen, 1969a, p. 81) He also reported similar findings on achievement tests. He explains this substandard performance as being due largely to genetic (hereditary) differences between blacks and whites. However, we have also discussed the damaging effects of stimulus deprivation in early childhood, which appear to be a function of social class. There are proportionately more blacks in the lower socioeconomic class than whites. It would be difficult, therefore, to accept Jensen's thesis without further investigation.

Is there, for example, a relationship between personality and cognitive characteristics and academic achievement which demonstrates racial differences? In a study of eleventh-grade black and white students of both sexes in a northern urban educational system, Green and Farquhar (1965) sought to answer this question. They found no correlation (−.01) between aptitude and achievement for black males, although scores for white males had a correlation coefficient of .64 for the same variables. However, they did find that motivation was a better predictor of achievement for black male subjects and concluded that this ". . . emphasizes the relationship between nonintellectual factors and school performance. It may well be that many black students (especially males) are being graded on other than academic performance (e.g., social desirability)." (Green and Farquhar, 1965, p. 243) If we turn to a study of the same age group in southern schools, we find that black and white students had no significantly different attitudes toward school, but that the black students had ". . . poorer academic morale in recently integrated schools than in segregated institutions. . . ." (Williams and Cole, 1969,

p. 75) This finding was attributed to competition in the integrated classes, low expectations by teachers, and the general sociological and educational poverty of the geographic area. We will examine the factor of teacher expectations later on, because there is some indication that this may be a major factor in the child's ability to perform as a learner.

Is the combination of low socioeconomic status with race the key to lowered intellectual performance? Kamii and Radin (1969) found, for example, that retarded black preschoolers had their greatest difficulties in the areas of verbal responses, abstract and spatial reasoning, and memorization on the Stanford-Binet test. These children were all from the lowest socioeconomic class. Their inability to respond to simple tasks and questions is almost unbelievable: ". . . of the retarded children with a mental age of 3, only 15 percent could look at a simple picture and select and label three items. Only 10 percent could answer either 'what must you do when you are thirsty?' or 'why do we have stoves?'" (Kamii and Radin, 1969, p. 286) Is this a matter of race or socioeconomic class or both? Surely black children, rich or poor, get thirsty, but why do these children not know the word for this need? It is possible that poor children, black or white, don't have a stove, or perhaps call it by another name that is not used on the test. The use of local idiomatic expressions instead of more generally used terms can obviously work to the disadvantage of certain subjects.

Related to the preceding study is another small study of black five-year-olds: 27 culturally deprived children attending a Head Start program, and 27 middle-class children. These youngsters were tested for verbal fluency, verbal expression, recognition of vocabulary (Peabody Picture Vocabulary Test), and grammar. The two groups were comparable on measures of fluency and expression, but the middle-class children had both more extensive vocabulary and better grammatical ability. This, the authors attributed to ". . . the opportunity for contact with adults who can provide verbal stimulation and grammatical patterning which will not ordinarily be obtained from peers." (Giebink and Marden, 1968, p. 367) The suggestion is made that Head Start teachers should emphasize training in grammar to reduce this difference. Notice, however, that this difference is relevant to social class rather than race.

There is a question that must be raised in connection with the studies that use intelligence tests. Does the race of the examiner affect the scores obtained? Using black preschoolers from low-income families, Moore and Retish (1974) found that it did. "The means obtained by the black examiner all fall within the average range of intelligence (90–109) while the means elicited by the white examiner are in the dull-normal range (80–89)." (p. 674) Even such young children are aware of racial differences and may react to a white examiner with fears of inadequacy, fears of the white race in general, and even hostility—all of which can depress test scores.

Is the decline in tested intelligence as children continue through the grades a matter of race? This is a finding in a standardization project concerned with the 1960 revision of the Stanford-Binet intelligence test. (Kennedy, Van de Riet, and White, 1961) The sample included 1800 black children, ages 5 through 13, from the bottom of the socioeconomic scale (about 86 percent of them), who tended to be from large families (about 60 percent lived in households of 6 or more). The mean IQ for the group on the revised test was 80.71, with a *standard deviation* of 12.48. (Note: the national mean for this test is 100 with a standard deviation of 16 points.) This is not the major point, however. Kennedy, *et al.*, found a consistently increasing gap

> . . . between the mental age and the chronological age in both sex groups and in the group as a whole. The difference is initially in a positive direction, that is, the mean mental age is 1.4 months higher than the mean chronological age. However, this difference is reversed, resulting in a difference of 57 months in a negative direction at the extreme. That is, by year 13 the mean mental age is 98 months and the mean chronological age is 156 months. (Kennedy, *et al.*, 1961, p. 90)

(This pattern is shown in Figure 3.1.)

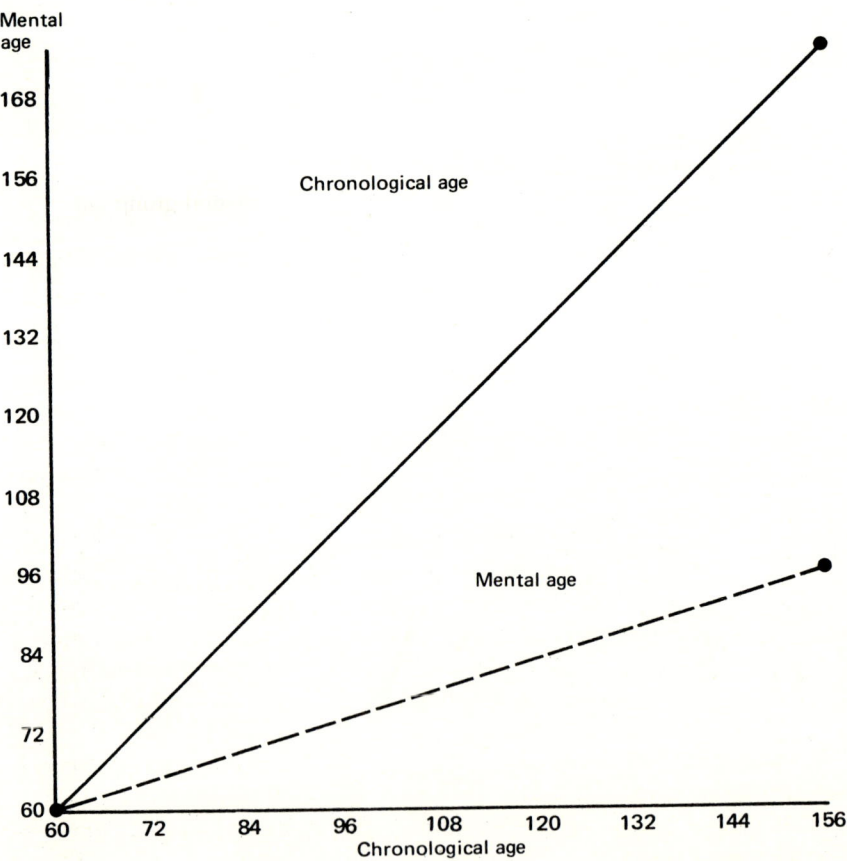

Figure 3.1 *Change in mental age with chronological age (after Kennedy, Van de Riet, and White).*

In studies of black intelligence such as this one, many variables are uncontrolled, despite the best efforts of investigators. These include: population sample, social status, definition of race, status and caste confusion, language usage, test motivation, quality of education, rapport with examiners, and selective migration. Kennedy, *et al.*, therefore concluded that "in view of these variables which have not been adequately controlled and in view of the present status of intelligence tests, it seems impossible to isolate the effect of race on intelligence test scores." (Kennedy, *et al.*, 1961, p. 143) The study and its conclusions have been criticized on the grounds of size and selection of sample. That is, the children tested ". . . at the lower ages were probably more intelligent and those at the higher ages were probably less intelligent than the total population of Negro children at these age levels." (Schaefer, 1965, p. 257) It is the critic's view that a low level of intellectual functioning was developed during the preschool years and simply maintained during the school years. Schaefer does not agree with the slow decline found by other researchers. (p. 259) The criticism seems somewhat naive since Kennedy, *et al.*, were working in a limited geographical area in which it would be difficult to select (intentionally or by chance) more intelligent younger children and less intelligent older ones. (Note: It is possible, you see, to criticize the critic.)

Focus 3–4

Again, we must ask if such a decline can be prevented, whether or not the differences are racial in origin. In a three-year prevention study, black children in a day-care center were divided into an experimental group and a control group. The program for the experimental group was designed ". . . to counteract the inhibiting effects of cultural deprivation on language and perceptual learning during the important formative preschool years, . . ." and included home visits, the use of Montessori materials in the third year, and emphasis on increasing listening skills and attention span as well as the expressive aspects of language. (McConnell, Horton, and Smith, 1969, p. 597) The curriculum leaders included a teacher of the deaf, three speech pathologists, and an elementary-level teacher. The pre-training and post-training IQs as well as mean changes for the two groups are shown in Table 3.4.

Obviously, intervention can be effective not only in halting an intellectual decline, but also in bringing about an increase in test score (although this may reflect a practice effect). If the increases in the experimental group were due solely to practice, however, one would expect to see similar positive changes in the control groups. It is also interesting to note, in the table, that the youngest experimental group, admittedly small in number, made the largest gain in IQ points.

The resumption of schooling, too, can have positive effects as Green and Morgan found in studying the black children of Prince Edward County (Va.) who had been denied public education for a four-year period. Part of the sample had had up to 1.5 years of schooling in that time. However, the children who had had no education for the four-year period made the only significant gain in measured IQ. "This finding suggests that even the most severely de-

Table 3.4 *The mean Stanford-Binet IQ levels for each of the designated populations following first nine-month experimental period.**

Group	N	Mean age	Mean pre-training IQ	Mean post-training IQ	Mean gain
I. *Experimental groups*					
1965–66	35	4–1	90.5	107.0	16.5
1966–67	54	4–1	93.8	109.4	15.6
1966–67	17	3–6	88.0	112.8	24.8
Total 1st year	106	4–0	91.8	109.2	17.4
II. *Control groups*					
1965–66	18	4–1	98.4	98.2	−0.2
1966–67	24	5–3	93.0	91.0	−2.0
Total	42	4–9	95.3	94.0	−1.2

*McConnell, et al., 1969, p. 601.

prived children can make significant gains when educational deprivation is altered." (Green and Morgan, 1969, p. 150) Such an optimistic view would be an argument in favor of early intervention, as in the Head Start programs, with continuation in the primary and middle grades.

Similarly, the use of more relevant material, as in the multiethnic readers, may help to reduce the loss in intellectual performance. The demand for a change in reader content has brought materials of varying quality to the classroom. It is hoped that more of the readers will be improved as they are oriented to the experiences of minority-group children. More meaningful and relevant texts have two purposes: 1) to reduce losses in intellectual performance due to lack of interest and 2) to change attitudes toward minorities on the part of majority-group children.

Puerto Ricans The consistent low ranking of Puerto Rican first-graders as seen in Table 3.2 may reflect more than ethnic-group and social-class differences alone. Like the Mexican Americans and exiled Cubans, these children bring to the classroom a language problem that is not easily overcome. We have been accustomed to substituting nonlanguage tests for the usual verbal tests where a language barrier exists, but there is some question as to whether the two types of tests actually measure the same intellectual functions. Further questions arise in testing bilingual children: 1) What kind of rapport is established in the testing situation between the bilingual child and an examiner of the same or different background? 2) What is the attitude of the bilingual child toward testing? 3) How competent is the child in either or both languages, even for understanding test directions? 4) Are there more personality problems among the bilinguals than among monolinguals that may further affect intellectual performance? 5) Do the apparent variations in ability patterns among ethnic groups help or hinder the child on nonverbal tests? 6) What standardization groups were used for the tests?

A classic study in this field was done by Anastasi and Cordova (1953) with Puerto Rican children in New York. The subjects were 176 children in grades six, seven, and eight in a New York City parochial school. They were given the Cattell "Culture-Free" Test, Forms 2A and 2B, with half the subjects taking the test first with instructions in English and the other half of the group having Spanish instructions first. At the second test session, the language in which the instructions were given was reversed for the two groups. The subjects were also given a questionnaire regarding the extent of their bilingualism. Results indicated that there was a large and significant practice effect, with both groups scoring much better at the second session, regardless of the language used. The language in which the test was administered apparently had no significant effect on the subjects' test performance.

The authors found that "The bilingualism encountered in this group appears to be of the bifurcated variety, the children's mastery of either language being restricted and inadequate. The teachers report that these children show a reluctance to speak English. Yet in Spanish, the majority are illiterate." (Anastasi and Cordova, 1953, p. 13) The authors also found that the children's attitude toward testing was atypical.

> A large number of factors, including lack of test sophistication, little or no motivation to excel in a competitive intellectual situation, and lack of interest in the relatively abstract and academic content of the test contributed to this attitude. The characteristic reaction to the testing was a mild confusion, followed by amusement and indifference. Such attitudes, moreover, are closely related to the poor emotional adjustment which this group makes to the school. (p. 15)

The children generally scored well below Cattell's norms because of these attitudes, language problems, and their low socioeconomic background. Here we have answers to several of the questions raised earlier. In Focus 3–5 these are confirmed and additional answers may be found.

Focus 3–5

Fifteen Puerto Rican children living in a suburban community near Philadelphia were tested by the author for placement purposes in their local school district. Their families lived marginally; that is, on welfare checks or the inadequate wages of their unskilled-laborer fathers. The families were large, with up to a dozen children in the home. Their parents had had little formal education, and only a few of the children had gone to school in Puerto Rico. The homes, although of better construction than those they had lived in in Puerto Rico, provided minimal comfort and were meagerly furnished.

With the assistance of the school district's bilingual reading teacher, each of the fifteen children was given the Spanish form of the Wechsler Intelligence Scale for Children. This test was standardized in Puerto Rico and Venezuela. In addition, nine of the group were given the Test Rápido Barranquilla, a Spanish-language verbal test, and ten of them were given the

> Bender-Gestalt Visual-Motor test, a nonverbal test. Instructions and questions for all three tests were given in Spanish and, on the latter two tests, occasionally repeated in English for those who had some competence in the latter language.
>
> These children, like those in the Anastasi and Cordova study, demonstrated little test sophistication, a strong desire to please the examiner, and little or no achievement motivation. They lacked understanding of basic directions (e.g., they did not know the meaning of *subrayar*—to underline) and had relatively low anxiety in the testing situation. Supposedly, their families had moved from the island in the late 1960s to improve their economic situation, but the motivation for improvement had apparently not been transferred to the educational realm.
>
> The school district tried to keep each of these children in a grade fairly close to his or her age-appropriate level, but this was difficult when the test scores ranged from mildly-retarded to dull-normal levels on both the Verbal and Full-Scale IQs. The district provided a bilingual remedial reading teacher and accepted tutoring assistance from high school and college students, yet little progress was made by the youngsters. Spanish was spoken almost exclusively at home, which offered more security, apparently, than the strange school where practically no one spoke Spanish. The functional illiteracy may also have resulted from perceptual problems, such as those seen on the Bender-Gestalt drawings.
>
> Whether the poor test performance stemmed from prenatal or postnatal deficiencies, mild retardation, or lack of experience is difficult to say. Some of the difficulties may have arisen in the socioeconomic background, since not all Puerto Rican children have the same learning problems. With the continuing shortage of bilingual teachers and appropriate learning materials, one wonders whether these children will ever find a better life in the English-speaking community, however well they might be able to function in their native rural communities with limited intellectual ability and training. (Note: Because of the small N in this study, the comments should be regarded as suggestive rather than definitive.)

A case study of a single family also demonstrates many of the problems and characteristics we have been discussing. In the Mendoza family, with eight children, none of those in school were achieving at an average level in reading or mathematics, and all of those tested had low scores in intelligence. The mother is described as completely illiterate, with no understanding of the educational process or the concept of learning disabilities.

> There is a striking similarity in the school reports of all the children. . . . The girls are noted as being, "shy, withdrawn, in need of encouragement, unassertive, passive, lacking in energy, and lethargic." The boys' records are replete with "does not get along well with others, resents control, temper out-bursts, requires much attention, . . . evades responsibility, shy, withdrawn, does not participate, . . . indifferent, unmotivated." The boys allow themselves to act out their feelings. They become difficult for the teacher to manage. (Elam, 1969, p. 623)

Much of this description is typical for children of this group. Part of the problem is the apathy of the parents, caught up in poverty, limited in the larger society by their own language and vocational deficiencies, and unprepared for an industrial- rather than an agrarian-oriented environment. Another part of the problem is, of course, the belated and often inadequate efforts of the community to integrate these families into the mainstream of American life through adult-education and positive human-relations training programs. Parents must be taught somehow to view the school as a helping agency rather than a negative authority force.

Mexican Americans

Let us turn now to the Mexican-American population, who share the same language with the Puerto Ricans, to see if they, too, experience learning problems in American schools. In measurement of intelligence, the Mexican-American children also tend to come off poorly. For example, Carlson and Henderson compared American children of Mexican parentage with a similar group of non-Mexican parentage and found that the former had consistently lower mean IQ scores than the latter. (Carlson and Henderson, 1950) Knowing that the Mexican-American parents have themselves had little education and live a marginal existence economically, we can assume that their disadvantage is not a genetic one. Education to the age of 14 or 16 has been compulsory in all of the United States since 1918, so that the non-Mexican parents have had at least this in their favor as they raised their children, while the Mexican parents may or may not. Often, the Mexican families are migrant farm workers, so that their children's education is frequently interrupted.

A more recent study of three generations of Mexican Americans (Anderson and Johnson, 1971) is quite revealing of the effects of home background on the learner's concept of his ability and academic motivation and achievement. Among the survey findings are these points:

1. Spanish is the dominant language in the home, even among three-generation families, with obvious difficulty in mastering English.
2. Male adults in all three generations have a low educational level and therefore low socioeconomic level, although as use of English improves so does occupational level.
3. "Apparently, the home background of the child has a differential influence on the child's success in various areas of school work. Success in English appears to be highly dependent upon the general educational background of the father and the patterns of language usage at home. . . . success in mathematics appears to depend more directly upon the student's desire to do well in school." (Anderson and Johnson, 1971, p. 304)
4. Mexican-American high school students are strongly motivated, and pressured by parents, to complete high school and attend college.
5. A negative self-image and low teacher expectancy for success of Mexican-American students begins to develop as early as first grade.

However, in a study of truly bilingual (as opposed to those suffering from bifurcation) Mexican-American children in Albuquerque, New Mexico,

Keston and Jiminez (1954) found somewhat different results. The 50 subjects they studied were aged 9–10 to 9–11 years, closer to those in the Anastasi and Cordova study. The children were given the Stanford-Binet intelligence test in English (Form **M**) and Spanish (Form **L**). On the English form, the mean IQ was 86.0, with a range of 58–121; on the Spanish form, the mean IQ was 71.8, with a range of only 62–97. The correlation coefficient between the two versions was .36, whereas Forms **L** and **M** in English have a correlation coefficient of .93. (Keston and Jiminez, 1954, p. 264) The authors attributed the higher English test scores to several factors: the children had had no formal instruction in Spanish after school entrance, had a higher level of development in English than in Spanish, were accustomed to classroom instruction in English, and found the Spanish translation of the test a poor "fit" to the Spanish-American idiom. (Note: The Spanish WISC presents similar translation problems, since local idioms often supersede "common" terms in the children's language usage.) In any case, most of the children in the Keston-Jiminez sample had below average intellectual functioning as measured by either version.

Comment: The Supreme Court decision in *Lau* v. *Nichols* (1974), that San Francisco's failure to provide special language instruction for Chinese-speaking students was a violation of the 1964 Civil Rights Act, is expected to affect Spanish-speaking students as well. Under this ruling, children must be taught in a language they know so that they can understand what they are being taught. An obvious effect of this ruling will be an increasing need for competent bilingual teachers.

Such teachers need to feel comfortable in both English and the foreign language. They should also be "at home" with the cultural practices, attitudes, and values of the non-Anglo group with whom they will be working. Relatively few colleges of education have programs specifically designed to prepare bilingual teachers, but interested students can arrange experiences and courses that will contribute to their competence in this role.

A comparison of teacher behavior toward chicano (Mexican-American) and Anglo (non-Mexican) students in integrated classes shows that there are enough significant differences in behavior to affect the academic achievement of chicano students negatively. (Jackson and Cosca, 1974) For example, teachers gave Anglos 35 percent more praise and encouragement than they gave to chicanos, and asked them 21 percent more questions. (p. 228) There was also considerably less acceptance or use of chicano students' ideas.

There are two reasons to suspect that the actual average disparities in teachers' behaviors toward chicano and Anglo students are even greater than observed in this study. First, most teachers knew the classroom observer was from a federal civil rights agency, a factor which probably influenced many of the teachers to be particularly careful about how they related to their minority group pupils during the period of observation. Second, the sample excluded schools in districts with records of federal investigation or prosecution for civil rights violations; on the average, these schools probably have somewhat worse disparities in teacher behaviors than those visited. (Jackson and Cosca, 1974, p. 227)

For many teachers, such biased behavior is unconscious. If so, they need to be made aware of it and then taught how to overcome it.

The problems encountered by Mexican-American children in learning are somewhat different from those of the Puerto Rican children because so many of the former are part of the migrant labor population. These children not only face language barriers, but also frequently interrupted and inconsistent episodes in education. California and Florida, the two states where the migrant laborers work most often, have developed programs that integrate the children into the schools quickly and keep their learning materials consistent and sequential from school to school. This is intended to reduce the negative effects of their frequent moves from one community to another. ("Kaleidoscope," 1972)

Efforts to convert Mexican-American children from potential dropouts to actual learners have ranged from using the bicultural and bilingual characteristics of these children as an asset (as resource persons in social studies) instead of a liability (MacRea, 1955) to teaching English as a second language (TESL programs) under Title VII, Bilingual Education Act) of the Elementary and Secondary Education Act of 1965. Up to now, relatively few of the approximately five million Mexican Americans living in the Southwest have gone on to college. Those who have graduated from high school find or feel that they are inadequately prepared in study habits, have insufficient guidance for the future, and are caught in the midst of a culture conflict that leaves them isolated in the school and at least partially rejected by their families and peers. Psychologically torn, they are hardly in a position to become successful learners.

American Indians

The problems of the American Indian also reflect culture conflict that inhibits achievement. In many tribes, cooperation is stressed and competition virtually eliminated. The American school, on the other hand, tends to reverse these emphases in practice. Even if intraclass competition does not exist, each child is supposed to compete with himself—"to do his best." Since the Indian youngster has been taught at home that it is incorrect to compete or to stand out from others, he finds it difficult to resolve the conflict between tribe and school. The result is that frequently these children drop out of school and return to their people's way on the reservation. In addition, the Indian, like the other groups mentioned, lives in poverty and apart from the largely industrial and technological society that surrounds him. His childhood experiences are rarely part of the "white man's" curriculum, a factor that also contributes to his feeling of alienation in the school. The result that has been observed is that academic achievement starts to slide in the upper elementary grades. By the high school years, the Indian youth tends to drop out as a result of frustration and failure.

Why should this crossover pattern occur? Is it because Indians have less inherited intellectual potential than whites? Is it because the political unimportance of Indians makes success in traditional tribal values more important, even for the children, than success in the white man's schools? Or is it, perhaps, a tribal value that dictates certain behaviors? Among the Dakota Indians, for example, according to Klineberg,

> . . . it is considered bad form to answer a question in the presence of someone else who does not know the answer. This creates a particularly difficult situation in school, where teachers find it difficult to induce children to recite in class. In the same group, custom forbids one to answer a question unless he is absolutely sure of the answer. The effect this would have upon intelligence tests, in which the subject is advised to "guess" when not sure and is urged to "try his best" on a difficult problem, can be readily foreseen. The child who refuses to give any answer unless he is certain of its correctness will lose many points that he might have earned through partial credits and chance successes. (Anastasi and Foley, 1958, p. 331)

Among the Plains Indians of western Oklahoma, adolescents face the tortured conflict of accepting the "white man's ways" and rejecting their native heritage or of rejecting what the schools have to offer and continuing to be powerless in American society. (Allen, 1973) With this dilemma, on top of the usual adolescent crises, it is no surprise that poor achievement, a high dropout rate, and emotional disorders are seen so often.

Question   *In what ways might the culture conflict be resolved and the resulting poor academic pattern be changed?*

A study of teenage urban Chippewa Indians in the Minneapolis area revealed that they had a strong interest in learning more about Indian history, culture, and language. (Harkins and Woods, 1969) Since this group resides in an urban area, its achievements, orientation, and goals differ somewhat from those of Indians living on reservations in the Midwest and Southwest. Nevertheless, the study pointed up the need for more native Indian teachers in both types of environment. One example of an effort to fill this need, although it doesn't supply native Indian teachers, is the program at Northern Arizona University where special courses and field work are offered in the education curriculum for prospective teachers of Indians. In another program, parent seminars and parent participation in all areas of schoolwork, in a Title VIII Dropout Prevention Program, helped to reduce the dropout rate from 30 percent to 15 percent over a four-year period among the Oglala Sioux. (Woodward, 1973)

Here again, however, the children suffer because of gaps in culture, economic orientation, language, and motivation between the tribes and the surrounding society. Not only must the opportunity to become educated exist, but also psychological changes need to occur within the tribes and on the part of educators. As appears to be true with other minority groups, there is a need to integrate school learning with subcultural experiences to achieve meaningful progress. We also need to ask the question of the extent to which it is desirable to "Americanize" the Indians. Will this help them to become more effective human beings?

Another highly visible minority group consists of Asian Americans, predominantly those of Chinese and Japanese ancestry. Much of the social structure and many of the mores and values of these groups are generally believed to be alien to their American counterparts. Yet both groups are seen as exhibiting industriousness and ambition for self-improvement, two characteristics held in high esteem by the American middle class. There is a low incidence of school dropouts and juvenile delinquency in both groups, contrary to what is seen in the subcultures already surveyed.

Asian Americans

In what ways will this child's ancestry affect her as a learner?

Studies of the Issei (Japanese-born Americans) and Nisei (first American-born generation) reveal that by 1947, despite wartime relocation from 1942–45, Japanese Americans could be counted among those highly motivated to achievement. The Issei had a median level of ten years of education, and the Nisei had a median level beyond high school graduation (Caudill and De Vos, 1956, pp. 1103–1104) In fact, it has been found that the occupational and educational attainment of the Issei is reflected in the achievements of second and third generation Japanese Americans. Members of this ethnic group were, and are, upwardly mobile. (Levine and Montero, 1973) Japanese Americans have long been oriented toward careers, small business ownership, and white-collar jobs, all of which require a certain amount of educational achievement and persistence of effort toward long-range goals. Caudill and De Vos found a "significant compatibility" which ". . . gives rise to a similarity in the psychological adaptive mechanisms which are most commonly used by individuals . . ." in Japanese-American and American middle-class society as these people go about the business of living. (p. 1107)

Self-motivation, for example, as measured by projective tests, was high for both Japanese-American and American middle-class groups, and we know that this is a trait highly desirable for learning and achievement. Although there are differences between Chinese and Japanese cultures, there are similarities in the values and learning behaviors of these two groups as well. As seen in the Lesser, Fifer, and Clark study (earlier in this chapter), the Chinese, too, tend to be learners and achievers.

Much of this positive picture for Chinese and Japanese students stems from their cultural groups' attitude toward education. All is not rosy, however. The texts they use in school tend to ignore their existence as a culture. David Sue (1974) recalled

> . . . searching through social science textbooks for any mention of the Chinese. At the most, the texts referred to coolies building railroads or to Chinatown in San Francisco. The people in my books behaved differently than my parents. They ate different foods and wore different clothes. There was very little that I could identify with. (p. 84)

For other Asian Americans—Koreans, Vietnamese, Indians, Filipinos, Malaysians, Thais—there is even less in texts or the curriculum with which to identify. Frequently, there is also a language barrier and perhaps isolation from the general community because there are fewer members of these national groups living in the Western Hemisphere. There are also fewer people in the schools prepared to understand the cultural values that distinguish these Asian Americans from the Chinese, Japanese, and American values. As is true for other groups discussed, such a situation can create negative self-images, culture conflict, and poor academic performance. Further, the problem of finding bilingual teachers and appropriate teaching materials is more difficult for these groups because there are comparatively so few of their nationals prepared to tutor or teach.

Jewish Americans

In looking at our last minority group, the Jewish Americans, we find them generally less "visible" and "different" from Americans as a whole, and more strongly motivated to achievement than most of the other groups discussed. The immigrant generation saw education as the means to a better life and urged their their children to read and learn as much as possible. In this, they resemble the Issei, but they did not attain for themselves the high level of education of the Issei. They did, however, fill adult-education classes in order to learn English and had a well-developed and literate society of their own. The first American-born generation tended to remain in school through high school graduation and then urged their children to attend and graduate from college. The traditional Jewish emphasis on learning, and respect for the scholar, provides an environment conducive to intellectual achievement. The results are seen in the high proportion of college students and graduates, scholarship winners, and recognized contributors to different professions.

Datta (1967), for example, studied the relationship between family religious affiliation and potential scientific creativity and found that on projects submitted to the Westinghouse Science Talent Search ". . . ratings of projects submitted by students from Jewish families were higher than were the ratings of projects submitted from Catholic, 'liberal' Protestant, and 'fundamentalist' Protestant backgrounds." (p. 626) The only statistically reliable relationship for this finding, however, is for subjects from communities of 500,000 *and under* populations, and *non*-upper-class environments. These are not the areas in which one would expect to find sufficient opportunities for the potential scientist to discover and explore his interests. Datta attributed some of the disproportion in scientific creativity to the subcultural emphasis on achievement of learning, which may be intensified in the less assimilated groups present in smaller communities. (p. 632) That is, pressures for success as learners may be strengthened as a defensive measure by parents in socially constricted circumstances.

For Jewish students, like some of those already mentioned, the curriculum provides little opportunity for identification. Some texts mention Haym Salomon (financier of the American Revolution), or the Jews' arrival during the great immigration period of 1890–1920 or before and after the second World War as refugees. Some attempts to integrate their beliefs into social science courses are seen, mostly where there are many Jewish residents, but, in general, education contributes to their alienation from their families and/or from the larger society.

Summary

In summarizing this section on ethnic influences on learning, we might consider several possibilities for positive change. Perhaps we should evaluate the efforts of compensatory education programs on the basis of growth in basic skills rather than IQ score changes. Or, perhaps, it might be more appropriate to change children's attitudes in our drive to reduce the negative effects of cultural differences. Gross states this point of view quite well when he shifts the focus of concern ". . . from lack of opportunity to lack of drive and appetite for intellectual stimulation. . . . If an individual is driven to educational attainment, he will overcome economic handicaps or massive physical and environmental obstacles. The heart of educational deprivation may be lack of internal need or drive, not insufficient opportunity." (Gross, 1969, p. 46) That is, it should not be the ethnic label that is important, but the individual himself.

A third possibility is to eliminate the choice that so many minority group children face when they enter the classroom. "Either they must betray family and heritage or they must settle for socioeconomic failure. How students respond to this crucial set of alternatives is . . . the most significant determinant of school performance, far outweighing such other variables as innate ability, linguistic background and pre-school environment." (Banks, 1973, p. 15)

Whatever the viewpoint of factors underlying learning, there are certain facts that must be faced. As our society grows increasingly demanding in terms of knowledge and skills, curriculum is being altered with more advanced material being taught at lower levels in schools than ever before. At the same time, we have become more aware of diverse elements in our society that are inadequately prepared to meet such a challenge. Even bright students frequently complain that too much new material is being taught too quickly with no time for them to absorb and integrate it into their fund of knowledge.

What can be done to minimize the effects of a head-on clash of these facts? Educational psychologists believe that elements of success for the learner must be built into the educational process. This can be accomplished by using current experiences to illustrate many concepts; by adapting text materials to the background, needs, interests, and achievement levels of the learners; by designing learning units which are relatively short with achievable goals; by correlating subject areas to increase meaningfulness and integration of knowledge; and by setting and maintaining realistic standards. For some of the culturally different, emphasis should be placed on orienting instruction to vocational goals, and on oral communication, although the ability to read directions is a necessity in almost any job. For these students and others as well, learning may be enhanced if they are seen as individuals rather than as group members or "numbers."

PEER GROUP INFLUENCES

Children tend to function socially within groups and to choose to belong to groups that have as members their peers who are compatible in a number of ways: age, sex, ethnic background, interests, abilities, and so on. The functions of a group are determined largely by the needs of its most dominant members. At the same time, the needs of the members are partly shaped by the characteristics of the group. One of the primary motives in a child's life, after all, is the desire to belong, to be accepted, to achieve eventually some degree of prestige and recognition in his relationships with others. His expectations or attitudes regarding his acceptance by others are related to his experiences with adults in early childhood, as we have already discussed, and with peers in middle childhood and adolescence. Security in the family relationship, approval by teachers, and acceptance by peers are all important factors in determining his self-image and long-range goals. Oversocialization, on the other hand, or an emphasis on adjustment to the group rather than combining the search for self-identity with the need for acceptance, can reduce the freedom of the individual, stifle his initiative, and stunt his productive growth. Since we are primarily concerned here with the interaction between peer-group pressures and the individual as a learner, it is appropriate to question the possible effects of such oversocialization on the educational aspirations of the individual.

Does adjustment to the group conflict with self-actualization?

For example, in a coeducational school, it is generally believed that a girl who wants to be accepted by her male peers should not exhibit her intellectual superiority—at least not in the classroom. (Out-of-school tutoring is apparently all right, since there is less "loss of face" by the boys.) If she desires group membership more than self-actualization, we can say that her learning is affected adversely to some extent. This situation may be equally true for a bright, academically-oriented boy in an athletically-oriented student population. While such predicaments arise beginning in the middle grades, they seem to become more important in the middle and later adolescent years when post-high school planning occurs. We will, therefore, focus on peer influences on the adolescent learner (or nonlearner).

We have all read of youth from slum neighborhoods who have achieved at a high level in some socially acceptable activity. They move from potential delinquency to championships or fame, despite the negative factors of race, socioeconomic level, and delinquent peers, and because of the intervening influence of helpful adults. Are they exceptions or examples? It is apparently more common for working-class youth with college aspirations to have had more contact with the middle class, including perhaps attendance at a dominantly middle-class high school. In a study of almost 400 working-class high school seniors, Krauss (1964) found that ". . . working-class students whose acquaintances plan to go to college are more likely to plan to go themselves." (p. 874) They were also more likely to have older siblings who had attended college and to have participated themselves in high school extracurricular activities. The upward strivings of these youths therefore began before they became involved with college-bound middle-class peers, but such strivings were positively reinforced by those associations.

Is the parental influence stronger for lower-class students than peer influence? On the basis of a study of 2337 lower-class urban and rural youths in the eastern part of the United States, we would have to say it is. Kandel and Lesser (1969) investigated triads consisting of a lower-class adolescent, his mother, and his best school friend and found that when the mother had college aspirations for her son and his best friend planned to stop formal education with high school graduation, the boy, in 49 percent of the cases, tended to have college aspirations. (pp. 216–17) On the other hand, if the mother had no such hopes for her son, only 21 percent planned to continue, even if the best friend intended to attend college. "That friends have influence beyond that of the mother is shown by the increase in college plans (to 83 percent) when both mother and best-school-friend have college plans." (p. 217) This is, of course, a "within-school" peer influence situation and may reflect the middle-class atmosphere mentioned earlier.

Question *As you look back on your own high school years, can you see any relationship between your aspirations and those of your friends?*

Does the neighborhood in which a youngster lives have a similar influence on his or her educational aspirations? That is, does the "street-corner gang" or the social clique push or pull the individual in a particular direction? Let's look first at the distribution of students with college plans from different types of neighborhood *and* with differing levels of intelligence.

You can see in Table 3.5 that as neighborhood status increases, for all the males and for the bright females, so does the percentage of seniors having plans to attend college. This is true also for all groups as intelligence increases. There are marked differences evident in college aspirations by sex, too, at all levels of neighborhood status and intelligence. However, when these differences and family socioeconomic status were controlled statistically, it was found that differences in neighborhood contributed very little to the differences observed. Sewell and Armer (1966) therefore concluded that ". . . past claims for the importance of neighborhood context in the development of educational aspirations may have been overstated." (p. 159)

Percentage with college plans by neighborhood status and intelligence, for male and female Milwaukee high school seniors* Table 3.5

Neighborhood status**	Intelligence			
	Low	Middle	High	Total
Males				
Low	15.9(195)	31.4(207)	52.5(122)	30.5(524)
Middle	24.5(212)	35.6(191)	55.3(255)	39.7(658)
High	37.6(109)	57.7(222)	77.6(241)	62.2(572)
Total	24.0(516)	42.1(620)	63.4(618)	44.3(1754)
Females				
Low	8.8(328)	26.6(256)	34.0(159)	20.3(743)
Middle	8.1(347)	21.7(240)	39.0(246)	21.1(833)
High	29.8(188)	55.5(245)	69.5(236)	53.2(669)
Total	13.1(863)	34.6(741)	49.0(641)	30.4(2245)

*Sewell, W. H., & Armer, J. M. Neighborhood context and college plans. *American Sociological Review*, 1966, 31, p. 165—Table 4. Copyright 1966 by the American Psychological Association. Reprinted by permission.

**Socioeconomic.

Reanalyses of the Sewell and Armer data (Spady, 1970; Smith, 1972) suggest that there may be a greater peer effect than Sewell and Armer found. Some of the differences in results have been explained as being related to the nature of the student body in the high school attended—lower-, middle-, or upper-class. The use of other statistical techniques also affected the later findings. An analysis of more than 25 studies dealing with peer influence, by Bain and Anderson (1974), suggests that educational goals depend on an interaction between the social-class composition of the high school and peer influence. (Note: The results obtained will vary to some extent with the number of high schools available in the community studied and any school desegregation programs in operation.)

However, if neighborhood peers have questionable amounts of influence on post-high school plans, who else might provide the motivation for academic aspirations? In a study at Stanford University of lower-class youth already enrolled, Ellis and Lane (1963) concluded that the mother was the primary influence for upward mobility, supported by one or more high school teachers. Also, as in the Krauss study mentioned earlier, it was found that lower- and lower-middle-class students in this sample formed close peer-group ties with the middle class while in high school. The upward mobility of this group of youth, then, ". . . is linked to a distinctive pattern of maternal authority within the nuclear family and to dependence upon the outside social structure for support." (Ellis and Lane, 1963, p. 743) McDill and Coleman (1963) came to a similar conclusion after analyzing data from students in six midwestern high schools, but added that ". . . college plans apparently derive from parent or peer socialization for those in the leading crowd but more often derive from an interest in the scholastic content of college for those outside the leading crowd." (p. 915)

It seems appropriate, then, to describe the role of the peer group as supportive with respect to educational aspirations. If there is already parental influence toward achievement at home, perhaps reinforced by teachers, the best the peer group can do is to support the learner in his plans. In the 1970s, peer pressure to "do your own thing" has also tended to help some wavering youths decide to move to less traditional studies, delay college entrance, or ignore parental goals altogether.

EFFECTS OF TV WATCHING

An environmental influence on the learner that is of relatively recent concern is television. Children born since 1945 have adopted it as part of their lives. Its "power" has been evident in the quick responses that follow the broadcast of student strikes, assassinations, revolutions, and other critical incidents.

Today, TV sets are found in homes of all socioeconomic levels, in all types of communities, virtually all over the world. Often, the TV set serves as an unpaid babysitter-entertainer for preschoolers while their parents are busy elsewhere in the home. Estimates of up to 50 hours per week of TV watching have been given for preschoolers. (Morrisett, 1973, p. 4) Even school-age children spend a large portion of their free time watching television.

What do they watch? Cartoons, quiz shows, commercials, reruns of old programs, and occasionally something "educational." What do they learn? It is alleged that children learn techniques and acceptance of violence. (Liebert, Neale, and Davidson, 1973) Certainly they are exposed to a great deal of violence in programs for which they are the principal audience. Research evidence is unclear as to the long-term effects of this exposure on behavior. Secondly, despite protests by women's liberation groups, they learn traditional sex-role stereotypes. (Sternglanz and Serbin, 1974; Frueh and McGhee, 1975) Few of the situation comedy programs offer psychologically healthy portraits of either males or females. And few programs show either sex in nonstereotyped occupations.

Occasionally, children learn constructively from television. *Sesame Street* was directed toward facilitating social and academic learning of inner-city preschoolers. Its brief segments, animation, humor, and repetition attracted millions of young viewers and taught them numbers, letters, English and foreign language vocabulary, social values, music, and humor. (Lesser, 1974) Psychological knowledge of early childhood development was applied profitably to this educational effort. The popularity and success of the program in the English version led to translated versions in Spanish and to modified versions in other languages around the world. It also led to the development of a more advanced program, *The Electric Company*, with a format similar to *Sesame Street*, but aimed at the young school-age child.

Effective teachers of the preschoolers.

News-type programs for young children have been introduced in late afternoon and Saturday morning programming. Using the example of *Sesame Street*, the segments are short, to the point, and interesting. They may touch on human interest stories, or explain current headlines so that an elementary school child gains some understanding of political, economic, religious, or social events. Television "specials," such as those filmed on Jacques Cousteau's expeditions or *National Geographic* field studies, are also directed in part to broadening the information experiences available to children. These programs have an adventurous quality that appeals to youngsters and frequently feature animals, which are also attractive to them. During the "space race" of the 1960s and 1970s, children learned a great deal about the work of the astronauts, outer space, mathematics and physics, and the vocabulary unique to space exploration. Much of the interest aroused by watching rocket flights was carried over to the classroom.

There is concern, of course, that children will watch television when they should be studying school work. There is concern that children will become too much the passive spectators instead of active participants. And there is dismay that children read less as they watch more, with negative effects on their potential as learners. Whether these anxieties of parents and educators are valid or not remains to be seen.

SUMMARY

In this chapter, we have explored the environment of the learner, moving from place in the family to place in the community. Within the family, there is abundant evidence suggesting that there is something "special" about the oldest child in a general sample of achievers, but that it is difficult to predict the influence of birth order in specific families. More important, perhaps, are the parental attitudes toward the child himself, toward education, and toward achievement in general. Again we have been impressed with the importance of adult-child interaction in the first six years of childhood. This can even outweigh peer-group influence in the adolescent years with reference to the individual's goals as a learner.

An examination of social-class differences indicates that there is a significant and positive relationship between social-class status and achievement. It is not the student's socioeconomic status, *per se*, that determines his intellectual functioning, but rather the self-image and the perception of him by others, such as teachers, as a member of that social class which seems to affect his performance. In measuring that performance, we have become increasingly aware that the measuring instruments known as intelligence tests have a strong middle-class bias and verbal emphasis that are inappropriate for children from lower-class backgrounds.

Social-class differences are often closely related to ethnic group membership as well. The pressures within minority groups for becoming a learner vary considerably. In many cases, the pressure is toward becoming a wage-earner as early as possible, because of the poverty extant in the family. In other instances, the problem is more psychological and cultural, particularly where a different heritage exists from the one dominant in the society. The effect of culture conflict was discussed in relation to black Americans, Puerto Ricans, Mexican Americans, and other minority groups. Language barriers in many cases not only inhibit but totally prevent learning in white, middle-class oriented schools. On the positive side, we discussed the achievement patterns of Asian-American and Jewish-American learners, which are generally above the national average.

Peer influence on the learner was presented with special reference to the educational aims of the adolescent. The conflicting results obtained in several studies led to the conclusion that peer influence interacts with other environmental factors in affecting these goals.

Finally, the role of television was discussed. The negative aspects of watching TV include poor program content and the excessive amount of time that children spend in viewing. On the positive side, several educational benefits were noted.

Throughout the chapter, as appropriate, constructive alternatives to negative environmental practices were offered. Preventive intervention efforts were seen as more desirable than emergency remedial projects.

Preview

INTRODUCTION

THE SELF-CONCEPT
    AGES AND STAGES
    SELF-ESTEEM
    SELF-CONCEPT AND ACHIEVEMENT
    ACQUISITION OF VALUES

MOTIVATION
    COMPETING MOTIVES
    INTRINSIC V. EXTRINSIC MOTIVATION
    ACHIEVEMENT MOTIVATION
    GRADES AND MOTIVATION
    SUMMARY

ANXIETY
    SOURCES OF ANXIETY
    ANXIETY AND ACHIEVEMENT
    ANXIETY AND SELF-CONCEPT

ACHIEVERS

UNDERACHIEVERS
    VARIABLE CRITERIA
    PERSONALITY TRAITS
    IDENTIFICATION
    REMEDIATION

SUMMARY

4

Psychological Factors and the Learner

INTRODUCTION

We come now to a look at the individual as a whole. He is a product of his genetic potential interacting with the forces in his environment, and develops a self-concept as a result of this interaction. What does this view of himself have to do with the openness to new experience that maximizes learning? How much of himself is he willing to invest in learning? To what extent is his behavior consistent or inconsistent with his self-concept? And, if inconsistency is the case, to what extent do the resulting anxiety and defenses against anxiety inhibit his tendencies toward achievement and fulfillment?

To answer these questions, we will now discuss three major psychological factors operating within the individual: self-concept, motivation, and anxiety. These are not the only psychological forces determining the individual's behavior, but they do have a strong effect on his learning. This will be clearly seen in the section on achieving and underachieving students at the end of the chapter.

THE SELF-CONCEPT

What is a *self-concept* and how does it develop? Without splitting hairs among psychological theories, a self-concept is the view of the self as the individual perceives his or her behavior, thoughts, and effect on others. It is not the ideal image of himself as he hopes to be or would prefer to be, but as he *is*, now. The self-concept arises from experiences in early childhood where the behavior of adults and older children in the environment first give the baby clues as to whether or not he is an acceptable and desirable human being. Through repeated exposures to the attitudes of others, he gradually develops a sense of personal worth or lack of it. The reactions of other people to his attempts to master developmental tasks and later on his self-evaluation of the results of such attempts contribute to his perception of himself as a success or failure.

To develop a healthy view of oneself, one requires parental love and acceptance, particularly in the early years, success experiences, and the opportunity to try out one's growing abilities. As organism and environment continue to interact, the self emerges and begins to evolve personal values and aspirations. One of the principal tasks of middle childhood, for example, is "To become an autonomous person, able to make plans and to act in the present and immediate future independently of one's parents and other adults." (Havighurst, 1952, p. 25) If the preadolescent child is to perceive himself as successful in meeting this task, he must be allowed to make increasingly complex decisions for himself and to have opportunities to make his own mistakes (within reasonable limits, of course). This is a function of home, school, and peer group. As the individual moves into adolescence, the task recurs at a more advanced level where he must become more independent of adults, but at the same time be able to maintain affection and respect for them. (Havighurst, 1952, p. 42)

Ages and stages

Erikson has written of these tasks in somewhat different terms, in which one can readily see how resolving conflicts in the stages of development contributes to the growth of a self-concept. There are five preadult stages which offer potential sources of conflict and choice for the youngster. They are:

1. *Development of trust v. sense of mistrust (birth to 1½–2 years).* In a nonverbal way, the infant begins to perceive his relationship with his parents as one in which they are dependable or not. If they are seen as dependable, the infant has a sense of being worthy of their attention. If not, then he may feel that people are untrustworthy, and that this is related to some deficit or lack of desirability in himself.

2. *Sense of autonomy v. shame and doubt (ages 2–4 years).* This is the age of growing mobility, independence, and language acquisition. The toddler/preschooler should be able to assert himself and to do some things for himself, or he develops feelings of shame and self-doubt because of the inadequacies he senses.

3. *Sense of initiative v. sense of guilt (4–7 years).* Curiosity and independence of action are normal behaviors at this age. Reproofs and punishment for these behaviors lead to a sense of guilt for having asked questions or acted without parental permission and guidance.

4. *Sense of industry v. inferiority (7–11 or 12 years).* The fourth stage, also referred to as the latency stage by psychoanalytic writers, occurs during middle childhood. According to Erikson, this is the time when the individual develops a sense of competence as a result of his efforts in learning, or a sense of inferiority in comparison with his peers and their capabilities and skills.

5. *Sense of identity v. identity diffusion (adolescence).* The adolescent is very concerned with determining "who" he is, and pulls together the self-concepts he has developed in the previous stages. The in-

ability to integrate his experiences and roles results in identity diffusion, or lack of a coherent self-concept. (Erikson, 1950)

A successful resolution of each stage will enable the individual to develop his self-identity better in the next stage. Again, this is an area where home, school, and peer group can contribute to a positive outcome. Every child can do something successfully and needs to have this recognized. The child in the lowest reading group may have the gift of making people about him feel better by a cheerful manner; the poor athlete may have artistic or musical talent; the nonscientific youngster may be particularly cooperative or diligent as a worker. Since we need all types of people in our society, who is to brand one as inferior and the other as a success? Rather, it should be pointed out that these different abilities are complementary, thus giving each youngster an opportunity to have a positive self-concept and to find self-fulfillment.

Growth and development do not cease with adolescence. The individual must continue to grow if he is to resolve the psychosocial crises of adulthood that Erikson has also discussed.

6. *Intimacy v. isolation.* The (young) adult must decide whether she or he can live happily with another person, sharing functions and values (even when there is some disagreement), or whether she or he is unable to do so. If the latter, the person becomes personally and socially isolated.

7. *Generativity v. stagnation.* If the young adult has opted for intimacy, there is a further choice to be made: Should growth continue through parenthood, with its implications for helping another generation to develop and grow? In a way, this is the person's opportunity to affect his society. The individual who chooses to be creative in this way, and finds fulfillment, is better prepared to face the final stage of old age.

8. *Integrity v. despair.* The individual who can look back on his life with satisfaction at having had productive years, at having been an emerging person throughout, can face death with greater integrity. His positive self-concept at this stage helps him to recognize the worth of his having lived. (Erikson, 1950)

Self-esteem

Related to this attempt to find a positive basis for the self-concept is Coopersmith's (1967) view of self-esteem as being the result of four factors: competence, significance to others, virtue ("doing the right thing"), and power. "Significance to others" in particular develops throughout the first six years of childhood and has great importance to the self-concept. The child who perceives himself as unworthy, insignificant, and/or unacceptable in the eyes of others, as a result of parental statements or actions, is unlikely to develop the measure of positive self-concept or self-esteem that will contribute to his functioning as a learner. Coopersmith believes that individuals who view themselves in terms of one or more of these negative factors may thereby create some of their own difficulties.

It may be, for example, that an individual may employ a basis in which he is markedly deficient—for example, he may be woefully incompetent—instead of employing a basis in which he is indeed worthy—such as his significance to others. Another individual may employ two bases that are mutually incompatible, thereby leading him to believe that he has failed to live up to one of them. (Coopersmith, 1967, pp. 262–63)

For many school-age children and adolescents, this sense of personal worth or positive self-concept is derived from opinions of them held by their peers and teachers. This has been found to be more true for children of average ability in fifth and sixth grades, for example, than for those in the same grades with superior ability. (Sears, 1963) The superior children in this study had self-concepts related to their sense of competence; the average children were much more dependent on interpersonal acceptance. This finding is highly relevant to our concerns with teacher-pupil relationships and "classroom climate," which we will discuss later in chapter thirteen.

In another study of fifth- and sixth-graders (Zirkel and Moses, 1971), it was found that ethnic group membership had a significant effect on individual self-concepts. The subjects were black, Puerto Rican, and white. The mean IQ in each group was at the low-average level (90.65–93.73). The test used to measure self-concept was Coopersmith's Self Esteem Inventory (CSEI). Although the authors suggest that their results need to be interpreted with caution, they did find that the self-concept of black children was similar to that of the white children. Puerto Rican children had a significantly lower self-concept than either of the other groups.

Question On which of Coopersmith's factors might the Puerto Rican children have felt deficient?

The Coopersmith scale (CSEI) was also used by Trowbridge (1972) in her study of self-concept and socioeconomic status. Her subjects were third- to eighth-graders. Those in the lower class scored significantly higher on the CSEI than the middle-class children. One reason for this, according to the children's teachers, was that the lower-class children had a lower level of aspiration and were therefore more easily satisfied with their school performance. Thus, they had feelings of competence. Secondly, these children did not tend to blame themselves for poor school experience as the middle-class children did. (Trowbridge, 1972, pp. 533–4) The development of a sense of industry and feelings of competence was apparently not proceeding positively with the second group of children.

Note: For further information on the CSEI and other measures of the self-concept, you are referred to Wylie (1974). In general, there is some question as to the validity of self-evaluation or self-descriptive scales. Children, especially, may tend to exaggerate their performance, positively or negatively. It is wiser to be cautious in interpreting the results of various studies that use such scales as a variable in their investigations.

Self-concept scales may ask the child to rate himself on various characteristics, for example, friendly, cheerful, lazy, studious, jealous, on the basis of "Yes, ?, No," or in terms of frequency (never, sometimes, always), or on a 1–5 scale as being least or most typical of himself. Sometimes the self-perception is fairly accurate, and at other times the individual may either deliberately or inadvertently misperceive his own characteristics. We do not, after all, find it easy to recognize or admit our own shortcomings. What we may negatively view as stubbornness in others, for instance, we may call persistence in ourselves. Furthermore, as Minuchin, Biber, Shapiro, and Zimiles (1969) point out, "The child's relationship to himself and his communication about himself are not necessarily the same thing. What he knows, thinks, and feels about himself is different from what he tells about himself, to an unknown degree. . . ." (Minuchin, et al., p. 290) Although many children tend to overevaluate some of their personality traits in order to make a better impression, there are others who underevaluate their qualities because they really feel unlikeable, incompetent, or otherwise "unworthy." Even gifted children sometimes underestimate their potential. Minority groups and otherwise disadvantaged children frequently make little or no effort to learn because of their negative self-concept and the belief that they can never achieve anything no matter how hard they try. (Their resolution of Erikson's fourth stage is clearly on the side of inferiority.) All of these possibilities pose a methodological problem that must be kept in mind when one is doing or reading research.

Self-concept and achievement

Exercising these cautions, let us look at some of the work being done in which self-concept is a central variable. Several investigators have attempted to discover some relationship between measures of self-concept and academic achievement or other factors. One of the more extensive studies is the project undertaken by Bledsoe and Garrison (1962). They gave a large battery of tests to 125 fourth-graders (65 boys and 60 girls) and 146 sixth-graders (76 boys and 70 girls), including language and nonlanguage intelligence tests, six achievement tests, an interest test, and the children's form of the Manifest Anxiety Scale. Although many of the correlation coefficients were statistically significant, the strongest relationship, .525, was found between the self-concept and English achievement level of fourth-grade boys. (This is not considered a really high correlation.) All of the correlations between self-concept and anxiety test scores were negative, as you might expect. Those who have a stronger self-concept have fewer feelings of inferiority or incompetence, which cause anxiety. Some of the differences in self-concept scores were attributed to the additional experiences which the sixth-graders had, leading to more independence and a lowered variety of interests. Other findings apparently reflected cultural differences between boys and girls, which we have previously discussed. In commenting on the development of an adequate self-concept, Bledsoe and Garrison suggested several factors that might interfere with the normal sequence of development:

1. teachers failing to recognize individuality
2. emphasis on objectivity in the classroom
3. possibly too many women teachers for the boys (who had significantly lower mean scores on the self-concept scale than the girls at each grade level), and
4. lack of acceptance at home or by teachers.

Whether these factors are also related to the slightly lower mean grade-level scores on achievement tests for the boys is not stated, but this result was obtained quite possibly because of alleged teacher bias in favor of girls, documented elsewhere.

Focus 4–1

> In another comprehensive study, Minuchin, *et al.* (1969), worked with fourth-grade children also, but these were in modern or progressive and traditional schools in New York City. Despite their caution about interpreting data from the self-concept material, they believed that the data represented an intrinsically interesting mixture of "inner reality and self-presentation." Again, sex differences were apparent. "The boys presented themselves more positively in the three spheres of work competence, sex role, and peer popularity.... In graphic presentation, however, girls projected the more confident and satisfied image." (Minuchin, *et al.*, 1969, p. 294) Although the home had primary influence on the children's perception of people and their view of their own social sex roles, the authors pointed out that schools also affect children's personality development, of which self-concept is a part, intentionally or not. They stressed the strong implication of this finding for further exploration of the relationship between educational approach and personality development. (pp. 400–401)

A similar acknowledgment of the importance of student self-perception in relation to learning and achievement is made by Yamamoto, Thomas, and Karns (1969). They studied the attitudes toward school courses and personnel of 800 children in grades six through nine. They concluded that,

> Wherever their origins may be, students' perceptions should not be ignored by curriculum planners since the meaningfulness and, hence, the motivation for learning will largely depend upon the psychological significance and interest each subject matter holds in students' minds at various levels of school life. Such inside-out view of school personnel and curriculum would add much to the traditional outside-in observations used in defense of either the *status quo* or any of the numerous proposed innovations.... No unilateral reshuffling of school organization and programs will be effective unless students' perceptions, which precede and accompany any desired behavior changes, are taken into consideration. (pp. 204–5)

Does this apparent correlation of self-perception and achievement continue in adolescence? Jones and Strowig (1966), following the lead of several other researchers, assumed that their adolescent subjects would reflect their self-concepts accurately. The subjects were 150 girls and 167 boys, all seniors in a rural Wisconsin high school. They were asked about their self-concepts and self-expectations. These test scores were then correlated with achievement test scores. The investigators found that "Adolescent identity, student self-concept, and self-expectations appeared to be positively related to scholastic achievement, although they are not equally effective predictors of achievement." (Jones and Strowig, 1966, pp. 62, 81) This is consistent with the positive correlation between self-concept and achievement test scores reported by Bledsoe and Garrison. Jones and Strowig also stress the importance of educators and counselors attending "... more directly and discriminatingly to the self-perceptions of boys and girls in high school. Perhaps it is in the realm of such non-intellectual variables that one's insights into the nature of other persons must become most meaningful for decision-making and accomplishment." (p. 81)

Focus 4–2

Many things contribute to the self-concept, as you are now aware. One event occurs virtually at birth and has persisting effects—acquiring a name.
What's in a name?
In a study with 80 female elementary school teachers (Md age = 30, $\bar{X}$ years of experience = 10) and 80 female freshman and sophomore psychology students (Md age = 20), 8 essays were evaluated. The essays were supposedly written by 10-year-olds, identified only by first name (Karen, Lisa, David, Michael, Bertha, Adelle, Elmer, and Hubert). The essays identified with the first four names were all ranked positively, while those identified with the last four names were ranked negatively. The effects of stereotyping were more apparent for the teachers than for the undergraduate students. (Harari and McDavid, 1973)

Questions

What self-concepts or stereotypes might go with the names Grace, Morris, Beulah, Todd, John, Leslie? How do you feel about your name? In what ways has your name affected your self-concept? Your behavior as a learner?

What all of these investigators are saying is that, in the light of the observed relationship between self-concept and achievement or learning, it is imperative that educational personnel take this relationship into consideration in their planning. If a negative self-concept detracts from learning, then measures must be taken to improve the learner's self-concept. This implies the use of positive reinforcement techniques, more individualized classroom assignments, and more realistic curriculum planning.

In the studies reported so far, the subjects were generally representative of the majority white population, some rural, some urban, and from different socioeconomic levels. The next logical question to raise would concern the validity of the cited findings for culturally different children. Caplin (1969) studied 180 children, matched for grade, sex, intelligence, and socioeconomic status, in the intermediate grades of three northern New Jersey urban schools. There were 30 white and 30 black children from each school. The base group was from a long-integrated school. The other two groups were from a *de facto* segregated school and a newly desegregated school. Caplin found, as did the other investigators, that the children with more positive self-concepts had higher academic achievement, although ". . . apparently school-related traits are more intimately related to academic achievement than are the generalized personal/social feelings about the self." (Caplin, 1969, p. 15) As might be expected, children in the segregated school had lower self-concepts on school-related traits than did children in other schools. He found no significant difference in self-concept between the sexes, but did report a significantly lower self-concept for the black children. (Note: This racial difference has not been found in all studies.)

All of this emphasis on the importance of the school's role in relation to the developing self-concept does not negate the parental role in the preschool and school years. It is an interesting phenomenon, however, that the teacher in the primary grades replaces the mother for several hours a day, and is looked upon by the young schoolchild as an even higher "authority" than mother. Somehow parents can say to a child that she's "stupid" (once or twice) and not necessarily damage her self-concept for life, although this isn't recommended. If a teacher says the same thing in the same tone, it has a ring of truth and finality which peals on in the child's mind throughout the school years. It is not helpful to the child to tell her she's a success, either, if she is not. On the other hand, neither should one brand her as a failure in general.

Helping a child to develop and maintain a positive self-concept so that she can and will learn requires a delicate balancing of realistic evaluation and good mental health practices. Tailoring school tasks to the individual learner's needs can at one time help her to experience success and avoid damage to her self-concept. Given the chance to direct their own learning, one teacher found that her previously troublesome sixth-graders had changed markedly. "I cannot explain exactly what happened, but it seems to me, that when their self-concept changed, when they discovered they *can*, they did! These 'slow learners' became 'fast learners'; success built upon success." (Rogers, 1969, p. 22)

Acquisition of values

Along with the growing self-concept, the individual begins to acquire a system of values. Initially, what is good or bad is told to him by others. "It is *good* to be honest." "It is *bad* to fight." In some situations, valuing is easy. In other instances, values are less clear. The adolescent, particularly, begins to question judgments of good and bad and on what they are based. This is sometimes referred to as moral or character development. It is really part of developing a *self*.

Who am I? Who do I want to be?

Another part of the evolving system of values consists of other questions: "Who am I?" "Why am I here?" "What do *I* want to be?" "*Who* do I want to be?" In seeking the answers, the individual begins to discover his identity. Maslow (1971) describes this as "... finding out what your real desires and characteristics are, and being able to live in a way that expresses them. You learn to be authentic, to be honest in the sense of allowing your behavior and your speech to be the true and spontaneous expression of your inner feelings." (p. 18) (Note: Most people are not prepared to receive such honest expressions of feeling, so that one must expect to pay a price for this freedom.)

Focus 4–3

The idea of being truthful extends also to curriculum. Content should be relevant to the life of the learner.

That means truthful and useful. For example, an activity in which a third-grade class learns how a voting machine works may fail the test

> of usefulness since such information cannot be readily employed in the children's near future. But if this third-grade class employs voting to decide whether money raised from their rummage sale should be used to have a party or given to UNICEF, the activity may meet both truth and use tests. (Hoffman and Ryan, 1973, p. 9)
>
> Truth and use (or meaningfulness) are tests applicable also to secondary and college level courses. A *suggested activity* is that *you* find at least 10 uses for your educational psychology course. Afterwards, review your feelings about the course.

Self-actualized individuals, according to Maslow, "seem to do what they do for the sake of ultimate, final values, which is for the sake of principles which seem *intrinsically worthwhile.*" (p. 190) They have chosen principles and values which they prize and on the basis of which they act. The emphasis is on the individual's efforts, not the imposition of values by some authority figure. (Simon, Howe, and Kirschenbaum, 1972, p. 19) This selection process, of which the individual is often unaware at the time, underlies his self-concept, his motivation, and his behavior. As we look at motivation and the learner, try to keep this in mind. The most desirable motivation for learning is the learner's interest in what he or she is learning.

MOTIVATION

It would be a gross error to say that a person is either motivated or is not. Rather, the individual tends to behave along a continuum. That is, on the positive side, there is little, some, or great motivation toward doing something. Frequently one must choose between two or more motives which have approximately equal strength.

Some activities are higher on the priority list than others. On a given day, for example, when you have no classes but do have an exam coming up in four days, a new suspense novel has just arrived in the mail, rain has cancelled a planned tennis game, and there's a good movie on television. What are you motivated to do?

Play tennis	Study	Watch TV	Sleep	Read
X	X	X	X	X

Your motivation to play tennis is very low due to the rain, but the other options, despite varying strengths, have to be evaluated in terms of long-range effects and short- versus long-range gratifications. If you are eager to prove your academic competence, you study, despite the more immediately pleasurable alternatives. If you don't particularly care about grades or are confident in your knowledge for the exam, your choice might be among the short-range gratifications. Perhaps you've already done considerable studying and are tired, or you feel entitled to some recreation. Will you have a sense of guilt if you choose not to study? Whichever choice you make, no one can say that you have *no* motivation for the alternatives. Rather, all things considered, you are most motivated toward your chosen activity at the time of choice. That is, motivation both directs the course of behavior and determines the intensity of that behavior.

When we discuss the motivation to learn, therefore, we must take into account several factors, such as competing motives, what is to be learned, and the past experiences of the learner.

Competing motives

> As Atkinson (1974) puts it, "Some college students do less well academically than someone might have predicted because they spend so much time doing other interesting things, not because they are deficient in either achievement-related skills or motivation, but because they have a variety of other strong motivations that have an equally important influence on their distribution of time among various activities." (p. 396)

An individual who wants to be able to speak a foreign language, but who has had failure experiences with such learning in the past, may elect to play basketball or study history, areas in which her competence is higher, instead of studying for a language exam. She makes this choice in spite of any anxiety about the exam, the obvious need to study, and the guilt feelings she may have because of her decision not to study and/or her lack of achievement in the foreign language course. Her motivation to study the language is simply not strong enough to compete with her other motives. This does not mean, however, that she has no motivation toward studying the language, as you can see.

Another way of looking at motivation, again using a kind of continuum, is Lewin's analysis of conflict. Lewin developed the concept that each person functions in a "life space" or psychological environment. In this life space, there are objects or events that create pressures which tend to attract or repel the individual. These pressures have positive or negative valences, thus:

Punishment (Avoidance)	Neutral	Praise (Approach)
+	+	+
×	−	+
	×	×

The further that objects are located in relation to the person in life space, the less the valence attached to them produces either approach or avoidant behavior. A remote goal, such as obtaining a high grade at the end of a semester, may have little effect on behavior, because the grade is so remotely related to the person within life space that it can do little to attract or repel. On the other hand, an object which is much nearer at hand, such as the praise a parent may give, may result in immediate approach behavior. (Travers, 1972, pp. 387–89)

Similarly, there can be a negative situation, one in which the person is motivated to avoid certain objects or events. When there are two or more motivations operating in the person's life space at a given time, he is in a state of conflict.

Focus 4–4

A few brief examples will illustrate the kinds of conflicts that may occur:
approach-approach: a person must select between equally attractive or positive alternatives, such as choosing which of two good job offers to accept; or between equally attractive but apparently incompatible career goals, such as law and engineeering.
approach-avoidance: a person must choose between objects or events, one of which has a positive valence and the other a negative valence, such as the bilingual youngster who wants to learn and achieve in English, but is equally anxious about appearing to reject his parents and native culture in so doing; or a desire to attain high grades but an unwillingness to do the work involved.
avoidance-avoidance: a person must select between equally unattractive alternatives, such as a student being obliged to elect one science course from a list when he feels totally incompetent in and has a distaste for any science courses; or a desire to avoid conformity v. a desire to avoid the penalties for nonconformity.
double approach-avoidance: a person can accept a fantastic job offer 2000 miles from home and loved ones, or he can stay home and accept a less attractive position.
The ways in which a person resolves these or similar conflicts depends on other forces operating in his life space, such as past experiences, parental or peer pressures, and other variables.

With respect to motivation and education, these concepts have been organized in another way, a social-psychological model, which intertwines many of the variables we have already discussed. Sewell, Haller, and Portes (1969) have assumed

> ... 1) that certain social structural and psychological factors—initial stratification position [socioeconomic status] and mental ability, specifically—affect both the sets of significant others' influences bearing on the youth, and the youth's own observations of his ability; 2) that the influence of significant others, and possibly his estimates of his ability affect the youth's levels of educational and occupational aspiration; 3)

that the levels of aspiration affect subsequent levels of educational attainment; 4) that education in turn affects levels of occupational attainment. (Sewell, *et al.*, 1969, pp. 83–84)

They found, in a longitudinal study of male rural high school seniors, that the effects were linear and the social-psychological variables performed "mediational" functions between background factors and later behaviors. In a state of conflicting motivations, for example, this whole chain of variables would affect the way in which the individual resolved the conflict.

Motivation is usually subdivided, in some fashion, into primary and secondary classes of motives. Maslow's breakdown is basically in three parts: survival motives (often called basic or primary needs), social or affiliative motives, and ego-enhancing motives. The survival needs may be subdivided into physiological needs (air, food, elimination, activity) and security needs. Social motives include the need to receive acceptance from others and to feel a sense of belonging. The need to be approved by others and by oneself transcends both the social-affiliation motives and the ego-enhancing motives, as is seen in the need to achieve. While it is quite true that the motive to achieve academically ultimately means getting a job that will supply the money needed to satisfy such survival needs as food and shelter, the need for academic achievement is more readily related to social and ego-enhancing needs. There is also a cognitive motivation, that is, learning for its own sake, which might properly be classified as self-actualization.

In the learning situation, as elsewhere, the individual can choose to move ahead and to welcome or seek new experience, or make a choice wrong for himself or herself, or virtually "stand still" to maintain safety and security. Humanistic or "Third Force" psychologists, including Maslow, Rogers, Combs, Purkey, and others, stress the self-actualizing tendency of people—the urge to experience or to be what we think we are. This is the highest level in Maslow's hierarchy, attainable only as the physiological, social-affiliative, and esteem needs are met satisfactorily. The process of moving toward self-actualization is itself seen as a realization of one's potential. To accomplish this, the motivation emphasis is on ". . . *intrinsic* learning; that is, learning to be a human being in general, and second, learning to be *this* particular human being." (Maslow, 1971, p. 168)

Intrinsic motivation is a pressure from within the person to behave in certain ways. *Extrinsic motivation* is an incentive provided from outside the individual to encourage him to behave in ways desired by the person(s) who provide the incentive. Learning can occur whether the learner is intrinsically or extrinsically motivated.

Intrinsic v. extrinsic motivation

Intrinsic motives include anxiety, the need to achieve, maintenance of the self-concept, and aspirations. Extrinsic motives include praise or acceptance by others and concrete rewards. Ultimately, of course, our goal is to develop the intrinsically motivated learner who finds learning a self-rewarding experience, whether or not he has power to direct the learning situation.

Now we know from considerable experimental evidence that there is an exploratory drive or motive in very young children which tends to peak in the preschool years. This might be considered an intrinsic motivation for learning. Many psychologists deplore the apparent loss of this intrinsic motivation as children progress through the early grades.

Focus 4–5

> Gardner Murphy, highly respected by his colleagues for his work in studying human personality and potential, has long been concerned with the disappearance of curiosity. He has placed on the community, school, and teacher the responsibility for providing an environment that includes those activities and opportunities which nourish a child's curiosity. From Murphy's point of view, such behavior is critically important for the development of self-motivated learning behavior.
>
> If we supply this kind of satisfaction for curiosity cravings, the child's curiosity will become more and more pervasive and enrich his whole personality. He will learn how to learn. By working on his vital concerns he will develop the habit of actively working on problems. In other words, he will generalize from the particular classroom material used to all sorts of other subsequent material both in his own personal life and in his community. (Murphy, 1970, p. 5)
>
> It is gross negligence and lack of foresight to ignore the relationship between curiosity and learning.

Question   *As a teacher, how would you stimulate curiosity?*

One of the harsher criticisms of primary education is contained in Elkind's statement:

> In the school . . . we do not permit children to become totally engrossed in any activity but rather shuttle them from activity to activity on the hour or half hour. The result is what might be called *intellectually burned children.* Just as the burned child shuns the fire so the intellectually burned child shies away from total intellectual involvement. (Elkind, 1969, p. 334)

Now Elkind, a leading contemporary psychologist, is well aware of the short attention span of most young children. Yet his statement has some truth because when a child, like an adult, is interested in what he is doing, he will persist in his activity for extended periods of time, even to the point where he ignores or rejects other equally attractive possibilities. The forced shift in activity may indeed stifle the child's intrinsic motivation for learning. This may be seen also if we examine White's theory of competence motivation which, he wrote, "... is directed, selective, and persistent, and ... is continued not because it serves primary drives, which indeed it cannot serve until it is almost perfected, but because it satisfies an intrinsic need to deal with the environment." (White, 1959, p. 318)

White rejects the possibility that the competence motive is wholly innate and postulates that much of humanity's desire to interact with the environment is learned. However, as the work of several conditioning theorists indicates, not only can this behavior be learned, but it can also be stopped by negative reinforcement or other conditioning techniques. A child who is constantly told that "curiosity killed the cat" or that it is forbidden to delve into nonapproved subject matter develops an avoidance motive toward learning that is stronger than his intrinsic need to know. What Murphy and Elkind have suggested is that, through these or other methods, intrinsic motivation for learning is stopped or stifled in the classroom.

As an illustration of the possible *mis*handling of this matter of intrinsic v. extrinsic motivation, let's look at a classroom situation. In recent years there has been much emphasis on reinforcing ("rewarding") learners for effort and/or achievement. This technique has been successful with many children who had been nonachievers.

Greene and Lepper (1974) have suggested, however, that if the reinforcement is given without discrimination, then the learner may soon work for the reinforcer rather than because of intrinsic interest in an activity. Then, when reinforcers are withdrawn, the learner loses interest in the activity. This is clearly an undesirable outcome. A balance is needed between extrinsic reinforcement and the encouragement of intrinsic motivation, and this may well differ among individuals.

Achievement motivation

From another point of view, omitting much of this background of the individual, deCharms and Carpenter (1968) have suggested that achievement motivation includes certain other aspects: personal responsibility, the nature of risk-taking strategies, and the use of feedback. In their conception, "The entrepreneurial spirit of achievement emphasizes self-reliance, the taking of calculated risks, careful planning and checking of progress with constant emphasis on the skillful use of one's abilities. These ... are the dependent variables that are related to the measure of achievement motivation." (deCharms and Carpenter, 1968, p. 34) Obviously, this interpretation of motivation would tend to discriminate between those who have high levels of motivation and those who have low levels of motivation, both within and without the educational scene. Put another way, the discrimination is also between those who have an internal locus of control and those who have an external locus of control. For some learners, there has been no opportunity to develop self-reliance. For others, risk-taking is an anxiety-producing behavior to be avoided. Still other learners have not developed the necessary skills for self-evaluation or profitable use of the evaluation of others. These negative aspects of achievement motivation appear to be learned as much as the positive aspects are.

In a study related to these concepts, Feather (1959) tried to weigh the relationship between motivation and choice behavior in situations where success (attainment of the goal object) was related to personal effort or to chance (risk-taking). His subjects were 192 sixth-grade boys. He hypothesized that when the subject is ego-involved because of the need to exert his efforts or skills to attain success, anxiety increases and motivation decreases as the probability of success declines. However, when success depends on luck rather than personal effort (therefore no ego-involvement), motivation increases as the probability of success increases. This is, in essence, the gambler's psychology. Feather found that the results of his study with the boys supported his hypotheses. The question of ego-involvement in determining behavior was also touched on by deCharms and Carpenter (*supra*) and Shaw (1967), who wrote that "Individuals who perceive a learning situation in which outside forces determine the reinforcements are less likely to raise their expectancies for future reinforcement, even following success. They are also less likely to lower their expectancies as much after failure." (Shaw, 1967, p. 571) The feeling of powerlessness, or external control, in this situation clearly affects motivation and subsequent behavior.

Is there, then some quality or personality, or a personality syndrome, that is related to achievement motivation? Major studies in this area have been conducted by McClelland and Atkinson for many years. They have used a variety of techniques to measure need-achievement. Other psychologists have attempted to test achievement motivation in conjunction with other variables. From their research at the Fels Research Institute, for example, Kagan, Sontag, Baker, and Nelson (1958) have found that children in the six-to-ten-year age range who have a high motivation to achieve, intellectual curiosity about nature, and competitive strivings tend to acquire the intellectual skills and knowledge that facilitate an increase in tested IQ. This suggests that there is a cluster of personality traits which includes achievement motivation and results in achievement in fact. Ringness (1965), in a study of bright ninth-grade boys, matched for IQ, sex, age, school, and academic load, attempted to differentiate between those who were academically successful and those who were not. He concluded that the difference lay in the nature of their motivation. That is, the most successful boys had a higher achievement motivation, while the less successful boys had a stronger affiliation motivation. If you will recall, in the exploration of sex differences in learning, we found that these two motives might conflict in the learner, especially in the female learner.

Interacting with motivation in the learning process is the attitude of the learner toward all learning or toward specific areas of learning. Attitudes are *constructs*, not directly observable phenomena, which are inferred from observable behavior. For example, we can infer a positive attitude on the part of the child as he hugs his mother, although no verbal communication has occurred. Or, we can infer attitudes from responses to questionnaires or rating scales. Although it is often difficult to evaluate the truth of attitude studies, the view that attitudes affect motivation and learning is generally accepted. Students tend to study more and achieve at a higher level in subject areas they like, as contrasted with those they dislike. More formally, we might say that their motivation is higher where their attitudes are more positive.

The positive or negative valence which subject matter has for an individual is learned, usually in casual ways. As a simple illustration of this casual learning, a parent who enjoys classical music, for example, exposes his child to it, comments favorably on it, and subtly or otherwise conveys the message that classical music is good and that to like it is good. If the child wishes parental approval, he perceives these cues over a period of time and acquires or learns to have a positive attitude toward classical music.

Other factors involved in the development of motivation include the need for peer acceptance, reinforcement, and anxiety-avoidance. In the learning situation, this results in the individual accepting a value, subject matter, or person ". . . to the point of being willing to be identified with it, . . . sufficiently committed to the value to pursue it, to seek it out, to want it." (Krathwohl, Bloom, and Masia, 1964, p. 145)

Grades and motivation

To too many teachers, motivation implies the use of external pressures (reward or punishment) to achieve some desired learning or other behavior. "Even if reward and punishment succeed temporarily, they do not supply the stimulation necessary for continued motivated learning." (Torrance, 1965b, pp. 340–41) That is, as we have already seen, reward and punishment do not create the intrinsic motivation so much desired in the learner. The extrinsic pressure usually applied in the classroom is the use of grades. On the one hand, some teachers believe that the promise of good grades will motivate their students. On the other hand, some teachers consider the threat of failure as essential as motivation, particularly in elementary education. In fact, many of them feel that several children must be failed every year as a double guarantee that high standards of achievement will be maintained and that the nonfailing children will feel obliged to work to capacity. (Glasser, 1972)

In Otto and Melby's study (1964) of second-graders, their goal was to determine whether the threat of failure actually was a meaningful source of educational motivation. At the beginning of a semester, half of the children were threatened with nonpromotion, and half were told they would all be promoted to the next grade. At the end of the semester, the entire sample was retested, and no differences in achievement were found between the threatened and nonthreatened groups. The teachers agreed with the finding that the absence of threat did not affect the quality of their pupils' work. (Otto and Melby, 1964, pp. 484–89) It may be that, despite the usual trusting acceptance of statements by the school authorities, these second-graders simply did not comprehend or did not believe the threat of nonpromotion. The nonthreatened group may have similarly been unconvinced. In fact, unless there were reminders about promotion throughout the semester, it is even possible that these young children forgot the threat altogether.

At the college level, several studies have been done in an attempt to discover the effect of grades on learners' motivations. Instructors know from experience that many of their students are motivated principally by external pressures or the desire to earn high grades, often illustrated by the prompt forgetting of subject content immediately after an examination. Other students are motivated more by the desire to *know* and are less concerned with grades. They may even comment that "I got a lot out of this course, even if you did only give me a C."

> *Note:* Such a statement has an internal inaccuracy, since students earn a grade rather than being "given" it by the instructor.

Many colleges and universities, and even some secondary schools, have recognized the problems that connect motivation and grades and have begun pass-fail or satisfactory-unsatisfactory grading systems to increase interest as a motive for taking a course. Such a system is also supposed to reduce dependence on grades as an attraction ("It's an easy 'A'!") or avoidance (anxiety-producing and grade point-reducing) mechanism. These systems have proved to be a mixed blessing, however. Admissions committees tend to prefer a grade point average on admissions applications to a list of courses passed or wordy teacher evaluations for each course.

The criticisms of grades as negative forces on motivation are seen at all levels of education. The critics say that grades reward conformity and punish creativity, damage the individual's self-concept, cause students unnecessary anxiety, do not accurately reflect what a student understands and has learned, and promote competition instead of cooperation. (Simon' 1970; Campbell, 1974)

> We have created, through competition, a system based on mistrust. In school the assumption is that no one learns without threats of grades, failure, being less than first, i.e., that these extrinsic factors are prime motivation for learning. . . . the whole frantic, irrational scramble to beat others is essential for the kind of institution our schools are, i.e., sorting, ranking, and labeling places. Winning and losing are what our schools are all about, not education. (Campbell, 1974, p. 145)

The most extreme example of this emphasis is seen in schools where class ranks are posted publicly, by name. Pity the poor student who sees his name as 87th on a list of 87 term after term! A few #87s will try to move up a rank or two; most of them will ask, "Why bother?"

To avoid or reduce negative effects of grading on motivation, some schools have adopted individualized instruction programs. Learners are then evaluated on the amount of progress they have made. This method stresses growth and is believed to increase achievement motivation and feelings of competence and personal worth. British primary schools, and their American counterparts, which stimulate and reward curiosity, and encourage self-direction in learning, are also seen as increasing intrinsic motivation to achieve. (King-Stoops, 1974) Computer-assisted instruction, in some formats, is similarly a possible stimulant to intrinsic motivation. The student begins to compete with himself in all of these settings, not against other students, nor for grades alone.

Summary

As you can see, motivation is both a cause and an effect of learning. Although extrinsic positive and aversive motivation should be used with moderation, they are needed at times, since one cannot always wait for the learner to become self-motivated before involving him in learning. Torrance asserts that

> ... many children and young people not now motivated to learn in school will become excited about learning and will achieve in line with their potentialities, if given a chance to use what is learned, if given a chance to communicate what is learned, if we show an interest in what is learned rather than in grades, if learning tasks are not too easy or too difficult, if there is a chance to use their best abilities and preferred ways of learning, if we reward a variety of kinds of excellence, and if learning experiences are given purposefulness. (Torrance, 1965a, p. 260)

If this sounds like a prescription for the more effective use of learning potential, it is. We might further organize it in this way: To increase classroom motivation,

1. utilize existing interests and motivations while developing new ones.
2. make the objective of the learning task as clear and meaningful as possible;
3. set task goals realistically, e.g., appropriate to each learner's level (as is done in some nongraded schools and individualized instruction programs);
4. help students to set realistic goals, evaluate their progress, and provide informative feedback as to their progress (i.e., not just a grade, but point out how and where they erred and were correct);
5. "... maximize cognitive drive by arousing intellectual curiosity, by using attention-attracting materials, and by arranging lessons so as to insure ultimate success in learning" (Ausubel, 1968, p. 393);
6. recognize and take account of individual differences and developmental changes which affect patterns of motivation.

In connection with the last aspect, it might be well to remember that everything discussed in the previous two chapters and the present one, to this point, has a bearing on the individual's motivation. There are also other emotional or psychological factors that affect motivation for better or worse. In the next section, we will be discussing one of them—anxiety—and we will demonstrate how this interacts with motivation in the learning process. Motivation will also be an integral part of the section on underachievers, students whose motives for not maximizing the use of their abilities in an academic way are often complex.

The use of reinforcement and behavior-modification techniques in the classroom for increasing learner motivation will be discussed in chapter eight, which is on learning theory. Evaluation of achievement is part of chapter seven, and the use of innovative approaches and their effects on learner motivation will be discussed in chapter twelve.

ANXIETY

What is anxiety? It is *not* fear, which is a specific reaction to a specific situation with a realistic basis. It *is* a diffuse feeling arising within the individual that may be realistic, in that it is related to a stimulus of some kind. Or, anxiety may be characterological, in that it is a general manifestation of individual temperament unrelated to any immediate or observable threat. Much of our concern about anxiety and the learner is of the latter type, which is often called neurotic anxiety. We should use caution with the term "anxiety," however. As Wertheimer (1959) has written, there are two types of anxiety: the capital T or tension-interfering variety that is parallel to neurotic anxiety and the small t or tension-driving variety. It might clarify things if the small t variety were called "yearning pressure," meaning the degree of tension necessary to motivate the individual to action. Yearning pressure is, for example, the tension inherent in doing statistical computations in order to learn whether experimental results support or refute one's hypothesis. Or, less seriously, it would be the tension aroused as one reads an espionage novel and becomes "anxious" to reach its climax. Yearning pressure supports motivation and learning. As we shall see, neurotic anxiety, the capital T variety, tends to interfere with motivation and learning.

Sources of anxiety   In cases of neurotic anxiety stemming from the child's own inner conflicts, constant direction and assurance may be sought if the child is ambivalent, unable to make up his own mind, and consequently highly dependent on the teacher. To Freud, Erikson, and others, latency, which corresponds to the elementary school years, is the period that is particularly characterized by the sense of industry. Yet, from a psychoanalytic point of view, the child at this stage may still be trying to resolve repressed psychosexual urges that arouse feelings of guilt and anxiety. Or, the child may perceive independent activity in the classroom as a rejection of his parents, with similar emotional reactions. These guilt and anxiety feelings in turn inhibit his adequate functioning. Anxiety may also be the result of an intense reaction to the birth process, according to Bergman and Escalona (1949). They found that infants who react to birth intensely seem to be characterized in later childhood by hypersensitivity and low frustration tolerance. With maturation, anxiety becomes an ego-controlled warning signal to avoid pain rather than an automatic reaction to danger.

Still another source of anxiety may be an overly permissive environment in which the child never experiences frustration of his desires, but is granted immediate gratification of all his wishes. The child is therefore unprepared to cope with the real world in which instant gratification is neither always possible nor always desirable. As Pearson (1954) wrote, this leads to minimal effort and underachievement in the classroom. In order to learn, the child must put forth effort, which is painful and pleasure-inhibiting for him. Anxiety is aroused whenever the child with this type of background has to work to attain a goal.

Anxiety is often accompanied by feelings of utter helplessness, which may lead to a negative attitude toward life. Such an attitude forces the child to interact with the environment in a way designed to reduce his anxiety. He may react to threatening situations, such as the learning situation, by becoming conformist and submissive, by acting out his anxieties in rebellious behavior, by rationalizing his actions, or by withdrawing emotionally. Children use all these techniques in combatting their anxiety, but one or another of them usually becomes a relatively characteristic pattern of behavior in the anxious child and may be inappropriate in some situations. Past history, if known, can help the teacher to be aware of situations that act as "triggers" for the onset of defensive behavior. Then the teacher can try to avoid, for example, creating excess frustration, or embarrassment, or anxiety. For some children, and adults also, psychological safety lies in infallibility. In the classroom, this may be demonstrated when a child known to be bright hesitates to answer a question for fear of being wrong. If the fear of being incorrect in responding is a usual behavior pattern of the child, her learning will be inhibited. She will become anxious in situations where she is not sure of what is expected or what is correct.

Fromm and others believe that the process of becoming an individual may be, as suggested earlier, a threatening or anxiety-provoking situation for the child. Moreover, the role of individual competitive success in our culture is often a dual one: It is a dominant sociocultural goal, and at the same time it is anxiety-arousing, both in the T and t senses. An illustration of this viewpoint is seen in the studies of Redlich, Seward, and others, who have studied ambivalence and status-striving in middle-class families. They found that approval is ". . . experienced by the child as being contingent on conformity and submission, though the verbal teachings in such an environment tend to stress independence and individualism." (Portnoy, 1959, p. 34) Conflict is thus aroused in the child. The constant threat to conform or be rejected hinders her self-realization and forms the basis for future neurotic conflicts and anxiety.

Put another way, Rogers (1969) asserted that

> *Those learnings which are threatening to the self are more easily perceived and assimilated when external threats are at a minimum.* The boy who is retarded in reading already feels threatened and inadequate because of this deficiency when he is forced to attempt to read aloud in front of the group. When he is ridiculed for his efforts, when his grades are a vivid reflection of his failure, it is no surprise that he may go through several years of school with no perceptible increase in his

reading ability. On the other hand, a supportive, understanding environment and a lack of grades, or an encouragement of self evaluation, remove the external threats and permit him to make progress because he is no longer paralyzed by fear. (p. 159)

Question *If the teacher wanted to evaluate this boy's reading ability, in what nonthreatening ways could it be done?*

The child who is emotionally upset, whether by his parents' conflicts or anxieties, rejection by peers, feelings of guilt and hostility because of which he feels anxious, or conditions in the larger society (war, bomb scares, kidnappings), finds it difficult to pay attention to the teacher and to learn. In such children, Watson (1959) wrote, ". . . the natural endowment will become inhibited and refractory to observing, conceptualizing, and thinking." (p. 483) That is, the neurotically anxious student cannot do his best as a learner.

The foregoing have all been theoretical explanations of the causes and effects of anxiety. What happens when the theory is tested on live subjects?

Anxiety and achievement

Some of the principal studies of anxiety in children have been carried out at Yale University by a team of psychologists, headed by Seymour Sarason. They have tested elementary school children here and abroad, developed tests of anxiety appropriate to this age range, and differentiated general anxiety from test anxiety. They are careful to point out that, in situations where cautiousness is permitted or encouraged (e.g., nonspeed or "power" tests), the highly anxious child is not put under pressure and therefore does not exhibit his anxiety. (Sarason, Davidson, Lighthall, Waite, and Ruebush, 1960, p. 186) Among other findings, the high anxiety (HA) boys asked many questions of the teacher as an attention-getting device. This dependence on the approval of others tended to occur more often in boys and tended to inhibit their spontaneity and flexibility in interpersonal behavior. On the Rorschach Test, Human Figures Drawings, and in learning studies with these same subjects, it was found that ". . . the child who scored high on the anxiety scales manifested greater interference in problem-solving than his peer who scored low despite the fact that both scored the same on an intelligence test." (Sarason, *et al.*, 1960, p. 166) The spontaneity and flexibility inhibited by anxiety are necessary ingredients in problem-solving as well as in other types of learning.

The Luchins and Luchins (1959) studies of rigidity in thinking emphasize the same difficulties that the Sarason team found in the anxious subject. Under stress-producing conditions, the anxious individual focused on his own personality, *his* inadequacies, and *his* tensions rather than the problem to be solved. (p. 130) Thus, an anxious subject could not shift his approach as needed in solving the experimental problem. The Luchins also hypothesized that a low degree of anxiety may be as conducive to rigidity of behavior as a high degree of anxiety. In this, they asked logically why an individual should change his behavior if he is not disturbed by psychological tensions. (p. 148) Along this same line of thought, Silverman and Blitz (1956) hypothesized that low anxiety subjects ". . . are those who have learned appropriate defenses against threat stimuli, (and they) would expect their performance to be improved by an avoidance condition but disrupted by a nonavoidance condition." (p. 301) On the other hand, the authors expected high anxiety subjects, who have not learned appropriate defense techniques, to react to threat by rigid behavior, with no difference in their responses to avoidance or nonavoidance conditions. They did indeed find that the performance of the high anxiety subjects was characterized by lack of flexibility and exploratory behavior. To Silverman and Blitz, the results ". . . suggest that anxious persons do not respond adaptively to threat. It appears that their anxious responses reflect either inappropriate defenses or defenses which are so firmly entrenched as to obviate sudden changes in response to the relatively mild threats of the laboratory situation." (p. 303) That is, the highly anxious individuals in this study tend to function in the same way as those of Luchins and Luchins and the Sarason team. They are so involved in, and possibly overwhelmed by, their anxiety, that they find it virtually impossible to concentrate on the requirements of the task at hand.

From another point of view, the assets of a *lack* of neurotic anxiety, Eiduson (1962) found that, as a group, her 40 scientist subjects had a lack of free-floating anxiety and fears. They tended to make "relatively constant, habitual adjustments in the face of problem or conflict situations, and these keep anxiety from getting so great that it interferes with performance." (p. 98) This confirms the laboratory results reported by Silverman and Blitz and suggests a reason for the difference in achievement between learners of apparently equal ability.

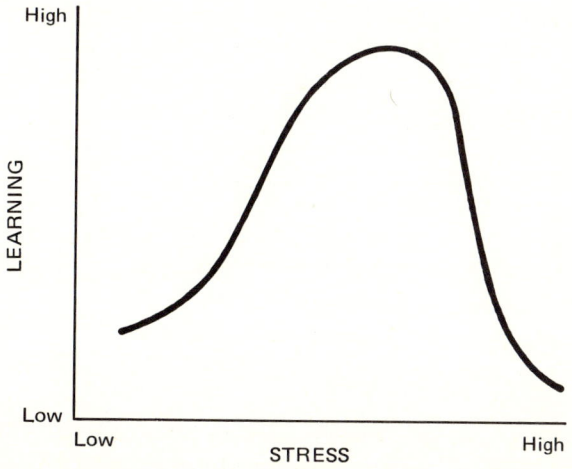

The relationship between stress and learning.   **Figure 4.1**

As Figure 4.1 suggests, less learning tends to occur when stress is very low or very high. This is a curvilinear relationship. That is, there is a negative correlation at some points and a positive correlation at other points. Some of the factors that affect the relationship between anxiety and learning are task complexity, for example, simple- or single-response learning v. multi-response learning; the nature of the task, for example, speed v. power requirements as noted in the Sarason team studies; intelligence; naturally-occurring stress as differentiated from laboratory-inducing stress; and experimental relief from anxiety. (Levitt, 1967, pp. 130–32) To this list, we might add sex differences and physiological changes, particularly those seen in the upper elementary and early secondary grades. Most people can tolerate *some* stress (anxiety, fatigue, environmental manipulation, physical discomfort, etc.), but, as stresses accumulate, or when external stress is added to existing internal stress, the total effect becomes overwhelming to the point where human performance is affected negatively. Very simply, as the learner's tolerance limit for stress is approached and passed, he or she tends to *learn less*.

The studies that follow have as variables one or more of these factors. The measures of anxiety used are generally one or more of the following: Taylor Manifest Anxiety Scale, General Anxiety Scale for Children, and Test Anxiety Scale for Children. The latter two were devised by the Sarason team and have built-in "lie" scales, using items like "I have never been afraid." Since it is unlikely that a subject has *never* been afraid, a positive answer would be credited to a "lie" score. This is generally higher for boys than for girls, while the anxiety scores are usually higher for girls. This sex difference has been confirmed in several investigations and is attributed to the pressure on boys to conceal their anxieties, while girls do not experience this pressure to the same degree. It is, in fact, thought to be quite feminine in some groups for girls to display their fears and anxieties.

One study which illustrates this point was done by Loughlin, O'Connor, Powell, and Parsley (1965), using over 5000 subjects in grades four through eight from urban and suburban middle-class backgrounds. They found that the girls had higher anxiety scores on all three anxiety scales used. Their results suggested that ". . . sex differences in anxiety manifest themselves early in children's academic careers, reach a peak in the fifth or sixth grade, and diminish considerably by the time the eighth grade is reached." (p. 214) Anxiety was also greatest in the average-achievement group, with the underachievers next and the overachievers last.

Question   Why do you think this order was obtained?

Hill and Sarason (1966) sought to test the stability of anxiety test scores by following 670 youngsters from grades one and two to grades five and six. These were suburban, middle-class children of above-average intelligence. They also tried to establish the relationship between test anxiety and test performance. As the experimental tasks became more test-like, Hill and Sarason found that the negative correlations between anxiety and test performance increased. (p. 59) The increases in test anxiety above grade two also contributed significantly to increasing differences in reading level between high and low anxiety pupils, with an average difference of 18.7 months at the grade five level. (pp. 69ff) The sex differences found here parallel those mentioned earlier. One cause for this consistent finding may lie in the differences in physiological maturity between the sexes at ages eleven and twelve. The imminent onset of puberty in the girls may cause an increase in general anxiety because of physiological instability. On the other hand, Jackson, Getzels, and Xydis (1960) have hypothesized that the preadolescent period is psychologically more difficult for boys, while the middle-adolescent period, with the rise of more complex social relationships, is more difficult for girls. In either case, the cumulative effects of stresses appear to be in operation here.

At the college level, too, there is evidence that anxiety interferes with learning. The magnitude of the correlation between anxiety and academic achievement varies, however, from study to study. Spielberger and Katzenmayer (1959) found a small inverse relationship between grade point average and scores on the Taylor Manifest Anxiety Scale for their subjects of average aptitude. However, "College work appeared to be too difficult for low aptitude students whose poor grades were unrelated to their MAS scores. High aptitude students tended to obtain good grades regardless of their anxiety level." (p. 278) The ability of high aptitude students to function well despite anxiety may be explained by the ability of some of them to suppress their anxiety and use their energies constructively in the pursuit of academic achievement. On the other hand, it is equally possible that they might be achieving at an even higher level if their anxieties were reduced. McKinnon (1967) illustrates this possibility in a small study of young college students who were unable to cope with their studies, but who also feared failure and therefore sought psychological help. They had not had learning difficulties in their precollege years. The therapy they received was psychoanalytic in orientation. Their problem was diagnosed as a depressive neurotic disorder. Apparently the therapy was effective, for McKinnon reported that the students moved from the status of helpless, angry children to that of more productive students. In a nonanalytic approach to this problem, one might suggest that the young college student felt inadequate in the face of course assignments and became angry with himself as he perceived this inadequacy. The student became more anxious as his inadequacy-anger pattern continued, until he did, indeed, become neurotically depressed. This often happens in the first term in college, because the freshman is ill-prepared for the independence of action and nature of self-responsibility that he must assume.

The factor of self-perception or self-esteem obviously cannot be overlooked, as the McKinnon study and our investigation of self-concept have shown.

Anxiety and self-concept

> From whatever source the self-concept is acquired, what is learned is a matter of the individual's own experience, not what seems to some outsider to be happening to him. A parent who scolds a child for not doing well in school may do so with the best of intentions, hoping to motivate his child to greater effort. To the child the meaning of this event may only be that he is stupid, unacceptable, or not much good. . . . Children learn about themselves, for example, from the atmosphere of the classroom, from the moods of teachers, and from the overt or covert indications of success and failure implied by approval or disapproval of teachers and classmates. This unplanned learning is likely to be much more significant and permanent than what the teacher taught. (Combs, Avila, and Purkey, 1971, p. 49)

Even at the upper elementary level, the self-concept is sufficiently well developed to have an effect on simple learning. A group of fifth- and sixth-graders, from all socioeconomic classes, was given a modified paired-associates learning task, with test instructions and game instructions. Apart from differences found between low-anxious and high-anxious subjects due to the type of instructions, the investigators found that "High self-esteem was positively related to performance for boys but not for girls. A negative correlation between self-esteem and test anxiety was found for boys." (Lekarczyk and Hill, 1969, p. 147)

College students, too, find themselves in a number of situations that are potentially stress-provoking and at the same time involve a great deal of self-esteem. Most of us feel somewhat ego-involved in writing answers to any test, but additional stress and ego-involvement are present when we must literally stand up and stand out from the group in making an oral report or in some other speech-type situation. Beam (1955) investigated three such situations: 1) presenting an oral report in class to meet a college course requirement, 2) taking an oral preliminary examination for a graduate degree, and 3) appearing before a large audience in a play. All three of these can provoke what is commonly called "stage fright." Beam's subjects were also tested under neutral or nonstress-provoking conditions. All subjects were to learn a standard list of nonsense syllables to the point where they had two consecutive errorless trials. Under stress conditions, the subjects made an average of 50 percent more errors (195 v. 127) and needed 50 percent more trials to meet the criterion than under the neutral conditions. Beam concluded that anxiety had an inhibiting effect on learning.

Epstein (1973) views the self-concept as a self-*theory* that has among its basic functions that of helping to maintain self-esteem and the organization of ". . . the data of experience in a manner that can be coped with effectively." He points out, however, that, under stress, theories tend to become restricted as a protective measure and ". . . individuals who, at one time, were highly anxious and learned to react to threat by restricting their self-theories may continue to react to minor threats with constriction, even though they no longer are highly anxious." (pp. 407–8) As noted earlier, it is sometimes difficult to change a pattern of behavior that has served one well, even when it is no longer appropriate.

The effect of stress or nonstress conditions may be seen in a more usual academic activity than in Beam's study. One of the characteristics of individual intelligence tests such as the Stanford-Binet or Wechsler scales is that items are arranged in order of difficulty and a stated number of errors must occur before the test can be discontinued. This often has a demoralizing effect on the test subject as he hears himself fumble with guessed or incorrect responses or an "I don't know." You might have had this sinking feeling yourself as the problems on a test looked more and more foreign to you. Hutt (1947) experimentally changed the usual easy-to-difficult order of Stanford-Binet items so that hard and easy items were mixed and each failure was followed by a more likely chance for success. He found that morale was maintained at a higher level when failures were partly erased by successes and that maladjusted (anxious?) children made definitely higher scores with the revised procedure, averaging an increase of four or five IQ points. There was no difference in scores for normally adjusted children with either the usual or revised procedure, thus ruling out the effect of practice. Hutt therefore concluded that anxiety, induced by recurrent failure, can result in lower scores on an intelligence test. One might go further and suggest that recurrent failure, in a single subject or in school work generally, is so discouraging as to impair future performance. Some students are motivated to improve after failure, but those who try harder and still fail to succeed after several trials may become convinced of their incompetence and dwell on that instead of on learning. Hutt's experiment is more similar to current learning theory, which stresses positive results and reinforcement, than it is to the traditional practices of the classroom.

Is it possible that part of learning failure is due to the presence of irrelevant information in a task which, combined with a high level of anxiety, makes it difficult for the individual to select the important factors needed for the problem's solution? Under such conditions, does he become confused to the point of inability to perform the task adequately? We have all been in situations where there were so many details that it was difficult to choose the key items needed to solve the problem. If we became excited, or panicked, it became harder and harder to solve the problem. West, Lee, and Anderson (1969) investigated this possibility. They used the Test Anxiety Scale for Children, and two forms of an achievement test, one form of which had no irrelevant information (Selectivity High) and a second form which contained irrelevant information in every item (Selectivity Low). They hypothesized that scores of subjects with high anxiety would be adversely affected by the condition of low selectivity (irrelevant information). "The results indicate that anxiety interacts with irrelevant information to produce a difficult situation for the problem solver." (p. 52) The achievement task in this study consisted of word problems in arithmetic, a source of difficulty for many students.

In another study involving arithmetic and anxiety, Zweibelson and Lodato (1965) hypothesized that

> Personal anxiety resulting from negative attitudes toward arithmetic produce a specific deterrent to arithmetic achievement. . . . specific enough to be called arithmetic anxiety. . . . It seems likely that these

negative attitudes toward arithmetic and the subsequent avoidance or fear of arithmetic may account for lack of achievement in number work. (p. 140)

Working with children as they moved from grade one to four, Zweibelson and Lodato found their hypothesis supported. The same kind of arithmetic anxiety has been observed in college students when they were asked to do basic statistics problems. The students would frequently say: "I can't do math." They could, but anxiety interfered with their performance of the task. In this study, as in many others, there is a negligible relationship between scores on an anxiety scale and intelligence test scores.

Considerations in studying the problem of anxiety and achievement include whether the type of anxiety measured on an anxiety scale is true to life. One also needs to know how sensitive an anxiety scale is to changes in the nature of the individual's anxiety and whether intervention in an anxiety-producing situation has any real effect. Hutt's study suggests that intervention does have an effect, but much more work needs to be done in this area with a variety of situations.

ACHIEVERS

Students all achieve at some level. Those who perform as well as expected for their ability are called achievers. Those with high ability and high achievement are considered to be successful learners. Those who achieve below their measured ability are called underachievers.

Questions *How would you define "overachievers"? Is it possible to have overachievers? What factors might make overachievement possible?*

A review of research on factors influencing achievement by Asbury (1974) revealed conflicting results. That is, no one factor *by itself* was generally agreed upon as affecting achievement for better or worse.

Kifer (1975) sought to show, however, that patterns of academic achievement (success or failure) are directly related to personality characteristics. His study confirmed the view that "With success in academic tasks in the school comes positive personality characteristics; with failure comes lower levels of regard for self and abilities. The relationships become stronger and more powerful as the success or failure becomes prolonged and as a consistent pattern of accomplishments emerges." (p. 205) Encouragement from home seems more important in the early grades and level of achievement in the upper elementary grades in the development of personality characteristics. There may be some cultural differences in this relationship, as pointed out by Kagan and Ender (1975), who studied the ways in which

American and Mexican mothers responded to their children's successes and failures.

Not only the home response is important, however. Interestingly enough, Harrison and Westerman (1974) found that public school teachers differentiate between the personality characteristics of the ideal child and the successful student. The ideal child is seen as one who is curious, sincere, humanistic, and creative and who has personal convictions and a sense of humor. The successful student, on the other hand, is competitive, conforming, obedient, and orderly. It is for these behaviors that teachers offer reinforcement in the form of social acceptance and high grades. The difference in desirability of student characteristics is attributed to the role of the public schools in "... preparing students to become economically successful in society *as it is, not as it should be.*" (p. 636) Similarly, Weiner (1972) has stated that "The main behavioral differences between individuals high and low in achievement needs are that individuals in the high motive group are more likely to *initiate* achievement activities; they work with greater *intensity, persist* longer in the face of failure, and *choose* more tasks of intermediate difficulty, than persons low in achievement needs." (p. 208) Again, these are behaviors that earn approval and high grades from teachers and are keys to success in the competitive business world.

In terms of personality, therefore, we see what tends to separate high achievers from low or underachievers. Obviously those high in ability and effort, who evaluate their performance themselves, and who perceive achievement in terms of their own needs and characteristics (inner locus of control), rather than external factors, will be achievers no matter what their teachers may think. The picture is somewhat different for underachievers who tend to be at the "mercy" of external factors and who have different personality characteristics.

UNDERACHIEVERS

Perhaps the best way of demonstrating the effects of psychological factors on learning and achievement is to present the case of the educational underachiever. By definition, underachievers are those learners who have ability and/or aptitude that is substantially higher than their performance level. For example, a youngster with a measured IQ of 100 or higher, and an achievement level one or two grade levels below his grade placement would be considered an underachiever. Considering the vagaries of IQ measurement, however, and of achievement levels, one must be quite cautious about pinning the label of "underachiever" on a student. It would be unwise and unprofessional to label a child an underachiever on the basis of a single test score or grade. Rather, we would expect that the underachiever would demonstrate a consistent pattern of high ability or aptitude and low performance. Most of the studies of underachievers seek to define the personality characteristics and to identify the learning patterns of the underachiever as a first step in identifying members of this group and as a preliminary measure to remedial procedures. As you will see, these studies involve the factors of anxiety, motivation, and self-concept, which we have already discussed, and tie them together quite neatly in the package labeled "underachiever."

Variable criteria   We might first consider some of the other problems surrounding underachievement. What is the frequency of underachievement in our schools? What are our performance criteria? How valid are our predictive measures of ability and aptitude? As several investigators and educators have indicated in the past several years, intelligence tests as now used are valid only for a segment of the population. We have already noted that they are generally invalid for the "culturally different" and educationally disadvantaged. They are also invalid when improperly administered or when administered under adverse conditions for the individual. We must assume, however, that conscientious investigators exercise appropriate precautions in test administration. Indeed, most of them are careful to remind their readers that the test results given are valid only for groups with the same background factors as their study groups.

Similarly, performance criteria vary from community to community, from school to school, and from teacher to teacher. You are all familiar with teachers who are "hard" markers and those who are "easy" markers. This is what Thorndike has called "criterion heterogeneity." He asks what is an "A" and where is this definition made and by whom? (1963, pp. 4–6) According to Thorndike, "Whenever we combine data from different schools, different programs, or even different teachers, we are likely to introduce heterogeneity into the criterion." (1963, p. 17) That is, the expectations of different people as to what constitutes satisfactory or outstanding performance differ enough to confound research results. This problem in turn helps to determine the frequency of underachievement.

In an affluent suburban school, students may have to meet a criterion that is higher for their grade level than that in an urban school and/or higher than published norms for an achievement test. We must also consider the possibility that a teacher may expect more than the students are able to produce in the belief, rarely justifiable, that all the students in the class are equally capable of learning. If the criterion level is too high, all or most of that teacher's pupils will be considered underachievers by the teacher. At a more realistic level, however, and with the use of objective criteria (National Educational Development Tests), Tolor found 26 percent of the tenth, eleventh, and twelfth-graders in a high socioeconomic level community to be underachievers. These were students with ". . . at least average current intellectual function . . ." as measured by a form of the Otis Mental Ability Test and a placement on the achievement tests of ". . . at least one standard error of estimate below expectancy . . ." based on their Intelligence Quotients. (Tolor, 1969, pp. 63–65) Tolor felt that his figure was a conservative estimate because of the relatively exclusive nature of the sample population and the limitations of the group-administered intelligence test. Even one-quarter of the student population is an alarming frequency of underachievement, however. In urban areas, the frequency is reputed to be two or three times as high. Obviously, something is wrong in the learning situation. At this time, we will look in one direction for an answer—toward the learner himself, although he is only one factor.

Who are the underachievers?

"A child with a failure identity, that is, one who lacks a concept of himself as a loved and worthwhile individual, will not work for any long-term goals. . . . his life is full of pain, and he lives in a haphazard, erratic struggle to get rid of the pain." (Glasser, 1972, p. 165) And, as Atkinson (1974) has pointed out, underachievers have in common weak motivation for academic work, be it daily tasks or achievement tests. (p. 401)

One of the difficulties to be recognized is that our schools are filled with competition—for grades, admission to programs, class rank, and approval. Where there is competition, there are winners and losers, with many more losers than winners. We practice, contrary to what we preach, negative criticism on a daily basis as papers are "corrected," and work is "corrected."

> In such a system the losers must . . . be tormented by envy and self-loathing; some sort of defense must be constructed against the assault of continued failure. It may take the common form of "turning off," non-involvement, don't-take-a-chance, keep-your-mouth-shut, or becoming a "discipline case," having a "learning problem," . . .
>
> . . . To survive 12 or more years of that sort of assault one must develop elaborate defenses, schemes and means for survival, along with a vast reservoir of smouldering hatred, resentment, need for revenge and for evening the score. (Campbell, 1974, p. 145)

In short, for many students who become underachievers, "Why try?" is their response to a situation that shrinks their self-esteem and batters their self-concept. They seem to share weak academic motivation as we have already noted. Do they share other behaviors and characteristics as well that predispose them to underachievement?

Personality traits

The bulk of the studies on underachievers have been done on boys because they appear to have learning problems more frequently than girls do. Havighurst, in a summary of a number of these studies, reported that the underachievers tend to be personally and socially maladjusted and that they share many of the following personality characteristics: (1964, p. 214)

1. They see themselves as inadequate;
2. They have lower aspirations than achievers;
3. They don't like school as much as achievers do;
4. They don't enjoy learning from books;
5. They have less popularity and lower leadership status among their peers;

6. They tend to come from homes that are emotionally inadequate or unstable and of low socioeconomic status;
7. They have poorer study habits than achievers do;
8. Their vocational goals are less clearly defined than achievers';
9. They have narrower interests than achievers do;
10. They are more poorly personally adjusted than achievers.

Jackson (1965) has applied this list to students who are malfunctioning in the motivation aspect of learning generally:

> The student who gets no pleasure from his own progress has devaluated the *intrinsic* reward system. Similarly, the student who doesn't care what the teachers or others think has devaluated the *extrinsic* reward system. . . . Devaluation (in form of student indifference) is often a reaction to the suspicion of unfairness or illogic in the handling of rewards. (p. 300)

The answer to why this suspicion arises in the first place may be found in the classroom situation itself or in the individual, as suggested by Havighurst.

From a study of fifth-grade underachieving boys, Morrison (1969) pinpointed hostility toward authority and passive aggression as two of the key personality characteristics of the underachiever group. Much earlier, Kimball (1953) had also found that the adolescent underachievers in her study (also all boys) were significantly more passive in their expression of their negative feelings than were their normally achieving peers. What does this mean? Consciously or unconsciously, the student may be trying to "get back" at his parents for real or imagined emotional injuries by failing to achieve. The parent who presses too hard on his child may bring on this type of behavior. That is, the parent may be saying in effect that nothing less than perfection is acceptable, which is interpreted by the child as being a case of "nothing less than perfection makes me worthy of my parents' love." Sometimes, poor performance is a passive form of rebellion against parental interests or goals, as when the parent wants his son to attend his alma mater or to be an engineer, and the boy would rather study elsewhere or become an historian. If he fails or does poorly in his math courses, he cannot become a successful engineer. While failing, he can plead lack of understanding of the course materials while at the same time he voices his attempt to comply with the parental wishes. A similar psychological process may operate at the precollege level.

Identification There have also been several attempts to find out how early underachievers can be identified so that intervention measures can be applied and the underachievement process stopped and reversed. Shaw and McCuen (1960) studied eleventh- and twelfth-graders for whom grades were available from their earliest school years and who had taken an intelligence test in the eighth grade. All of their subjects had IQs over 110, but the underachievers in their sample had a grade point average below the mean of their class. Shaw and McCuen found a significant difference in achievement among the boy achievers and nonachievers, as measured by grade point average, from the third grade on, and among the girls beginning at grade six. In a similar longitudinal study, Fitzsimmons, Cheever, Leonard, and Macunovich (1969) examined the records of middle-class suburban secondary students who had had three or more Ds or Fs during their high school years. "Of these students, 3 out of 4 had already demonstrated poor performance in the fourth grade, and by the seventh grade, 9 out of 10 had performed poorly." (p. 137) They found that the pattern of failure in this group tended to start with poor performance in reading in the early grades and that this later spread to other subjects such as English, social sciences, and science. This finding underscores the importance of reading ability as a key to other subjects. Not only does the early failure in reading contribute to the child's sense of personal inadequacy, but his inability to read quickly and/or with comprehension makes it more difficult for him to read books or problems in almost any other subject with success.

> *Note:* Even first-graders are aware of how well they read in comparison with their classmates, whether reading groups are called "high, medium, and low" or "Bluebirds, Cardinals, and Robins." They perceive the differences in level of difficulty of the readers, page numbers, and book bindings.

Remediation

What does this accumulation of information suggest to us? Obviously, classroom teachers are not psychotherapists and therefore cannot effectively intervene in parent-child relationships in any depth. They *can* suggest more realistic expectations to the parents, or a modification of parental reactions to poor grades. They *can* work with the learner to modify poor attitudes toward learning and poor self-concept as they try at the same time to improve study habits and competence in school subjects. Equally obvious, moreover, is the need for early intervention to prevent the development of the failure pattern at all. Ideally, appropriate individualized instruction should be the rule from the first day of school. Failing this, however, remedial and supportive programs in reading and arithmetic should be introduced as early as possible, with emphasis not only on changing performance levels, but also on changing attitudes toward school. (Fitzsimmons, *et al.*, 1969, p. 146) These programs should not be "blanket" programs where all children are given the same kind of assistance; they should ideally be diagnostic and prescriptive, so that each faltering learner is given the specific help that he needs.

You are aware by now that all children differ in what they bring to learning and in how they respond to the learning situation. It may even be that ". . . instructions that produce motivation and improved performance in good achievers may provoke anxiety and poorer performance in poor achievers." (Otto, 1965, p. 207) Or, it may be that the extrinsic reward system is not operating for a given child, either because it is misapplied or not applied at all or not right for that child. After all, not all children like lollipops or gold stars to the same degree. Therefore, ideally, the teacher who uses extrinsic rewards or concrete reinforcements needs to find out which one is meaningful to each of her pupils and award them accordingly. A nonmeaningful reinforcement has no effect on the learner. The teacher must try to find enough successes for the child to feel that he is acceptable and adequate. The school needs to identify and assist poor achievers early in the school years and do something to help them *then*, not when it is too late or more difficult to reverse the pattern of failure. All of these suggestions hold true, also, for children with learning disabilities whose underachievement is caused primarily by neurological involvements. (Their needs will be discussed in a later chapter.)

There should be recognition by teachers, also, that learners vary in their abilities. Few students are underachievers in every subject, although they are often treated that way. With a different teacher, or a different teaching method, or even a different mode of assessing achievement, the underachiever may "bloom." Each of these variations brings forth a different group of "star" learners or achievers, and the opportunity to be an achiever evokes its own push toward continued achievement as well as modifies the negative self-concept of the underachiever.

SUMMARY

This has been a chapter devoted to studying the effects of psychological factors on the learner. Beginning with the student's view of himself and how it develops, we have discussed motivation and anxiety, and, finally, how all three factors interact in the underachiever. There is no escaping the influence of parents on the child, for it is the parents who initially and continually shape the child's self-concept. At the same time, however, teachers, too, have an effect on the child's self-concept, with particular emphasis on the realm of learning. The first teachers a child has in school contribute greatly not only to his self-concept in relation to learning, but also to his attitudes toward school and himself generally. Thus, we might consider a feeling of acceptance as the primary need of the learner—acceptance for himself at home and at school. The studies reviewed indicate these tendencies: if the child feels that he is acceptable to his parents, his anxiety is reduced; if he feels that he is acceptable to his teachers, his motivation is increased and his attitudes toward school are positive.

On the basis of the work of Lewin and others, we have said that motivation is not an all-or-none phenomenon or concept, but rather that it can be demonstrated on a continuum of different levels of motivation. Our primary concern is with the development of intrinsic motivation, or working toward self-set goals for one's own satisfaction. When focused on achievement motivation, this concept implies realistic goal-setting, persistence, personal responsibility, optimal use of feedback (in the nature of teacher- or self-evaluation), and positive attitudes toward learning. We also discussed the effects of grades as causes and effects of motivation and found that grades are not universally effective as reinforcements, threats, or stimulants from the earliest grades through the college years.

At times, motivation is inhibited by anxiety, and at other times, anxiety increases motivation. The difference lies partly in the nature of the anxiety. Sources of anxiety, as well as differentiation and effects of different kinds of anxiety, were discussed in this chapter and illustrated by a number of research studies. Again, this psychological factor was presented in relation to learners of all school ages.

The ways in which psychological and other factors affect the learner with respect to achievement were discussed in terms of those who are successful and those who do not achieve as well as might be expected. The characteristics of the underachiever generally include both a high level of tension-interfering anxiety and a low level of academic achievement motivation. Naturally, the results of studies can be applied validly only to groups similar to those populations used in the original research, but these results do give direction to our thinking. Research on the underachiever, in particular, has guided us to practical techniques for reducing anxiety and underachievement and maximizing self-concept and motivation. The frequency of underachievement in our schools is so high that we must begin to use those techniques as early as possible for every needy learner.

In closing this chapter, we are also closing our formal investigation of nonintellectual influences on learning and the learner. The interaction of physiological, sociological, and psychological factors have been shown to affect both the normal and the exceptional child, although they are more easily demonstrated in the latter. It is difficult, if not impossible, to divide the effects proportionately among these three areas, for they are complexly interrelated. Given a child whose development has been normal physiologically from the prenatal period on, we can ascribe poor or good performance largely to the influence of his parents in the preschool years. As we have demonstrated, however, this influence has been developed itself in relation to ethnic and socioeconomic attitudes and mores, and it depends, too, on the emotional stability and the expectations of the parents. Once the child is in school, the teacher adds his or her influence to the personality of the developing learner. It is not enough, obviously, to say that the child is or is not a learner. We need to study him as a unique personality, to study his home and family, to consider at least the impact on him of his environment, and to discover his strengths and weaknesses—all with the goal of helping him to be a successful learner. For him, Maslow says: "Education is learning to grow, learning what is desirable and undesirable, learning what to choose and what not to choose." (1971, pp. 178–79)

Part Three

Intelligence and Evaluation

If a dog learns to fetch his master's paper, does this mean that he has intelligence? If a child learns to swim, is he intelligent? In both cases, we would have to answer affirmatively, for definitions of intelligence commonly state or imply the ability to learn as one of the requisites of intelligent behavior. The strength of the affirmative response would depend in some ways on whose definition of intelligence you use, for not all the theorists include nonacademic types of behavior as part of intelligence.

In the next three chapters we will focus on the themes of intelligence, mental growth, individual differences, and evaluation. The emphasis in discussing intelligence will be on definitions of the term, theories of intelligence, and tests designed to "measure" this characteristic. Our concern with the patterns of mental growth and individual differences is with what these mean in terms of ability to learn. An essential part of this section is a consideration of the application of the concept of intelligence in terms of its effect on the learner. This includes interpretation of intelligence test results; views of mental growth, particularly as they affect older learners; and teacher expectations.

There are means of evaluation other than intelligence tests. These include other types of tests (aptitude, achievement, attitude, interest). The tests, their interpretation, and the uses of this information are the content of the third chapter in this section.

Preview

THE NATURE OF INTELLIGENCE
   INTRODUCTION
   WHAT IS INTELLIGENCE?
      Binet
      Terman
      Spearman
      Thurstone
      Cattell
      Thorndike
      Wechsler
      Piaget
      Guilford
   CONCLUSIONS

TESTS OF INTELLIGENCE
   INTRODUCTION
   THE BINET-TYPE TEST
   THE WECHSLER TESTS
   GROUP TESTS
      Teacher Expectations
   "CULTURE-FAIR" TESTS

A CONTEMPORARY LOOK

SUMMARY

5

Intelligence: Theories and Tests

What is "intelligence" or "intelligent?" And, if we manage to define these terms, how do we measure them? Part of the answers to these questions lies in the nature of the culture where the answers are to be found. For example, a brilliant Latin scholar (brilliant by general American standards) in a primitive civilization will find little use for his Latin and will retain his reputation for high abilities only if he is able to perform at a superior level in the skills of that civilization. Similarly, a poorly educated village child may function quite adequately in his native setting, but may be considered mentally retarded when compared with children in a more urban environment. An example of this situation was seen in a "Focus" segment in chapter three. In other words, we need to decide not only what intelligence or intelligent behavior is, but also by what criteria we will measure it.

THE NATURE OF INTELLIGENCE

In what ways do you define intelligence? (Write out your definition at this point.) — **Question**

An examination of definitions of intelligence in standard psychological dictionaries reveals little more than the fact that several definitions have been offered through the years by several noted psychologists, each of which is quoted briefly. Let us turn, then, to a contemporary general dictionary in which intelligence is defined as: "a. The capacity to acquire and apply knowledge. b. The faculty of thought and reason. c. Superior powers of mind." (Morris, 1969, p. 682) Does this definition fit *your* conception of intelligence? We might generally agree that an intelligent person can acquire knowledge and that he is somewhat more intelligent if he can also apply — **Introduction** this knowledge. The next phrase, however, "the faculty of thought and reason," is out of keeping with the twentieth-century deemphasis on "faculties of the mind." That was a nineteenth-century concept in which the "mind" was divided into faculties (thinking, feeling) and subfaculties (memory, numerical ability), which it was thought could be precisely located in the brain. This concept led to the development of difficult curricula designed to exercise the mental faculties, much as stretching and bending are used to exercise the muscles of the body. The third part of the dictionary definition implies that people who do not have superior mental powers, whatever that may be, are not intelligent. Again, by experience, we are forced to use a continuum to indicate that people exhibit various levels of intelligence, for it is virtually impossible (with some rare exceptions) to describe a person as having *no* intelligence. A look at the diagram of the normal curve reminds us of how intelligence is distributed along this continuum in a normal population.

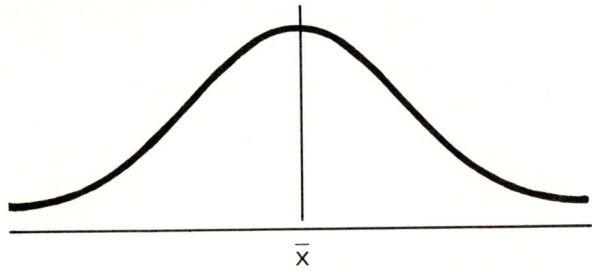

Figure 5.1   *Distribution of intelligence along the normal curve of probability.*

Individuals function with a greater or lesser degree of intelligence, which may vary according to measuring standards used.

Having found the dictionary definition of intelligence wanting in several respects, we need to find another route to a more satisfactory definition. Is intelligence a unitary concept, such as a general ability? Is it an additive concept, in which several different abilities are summed up to reach an intelligence "score"? Is it more of a Gestalt concept, a functional composite in which the whole is greater than the sum of its parts? Are there different kinds of intelligence that interact to form unique patterns of intelligent behavior? Or simply, are there different kinds of intelligence? Obviously, there is a choice of routes. Psychologists in the United States and other countries have sought the correct one throughout this century. Each psychologist, of course, believed or believes that his or her analysis of what constitutes intelligence is the most satisfactory explanation. These psychologists designed tests in an attempt to define intelligence. From the results, they developed theories that were significant contributions to psychology. These psychologists can be grouped according to their overall point of view as to the nature of intelligence, and this is what we shall now do. After discussing various approaches to the definition of intelligence, we will examine several types of tests that are currently used to measure intelligence. Whether "intelligence is what intelligence tests measure," as some say, remains to be seen.

One group of psychologists stresses adaptation to the environment as the primary characteristic of intelligent behavior. A second group emphasizes that intelligence is the ability to learn. A third contingent defines intelligence in terms of the ability to do abstract thinking. Actually, as Freeman (1950) points out, ". . . a definition of intelligence as the capacity to behave appropriately and effectively in new situations and a definition that intelligence is the ability to learn are in fact two aspects of the same process." (p. 69)

What is intelligence?

Binet

The father of intelligence testing, Alfred Binet, worked for about ten years at the turn of this century to determine the differences between "bright" and "dull" children. He worked under the auspices of the French government, which wanted a means of predicting probable educational achievement. Part of this purpose was served by differentiating the retarded from other learners through psychological tests. From his studies, Binet developed a conception of intelligence which defined it as ". . . the tendency to take and maintain a definite direction; the capacity to make adaptations for the purpose of attaining a desired end; and the power of auto-criticism." (Terman, 1916, p. 45) Ah-ha! We have here something quite different from our dictionary definition, a viewpoint which combines different functions. Binet, and others after him, tended to see intelligence as a general ability. In a discussion of the term "intelligence," Binet and his colleague, Simon, wrote that

> It seems to us that in intelligence there is a fundamental faculty, the alteration or the lack of which, is of the utmost importance for practical life. This faculty is judgment, otherwise called good sense, practical sense, initiative, the faculty of adapting one's self to circumstances. To judge well, to comprehend well, to reason well, these are the essential activities of intelligence. (Binet and Simon, 1905/1961, p. 886)

His definition is certainly a functional one, if you consider that it describes how an intelligent individual functions. The capacity for adaptation, included by Binet, is one aspect of intelligence which is, as we have seen, still believed to be an essential ingredient of intelligent behavior. It is, however, regarded by some psychologists today more as evidence of problem-solving ability (which may or may not itself be part of intelligent behavior). The power of self-criticism becomes involved with emotional factors, which Binet may or may not have recognized. An egoist, or a highly defensive individual, for example, may not be able to allow himself to indulge in self-criticism. Such behavior might cause overwhelming anxiety. On the other hand, the ability to criticize one's own work, to be able to recognize and acknowledge one's own successes and errors, does require a certain level of intellectual maturity, standards by which to evaluate one's efforts, and sufficient emotional stability to carry out the evaluation.

Alfred Binet: Father of intelligence testing.

It is the first part of Binet's definition that really affects the learner, however. To be able to select and maintain directed effort means that the learner must have certain abilities: memory, focused attention, adaptation (for learning implies adaptations or changes in behavior with new experiences and/or increased maturity). Those children who exhibited little evidence of these abilities were called "dull" and were not expected to profit much from classroom instruction. Those who could "take and maintain a definite direction" were considered bright by Binet. Possibly this was a crude distinction, but it was the first modern move toward fitting learners and learning together with some degree of appropriateness. By 1909, Binet had revised his original definition of intelligence somewhat as a result of his experiences with classes for retarded children and the teaching techniques used in them. This definition of intelligence viewed it as a ". . . union of all the little functions of discrimination, observation, retention, etc. . . ." which can be developed to an upper limit with practice, training, and proper methods. (Binet, 1909/1969, p. 69)

Terman

Lewis Terman, who translated Binet's work into English and revised it for American use as the Stanford-Binet test, supplemented Binet's definition by including as part of intelligence "the ability to do abstract thinking." This is the ability to do one's work by means of symbols rather than by using concrete objects. We expect all school-age children to be able to do some abstract thinking, even at the simple level of adding $1 + 1$ without having two objects in view or in hand. At a later age, abstract thinking includes the ability to hypothesize alternative solutions to a problem, think them through, evaluate them mentally, and select the one with the highest probability of success, all without actually working each one out on a trial-and-error basis. Some individuals obviously are more capable of mentally manipulating symbols (numbers or words) than others. Terman stressed the numerical score derived from the Stanford-Binet test as evidence of mental superiority or inferiority, leaving little room for Binet's more clinical evaluation, which included the influence of personality and emotional factors on intellectual functioning. Unfortunately, even today, too many people assess a child's ability to learn solely on the basis of an IQ score, omitting consideration of the other psychological factors discussed in earlier chapters.

Spearman

Both Binet and Terman saw intelligence as a union or "ensemble" of abilities. This was a theory proposed also by Charles Spearman, an eminent British psychologist. He believed that intelligence was a general ability, which he called *G*. However, this general ability of *G* incorporated many specific or *s* factors, such as mechanical abilities, reasoning, logic, and so on. A diagrammatic representation of Spearman's approach is presented in Figure 5.2.

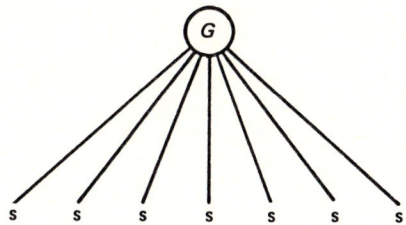

Representation of Spearman's early definition of intelligence. **Figure 5.2**

However,

whereas Binet had been willing to consider personality and emotion as contributing to intellectual functioning, Spearman sought to isolate the purely intellectual element, i.e., to observe "mind" in its strictest sense. While some useful reasoning tasks were devised by Spearman and his students, their more fundamental influence was on the aims of testing and on test interpretation. In particular, their work encouraged 1) a sharp separation of intellectual powers from acquired understandings and from emotion and temperament; 2) ranking persons along a single dimension; and 3) interpreting the score as a measure of pure intellectual capacity. Only gradually have psychologists broken away from this thinking. (Cronbach, 1970, pp. 202–3)

The basis for Spearman's conclusion that there was a general ability factor of intelligence was his finding on the tests he constructed that there was a moderate to high positive correlation among different intelligence tests. The fact that this correlation was not a perfect one ($r = 1.00$) was explained by the presence of the specific factors called forth in the various tests. By 1927, Spearman had further refined his theory of intelligence to include major group factors such as verbal, numerical, and spatial abilities. (Spearman, 1927) The illustration of this revised conception is shown in Figure 5.3.

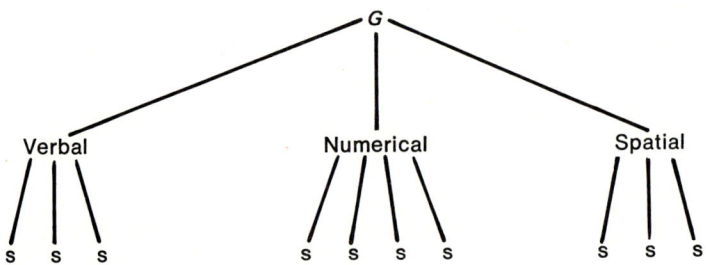

Figure 5.3   *Representation of Spearman's later definition of intelligence.*

Later British psychologists, such as Burt, Thomson, and Vernon, have continued along this line of thinking in their views of intelligence. However, they have placed more stress on factor analysis, which minimizes the importance of Spearman's G.

Thurstone

Factor analysis, a statistical approach to the task of defining intelligence, is perhaps best exemplified by the work of Thurstone and Thurstone. Their emphasis is on group factors rather than the specific factors first hypothesized by Spearman. They concluded, again on the basis of tests they constructed, that certain mental operations are united in clusters or groups, each of which has a primary unifying factor that differentiates it from other groups of mental operations. Through factor analysis, they have clearly defined seven "primary mental abilities," with an eighth tentatively defined. (Thurstone, 1955) These are:

1. **V** verbal comprehension
2. **W** word fluency
3. **N** number
4. **S** space visualization
5. **M** rote or immediate memory
6. **R** reasoning
7. **P** perceptual speed
8. **D** deduction

Items testing most, if not all, of these abilities are included in most contemporary tests of intelligence. On the Thurstones' Test of Primary Mental Abilities, however, each ability is considered an element of a profile of scores rather than as contributing to a single overall intelligence score.

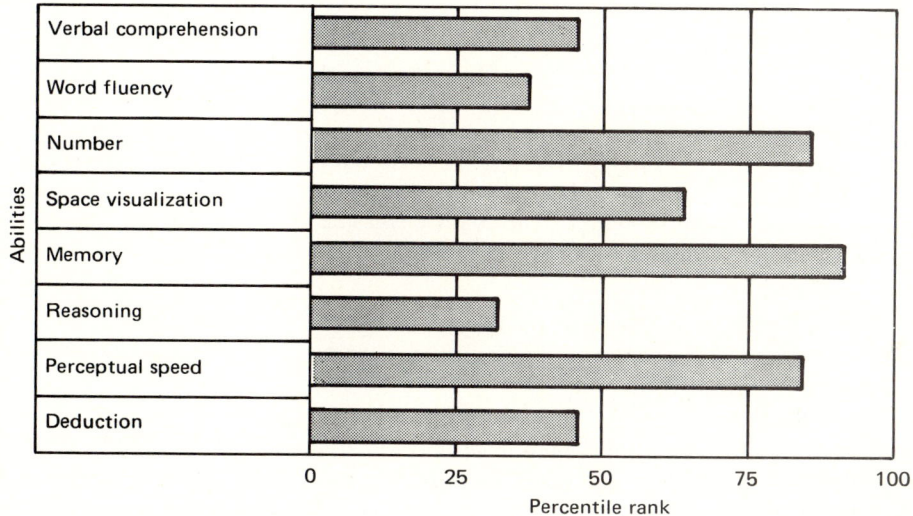

*Test of Primary Mental Abilities.

A sample profile of "primary mental abilities."   **Figure 5.4**

Such a profile tends to be more useful to a teacher than a single score. The profile permits the teacher to see immediately where the learner's strengths and weaknesses are, as well as the learner's achievement in comparison to his grade-level peers.

The difference in interpretation of test scores, however, does not negate completely the concept of a general ability. As Cattell and Butcher (1968) have pointed out, the relationship of Spearman's "G" to Thurstone's "primary mental abilities" might well be explained as the existence in every individual of "... an inborn general ability, which, by practice and experience, becomes directed in different degrees to different areas." (p. 16)

Cattell

Cattell, himself, also using factor analysis methods, has attempted to reconcile these two points of view by distinguishing two kinds of general ability, fluid and crystallized. Fluid intelligence is seen as the capacity for learning and adaptation, which is relatively independent of education and experience. It is what we have previously considered the inherited intellectual potential. Crystallized intelligence, on the other hand, is the result of experience—acquired knowledge and the development of intellectual skills. (Cattell, 1963, pp. 1–22) The two are necessarily related in the learner. In a later work, reflecting further research with this approach, it has been shown that

> Crystallized ability . . . loads more highly those cognitive performances in which certain initial intelligent judgments have become crystallized as habits. . . . Fluid general ability, on the other hand, shows more in tests requiring adaptations to entirely new situations, where crystallized skills are of no advantage because they do not apply to the particular data.
>
> Before biological maturity (fourteen to eighteen years), individual differences between g_f and g_c will mainly reflect differences in cultural opportunity and interest. Among adults, however, these discrepancies will also reflect differences in age, because the gap between g_c and g_f will tend to increase with experience, which raises g_c, whereas it has frequently been shown . . . that with increasing age some decay of g_f occurs. (Cattell and Butcher, 1968, p. 19)

For the moment, we will postpone discussion of the stability of intelligence or some of its aspects and concentrate instead on the implications of Cattell's two-pronged theory.

He has postulated that fluid intelligence is, in effect, an innate potential and that crystallized intelligence is essentially shaped by environmental opportunities. Since we do not know anyone's upper limit of intellectual potential as a certainty, we are obligated to question what opportunities the learner may have had or lacked that affected his ability to learn, and also what experiences should be included in the learner's life to maximize the use of whatever fluid intelligence he may have. Thus, Cattell's theory is highly relevant to our earlier discussions of the effects of ethnic group affiliations, stimulus deprivation, critical periods for learning, socioeconomic status, and so on. This is reflected in the types of tests that Cattell sees as appropriate for measuring his two aspects of intellectual functioning. Fluid intelligence

> . . . will be measured most purely when task materials are culture fair; that is, the fundamentals are either novel for all persons being measured or else are extremely common, over-learned elements of a culture, and the aids needed to attain solutions are not those made available, by favored educational opportunity, to some persons and not to others among those measured. (Horn and Cattell, 1966, p. 255)

Such a test for g_f would include items measuring the factors of reasoning, induction, memory span, associative memory, and simple clerical speed. To test crystallized intelligence (g_c), which reflects experiential-educative-acculturation influences, on the other hand, one would include items relevant to the factors of verbal comprehension, judgment, evaluation, and mechanical knowledge. After a number of studies in this area, Cattell found himself "... forced to a definition of intelligence as *the capacity to perceive relationships (regardless of content)*." (Cattell, 1971, p. 17)

Thorndike

A somewhat different multifactor theory of intelligence was developed by E. L. Thorndike more than half a century ago. (1920) Despite its age, his theory still has its proponents. Thorndike hypothesized that there were actually three kinds of intelligence: social, abstract, and concrete. Although these are somewhat interrelated within the individual, each kind of intelligence has a different function. Social intelligence, for example, refers to the ability to understand and deal with people. A person scoring high in this area would be able to understand people's motivations, perceive social relationships, comprehend everyday problems, and the like. He would, very simply, be able to get along well with others. There are few estimates of how much of this ability is innate and how much is learned, and any attempted interpretation would tend to reflect theoretical psychological biases (psychoanalytic, developmental, learning, etc.). It is quite possible that an individual may be high in social intelligence without having comparable abilities in abstract and/or concrete intelligence.

Abstract intelligence implies the ability to understand and deal with symbols, which is similar to Terman's view that intelligence is the ability to do abstract thinking. This is the kind of intelligence the learner needs in greatest abundance for success in the school situation and is also the kind most commonly measured by intelligence tests. Included in Thorndike's own test (the CAVD test of intelligence) are items in which the subject has to deal with sentence completion (C), arithmetical reasoning (A), vocabulary (V), and following directions (D).

> It is not claimed by Thorndike that these four sets of items encompass the entire range of abstract intelligence. They represent and sample only certain parts; but because of the very significant correlations between all types of measures within the tested range, it is held, the other aspects of abstract intelligence can be estimated with satisfactory accuracy from those portions that are actually measured by this test. (Freeman, 1950, p. 81)

As for concrete intelligence, an individual who scores high in this area would tend to be competent in dealing with objects. Again, it is possible for a person to be concretely quite intelligent but not high in abstract and/or social intelligence. He would probably be a good technician or mechanic, able to follow blueprints, for example, but not necessarily capable of originating their designs.

Thorndike's three kinds of intelligence are not mutually exclusive, but neither are they interactive or intercorrelated to a high degree, as has been already suggested. The difficulties for learners whose strength is not in abstract intelligence may be reduced if they have a high level of concrete intelligence, for they can study in vocational or technical education programs. For those whose greatest strength lies in social intelligence, there may be greater problems during the school years if this capacity is not supported by average or above-average abstract intelligence. As adults, they may succeed in any of several types of interpersonal positions, but as elementary and secondary school students they would probably experience learning difficulties. Thorndike's concept of intelligence is perceptive of inter- and intra-individual differences and is particularly useful as a guidance tool.

Wechsler

Among the more widely used individual intelligence tests are those devised by Wechsler. He summarizes his views of intelligence as ". . . the overall capacity of an individual to understand and cope with the world around him." (Wechsler, 1974, p. 5) He stresses the overall or global quality of what is inferred from the variety of behaviors exhibited by an individual, rather than a single factor. He also recognizes the role of nonintellective factors (e.g., motivation, aptitude) in intelligent behavior. The validity of including these factors has been questioned, but as we saw in chapter four, there is no doubt that they have an effect on behavior in the academic realm. The poorly motivated but highly intelligent learner is frequently an underachiever; the highly motivated but not as intelligent learner can often be an above-average achiever.

Focus 5–1

The most comprehensive of these "traditional" definitions of intelligence is probably the one offered by Stoddard:

Intelligence is the ability to undertake activities that are characterized by 1) difficulty, 2) complexity, 3) abstractness, 4) economy [efficiency], 5) adaptiveness to a goal, 6) social value, and 7) the emergence of originals, and to maintain such activities under conditions that demand a concentration of energy and a resistance to emotional forces. (1943, p. 4)

Stoddard's definition implies qualitative differences in intellectual functioning that incorporate two of the characteristics of creative thinking, flexibility and originality, as defined by Guilford and Torrance, as well as the more traditional concepts of abstract thinking, adaptation, varying levels of difficulty, and the goal-direction and motivation which Wechsler included. The inclusion of "social value" as a criterion of intelligent behavior is open to debate, for not all intelli-

David Wechsler: Designer of individual intelligence tests.

gent behavior has this characteristic at the time it occurs. By what or whose standards may behavior be judged as having social value? Many of our greatest inventors have been criticized as nonintelligent "tinkerers," or worse, because their work did not meet this criterion; yet today their visionary efforts provide many of society's necessities as well as luxuries. (This same criticism recurs in defining creativity and is subject to the same debate.)

Piaget

Two other contemporary psychologists, Piaget and Guilford, have approached the task of defining intelligence from rather nontraditional vantage points. Piaget, for example, has observed and tested children for nearly half a century with the goal of discovering how their mental processes develop. A major American interpreter, Elkind, expounded Piaget's view of intelligence as

> ... an extension of biological adaptation which, in lieu of the instinctive adaptations in animals, permits relatively autonomous adaptations which bear the stamp not only of our genetic endowment, but also of our physical and social experience. On the plane of intelligence we inherit the processes of assimilation (processes responsive to inner promptings) and of accommodation (processes responsive to environmental intrusions). Assimilative processes guarantee that intelligence will not be limited to passively copying reality, while accommodative processes insure that intelligence will not construct representations of reality which have no correspondence with the real world. (1969, p. 329)

Piaget therefore includes both the qualities of adaptation and intrinsic motivation in his definition.

Since Piaget sees intelligence as developing from motor activity, this would be the area where experience should be stimulated, for, ". . . the wider the range of the activity, the more diversified will be the intellectual operations of the developing child." (Rowland and McGuire, 1968, p. 51) Active interaction between the child and his environment is essential for the evolution of his intelligence, and adult intervention can encourage this interaction. A lack of opportunity for the child to interact with the environment, as we saw in our study of the effects of stimulus deprivation in early childhood, will necessarily slow down the evolutionary process.

Piaget divided the development of intelligence into four major stages: sensorimotor (birth to age two), preoperational (ages two to seven), concrete operations (ages seven to eleven), and formal operations (ages eleven to fifteen). He further distinguished between intellectual structures, the changes in intelligence that occur in these stages, and intellectual functioning, which is a continuing process. The two *functional invariants,* or continuing characteristics of intellectual functioning, are organization and adaptation. Organization implies the coordination of intellectual acts and is largely internal, while adaptation implies the balance of assimilation and accommodation (Flavell, 1963, pp. 47–48) *Assimilation* occurs whenever the organism utilizes something from the environment and incorporates it into his behavior (as in play). *Accommodation* is the "adjustment" of the organism to new information (as in imitation). These two aspects of functioning, along with organization, are seen throughout the intellectual behavior of human beings.

The development of intelligence, utilizing the functional invariants, proceeds in orderly fashion from stage to stage, according to Piaget, as follows:

1. Sensori-motor period

    a. reflex behavior (birth to one month): the neonate has no voluntary control over his responses to stimulation

    b. primary circular reactions (one to four months): the baby looks about aimlessly at first and then "looks to see" (i.e., looks about purposefully). This implies that he must have something at which to look, be it his mother's face, or a dangling toy

    c. secondary circular reactions (ages four to eight months): the infant includes his earlier responses in repetitive and self-reinforcing activities, for example, he shakes a rattle in order to hear the noise

d. coordination of secondary schemata (ages eight to twelve months): at this plateau, as he coordinates what he has already experienced, the baby is becoming more capable of acting purposefully, of separating means and ends (this is the beginning of an awareness of causality or the relationship between cause and effect), and is taking more interest in objects and events generally

e. tertiary circular reactions (ages twelve to eighteen months): the child begins to "experiment" to discover new properties of known objects and events, learns to use simple "tools" with the awareness that they are not part of or extensions of himself but are something different from himself, and engages in deliberate acts. He is mobile enough to move forward or away from a person or object voluntarily and to select acts appropriate to some situations, as when he says "bye-bye" when his mother puts on her coat.

f. invention of new means through mental combinations (ages eighteen to twenty-four months): now a toddler, the child is gaining object permanence (i.e., he can follow the displacement of objects and will look for the hidden object), gives considerable effort to conscious imitation, increases his use of symbolism as in using words to represent something concrete. He is, basically, creating new relationships among already existing elements of his experience

2. Preconceptual or preoperational phase (ages two to seven years)

   a. increasing internalization and manipulation of symbols

   b. shift from physical action to verbal explanation as the child develops increasing facility with symbols which he can manipulate and communicate with others

   c. growth of language, starting with "one-word sentences" such as "Eat!" for "I want to eat," and progressing through garbled syntax ("Let me key the door," "It's raining and winding out") to a quite comprehensible, almost adult use of language structure with rapidly increasing vocabulary

   d. intellectual behavior characterized by:

      1) concreteness

      2) irreversibility (e.g., $2 + 3 = 5$, but $5 - 3 = ?$ is not seen as its inverse)

      3) egocentrism of thought

      4) centering—or the inability to shift from one point of view to another

5) states v. transformations—the inability to see an action sequence (e.g., child can see a stick as vertical and then horizontal, but not follow its different angles as it falls)

6) transductive reasoning—in which he can relate particular to particular (e.g., A causes B, therefore B causes A)

3. Concrete operations (ages seven to eleven years)

   a. acquisition of concepts of conservation of number, quantity, weight, volume, time

   b. understanding of simple relationships

   c. ability to arrange items in a series according to a rule such as height or weight

   d. complete operations and reverse them (now the child can relate $2 + 3 = 5$ to $5 - 3 = 2$ and $3 + 2 = 5$)

   e. classification of items at an elementary level (e.g., house, stable, garage, and tent may all be considered some kind of "home")

4. Formal operations (ages eleven years and up)

   a. ability to develop hypotheses and alternatives mentally and to evaluate them systematically

   b. reflective thought, enabling the adolescent to make conjectures about the future although he may not always be very practical in his planning

   c. classification of objects at an increasingly abstract level

   d. less egocentric in his point of view

   e. can follow the form of an argument at an abstract level, discarding specific content while comprehending the principles involved.

The last two stages are, of course, the most relevant to examining the child as a learner in the school situation. In practice, we can see children and adolescents operating with considerable overlap among these stages, although they have been presented as distinct. Piaget has been criticized both for his research methods, which are not considered experimentally sound by many American psychologists, and for his apparent lack of awareness of inter- and intra-individual differences in patterns of development. Many facets of his developmental theory have been substantiated, however, in controlled research situations. We will examine a number of such specific instances in our discussion of thinking in chapter nine.

Guilford

The other "nontraditionalist" with whom we need to be concerned is J. P. Guilford. He has developed a "unified theory of human intellect, which organizes the known, unique or primary intellectual abilities into a single system called the 'structure of intellect.' " (Guilford, 1959) The existence of these factors has been determined by factor analysis, and "each intellectual component or factor is a unique ability that is needed to do well in a certain class of tasks or test." (p. 470) The factors can be grouped in three ways: as processes or operations, as materials or content, and as products. Each of these categories can be further divided into smaller units which still group the intellectual factors, as shown in Figure 5.5.*

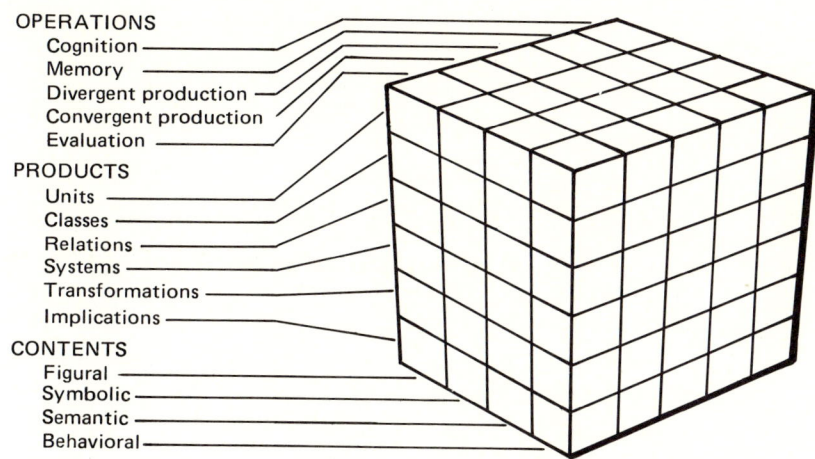

*Guilford, J. P., Intelligence: 1966 model. *American Psychologist*, 1966, *21*, 21. Copyright 1966 by the American Psychological Corporation. Reprinted by permission.

Model of the structure of intellect. **Figure 5.5**

Guilford has identified at least 120 distinct abilities which may be broadly classified as concrete, symbolic abstract, semantic abstract, and social intelligence. He differentiates symbolic from semantic abstract intelligence in educational implications by saying that

> Symbolic abilities should be important in learning to recognize words, to spell, and to operate with numbers. Language and mathematics should depend very much on them. . . . Semantic intelligence is important for understanding things in terms of verbal concepts and hence is important in all courses where the learning of facts and ideas is essential. (Guilford, 1959, p. 477)

Again, a detailed analysis of the individual and minor group factors Guilford has found must wait for our chapter on thinking. However, he does perceive intelligence as the function of the interaction of (five) operations, (four types of) content, and (six) product categories. In a later article, Guilford shifted from the cube model in Figure 5.5 to a more computer-like model of intellect. This more recent conceptualization utilizes the ideas of input, filtering, cognition, evaluation, and memory storage, which are terms and concepts we associate with mechanically complex computers. Essentially, then,

Guilford appears to see the mind functioning intellectually somewhat like a computer, but with added flexibility and the capacity to create original responses.

In this later model, Guilford stresses the arousal of attention, or "filtering," the dependence of the individual on his memory storage, and evaluation *during* the problem-solving operation, rather than solely at the conclusion of the process. It is possible that, from this point of view, the more intelligent individual is the one who makes most effective use of both his memorative and evaluative thinking abilities as he goes along. No distinction is made between convergent and divergent production. Rather, Guilford wrote that

> which kind of productive activity occurs will depend upon the kind of search model that is set up consequent to cognition of the problem structure. If the structuring is complete and if enough information is available and is used, the production should be convergent; if there is not enough information for determination of the answer or if the problem is incompletely structured, the production is likely to be divergent. (1966, p. 25)

Among the many studies that this approach has generated is one concerning the comparative structure of intellect in four-year-olds of different racial and socioeconomic backgrounds. One hundred white and black children were tested on six of Guilford's ability factors, and the results supported the hypothesis that the most significant differences between races and between classes would be on the factor of cognitive semantics (or verbal comprehension). That is, ". . . class and race differences seem limited to the functions that use Standard English . . . and are not found in expressive language or in memory or figural activities. This finding is the more impressive when it is recalled that the sample of [black] children was not entirely equivalent to the white in class status. . . ." (Sitkei and Meyers, 1969, pp. 600–601) To give you an idea of the types of ability factors for which individuals may be tested under Guilford's theory, here are the ones which Sitkei and Meyers included in their test battery:

1. CMU—cognition of semantic units (verbal comprehension)—relating a picture to a given word, answering simple questions ("What runs?"), understanding questions
2. DMU—divergent semantic units (ideational fluency)—describing pictures, multiple uses of items, naming as many items as possible in a category
3. EFU—evaluation of figural units (perceptual speed)—color-form matching and figure matching, as quickly as possible
4. NF—figural convergence (figural or spatial reasoning)—picture completion and selection of the "different" item in a series or group of items
5. MSS—memory for symbolic systems (auditory memory span)—repetition of numbers, letters, and sentences

6. MMU—memory for figural semantic units (object-picture memory)—memory for names of objects or pictures. (pp. 600–601)

Further illustration of Guilford's ability factors will be given in the section of this chapter dealing with intelligence tests.

Conclusions

We have considered a number of different approaches to the definition of intelligence. Other than deciding that psychologists are "hairsplitters," to what conclusions can we come? We might easily agree that intelligence is a multifaceted concept, derived from both hereditary and environmental sources, which describes an individual's level of functioning in several areas of behavior. We might further agree that what appears to be an overall "intelligence" actually is a *construct* (a nonobservable entity) composed of abilities in these different areas, and that the abilities are themselves determined by specific skills or bits of information. That is, logically, a hierarchical model might best serve our purposes in attempting to describe and define intelligence. Such a model, combining the thinking of several theorists, is shown in Figure 5.6.

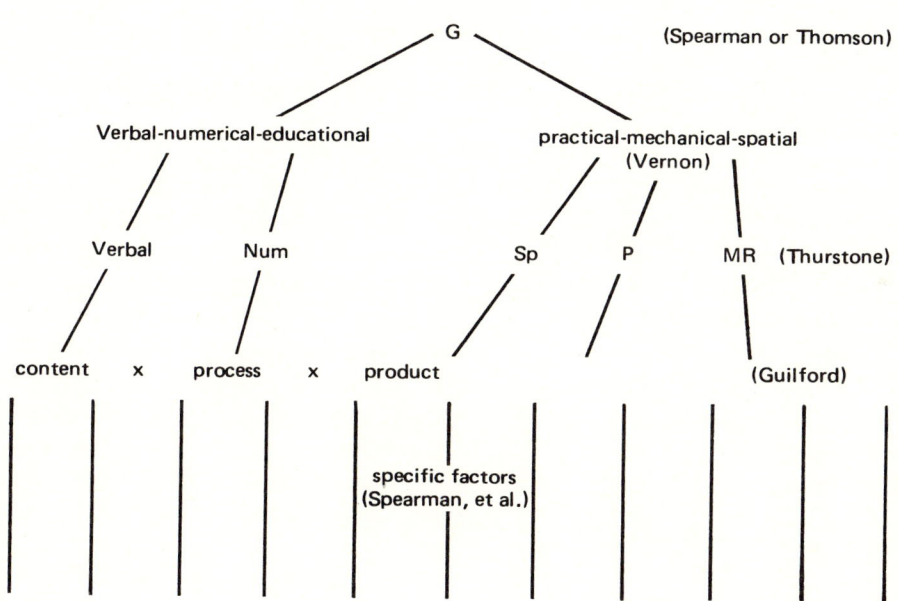

A hierarchical model of intelligence.   **Figure 5.6**

Vernon is a British psychologist who theorized that the major group factors are 1) verbal-numerical-educational and 2) practical-mechanical-spatial-physical. (1950) He does not include Thorndike's social intelligence, although this might be subsumed under the second major group of factors (which Thorndike would call "concrete"). Vernon and other British and American psychologists tend to view "G" as determined by overlapping bonds among the group abilities rather than as an all-encompassing unitary concept. Whether you agree with this hierarchical point of views depends on the conclusions you draw from evidence available from research with the various tests that were designed in accordance with each theory.

Hunt, a prominent psychologist, conducted studies of Piaget's theory, computers, and neuropsychology. On the basis of these studies, he concluded that intellectual capacities, or intelligence, are based on processes within the brain that function in ways similar to electronic computers. (1961, p. 362) Hunt further believes that concepts of mental age, IQ, and general or "g" intelligence "... have stood in the way of serious consideration of the concept of intellectual development as a hierarchy of learning sets which underlie a sequential [development] in the structure of information processing." (Hunt and Kirk, 1971, p. 286) He does not believe that intelligence is fixed or that it is predetermined by heredity.

Also important as a view of intelligence is the associationists' idea that the more associations a person can make to a stimulus, the greater potential intelligence he may have. This is because he can adapt to his environment (one definition of intelligence) in a larger variety of ways.

Questions *On the basis of your reading, would you now wish to revise your earlier definition of intelligence? Do you think that "intelligence" can be taught?*

The importance of being aware that there *are* different viewpoints about intelligence is obvious if you are going to be involved at all with interpreting the results of intelligence tests. You need to know the bases on which the test was constructed—factor analysis or theoretical construct. You need to know what the test conductor was attempting to measure—general information in one or more areas of functioning, aptitude in one or more areas, or specific skills. You need to know, for example, that you cannot obtain a single "intelligence quotient" from Thurstone's Primary Mental Abilities Test and why this can't be done. In the preceding pages, such theoretical differences have been presented. In the next several pages, we will see how these theories are implemented in tests.

TESTS OF INTELLIGENCE

Introduction Basically, intelligence tests may be grouped in two ways: individual or group, and verbal or performance. Historically, the modern intelligence tests developed from Binet's individual verbal tests. Group testing began in World War I, when it became necessary to classify large numbers of draftees for military service. When it was found that many were functionally illiterate, performance or nonverbal tests were devised. After this initial development of group tests for military purposes, the tests were reworked for application in the field of education. As with any innovation, they were used abundantly and abused frequently, until in recent years, negative attitudes toward intelligence testing have increased markedly. Although the tests have been refined as our knowledge of human behavior expanded, and although the need for some evaluation of intelligence for certain purposes is conceded, many large urban school districts have decided to discontinue the use of intelligence tests.

What about the tests has caused this turnabout? There are a number of reasons, some of the major ones being that the test results have been too often misinterpreted, considered "sacred," or considered definitive and fixed, and misused.

Focus 5–2

> As an example, take a first-grade boy—Bobby by name, new to formal education and away from home all day for the first time. At home, he left Mother taking care of a brand new baby sister. A group intelligence test is given on which he achieves an "intelligence quotient" of 90. That is, his chronological age exceeded his mental age. His teacher mentally labeled him as a slow learner and treated him accordingly, expecting low-average achievement. Five or six years later, his current teacher took the time to examine his school record and discovered that this slow learning boy had earned mostly As and Bs in his school work. How could this be? Had he suddenly grown smarter? Was he an "overachiever"? On a retest, Bobby achieved an IQ of 127, in the bright or superior range (mental age now exceeded chronological age). Only then did the school become aware that he had been bright all along, but that his emotional crises in first grade had hindered his performance at that time. Subsequently, Bobby completed grades seven through nine in two years under a rapid advance junior high school program then in existence in New York, was graduated from high school at age 16, was graduated from college, and as an adult is a highly successful business executive.
>
> The point of this and many similar examples is that too often such children are retained in slow-learning classes throughout their school years, particularly where insufficient psychological staff (or uncaring teachers) is a problem, and are never given the opportunity to overcome the original label. Parents are advised not to expect too much of the youngster, and his personality development as well as his academic development may be affected adversely.

A second major area of reasons for the negative attitudes toward intelligence tests is that they are considered biased in favor of the majority middle-class culture and are therefore unfair to the "culturally different." It is largely for this reason (better sampling) that the Stanford-Binet test was revised in 1960, using white and black, rural and urban, and all socioeconomic class subjects as the bases for new norms. (Illustrations used in the test also needed updating, however.) Several psychologists have also been trying to develop "culture-fair" tests to eliminate the middle-class bias. These are usually nonverbal tests and so far have not been perfected.

152 INTELLIGENCE AND EVALUATION

What constitutes intelligent behavior is, after all, a cultural value judgment, and a satisfactory differentiation of the more intelligent from the less intelligent will depend on the criteria established by someone who is a member of some culture. Liverant suggested that this be recognized in interpreting and using intelligence tests, by regarding them as aptitude tests which measure cultural expectations of academic preparation and which involve also a number of psychological or emotional variables in their results. (1960, p. 24) The unfortunate problem, of course, is that too few teachers or administrators recognize that test scores are a reflection of preschool experiences interwoven with psychological factors.

The Binet-type test

The term "IQ" or "intelligence quotient" has been used frequently in these pages. Since this is ultimately the single aspect of intelligence testing that is most abused, we might profitably look at its derivation and meaning. Fundamentally, the IQ describes the relationship between *mental age* and *chronological age*. This permits the comparison of a subject's intellectual level with that of other subjects of the same chronological age. The basic concept of a mental age was developed by Binet, and the procedure he used to compute the mental age was followed on the Stanford-Binet tests until the 1960 revision. This involved finding a basal year (i.e., the year level below which all tests were passed) and then adding additional credits in months for tests passed above that level. It should be noted that the Stanford-Binet tests are arranged by age levels: Year III, Year VII, and so on.

> The six tests under the heading year V cover the period from IV-6 to V; the six tests under the heading year VI cover the period from year V to year VI. Since the age periods are divided into six months intervals from years two to five, we count one month toward mental age for each of the six tests at a given level in this part of the scale. From year six to fourteen each year group represents an interval of twelve months and we therefore count two months toward mental age for each of the six tests at these levels. (Terman and Merrill, 1937, pp. 65–66)

The mental age is therefore computed in months as seen in this example.

Focus 5–3

For a child with a chronological age (CA) of eight years, four months (8-4), scores obtained on the Binet test are:

	Years	Months
Year VII, all passed. Basal year	7	
Year VIII, 4 tests passed at 2 months		8
Year IX, 2 tests passed at 2 months		4
Year X, 2 tests passed at 2 months		4
Year XI, no tests passed. Upper limit		0
	7	16

(7 years-16 months = 8 years-4 months, or 100 months mental age)

Age scores are converted to months, as above, for easier computation. Since the child has a mental age of 8 years, 4 months or 100 months, and a chronological age of 8 years, 4 months or 100 months, these figures are substituted in the ratio formula:

$$\frac{\text{Mental Age}}{\text{Chronological Age}} = \text{Intelligence Quotient}$$

That is, 100/100 = 1.00. The result of the division is multiplied by 100 to eliminate the decimal point, which in this case would yield an intelligence quotient (IQ) of 100. Suppose the same subject had instead passed tests at these levels:

	Years	Months
Year VII, all tests passed (Basal year)	7	
Year VIII, 5 tests passed		10
Year IX, 3 tests passed		6
Year X, 2 tests passed		4
Year XI, 1 test passed		2
Year XII, no tests passed		0
	7	22

The ratio of mental age (106 months) to chronological age (100 months) would then be:

$$\frac{106}{100} = 1.06 \ (\times 100 = 106 \text{ IQ})$$

If, on the other hand, the same subject had the following scores:

	Years	Months
Year VI, all tests passed (Basal year)	6	
Year VII, 4 tests passed		8
Year VIII, 1 test passed		2
Year IX, no tests passed		0
	6	10

154 INTELLIGENCE AND EVALUATION

> The ratio of his mental age to his chronological age would be:
>
> $$\frac{82}{100} = .82 \; (\times \, 100 = 82 \, \text{IQ})$$
>
> It became a difficult matter to use this formula, however, when testing individuals over ages 13–16, when it was assumed that intelligence or mental age stopped increasing.

In the pre-1960 Stanford-Binet tests, all adults were given a chronological age of sixteen years. Even this was inadequate, however, so in the 1960 revision the technique of finding a deviation IQ was adopted. Wechsler had used this approach in his tests for both children and adults with more satisfactory results than the ratio formula provided.

The Wechsler tests

The *deviation IQ* is based on a mean scaled score of 10 for each test at each age level and units of standard deviation from the mean. Raw or actual scores are converted into "scaled scores" by examining the table appropriate to the subject's chronological age, as in this example:

A boy, 11 years, 10 months (11–10), was given the Wechsler Intelligence Scale for Children-Revised, or WISC-R. To convert his raw scores on each subtest to scaled scores, we look at the table for children aged 11–8 to 11–11 (reproduced here as Table 5.1).

Drawing on the table, the boy's scaled scores would be:

	Raw score	Scaled score
Verbal tests:		
Information	23	14
Similarities	22	15
Arithmetic	14	11
Vocabulary	44	13
Comprehension	27	14
Digit span	12	10
Performance tests:		
Picture completion	19	10
Picture arrangement	12	5
Block design	32	10
Object assembly	21	9
Coding	43	9

Since each age has a mean scaled score of 10 for each subtest, it can be readily seen that this particular youngster is above the average for his age group in

11 yrs. 8 mos. 0 days
11 yrs. 11 mos. 30 days

Scaled score equivalents of raw scores—Wechsler Intelligence Scale for Children—Revised*.

	Verbal							Performance					
Scaled score	Information	Similarities	Arithmetic	Vocabulary	Comprehension	Digit span	Scaled score	Picture completion	Picture arrangement	Block design	Object assembly	Coding	Mazes	Scaled score
1	0–6	0–3	0–4	0–15	0–4	0–3	1	0–6	0–4	0–5	0–6	0–21	0–6	1
2	7	4–5	5	16–17	5–6	4	2	7	5–6	6	7–8	22–24	7–8	2
3	8	6	6	18–19	7	5	3	8–9	7–8	7–8	9–10	25–27	9–10	3
4	9	7	7	20–21	8–9	6	4	10–11| 9–11	9–10	11–12	28–30	11–12	4
5	10	8	8	22–23	10–11	7	5	12–13| 12–14	11–13	13–14	31–33	13–14	5
6	11	9–10	9	24–25	12–13	8	6	14–15| 15–17	14–17	15–16	34–36	15–16	6
7	12	11	10	26–28	14–15	9	7	16	18–20	18–21	17–18	37–39	17–18	7
8	13–14	12	11	29–30	16–17	10	8	17	21–23	22–25	19–20	40–42	19–20	8
9	15	13–14	12	31–33	18–19	11	9	18	24–26	26–29	21–22	43–45	21–22	9
10	16–17	15–16	13	34–36	20–21	12	10	19	27–29	30–34	23	46–48	23	10
11	18–19	17	14	37–39	22–23	13	11	20	30–32	35–38	24	49–52	24	11
12	20	18	—	40–42	24	14–15	12	21	33–34	39–42	25–26	53–55	25	12
13	21–22	19–20	15	43–44	25–26	16	13	22	35–36	43–45	27	56–59	26	13
14	23	21	—	45–46	27	17	14	23	37–38	46–48	28	60–63	27	14
15	24	22	16	47–48	28	18	15	—	39–40	49–51	29	64–67	28	15
16	25	23	17	49–51	29	19	16	24	41–42	52–54	30	68–70	29	16
17	26	24	—	52–53	30	20	17	—	43–44	55–56	31	71–73	—	17
18	27	25	18	54–55	31	21	18	25	45	57–58	32	74–76	30	18
19	28–30	26–30	—	56–64	32–34	22–28	19	26	46–48	59–62	33	77–93	—	19

*Wechsler, 1974, p. 135. Reproduced by permission. Copyright © 1974 by The Psychological Corporation, New York, New York. All rights reserved.

Table 5.1

verbal tests, except for Digit Span or immediate memory where his score is average, and tends to score below average to average on performance tests. These observations are confirmed by a verbal IQ of 119 and a Performance IQ of 90, both obtained from tables in the test manual.

Knowing the raw scores alone is meaningless, as you can see in Table 5.2, which shows the same raw scores as in the previous example, but for different age levels for the single set of scores. Even one year's difference in age yields scores sufficiently different to warrant different interpretations of a youngster's abilities (if someone interprets strictly according to scores).

Table 5.2   *Standard score equivalents for a single set of WISC-R raw subtest scores for ages 10–10, 11–10, and 12–10*

Subtest	Raw score	10–10	11–10	12–10
Information	23	16	14	13
Similarities	22	16	15	14
Arithmetic	14	12	11	10
Vocabulary	44	15	13	12
Comprehension	27	16	14	13
Digit span	12	11	10	9)*
Verbal score		130	119	113
Picture completion	19	11	10	9
Picture arrangement	12	5	5	4
Block design	32	11	10	9
Object assembly	21	9	9	8
Coding	43	10	9	8
Performance score		93	90	84
Full-scale IQ		114	105	99

*If all 6 Verbal subtests are given on the WISC-R, the Digit Span score is not included in computing the Verbal Score. (Manual for the Wechsler Intelligence Scale for Children—Revised, 1974, p. 114)

Although obviously the IQ is still tied to chronological age, it is no longer necessary to give adults an artificial age since deviation IQs have also been derived for adult age groups on both the Stanford-Binet 1960 Revision and the Wechsler Adult Intelligence Scale.

In group testing, similarly, norms are established for the various age groups on the basis of extensive testing with standardization groups. Scorers may then look in the published tables for mental age or grade level equivalents of the raw scores obtained by test subjects. However, there is one problem with almost all intelligence tests: they have an upper limit. If someone earns a maximum score, you can only estimate how much more intelligent he is.

The WISC-R provides overlap with both the Wechsler Preschool and Primary Scale of Intelligence (WPPSI), designed for children aged 4 to 6½

INTELLIGENCE: THEORIES AND TESTS 157

years, and the Wechsler Adult Intelligence Scale (WAIS), since the age limits for the WISC-R are 6–0 to 16–11. In the *Manual*, correlations for Full-Scale IQ are reported between the WPPSI and WISC-R at age 6–0 as .82 and between the WISC-R and WAIS at age 16–11 as .95. (Wechsler, 1974, pp. 48–50) Relatively small differences in mean IQ between tests are attributed to different population samples and learning opportunities over the years between standardizations.

Intelligence tests are used in an attempt to measure verbal ability, predict school achievement, and evaluate performance at a given point in development. They cannot yet measure innate or inborn potential.

Focus 5–4

What kinds of questions might be asked on an individual test? The WISC format may serve as a model. As noted earlier, there are six verbal and six performance tests, although only four or five of each may be used in an individual case. Items similar to those on the Wechsler Intelligence Scale for Children, in the different subtests, follow:

General Information:

1. How many wings does a bird have?
2. How many nickels make a dime?
3. What is steam made of?
4. Who wrote "Paradise Lost"?
5. What is pepper?

General Comprehension:

1. What should you do if you see someone forget his book when he leaves his seat in a restaurant?
2. What is the advantage of keeping money in a bank?
3. Why is copper often used in electrical wires?

Arithmetic:

1. Sam had three pieces of candy, and Joe gave him four more. How many pieces of candy did Sam have altogether?
2. Three men divided eighteen golf balls equally, among themselves. How many golf balls did each man receive?
3. If two apples cost 15¢, what will be the cost of a dozen apples?

Similarities:

1. In what way are a lion and a tiger alike?
2. In what way are a saw and a hammer alike?
3. In what way are an hour and a week alike?
4. In what way are a circle and a triangle alike?

Vocabulary:

This test consists simply of asking, "What is a _____?" or "What does _____ mean?" The words cover a wide range of familiarity or difficulty.

Digit Span:

This test consists of having the test subject repeat a series of numbers immediately after the examiner says the series. Each series of numbers is a different length.

Performance Tests:

In addition to the above verbal tasks, there are a number of performance tasks involving the use of blocks, cut-out figures, paper and pencil puzzles, etc. These are generally tasks with a time limit. Their titles include: Picture Completion, Picture Arrangement, Block Design, Object Assembly, Coding, and Mazes.

These tests are all timed, with bonus credits given for quick and accurate performance. (Wechsler, D. *The Wechsler Intelligence Scale for Children.* New York: Psychological Corporation, 1949. Paraphrases approved by the Psychological Corporation.)

The Verbal subtests (except for Digit Span) tend to depend heavily on learning opportunities. The Performance tests generally do not, although Picture Completion appears to require at least some familiarity with the objects shown if one is to perceive what is missing. Criticisms of the original WISC have been answered in the 1974 Revision. Out-of-date content in test items has been removed. Verbal and Performance subtests are given alternately (reducing feelings of tension in the subject), culturally unfair or relatively unimportant items have been eliminated, and administration procedures have been modified to promote understanding by the child being tested. On the other hand, questions are still raised about the artificial quality and irrelevance of some tasks, such as Digit Span recitation, mental arithmetic problems, and completing pictures.

Basic differences between individual and group testing lie in the types of questions that can be asked, the nature of test administration, the number of subjects involved in a single testing session, and the relative accuracy of the task. An individual test is obviously designed to be given to one person at a time, while group tests may be given to one or more subjects simultaneously. In individual test administration, the examiner asks the questions aloud and is frequently able to ask the subject to "explain further" or elaborate on his or her responses. Group tests typically require that the subject be able to read the questions, as well as the several choices of response, and to indicate his or her choice either in the test booklet or on a special answer sheet provided. On this basis alone, another distinction can be made: a blind person could be tested individually but not on a group test, unless he was given the test on an individual basis with choices read aloud. As to the types of questions that may be asked, the individual test may require the subject to repeat from memory a sentence (as in the Stanford-Binet test) or a series of numbers (as in the Wechsler tests), which cannot be done on group tests. Non-language items, such as copying designs with blocks, or stringing beads in a prescribed pattern, are also obviously possible only with an individual test. Binet recognized the value of moving from simple to difficult tasks by very gradual steps and did this in his test by having tasks divided by age level. Wechsler also follows the easy-to-difficult pattern, but does this within areas of inquiry. Binet anticipated the current stress on positive reinforcement by stating that subjects' successes should be reinforced (Binet, 1969, p. 75), and again this is a practice generally possible only with individual tests. The validity of both of these individual intelligence tests, assuming optimal testing conditions and correct administration, is considered to be much higher than that of group tests. As a rule, group tests are given in the schools periodically, and children with scores at the extremes of the distribution or whose scores have changed markedly since a previous test may be retested by the school psychologist, using either a Stanford-Binet or Wechsler individual test to confirm or refute the group test score. The stability of these two tests has been shown to be equal over a four-year interval ". . . as determined by comparisons between mean scores, test-retest correlations, and intercorrelations of major parts" for 60 fifth-graders who were retested in ninth grade. (Gehman and Matyas, 1956, pp. 150–52)

Group tests

By contrast, group tests neither require the same memory abilities nor provide the same opportunities for individual differences that individual tests do. Since they are designed for large-scale group administration and frequently for machine scoring (or rapid hand-scoring with the help of a master answer key), subjects must choose the correct response from four or five possibilities, a much easier task than having to use total recall abilities. For example, the first WISC Information question asks how many wings a bird has. The subject must know the answer "2," but on a group test would be able to choose from a) 1, b) 2, c) 3, d) 4. Or, compare a Comprehension or Similarities question on the WISC, where it is possible to give a 1-point or 2-point response, with the task on a group test of merely selecting a single response from several choices. Although, in your own experience with tests, you may have found that it is sometimes quite difficult to choose between two of the four or five possibilities, wouldn't you agree that having to provide the complete answer to an essay question is *more* difficult? This is, essentially, the relationship of group test questions to individual test questions.

As an example, the types of questions that Guilford poses to test intelligence are utilized in his own group tests and have been adapted in others as part of verbal measurement. To evaluate two aspects of cognition of semantic units, he has the Disemvoweled Words test ("Put vowels in the following blanks to make a real word": h p) and the Omelet test ("Rearrange the letters to make a real word": LCTO). (Guilford and Hoepfner, 1971, App. B) His vocabulary test resembles others and could conceivably be presented in a "free-response" (individual test) or multiple-choice (group test) format. The ability to see relationships is measured by a variety of analogies tests in which the subject must choose the correct item to complete the analogy, for example:

night:day: : timid:?_____
a. brave b. bold c. afraid d. fearful e. strong
(Guilford and Hoepfner, 1971, p. 489)

His more unique items, however, are concerned with divergent thinking abilities such as word fluency (give as many words as you can beginning with the letter "r"), ideational fluency (list as many objects as you can which are edible and round), spontaneous flexibility (give all the uses you can think of for a tin can, with frequent shift of classes of items), and so on. Convergent production and evaluative abilities are tested with other types of questions, using figures or words.

Although there are several group tests in use, perhaps two of the most frequently used are the Lorge-Thorndike Intelligence Test and the California Test of Mental Maturity. Both of them have several forms, geared to different age levels. As you can see from the nonverbal examples in Figures 5.7 and 5.8, many of the questions are based on what are assumed to be "common" or universal learning experiences.

It is this assumption of universal experience that disturbs both educators and parents in relation to intelligence tests. Marland (1969), for example, has emphasized the need for inventing a new way of providing a profile of the child's ability and performance against the background of the environment in which he works and lives. Such a profile should be constructed so that it is easily communicated to counselors and teachers, allowing for their degrees of expertise, and also to parents and children. (p. 106) Part of Marland's proposal is directed toward the development of a truly culture-fair test. Despite the efforts of Davis and Eells, Cattell, and others, no really successful such test is yet generally available. There have been attempts also to use projective tests, such as the Draw-a-Person test, as an estimate of intelligence because of experience gained in cross-cultural research. However,

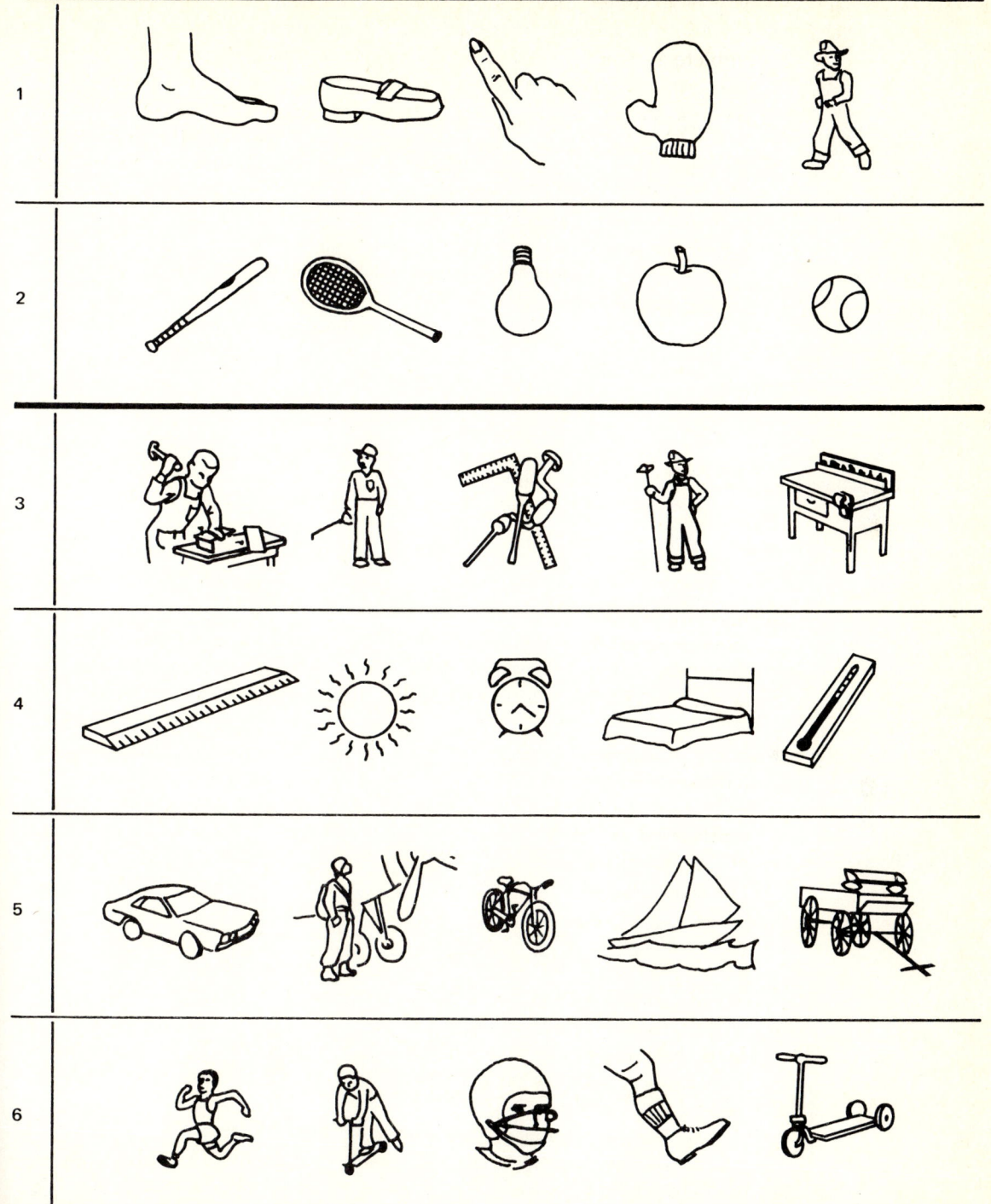

Level 2—Form—Primary Battery of the Lorge-Thorndike Intelligence Test. Child is directed to draw a ring around one of the items. © *Houghton Mifflin Co.*

Figure 5.7

The **quantitative section** is comprised of three item types.

1. In the *number series,* items were developed following familiar models with difficulty introduced by the complexity of the relationships involved among the numbers of a series.
2. Items for the *quantitative relations* or "greater than or less than" subtest are of the type in which two quantities are presented to the examinee (e.g. one quarter and 25 cents) and he has to indicate whether the first quantity is greater than, equal to, or less than the second quantity.
3. The third item type for the quantitative test, *equation building,* consists of items of the sort shown below. The examinee is asked to arrange the numbers and signs in such a way (i.e., in an equation or number sentence form) as to produce one of the lettered answers.

Example:

					A	B	C	D	E
2	4	8	−	+	4	8	10	12	14

The number and difficulty of items to be included in the final test were determined after extensive tryouts. A similar type of item, but in open-ended format rather than multiple-choice, had been used in previous tests.

The **nonverbal section** consists of two familiar item types, *figure analogies* and *figure classification.* Factor analyses of our own and by others indicate that these share a common factor, perhaps of nonverbal reasoning, that is distinct from though correlated with the factor in the verbal tests.

1. In order to maximize the reasoning component, the graded difficulties of the items rest on the complexity of the relationship involved in the case of the *figure analogies,* or the definition of the category in the *figure classification test,* rather than on fine perceptual discriminations and visual acuity in perceiving the figures that are provided for the items.
2. The last nonverbal item type, *form synthesis,* provides a task of the sort illustrated below, in which the examinee must judge for each response figure whether it can be produced by putting together the part figures that are provided as stimulus material. Again, in building items, degrees of difficulty are produced through complexity of analysis of the total figure rather than fine visual discriminations. Experience gained from tryouts determined the level of complexity and subtlety of these items for use at the various grade levels.

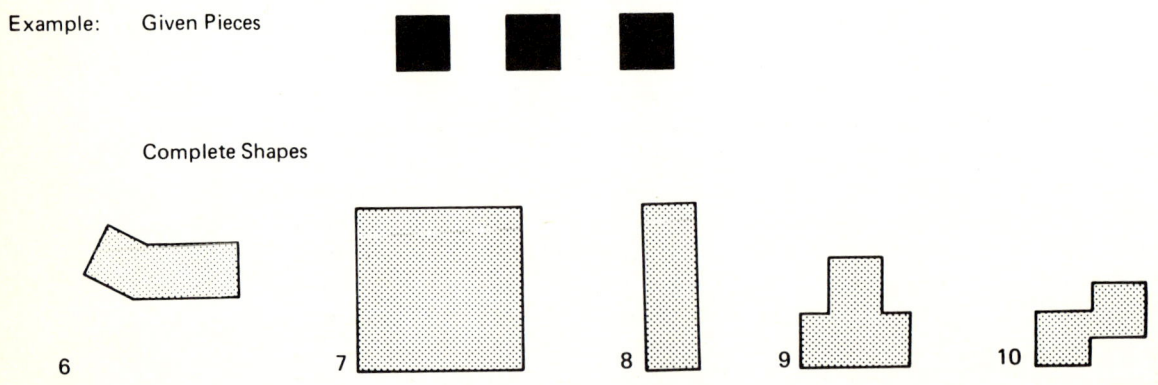

Figure 5.8 *Cognitive Abilities Test.* © *1971 Houghton Mifflin Co.*

the scores obtained tend not to be precise but rather to provide categorical estimates of "slow," "average," or "bright."

An alternative to even this type of intelligence testing is the suggestion that achievement test measures be substituted for intelligence tests. They are both less susceptible to misuse and misinterpretation and more easily improved by mutual pupil and teacher efforts. (Yourman, 1964) Achievement tests would show what a child has learned and indicate at which level instruction should be begun or resumed. They would thus meet the need to evaluate functional capacity at a given level of development better than our present IQ tests.

Misuse of intelligence test results, pointed out by Yourman and so many others, has been demonstrated frequently in classroom settings. Children are placed in homogeneous groups according to their IQs (and possibly reading achievement scores), and an IQ of 129 may well keep a child from being in the accelerated class for which the admission criterion is an IQ of 130. Or, lulled by labels, the teacher may expect too little of youngsters who score low on the test, and thus help to maintain their low score.

Teacher Expectations

In their study of the role of teacher expectations in relation to pupil performance, Rosenthal and Jacobson cited the influence of the "halo effect" that often leads to self-fulfilling prophecies. Specifically, they assert that "Sometimes the teacher recognizes disadvantages and perhaps, sometimes, she creates them. An evaluation of a child, lowered or raised by halo effects, may lead to a specific expectation of performance which is communicated to the child who then may go on to fulfill the teacher's prophecy." (Rosenthal and Jacobson, 1968, p. 55) They tested this hypothesis in a California elementary school, the population of which was largely lower-class and culturally deprived, and which was one-sixth Mexican-American. Teachers were told that certain children in their classes, experimentally designated, could be expected to have an academic "spurt" in the coming year. Changes in IQ score after one year are shown in Table 5.3 and demonstrate the particularly strong effects of teacher expectations of prophecy in the lower grades.

Several possible interpretations of the greater effect of expectations on the younger children are offered by Rosenthal and Jacobson. Apart from possible differences among the teachers themselves, two interpretations that offer much food for thought are: 1) ". . . younger children show greater gains associated with teacher's expectancies not because they necessarily *are* more malleable but rather because they are believed by teachers to be more malleable," and 2) ". . . younger children are more sensitive to and more affected by the particular processes whereby teachers communicate their expectations to children." (Rosenthal and Jacobson, 1968, p. 83) Retesting two years after the initial pretesting showed the original experimental fifth-graders to have maintained the greatest expectancy advantage, a phenomenon for which the authors could develop no satisfactory explanation. Overall, they concluded that the teacher, by various subtle interpersonal means,

... may have communicated to the children of the experimental group that she expected improved intellectual performance. Such communications together with possible changes in teaching techniques may have helped the child learn by changing his self-concept, his expectations of his own behavior, and his motivation, as well as his cognitive style and skills. (p. 186)

Table 5.3 Mean gain in total IQ after one year by experimental and control group children, gr. 1–6.*

Grade	Control		Experimental		Expectancy advantage IQ points	p
	N	Gain	N	Gain		
1	48	+12.0	7	+27.4	+15.4	.002
2	47	+ 7.0	12	+16.5	+ 9.5	.02
3	40	+ 5.0	14	+ 5.0	0.0	
4	49	+ 2.2	12	+ 5.6	+ 3.4	
5	26	+17.5(−)	9	+17.4(+)	0.0	
6	45	+10.7	11	+10.0	− 0.7	
Total	225	+ 8.42	65	+12.22	+ 3.80	.02

*From Pygmalion in the Classroom: Teacher Expectation and Pupils' Intellectual Development by Robert Rosenthal and Lenore Jacobson. Copyright © 1968 by Holt, Rinehart and Winston, Inc. Reprinted by permission of Holt, Rinehart and Winston, Inc. (p. 75)

The investment and perception of oneself in learning, as we have noted repeatedly, is indeed a critical factor in such efforts.

There have been several criticisms of the Rosenthal-Jacobson study, notably one by Robert L. Thorndike. He is particularly critical of two facets of the study: 1) the conclusion of the "prophecy" effect based on the gains of only nineteen children in grades one and two and 2) the adequacy of the data-gathering and analysis procedures. (1968, pp. 708–11) Gephart (1970) has stressed the high probability of experimenter bias effect (EBE) operating in the report of the study. That is, "... the data have been re-examined as if the experimenter was compelled to find what he expected." (p. 474) The criticisms, as you can see, are directed at the research procedures and data analysis rather than at the concept of teacher expectations affecting behavior. In a longitudinal study, Rist (1970) found confirmation of this concept in the subtle and subjectively based teacher expectations of kindergarteners from different socioeconomic classes. Achievement expectations were based on various types of social information, and subsequent teachers accepted the evaluations so derived. The deception used in the study is also viewed as contrary to professional ethics in testing.

Although few studies have shown the same results as Rosenthal and Jacobson obtained, the idea persists that teacher expectations do affect pupil performance—even on intelligence tests. Finn (1972) suggested that teacher expectation, itself shaped by many factors, is only one influence on the learner. Other influences that he named included the physical setting within the classroom, familial and peer expectations, self-concept, and the shaping of learner expectations over a period of several years. Rappaport and Rappaport (1975) have experimentally supported some of Finn's suggested influences. They found, with five- to six-year-old black children in a compensatory education program, that if positive expectancy could be induced in the *child*, there were marked gains in performance. There is reason to accept this finding, for, if we believe that others think highly of us, we try to live up to their evaluation.

Rosenthal himself (1973) reviewed several studies that supported his argument on teacher expectancy effects. He attributed the effect to four factors.

> People who have been led to expect good things from their students, children, clients . . . appear to:
> —create a warmer social-emotional mood around their "special" students (*climate*);
> —give more feedback to these students about their performance (*feedback*);
> —teach more material and more difficult material to their special students (*input*); and
> —give their special students more opportunities to respond and question (*output*). (Rosenthal, 1973, p. 60)

In discussing these factors, Rosenthal demonstrated several times that teachers who "demanded" more of their students because they believed that the students could do the work did indeed get higher levels of performance, on intelligence tests as well as class work.

A related study, but one which points up the opposite expectancies, was conducted by Nalven, Hofmann, and Bierbyer (1969) with clinical and school psychologists. They were to evaluate WISC IQs for their validity. That is, they were asked to determine whether the obtained full scores were accurate estimates of the true potential of children whose IQ scores were sent to them. The test records were all "manufactured" for the purpose of the study and included various combinations of "children" of both sexes, age eight or fourteen, white or black, and low or middle socioeconomic status. Sex and age apparently had little effect on the psychologists' judgments.

> In contrast, a child's social class background, to a great extent, and his race, to a lesser extent, significantly shape psychologists' judgments as to whether his obtained IQ scores are representative. The results point to the fact that psychologists assume that lower class and Negro children's obtained WISC IQ scores represent significant underestimates of their true intellectual capacities. (Nalven, et al., 1969, p. 274)

This variation in perception of the "true" abilities of culturally different children can in itself be a self-fulfilling prophecy when real children are tested, for psychologists, who are also human, may give the child barely perceptible nods of encouragement that the child correctly interprets as "being on the right track." This is possible, obviously, only in the individual testing situation. The point is, however, that psychologists tend to view test scores as underestimates of ability, particularly for the "different" child, while the teacher tends to view test scores as hard realities. This difference in viewpoints can obviously affect performance expectancies.

"Culture-fair" tests

Mention was made earlier of culture-fair tests of intelligence that might resolve this problem. Since a number of them do exist, it is worthwhile to consider them briefly. There are several that are being given experimentally. The best known, possibly, are the Davis-Eells Games, which are nonreading tests designed for children of different socioeconomic levels. They do, however, require auditory comprehension (as do the nonverbal test items shown in Figures 5.7 and 5.8). In one large-scale study with the Davis-Eells Games, Love and Beach (1957) found high positive correlations between reading achievement scores and IQ on the Kuhlmann-Anderson intelligence test and the Davis-Eells Games tests, except for the lowest socioeconomic group on the Davis-Eells test, where reading ability was only slightly related to the score. However, the distribution of means on the Davis-Eells and the Kuhlmann-Anderson also indicated that the Davis-Eells Games yield means 10–15 IQ points lower than the Kuhlmann-Anderson. There is, therefore, some question as to the helpfulness of this nonverbal test in resolving the teacher-expectancy problem.

Raven's Progressive Matrices, nonverbal tests of figural reasoning, supposedly test "g" or general intelligence. The Goodenough-Harris Draw-a-Person test, which is a well standardized, nonexperimental test, simply requires the subject to draw one or more human figures, and is scored in terms of details included rather than artistic ability. In this test, frequently used in cross-cultural studies, the examiner must be aware of unique characteristics of the culture from which his subjects come because of varying attitudes toward parts of the body and/or tabus that would affect the details included in the drawings. Rulon's Semantic Test of Intelligence does not require language comprehension since it is administered in pantomime, but does need the same caution about cultural differences (this time in terms of hand and head movements) as the Goodenough-Harris test. (Lambert, 1964) In the mid-1970s, these difficulties continued.

There are problems in administering even these tests to culturally different children. The language used in giving directions may be totally unfamiliar or may include words that the child is accustomed to hearing in other contexts. The whole idea of "do your best" may be foreign to the children. Time limits may be unrealistic or unimportant. If the examiner is a stranger, or of a different race or sex, this may upset the children who are not used to dealing with such differences. Perhaps the younger children have never had the opportunity to draw with a pencil, look at pictures, or participate in other activities that we consider "normal" for the preschooler (although some of this problem is reduced by exposure to good, children's programs on TV, if a TV is in the home and available to the child).

Because of the experimental stage of development of these tests, and the cautions to be observed with several of them, there is doubt at this time that they are the answers to the needs of the culturally different in the school situation, or to the problem of halo effects in teacher expectancies. Obviously, this is an area for continuing research.

In what ways might you test culturally different children?   **Question**

A CONTEMPORARY LOOK

In looking back at both theories and tests of intelligence, one sees many problems. Not only do we have disagreement as to the nature of intelligence, but there are also many doubts about the value of the tests. Several psychologists have written their ideas of how to reduce these problems in size and quantity.

McClelland (1973), for example, points out that IQ test scores and job success are not as clearly or strongly related as people have assumed. He reminds us that job success is based on many other factors as well: socioeconomic class, opportunity, "pull," appearance, and so on. Further, he suggests that intelligence tests be replaced by tests of competence. These competency tests would be directly related to the task to be done. In criticizing intelligence tests as they *are*, McClelland urges that test items presently used be replaced by items that more truly reflect real-life situations and that have the test subject actively doing something rather than passively responding to artificial multiple-choice questions.

Echoing the plea to move away from academically oriented measures of intelligence, Allen (1975) has suggested that the Rorschach Psychodiagnostic Inkblot Test be used to find out how the child copes with unfamiliar and unstructured problem situations (the inkblot cards). The focus is then on how the child perceives, organizes, and responds to these situations. It is Allen's contention that this information would tell us more about the individual's ability to adapt to his environment (remember *that* definition of intelligence?) than an IQ test score can.

Finally, Thorndike (1975) reminds us that

> Binet developed his scales 70 years ago in a France that was ethnically and culturally relatively homogeneous for a school system generally elitist in its orientation and unsympathetic and unresponsive to individual variability.... When Terman adapted the scales for use in this country, completion of high school was still the exception rather than the rule here, and schooling through most of the country was oriented toward the white English-speaking majority....
>
> ... How must our conception and use of Mr. Binet's test be modified for the educational scene of 1975?

> Clearly, the normative interpretations must be adjusted to the changing times. But it seems equally clear that the prognostic interpretations must be adjusted to the particular place—that is, the setting and subculture in which a child has been reared and educated. . . . Binet's test—or any other—must guide, and not replace informed judgment. (pp. 6–7))

One must be careful not to throw out all intelligence tests because of dissatisfaction with test items or test results. Rather, there is need to be more selective in the use of intelligence tests, more competence-oriented in designing test items, and more cautious in interpreting test results.

SUMMARY

What is intelligence? How do we measure it? These are the two questions that we have sought to answer in this chapter.

An extensive survey of definitions of intelligence revealed that most of the definitions are related to academic learning potential and ability, with some focusing also on the ability to adapt to the environment. Another method of classifying the definitions is to divide them according to whether they stress a unitary concept of intelligence or a multifaceted concept. Binet, Spearman, and Terman are among those who view intelligence as a general ability. Cattell, using factor analytic techniques, has distinguished two kinds of general ability. Thorndike, the Thurstones, and others, by contrast, perceive intelligence in terms of several different group abilities that are sufficiently different from each other that they cannot be subsumed under a single label such as "intelligence quotient." We also discussed two approaches to intelligence that do not readily fall into either camp: Piaget's developmental approach and Guilford's "structure of intellect," which employs a cubic model emphasizing the interaction of specific factors. A hierarchical model of intelligence was presented as a possible all-encompassing point of view.

The second area of focus in this chapter was the measurement of intelligence. Positive and negative attitudes toward testing were discussed before we presented various intelligence tests. Derivation of the intelligence quotient was demonstrated through both the ratio and deviation (or scaled score) methods, using Binet and Wechsler scores as examples. Differences between individual and group tests were illustrated by samples of the kinds of questions and format for answers from various intelligence tests. We also looked at illustrations from nonverbal group tests and considered several attempts to construct related "culture-fair" tests.

As was demonstrated several times in this chapter, the interpretation and use of testing results make an understanding of the concept of intelligence and of appropriate measurement techniques imperative. The damage that can be done by psychologists' or teachers' biases may be extensive and/or permanent. The influence of teacher expectations on pupil performance has been shown in some of the research cited. Despite the number of negative comments necessarily made about intelligence tests, they are useful if used properly. Initially, the tests must be properly administered, following directions given in the test manual. Nonconformity to the directions invalidates test results. Giving students samples from a test as a means of preparing them for it similarly invalidates the results. (This does not include using items from similar tests for familiarization purposes, such as learning how to handle analogy questions and the like.) Intelligence tests do tell us at what level the individual is functioning at a particular point in time. If the scores seem too different from the learner's classroom performance, or from other indicators of his intellectual level, a retest may be in order as well as a careful examination of where he made errors on the test. It is not always the tests themselves that are "bad," but rather the way in which test results are interpreted and applied.

Constructive suggestions for other ways in which intellectual performance can be evaluated were also presented. These included tests for which competence is the criterion and vague or unstructured tests on which the learner can demonstrate his adaptability to strange situations.

None of the foregoing is an attempt to deny that individuals do differ in level or kind of intelligence. That, however, will be discussed in the next chapter, which focuses on individual differences and mental growth.

Preview

INTRODUCTION

THE CURVE OF MENTAL GROWTH
    AGING AND IQ
    ADULT STUDENTS

THE STABILITY OF MENTAL GROWTH
    SUMMARY

CLASSIFICATIONS OF INTELLIGENCE
    THE RETARDED
    THE AVERAGE
    THE GIFTED

HANDLING INDIVIDUAL DIFFERENCES
    A CONTROVERSIAL ISSUE
    POSSIBLE SOLUTIONS
    SUMMING UP

SUMMARY

6

Mental Growth and Individual Differences

INTRODUCTION

Binet introduced the concept of mental age and then developed the ratio technique of deriving the intelligence quotient:

$$\frac{\text{Mental Age}}{\text{Chronological Age}} = \text{Intelligence Quotient}$$

He believed that the rate of mental development was consistent throughout childhood; that is, that mental development had a linear relationship to chronological age. In testing adults, however, he found the linear trend did not continue as before. This led to the erroneous assumption on the part of many psychologists that no intellectual growth occurred after adolescence. Although it is true that we cannot measure a mental age of thirty, forty, or fifty years, it is equally true that we do not remain intellectual adolescents throughout our lives. What happens to intellectual development in adulthood? This question is particularly important today because of the growing emphasis on lifelong learning and the increasing number of adult education programs. The curve of mental growth, the difference between quantitative and qualitative changes in the intellect, and viewpoints concerning mental growth are our first topic in this chapter. Closely related to this question is the stability of mental functioning. That is, do we maintain our level of ability throughout our lives? Is an IQ or other score the same year after year? These questions are the second topic of this chapter.

We know that Binet developed his intelligence test for the purpose of differentiating the educationally capable from those less likely to profit from traditional education. Ultimately, several grades or classifications of ability were distinguished, and intelligence quotients were set into scale form. This is the third principal area to be discussed in this chapter: individual differ-

172 INTELLIGENCE AND EVALUATION

ences in intelligence. Relevant to such differences are the arguments regarding "grouping" for classroom instruction as a technique for coping with individual differences in learning ability.

This is, therefore, a chapter that enlarges upon the theories presented in the previous chapter and also provides a foundation for more focused study in material to be discussed in later chapters.

THE CURVE OF MENTAL GROWTH

We are well aware that the child grows more physically in the first year of life than in any other single year. For example, he triples his birth weight by

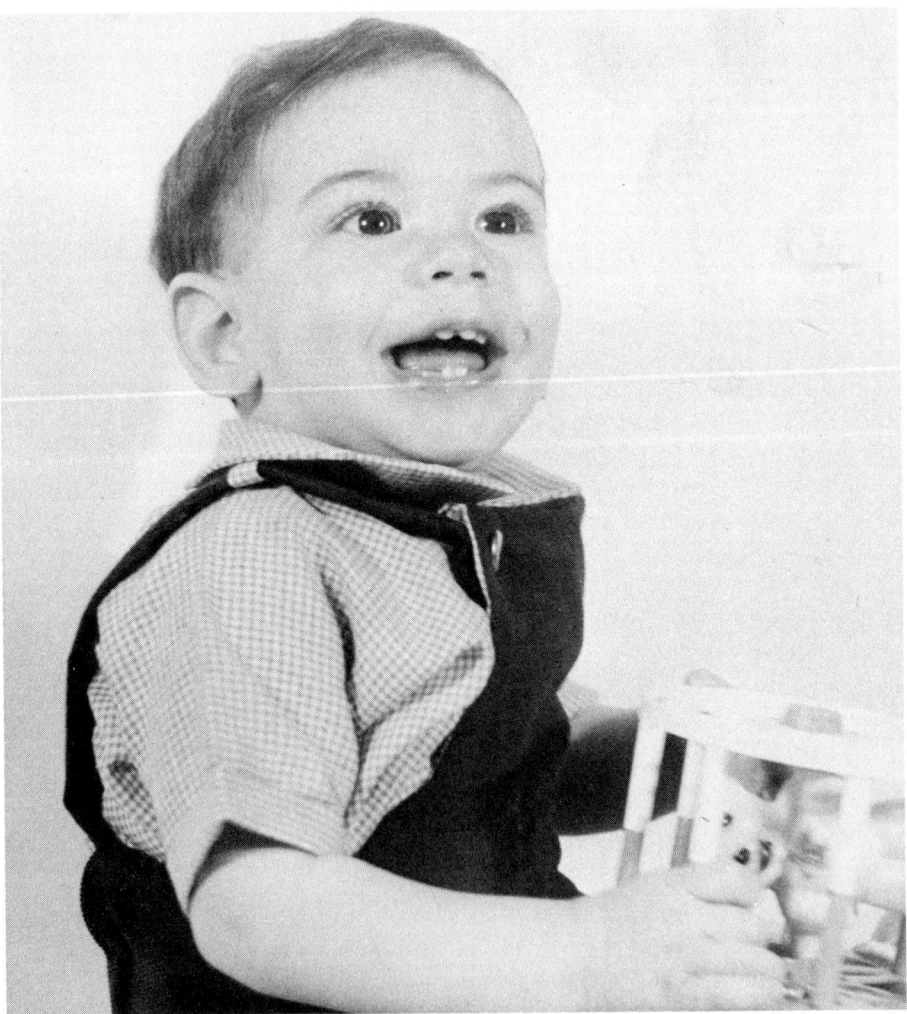

Figure 6.1   *Shown this picture . . .*

age one. Similarly, research indicates increasingly that mental growth in the first six years of life is normally greater than in any similar time span after the age of six. Just think of the newborn infant who has functioning abilities relevant only to his basic biological needs: breathing, sucking, swallowing, elimination, and sleeping. Look at the same child on his sixth birthday. He can speak in understandable sentences of fairly good grammatical construction, comprehend most of what is said to him, has an elementary knowledge of numbers, can associate objects and symbols mentally in many situations, may be able to read a few words, has the ability to remember and to project somewhat into the future, has developed a rudimentary sense of morality, and has matured considerably in other areas as well, such as in social development, motor development, and perceptual development.

Can the school-age child recognize his earlier "ignorant" status? **Figure 6.2**

As Terman and Merrill pointed out in their introduction to the 1937 Revision of the Stanford-Binet Tests, the mental age unit

> ... appears definitely to decrease with age, if we can judge by the ease or difficulty with which adjacent mental ages can be discriminated. For example, the difference between one-year and two-year intelligence is so great that anyone can sense it, while even a psychologist might have difficulty in discriminating between the mental levels of twelve years and thirteen years on the basis of ordinary observation. (Terman and Merrill, 1937, pp. 25–26)

Aging and IQ   In a quantitative sense, the amount of measurable mental growth in adulthood is relatively small. Individual decreases in intellectual functioning are attributed to slower reaction time in old age and organic dysfunction. This is illustrated in Figure 6.3, which shows the total standard score needed to earn a full-scale IQ of 100 on the Wechsler Adult Intelligence Scale (WAIS) at different ages. (The decline in the curve after ages 25–34 actually reflects greater decrease in timed nonverbal performance than in verbal levels required to maintain a full-scale IQ of 100 on the WAIS.)

> If changes in measured intelligence are part of a process of primary biological aging, every individual would be expected to show some change during the second half of life. The fact that some individuals beyond the age of 70 show large changes and others show none at all suggests that the terminal or near terminal phases of the life span can be accompanied by unique and relatively rapid or precipitous changes in individuals when their health fails. . . . There is the possibility that the psychological norm for the species is one of little change in intellectual functions in the years after 65, given good health. (Birren, 1970, p. 125)

This is borne out in several studies. Owens (1966), in a longitudinal study of 96 subjects who were initially tested with the Army Alpha as college freshmen in 1919, was able to retest the men with the same instrument in 1950 and 1961, or at average ages of 19, 50, and 61.

> Results obtained indicate a substantial and significant increment in test scores over the years. . . . and that such variables as amount of education, field of college specialization, rural to urban migration, numbers of hobbies and recreational activities, and earned income are important correlates of temporal shifts in test score. (Owens, 1966, p. 311)

This study also substantiates Piaget's view of mental growth as a qualitative rather than solely a quantitative concept. The influence of the kind of life one leads as an adult cannot be underestimated in evaluating adult intelligence. For example, the adult who lives in an environment that provides little stimulation, opportunity for conversation, or other limitations, may ex-

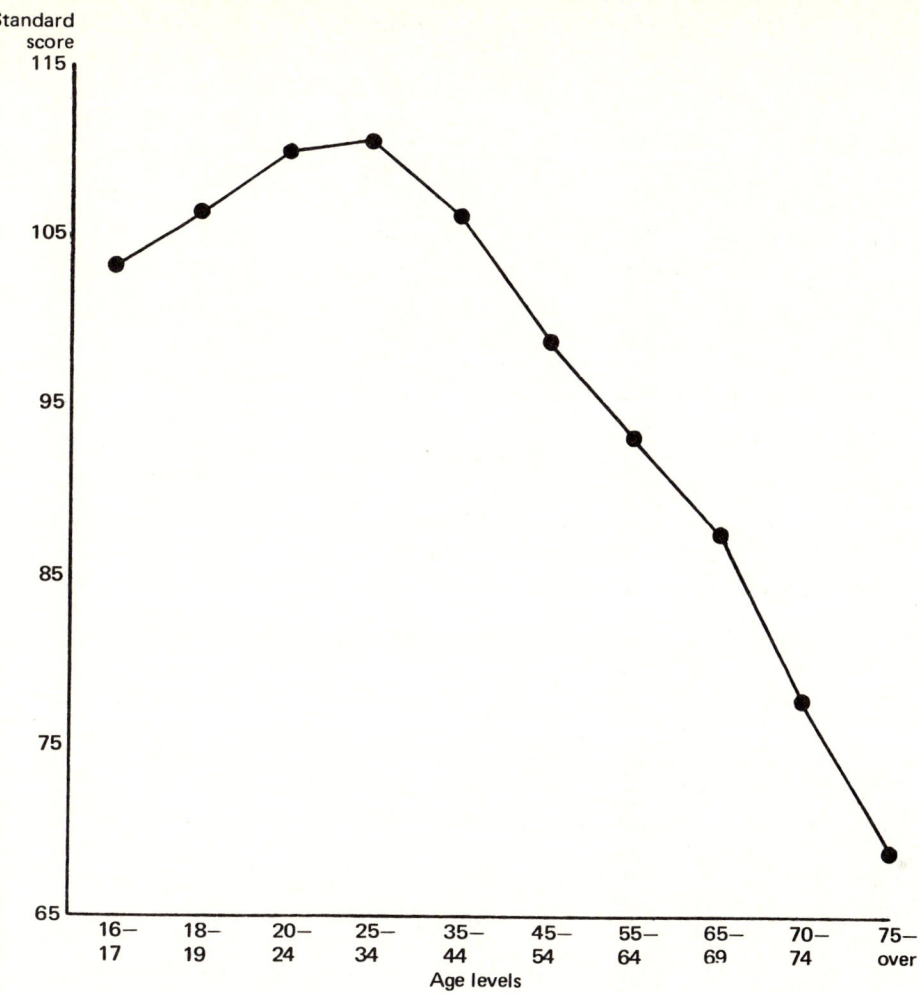

*After Wechsler, 1955, pp. 79–97.

*Standard score equivalent of full-scale IQ = 100 on the Wechsler Intelligence Scale at different ages.** **Figure 6.3**

perience the same kind of stunted intellectual growth as the infant in a similar situation.

What is being said here is that, although changes in the *amount* of mental growth may be relatively insignificant after early adulthood, changes in the *nature* of mental growth *are* meaningful. If we look back at childhood and adolescence, particularly in the framework of Piaget's work on cognitive development, we can see quite easily that not only does the six-year-old have many more intellectual abilities than the four-year-old, but also that they differ in kind. Elkind (1967) has also suggested that changes in mental structure in adolescence, such as the capacity for combinatorial thought, the capacity for introspection, and the capacity to construct ideals, all are reflected in behavioral changes at this stage of development. Again, these changes represent qualitative differences rather than merely quantitative differences in the size of vocabulary, amount of information known, or ability to repeat digits from memory.

Denney and Denney (1973), for example, tested ten women aged 26 to 46 years and ten women aged 75 to 90 years to find out whether they used logical classification for problem solving. The two groups were comparable in level of education (ninth to tenth grade) and current/former occupation (housewife). The elderly women asked many more questions, with less use of classification, than the younger women. This may be because they felt less pressured to arrive at a solution efficiently rather than simply because of their age. The elderly have more time available for fewer tasks.

Questions *Try to think of elderly people you know, such as grandparents and neighbors. Do those who are retired handle problems in the same or different ways from the nonretired? Do the elderly handle problems in the same way as people in their 40s and 50s?*

Green (1969) has suggested that, where marked intellectual declines are found after middle age, this may be due to the smaller amount of formal education received by the subjects in their youth. This is logical if the curves of mental growth are based on cross-sectional studies rather than longitudinal data. People now past age sixty are less likely to have had as much formal schooling as their children's generation or the present generation of youth. This is partly due to economic changes within families but is more largely a result of the increased emphasis upon and availability of higher education since 1945.

Add to these experiential differences the possibility that IQ tests may be biased against the aged. The content of questions tends to be more relevant to adolescence and early adulthood than to later years. Recall also that the elderly tire more quickly and react more slowly than the young. Further, the aged tend to live in less stimulating environments than younger people. All of these factors can contribute to lowered test scores. (Baltes and Schaie, 1974)

Differing educational opportunities and current health and environmental factors are to be considered essentials in interpreting test scores of older people. However, the importance of practice for maintaining intellectual skills must be emphasized, just as it is necessary for the maintenance of motor skills. In a longitudinal study of average adults (Army noncommissioned officers with 20 years of service), comparison of retest scores on the Army General Classification Test after an average of 13 years since the original test administration yielded a "barely measurable decline . . . during the two decades from the early twenties to the early forties. . . . Only on a test of perceptual reasoning was there a mean decline significant at the .01 level.

This last scale, in contrast to the verbal and arithmetic measures, poses novel demands unlikely to be encountered in daily life." (Tuddenham, Blumenkrantz, and Wilkin, 1968, p. 662.) This implies, perhaps, a decline in flexibility, or a shift in mental activities, with age.

Another factor in the downward curve of intelligence in middle and late adulthood may be emotional disturbance, according to a study at the Menninger Clinic. A number of emotional problems arise in these periods as people face marked changes in their lifestyle and physical condition. In research with adult psychotherapy patients at the clinic, subjects were given the Wechsler-Bellevue Intelligence Test (ancestor of the WAIS) when they entered therapy, terminated therapy, and two years after terminating therapy. There was a tendency for intelligence test scores to rise during or after psychotherapy, even after allowing for practice effects. (Applebaum, Coyne, and Siegal, 1969) The negative, or inhibitory effects of anxiety or other emotional problems on intellectual performance, which are demonstrated in this study, have already been presented in some detail in chapter four.

Adult students

With many adults taking courses in a variety of educational settings today, it is reasonable to ask how well they can function as students. They come to class with strong motivation for learning (Schwartz, 1975c), but with varying backgrounds, degrees of self-confidence, and needs.

> The object of learning or change is heavily influenced by the centrality of that change. Are the changes essential for personal, social, civic, religious or career well-being? Are they of mediocre importance? Only the adult can weigh the centrality of an anticipated change. (Snyder, 1975, p. 20)

The adult student tends to be more interested in specific learning experiences, whether enrichment- or degree-oriented, than younger students. He or she is generally capable of handling long-term assignments effectively and may become impatient if the course objectives are not made clear at the outset.

Not all adults are attending college classes or evening sessions. Some school districts welcome senior citizens to high school classes on a space-available basis. In this case, there are needs to make them feel comfortable among their adolescent classmates, to respect health or other problems that may interfere with their learning, and to use their accumulated experience or expertise as a resource in the class. As teacher of a class with older students, you may find their questions more to the point and more penetrating than those of the usual high school student, so that you will have to be better prepared than you might expect in order to give meaningful answers.

THE STABILITY OF MENTAL GROWTH

The implications of longitudinal studies of intelligence are further seen in considering the stability of mental growth. That is, do bright people continue

Adults, as well as children, take tests.

to be bright throughout their lives? Or, are there changes in individual patterns of mental growth as compared with peer patterns?

For most people, levels of competence in different skills vary along a continuum from weak to strong. Although their overall performance may remain at about the same level, there may be variations in particular areas depending upon interest, training, or other factors. For some individuals, even the general intellectual performance level may change from time to time, frequently as a result of changes in the person's psychological or emotional status (and this may be negative to positive or positive to negative). Environmental factors, as we have already seen, also are potent forces affecting intelligence. All of these possibilities must be considered when dealing with the concept of stability of mental growth.

The question of stability is usually investigated by studying a population sample longitudinally, as in Terman and Oden's four-decade study (1947) of geniuses, or Bayley's thirty-six year study (1968) of "full-term, healthy, hospital-born babies of white, English-speaking parents" from a broad socioeconomic sample. Bayley found that many personality variables in mental abilities remained stable throughout this period, although "... the females' mental abilities stabilize at an earlier age, while the males exhibit greater stability later." (p. 15) In fact, of the six factors derived from Bayley's First-Year Mental Scale scores, only one, which was called "Vocalizations," showed a long-term clear correlation with later intelligence. Even "... this relationship after 3 years of age is found only for the girls and not for the boys." (p. 2) Now, the question arises whether such results stem from instability of mental growth or from inadequacies of the measuring instruments.

Bayley, Gesell, Psyche Cattell, and others have developed infant tests of "intelligence" which show varying correlations with tests at later ages. The general conclusion is that, in early childhood, the IQ is *not* constant, but that it becomes increasingly stable as children approach school entrance age. This reflects, in part, the fact that tests in early infancy stress sensorimotor skills, while tests at later ages include verbal behavior. (McCall, Hogarty, and Hurlburt, 1972, pp. 728–48) Several studies may be cited to support this assertion.

Honzik, Macfarlane, and Allen (1948) tested their matched "Guidance" and "Control" groups annually from the preschool years through age eighteen. The tests used were the California Preschool Schedule (ages twenty-one months to five years), the Stanford-Binet (ages six to fifteen years), and the Wechsler-Bellevue (ages sixteen to eighteen years). In Table 6.1, the relative stability or variability of IQ of their subjects during the school years is shown.

Table 6.1 *IQ changes between 6 and 18 years.**

IQ changes between 6 and 18 years	Guidance N = 114 %	Control N = 108 %	Total N = 222 %
50 or more IQ points	1	—	.5
30 or more IQ points	9	10	9.
20 or more IQ points	32	42	37.
15 or more IQ points	58	60	59.
10 or more IQ points	87	83	85.
9 or less IQ points	13	17	15.

*Honzik, Macfarlane, and Allen, 1948.

The changes are slight from one age period to the next, but, if consistently moving in one direction, could go as high as +50 points in the twelve-year age span, as seen in the table. As Honzik, et al., pointed out, there is great potential variability in intelligence test performance. Therefore, cautions must be observed in using a test score, particularly one obtained at an early age, as either definitive or predictive.

Sontag, Baker, and Nelson (1958) followed their sample population from age three to age twelve. Some children had a fairly steady increase in mental growth, others had a fairly steady downward trend, but the majority (almost two out of three) of subjects changed more than 15 IQ points in either direction over the period of the study. This marked, and often irregular, fluctuation occurred despite careful design to rule out most errors in measurement.

Generally, however, individuals tend to perform at a fairly consistent level once they reach school age—if there are no traumatic events that intervene. There may be, however, changes in particular school-related skills, such as a spurt in vocabulary development, but not in other subtest areas, from one testing time to another. These can result in stable overall performance as seen in a fairly stable IQ figure, but with varying subtest scores. That is, qualitative changes seem to be greater than overall quantitative changes. Such a situation is illustrated in the following Focus.

Focus 6–1

Recognizing the fact that skills and areas of competency develop at different rates, let us look at the changes that occurred in the test scores of a young boy, Ray, over a three-year period. The same examiner tested Ray each time with the Wechsler Intelligence Scale for Children. The scores given below are scaled or standard scores, with 10 the average scaled score at each chronological age.

Table 6.2

Scaled scores on the Wechsler Intelligence Scale for Children for one boy, ages 7–4, 8–0, and 10–5.

Subtests	Age 7–4	Age 8–0	Age 10–5
Information	11	12	12
Comprehension	16	14	13
Arithmetic	9	11	11
Similarities	9	11	13
Vocabulary	10	9	10
Digit span	12	9	9
Picture completion	7	13	11
Picture arrangement	8	9	11
Block design	11	11	8
Object assembly	13	13	12
Coding	16(A)	11(B)	9(B)
Verbal scale IQ	108	106	109
Performance scale IQ	107	110	101
Full-scale IQ	108	109	106

As you can see, the Verbal Scale IQ stayed remarkably constant, which also contributed to the stability of the Full-Scale IQ. Performance Scale IQ varied, however, from the second testing to the third. The specific drop in the Block Design and Coding scores (Forms A or B) was later found to be due to an uncorrected visual problem. Additional causes of variability in subtest scores for Ray, as for other children, are school learning, attention span, test anxiety, and maturation. The varying ranges in standard scores at each age further reflect differential rates of development within an overall picture of stable mental growth. (Note: From the author's case files)

It is also true that when IQs change, the changes tend to be positively correlated with parental socioeconomic status and educational level. Honzik, et al., reached this conclusion, and it was confirmed in a study by Stennett (1969), as well, working with Canadian children. He had test scores available for 882 ninth-graders from their first year in school through ninth grade. The tests used were: Kindergarten/grade 1: Pintner-Cunningham; grade 3; Otis Quick-Scoring test of intelligence; grades 7 and 9: Dominion Intermediate Test. In Figure 6.4, the pattern of changes for the subjects, by sex and socioeconomic status, is shown in terms of "z" or standard scores to eliminate the problem caused by having different scoring systems on the three tests.

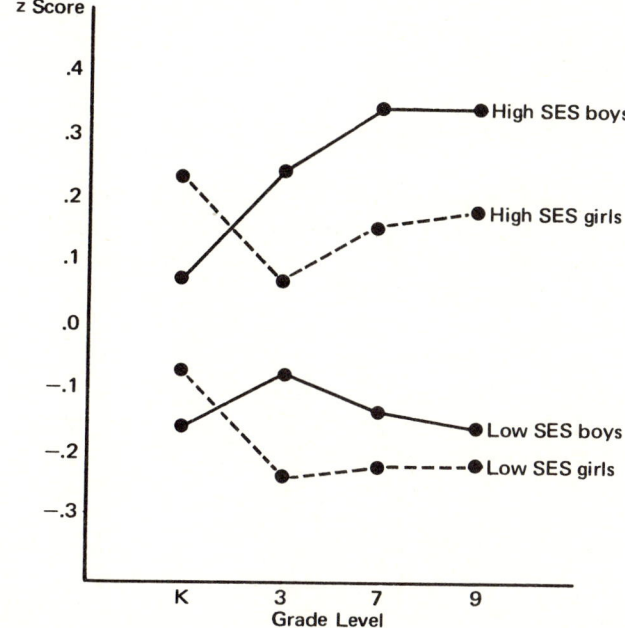

*Stennett, 1969, p. 389.

Mean z scores for four sex-SES groups of 200 cases each. **Figure 6.4**

Except from the first to second tests, the pattern of decreases among lower socioeconomic class children and increases among upper socioeconomic class children appears to be clearly demonstrated.

We have already discussed the possible relationship between socioeconomic status and IQ, as well as sex differences and IQ. Here, we are primarily concerned with these factors on a long-term basis as they affect the stability of the IQ. Because of environmental differences, later performance may be inconsistent with earlier performance, suggesting an *unstable* level of intelligence. Moreover,

> It should be emphasized that an IQ score is not an absolute measure of potential and is greatly influenced by the items and construction of a particular test. Furthermore, since different intelligence tests measure different samples of skills which are thought to be aspects of the total capacity to learn, some changes in IQs should be expected from test to test and accepted far more readily than they are by both educators and laymen. (Kraus, 1973, p. 30)

Summary In summary, we may draw several conclusions. Quantitative changes in intelligence are observed most in the early years of childhood, and the measurable amount of learning (i.e., change) tends to decrease as adulthood is approached. Qualitative changes in intelligence, however, tend to increase throughout the school years and continue in adulthood. Individual performance levels tend to be stable, but traumatic events (injury, emotional disturbances, etc.), sex, and socioeconomic status can reduce this stability.

Some teachers prefer not to look at past performance records of their students until several weeks of the term have passed by. In this way, they feel, they can deal with each child as he or she is functioning at present rather than prejudging him or her on the basis of earlier test scores or teachers' reports. This practice, in effect, gives each student a chance to make a new start, unhampered by previous interpersonal relations and "unlabeled" by test results. If, on the other hand, the teacher reads through each student's file before the start of a school term, the teacher will have a better knowledge of the general ability level and character of the class. He or she may also tend, however, to classify students without giving them a chance to demonstrate whatever personal growth may have occurred since leaving earlier teachers. (This was one of the problems that Rist noted in his study of teacher expectancy, as cited in chapter five.)

CLASSIFICATIONS OF INTELLIGENCE

Intelligence tests are given for a variety of purposes: evaluation of individual abilities, prediction of future performance, grade and/or section placement, matching groups of experimental and control subjects, and so on. Properly standardized tests base their scoring systems on a broad sample of the population and thus try to reflect a normal distribution of abilities in the population. In keeping with this practice, we should be able to classify groups in terms of their position under the normal curve. An IQ of 100, derived from Binet's original ratio concept, is considered to be the average IQ—the mean of the normal distribution. As the curve tapers downward on each side of the mean, fewer people fit into each category. In actual practice, Wechsler, for example, classified intelligence test scores (IQs) on his children's test in just this way.

*Classifications of intelligence by percent of the population in each category.** Table 6.3

IQ	Classification	Percent
130 and above	Very superior	2.2
120–129	Superior	6.7
110–119	High average (Bright)	16.1
90–109	Average	50.0
80–89	Low average (Dull)	16.1
70–79	Borderline	6.7
69 and below	Mentally deficient	2.2

*Wechsler, 1974, p. 26.

Thus we see that half of the population is expected to be of average intelligence, 25 percent of better than average intelligence, and 25 percent of less than average intelligence. The lowest category (Mentally Deficient) is usually further broken down for diagnostic and educational placement purposes to: 1) Mentally Retarded—Educable (IQ 50–70); 2) Mentally Retarded—Trainable (IQ 25/30–50); and 3) Mentally Retarded—Custodial (IQ 25/30 and below). We will discuss each of these classifications separately, principally to illustrate their significance for the learner in the classroom with respect to the learner's vocational aspirations. It might be helpful, initially, however, to examine the comparative strengths and weaknesses of these assorted groups.

Focus 6–2

Since we are primarily concerned with the learner, it is most appropriate to compare children in different intelligence classifications in terms of their academic or abstract mental abilities, rather than on some other basis. A study by Gallagher and Lucito (1961), using scores on the Wechsler tests, illustrates one method of making such a comparison. They used data collected by themselves and others, principally the original standardization data for the Wechsler Intelligence Scale for Children, on both children and adults who were bright (Full-Scale IQ 125–145), average (90–110), and retarded (40–75). As you can see in Table 6.4, these data are compared in terms of the three highest and three lowest subtest scores for each of the three groups.

Perhaps the most obvious pattern seen here is the relationship between high and low subtest scores for the gifted and the retarded. It is a strong inverse relationship, with the gifted scoring high on tests of verbal comprehension, and the retarded scoring low on the same subtests. By contrast, the gifted score low on tests of nonverbal abilities and the retarded do best on these subtests. The average group does not follow consistently either pattern, as might be expected. Gallagher and Lucito suggested that these differences

Comparison of groups of gifted and mentally retarded on high and low subtests of the Wechsler Scales. *

	Gifted		Average		Mentally Retarded	
	Children	*Adults*	*Children*	*Children*		*Adults*
	Lucito and Gallagher	Psychol. Corp.	Norman	Psychological Corporation	Psych. Corp.	Carleton & Stacey	Gill & Stacey
N =	50	43	38	565	52	150	172
CA Range =	7–11	7–11	15–29	7–11	7–11	7–16	16–58
Three highest subtests	Similar.	Vocab.	Similar.	Arithmetic	Object Assembly	Object Assembly	Object Assembly
	Informat.	Inform.	Bl. Design	Digit symb.	Dig. span	Picture complet.	Digit symbol
	Vocabulary	Similar.	Vocabulary	Pict. arrgt.	Pict. com.	Dig. span	Pict. c.
Three lowest subtests	Pict. com.	Pict. com.	Dig. symb.	Bl. design	Vocabulary	Inform.	Dig. sp.
	Pict. arr.	Dig. span	Pict. arr.	Information	Inform.	Vocab.	Inform.
	Dig. span	Dig. symb.	Dig. span	Similarities	Pict. arr.	Arithm.	Arithm.

Gallagher and Lucito, 1961, p. 481.

Table 6.4

> in intellectual patterns be considered in planning curriculum and teaching methods for the three groups. We do emphasize the use of concrete visual materials and limited verbal curricula for the retarded, but relatively few schools or school systems make provision for the strengths of the gifted in abstract thinking and verbal abilities. As the authors suggested, perhaps the gifted need a different curriculum and approach from the average, for they may not need as many cues to learning concepts as even the average learners.

It should also be remembered, and can be seen in Table 6.4 as well, that learners vary within themselves. Such individual patterns of abilities were shown in Focus 6–1. The gifted, for example, tend to do very well in verbal and abstract thinking areas, but some may be better performers with mathematical-spatial concepts than with strictly verbal concepts, despite the fact that they are above-average achievers in both areas. The implication for education here is quite clear. In planning a course of study for each youngster, recognize *intra*-individual differences as well as *inter*-individual differences in learning ability.

As much as one may wish that every learner might function at the same level, a realistic appraisal of individual differences demonstrates that this is unlikely to occur. Nevertheless, many schools still expect all learners of a given age and/or grade level to study from the same books and to learn in the same ways. As Bereiter (1969) stated, such an approach magnifies rather than equalizes individual differences.

> Tools . . . may act as amplifiers or equalizers with respect to basic human capabilities. . . . The equalizing effect of sophisticated tools is gained by having intelligence take over the function of other abilities. Intellectual tools . . . appear in the long run always to function as amplifiers rather than equalizers of intelligence and, thus, to magnify rather than nullify individual differences in ability. . . . Every tool requires certain minimum abilities of a person in order for him to use it at all. Accordingly, each new tool drives a wedge between those who can learn to use it and those who cannot. (pp. 311–12)

Essentially, Bereiter, too, is calling for recognition of individual differences in learning abilities and implementation of varied curricula and materials to meet these differences.

In what ways might you vary a laboratory assignment? A spelling lesson? Is variation in materials necessary or practical in higher education as well as basic education? **Questions**

Let us look first at the retarded learners. What does it mean to be retarded? We usually think of the retarded as being unable to learn what the average **The retarded** person learns, or as learning at a slower than average rate, as needing some supervision to protect them from the hazards of daily living, and as being perhaps more incompetent than some of them really are. These words describe their present condition in the layperson's mind. But what does retardation really mean? The term retardation implies delayed or slowed development, and this is indeed the case in many areas of development and functioning. Mental development in the intellectually retarded either proceeds at a slower-than-usual pace or stops short of complete development (is "arrested," to use a more precise term). The causes of retardation may be *endogenous* (genetic) or *exogenous* (illness, injury, or environmental deprivation).

Endogenous factors in retardation include the presence of a single dominant gene which can be traced in the family history, a genetic mutation in families that have had no previous known instances of retardation, or the matching of two recessive genes. In families where there are, or have been, several retardates, it is sometimes difficult to be certain whether a child is retarded because of a genetic factor or because of the negative factors in the family environment.

Exogenous factors are those which are environmentally produced, although some of them may occur in the prenatal or perinatal environment, as noted in chapter two. As we discussed earlier, pseudo-retardation may also be induced, and may result in permanent retardation, by stimulus deprivation, or possibly by families with several retarded members. That is, children who are born intellectually normal may become retarded because of the lack of opportunities for normal intellectual growth in their immediate environments during the preschool years. Another cause of pseudo-retardation is a severe psychiatric problem, such as infantile autism, where the child behaves like a severely retarded individual in his lack of response and communication.

Suspicions of retardation may occur in early childhood when the baby or preschooler lags considerably behind his age-peers in language, adaptive, motor, or personal-social development. Such suspicions may be confirmed or refuted by observing and testing the child. The examining physician or psychologist takes a complete medical and family history while performing an intellectual evaluation. In addition to the IQ of the child, he would also consider the youngster's social adjustment, emotional reactions, and his general behavior during the evaluations. Three descriptive levels of retardation are usually employed, based on IQ scores as mentioned earlier in this chapter: educable (mildly mentally retarded, IQ 50–70; trainable (moderate) mentally retarded, IQ 25/30–50; and custodial (severely) mentally retarded, IQ below 25–30. Both the trainable and educable retarded can be taught in special education classes, with the curriculum, methods, and pace adjusted to their needs and abilities. The severely retarded are primarily taught self-help skills at home or in institutions. We will discuss the specific educational adjustments for the retarded in chapter twelve.

The average   Under the normal curve, approximately 95 percent of the population fits between plus and minus two standard deviations from the mean. These are the intellectually "normal," although it is obvious that those at the lower end of the distribution, IQ 70–80, may resemble the retarded in some ways more than they do others in the average range, while those at the upper end, IQ 120–130, may appear to be more like the gifted. Those who are classified simply "average" without modifiers, usually have IQs in the range 90–110. In most schools, education is geared to this level of ability and to the "average rate" of progress. It is obvious, however, that the "average" child may not always learn at an "average" rate for a variety of reasons: the child may be poorly motivated or highly motivated toward achievement; the instructor may or may not use effective teaching techniques; the child may have emotional problems to some degree; he or she may have organically based learning disabilities; and so on.

The child with specific learning disabilities is a special example of the child with "average" intelligence. In fact, through naive error, he may be treated as retarded rather than average. Usually, his disabilities are rooted in perceptual-motor dysfunctions which cause him to have difficulty in reading (dyslexia), spelling, penmanship, speech, physical coordination, and/or arithmetic. In some cases, the learner can comprehend what he is being taught, but cannot express it correctly in speech or writing. Other such learners have difficulty in comprehension or reasoning—deriving abstract principles from specific examples, or applying what has been memorized by rote—and appear to be retarded. Frequently these children cannot perceive errors they have made, a symptom best observed through the use of individual intelligence tests and visual-motor tests.

In general, however, the learner with average intellectual ability progresses through the school years at the rate of one year's achievement for one year's attendance. Each learner, of course, has some studies in which he achieves more than in others. Interest as well as ability help to determine academic strengths and weaknesses.

Some difficulty for the average child may arise in schools or school districts where "average" is defined for their student populations as 120 or 125 IQ. The standard of expected achievement in such a situation can lead to continuing frustration and a negative self-concept.

If you were a student in such a school, how might you cope with these expectations? As a teacher, what could you do to reduce the negative effects of the situation while being "fair" to all your students? **Questions**

At the upper end of the intelligence distribution are the gifted, some of whom are referred to as "geniuses." In the schools, there are usually learners who have IQ scores of 125, 130, or 140 and higher, depending upon the standards of the individual school district or program. According to a recent survey of the literature on "geniuses," the concept of genius ". . . not only has been used to anchor the extreme ends of both intelligence and creativity, but there has been a continued, relatively unchallenged acceptance of the earlier ideas **The gifted** that genius or a genius is basically 'mad,' inspired, or so distinctly peculiar as to be hardly understandable through behavioral and social science techniques." (Albert, 1969, p. 744) In the period of 1927–65, 135 papers were published in professional journals dealing with this topic, which emphasized psychopathology of genius (22%), conditions and characteristics related or contributing to genius (19%), and the background of genius, e.g., heredity (13%). (Albert, 1969, pp. 745–47) As Albert said, the stress was placed on recognizing geniuses rather than on understanding their development. However, other studies of the gifted, notably the longitudinal research of Terman and Oden (1947), have found the gifted to be characterized by good mental and physical health, with few "peculiarities," except among those of extremely high intelligence (IQ 150–160 and higher). More recent research (Halpin, Payne, and Ellett, 1975) confirms the *lack* of psychopathology among gifted adolescents.

As learners, the gifted tend to be highly competent in verbal skills (although some are stronger in the mathematics-science areas instead), above average in abstract reasoning, very high in intellectual curiosity, and self-motivated.

Focus 6–3

Examples of these characteristics may be seen in the following description of children at the Hunter College Elementary School, a laboratory school for gifted children (IQ 130+) in New York City:

... a 9-year-old showed encyclopedic knowledge of science amassed through diligent reading on his own initiative and questioning of adults who could answer his queries. ... On learning that plants drink water, the child did not rest until he discovered for himself how this phenomenon takes place.

An 8-year-old highly gifted child became an expert on dinosaurs as a result of his intense interest in this subject which led him to spend all his Saturdays at the city museum, attending classes, poring over books on the subject, and making his own large watercolor drawings of prehistoric monsters. (Hildreth, 1952, pp. 1–2)

As with the mentally retarded and the average children with learning disabilities, the gifted learners profit from special teaching techniques. Several of the placement methods that have been used with them over the years are acceleration, special schools, homogeneous grouping for all subject classes, special classes in major subjects, and, more recently, individually prescribed instruction. Although these methods and techniques will be discussed more fully a bit later, let us look briefly here at a group of gifted first-grade children (IQ 133+) learning problem-solving techniques via programmed instruction. Using experimental and control groups, Anderson (1965) found that the experimental group learned, retained, and transferred problem-solving skills which Piaget had found to appear naturally in children of fourteen to sixteen years, or twice the age of the gifted children involved. (p. 285) The point demonstrated so clearly here is that, given the opportunity, gifted children are able to learn at a much faster than average rate. At the secondary level, such learners are often allowed and encouraged to take "advanced placement" courses that are given college credit, thus permitting them to accelerate their higher education.

What are the implications for teachers of individual differences in intelligence? **Question**

First of all, the teacher should provide a school environment where the learner, at any age, can find appropriate experiences of many kinds and at varying levels of difficulty. Secondly, the teacher needs to provide an atmosphere adequate to the needs of all her students, adjusting her expectancies realistically to the level and pattern of growth of each child. These are difficult tasks, requiring effort on the part of the teacher, and cooperation from her supervisors in the school district. Some of the ways in which the tasks have been approached have aroused controversy. That controversy is the next topic we will consider.

HANDLING INDIVIDUAL DIFFERENCES

As recognition of individual differences has grown, educators have become increasingly aware of the fact that children differ not only among themselves, but also *within* themselves. On various tests, as well as in classroom performance, it has been amply demonstrated that the individual child varies greatly in his abilities, interests, and other characteristics, so that he neither excels nor lags in *every* field, but does better in some than in others. It is this fact of intra-individual differences that underlies Conant's (1959) proposal for a flexible tracking system, a proposal he made after investigating American high schools. As we have read in the writings of eminent Americans from Jefferson to Gardner, equality of opportunity, as stated in our national documents, implies that each individual has an equal right to have the opportunity to go forward to the limits of his abilities.

Social theory began to take account of individual differences as part of the reaction to the immobile, feudal, deterministic, caste society that arose in the Middle Ages, when the Industrial Revolution almost completely destroyed economic feudalism and social caste systems in the nineteenth century. Some educators and philosophers have contended that ability grouping represents a return to feudal determinism. Others interpret ability grouping as a recognition of and respect for individual differences, which should permit greater social mobility and maximum individual development. *A controversial issue*

The increase in industrialization and urbanization, which began in the 1800s and continues to this day, has affected education in its organization, expansion, and curriculum. With the advent of compulsory education laws and new waves of immigration, persons of widely varying backgrounds, abilities, and goals came into the schools. Provision for these differences had to be made and was accomplished largely through a vastly increased variety of courses offered and refinements of the grading system, among which was the practice of homogeneous grouping.

The most frequent objection to ability grouping is that such a procedure is not consistent with democratic principles. It is not the grouping procedure, per se, that is undemocratic. It is the way in which grouping is handled. The ideology that pervades the school system, and the government, affects all students whether or not they are in homogeneous groups.

In this country, for example, we have had two seemingly inconsistent traditions that have dominated our approach to the individual, to education, to economic life, and other activities: rugged individualism and cooperation for community welfare. They are not incompatible, however, as we can see in other systems of education. Russia has competitive individualism in a socialized economy and adopted this system when it was found that progressive education, with its emphasis on cooperation, could not produce the skilled workers and intellectual leaders needed to elevate the Soviet Union from its primitive condition. The same competitive individualism in France has resulted in neither a communistic nor a particularly stable society. In the Netherlands and Switzerland, the competitive educational systems, which like other European systems have ability grouping, have produced leaders for stable and highly respected societies. Certainly some of our most rugged individualists, past and present, have not favored social welfare programs, but others who have risen to success through their own efforts have been more than willing to help those who could not help themselves. Competition and cooperation are not as completely "either-or" principles as some people assert. Therefore, academic competition as seen in grouping practices is not as inimical to democratic cooperation as is alleged.

No objection to homogeneous grouping was raised when special classes for exceptional children were established, or the grading-by-age system, or the development of vocational schools, division of larger classes into smaller ones by some criterion, and so on. In recent years, opposition to entrance requirements for college admission has arisen, not because of sudden negative feelings toward homogeneous grouping (which selection for college admission is, in a way), but because that practice is alleged to be discriminatory to minority groups.

Possible solutions

If you have a school of a dozen children, you will find no consistent uniformity in their interests, abilities, or attitudes over a period of time. Therefore, some kind of structure has to be introduced into the organization of the classroom. This is even more true when you multiply the dozen learners by 10, 20, 50, or 100. The use of one criterion to promote homogeneity still leaves a heterogeneous group by other criteria. With 60 independent criteria, the probability that any individual will be in the median 50 percent on all the measures is, according to one estimate, about one in one quintillion. (Williams, 1957)

Several plans have been proposed and tried, therefore, in attempts to cope with individual differences: age-grading, nongraded schools, diversified activities in the heterogeneous class, homogeneous grouping on rigid or flexible bases, special schools, and acceleration or retardation. They narrow down, basically, to adaptation, segregation, and grade adjustment. Let's examine each of these options briefly:

1) The technique known as age-grading, or less kindly as the "lockstep," does not really take individual differences into account. It is a minimal attempt to achieve order in the heterogeneous group of all school children—a step beyond the old one-room school. In this system of organization, as you know from your own experience, children enter first grade at age six, and are graduated from high school twelve years later at age eighteen. The concern here is with the supposed equal social and intellectual maturity of children of the same chronological age. The fact is, of course, that children of the same chronological age vary greatly in physiological maturity, social maturity, emotional maturity, and intellectual maturity.

2) Nongraded plans are seen in operation most frequently at the primary level, as in Philadelphia, where there are no official divisions into first, second, and third grades. In these programs, the goal is the continuous progress of each pupil at his or her own pace. Some plans permit the academically gifted child to complete the three-year sequence in two years, while the slow learner may remain in the program for four years without stigma. The Continuous Progress Plan tried in Appleton, Wisconsin, extended the plan to a seven-year situation. Following one year of kindergarten, children entered a three-year primary bloc, then a three-year intermediate group. Entrance to the junior high school usually followed, but it was possible to retain learners who were immature or academically deficient in either the primary or intermediate bloc for an extra year. Articulation was maintained with the junior high school to permit each learner's continuous progress. Combined with the nongraded plan, Appleton had mixed or heterogeneous grouping by ages and abilities. (Morse, 1960, pp. 30–31) At Melbourne High School in Melbourne, Florida, the nongraded concept was successfully extended to the senior high school. (Brown, 1965) Students are allowed to progress at their own rate of learning and frequently complete college-level courses in mathematics, English, science, and other subjects, before they are graduated. Ideal as the nongraded plan seems, its wider adoption has been slowed by the admitted administrative difficulties imposed by the flexible approach.

3) Perhaps the most common way of dealing with individual differences at the elementary school level is through subgrouping within the heterogeneous class. The children are divided into three to five groups according to reading ability, for instance, with each little group reading at its own speed and, frequently, from different books. In the area of social studies, project groups may be so arranged that the most able readers do the research reading, while the less able readers find or create illustrative materials. This approach does attempt to recognize individual differences in academic ability,

but, being allied with age-grading, may not provide adequate recognition of other differences among the learners. Extra effort is involved in this approach, not only in lesson preparation, but in planning a variety of meaningful learning tasks for the children with whom the teacher is not working at a given time.

4) Homogeneous grouping may be accomplished in several ways and on the basis of varying criteria, as has already been suggested. Some school districts establish groups on the basis of IQ test scores, others on the basis of achievement test scores, and still others according to combinations of these and/or other criteria. One question that immediately comes to mind is whether there is a real difference between IQ 89 and IQ 90, or between IQ 129 and IQ 130, assuming that 90 and 130 are cut-off criteria. Grouping may be rigid and across-the-board, or flexible. Where it is rigid, all students with IQs of 120 or 125+ are placed in the fastest section in every subject. In a more flexible arrangement, each student is placed for each subject according to his performance in that subject, and shifts from one section to another during the school year according to the learner's progress may be possible.

For very slow learners, ability grouping often provides smaller classes and even specially trained teachers. A major goal for these students is a sense of accomplishment, which might be unattainable for them in heterogeneous classes. On the other hand, the absence of brighter students may reduce the variety of stimulation that they would have experienced in heterogeneous classes.

Many elementary schools now have within-grade grouping where children move from one teacher to another for instruction in reading or arithmetic, with the groups divided by achievement in that subject. At the secondary level, there are frequently several sections for each major subject at each grade level, with different rates of progress and different levels of instruction. These are rarely flexible section assignments, since the student stays in the same section throughout the year regardless of any change in his learning pattern. Adjusting for individual differences, ideal as it appears, however, is a complex administrative task.

5) Special schools, or segregated educational facilities, are found mainly in large urban school districts where their cost can be justified by the number of academically gifted or other special learners in the school population. Examples of special schools for the academically talented are Hunter College Elementary School, Hunter College High School, Bronx High School of Science, High School of Music and Art—all in New York City—the Lowell School in San Francisco, and the Masterman Elementary School in Philadelphia. In addition, many districts have vocational schools for students not bound for college; these schools specialize in preparation for certain trades, such as aviation mechanics, fashion design, printing, and the restaurant field. Sometimes several such programs are housed in a single vocational-technical high school. This is the avenue often taken by several small school districts, which unite their funds, students, and teachers to provide such education.

A modification of the segregated school concept is the use of special classes within a regular school. Again, these are more commonly found in urban areas, but are now being established on a cooperative basis by several adjoining school districts. In such cases, a single district may not have sufficient pupils to warrant setting up a special class and/or may not be able to finance such a class in terms of special personnel and materials. The cooperative effort pools both the pupils and the financial resources. Special classes are provided for the academically gifted in some areas, but more often for the educable and trainable retarded, or children with learning disabilities.

6) Acceleration for fast learners and retention in grade for slow ones were more commonly practiced when semiannual promotion was the schools' policy and ability-grouping was frowned upon. Acceleration involves double promotion of a student, or "skipping" as it is also called. Although some schools have accelerated pupils mainly on the basis of IQ test scores and achievement test scores, it is more usual today to include levels of physical and social maturity as well in making such a decision. A bright child may be able to compete successfully on an intellectual level with pupils one to three years older than himself, but may suffer in his or her social development and peer contacts because he or she is ill-equipped emotionally and/or physically to meet the social demands of the older group. If a short, somewhat baby-faced, eleven-year-old boy enters seventh or eighth grade, for example, he is a likely candidate to teasing in which his academic prowess is of little aid. Of course, many gifted children are well-developed physically and socially as well as intellectually, and thereby avoid these problems. Some of the difficulties discussed in relation to rigid homogeneous grouping, as uneven readiness in various subjects, also present problems in acceleration. This is, therefore, an infrequently used method of resolving individual differences in ability.

Some specially planned programs that are very selective, however, have been successful for some intellectually precocious young adolescents. A combination of acceleration in grades 7–12, advanced placement credits, part-time college courses, and early admission to college have enabled students as young as 11½ years to enter college and succeed academically. According to a report by George and Stanley (1975), these early entrants have not met any unusual social or emotional difficulties. (Note: For a fuller description of the Johns Hopkins program, see Stanley, Keating, and Fox, 1974.) A less extreme program practiced by many colleges permits gifted learners to enter college after eleventh grade and has similarly not caused any undue problems.

Repetition of a grade offers other challenges. The repeating pupil may become the bully of the class because of his physical size and because of his feelings of hostility and frustration at having been "held back." He is branded a failure in the eyes of his peers and family, and frequently suffers considerable and possibly irreparable damage to his self-concept. Since research findings have indicated that the repeater learns little more in his second go-round in a grade than he did in his first attempt, retention, too, has become more of a rarity in recent years. Remedial instruction, subgrouping in regular classes, and special curriculum units are among the substitutes for retention in grade.

Summing up   These, then, are several of the possible approaches to the problem of how to deal with individual differences in learning abilities. The position one takes on whether or not to group depends upon one's own academic experiences, philosophy, and interpretations of the goals of education. Critics of ability grouping fear the creation of both an intellectual aristocracy and a demoralized and undereducated low-ability group, divided in their educational paths from preadolescence on, as is done in Western Europe. The arguments against ability grouping stress, as previously mentioned, its "undemocratic" basis, its lack of contact with reality, the potential dangers to the personalities of the less able, the difficulties of scheduling involved, and concern about the nonacademic (e.g., personal-social) aspects of the child's development. They are further in favor of the challenge presented by bright pupils to the slower ones in the heterogeneous classroom.

The proponents of ability grouping argue that, in adult life, people do tend to "segregate" according to their interests and abilities, that dull students are not constantly frustrated and overshadowed by their brighter peers in the classroom, that the range of teaching and learning problems faced by a teacher at one time is reduced, and that each ability group (slow, average, and rapid) can move at its own pace and to its own depth of comprehension. They also emphasize that if pupils of similar ability levels work and progress together, all individuals in the group will benefit.

Since studies of homogeneous grouping programs tend to show questionable benefits for the learners, it has been suggested that ". . . bringing together children who vary with respect to attitudes, learning styles, ethnic and socioeconomic background, and so forth, *within a structure which encourages flexibility in arranging instructional experiences*, could serve as the foundation for innovative and successful approaches to improving and equalizing educational opportunity." (Esposito, 1973, pp. 174–75)

Some of the arguments on both sides of this issue are valid and convincing. The dilemma appears insoluble, unless one plans education for each individual. To Vernon, in 1958, this seemed undesirable as well as impossible, because

> education implies not only individual development but also the training of different individuals to conform to society's pattern of intellectual and social norms. Thus there are positive advantages in educating diverse individuals in groups. Nevertheless, there must be some restriction of their heterogeneity, otherwise the educational process becomes inefficient and frustrating to the students as well as to the teacher. (1958)

While Vernon's point of view about relative desirability may still be valid, it is no longer impossible to design individual educational programs. Individualized instruction depends, however, on diagnostic skills as well as expertise in curriculum design, as the following example shows.

> Evidence of Eskimo figural skills suggests that the use of Guilford's structure of intellect model may be appropriate for discovering the Eskimo's abilities and the implications of testing for occupational guidance. Some possibilities suggested involve fields demanding clerical accuracy, technical ability, and mathematics and physics. ". . . Eskimos themselves tend to evidence a pattern of high figural ability and low English verbal ability. Thus, the educational question is whether new forms of instruction can be devised which build on Eskimos' intellectual strengths to increase their achievement, especially in their areas of academic weakness." (Kleinfeld, 1973, pp. 354–55)
>
> Ability grouping or differentiating instructional techniques in the usual sense may be inadequate as responses to this need. The designer of a curriculum for the Eskimos would have to consider how to combine the assets of the Eskimos with the needed verbal instruction in a way that would help these people to accomplish their own goals as well as the educational goals being imposed upon them.

Focus 6–4

The advent of computer-assisted and other programmed instructional modes and the flexible programming of the "open classroom" have made individualized instruction and progress a reality. These approaches to meeting individual needs will be discussed in chapter eleven.

SUMMARY

The initial emphasis in this chapter was on the patterns and nature of mental growth. Demonstration of the shift from mainly quantitative growth in childhood to principally qualitative changes in adolescence and adulthood was a major consideration. This led to discussion of the questions of whether mental ability is stable and whether mental differences are stable. Are the "bright" consistently bright? The answer: a qualified "yes." Are individuals who are above average in one area of mental competence above average in all areas of mental competence? The answer, "sometimes." It was shown that the total picture of an individual may appear to be consistent, but that the patterns of competence within the individual may change from time to time. This is particularly important when we work with adults returning to the classroom.

A major portion of the chapter dealt with individual differences in intelligence. First, we considered the several categories of intelligence, as measured by intelligence tests, and their relationship to learning. This revealed inter-individual differences in learning abilities. Quite naturally, we then had to raise the question of how to deal with these differences in the classroom. A discussion of several approaches to individual differences in the classroom illustrated a variety of potential answers to this question. The approaches included: age-grading, subgrouping in heterogeneous classes, homogeneous classes, and flexible scheduling and individualized instruction.

Preview

INTRODUCTION

EDUCATIONAL ASSESSMENT
- PRINCIPLES OF TESTING
- APTITUDE, ACHIEVEMENT, AND ATTITUDE TESTS
- CRITICISMS OF TESTING
- NATIONAL ASSESSMENT
- TEACHER-MADE TESTS
  - Mastery Learning

EDUCATIONAL EVALUATION
- GRADING
- SELF-EVALUATION
- PROMOTION POLICIES

GUIDANCE AND COUNSELING
- APTITUDE, PERSONALITY, AND INTEREST TESTS
- GUIDANCE PROGRAMS AND COUNSELOR FUNCTIONS

SUMMARY

7

Assessment and Evaluation

INTRODUCTION

Once out of school, there is a tendency to forget or minimize test anxiety, report card anxiety, and promotion anxiety—all very real sources of threat when they occurred. Assessment and evaluation may be less formal in the adult world, but virtually everyone is measured in some way, as a competent clerk, a talented architect, a gifted teacher, a good housekeeper, a gourmet cook, or as the reciprocal of one of these. In a paid position, such an evaluation bears heavily on whether or not one keeps a job. Even in marriage, too many negative evaluations lead to the loss of that position through divorce. In the school years, however, assessment and evaluation are constant companions of the learner and strongly influence his development and progress.

In this chapter, we are primarily concerned with these factors. We will look at the various measuring tools (tests) that are used to assess the learner's status, aptitude, or progress, as well as the National Assessment of Educational Progress, which seeks to evaluate the schools in which he learns. Related to these are considerations of test norms, interpretation, and construction. We will not focus on these at a high level of sophistication, for the purpose here is not to make test experts of you, but we will survey these items simply to make you aware of them and familiar with a number of problems in these areas.

Test scores are often used as contributors to an overall evaluation of the learner and for the purposes of appropriate placement in the school. Such uses have provoked educational controversies about "grouping," grading and the reports to both learners and their parents, and promotion policies. Each of these questions arouses heated arguments whenever parents, teachers, or students gather to discuss them. We have already seen evidence of this in the discussion of handling individual differences in chapter six.

Test scores are also used in the school guidance office. We shall look not only at the use of test scores and other assessments of the learner as they are employed in counseling and guiding him, but also at the functions of the guidance counselor as well. Psychologists and teachers both contribute to the efforts of the guidance counselor, so it is appropriate for educational psychology students to learn something about this field.

Apart from these evaluations by others, it is important for the individuals to learn to evaluate themselves and their performance. Ultimately what *they* think is most important—their criteria, their goals, and their achievements.

EDUCATIONAL ASSESSMENT

There are a number of ways in which learners may be assessed. With regard to academic performance, specifically, the learner may take an achievement, aptitude, and/or attitude test. Other measures that may be used are interest and personality tests, but these contribute more to overall evaluation than to academic considerations. Any or all of these tests may be used to select and classify individual learners, facilitate student learning experiences, create more effective teaching techniques, appraise curricula, assist in the individualization of instruction, or aid in guidance and counseling.

Another way of dividing tests is to classify them as measures of status (that is, where the learner is *now*), or as predictive instruments. Achievement tests, like intelligence tests, usually fall into the category of status measurements. Like the intelligence tests, however, they are also used as bases for estimates of future performance, or predictors. In their original purpose, achievement tests were and are designed to measure the amount or kind of learning that took place as a result of instruction or experience. Teacher-made tests obviously fit these purposes as readily as do standardized published tests. Aptitude tests, on the other hand, are clearly predictive instruments, for they are administered before the learner embarks on a course of study. Attitude tests are categorized as measurements of status, that is, what the person's attitudes are at the time of taking the test. They can be used as part of a battery of tests to predict potential success in certain fields. Indeed,

> Prediction is a tool of educational guidance; as such, it depends on the educational system and the values implicit in educational goals. We have also recognized . . . that achievement should comprise achievement in school subjects, in the development of personality and character, and also achievement in later life as a citizen, which includes far more than occupational success. (Cattell and Butcher, 1968, p. 8)

All predictions, however, have a component of error. Since all behavior is multiply determined, it is grossly unwise to make firm predictions of future performance on the basis of one or two tests, no matter how valid and reliable the tests may be.

Principles of testing

Before discussing the various kinds of educational assessments further, we should review briefly certain basic principles of testing. Most fundamental is that the test be appropriate to the person(s) taking it. Then, to be useful, a test should be both reliable and valid. That is, it should yield consistent scores (reliability) and the scores should have a high positive correlation with a criterion measure (validity). Published tests should be administered in accordance with directions given in the accompanying manuals, following all of the stated time limits, examiner behavior, and so on. The room in which the test is given should be comfortable in temperature, have adequate lighting, and be free of noisy distractions. All persons taking the test should have the appropriate supplies and clearly understand the task ahead. Ideally, anyone taking a test should be in good health, sufficiently rested, and relatively free of test anxiety. For practical reasons, however, these ideal personal factors are rarely checked in group test administration. In individualized testing, the examiner can reduce anxiety and arouse motivation in the process of establishing rapport with the subject.

Teacher-made tests, of course, usually do not have formal instructions in a manual. In this case, the teacher or proctor should provide clear, preferably concise, directions orally or in writing, making certain that all the students have the necessary answer sheets or essay booklets, pens, pencils, or other tools and that everyone in the class abides by the stated time limits. Again, classroom conditions in terms of noise and temperature should be controlled as much as possible.

Once the test scores have been derived, they must be interpreted. A score may be compared with that of other students who have taken the same test (norm-referenced) or with the body of knowledge that the learner has studied (criterion-referenced).

Test manuals include information on the scores of population samples on whom the test was standardized. These are known as norms. If students in a school district consistently score above or below the norms over a period of years, however, it is often appropriate to develop local norms. Students in that district are then compared with students who have previously taken the same test under similar conditions of learning and socioeconomic background.

Norms are helpful in educational placement, since a learner can be compared with his or her peers, and can also be of value in evaluating educational programs. A caution from Cronbach is that "Norms are not 'standards.' A common mistake is to assume that all pupils in the ninth grade should reach the ninth-grade norms. This is of course a fallacy; 50 percent of the pupils in the standardizing sample fall below the norm. Furthermore, the test shows only what schools are doing at present." (Cronbach, 1970, p. 107) The public, and educators, have reason to become concerned, however, when substantially more than 50 percent of students are below the average for a grade. This situation has been recurring annually in large cities such as New York and Philadelphia where 55 percent or more of students have been scoring below grade average on reading tests.

Criterion-referenced measurement, on the other hand, is useful in ". . . the more hierarchically organized subject matter areas, such as mathematics and the physical and biological sciences." (Carmody, 1974, p. 363) In the classroom situation, the criterion may be that the student can complete 50 mathematics problems in 20 minutes with no more than two errors. Or, a typing student may have to be able to type at a speed of 60 words per minute with no more than three errors.

"Two immediate advantages come about from the use of criterion-referenced testing: (1) specific skills are identified and *must* be mastered to 'criterion' before the student works on the next skill area, and (2) the success of some students does not automatically mean that others will do poorly." (Good, Biddle, and Brophy, pp. 155–6)

Ebel (1975), however, has criticized criterion-referenced testing because of the special problems it creates. His specific points include:

1. "selecting and later defending a unique set of ideas and abilities which each student will be expected to learn";
2. "rational definition of a particular level of test performance which will indicate attainment of each objective";
3. "repeated testing of students and the need to construct multiple parallel test forms for this";
4. "reporting only two levels of an achievement that exists at many different levels"; and
5. "producing, distributing, and using detailed, bulky, and quite ephemeral reports on which objectives a particular student achieved and which he did not." (p. 85)

Even with the problems suggested, criterion-referenced testing is being used more widely at all levels of education. One reason for increased usage is that this type of measurement is frequently tied to educational objectives and individualized instruction (see chapter eleven).

Suggested Activity

Develop a list of criteria for an area in which you expect to teach. (If you are not planning to teach, develop such a list for a course you are now studying, perhaps even your educational psychology course.) Are your criteria specific and clear?

The major criteria for a useful test are, then, reliability, validity, and appropriate norms, or meeting stated criteria. To interpret the scores obtained on a test, the teacher must ask himself what kind of test it is (achievement, aptitude, personality, and so on), how the individual learner scored in terms of some criterion, and in what ways this information helps him to understand the learner. Care must be taken in interpreting the test scores to parents or to learners, for while norms may be valid for groups, there is considerable room for error in individual cases. This is, indeed, one of the primary reasons for introducing criteria-based evaluations. Then, students and their parents can know specifically what the student is able or not able to do.

Aptitude, achievement, and attitude tests

Now, let us look first at academic *aptitude* tests. These are generally administered to candidates for admission to a program at the college or graduate school level, but may also be used for selection of students to special classes or schools at the secondary level. Examples of these tests are the Modern Language Aptitude Test; the Miller Analogies Test, Graduate Record Examination, Law School Admissions Test, and Differential Aptitude Tests. Each of these taps abilities relevant to the course to be pursued, such as verbal fluency, verbal reasoning, mathematical reasoning, auditory memory, clerical speed, mechanical comprehension, spatial relations, and so on. From the level of success attained on each ability test, one can predict with some certainty whether the learner is likely to profit from instruction in a given field. A student with poor scores in verbal fluency and auditory memory, for example, would be unlikely to do well in studying languages. On the other hand, one with high scores in verbal fluency and reasoning might be a good candidate for law school admission.

Aptitude tests should not be confused with *pretests*, which are often given before a course begins or a new unit is started. These are essentially status tests to find out how much the students know before they start a course. The main purposes of pretests are 1) to have a baseline against which to measure change and 2) to eliminate repetition where content has already been acquired. Of course, if a student attains a high score on a pretest, it might be reasonable to predict high achievement in learning additional content that is dependent on his knowledge. In some instances, where a student has an extremely high score on a pretest, it might be wiser to advance him to the succeeding course rather than bore him by attempting to teach him what he already knows.

Achievement tests are taken after completing a course of study. They may be classroom tests, for example, unit or final exams, or standardized tests, such as those offered by the College Entrance Examination Board. In any case, they are intended to measure what the student knows after a period of learning. If the teacher has stated her educational objectives, the achievement test should indicate to what extent the student(s) met the objectives. These may reflect changes in attitude, skill level, perception, or information. Despite known limitations of pretest-posttest measures, measurements of change are ". . . usually obtained by observing the difference between scores on a pretest and a posttest." (Sjogren, 1970, p. 370) The achievement test may also reflect level of mastery. As noted earlier, achievement test scores are frequently used as predictive measures and may, if designed for the purpose, serve in a limited way as diagnostic tests. College admission boards include achievement test scores in considering an applicant's potential for future learning, and graduate school admissions officials do the same at that level. The Scholastic Aptitude Tests, administered by the College Entrance Examination Board, are a good example of this combination of functions, for, in reality, the questions asked refer to content learned up to that point *in school*, and thus are achievement tests as well as aptitude tests. A caution should be observed, however, in using the SAT or other achievement predictors, according to Cronbach.

> There can be little long-range differential prediction before grade 11. In grades 7–10, aptitude tests suggest strong points; the pupil will be

A situation familiar to almost all students.

encouraged to enroll in courses in which these assets will be developed. Low points in the profile need not be taken seriously at such an early age except when, as in numerical or spelling tests, remedial instruction can raise the score. By midadolescence the aptitude pattern is reasonably stable, but even at this age irreversible decisions should be avoided. Later courses and job experience may alter the profile and will certainly add to the student's knowledge about his capabilities and interests. (Cronbach, 1970, p. 371)

Not only may courses and job experience alter aptitude patterns, but also the late-blooming adolescent may suddenly find motivation to learn late in high school or early in the college years. An inspiring teacher may cause a student to begin using latent abilities that improve her performance or may stimulate a student's interest in a particular career, one that she may not have considered previously. Changes in the home situation may also affect achievement. It is hoped that such possibilities are considered by admissions staffs. Cronbach has warned us to avoid the pattern that prevails in European schools, where determination of future schooling, and therefore future occupational status, takes place at age eleven, twelve, or thirteen, ages that are preadolescent and frequently presecondary school level.

Attitude tests are something quite different from either aptitude or achievement tests. These tests attempt to measure the positive or negative feelings of individuals toward a particular problem, event, person, course, and so on. More than the other types of tests, attitude tests lack reliability, for the subjects can "fake" their answers. If you assume that the examiner will, for example, select people for a job or class on a certain basis, it is quite simple to respond to the questions with the kind of answer you think the examiner wants.

Focus 7–1

"Students will be nominated for faculty-student committees on the basis of their attitudes toward educational policy," reads the handout. Now the trick is to discover whether this means that the school administration will choose students who can be manipulated easily by the faculty, or students who are less conforming but willing to work within the system, or students who are innovative but may "fight" the faculty. Consider questions that might be on an attitude test and how students in each category might answer them.

1. Students should have a voice in determining curriculum.
   Agree / / / / / Disagree

2. Students should be able to recommend dismissal of poor teachers.
   Agree / / / / / Disagree

3. Students should abide by administrative rulings without question.
   Agree / / / / / Disagree

The bias of the test-maker may show in "loaded" questions, or in those that force the respondent to choose a position that is only partially true for him, as in cases where there are only two or three choices.

Criticisms of testing

Depending upon the circumstances involved, testing can be criticized on many counts. A major concern is that highly anxious students tend to perform on tests below their capabilities because of this anxiety and the stress situation presumably evoked by taking a test. At least two recent studies question the validity of this hypothesis, one at the college level and the other with sixth-graders. (Marso, 1970; Allison, 1970) The investigators in both studies found that stress conditions (or lack of them) did not affect high-anxious subjects adversely. However, they also commented that individual anxiety problems might have been hidden in group statistics. This seems to be a logical explanation if classroom experience is any guide. Although exam scores may be high for a class, and even for a specific student, said student may truthfully tell the instructor that he knew the material being tested but did not answer properly because he "drew a blank," or misread the question in his anxious state. It is also possible that a curvilinear relationship exists between anxiety and test scores, as a number of studies have shown. Here, students with very low anxiety or very high anxiety, but with equal learning ability, may achieve similarly low test scores in a stress situation (for example, a timed test) or high scores in a nonstress situation.

A second criticism is that many of these tests reflect the student's performance at an isolated point in time, and that, at that point, the student may have been poorly motivated, examined under adverse conditions, or otherwise at a disadvantage.

A third criticism is often leveled at the tests themselves. Were the questions appropriate to the test population in terms of language used, content included, and level of difficulty? This criticism has been directed most often at the intelligence tests, but can hold also for other tests, both standardized and teacher-made. Is there allowance for creative or nonconformist answers?

Another negative aspect of testing programs is the amount of time spent in administering and scoring tests. It is not unusual for three or more days each spring to be consumed in administering achievement tests at the elementary school level. Classroom tests take additional hours each term or school year.

Item: A field-work supervisor tried in vain for three successive Fridays to visit a school in which one of her students was acting as a teacher aide. Each Thursday, when she called the school, she was informed that the children were taking achievement tests, and therefore the visit would need to be postponed. Finally, on the fourth Friday, she was allowed to visit.

Item: In a ten-week term of thirty class meetings, each hour exam given significantly reduces the teaching time available. The result: only midterm and final exams are given. More frequent evaluations would "cost" too much.

Additionally, testing may be used for other than its original purposes. In some instances, diverse uses are legitimate, as when test profiles are examined with an eye toward possible needs for remedial instruction or to provide the student with information for the purposes of guidance. Criticism arises, however, when test scores are used to "group" pupils in what is supposed to be a heterogeneous school system. Criticism also is aroused when tests are used to evaluate teachers and/or curricula. The practice of keeping cumulative records, including test scores, for each pupil can be criticized because of the prejudice that can be aroused in a teacher before he sees the student. The impact of teacher expectations, influenced by past test scores, on current performance cannot be totally discounted.

A major question that has come up in recent years is whether or not test results, particularly those on achievement tests, should be publicly disseminated. There is a concern whether the publication of test results by school or by district is either desirable or ethical.

Questions *What purposes does such publication serve? If you were a teacher in the school where test results were poor, how would you feel? How about if you were a parent?*

On an individual basis, test results (and other information directly related to the student) are more closely guarded. The General Education Provisions Act (the Buckley Amendment) protects the privacy of such records. The law

> ... prohibits schools from transferring data from education records to third parties without first making announcement of the intention to do so, stating the purposes for which the data are being released, and obtaining the parents' or students' written consent for release. (Davis, 1975, p. 11)

The effects of this law on educational research projects remain to be seen, but the effect on teachers is much clearer. Teachers are still able to see test scores, but find other comments much scarcer in pupil personnel folders. (Note: A highly informative presentation of the issues is contained in J. W. Rioux and S. A. Sandow, *Students, Parents, and School Records.* Columbia, Md.: National Committee for Citizens in Education, 1974.)

On the other hand, testing does have positive aspects if handled carefully. As schools exist today, some indication of achievement is desired for measurement of learning. Aptitude, achievement, and attitude test scores do help in guiding the individual for the future. Weaknesses can be observed in test score profiles, and needed remedial instruction given. Test contents are being modified to permit the abilities of the thinking student to come through, as well as those of the memorizing learner. Recognition of cultural differences has led to the abandonment of intelligence testing in many cities, noted earlier, and to the use of multilingual achievement and aptitude tests in other school districts. Researchers are also more aware that teachers "teach the test" before achievement tests are given, or manipulate the testing conditions. This has resulted in attempts to achieve tighter control of the testing situation.

It has been proposed that improvements in secondary education, particularly, could be made for students and schools alike if changes were made in the measurement system used. Lohnes (1967) suggested two purposes for a revised measurement system: 1) "We need a school measurement system that makes it impossible for teachers to type students. The system would treat each student as a unique person. . . ." and 2) ". . . the second is to inform students about their potentialities vis-a-vis self-posited goals." (p. 105) The guidance purpose has already been discussed. The attempt to remove or minimize teacher influence will be explored in discussing grading.

In contrast to the individual testing such as we have been discussing,

National assessment

there are other testing situations in which the individual's score is *not* of primary importance. A major example of this is the National Assessment of Educational Progress.

The National Assessment of Educational Progress (NAEP) was originated in 1964 for the purpose of gathering data on the effectiveness of expenditures in the field of education. Tests are administered in ten subject areas, divided into two testing cycles, to large samples of nine-, thirteen-, seventeen-year-old, and young adult age groups. Knowledge, skills, and attitudes are assessed. Except for reading tests, all group-administered tests are presented on tape to standardize testing procedures and minimize reading problems. The scores are reported in terms of geographic regions, type of community, sex, race, and level of education of the subjects' parents. If the project reaches its goals, it will serve to inform educators and the public where greater emphasis and expenditure is needed in the curriculum. On the other hand, substantial criticism has been made of the stated objectives and the questions asked. Katzman and Rosen (1970) condemn the goals as unimaginative, a blend of "momism" and "apple pie," and the test exercises as a test of children's abilities ". . . to memorize tidbits of information rather than any ability to process information or solve problems." (p. 583)

Focus 7–2

In the Reading and Literature tests, administered in the period October 1970–August 1971, the following questions are samples of the type asked of 17-year-old subjects. (Demonstration Package Year 02, NAEP)

Item: A compound word is made by putting two words together. Fill in the oval beside the compound word in the list below.

◯ car
◯ elephant
◯ football
◯ table
◯ I don't know

(The author's son was learning this concept in second grade in October 1970.)

Item: Here is something you might read in the index of a book. How are the headings under "Automobiles" arranged?

Automobiles
  history of,   144–149
  making of,   149–153
  manufacturers of,   147
  materials used,   149–151
  styles of,   157–161
  uses of,   145;154;164–167

> Fill in the oval beside the BEST description of how the headings are arranged.
>
> ○ In numerical order
> ○ In alphabetical order
> ○ By importance of the heading
> ○ In no special order
> ○ I don't know

Findings from NAEP studies are interesting. In one, for example, it is revealed that ". . . 13-year-olds from affluent suburbs consistently outperform their rural and inner-city peers . . . [and] that parents who have the advantage of training beyond high school pass on that advantage to their children." (Justus, 1973) Another study, surveying social studies, showed that "Only 41 percent of the 17-year-olds and 44 percent of the 26 to 35 age group can correctly use a simple ballot containing nine candidates' names." (Vandermyn, 1974, p. 22) A more alarming conclusion was drawn from the second round of assessments in knowledge of scientific principles and facts. It was shown ". . . that science knowledge is declining in American schools in virtually all types of socio-economic communities." (Beshoar, 1975, p. 6) This conclusion is the more disturbing because school districts with a poor showing on the first science assessment *had* attempted to improve the quality of science education they provided. Specific recommendations had been made after the first assessment to guide the correction of educational inequities and curriculum weaknesses. (p. 11)

What causes can you suggest for a decline in scientific knowledge between 1969 (first round of testing) and 1973 (second round)? — ***Question***

Those opposed to the NAEP program fear that national evaluation will lead to nationalization of education. (Saylor, 1970, p. 596) The United States is one of the few countries in the world that does not have a national system of education, and the desire to maintain state and local control of curriculum and standards is a very strong one. Nationalization was not part of the original charge to the committee that developed the exploratory program leading to NAEP.

The assessment program involves status tests on the achievements of the different samples of the population over a period of years. These tests do not cover the same ground that the College Boards or similar nationally administered tests do. They do not give individual school districts or states the same kind of information that a national testing program can. They only indicate that a given percentage of a certain population sample can answer certain questions. This may contribute to schools reevaluating and reformulating their goals, possibly on a more uniform basis, or the tests may be, as some critics charge, a complete waste of time and money.

An alternative to the National Assessment Program, and one that serves somewhat different purposes, is a statewide evaluation program. Henry S. Dyer, of the Educational Testing Service, believes that statewide evaluation could aid the student in understanding his or her educational needs and personal and career goals, assist local school personnel in evaluating the effectiveness of their performance as compared with similar schools in the state, provide the state authorities with adequate information for the appropriate allocation of resources to each school system, stimulate research and experimentation designed to elevate the quality of education, and inform the public of the educational benefits its tax dollars support. (1970) Pennsylvania has such an evaluation program, although not on as large a scale as Dyer suggests, and not listing all the priorities he cited. New York has long had Regents' Examinations and state scholarship tests, which serve as statewide evaluations at the secondary level. School personnel can infer from the scores of their students how well their performance compares with that in other areas of the state. These are only beginnings of a comprehensive state evaluation program.

Teacher-made tests

Let us turn briefly to teacher-made tests, for you will deal with these more frequently than with standardized tests. The basic motivations for giving your class a test are 1) to measure student progress, and 2) to diagnose strengths and weaknesses. In designing a test, you must know what information you are seeking and also how you intend to obtain it. There are two fundamental test formats: essay and objective. Which you use depends on what you want to measure—ability to see trends, recall of facts, recognition of information, and so on—and, in a very practical way, on the number of students who will be taking the test. It is difficult to grade effectively or with equal judgment 150 students on an essay test.

Essay tests have advantages over objective tests in estimating the learner's comprehension of what he has been taught, or his ability to apply new knowledge to unfamiliar problems. Essay papers and tests are specific targets of the anti-grading movement, because the evaluation of them is so subjective. In a study by Huck and Bounds (1972), the results indicated that "... graders who have neat handwriting are biased by the neatness of an essay—biased in the direction of giving lower grades to essays that contain messy handwriting. Graders who have messy handwriting, however, are not influenced by the neatness of essays." (p. 282) There are other teachers who downgrade essays because of poor spelling or poor grammar.

Objective tests, on the other hand, are easier to grade, less subject to bias in grading, and permit a wider sampling of what has been learned, as shown in Focus 7–3. It is difficult, however, to write multiple-choice questions, for example, with almost equally plausible choices of response. True-false questions (alternative-response type) may be unclear or too clearly one or the other. Recall items must ask for the most important information without giving too many hints as to the desired response. In other words, writing test questions is a tricky task.

Focus 7–3

Comparison of objective and essay tests.

Trait	Objective test	Essay test
1) Type of structure	The pupil operates within an almost completely structured task	The pupil organizes his own response with a minimum of constraint
2) Type of response	The pupil selects one of a limited number of alternatives or recalls a short answer	The pupil uses his own words and expression in his response
3) Sampling of knowledge	The pupil responds to a relatively large number of items (extensive sampling)	The pupil responds to a relatively small number of questions (intensive sampling)
4) Credit in scoring	The pupil receives a score for each answer according to a predetermined key (usually right or wrong with no partial credits)	The pupil receives a score for each question depending upon the degree of completeness and accuracy

Lien, 1967, p. 65.

Obviously, your choice of test format and types of questions asked depends on the amount of material you wish to include, your desire to measure recall, recognition, or understanding, and whether you want to grant partial credit for partially correct responses. One solution, of course, is to give tests that are partially objective and partially essay. This practice is more flexible and also offers a more equal chance for success to learners who "understand" as well as those who memorize.

Focus 7–4

In what category—essay, objective recall, objective recognition, association—would you place each of the following questions?

1. An event that follows a response and gratifies a need is called:
   a) responsiveness
   b) motive
   c) reinforcement
   d) incentive
2. Discuss briefly the relationships between anxiety and curiosity.
3. Compare the viewpoints of Behaviorists and Field Theorists with respect to learning.
4. The concept of "Life Space" is associated with _____.
5. Match capital cities with their states:

   _____ 1. Alaska   a. Albany
   _____ 2. Florida   b. Atlantic City
   _____ 3. New Jersey   c. Fairbanks
   _____ 4. New York   d. Jacksonville
   _____ 5. Oregon   e. Nome
                              f. Salem
                              g. Tallahassee
                              h. Trenton

Suggested Activity Write five multiple-choice questions based on the content of this chapter. Compare questions with your classmates to see which points most members of the class consider important. Which questions would you consider petty? Why?

Other considerations in test construction are level of difficulty and time. The test should be of a length that will permit most of the class to complete it in the allotted time period. If the test is too difficult for the class, not only will most students fail it, but also relatively few will complete it. Conversely, a too-easy test will not give you a true indication of "who" has learned "what." That is, it won't discriminate effectively between those who have profited from instruction and those who need remedial help. It is no favor to the learners to give a test for grading or diagnostic purposes that they could have answered before taking the course. (There are occasional exceptions to this statement, particularly in research situations.)

Tests are not limited to strict essay or objective formats. There are open-ended questions that may have no single correct answer, but that are evaluated on the basis of the student's support of his or her point of view. Such questions permit the thoughtful, the creative, the nonconforming learner to say what *he* thinks and "back it up" rather than what someone else *tells* him to think. There are, also, of course, nonwritten tests. Oral exams are one example. Performance tests are used in music, art, driving, laboratory courses, and the like. Tests of skill are common in physical education, typing, shorthand, mechanical, and technical courses.

Teacher-made tests that measure an individual's achievement in a given subject are obviously not norm-referenced. There are, however, methods the teacher can use for comparison of the individual's score with those of the rest of the class. Noting where his score falls within the *range* of the class's scores, whether it is above or below the class mean, or which *quartile* or *quintile* it is in gives a general indication of comparison. More indicative and more frequently used in the classroom is a *percentile score,* which indicates the percentage of scores that falls below that student's score. Still more precise (and often used in research) are *standard scores:* z scores and T scores. They describe the score's distance above or below the mean for that class. (For details in the calculation of these measures, see the Statistical Appendix.)

Mastery Learning

One of the main reasons for measuring the individual by using tests is to assess his progress toward an objective, whether it be a level of mastery, a specific goal (as in the quantity of push-ups in a physical fitness program), or one of the general objectives associated with education (for example, "development of the individual as a citizen"). Learning for mastery is a concept being adopted by more and more teachers. Its underlying philosophy is that most students can learn subject matter at a very high level of mastery if given enough time. After all, one would rather cross a bridge built by an engineer who scored at 95 percent in his professional studies than by an engineer who graduated on the basis of a 70 percent average in the same courses.

To teach, using the mastery concept, the teacher must first define what the students are expected to learn. Then he must decide the standard of performance (criterion level) to be achieved by the students in learning this material. Usually the teacher breaks the course goals down into units of work, each of which could be completed satisfactorily in a week or two, but could take longer for an individual student. Progress tests are scheduled at the end of each unit. If the student passes at the criterion level, he moves on to the next unit. If he fails to meet the standard, perhaps 9 out of 10 units correct, he is given the opportunity to approach the material from a different angle and then take another progress test. Learners who complete the required number of units at criterion level and/or a final examination at criterion level earn an "A." The final test would be *summative* and criterion-referenced. (Block and Anderson, 1975)

EDUCATIONAL EVALUATION

As a result of the measurement process, a grade is usually assigned. Measurement is also an aid to educational placement, in ability groups or grade levels. A look at these evaluative policies as they are practiced in the schools is our next logical area for discussion.

Educational evaluation is seen as incorporating the various assessments made of the learner's performance on tests and in the classroom. Such evaluations are basic to the problems of giving grades (and reporting them to parents), whether or not to group learners by ability and promotion policies. These problems have been the subject of animated discussion in the popular press as well as in professional journals, in educational meetings as well as social gatherings. Parents are vitally concerned about these problems, as they should be, because of the effects of evaluations on their children *and* because too often they see evaluations of their children as evaluations of themselves. Parental egos are easily damaged in this area. Educators, too, are vitally concerned as they try to foresee the academic and emotional effects of given policies on individual learners. As recognition of individual differences has grown, educators have become increasingly aware that children differ not only among themselves, but within themselves (see chapter five).

Grading

No matter whether homogeneous or heterogeneous grouping is followed, there must be some evaluation of what progress the learner is making. Despite recurrent student pressures for doing away with grading, even a "pass-fail" system means that the teacher has to estimate whether or not the student has learned enough to complete the course satisfactorily. Grading has been supported on several grounds: administrative need, informative, and motivational. As noted in chapter four, however, students vary widely in their views as to whether grading is a motivating force. In another study with college students, Goldberg found ". . . that five different grading policies had little differential effect on subsequent test performance. . . ." (Goldberg, 1965, p. 22) For some students, grades are the "carrots" that encourage them to study harder. For other students, grades are the "sticks" that prod them and keep them from failing. Both of these are examples of the motivational force of grades. To many others, however, the grade they earn is not as important as *what* they learn. For these students, grades are important only in an administrative sense, in case of application to graduate school or transfer to another college. Even the information function of grades, that is, feedback from the instructor, is relatively unimportant to the non-grade-oriented learner. Simon (1970), an arch-opponent of the grading system, has enumerated five reasons why grading must be eliminated.

1. Grades prevent effective and real communication between teachers and students because the two groups must be divided by the grading or evaluation process.
2. Grades tend to reward the best memorizers rather than the best learners and doers, while punishing those who do not conform to the "system."
3. Grades misdirect learning, in that students tend to select easier courses and/or instructors in order to maintain a high average, rather than taking courses that interest them or are likely to have future usefulness for them.
4. Grades reinforce competitiveness, especially where "curved" grades are given. (Among other things, this practice also encourages cheating, which is hardly what we want students to take from school to their adult lives.)
5. Grades frequently mutilate the person's concept of his own worth.

It is Simon's last point that is, perhaps, most relevant to the learner in the precollege years. At a time when so much emphasis is being placed on mental health and individual worth, how can grading be justified and how can it be handled in order to reduce its injurious psychological effects?

Many schools are attempting to evaluate students on the basis of what is essentially a double standard. That is, the learner is graded in terms of his or her own ability and also in comparison with grade norms as given in terms of average expectations for achievement in a given grade, scores on standardized tests, or teacher standards of performance. This plan has more merit than a single competitive grading system if only because the diligent efforts of slower learners can be reinforced by an "A" or "B" in terms of the individual's ability, rather than the constant "D" or "F" in terms of class norms.

In other schools, no grades are issued to parents or students, but written commentaries and/or parent-teacher conferences replace them. In this procedure, there is still a question of whether or not the student is learning enough to go on, is making average progress, and so on, but there can be fuller explanation of strengths and weaknesses and of areas in which remedial help will be appropriate.

There is much debate about what grades really mean, or should mean. There are articles in the public press deploring "grade inflation." The two items are closely tied. Ladas (1974) defined a grade as ". . . a measure of academic achievement using an explicit standard." (p. 185) He further wrote that grades should not be awarded merely for attendance or effort, professed need, to bolster self-concept, or to avoid conflict with the student. (pp. 185–86) Those who criticize grade inflation allege that these are the reasons why students are graduating from school with higher averages but less knowledge. Traditionalists tend to favor grading on a curve, that is, a limited percentage of As, a larger percentage of Bs, perhaps 50 percent Cs, a stated percentage of Ds, and a limited percentage of Fs. Reformers argue that this dooms some learners to failure and increases the probability of cheating as students compete for the few high grades available.

Do you believe that grading is necessary? Why? Do you favor curve grading or criterion grading? **Questions**

Another approach to evaluation is *self*-evaluation. Rogers (1969) was one of the strongest proponents of this approach, stressing that **Self-evaluation**

> The evaluation of one's own learning is one of the major means by which self-initiated learning becomes also responsible learning. It is when the individual has to take the responsibility for deciding what criteria are important to him, what goals he has been trying to achieve, and the extent to which he has achieved those goals, that he truly learns to take responsibility for himself and his directions. (pp. 142–43)

Students as young as those in elementary school are capable of developing criteria, possibly with the teacher's guidance, for evaluating their own work. Rogers suggests that criteria be grouped under those that are personally most meaningful, and those that are imposed by others or from past experience. (p. 92)

If the student uses criteria that have personal meaning to him, it is possible that negative self-concepts aroused by outside evaluations will be reduced. As Purkey (1970) commented, "When the student has a say in his own development and is given personal decisions to make, he develops faith in his own judgments and thoughts." (p. 51) Self-evaluation gives the learner a chance to grow in the directions *he* chooses.

Some of the criteria a learner may adopt include:

1. Having the skill(s) necessary to do the task
2. Profitable use (comprehension, application) of resource materials

3. Amount of effort put into the task
4. Increase/decrease of interest in content of the task
5. Sense of having learned something from completing the task
6. Recognition of problems met in doing the task
7. Meeting the objectives of the task as assigned by the teacher.

Questions *Do these criteria meet your needs? If not, what criteria would you use in evaluating your work?*

The student would then confer with the teacher about what the grade for the work should be. If the two differ, they would each reevaluate the work before determining a grade.

Promotion policies Inevitably, evaluation affects decisions on promotion. Should all students be promoted annually, regardless of their rate of progress? This is "social" promotion, and it is widely practiced in the schools. It implies, to some, a lack of standards in pupil evaluation and leads people to question the meaning or worth of a high school diploma. While no parent likes to see his child held back, nor do most school officials enjoy having to do this, is it fair to the child to keep pushing him ahead when he is genuinely unable to keep up with his peers? Is it possible, or desirable to combine uniform or social promotion with remedial skills classes to help weak students to become more effective learners? Might it be more important, as Chansky (1964) has suggested, to choose the best or most appropriate teacher for the child rather than to determine whether to promote or retain a poor student?

Nonpromotion is a policy that permits retention of a child in a grade for a second year. "Causes of non-promotion might . . . be summarized into four major categories: 1) Administrative decree; 2) Material beyond the capacity of the child, especially reading ability; 3) Environmental factors; and 4) Teacher-pupil personality conflicts." (Gorton and Robinson, 1970, p. 265) When a youngster is not promoted, or even if he is promoted but is consistently "low man" in the class, he perceives himself and is perceived by others as a failure. He is punished at school and at home. He punishes himself. "As dissatisfaction with school increases, such a pupil evolves from dolt to truant to dropout. The understanding he needs is seldom forthcoming because teachers, as a rule, have not had personal failure with academic work." (French, 1965, p. 379) Perhaps the youngster suffers from having found a safe niche in which she need struggle and compete no more, as suggested in the discussion of underachievers in chapter four. Perhaps she has a communications or perceptual disorder that has gone undiscovered. The result, however, is the same. She considers herself a failure and drops out of the field.

It is quite true that as adults we live in a world where people are in constant competition and have varying abilities. Most people fail at something, sometime, and it may be wise to have children experience this early in their school years rather than as adults. "Through failing an individual learns what he can and cannot do. Therefore, adjustment after a failure is a must for living, for mental health. Also, it is through failing that a person is toughened, develops courage and stamina. Success derives its joys from overcoming previous defeats." (French, p. 378) In the 1970s, this may appear to be an "old-fashioned" way of looking at failure, one that is out of tune with the times. Yet, in the most idyllic society, can everyone experience success all the time? There would be no purpose to sports events, for example, if every team or every competitor were a winner—unless there is an earthshaking transformation of attitudes to the point of view that it's not important whether you win the game, but only that you play it. It is apparent, then, that there is no ready answer to the question of promotion v. nonpromotion. What *is* important is how the learner is treated. He is not to be branded a chronic failure, not to be compared with others who are not really his peers, is to be helped and listened to, and should be encouraged and understood rather than "beaten down" more and more at home as well as at school. Overdependence on test scores, particularly group test scores, is also unwise in dealing with the failing student.

Wisest of all possibilities is to develop or find measures to prevent failures in learning. Ideally, each learner should be placed with the teacher with whom he or she can interact most effectively. Whether in second grade or eleventh grade, the positive effects of such interaction can bring about remarkable changes in a student. A college student may feel he or she needs an "inspiring" teacher to be an effective learner, but most younger ones will respond to teachers who accept them as capable individuals who can learn in some way. Again, we must point to the teacher as the member of this dyad who needs to be flexible so as to provide maximum opportunity for each pupil. Flexible scheduling with some attention to ability and interest differences may also help the learner, for at least he may then feel that he "has a chance" to achieve well. Much more attention to basic learning skills is important in both regular and remedial classes to enable the pupil to learn and to avoid chronic failure. Evaluation of the learner must be total, rather than solely in terms of assessment measures, if realistic and mentally helpful judgments are to be made. This kind of evaluation often demands consultation with psychologists or school counselors, but forms only a part of their job functions.

GUIDANCE AND COUNSELING

Let us first look at the varied activities of guidance and counseling personnel. They are usually thought of in terms of helping the learner to choose future courses in accord with abilities and interests. They may even administer tests to determine interest and nonacademic aptitudes. They advise the prospective high school graduate of college or other advanced training possibilities.

INTELLIGENCE AND EVALUATION

They confer with teachers about students' progress and often mediate between teachers and parents where conflicts arise. In the absence of a school psychologist, they may recommend private diagnosis or therapy, special class placement, or other measures designed to assist the learner. Much of this area of functioning depends on the individual's test scores as well as his or her classroom performance grades. Frequently, the guidance counselor is called upon to predict future academic performance based on these same criteria. Can this be done?

Aptitude, personality, and interest tests

At the first-grade level, predictions for success in reading are often based on either intelligence or reading readiness test scores. Hopkins and Sitkei (1969) investigated this procedure by administering both types of tests to all children entering first grade in two lower-middle class schools. The test scores were correlated at the end of the year with scores on a standardized reading test and final teacher grades. Both tests were moderately successful predictors, but the authors concluded that the reading readiness test was preferable to the intelligence test because: "(a) it requires considerably less testing time, (b) it is more easily and meaningfully interpreted, (c) the effects of improper interpretation are much less serious to the pupil, and (d) it is less expensive." (p. 33) Each of these considerations is a source of legitimate concern to the guidance counselor or other individual who has to decide which tests to use for which purposes, especially the effects on the learner.

At a much higher level, Gardner and Lambert (1965) tried to determine what relationship, if any, measures of intelligence have to language aptitude and second-language learning. Their subjects were 96 students from English-speaking homes, who were studying the first or second year of French in high school. These investigators found that "intelligence" and verbal knowledge were unrelated to either aptitude or achievement for these learners. Linguistic Reasoning and French Vocabulary Knowledge, however, were two factors identified as related to achievement in French. This should suggest to guidance counselors that perhaps students who don't score well on intelligence tests may be able to learn a second language despite their "IQ." At least, they should be given a language aptitude test, and if they appear to possess linguistic reasoning abilities and are able to learn the test's artificial vocabulary and grammar with a fair amount of ease, they should be permitted to roster a foreign language course. Conversely, there are many so-called bright students who do not have these abilities and find second-language learning a very painful experience.

Another function of the guidance counselor has been the administration of personality and interest tests. Stroup (1970) reported on a long-term investigation that used the Scholastic Aptitude Tests and California Psychological Inventory as possible predictors of freshman grade point averages. Although SAT scores were more highly correlated with grade point average than any of the personality test variables, since SATs *are* academically oriented tests, Stroup found that SAT plus three personality scales increased prediction power slightly. For both sexes, Socialization and Flexibility were effective additives to SAT Math and Verbal scores. In addition, for women, achievement through conformity, and for men, femininity, were significant variables. As noted much earlier in this text, conformity and feminine behavior both found favor with teachers, creating a "halo effect" that had positive effects on teacher evaluations and learner achievement. It is quite interesting that these variables should reappear at the college level. However, the principal merit of this study for us is to create an alertness to the influence of personality variables on achievement—whether as college freshmen or earlier in school life.

If the usual pen-and-paper personality tests are given, they should also be interpreted with caution, for it is easy for the test subjects to modify their answers to suit the purpose of the occasion, and the wording of some questions is highly ambiguous. This is much the same story as in the case of attitude tests.

Focus 7–5

How would *you* answer the following questions, drawn from a variety of self-report personality inventories?

1. I frequently have headaches.	True	False
2. I worry a lot.	True	False
3. I am a good mixer.	True	False
4. I enjoy studying.	True	False
5. I always tell the truth.	True	False
6. I am self-confident.	True	False
7. I am afraid of the dark.	True	False
8. I often cannot control my impulses.	True	False

Ambiguity stems from the possible interpretations by test-maker and test-taker of words like "frequently," "a lot," "often," as well as the magnitude of "good," "afraid," "worry." Further problems are introduced when a third party, such as the counselor, interprets the responses.

Personality rating scales, on which teachers are asked to rate students in terms of dependability, responsibility, honesty, sociability, leadership, and so on, are similarly subject to rater interpretation and bias, further confounding the possible usefulness of such evaluations. Of course, consistent ratings over a period of time or by a number of independent raters will have some contribution to make when the counselor attempts an overall evaluation of a student.

Interest tests, such as the Kuder Preference Record, Strong Vocational Interest Blank, and Thurstone Interest Schedule, are often as valuable for what they contraindicate as for what they suggest as possible career goals. Frequently, students have average or below-average scores in all of the several potential interest areas, but there are almost always some peaks and

218 INTELLIGENCE AND EVALUATION

valleys in their score patterns that suggest to the counselor possible directions for discussion. In some interest tests, subjects select the more preferred of two occupational choices (often the lesser of two evils in the subject's view). In other tests, they are asked to indicate their preferences among three or more activities in rank order, thus:

1. planting rose bushes ____
2. conducting a survey ____
3. painting a portrait ____

If there are enough opportunities, or groups of items, in the test, the scores should be a reliable indication of the student's interests at that particular time.

Guidance programs and counselor functions

What happens when the counselor puts all this information together? Can achievement, personality, and interest test scores reveal anything substantial? Can they be used, in other words, for effective guidance of the learner?

Focus 7–6

> Henry was in the second half of tenth grade when he went to see his counselor. His parents were concerned both about his current academic achievement and his occupational potential. Examination of the tenth-grade report card plus additional testing were believed appropriate procedure in answering his parents' questions.
> Report card grades through the fifth and sixth marking period in the tenth grade revealed a dismal picture:
>
> English: C–E range, with 3 Ds
>
> World History: D–E range, with 3 Es
>
> Mathematics: D–E range, with 3 Ds
>
> French: D–E range, with 3 Es
>
> Biology: D–F range, with 4 Ds
>
> All teacher comments indicated poor study habits and often a lack of preparation.
> On the Wechsler Intelligence Scale for Children, Henry scored:
>
> Verbal Scale—108 IQ
>
> Performance Scale—96 IQ
>
> Full Scale—102 IQ
>
> On the verbal subtests, he was considerably above average in Similarities (abstract relationships), and above average in Information and Vocabulary, all areas needed for academic success. His National Educational Development

Test scores (tenth grade, Spring, norms) were also generally above average, with one exception:

English Usage—33rd percentile

Mathematics Usage—67th percentile

Social Studies Reading—71st percentile

Natural Science Reading—71st percentile

Word Usage—71st percentile

Composite—62nd percentile

On the Differential Aptitude Tests, Henry was again above average in Verbal Reasoning, and, despite a low Numerical Ability score, was within the average range of tenth grade boys' scores. Obviously, he had at least average academic potential.

Henry's interests were strongest in the areas of Executive, Language, and Business on the Thurstone Interest Schedule, a forced-choice preferential test. His above-average scores on verbal tests supported these interests.

In answering his parents' concerns, the counselor could reassure them that Henry had at least average abilities, but needed to learn and use better study habits, if his academic work was to improve and reflect these abilities. As far as future planning was concerned, the counselor had to consider not only measured abilities, but also his actual school performance and indicated interests. Henry's grades would weigh heavily against admission to a four-year college unless there was a radical improvement in the eleventh and twelfth grades. Considering all aspects of the evaluations, the counselor recommended planning toward a business administration course in a two-year college.

Follow-up information revealed little improvement in grades by graduation and admission to a two-year community college where Henry achieved much better grades and began to gain some self-confidence academically. He did sufficiently well to be admitted as a third-year transfer student to a four-year college from which he has now graduated. This happy ending may seem inconsistent with the counselor's earlier recommendations, but it must be remembered that the counselor can deal only with past and present information. Counselors are not clairvoyants and therefore cannot make recommendations based on events, for example, changes in motivation, which have not yet happened. (From the author's case files)

Teachers and guidance counselors can work together in cases where learning problems exist. Teachers, because of their daily contacts with students, are generally capable of contributing information that is rarely measured on tests, such as shyness, degree of self-confidence, degree of effort, emotional problems, as well as diagnosing assets and weaknesses in different areas of learning. Guidance counselors are the source of assistance for improvement of study skills and interpreting test scores, academic achievement, and interests in terms of a total evaluation.

The work of guidance counselors, formerly confined to secondary schools, now is expanding to the elementary level. This seems highly appropriate, since guidance and counseling early in the school years may prevent later problems. Teachers in elementary schools that have had counseling programs for two or more years have been found to have significantly more positive attitudes toward counseling and guidance than their colleagues in the same community who have not had such programs in their schools, although there is some question as to whether this is due solely to the presence or absence of the programs. (Axelberd, 1969) A survey of elementary school guidance programs reveals that different approaches are being used. Several schools employ group guidance programs, where up to 25 or 30 children work together in discussing values, attitudes, feelings, and academic problems. Other schools center guidance activities around the teacher, but with assistance as needed from social workers and psychologists in the school system. The emphases at the elementary level tend to be on preventive guidance, mental health, and facilitation of learning rather than on remediation of accumulated problems. Testing and evaluation are part of these programs, but are not their sole reason for existing.

At the secondary level, the counselor becomes more involved with other types of problems, many of them accumulated during the elementary school years: what to do with the nonacademically skilled student, college and career planning, overpressured students, frightened students, misbehaving students, teacher-student conflicts, potential dropouts, parent conferences, scholarship aid, and so on. (Faust, 1968) Basically, a guidance counselor's activities include collecting and disseminating information relevant to educational and vocational decisions, evaluating student progress, and transmitting the appropriate end results of findings in both areas to students and parents. In practice, it can be seen that "something" *does* happen as a result of counseling: students apply to and are accepted by particular colleges; students change their study habits and improve their academic performance; students and their parents gain a more realistic perception of a youth's abilities and potentials. There are failures, too, where the counselor evaluates in error or the student rejects the counselor's advice.

Some of the innovations being introduced in guidance and counseling include the application of behavior theory to counseling and the use of computers to define specific educational programs for each student. More attention is being paid, at least in principle, to the needs and personal worth of the individual student. The conscientious and well-trained guidance counselor makes a sincere effort to handle his counselees in a human rather than a mechanical way, despite reliance on technological aids and standardized tests. If given a reasonable number of students with whom to deal, he can be an effective guide for the learner, basing his educational evaluations on valid assessments and sound judgment. A major problem, however, is that counselors usually have too many students assigned to them to be optimally effective.

To develop a more effective high school counseling and vocational guidance program, Holland (1974) has suggested introducing a Placement and Work Experience Service open to all students, the use of "troubleshooters" to help students who cannot use standard services, and a consultant to help students in their self-directed and exploratory searches for occupational information. These practices may help to reduce the counselor's overload.

As affirmative action programs go forward, the counselor also needs to change some attitudes. More girls expect to work before marriage and at various times during their marriage than was true a decade or two ago. Furthermore, regulations under Title IX of the Education Amendments of 1972 prohibit

> . . . schools and colleges from restricting various courses—including (among others) courses in the industrial arts and in business, vocational, and technical education—to members of a particular sex. Another [regulation] prohibits schools from using testing or other counseling methods or materials that have the effect of distinguishing between the sexes in charting potential career opportunities. No longer, in short, may a girl interested in medicine be given the impression that the only field open to her is nursing, nor may girls of a mechanical turn of mind be excluded from a course in shop. (Lederer, 1974, pp. 8–9)

Through the career education program, beginning at the primary level, students will be helped to find their occupational goals without regard to sex-role stereotypes. Counselors are deeply involved in guiding and providing information to such programs. Their roles are being enlarged as our world becomes more complex. The danger to which they need be alert is becoming more involved with programs and roles than with individual learners.

SUMMARY

Assessment and evaluation of learners are two major activities of educational psychologists, whatever their job titles may be. In this chapter, we have discussed several means of assessing learning and several applications of the knowledge gained therefrom. The applications include placement of the individual student (grading and promotion) and guidance for the future. We discussed large-scale assessment programs, which serve purposes other than placement and guidance, but which are nevertheless important to education generally and ultimately to all learners. Functions of guidance counselors, traditional and innovative, were discussed, with examples of the types of problems with which they deal.

Overall, it has been the purpose of this chapter to emphasize the role of measurement and evaluation in facilitating student learning, increasing the effectiveness of teaching, appraising curricula, and assisting in guidance counseling. The avenues for growth provided by student self-evaluation and self-directed activity were discussed at some length. The role of the teacher as an active participant in these activities has been stressed, too, for the teacher is in a position to have much greater impact on individual learners simply by frequency of contact than is the counselor. The teacher is also expected to contribute meaningful information to the counselor to improve the counselor's effectiveness in aiding students.

Part Four

Learning about Learning

Since very shortly after your birth, you've been actively learning. You've learned how to eat from a spoon (held by someone else) and with a spoon (held in your own hand); how to distinguish colors and shapes; how to speak, to ride a bicycle, to read, to study, to do most of the things you are doing right now. Why, then, do you now have to learn about learning?

There are many theories about how, what, why, and when we learn. Since the theories underlie teaching techniques, it is helpful if you are aware of and understand them. As a professional educator, a knowledge of learning theories will also enable you to comprehend and evaluate reports in the professional literature and arguments presented on controversial issues. Chapter eight presents these theories, additional variables affecting the learner as he learns, and classroom applications of theory.

A second area of learning involves communication and comprehension of ideas. In chapter nine, therefore, we will discuss concept formation, thinking, and language. Special attention is paid here to the assets and problems of bilingualism. Two aspects of thinking, productive and evaluative thinking, are keys to problem-solving and creativity. These latter activities are regarded by some as the highest level of application of learning. Contemporary emphasis in the schools on the ability to apply cognitive skills warrants the close examination of problem-solving and creativity to be found in chapter ten.

As you can see, there is a great deal to learn about learning. There are also many reasons to become involved in this aspect of educational psychology, most of them directly applicable to your future work on the teacher's side of the desk. Many of the ideas will also be helpful to you in your current and future studies.

Preview

INTRODUCTION

WHAT IS LEARNING?
   DEFINITIONS OF LEARNING
   LEARNING GOALS
   "LAWS" OF LEARNING

THEORIES OF LEARNING: THE ASSOCIATIONISTS
   CLASSICAL VIEW
   E. L. THORNDIKE'S WORK
   PAVLOV'S CLASSICAL CONDITIONING
   SKINNER'S OPERANT CONDITIONING

THEORIES OF LEARNING: THE COGNITIVE THEORISTS
   GESTALT PSYCHOLOGISTS
   PIAGET'S APPROACH
   BRUNER'S VIEWPOINT

THEORIES OF LEARNING: TWO TAXONOMIES
   GAGNÉ'S TAXONOMY
   BLOOM

SUMMARY OF LEARNNG THEORIES

VARIABLES AFFECTING LEARNING
   STIMULATION AND ATTENTION
   EXPECTANCY
   RETENTION
      Aids to Memory
      Mnemonics
      Forgetting
   "TRANSFER OF TRAINING"
   LEARNING SKILLS
   LEARNING ENVIRONMENT

CLASSROOM APPLICATIONS
   PREPARATION
   PRESENTATION
   ASSOCIATION
   GENERALIZATION
   APPLICATION

SUMMARY

8

Learning: Theories and Variables

INTRODUCTION

Before we can consider the various theories of learning, we need to know what is meant by the word "learning." What is involved in learning? Are there different kinds of learning? Then we can proceed more intelligently to a discussion of the positions of the associationists and the cognitive theorists, the two major groups of learning theorists. You will recognize many of the names mentioned, such as Thorndike, Skinner, Piaget, and Bruner.

As you can imagine, theories are one thing and their operation is another. For this reason, we will consider a number of the variables affecting learning, this second look at such factors being somewhat different from the extensive discussion in chapters two to four. For example, we will include a brief look at memory and transfer of training. We will also investigate the applications of the theories of learning in the classroom.

WHAT IS LEARNING?

We usually define learning as a relatively permanent change in behavior that is not due to maturation, the effects of drugs, or physiological states. It is, in general, a change in behavior resulting from experience and is often affected by practice. A number of factors are involved in such changes in behavior: *learning set,* or the abilities the learner has at a given point in the learning task; *learning to learn,* or the acquisition of skills and abilities that are basic to further learning; *learning abilities,* or the ways in which the learner approaches learning; and *learning styles,* in terms of selection strategies and speed of decision-making. Many of these factors are themselves changes in behavior brought about by experience (learned), such as being able to evaluate what is read, or discovering that in one situation impulsive decision-making is appropriate while deliberation is necessary in another situation. Learning style is also acquired by imitation of those whom we admire and becomes a personality characteristic.

Definitions of learning

There are several types of learning that occur. Different psychologists group them in different ways. Ausubel (1968), for example, distinguishes four types: reception, discovery, rote, and meaningful. (pp. 21–26) *Reception learning*, that is, being presented with content in its completed state, may be rote or meaningful. *Discovery learning*, which requires the learner to complete the content, may similarly be rote or meaningful, although at first the emphasis may be on the meaningful aspect. An example of rote discovery learning might be seeking the single correct completion for an incomplete sentence in a chapter, such as "The Declaration of Independence was signed in _____." Meaningful discovery learning, on the other hand, would involve seeking a basic principle through experimentation or through the reorganization of known facts. *Meaningful learning* can be further subdivided into representational (understanding single symbols, such as words), propositional (comprehending ideas as conveyed by sentences), and concept learning (distinguishing the critical attributes of a concept). (pp. 42–44) Ausubel illustrates these, respectively, by vocabulary learning, learning to read, and learning second languages. His analysis of learning is principally concerned with cognitive learning, or the acquisition of knowledge.

Lewin (1942), a field theorist, also saw four types of learning, but described them somewhat differently. His list included: 1) a change in cognitive structure (knowledge), 2) a change in motivation (learning to like or dislike), 3) a change in group belongingness or ideology (cultural growth), and 4) voluntary control of body musculature (acquiring motor skills). In the first type, the individual's behavior is restructured, psychological directions are gained, and meaning is found. This appears to include the other three types of learning, since a gain in knowledge will affect changes in attitude, cultural growth, and the acquisition of skills.

Question

Can you give an example of how knowledge affects learning in each of these three areas?

Lewin believed that learning had occurred when the number of repetitions necessary for a particular behavior was reduced. An analogy to this statement might be seen in the changes in behavior that occur after one travels from point *A* to point *B* for the first time, carefully checking landmarks and mileage. Later journeys over the same route require little conscious attention to the same details, for the route has been learned.

If these are adequate descriptions of types of learning, what is the role of the teacher with regard to learning? Ausubel (1968) says that the principal function of the teacher is ". . . to bridge the gap between what the learner already knows and what he needs to know before he can successfully learn the task at hand." (p. 148) Some contemporary psychologists, particularly those who work in behavioral conditioning situations or with programmed instruction, are saying essentially the same thing when they speak of "entering behavior" and desired "end-behavior." The role of the teacher in this approach is to modify behavior until the new desired behavior is attained.

How would you define learning? — **Question**

To facilitate the process of learning, certain elements should be included, or at least considered. The first of these, mental set or attitude, must obviously be oriented toward the learning task or learning will become difficult, if not impossible. A second element to be considered is the similarity of the new learning task to what has already been learned. If the new learning task is simply a new application of a previously learned concept, this should be clearly demonstrated in the new presentation. If, on the other hand, the new material contradicts or otherwise interferes with previously learned material, this, too, should be made clear in the initial presentation. A third factor is the desired degree of learning. Is there room for error or must the new concept or skill be learned to perfection? Naturally, we would prefer that everything we teach be learned perfectly. However, it is unrealistic to believe that the retention of learned material over a period of time will be at the 100 percent level. Certain skills must be learned perfectly and retained perfectly for safety's sake or the sake of accuracy, such as how to fly a plane or how to add up a bill. On the other hand, errors in the exact dates of historical battles are, for most people, going to be neither fatal nor catastrophic. It is also important to consider the "learnability" of concepts and skills. How much time is available for teaching and learning? How new is the material? How frequently will the concepts or skills be used? Can they be presented vividly or in contrast to some previously learned material? In today's idiom, is this learning relevant? — **Learning goals**

Once these elements have been decided, it is time for the learner to decide how he or she is going to meet the stated learning goal. (One assumes that the learner accepts the goal. If he does not, then the assumption is that he either works out a mutually acceptable alternative goal with the teacher, or accepts the responsibility for his failure.) The learner needs to be able to recall either concepts or skills on demand. This necessitates practice, or review. The most effective way to review most material is to distribute practice over a period of time. "Cramming," or massed practice, is generally not effective in meeting the goal of prolonged recall—that is, beyond the next exam. Even with a highly limited study time, as when a new skill must be learned in 24 hours, it is more advisable to have several short periods of practice than to have an extended single practice period. It is also good to "overlearn" new material. In "overlearning," one recites or performs a task correctly 10 times before stopping review, rather than stopping after the first perfect recitation.

"Laws" of learning

Several elements or considerations in the learning process have been stated so frequently that they are considered to be psychological "laws." E. L. Thorndike was one of the first to state these learning principles as laws. These included the laws of:

1. exercise—which relates to the nature and amount of practice;
2. effect—in which what is rewarded tends to be learned better than that which is not rewarded or that which is punished;
3. readiness—which refers to the abilities the learner brings to the learning task, and;
4. belonging (or identical elements)—which deals with the relationships between what is known and what is to be learned, and the contexts in which learning takes place.

The ways in which these laws have been applied, and their validity in education today, will be discussed more fully as we look at Thorndike's work shortly.

Suggested Activity

Before turning to Thorndike's work, try to develop a means of studying each of these laws. For example, in what ways could you demonstrate the law of readiness?

At several points in this book we have also looked or will look at learning from the learner's point of view. The concepts of readiness, motivation, intellectual ability, and personality factors have already been discussed. Still to be considered are the various kinds of instructional materials, social factors in learning, and characteristics of the teacher. These will be discussed toward the end of this chapter as variables affecting learning. First we should examine the theoretical positions about learning. According to Hilgard, ". . . a comprehensive learning theory ought to answer the questions which an intelligent nonpsychologist might ask about the sorts of learning which are met in everyday life." (1956, pp. 6–8) The questions he suggests are:

1. What are the limits of learning?
2. What is the role of practice in learning?
3. How important are drives and incentives, rewards and punishments?
4. What is the place of understanding and insight?
5. Does learning one thing help you learn something else?
6. What happens when we remember and when we forget? (p. 708)

Our discussion will seek to focus on the major elements of different approaches to learning as we seek to answer these questions.

THEORIES OF LEARNING: THE ASSOCIATIONISTS

Associationism is at once the oldest and the simplest theory of learning. Aristotle observed that there were relationships between ideas and between events. Later philosophers similarly developed laws of association based on their perceptions of relationships. Experimental psychologists in the nineteenth and twentieth centuries further developed their theoretical approach as they studied learning, memory, and the physiological processes underlying behavior. Certain principles were developed which are still held as valid today: 1) association by *contiguity*—the association of objects, ideas, and/or events because they occur together; 2) association by similarity—the association of events, objects, and/or ideas because they resemble each other; and 3) association by contrast—the association of objects, ideas, and/or events because one of those stands out in contrast to its surroundings and is associated with the related circumstances because of its startling difference.

Classical view

In addition to these classical association theories, in which the associations are between two or more responses, a newer approach developed as physiological experiments were conducted. These tested the relationships between stimulus and response. The name most closely associated (by contiguity) with these studies is that of Edward Lee Thorndike. His theory has been particularly influential in educational practice. He emphasized that learning was based on the associations ("bonds," "connections") between sensory impressions and behavioral responses. The strengthening or weakening of the associations makes or breaks habits or learned behavior. Because of this emphasis, the whole associationist approach is sometimes referred to as the S-R (stimulus-response) theory of learning.

E. L. Thorndike's work

In his early work, Thorndike stressed the principles of readiness, exercise, and effect as the bases for human learning. He also introduced experiments on trial-and-error learning (learning by selecting and connecting).

His law of readiness was not quite the same as the concept of readiness

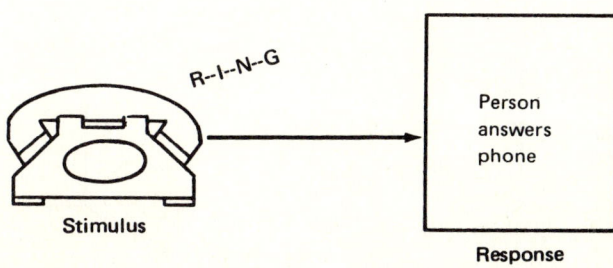

The association of stimulus and response. **Figure 8.1**

or maturation that is used in modern education, but rather reflected a physiological state of preparation or anticipation. It is more a state of neural readiness than psychological readiness. The law of exercise referred to the strengthening or weakening of connections in relation to practice ("use" and "disuse"). That is, Thorndike initially believed that connections between stimulus and response are strengthened by repetition and that those connections that are not practiced will be forgotten. This is a theory that Skinner has modified in *his* statement of how learning occurs (operant conditioning). Thorndike, however, after continued experimentation, altered this law when he found that there were circumstances in which it did not apply. For example, attempting to walk a straight line while blindfolded might not be significantly more successful even though the act was practiced for several hours.

His law of effect stated that a connection could be strengthened or weakened depending on its consequences. Again, this is used as an element in Skinner's theory. For both, theoretically, connections are strengthened when they meet with reward (reinforcement), and weakened when punished. When the connection between the English "to be" and the French "être" is made successfully and rewarded by the teacher's "Bon!", it tends to be retained and repeated. On the other hand, the connection between the heat of a fire and a finger in the fire tends to be weakened by the punishing consequences of pain. Again, after further study, Thorndike modified this law by saying that reward and punishment did not have equal consequences. However, he did find that effects spread, or generalized, to situations other than the immediate one. Through this discovery, he attempted to show that subsequent connections were rewarded or punished, in diminishing amounts, depending upon the consequences attached to the original connection or association. Thorndike's basic design was invalid, according to many of his critics, because he overlooked a number of sources of error such as bias, extraneous effects of probability and isolation, and so on. However, "Even those who denied reinforcement as a law of learning have generally accepted the principle that learning depends upon feedback or knowledge of results. . . ." (McKeachie, 1974, p. 8)

Trial-and-error learning, or the selection and connection of the correct response to a stimulus, is yet another of Thorndike's theories. It is related to the law of effect because producing a satisfactory response is rewarded in some way, and the reward encourages repetition or practice of the new

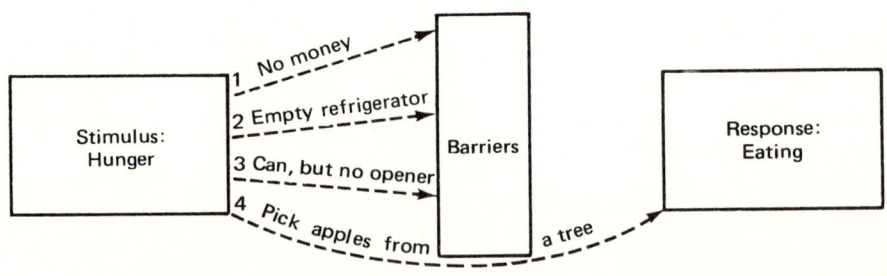

Figure 8.2   *Diagram of trial-and-error learning.*

connection. Trial-and-error learning is, of course, a vital component in problem-solving, although many contemporary psychologists would aver that, as stated by Thorndike, it doesn't go far enough in its explanation.

Thorndike also suggested some aids to cementing the associations between stimulus and response, or aids to improving learning. He included interest in the work being done, interest in improvement, and the absence of irrelevant emotion and worry. Other aids in learning that he suggested are the significance of the problem, the learner's attitude toward the problem, and attentiveness. We would now call these concentration, organization, memory, motivation, and the absence of interfering personal problems. What Thorndike called "associative shifting," we would now call classical conditioning, or partial substitution of one set of connections by another.

Another expression of Thorndike's work with associationism is shown in Miller and Dollard's "drive-cue-response-reward" theory of learning (1941), which includes motivation and reward as important components in learning or changed behavior.

Drive ⟶ Cue ⟶ Response ⟶ Reward
(Fluid deficiency in tissues) (Thirst sensation) (Drink liquid) (Relief of thirst)

Illustration of Miller-Dollard Theory. **Figure 8.3**

This is similarly based on a physiological process and encompasses S-R, trial-and-error learning (until the organism learns that drinking liquids relieves thirst), and the law of effect. As with other aspects of Thorndike's theories, it is insufficient by itself as an explanation of all learning.

More familiar as an example of association theory is the work of Pavlov. His approach to learning, called classical conditioning, also involves the organism as a receptor responsive to changes in the environment. It also applies the theory of learning by contiguity.

Pavlov's classical conditioning

As you can see in Figure 8.4, classical conditioning is essentially stimulus substitution, learned over a period of time. The crucial element is the

Step 1. Unconditioned stimulus ⟶ Organism ⟶ Unconditioned response
(meat powder) (dog) (salivation)

Step 2. Conditioned stimulus
  ↘ (bell) ⟶ } Organism ⟶ Response
Unconditioned stimulus ⟶

Step 3. Conditioned stimulus ⟶ Organism ⟶ Response

Diagram of Pavlov's theory. **Figure 8.4**

temporal contiguity (association in time) of the new (conditioned) stimulus and the old (unconditioned) stimulus in the second step. The arrow between the conditioned stimulus and the unconditioned stimulus in step 2 stresses the time factor in conditioning. The two must occur almost simultaneously if conditioning is to occur. Both stimuli yield the same response, one that is generally involuntary.

In the classroom, this can be demonstrated by the teaching of foreign language vocabulary:

Step 1. *Teacher to pupil:* "Sit down." Pupil sits down.
Step 2. *Teacher to pupil:* "Asseyez-vous."
    Pupil sits down.
  "Sit down."
Step 3. *Teacher to pupil:* "Asseyez-vous." Pupil sits down.

We then say that the child has "learned" the meaning of this French phrase. Or, the same steps may be used to teach different ways of reaching the same sum or product in arithmetic:

$$6 \times 2 = 12 \qquad 6 + 2 = 8$$
$$3 \times 4 = 12 \qquad 5 + 3 = 8$$
$$6 \times 2 = 12 \qquad 6 + 2 = 8$$
$$3 \times 4 = 12 \qquad 5 + 3 = 8$$

The second step usually needs to be repeated several times, depending on the learner, in order to strengthen the new association. Obviously, this approach to learning is still in use. Just as the child learning the new arithmetic concept is rewarded or reinforced with a "Right!" from the teacher, presumably Pavlov rewarded his dogs with some of the meat powder or a pat on the head or a "Good dog!" According to Thorndike's law of effect, the newly learned association will be strengthened by such rewards.

Skinner's operant conditioning

The newest, and currently most popular, theory of association owes much to the earlier work of Thorndike that we have just surveyed. Skinner's operant conditioning includes his modifications of the laws of effect and exercise, an emphasis on contiguity, plus his own distinctions of "respondent" and "operant" behavior. All that we have discussed before properly comes under the heading of respondent behavior, or responses aroused by known stimuli. These did not, however, explain the appearance of behaviors for which there were *no* known stimuli. Such responses or behaviors, according to Skinner, are operants. This distinction pays attention to such behaviors as spontaneous changes in activity by the organism when no stimulation is apparent. The organism voluntarily is *operating* on the environment rather than merely responding to it. Hence, the name "operant conditioning" for Skinner's approach.

Very important to Skinner's theory of learning is the role of reinforcement. Those responses that are reinforced tend to occur more frequently, that is, are strengthened. This point has been amply demonstrated in Skinner's work with pigeons, for example, who were given a grain of feed every time they pecked a colored disk correctly. Equally important, however, is the fact that no response can be reinforced until it appears. The difference between Skinner's reinforcement and "bribery" might be clarified here: reinforcement occurs only after a response is emitted, while bribery occurs before the response is emitted and is an attempt to get the organism to emit the response. The distinction may be seen in these two brief examples:

Example 1: Teacher to class: "I'll give you an extra 15 minutes at recess if you all get 75 percent or better on this week's math test." (bribery)

Example 2: Teacher to class: "You all worked so hard and did so well on this week's math test that you may have an extra 15 minutes at recess." (reinforcement)

In contrast to Pavlov's stimulus substitution, Skinner seeks to change responses. This can be done simply, by reinforcing correct responses and ignoring incorrect ones, or through shaping behavior over a period of time. Shaping is accomplished by reinforcing closer and closer approximations to a desired response. A "focus on the learner" segment shows the first approach.

Focus 8–1

Mark, an active five-year-old, was a nonconformist in kindergarten. When the children were supposed to be sitting at tables drawing, Mark sang or walked around. When it was time to sing, he rode the tricycle. When a story was being read to the group, he constantly interrupted the teacher. The teacher responded to these behaviors by talking to him, scolding him, having him sit next to her, and similar techniques. All of her efforts were fruitless as far as changing Mark's behavior was concerned.

The psychologist who was consulted drew her attention to the fact that she was being manipulated by Mark's behavior. He obviously wanted her attention and didn't care what means he used to attain his goal. The psychologist suggested that she keep a daily record of the frequency of Mark's acceptable and nonacceptable behaviors for the next week. It looked like this:

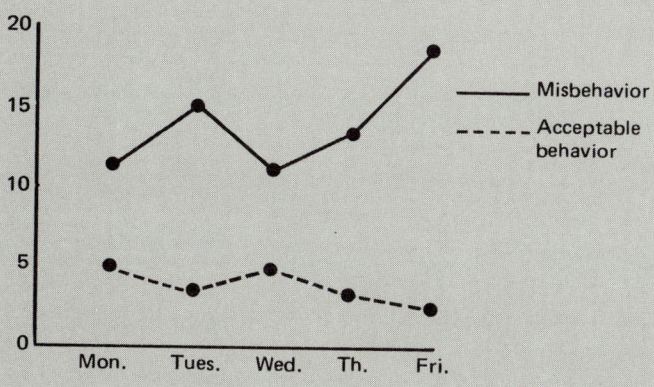

The frequency of Mark's nonappropriate behavior varied from day to day, but was consistently high.

For the following week, the psychologist recommended that the teacher ignore the misbehavior (unless it was potentially dangerous to Mark or someone else), but immediately reinforce Mark's appropriate responses by a word of approval or a pat on the head. The result is shown below.

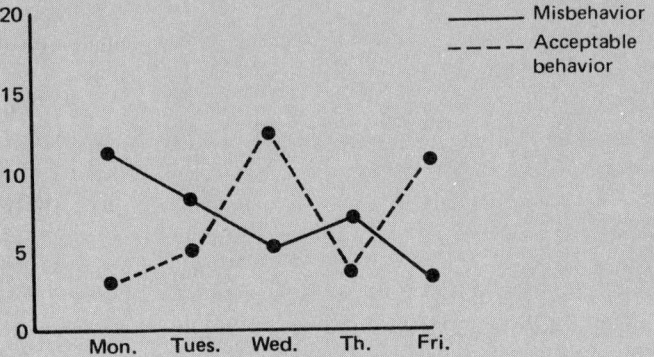

It is obvious that Mark was finding more appropriate ways by which to attract his teacher's attention. Continued over a period of time, his classroom behavior consistently improved.

Now who is manipulating whose behavior? (Note: From the author's case files)

The "Focus" also illustrates a number of elements in the application of Skinner's theory. It is necessary to know the frequency of the desired response to begin with if you are going to be able to ascertain whether learning has occurred. This provides a "baseline." By joining the two curves for appropriate behavior in the "Focus," perhaps this will be clearer to you.

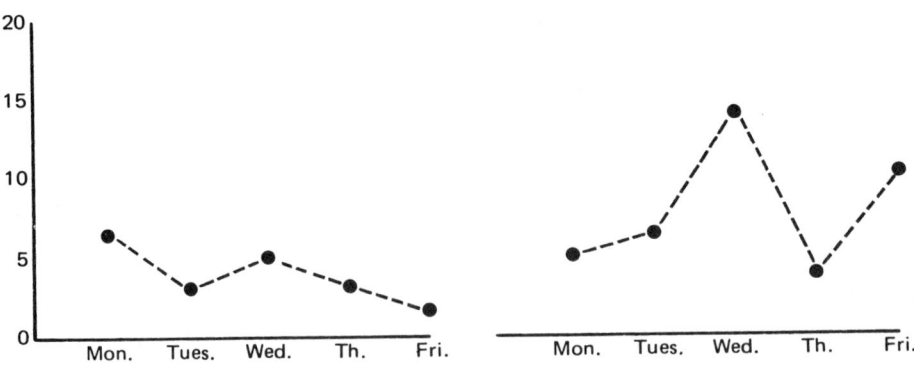

Figure 8.5 *Changes in frequency of appropriate behavior.*

In Figure 8.5, it is apparent that some changes in behavior, that is, learning, did occur when the teacher changed *her* behavior during the second week. True, the changes were not yet consistent, but they did appear, and better behavior occurred with greater frequency as it, rather than nonappropriate behavior, was reinforced.

The second technique of learning, shaping behavior, which involves reinforcing approximations of the desired response, can be illustrated also by classroom applications. For example, in elementary school, it is common practice to assign a 10 to 20 word spelling list on Monday, on which students will be tested the following Friday. Some students usually learn all or most of the words, and some students learn relatively few of the words correctly. (A similar example could be given for learning geometry theorems in high school or lists of names and dates for a history course.) To increase the frequency of correct responses, the teacher decides to give daily quizzes in preparation for Friday's test. Her goal is to have all students learn the correct responses at a level of 90 percent or better. She sets up the daily goals that bring the students closer to her ultimate goal by gradual steps, or approximations:

	Before	After
Monday	List distributed	List distributed
Tuesday		Quiz 30% is passing
Wednesday		Quiz 50% is passing
Thursday		Quiz 70% is passing
Friday	Test 70% is passing	Test 90% is passing

Under the first system, perhaps two-thirds of the class passes the test, but only 10 percent of the students learn 90 percent of the spelling words correctly. Under the second system, two-thirds of the class may pass the test with 90 percent of the spelling words correct. The original approach, as you see, is an "all-or-none" situation. The approximations or shaping approach not only secures a high percentage of the students passing the test, but passing at a higher level. More students master the assigned task, which is, after all, one of the goals of teaching. The effect of increased and spaced periods of practice is also apparent in the shaping system. The approximations approach also underlies much of programmed instruction, which is designed to have more people learn at a higher level of competence by using small steps of information rather than large chunks. It, too, is a technique that encourages mastery rather than mediocrity.

There are different schedules of reinforcement that may be used to reinforce correct or desired responses. These are:

	Fixed	Variable	Intermittent
Interval	every 10th second	about every 10 seconds	occasional
Ratio	every 10th item	about every 10 items	occasional

When a new learning project or task is undertaken, the teacher might find it advisable initially to reinforce *every* correct response. Later, however, a variable schedule may be preferable, since this tends to keep the learner working harder than a fixed schedule. When the task has been learned, intermittent reinforcement helps to maintain the desired behavior. To illustrate: first stage, the teacher reinforces every correct response to every math problem as it is answered; second stage, the teacher reinforces correct responses after every five to ten problems have been answered; third stage, the teacher reinforces correct responses on some days but not others. All of the foregoing is related to individual rather than class or group reinforcement.

The reinforcers used in schools—checks, stars, verbal approval, and grades—tend to be secondary reinforcers. That is, they do not satisfy a basic need. Primary reinforcers usually are food in the form of pellets, or lollipops, or candy, or other concrete objects. Even chimps, however, can be taught to accept tokens (secondary reinforcers), which can then be used in a "chimp-o-mat" or vending machine to obtain bananas (primary reinforcers). The price of obtaining the primary reinforcer, or number of tokens needed, can be altered to increase the frequency of occurrence of the desired response. The learner's correct responses can similarly be rewarded with tokens, which may be accumulated and then traded for a desired object or privilege after enough tokens are earned.

In setting up a token economy of this type, certain cautions need to be observed. "The prices should be set in terms of . . . accessibility and student preference. The greater the desirability of the reinforcer, the higher the value. . . . By raising the price of finger paints and keeping the price of regular paint at the same level, the finger paints will be bought only by those students who are willing to forego other purchases." (Givner and Graubard, 1974, p. 51) As student preferences and performances change, the exchange rate of tokens for reinforcers must also be changed.

Does the reinforcement technique create new problems? It may. There appears to be a need, particularly with younger children, to modify the reinforcement schedule and change the reinforcers from time to time in order to maintain interest. Eventually, the reinforcement system should be taken over by other reinforcers and evaluators. In a study of the long-term effects of a reinforcement system, Dickinson (1974) found that the "contrived" rewards were replaced by parental, peer, or self-praise, or simply grades and comments, two years after the learners studied had been in the reinforcement program. Further, "The students who had been on a reinforcement program some 2 years earlier made significantly greater growth in reading achievement between the sixth and eighth grades than students who had never been in a formal reinforcement program." (p. 160)

Although Skinner expanded the limits of association theory, he still did not include understanding as part of learning. Like other associationists, he emphasizes the role of motivation through reinforcement. Operant conditioning, therefore, remains a more sophisticated but still mechanistic theory of learning. This is not a condemnation, except by cognitive theorists, who would criticize any of the theories of association as a basis for learning on the same grounds. Associationists, or S-R theorists, are primarily concerned with the organism's response to stimulation as the basis of learning. This is frequently seen as a physiological process, and tends to ignore such factors as motivation (other than in connection with reward), varying circumstances, emotions, and capacity of the organism.

THEORIES OF LEARNING: THE COGNITIVE THEORISTS

What are the differences between association theories and cognitive theories? The first, as we have seen, emphasize responses or movements in relation to stimulation on an almost automatic basis, the strengthening of some responses until they become habits, and trial-and-error learning. The second group of theorists stresses the action of mental processes in learning, based on the acquisition of information, and the ability to perceive structure or underlying relationships. These perceptions lead to "insight" and the solution of problems (learning). Cognitive theorists tend to be more concerned with a *molar* view of behavior; the associationists tend to have a *molecular* view. That is, the cognitive theorists don't believe in "chance" solutions reached by chance actions in little bits. Rather, insight is defined as ". . . the appearance of a complete solution with reference to the whole lay-out of the field." (Köhler, 1959b, pp. 169–70) Köhler also defined insight as an awareness of a relation ". . . that follows from the characteristics of the objects under consideration." (1959a, p. 729) In other words, Gestalt psychologists and other cognitive theorists believe that perception of structure and an understanding of the relationships underlying that structure are essential to learning. The key, then, to cognitive theory lies in a mental process rather than a simple response to stimulation. Köhler has written at some length (1959b) of the variable sensations with which the organism experiences or perceives stimuli, depending upon saturation of the organism with the specific stimulus, awareness of sensations, and the organism's organizational processes. What he has said is that the organism responds in a total field or setting and not simply to an isolated stimulus.

The Gestalt psychologists, among whom Köhler was a leading figure, are perhaps the most prominent of the cognitive theorists. Not only do they view behavior in a total context, but they recognize that people act purposefully and that this aids in the development of insight. Their theory was originally developed in terms of perception, but the laws of organization that they

Gestalt psychologists

developed also apply to learning. They demonstrated that perception was based on past experience and that such past experience left "traces" that persist and that aid in ongoing cognitive processes. Individual "traces" become part of "trace systems" and are destroyed as repetition consolidates the "trace system." If such consolidation is overdone, however, as in excessive drill or rote memorization, the trace system becomes *too* available for one learning process and unavailable for others. That is, it is narrowing and rigid, thus inhibiting a broader use of the past experiences.

Focus 8–2

This is an important consideration in problem-solving and creative thinking. If an individual depends too heavily on memorized patterns, she tends to be less flexible in her approach to new tasks. Possible solutions to problems are less accessible.

Problem: Using the materials shown, affix the candle to the wall so that it will burn properly and the wax won't drip on the floor.

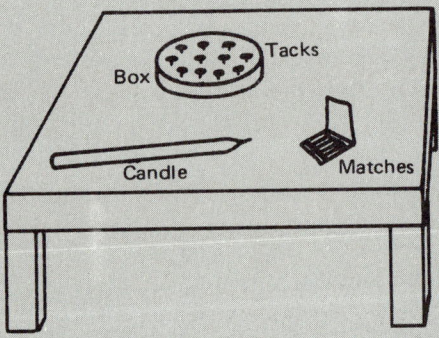

Duncker (1945) found that subjects who saw the objects with labels solved the problem more readily than those who saw the objects without labels or with only the tacks labeled. Inability to shift the box from its usual function of being a container for tacks was called functional fixedness. (Solution: tack the box to the wall as a candleholder.)

Although the Gestalt psychologists have presented ample evidence for their theory of traces and trace systems, some psychologists criticize this concept altogether.

The importance of the Gestalt point of view lies in its practical application in the classroom. Gestalt and other cognitive theorists believe that understanding relationships aids retention more and can be applied in more situations than trial-and-error learning or S-R learning. Indeed, much of the "new math" and other recently revised curricula are attempts to implement this viewpoint in the classroom. Understanding relationships occurs as perceptions change, and this is seen as learning.

In modern terms, one would say that learning involves changes in the phenomenal field. In popular terms, one would say that the world as it is perceived changes as learning occurs. Consider, for example, a child learning to read. The child perhaps has previously seen many of the words which he is to master in the early stages of reading. He has seen the word "man" many times, but this has not had any meaning for him, and it has been seen just as a jumble of meaningless lines. However, as he learns to read, the word "man," when it appears in his phenomenal field, tends more and more to stand as a figure against a ground, and it comes to evoke in him the concept of a man. The printed word has changed in significance in his phenomenal field, and learning has occurred only because it has changed. (Travers, 1963, p. 449)

Piaget's approach

One of the most eminent of modern psychologists is Jean Piaget. In the context of this chapter, let us consider only his relationship to associationist and cognitive theory. The early circular reactions of the sensorimotor stage that he has described depend upon the stimulus-response principle and the chaining of such S-R behavior into sequences. This is clearly associationist theory. However, by the stage of concrete operations (ages seven to eleven), the child is able to exercise rational coordination, to coordinate the perspectives of different individuals and of different aspects of individual experience. This is logical thinking and implies some understanding and manipulation of information—or cognition. (Piaget, 1937, pp. 32–48) Further intellectual development in the formal operations stage, beginning at about age twelve, is more and more a matter of cognitive learning. Interestingly enough, at least one contemporary psychologist perceives Piaget's thinking to be closer to Gestalt theory than to any other theory, although some differences are admitted. Muuss commented that:

> His kinship with Gestalt psychology lies especially in his emphasis on the patterns of organization, the structural whole and the total system. Similar to Gestalt psychologists Piaget is concerned with the relationship between the parts and the whole. However, . . . Gestalt principles do not seem to be applicable to explain the "logical operations in thought" which Piaget attempts to discover. Furthermore, he emphasizes structural changes as a function of development, while Gestalt psychology maintains that the "laws of organization" and "perceptual structure" are independent of age. (1967, p. 286)

The anchoring of stages to age is, of course, one of the major criticisms of Piaget's theory.

In a more recent publication, Piaget wrote that ". . . knowledge is derived from action, not in the sense of simple associative responses, but in the much deeper sense of the assimilation of reality into the necessary and general coordinations of action. To know an object is to act upon it and to transform it. . . ." (1970, pp. 28–29) That is, as one acquires information, he acts upon it in order to organize reality, not merely to copy it.

Jean Piaget, whose work has strongly inflenced modern classroom practice

Bruner's viewpoint

Jerome Bruner, strongly influenced by Piaget's work, emphasizes the mastery approach and integration of past learning. He has written that cognitive growth depends upon the mastery of techniques—imagery, action, and language—and of integration, ". . . the means whereby acts are organized into higher-order ensembles, making possible the use of larger and larger units of information for the solution of particular problems." (Bruner, 1964, p. 1) Granted that Bruner is discussing cognitive growth or intellectual development, not a narrow definition of learning, we must assume that he accepts association as the basis for future learning or growth and simply begins his theory at a higher level of entering behavior. He has listed several criteria for his theory that bear repetition:

1. Growth is characterized by increasing independence of response from the immediate nature of the stimulus.

2. Growth depends upon internalizing events into a "storage system" that corresponds to the environment.

3. Intellectual growth involves an increasing capacity to say to oneself and others, by means of words or symbols, what one has done or what one will do.

4. Intellectual development depends upon a systematic and contingent interaction between a tutor and a learner.

5. Teaching is vastly facilitated by the medium of language, which ends by being not only the medium for exchange but the instrument that the learner can then use himself in bringing order into the environment.

6. Intellectual development is marked by increasing capacity to deal with several alternatives simultaneously, to tend to several sequences during the same period of time, and to allocate time and attention in a manner appropriate to these multiple demands. (Bruner, 1966, pp. 5–6)

Several items are apparent in this list, particularly the relation of Piaget's work to Bruner's thinking. Language is a key to learning. Without language, the symbolic representation of thought, there is no learning. Even the infant soon learns that the vocal stimulus "Mommy" represents his or her primary caretaker. Language can be verbal, pictorial (for we translate images into verbal symbols and vice versa), or even physical (such as a gesture or a tic or a wink, all of which may imply many words). Cognitive growth depends also upon memory, but ". . . the most important thing about memory is not storage of past experience, but rather the retrieval of what is relevant in some usable form." (Bruner, 1964, p. 2)

Focus 8–3

> Consider this point for a moment. You may recall reading or hearing of "idiots savant," mentally retarded persons who have, for some unknown reason, been able to memorize a list of national capitals or the names of all the Holy Roman Emperors in sequence or who can give the day of the week on which a given date occurred or will occur in a particular year. Certainly such individuals have memory, and they can retrieve items from it, but are they relevant and usable? A computer can do as much and more, providing retrieved information that is both relevant and usable, but, not being human, it cannot construct original concepts in the way a human being can (despite the encouragement of science fiction writers).

Another important point is the development of ability to deal with abstractions, not to be stimulus-bound, which is one of the main themes of Piaget's studies. Indeed, Bruner's sixth criterion reflects the highest level of Piaget's stages of development, formal operations. Bruner cites the example of the game of "Twenty Questions," in which the item being thought about is discovered by implication and elimination. That is, the player asks, "Is it a living animal?" If the answer is affirmative, he eliminates all vegetable and mineral items as well as dead humans and other animals from further consideration. If the answer is negative, it implies 1) that the item is dead and possibly animal or 2) that the item is not animal, but is vegetable or mineral.

In his emphasis on language as a key to intellectual development, Bruner names three stages of using past experiences and present thinking. These are:

1. *enactive* representation, in which the child reconstructs events through motor responses;

2. *iconic* representation, which involves organizing percepts and images for use; and

3. *symbolic* representation, which is the use of meaningful language.

He believes that the transition from iconic to symbolic representation occurs in the five-to-seven-year age period. This crucial transition makes it possible for the child ". . . to represent and systematically transform the regularities of experience with far greater flexibility and power than before." (1964, p. 13) Many educators working with children from the poorest socioeconomic families believe that, not only do such children lack sufficient experiences on which to base formal learning at school entrance, but also they have not advanced beyond the enactive or possibly the iconic level when they enter school. Since language is seen as the key to learning, the negative effects of such a deficit are immediately apparent.

TWO TAXONOMIES

One of the ways in which we can discover how someone learns something is to imagine a pyramid, in which each layer builds upon the ones below. This is sometimes called a taxonomy or a hierarchy. In many such taxonomies, the theorist describes what is, in effect, a combination of the associationist and the cognitive viewpoints. In others, the pyramid model illustrates qualitative differences that are primarily cognitive and depend minimally on the associationist theories. Let us look first at a dual approach, that of Gagné.

Gagné's taxonomy

Gagné's taxonomy

> . . . is the hierarchy in which the most complex form of learning, problem-solving, requires the learner to have mastered the appropriate subtasks in the next lower level, principle learning. . . . One important consequence of arranging all learning tasks in a hierarchical system is that failure to reach the criterion on a task implies that tasks above the failed task in the hierarchy will also be poorly learned. (Byers, 1967, p. 494)

How would this description fit our pyramid? Suppose we enter the pyramid at level 4, "verbal association," which involves the chaining or linkage of verbal responses. Simple counting in sequence might be the entering behavior. At level 5, multiple discrimination, the learner is expected to be able to give differential responses for similar stimuli, such as the sum of 4 apples + 3 apples, and the product of 4 sets of 3 airplanes. Obviously, one must be able to count in sequence before one can add, a basic mathematical skill. At level 6, our budding mathematician does not need pictures of objects to help her add, but can deal abstractly with numerical concepts. Level 7, principle learning, involves two or more concepts, or evolving chains of concepts. In other words, the learner must develop "rules." Such a rule or principle might involve the reversibility of a mathematical operation, for example, if $6 + 2 = 8$, then $2 + 6 = 8$, and $8 - 6 = 2$, and so on. The highest level of concept learning in Gagné's taxonomy, level 8, involves the use of principles to reach a goal by evolving a higher principle from a combination of lower-order principles. An example of this would be the proof of a geometric theorem that depends upon uniting earlier learned skills and principles. Gagné is thus saying that problem-solving involves thinking and a restructuring of previously learned rules. However, such a capability rests upon mastery of basic mathematical skills, which in turn rest on the simple ability to count in sequence. (Gagné, 1965)

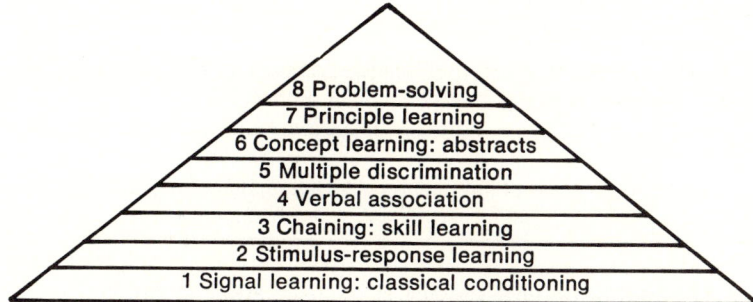

Pyramid model of Gagné's taxonomy. **Figure 8.6**

As you can see in Figure 8.6, the base of Gagné's pyramid or hierarchy is a strictly associationist point of view. However, at the upper end, one moves away from this and over to the concept, or cognitive, approach to learning. Indeed, more recently, Gagné has reemphasized this building-block arrangement in applying learning to instructional design. He supports the principles of contiguity, repetition, and reinforcement (all associationist) as basic learning principles, but adds internal learner factors that are crucial. These include previously learned capabilities of the learner, motivation, and self-confidence. "An act of learning is greatly affected by these internally generated processes. In particular, new learning is influenced by the recall of previously learned information, intellectual skills, and cognitive strategies.... These varieties are learned capabilities, and the conditions for their learning constitute the basis for instructional planning." (Gagné and Briggs, 1974, p. 17)

From a different vantage point, a group working with Bloom prepared two taxonomies of educational objectives, one in the cognitive area and the other

Bloom's taxonomy

in the affective domain. These are actually applications of learning theory to the learner and to the classroom situation.

The cognitive educational objectives specify the ways in which learners are expected to change their thinking as a result of the educative process. (Bloom, 1956, p. 26) The development of such objectives must include consideration of the learners' characteristics, the nature of the subject matter, the philosophy of education, and the psychology of learning. Weighing all of these factors and goals, the conferees developed a taxonomy or system of classification in the cognitive domain that is hierarchical in nature, with knowledge as the basis for all other objectives.

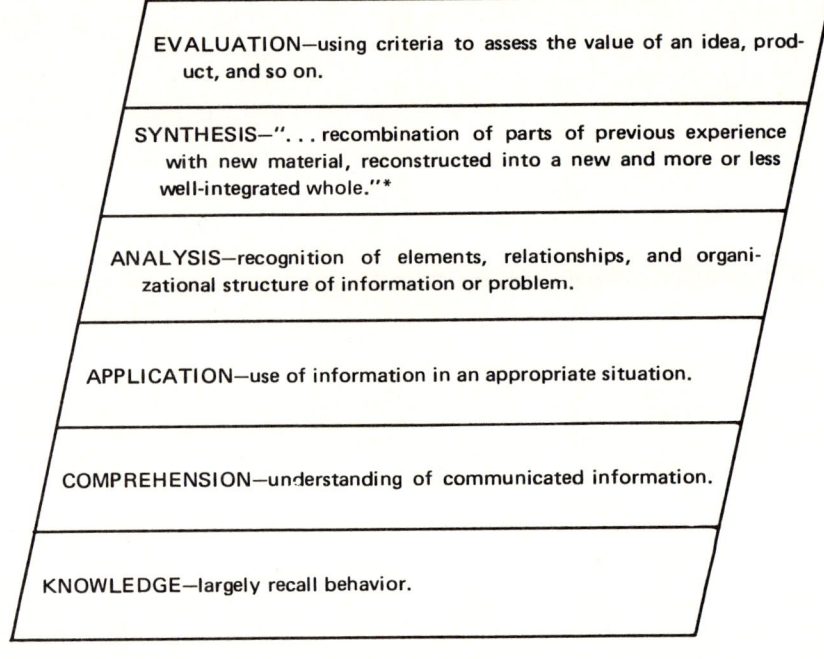

Bloom, 1956, p. 162.

Figure 8.7   *Hierarchy of cognitive education objectives.*

In the handbook, Bloom and his colleagues thoughtfully analyzed each of these objectives into specific elements and included illustrative test questions in various content fields to demonstrate how one can measure whether or not the student has met a particular objective. Although the idea of objectives is not new, it is only within recent years that educators have seriously introduced them into the schools.

A few examples will illustrate the ways in which objectives may be stated:

> *History unit:* The student will be able to list 4 of 5 causes for the Civil War to the teacher's satisfaction. (Knowledge)

Arithmetic unit: The student will be able to perform correctly the arithmetic operations needed to solve 8 of 10 word problems. (Comprehension)

Science unit: The student will be able to apply the law of refraction in 2 of 3 problem situations set by the instructor. (Application)

In the affective domain, objectives are also arranged as a hierarchy, but may be shown on a continuum. As a student or as a teacher, you can recognize that if any changes in the learner are to take place, he must first pay attention to (*receive*) the stimulus or phenomenon that is occurring. *Responding* implies the active participation of the learner in the learning process. In *valuing*, the learner develops a consistent behavior pattern that reflects beliefs, attitudes, or commitments toward objects or phenomena. "As the learner successively internalizes values, he encounters situations for which more than one value is relevant. Thus necessity arises for (a) the organization of the values into a system, (b) the determination of the interrelationships among them, and (c) the establishment of the dominant and pervasive ones." (Krathwohl, Bloom, and Masia, 1964, p. 154) Thus, *organization* involves the development of a system of values. Beyond this comes the development of a philosophy of life, which, as Krathwohl, et al., point out, is rarely set as an educational goal. This may be an effect of the need to mature and broaden one's experience that generally occurs after the completion of formal education.

| Receiving (attending) | Responding | Valuing | Organization (value system) | Characterization by a value or value complex |

Continuum of affective educational objectives. **Figure 8.8**

Affective objectives are clearly more difficult to define, to evaluate, and to include in curriculum outlines than are the cognitive objectives. They are, however, communicated to the learner through the teacher's own behavior toward students and toward the material being taught. Greater emphasis will be placed on these educational objectives in a later discussion of teacher-pupil relations.

Take subject matter from the grade level at which you expect to teach, and develop both cognitive and affective objectives appropriate to the content. **Suggested Activity**

SUMMARY OF LEARNING THEORIES

To what conclusions can we come now as to the correctness of the theories of learning? There seems to be no doubt that each theorist has something credible to contribute to our thinking. From our own casual observations, it is obvious that the youngest infant learns to respond to stimuli in a consistent way. Kantrow (1937), for example, demonstrated that newborns could be conditioned to suck in response to a buzzing sound through classical or stimulus-substitution techniques. We learn language, too, through associationist or S-R techniques. Operant conditioning is evident in the many experimental and therapeutic situations where psychologists are attempting to modify behavior, ranging from the elimination of stuttering or other aberrant behavior to programmed instruction and its elaborations. *But*, it is equally true that we humans put together what we have learned in these ways into patterns or structures, and thus exhibit cognitive learning. The ability to read this page is, for example, the result of 1) S-R learning at the auditory level, where we learned what each word sound meant or symbolized, 2) S-R learning involved in the mechanics of learning to read (alphabet, association of printed squiggles with known words), and 3) cognitive learning in what we read and comprehend thought by thought rather than in isolated words without context. In certain instances, one theory may dominate the learning situation, as in behavior modification, but other theories enter the picture as well. An eclectic approach to learning, which is recommended here, will draw from each theory what is applicable to a particular student and the subject matter with which he is dealing. The instructor, too, must be comfortable with the learning theory she applies, or her effectiveness will be reduced.

VARIABLES AFFECTING LEARNING

Theories of how we learn are very useful in themselves, but in practical terms we must consider that certain other factors enter into the learning situation. As indicated in the introduction to this chapter, the present discussion of such factors excludes socioeconomic status, emotional problems, and similar variables that have been amply discussed earlier. Variables affecting learning can be listed without end, but some to consider include:

1. attention
2. interest
3. level of difficulty of material to be learned
4. level of difficulty of presentation of new material
5. breadth of prior experience
6. communications ability of teacher
7. freedom of inquiry
8. memory and forgetting
9. capacity for mental imagery
10. expectancy
11. physical conditions in the classroom
12. informational feedback availability

This is obviously not an all-inclusive list, but it should give you some idea of the numbers of things that can contribute to or inhibit learning. Age, intelligence, sex, motivation, and level of aspiration have been brought to your attention already. Freedom of inquiry, which is important to intellectual curiosity, we will discuss further in chapter ten. So, to begin with, let's look briefly at the variable of attention.

You would probably agree that, if a learner is paying close attention to what is being taught, she should grasp the concept or skill readily (assuming that she had any necessary prior experience or knowledge). On the other hand, if she is not paying close attention, what *is* she learning? Is she experiencing incidental learning? That is, is she gaining information of which she is unaware at the time? It is sometimes difficult, when reading, for example, to shut out completely background voices or other distractions. On the other hand, if we are deeply interested in what we are reading or hearing in a lecture, we are less likely to become distracted. Attention, then, may vary from person to person and from time to time. It is possible that the degree of attention may be related to age and/or reading ability, according to a study by Siegel (1968). In a study with eight and fourteen-year-olds, he found that the older subjects were better able to control their concentration, resulting in less incidental learning. He also found that there was a negative correlation between the amount of incidental learning and reading ability in one of his eight-year-old groups. Siegel concluded that "It could be argued that better readers are able to inhibit attention to (i.e., ignore) irrelevant stimuli more quickly (and thoroughly) than do poorer readers. As a consequence, the better readers demonstrate a lower incidence of IL [incidental learning]." (p. 968) As far as the age factor is concerned, one *would* expect older students to be able to concentrate for longer periods and to a more intense level than younger learners as a result of experience and growing maturity. Confirmation of the relationship found by Siegel between attention and learning is seen in the learning difficulties of many brain-damaged youngsters who are easily distracted by external stimuli. One cannot say definitely that they are not learning at all, however, as incidental learning rather than specifically assigned learning may be taking place.

Stimulation and attention

There is another consideration, moreover, in terms of the role of stimulation in perceptual learning. According to Gibson and Gibson, all theories "... have at least this feature in common: they take for granted a discrepancy between the sensory input and the finished percept and they aim to explain the difference." (1955, p. 33) On the basis of their experimental research, they concluded that learning is the result of greater discrimination among previously vague, undifferentiated impressions, and that this comes about from greater stimulation. While this appears to be true in terms of much perceptual learning, there is a question of timing involved in when and how this stimulation occurs and whether it interferes with other forms of learning while contributing to greater differentiations in perceptions.

Another of the variables affecting learning is expectancy. By "expectancy" we mean the mental set or attitude with which the individual prepares to

Expectancy

meet his environment. There are adults, for example, who, because of narrow-mindedness or prejudice, find knowledge a threat. Therefore, they refuse to learn, or sometimes even to be exposed to new information. Expectancy is based on past experiences with the same or similar situations. It also reflects learning that has taken place since the last previous experience with the same phenomenon. Rotter (1954), a social learning theorist, associates expectancy with what he calls "freedom of movement." If freedom of movement is low, the individual restricts his activities because he expects failure or punishment to be the result of his efforts to satisfy a particular need. "Low freedom of movement or low expectancy for success or gratification may also be spoken of as high expectancy for punishment." (Rotter, 1954, p. 237) The learner who has such a high expectancy for failure or punishment, which in other psychological schools may be called anxiety, will be likely to learn less than the one with a high expectancy for success (which conversely implies a low expectancy for failure or punishment). Motivation, which Atkinson views as being a function of the strength of the motive interacting with expectancy of success or failure and the value of the incentive, is another related variable affecting learning.

Focus 8–4

As a simple illustration, let us look at a student who, because of past learning experiences, has a low expectancy for success (high expectancy for failure) in science courses. He is not generally oriented toward grades (low incentive value) beyond earning a passing mark, if that is possible. Although he may be mildly interested in the content of the course, the interaction of this relatively weak motive with the other factors will result in generally poor motivation and little learning. If we tried to put this idea into a formula,

$$\text{Motivation} = f \text{ (level of expectancy of success} \times \text{strength of motive} \times \text{value of incentive)},$$

with each factor assigned a numerical value from 1 to 5 (low to high), the result might look like this for the poorly motivated learner:

$$\text{Motivation} = f (1 \times 2 \times 1)$$
$$\text{Motivation} = 2 \text{ (of a possible maximum of 125).}$$

Is it possible to change this situation? Of course it is. In line with the reinforcement aspects of operant conditioning theory, Brackbill and Jack (1958) offered their subjects a choice of reinforcers in a study of the effects of reinforcement on learning. They found that 1) allowing the subject to choose his reinforcer or incentive goal tended to maximize motivation and 2) different reinforcers may vary in effectiveness at different ages. The moral of the study is, therefore, to know your learner before selecting his reinforcers, and preferably, to allow him to select the reinforcer himself. Changing the value of the incentive in the formula above for the same learner would result in a change in motivation:

$$\text{Motivation} = f (1 \times 2 \times 5), \text{ or}$$
$$\text{Motivation} = 10 \text{ (a quintupling of the previous level).}$$

If the method of teaching is changed from involved prose to a programmed instruction format, it might be possible to raise the level of expectancy for success to a "2" or a "3," thus doubling or tripling motivation again. Changes in intensity of interest or strength of motive would yield further increases in motivation. Motivation, to go full circle, will itself affect the amount of attention one pays, presumably the more one learns, which increases the expectation of success, which contributes to greater motivation, and so on in a cycle.

Can you think of other ways in which expectancy could be changed? **Question**

Certain other variables affecting learning are related both to the original acquisition of knowledge or skill and to its retention. You would probably agree that memory, or the ability to remember, is important to both aspects of learning. A child who cannot remember which combination of lines and curves represents which letter of the alphabet cannot learn to read. This may be obvious to you, but it doesn't say how or why we remember.

Retention

There are many hypotheses about the nature of the ability to remember. These include structural changes in the nervous system ("memory trace"), memory storage resembling the computer bank process, and genetic transmission in which "inherited" information is matched with acquired experience. Whatever the eventual outcome of scientific investigation of these theories, we must acknowledge that there is such a thing as memory, that there are aids to memory, that people differ in their ability to remember, and that memory is essential to learning.

Aids to Memory

One of the aids to memory is repetition. We can immediately ask why this is so. It may be that repetition "engraves" the material to be remembered more deeply into the memory mechanism, although we remember a great many things after merely one exposure. It may be that the increased familiarity of the material makes memory easier. As a result of his experiments dealing with the relationship between learning and organization of material, however, Tulving assumes ". . . that the success of retention and recall is to a large extent determined by what the subject *does* with the material he is to memorize, by the methods he uses to organize the material, and by the cues that he uses to effect the recall of retained material." (Tulving, 1968, p. 4) In order to test this assumption, Tulving asked two groups of university students ($N = 80$) to learn a list of 22 nouns, each beginning with a different letter. For the first three trials, both groups received identical instructions for free-recall of the listed nouns. Before the fourth trial, one group received a written repetition of these instructions, but the other subjects were instructed to try to organize the recalled words alphabetically. Eight trials followed, with the results seen in Figure 8.9.

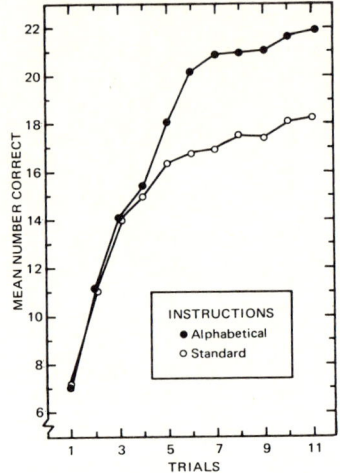

Figure 8.9   *Tulving, 1968, p. 6.

You might try a similar experiment with classmates or friends, asking them to remember as many familiar items in an unfamiliar set as possible in any order, and then instructing them to organize the list alphabetically, or in categories of some kind. Extrapolating from his experimental evidence, Tulving suggests that it may be more important to teach students *how* to learn and *how* to remember, than to put so much stress on methods of teaching.

> According to Tulving, "A good teacher may be successful because, among other things, he organizes the material to be learned for the learner, but a good learner is likely to be more successful because he can organize the material on his own even if it is not optimally structured by the external environment." (p. 12)

To Ausubel, retention refers ". . . to the process of *maintaining the availability* of a replica of the acquired new meanings." (1968, p. 98) He believes that both early review and delayed review aid retention, the former for its immediate advantage of consolidation and the latter because the learner is relearning material that has been partly forgotten. Spaced review, too, is advantageous to remembering what has been learned, since it provides both the early consolidation and the relearning features of retention.

Most of the experimental studies of retention test recall of lists of words, nonsense syllables, or some other controllable material. Shuell and Keppel (1970), for example, used a list of 30 words (simple nouns) to study individual differences in learning ability and retention on an immediate basis, after 24 hours, and after 48 hours. A pretest was used to establish fast- and slow-learning groups in their fifth-grade sample. In the first part of their experiment, they found that "... fast and slow learners recall, on the average, the same number of words after a single presentation of the list if the list has been presented at a 1-second rate for the fast learners (10.17 words) and a 5-second rate for the slow learners (10.8 words)." (p. 61) These differences were not as apparent in the other two portions of the experiment. The minimal differences in longer retention, or similarities in rate of forgetting, were explained in terms of the differences between short-term memory and long-term memory. (p. 64) In a related article, Rock (1958) contended that the length of the material to be learned causes differences in rote memory. For instance, too long a list of syllables, or whatever is to be memorized, causes interference and increases the need for repetition. Over-learning, or repeated exposure beyond the first correct recall, on the other hand, minimizes forgetting.

Rock applies this to classroom learning in the following way: "A teacher who is introducing the multiplication table, for example, might do well to present only a few numbers each day.... If the teacher took this approach to other rote subjects (spelling, for instance) she might devote shorter periods each day to a greater variety of subjects." (p. 72) In addition, Rock believes that the Gestalt theory of insight may explain some aspects of retention, since "... a number of experimenters have found that associative learning often involves the sudden discovery of some mnemonic device for linking together two items by means of some intermediate data." (p. 72)

Mnemonics

A *mnemonic device?* "What's that?" you ask. Suppose someone asks you how many days there are in the month of May. Unless it is May or early June, you may resort to the familiar "Thirty days hath September..." in order to give the correct answer. That little verse is a mnemonic device, or artificial aid to memory. Students in many eras, and at a variety of grade levels, have used mnemonic devices to help them recall the colors of the spectrum, the cranial nerves, historical names and dates, and so on. Mnemonic devices are not the only illustration of insight in relation to memory or learning, however. In problem-solving of any magnitude, insight is a sudden "flash" of the solution—the "Eureka! I've got it!" experience. As you will see when we discuss problem-solving, such insight is actually the result of mulling over a problem until the correct association of ideas (i.e., solution) appears.

Develop simple mnemonic devices that would help learners of different ages to remember information that they are studying in school.

Suggested Activity

Forgetting

Should insight fail to occur, Gestalt psychologists would expect forgetting to happen. Forgetting may also occur for other reasons: lack of motivation to remember, inadequate discrimination between known and new material, insufficient practice, or various types of interference. The types of interference are *retroactive inhibition* and *proactive inhibition*. The learning of foreign languages provides a good illustration of these two types. Let us suppose that you study Spanish and French, two Romance languages that have many cognate words although disparate pronunciations. You take Spanish first, and a year or two later begin to study French. In retroactive inhibition, as you learn French words, you forget the earlier learned matching Spanish words. In proactive inhibition, the Spanish words, which were learned first, interfere with your learning the appropriate French words. Ceraso (1967) cites a number of theories that attempt to explain these events. McGeoch, for one, asserts that retroactive inhibition occurs, not because of a forgetting process, but because responses compete and the wrong response "preempts" the place of the correct one. In a second theory cited, Melton assumes that some mechanism operates to suppress recollection of earlier learned material (i.e., it is unlearned) as new learning occurs. Underwood, in a third point of view, believes that in proactive inhibition "spontaneous recovery" overcomes the suppression of earlier learned material after a period of time and then interferes with the recall of later learned material, Ceraso himself supports a theory of "crowding," that is, the merging of earlier and later learned material that is counteracted by the spontaneous recovery of which Underwood wrote. Ceraso states further that forgetting is due to either loss of availability of the learned material or loss of associations connected with it. It is difficult to say which of these psychologists is closest to the truth in his theory, for the techniques needed to make a definitive study have yet to be developed.

"Transfer of training"

Still another variable in learning is the idea of "transfer of training."

> *Transfer* concerns how previous experience affects the *acquisition* of some specific material. *Proaction* and *retroaction* refer respectively to how the *retention* of material learned at some time may be affected by prior learning or subsequent learning. Since performance on one task can be either helped or hindered by the existence of other things learned, we have the following possible effects: in retention we can have proactive or retroactive facilitation and proactive or retroactive inhibition. In acquisition we can have positive or negative transfer. (Hulse, Deese, and Egeth, 1975, p. 340)

The inhibition effect has already been discussed with reference to forgetting. Positive transfer, on the other hand, or facilitation, helps one to learn and remember.

This concept implies that learning should be useful or applicable in situations other than the one in which material was originally learned. You will recall the earlier mention of Thorndike's theory of identical elements. In it, Thorndike expressed the belief that the more elements two sets of material had in common, the more easily the second could be learned, after the original learning took place.

If we use the illustration of foreign language study again, you can see that for an English-speaking person it might be easier to learn certain German words than their Spanish or French equivalents:

	House	White	Good	Morning
French	maison	blanc	bon	matin
German	hus	weiss	gut	morgen
Spanish	casa	blanco	bueno	mañana

This happens because of the similarities, or identical elements, between *these* German and English words. Other examples could be given of identical elements in French, Spanish, or other languages, and English.

During the era when formal discipline theory was dominant, difficult courses comprised the curriculum both for the "exercise" that they provided for the various mental "faculties" and their supposed transfer value. That is, since geometry required training in reasoning, it was believed that reasoning powers in general would be benefited if one studied geometry. The memorization of lengthy poems and speeches was similarly believed to strengthen one's memory powers in other fields. At the beginning of the twentieth century, however, as more and more psychologists questioned the faculty psychology-formal discipline approach to learning, several studies were made that demonstrated that there was little actual transfer from geometry to general reasoning, Latin to English, and so on. The two psychologists who did the most to disprove the effects of formal discipline in relation to transfer of training were Edward Thorndike and Charles Judd.

Thorndike, in an extensive study involving over 8000 high school students, found that the classical subjects favored by formal discipline proponents did no more for selective and rational thinking than did the practical courses such as woodworking, bookkeeping, and home economics. (1924) Years later, Travers (1972) wrote that

> Thorndike's work on transfer of training provided an entirely new basis for curriculum planning. No longer could subjects be included in the curriculum because of a belief that they were generally beneficial as devices for training the mind; a school subject had to be justified because of the *specific* skills, knowledge, and understanding it provided. The early research on transfer of training provided a revolutionary new basis for selecting subjects for inclusion in the curriculum. (p. 182)

Judd (1908), on the other hand had earlier demonstrated that transfer could occur through studies of his theory of "generalization." This was shown in an experiment where one group of subjects was taught the principles of refraction, and a second group was not given this instruction. Although boys in both groups were able to hit an underwater target with darts with approximately equal ease on the initial trials, movement of the target to a new position led to greater success in a shorter period of time for the boys who had been trained in the principles of refraction. Judd concluded that the principles learned had been applied, or generalized, to a new but similar situation. This is a cognitive theory of transfer, since associations were established that resulted in new cognitive patterns.

In a more contemporary study by Overing and Travers (1966), using a task similar to Judd's, it was found that transfer is facilitated by "... (a) training in the presence of irrelevant information, (b) establishing a set relating the material to be learned to a practical situation, and (c) verbalization of knowledge prior to its application." (p. 179)

In a slightly different but related concept, the Gestaltists' "transposition theory" emphasizes the "... *perception of the relationship between principles and specific instances* in the training situation rather than the *process of generalization.*" (Ausubel, 1968, p. 162) A study by Reynolds (1966) supports this approach. He hypothesized that new learning is easier if it is integrated into a meaningful structure. Reynolds had 60 college students learn part-nonsense syllables under differing conditions and found that positive transfer occurred only when separate components in the first stage of the experiment were organized as a whole. That is, the transfer occurred when relationships between specific items and a principle were perceived.

John Dewey, probably the foremost American educator in the first half of this century, stressed substantially this idea of applicability in his curriculum revisions and emphasis on "learning by doing." The Montessori approach to preschool and primary education also emphasizes learning through application. Increasingly, today's students demand relevancy in their education, which is their way of saying that they want to be able to transfer the information and techniques learned in the classroom to the practical situations of everyday life. However, one-to-one transferability is virtually impossible because we don't know what problems anyone will have to solve tomorrow, and we cannot possibly teach solutions to all of today's. Despite such practical problems, however, it is obvious that the emphasis in curriculum design has been shifted from the formal discipline approach to one in which the applicability of one subject to another is demonstrated and stressed. For example, Latin used to be included in the curriculum to improve one's memory and one's use of English, although the specific links between Latin and English were themselves rarely taught. Today, the relationship between English words and their Latin roots is part of the course content, since one of the modern goals of teaching Latin is to improve one's English vocabulary. It is recognized now that, for this transfer of knowledge to occur, it must be specifically taught rather than presumed to happen by some mysterious process.

Focus 8–5 Transfer can be taught with regard to things other than information and vocabulary. If cognitive skills are taught until mastered, learners can then be shown how to use these skills in a variety of subject fields. At first, for example, techniques for using library card files may be taught for their own sake, and then applied in the research for a history project or report. Obviously, once these techniques have been mastered, use of these skills can be transferred to any subsequent field.

Similarly, the basic steps in problem-solving, once mastered, can be applied to any problem. Students can be given problems to solve in class, at which time they are to hypothesize a solution based on the problem-solving steps. They can also be encouraged to report on their use of the steps outside of school. In all sorts of problem situations, they can learn to ask themselves certain questions:

1. What is the problem?
2. What information is needed to reach a solution?
   a) How much of this information do I already have?
   b) How do I find additional needed information?
   c) Have I ever solved a similar problem, and, if so, how?
3. What plan shall I carry out? (Can the steps be checked?)
4. Is the solution reached the correct one? Is there a more suitable solution? etc.

Obviously, information-processing skills, application of principles, and other bits of knowledge can also be demonstrated as transferable to a variety of events.

Negative transfer of training occurs when previous learning interferes with new learning. Thus, American drivers are prone to difficulty and accidents when they try to drive in the few countries where one drives a car on the left-hand side of the road rather than the right.

Contemporary research seems to indicate that learning will be more functional (relevant) if it is originally presented with as many applications as possible. These should be organized so that they are available for future use. Again and again, this emphasis on the need for organization in learning appears. Clearly, it is an important variable in learning. An example of such organization might be the statement in psychology that "frustration leads to aggression." Under such a general statement, you might list several demonstrations of the concept in widely varying situations. These could include, for instance: 1) a dog restrained from reaching his dinner; 2) an individual whose employer has unjustly criticized her; 3) a nation with inadequate natural resources. Such instances would provide clues to the general principle and possibly to the appropriate behavior when you yourself are in a frustrating situation or give you an idea of what to expect when your behavior frustrates someone else. As a teacher, the latter instance may occur more often than you'd like as you set limits for acceptable behavior in the classroom, focus on a less well-received topic in lessons rather than a "popular" one, or have to give negative criticism.

Learning skills In the Overing and Travers study cited earlier, one of the findings was that verbalization tended to increase transfer of training. This is part of the larger question of active versus passive participation in learning, a factor that we need to consider. Several studies support the greater effectiveness of overt responses in certain learning situations and with certain students. Overt responses include those in which the individual actively writes out or marks a response, rather than simply making a mental choice or just reading on before continuing the program. In nonprogrammed learning, overt responses may include reading a problem aloud to clarify what is asked, doing math problems, or rewriting a passage in one's own words to demonstrate comprehension of its concepts. Goldbeck and Campbell (1962) found that overt responses were more effective than covert responses for students dealing with difficult (rather than easy) programmed material. This conclusion is contradicted by Crist's findings (1966) of virtually no differences in scores between overt- and covert-response groups at the second- and sixth-grade levels, on immediate or delayed posttests. Differences in methodology, task difficulty, and subjects help to explain the conflicting conclusions.

Learning is aided also by the use of certain other skills. As the learner enters the middle and upper grades, particularly, she is expected to be able to use those skills she has previously learned as tools for new learning. The ability to read accurately and with comprehension is basic to every subject. She should be increasingly able to discriminate items of greater importance from those of lesser importance. She should be able to scan the pages of a book or article to locate the information or answers she needs. Such visual search skills can be improved with practice, according to research reports.

> In these studies, as in many others in the perceptual area, the effective use of sensory information requires extended practice of a kind that is not provided by ordinary daily life. The implication is that, unless the schools provide opportunities for students to undertake visual search tasks, little skill is likely to be acquired. A second finding of interest is that the efficiency of visual search can be improved by searching for more than one category at the same time. (Travers, 1967, p. 606)

Application of the visual search skill is seen even in learning to read, where the task is mainly form discrimination and recognition. Several psychologists have found that young children perceive parts before wholes, suggesting that letter recognition should come before word recognition, a reversal of the "look-say" method of teaching reading.

Learning environment There are factors in the classroom setting itself that also need to be considered as variables in learning. Is there appropriate lighting? Is the room too cold, too warm, or just right in temperature? Are the desks and chairs of a size comfortable for the learner? Is construction going on nearby which makes it difficult to hear and listen? Naturally, not all of these factors can be controlled ideally all of the time, nor do they affect all learners in exactly the same way, but physical comfort/discomfort does play a role in the learner's ability to do her job. Modern school construction experts are aware of this and accordingly design schools with climate control, up-to-date lighting arrangements, and consideration for the students who will be using the school facilities.

In addition to the physical setting, we should remember that the emotional climate of the classroom is also important. Although teacher-student relationships will be discussed in chapter thirteen, we might note at this point that the student who is afraid of the teacher (and probably any authority figure) will find it more difficult to concentrate on what she is supposed to learn. A teacher who has earned the dislike and/or distrust of his students will find it more difficult to teach effectively, thus creating a negative atmosphere for learning. Students who are more anxious about peer disapproval than teacher disapproval will similarly have problems in learning.

Gagné's observations (1973) of classes, grades 1–12, suggest several factors that affect learning. These involve the learner, the teacher, what is to be learned, and evaluation of learning combined with feedback. Further, he found that the ways in which these factors interact vary from the lower to the upper grades.

As you can see, learning is not a simple matter. Learning theory suggests methods of teaching. The learner herself must have the cognitive capacity plus accrued experience, that is, readiness, to profit from instruction. The material to be learned should have intrinsic interest wherever possible. The climate for learning should be a healthy one, physically and emotionally. We need to amplify these terse statements, however, if you are to accept them as practical. This is what we shall do in the next section.

CLASSROOM APPLICATIONS

Herbart, in the nineteenth century, introduced a five-stage program for teaching new material, the "Five Formal Steps of the Recitation." They are: 1) Preparation, 2) Presentation, 3) Association, 4) Generalization, and 5) Application. (Mulhern, 1959, p. 470) The steps represent one of the earliest modern applications of psychology to the classroom learning situation. Although Herbart's program is now about 100 years old, we still use this basic format. It is applicable to most learning theories and includes within it the concepts of motivation, association, and transfer. Let's take these steps one by one and see how they relate to theory and instruction.

Here we wish to arouse the learner's attention, interest, or motivation, which we are well aware is necessary for effective learning. At the primary level, the teacher can, for example, display groups of items in different places around the room. As the children look at and handle the displays, one expects that they will ask questions of the teacher, who can then respond with a brief introduction to the idea of sets and elements of sets. In science classes, similarly, displays of apparatus available for manipulation, posters depicting biological

1. Preparation

processes, chemical formulae, and the like can be available in the classroom at the beginning of the course or section of the course. Again, these should arouse curiosity in the students, which will prepare them for learning something new. Furth (1970), in his attempt to make Piaget's theories applicable to the classroom, urges "schools for thinking." He suggests how children would learn to read in such a school.

> The teacher would encourage the child's interest by reading from books, by writing during other activities, by exposing him to rhythmic and poetic qualities of language, and so on. She would use some of the excellent self-training materials on the market today, but without pushing him. If the child shows interest, there is every reason to think that he is ready and will succeed. (p. 149)

Furth and other Piagetians appear to be willing to wait a few years for the child's spontaneous interest to develop, which most other educators are not. Nevertheless, the ideas demonstrated in this passage are applicable to the stage of preparation.

Similar demonstrations in a wide variety of courses can be accomplished through the use of visual aids (films, filmstrips, graphs, displays of finished products) and audio aids (records, tapes, and guest speakers). Such introductory measures can apply no matter which modern learning theory you are using.

2. Presentation

The method in which the new material to be learned is presented will reflect learning theory more than the preparation phase does. If one is committed to the old "formal discipline," then rote memory is stressed, from the multiplication tables to Shakespeare's plays to historical information. Reasons for learning the new material tend to center on the intrinsic value of the new information and the idea that "it's good for you." We are then exposed to a multiplication table to be memorized by the next day or the day after next. True, it is important to be able to multiply correctly and speedily for efficiency's sake, but not simply for the exercise of memory. A more contemporary approach to teaching this material is to present a partially completed multiplication table puzzle and have the children discover multiplication facts for themselves. (See Figure 8.10.) Practice will ensure retention of the facts.

Another method of presentation involves Thorndike's "identical elements" theory. This has already been illustrated in the case of foreign language instruction where cognate or very similar words exist in both languages. It is used also in the phonics approach to reading instruction where "word families" are taught. One first-grade teacher, on the opening day of school, depended on the observation and incidental learning powers of her new pupils to teach them their first word, using the principle of "identical elements" (see Figure 8.11).

The same principle may be applied in teaching elementary algebra, especially since first-graders now learn that $1 + \square = 3$. You recall that early step to your algebra class and demonstrate that $1 + x = 3$ is the algebraic

X	1	2	3	4	5	6	7	8	9	10	11	12
1	1	2	3	4	5	6	7	8	9	10	11	12
2	2	4	6		10			16				
3	3	6	9	12			21			30		
4	4	8	12		20				36			48
5	5	10			25	30				50	55	
6	6	12			30			48				
7	7			28			49				77	
8	8	16			40				72			96
9	9		27			54		72				
10				40						90		110
11		22				66					110	
12	12			48					96			132

A multiplication table puzzle.   Figure 8.10

formula that makes the same statement. In social studies courses, you can show that similarities of climate, topography, and economic resources have certain common effects on the dress, diet, economy, and history of different countries. Using both the identical elements and discovery methods, you can demonstrate, for example, why wars are started or why dictatorships flourish.

Teaching the first word.   Figure 8.11

Simulation games, using the identical elements principle, contribute to the discovery of the desired new information. All of these ideas involve learning by association in some way. The application of Skinnerian theory was also shown in the teaching of required spelling lists.

From the cognitive point of view, emphasis in presentation of new material would be placed on the relationships between known and unknown and on problem-solving as a way of learning. Instead of presenting facts and formulae in a chemistry course, for example, the presentation might be in the form of an experiment to be done by the students under your guidance. Given the chemicals and appropriate apparatus, they would discover for themselves the relationship between acids and bases, or the importance of proper proportions in a formula. Other aspects of concept learning are apparent in every school subject. At the secondary and college levels, particularly, we expect students to discover principles based on information presented in text or class, and increasingly to experience the flash of "insight" as they solve problems.

3. Association

Wherever possible, the new material should be assimilated with previously learned material. The cognitive theorists emphasize this principle. Bruner's "spiral curriculum," which presents abstract concepts in simple concrete terms at the youngest levels, and repeats them in successively more complex terms at the intermediate and upper school levels, is one way of integrating past and present learning. Another method is to use personal past experiences of the students as they relate to new information, which should broaden their perceptions of the situations or events experienced. Here, one must assume that the students have had the desired kinds of previous experiences.

In teaching psychology, for example, it is often required that students take a course in introductory psychology before studying more specialized areas in the field. Having had that experience, the instructor should then be able to draw upon this earlier learning, as it relates to children, for instance, in developmental psychology. However, how much individual students have retained from that initial psychology course is debatable, for few students review old notes in preparation for a new course.

4. Generalization

Here is an opportunity to use the "trial-and-error" or "discovery" method to good advantage. The students have now become involved with new information and have been shown (or found out for themselves) its relation to previous knowledge. They are ready to climb higher on Gagné's pyramid by evolving a concept or rule or general idea or definition that is of a higher order of thinking than memorization or practice. This stage is also one in which there is an opportunity for creative thinking, in that students might be asked to hypothesize certain "rules," given specific facts that they have learned.

The integration of foreign language learning into English vocabulary and grammar study can also lead to the development of generalizations. If you teach a number of prefixes and suffixes, with their translations, for example, using familiar words, it is quite reasonable to ask students to develop "rules of thumb" that might guide them in their use of nonfamiliar words as well. The study of grammar in another language, also, has frequently led students to the formulation of principles for use with English.

5. Application

Ultimately, the goal of learning is to be able to use what is learned, whether in appreciating the subtle differences in artistic techniques, building a house or something smaller, comprehending current events, or performing more effectively in one's occupation. The application of what has been learned can be accomplished in many ways: directly, through lectures, texts, experiments, or other laboratory work; or indirectly, through events outside the classroom, creative imagination tasks, or perhaps not until years later when an unexpected opportunity to use the information arises.

The application of learned material is also related to the contemporary question of relevance in education. Why should a girl who plans to be a homemaker, and not a scientist, study chemistry? Use of common household cleaning compounds in the chemistry laboratory will demonstrate the wisdom of her knowing the potential effects of combinations of certain chemicals, or of a single chemical element on a particular household problem, such as removing stains or paint, dyeing fabrics, and so on. A knowledge of how to measure correct portions in following a formula can be transferred to the similar task in following a recipe. Studying physics has similar prospects for applying "laws" of mechanics, electricity, and so on, in the home. Why study ancient history? For one thing, we can, theoretically, learn from the mistakes of the past as well as from the successes. Are the factors that precipitated the fall of the Roman Empire occurring again in contemporary society? What can we learn from Roman times that will help us to prevent the collapse of our civilization? How does Thoreau's civil disobedience relate to today's anti-establishment activities? In another area of learning, courses such as educational psychology are designed to apply the principles of psychology to a specific field of endeavor, education, and to prepare the prospective teacher to meet a variety of problems with higher probabilities of success by applying those principles.

These steps of Herbart's are bound to no one theory of learning. They focus on the material to be taught and on the learner. At each step, it is possible to use information acquired in a study of theories, considering also the abilities of the teacher and the variables affecting the learner. The teacher should have the goals of learning specific information firmly in his or her own mind while preparing to implement the steps with appropriate methods.

SUMMARY

From the question "What is learning?" we have moved in this chapter to a study of the theories of how learning occurs. We presented the viewpoints of both the associationists and the cognitive theorists. An overview of each approach was discussed, together with examples based on the work of specific theorists.

Theory tells us how learning is believed to take place, but, since learning occurs not in a vacuum but within a human being, we had to consider a number of variables that affect the learner as he or she learns. Particular emphasis was given to attention, expectancy, motivation, retention, transfer of training, review, and classroom "climate."

The final section of the chapter was concerned with applying what came earlier. Specific suggestions for classroom techniques as related to the several theoretical orientations were presented within the framework of Herbart's five steps in teaching: preparation, presentation, association, generalization, and application.

As a whole, this chapter was designed to lay a theoretical and practical ground for examination of how the learner learns. Throughout, it is stressed that each point of view makes a unique contribution to our knowledge, but that none has a monopoly on teaching techniques or learning effectiveness. It is expected that this new learning will, however, enable the teacher to choose more selectively and predict more accurately the effect of teaching methods on the goals of learning. A leader among educational psychologists, Lloyd Humphreys (1970), has stated several principles of classroom learning that effectively and succinctly summarize the message of this chapter:

> Children do not learn something unless they have been exposed to the appropriate content. . . .
>
> The second principle of classroom learning is summed up under the rubrics of motivation, interest, and incentive. Students do not learn, even if exposed to the right curriculum content, if they go to sleep on every exposure. The motivation of the learner is essential for classroom learning. . . .
>
> Within the average classroom intelligence does not make the all-or-nothing contribution to variance that the right curriculum or its absence, or motivation or its absence, make, but the contribution is still very large. It is very difficult to prevent bright, motivated students from learning while the evidence that superior teaching makes much difference with such students is very slender indeed. . . .
>
> My evaluation of the effects of teaching methods on proficiency in subject matter leads to a further generalization: the highest payoff from the use in the classroom of knowledge of learning principles comes from applications to motivation of individual students and to management of the classroom of students rather than to the teaching of subject matter per se. . . . (pp. 1, 9)

Preview

INTRODUCTION

CONCEPT FORMATION
    ACQUISITION OF CONCEPTS
    STUDIES IN "CONSERVATION"
    NEW APPROACHES TO CONCEPT DEVELOPMENT
    MINI-SUMMARY

THINKING
    SUBJECTIVE AND OBJECTIVE THINKING
    RANDOM AND SYSTEMATIC THINKING
    COGNITIVE, MEMORATIVE, AND EVALUATIVE THINKING
    PRODUCTIVE THINKING

LANGUAGE DEVELOPMENT
    ACQUISITION OF LANGUAGE
    ABSTRACT AND CONCRETE LANGUAGE
    INTERPRETATION OF LANGUAGE
    BILINGUALISM

SUMMARY

9

Concepts, Thinking, and Language

INTRODUCTION

The title of this chapter might simply be "Thinking," as the formation of concepts and the use of language are both elements in the larger set called thinking. However, people commonly perceive these aspects of thinking as separate entities, and such a division, in approaching the chapter, permits us to justify the emphasis placed on each aspect. We use language to express our thoughts, and thinking is necessary if we are to develop ideas. The objectives of this chapter are to explore the ways in which thinking develops (as in concept formation), to illustrate different modes of thought, and to demonstrate the application of these thought processes.

It is possible to develop concepts without language, for concepts are defined in *Webster's Distionary* as mental images formed by generalizations from particulars. We can, indeed, form a mental image for something without having a verbal label for it, and this *is* thinking. On the other hand, it is virtually impossible to speak a language without having conscious or unconscious thinking in operation, or to solve problems without some thought (although the actual solution may occur serendipitously). To explore how thinking develops, we will need to begin in very early childhood where the infant begins to anticipate events, to comprehend words (first by intonation and later by significance), and to form those mental images mentioned earlier. When one learns a concept, he is learning certain signals by which to bring order into his experiences. That is, he begins to categorize objects as he encounters more of them. Then he gradually learns to select certain attributes of objects as he expands his experiences so that he can identify objects with common properties as fitting or not fitting into a category. Finally, he perceives relationships among objects or classes of objects, thus ordering his world still further. Much of the research and theorizing in this area of concept formation has been done by Piaget, by students inspired by his work, and by Bruner and others in this country.

In considering the development of language, we shall look at the growth of vocabulary and the learning of grammar at different ages, as well as the relationship between changes in vocabulary as concepts change. Certain advantages or complications may arise where a child is truly bilingual, so we'll have a look at these, too, in terms of concept formation. Second-language learning will also be considered here briefly.

A third portion of this chapter will be focused upon different kinds of thinking. Does it seem strange to you to be told that there are several kinds of thinking? There are, for example, daydreams, which are primarily randomly associated thoughts, and evaluative thoughts, used when you judge correctness or quality. Convergent and divergent thinking are related to finding answers or solving problems. Directed thought may include all or any of the last mentioned thinking processes.

A major corporation has used the single word "THINK" as an inspiration, a caution, and a guideline for all of its employees. Let's find out what

T H I N K

really means.

CONCEPT FORMATION

What is a concept? We have already defined it as a mental image formed by generalizations from particulars. How is it developed? Concepts appear to be based on experience, with continued interaction with the environment modifying concepts over a period of time. Piaget has demonstrated such modifications at different ages or stages of development, and it is his research that will be used principally to show the changes in concepts of space, number, and so on, in this chapter. Two processes occur in the modification of concepts: assimilation and accommodation.

> Assimilation is simply the application of an established behavior pattern to a familiar or new situation. If the behavior is successful, the child is not forced to change his behavior in the new situation. However, if the behavior is not successful, the child must adapt or change his behavior to the new situation. Accommodation is changing an existing behavior pattern that does not work in the new situation. (Birns and Golden, 1973, p. 127)

A child who is accustomed to playing with containers in her sandbox can readily transfer her play activity to the larger expanse of sand at a beach. That is, she assimilates the new setting into her perceptions. On the other hand, if the child is visiting a family that eats its main meal at noontime rather than in the evening (her usual dinner hour), she must change her eating behavior to conform to her hosts' pattern. This is accommodation.

The practice of providing experiences and opportunities, rather than the concepts themselves, actually demonstrates the respect of the teacher for the development of the child's thinking processes and indicates the awareness of the teacher that this is a continuous process. Although Piaget is not usually considered to be a behaviorist, he does agree that the child has to be an active participant in his or her own mental growth, as the behaviorists believe. Elaborating on this theme, Lovell, a follower of Piaget, points out that, while a child needs a growing variety of experiences and objects to stimulate his intellectual growth, the size of the gap between the child's present level of knowledge and the demands of the new situation remain vague. "This is where the intuitive skill of the teacher is called for. It is his task to arrange, or find in the environment, problems which call forth the schemas of the child in new and novel ways." (Lovell, 1968, p. 19) Teachers who function in this way operate an "open" classroom. The technique is associated with British infant and primary schools, but is also practiced here (see chapter eleven).

The child comes to school with some concepts. She has usually experienced some contact with animals, cars, and families, which enables her to classify at an elementary level objects, events, or people into those which fit into her concepts and those which don't. The ability to categorize and classify is an important achievement. Bruner, Goodnow, and Austin (1956) suggest that such an accomplishment does the following:

1. reduces the complexity of the environment
2. assists us in identifying the objects in our environment
3. reduces the need for constant learning
4. provides direction for instrumental activity, and
5. permits the ordering and relating of classes of events. (pp. 12–13)

The ability to classify is thus a labor-saving device, one which permits us to perform more efficiently. The young child has some conception of space, mass, volume, number, and so on, both as to their nature and their conservation. According to Piaget's descriptions, these are usually subjective, or self-oriented, concepts. It is not until the child is at the primary school level, ages six to eight, and entering the stage of concrete operations that he dissociates himself from these concepts and can really organize his thinking.

Acquisition of concepts

A major question is how children acquire these concepts. Four theories that have been advanced are nativism, learning theory, maturation, and equilibration. Nativism presents the viewpoint that ". . . even very small children are always logical *within those limited areas where they have sufficient knowledge*" because of the organization of the human nervous system. (Smedslund, 1961, p. 12) However, Smedslund argues that irrational conclusions drawn from sufficient knowledge tend to invalidate this theory. Learning theory assumes ". . . that the child acquires the concepts of conservation as a function of repeated external reinforcements." (p. 13) This point of view is seen as inadequate and inconsistent because of the absence of direct training in conservation concepts, for instance, in the home with a resultant lack of opportunity for reinforcement. Maturation theory, as one might expect, asserts that concepts develop gradually as a result of maturation of the nervous system and independently of external experience. Smedslund criticizes this theory because it fails to explain the time lag between the acquisition of different concepts of conservation and the effects of the environment. Finally, equilibration theory, which is associated with Piaget and others, asserts

> . . . that logical structure is not originally present in the child's thinking, but that it develops as a function of an internal process, equilibration, which is heavily dependent on *activity* and *experience*. This point of view differs radically from that of learning theory, since practice is not assumed to act through external reinforcements, but by a process of mutual influence of the child's activities on each other. . . . The process of equilibration is not identical with maturation, since it is highly influenced by practice which brings out latent contradictions and gaps in mental structure, and thereby initiates a process of inner reorganization. (p. 13)

As Smedslund points out, these theories are not mutually exclusive. Nativism and learning theory, which appear to be so opposite, actually see children and adults thinking in substantially the same way. When a child has enough information, according to these theories, he or she thinks like an adult. Conversely, a poorly informed adult thinks like a child. Smedslund concludes, therefore, that equilibration theory offers the best explanation for those facts known about concept development.

Studies in "conservation"

Piaget devised a number of experiments to test his theories of concept development. Perhaps the most familiar to you is the test for the conservation of mass. In this experiment, the child is given two equal balls of clay and is told that they are equally heavy. One of the balls is then changed (in the presence of the child) into another shape (e.g., a sausage), and the child is asked whether the ball has more clay than the sausage, or the same amount, or less clay, as a test of conservation of mass, or substance. Similar questions are asked about the conservation of weight. After responding, the child is asked why he thinks the way he does. Children with a grasp of conservation answer that amount and weight are the same in both shapes, while those without it answer in a way indicating their reliance on the perceptual features of the objects. Piaget and Inhelder reported as early as 1941 that the concept of conservation of mass is attained at about seven or eight years, followed by conservation of weight at about nine to ten years. These findings were confirmed in later studies, but Smedslund found that socioeconomic status had an effect on the transition ages, that is, earlier transition ages among children from a socioeconomically superior environment. He has also cited additional related support for the hypothesis that the rate of development of the concepts of conservation is influenced by environment. (p. 12)

CONCEPTS, THINKING, AND LANGUAGE   271

If one wishes to include training and experience as part of environment, which we must do since they are obviously not maturation factors, there is further confirmation of the influence of environment on acquisition of concepts. Suppes (1966), for example, working with youngsters on the formation of mathematical concepts, concluded from his experiments that concepts are formed by experience: "With the exception of a few salient features, new concepts may be formed by random choices, and only after one or more instances of the concept have been reached or put together by accident or chance is the new concept *recognized*." (p. 150) Piaget, too, has indicated that experience is necessary for concept formation, but has not considered whether the opportunity for experience exists for all children.

Let us look at some concepts. Research subjects in studies of concept formation tend to be young because a major shift in thinking patterns occurs at ages four to eight years. Since we have just cited Suppes' research, we can begin with mathematical concepts. Piaget avers that children aged five to six years can count numbers by rote or by pointing, but that, if items are disarranged, they become confused. If you ask a five-year-old, for example, whether the number of items in line B is the same as, less than, or more than the number of items in line A _____

A. ☐ ☐ ☐ ☐ ☐ ☐ ☐

B. ☐ ☐ ☐ ☐ ☐ ☐ ☐

Piaget believes that the child will respond that line B has more items. Therefore, a child of this age cannot be said to have conservation of number. Piaget believes that conservation of quantity must occur before conservation of number and that the latter does not appear before six and one-half to seven years. (1953) He came to this conclusion after experiments with children aged five to twelve years old. Piaget concluded that discoveries of different types of conservation occurred at different ages: number at six and one-half to seven years, mass at seven to eight years, weight at ages nine to ten, and volume at ages eleven to twelve.

Try the problem of conservation of number, using buttons or small candies, with a few children in the four to eight year age range. You might also try the conservation of mass problem (in the next paragraph), with clay or Play-Dough,® with the same children. Write a brief report summarizing your findings and comparing these with the studies reported by Piaget.

Suggested Activity

Elkind (1961b) replicated Piaget's work with 175 children in grades kindergarten through six. The material used in both situations was two clay balls, one of which at times was rolled out like a hot dog or sausage, as mentioned earlier. Elkind's work confirmed Piaget's findings and also pointed up the perceptual domination of the younger child's thinking. Siegel and Goldstein (1969) also tested Piaget's assertion that young children do not show conservation of number until age six or seven. Their conclusion, which also confirmed Piaget's work, is almost as amusing as it is interesting: "Most children younger than 5 years and 7 months do not have conservation of number. Instead of choosing the correct rational alternatives [more, less, same] or showing conservation of number, young children systematically exhibited recency response strategies by choosing the last of two alternatives offered them." (p. 128)

What does this mean in the classroom? Children who have learned to count to 10, 20, or 100 by rote before entering first grade need to be exposed to "proof" that seven items remain as seven items whether spaced close together or far apart, or grouped in three sets of $2 + 1$, or as $3 + 4$, $5 + 2$, and so on. Once they have accepted this experience, they can be said to have acquired conservation of number and are ready to learn various elementary arithmetic concepts. Several of the "new math" programs provide opportunities for the acquisition of this basic concept in the early sections of their material. There has been a question, however, whether the new math is more appropriate and effective for communicating such experiences than the more traditional math techniques. Can it help the characteristics of concrete operational thinking (identity, classification, seriation, conservation, and understanding of numbers) to develop? (Schwabel and Raph, 1973, pp. 26–30)

Focus 9–1

In a three-year study of arithmetic instruction techniques, Spears and Dodwell (1970) had two questions that they sought to answer: 1) were "new math" techniques more effective in communicating the concepts of arithmetic than the traditional methods, and 2) did any of the methods used have a discernible effect on the development of number concepts from a Piagetian viewpoint? The different approaches studied were traditional drill and rote learning, the Cuisenaire system (learning through activity), Suppes' sets and numbers, and patterns in arithmetic (stress on understanding through insight, intuition, and limited drill). The subjects were first- to third-graders in the Kingston, Ontario, city and township schools, with mean IQs ranging from 100–115, comparable socioeconomic backgrounds, and teachers of similar ability.

The findings did not support any one method over another in terms of effectiveness in teaching arithmetic in the early grades. They also did not show that any one method contributed to a greater understanding of number and related concepts in the Piagetian sense, nor did development of these children follow the sequences delineated by Piaget with any significant regularity. Those differences that were significant between classes taught by the same method appeared to be related more to differences in teacher characteristics rather than any other variable. Incidentally, this is frequently the conclusion reached by other researchers.

Other concepts stem from conservation of number and its related arithmetic operations. Smedslund, for example, says that equilibration theory (i.e., Piagetian theory) ". . . assumes that conservation of weight results from an organization of the operations of addition and subtraction; adding means more weight, subtracting means less weight, no adding and no subtracting must mean no change, i.e., conservation." (1961, p. 71) Again, the balls of clay can be shown to be of equal weight. If one ball is subsequently shaped into a hot dog, the child can be asked whether it is lighter than, heavier than, or equal to the clay shaped like a ball. In a five to seven age-group, Smedslund found that 20 percent of his subjects knew conservation of weight and could explain satisfactorily that no weight had been added or subtracted. (p. 74) He did not report a finding similar to that of Siegel and Goldstein.

Another concept that has its roots in conservation of number is that of measurement. Certainly, one needs to be able to measure for arithmetic and other studies by the third grade, and sometimes earlier. Piaget found that children began to understand that measurement involves two and three dimensions by age eight or nine. Bearison (1969), on the other hand, questions whether this comprehension *cannot* occur until this age, or whether it can occur earlier.

Focus 9–2

Bearison had a small sample of 34 white, middle-class children, with a mean age of 5 years, 10 months. He trained part of the sample group in measurement of liquids. The children were tested one month and again seven months after training, as were the control subjects. He found that the experimental subjects showed better conservation concepts than the control subjects and also retained and generalized what they had been taught. These data led Bearison to the conclusion that measurement precedes conservation rather than following it, as Piaget had said. Whether these results and conclusions will be confirmed with larger samples and other groups of subjects remains, of course, to be seen.

You may recall that conservation of volume, according to Piaget, does not occur until age eleven or twelve years. This, too, can be questioned, as the acquisition of other concepts has been. Can training in the conservation of continuous quantity and volume make these concepts appear earlier? Bruner, you will recall, has expressed the belief that young children can be taught rather complex concepts in rudimentary form and gain some comprehension of the information. Further, Siegler and Liebert (1972) suggest that training, rule presentation, and feedback may enable children younger than Piaget has averred to acquire concepts of conservation.

Focus 9–3

Not all studies conflict with Piaget's findings. Elkind, perhaps the leading American researcher working with Piaget's theories, investigated the development of quantitative thinking of 80 children aged four to seven years. (1961a) He divided quantitative thinking into three types:

1. gross—the perception of single relations between uncoordinated objects (longer than, wider than)
2. intensive—the perception of quantity relationships taken two by two (longer and wider, taller and thicker)
3. extensive—the perception of unit relations between objects, which must be attained by abstraction or reasoning (e.g., $x = \frac{1}{2}y$).

Sticks, liquids, and beads were the materials used to test quantitative thinking levels. The children were also tested with the Wechsler Intelligence Scale for Children. Elkind found high correlations between their levels of quantitative thought and their scores on the Picture Arrangement, Arithmetic, and Coding subtests, which also require conceptual organization.

Elkind set different minimum requirements for success at each of three stages: comparisons of gross quantity; comparisons of gross or intensive quantity; and comparisons of gross, intensive, or extensive quantity. Children at age four tended to succeed at the first stage, the five-year-olds usually succeeded at the second stage, and the six- and seven-year-olds usually succeeded at the third stage. These results suggest an orderly progression in the development of quantitative thinking and confirm Piaget's earlier results.

Suggested Activity

Devise tests for quantitative thinking, using sticks, liquids, and beads as Elkind did. Try your tests out on children in the four to eight year age range. If your results do not agree with Elkind's, discuss some possible reasons for the differences.

New approaches to concept development

A point that disturbs a number of students and teachers when reading about Piaget's theories and the studies that support (or refute) his findings is that there seems to be great emphasis on the relationship between concept attainment and particular ages. There seems to be too little latitude allowed for individual differences in intelligence, interests, and experiences. We have all known young children who appeared to be unusually perceptive for their age about relationships between people or objects and were able to proffer a realistic solution to problems that adults could not see. We also have known older children, exposed to similar influences, who lacked such abilities. This practical experience seems to be at odds with the Piagetian timetable and sets up a disharmony within us.

Two approaches will be used to demonstrate how this disharmony can be investigated and reduced. Both deal with logical thinking or the stage of formal operations, which Piaget has said occurs in early adolescence. Muuss (1967) believes that this stage is related primarily to the maturation of the nervous system that accompanies puberty, although interaction experiences with physical realities and influences of the social environment on the adolescent are also important. Individual differences in logical thinking, then, could be explained in large part by individual differences in maturation, which is a genetic point of view not too far from Piaget's own. Yudin (1967) postulates, however, that intelligence needs to be considered as it is related to mental age, and this is not the same as maturation of the nervous system. He tested twelve- to sixteen-year-olds of varying intelligence levels and found that both age and intelligence affected the level of logical thinking.

> ... For the individuals less favorably endowed, the sequence of development indicated no significant changes from age 12 to age 14, but significant changes from age 14 to age 16. For the high intelligence sub-group, the results pointed to almost linear development with increasing age being positively correlated with increasing efficiency. Thus, even at age 12, the high intelligence sub-group was functioning at or above the level that the middle intelligence sub-group failed to reach until age 14. (pp. 144–45)

The recognition of individual differences in intellectual ability appears to be a more all-encompassing explanation for differences in adolescent thinking than the more simplistic developmental view and may be a more satisfactory explanation, as well, for experiment results that refute Piaget's theories. Even with younger children, divided by age (6, 10, and 14 years) and intelligence (IQ 90–109 and 110+), differences in concept attainment as a function of intelligence rather than age have been demonstrated. (Osler and Fivel, 1961) Freyberg (1966), too, found that concept development, particularly as related to arithmetical computation, problem-solving, and spelling, was more highly correlated with mental age than with chronological age, six to nine years.

This is not to say that age has no bearing on concept attainment. Sigel (1959), for example, differentiates between the *perceptual* or sensorimotor abstract behavior of young children and the *conceptual* or organized behavior of older children. Studying lower middle-class boys aged seven, nine, and eleven years, Sigel gave them a variety of sorting tasks to perform. There was a distinct and significant trend for a decrease in perceptual organization and an increase in conceptual behavior to occur as age increased. Nor can we deny the role of experience in concept attainment. Indeeed, greater progress results when the learner discovers the link between events than when he is informed of it. (Sinclair, 1973) Goodnow (1969) demonstrated that kindergarten children permitted to look at and handle objects were more able to give "nonstandard" uses for the objects than the children permitted only to look at them. Her subjects were 48 upper middle-class children in a private school and 80 children from various socioeconomic backgrounds who attended public schools. The stimuli were a fresh piece of Kleenex, a large new paper clip, and a new eight-inch screwdriver with a yellow plastic handle. Standard responses concerning the paper clip, for example, involved its function of holding items together, where as the "nonstandard" uses included using the clip as a piece of wire or bending it into other shapes to construct things. As Goodnow concluded, "The results raise questions about the effects of various modes of contact with stimulus material in any study of thinking and the role of manipulative activity in development." (p. 201) Manipulation apparently encourages greater fluidity of thought, while looking and verbal description appear to restrict thinking. (p. 211)

Focus 9–4

In accord with Goodnow's study is the proposition that children can learn quite "advanced" concepts if given the opportunity to do so at a manipulative level initially. A beautiful demonstration of this is given by Bruner (1966), citing a small-scale experiment in which four bright eight-year-olds learned quadratic equations with the aid of manipulating building materials. Many of the newer mathematics programs provide similar opportunities as early as first grade, depending on the ability of the young learner to master concepts first at a concrete level and somewhat later at symbolic levels. Notations in primary workbooks such as $3 + \square = 7$ or $8 + 7 = 8 + (2 + 5) = \square$ illustrate this point.

Social studies, too, can be presented to elementary school learners in such a way that concepts not ordinarily developed until middle or late adolescence are formulated much earlier. A case in point is a course for fifth-graders called "Man: A Course of Study" (MACOS), developed by Bruner and others at Harvard. Four techniques were used, as Bruner put it, to ". . . rescue the phenomena of social life from familiarity, without at the same time making it all seem 'primitive' and bizarre." (p. 92) These included contrast, an old but valuable method; "stimulation and use of informed guessing, hypothesis making, conjectural procedures"; active participation through simulation groups and games; and the stimulation of self-consciousness as part of thinking. (pp. 92–93)

An unsolicited testimonial for this approach came from the writer's son when he was participating in the MACOS program. The testimonial took the form of frequent, rather excited comments about the material presented, often accompanied by rather wide-eyed wonder that the Eskimos have much in common with us. Motivation for further learning was unusually high, a clear affirmation that the goals set by the Harvard team had been met, at least with one student.

Despite the positive response of students to the MACOS program, some of its components were strongly criticized in the mid-1970s. These included highly structured directives in the teacher's manual and descriptions of infanticide and shabby treatment of the aged Eskimos in the content. Further, Weber (1975) charged that ten-year-olds were too young to understand the concepts of man and society presented in the program.

Mini-summary

To summarize the development of concept formation, we might go back to infancy where the world is a confusion of visual, auditory, tactual, olfactory, and other stimuli. Through maturation and learning, the infant begins to sort out some stimuli from others, categorizing those to which he listens, those at which he looks, the edible from the nonedible, and so on. This is the most fundamental stage of concept formation. Through experience, which is learning, and with the growth of language, he begins to develop concepts of weight, number, space, and so on. Piaget, in his experiments, found that the level of concept attainment appeared to be related to age. Other researchers later questioned his results, for, as we have seen, they found that concept attainment appears to be related to mental rather than chronological age and also varies with the opportunities for experiences necessary to formulate the different concepts.

It is obvious, therefore, that there is a need to expose the child to a wide variety of stimuli during his early years if he is to have a foundation upon which to build concepts. Several researchers have gone so far as to say that, if the child lacks these opportunities at various critical stages in his first six years, he may never "catch up" or will at best be retarded in his thinking abilities at school entrance and for several years more.

To teach these various concepts to learners, you can provide a multitude of materials for manipulation and subsequent "discovery." Questions to learners about how two or more items are related will also help them to develop concepts. Demonstrations, with weights and scales, for example, provide another means of helping learners to acquire concepts.

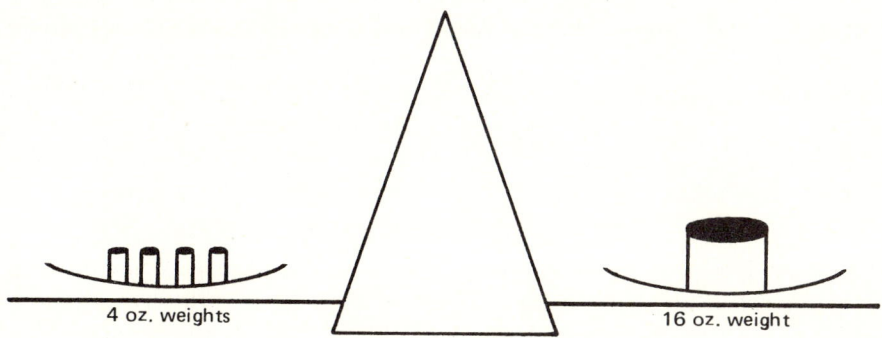

Conservation of weight demonstration. **Figure 9.1**

In Figure 9.1, some children might initially say that the 16-ounce weight is heavier than the four smaller weights together because of its size. Other children might say that the four weights are heavier because there are more of them. If, instead of weights, you wanted to be more concrete, you could use a pound of butter, divided into quarters, to demonstrate the point.

Bruner and others, while supporting much of Piaget's work, nevertheless assert that it is possible to teach young children complicated concepts in a simple manner without waiting for a magic number of years to pass to bring the child to a stage of logical thinking. The concept can be reintroduced in later years, in more and more complex fashion, as the child is better able to deal with more factors at a single time. Such a "spiral curriculum" was demonstrated in the fields of mathematics and social sciences in this section.

Teachers should recognize, also, that some children tend to be abstract thinkers while others remain more concrete in their thinking, even in higher grades. The ability to deal with abstract or complex concepts tends to increase as children move from grades four to eight (Meinke, George, and Wilkinson, 1975), but pupils differ in their basic conceptual style. If teachers are aware of these differences, they can use this knowledge in planning individualized instruction and other curriculum needs.

As adults, we tend to be able to verbalize our concepts. We can classify objects, ideas, people (sometimes being rather rigid in our "pigeon-holing") and can usually perceive that change in shape, for example, is only an illusion in relation to mass or weight. To be able to think about or to state these concepts and "conservations" in words is an achievement in itself.

THINKING

We may regard thinking in a number of different ways. There is general agreement that thinking is a symbolic activity and that it may be verbal or nonverbal. Thinking may also be dichotomized as subjective (egocentric) or objective, or as random or systematic. It may also be qualitatively differentiated as cognitive, memorative, evaluative, convergent productive, and divergent productive. Let's look at these diverse descriptions a bit more carefully.

Clearly verbal thinking involves the use of language. However, prelinguistic children, those who are very young, also appear to think. In fact, one often hears the comment that you can almost "see the wheels going round." in a tot's head as he prepares to engage in some activity (frequently a bit of mischief). Such littles ones apparently "think" in terms of picture-images. Sometimes adults think this way, too, when they "see" pictures in their minds, which are frequently followed by the use of language to describe them.

Subjective and objective thinking

Subjective or egocentric thought involves relating what is being thought about to oneself, either in terms of how one feels about an event or person, or how it affects the self. It is a kind of autistic thinking that is not necessarily abnormal and that is engaged in at various times by almost everyone. It is, for example, more concern with how a relative's illness affects oneself than with its possible effects on the sick person. If the teacher appears to be in a "bad mood," the ecogentric thinker wonders how this will affect him rather than why the teacher is grumpy today or how the mood can be changed. Objective thinking, on the other hand, divorces the self from the problem. An example of this distinction might be seen in the responses to a word-association test, where the subject is asked to respond to stimulus words with the first thought that comes to mind.

Stimulus word	*Subjective*	*Objective*
lamp	my desk	light
boy	dirty	young
mother	loving	woman
book	boring	reading

Children generally think in egocentric terms, as do some adults who have never outgrown the practice. Adolescents and adults, however, should be able to focus on the task at hand in a more objective way when there is no need to relate the task to themselves.

Random thinking is also known as associative thinking and/or daydreaming. The psychoanalyst asks his or her patient to think in this way because one random thought leading to another frequently evokes an important, but repressed, situation that has influenced subsequent behavior. It is also the kind of thinking that we associate with relaxation (as in lying on the grass contemplating a beautiful summer sky) and that we enjoy for its own sake. It *can* lead to systematic or ordered, directed thinking, when we are seeking solutions to a problem. Generally, however, the latter thinking process proceeds at a higher level of consciousness than associative thinking because we are progressing, for example, by steps: "First this happens. Second, we respond in this way under one set of circumstances or in another way under another set of circumstances. Third, the outcome of this action would be . . ." and so on.

Random and systematic thinking

Cognitive thinking is also related to consciousness in that we *know*, are aware of, recognize, what is happening. Concept formation is one form of cognitive thinking. Symbolic representation and mental manipulation of objects or situations are also forms of cognitive thinking. Memorative thought, on the other hand, involves recall of past experiences and past learning. It is the kind of thinking most frequently demanded on exams and in the classroom. Evaluative thinking, another intellectual operation, concerns judging, comparing, assigning values, and similar activities, all of which appear to be learned through experience. Collectively, these three types of thinking are probably the most common kinds of thinking that occur in schools. We read or listen and acquire information (cognitive), then we recall the information upon request (memorative), and at times we may be asked to consider its effects on some other bit of information (evaluative). These are legitimate, necessary activities in the classroom, but they are not the only ways in which thinking can be used to become an "educated" person.

Cognitive, memorative, and evaluative thinking

In what ways could you explain cognitive, memorative, and evaluative thinking to an interested high school student?

Question

Productive thoughts, both convergent and divergent, on the other hand, are not as frequently encountered in the population generally or among student assignments specifically.

Productive thinking

Convergent and/or divergent thinking may be used in problem-solving. In both cases, the problem-solver needs to have a variety of experiences on which he may draw to find possible solutions. He also needs to have cognitive flexibility, that is, the ability to shift from one track of thought to another. However, there is a difference between convergent and divergent thinking. In the former, the resources of information, experience, and flex-

Focus 9–5

ibility are brought to bear to find a single correct answer. To illustrate, let us use the example of a crossword puzzle.

        1. Rock ☐☐☐☐

There is only one "right" answer that will fit, although many definitions and associations come to mind. These might include:

stone	N'Roll
swing	crag
Hudson	agate
candy	Gibraltar, etc.

Some are rejected because they have the wrong number of letters, others because they don't mesh with other words in the puzzle.

In divergent thinking, by contrast, there are many possible correct responses to the stimulus or problem. In fact, with practice and effort, one can increase the frequency or quantity of such responses. Taking the same stimulus word, "rock," we can ask: "How many uses are there for a rock?" and proceed to enumerate:

weight—hold papers down, keep car from rolling

weapon—break glass, throw at attacker

ornament—decorate garden, floor of aquarium

construction—build stairway, shelter, wall, outdoor fireplace

heat to keep feet warm

as a headrest

etc.

Diagrammatically, we might represent the difference in these two types of productive thinking in this way:

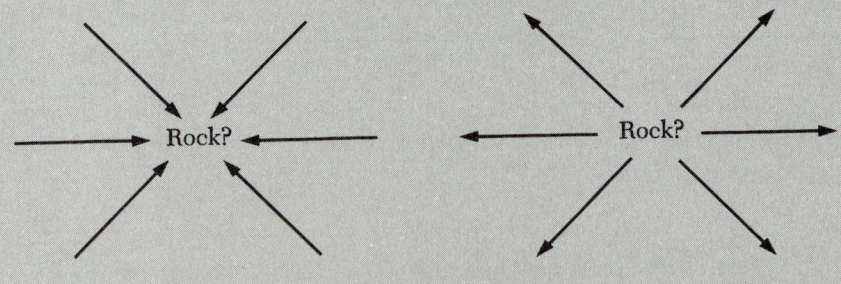

Convergent   Divergent

In terms of teacher-pupil relationships, you will often find the convergent thinker more acceptable in most classrooms. This student, according to many psychologists, is more docile, more retentive, and tends more often to seek the single "correct" answer to intellectual problems. He also tends to achieve better on standardized and teacher-made tests that are designed to have a limited number of correct answers. Although convergent thinking is useful and appropriate in many learning situations, it is also dangerous in that it can inhibit students from trying to find new ways to interpret or relate information. The divergent thinker, on the other hand, is often perceived as a daydreamer or as a troublemaker. She is so concerned with finding novel, experimental, or multiple answers to intellectual problems that she bombards the teacher with questions and may choose less obvious but more original and correct answers to test questions, which are then marked "wrong." Divergent thinkers generally are more fluent and more flexible than most of their peers and hence may be more creative. The threat to the status quo in the classroom in such cases is obvious, particularly where the teacher is less than comfortable with novelty or originality.

The difference in test performance and other variables as related to these two types of thinking has been demonstrated in several studies. Clark, Veldman, and Thorpe (1965), for example, studied the test and personnel records of 192 bright junior high school pupils. The California Test of Mental Maturity was used as a measure of convergent thinking (group test, multiple-choice format), and the mean IQ for the subjects was 124. A composite measure was used to assess divergent thinking ability. Among other findings, Clark, et al., discovered that the subjects high in divergent thinking scored higher on tests of word fluency and reading ability. Biographical data, however, indicated that those high in convergent thinking had higher grades, less trouble with schoolwork, and more parental interest in their attending college. It is apparent from this study that high scores on tests of one kind of thinking do not necessarily mean high scores on tests of other kinds of thinking, and it is possible that those with higher scores on tests of convergent thinking were more acceptable to their teachers and their parents in academic realms. The divergent thinkers may simply be too involved with thinking round and round a specific problem to focus on the "right" answer.

You are well acquainted with test-taking atmospheres—time limits, tensions, and anxieties abound. Might these explain the disparate performance of the creative? Adams (1968) studied the effects of a variety of test-taking settings in relation to one aspect of divergent thinking—spontaneous flexibility. He had 112 subjects, aged 14–16 years. The experimental testing conditions, each with its own test instructions, were competition, free of competition, and free of competition with open receptivity to ideas. The pretest included standard creativity subtests: Consequences, Unusual Uses, Object Naming, and Uses for a Brick, as measures. In discussing the results, Adams wrote, "The indications are that the competitive-evaluative atmosphere commonly found in the classroom does not allow for flexibility in thinking but requires rigidity and conformity toward *right* answers if approval and reward are to result." (p. 191–92) Freedom from competition resulted in significantly improved performance on the flexibility tests, particularly when coupled with open receptivity. This is not to be construed as saying that students do not have to learn "right" answers. There is no question, for example, that pure water is composed of 2 atoms of hydrogen plus 1 atom of oxygen, or that, in base ten, $2 + 2 = 4$. It is in the areas of interpretation of literature, or hypotheses concerning causes of historical events, or exploration of unmapped scientific problems, that open receptivity to ideas becomes important. This is where the creative student should be able to achieve. If asked to list six causes of the American Revolution, he should be able to give six thoughtful reasons without losing credit because his six do not exactly match his teacher's six. Who can say that his six are less correct, if based on rational thought, than someone else's six reasons?

It might be appropriate to consider here another approach to the relationship between divergent thinking and academic performance. Smith's paper on IQ, creavitity, and cognitive learning examines the relationships among Bloom's six cognitive processes (*Taxonomy of Educational Objectives: Cognitive Domain*), intelligence, and creativity as found in eleventh-grade students of varying intelligence (67–143 IQ). His hypotheses state that ". . . intelligence is sufficient to account for the observed variation on the Knowledge, Comprehension, Application, and Analysis subtests, while intelligence *and creativity* [italics added] are necessary to explain performance on the Synthesis and Evaluation subtests." (Smith, 1970, p. 58) The statistical analysis supported the hypotheses. The first four cognitive objectives are commonly tested in the classroom and on achievement tests. Synthesis and Evaluation, however, are more rarely evoked, to the apparent detriment of students who go beyond the usual in their thinking. Smith suggests that standardized achievement tests may ignore these two processes, which would explain the weak relationship between creativity and achievement. (p. 60) One might go a step further and hypothesize that teacher-made tests tend to follow the same pattern with similar negative effects on the grade point average. In an earlier study, Westcott (1962) indicated that he was thinking along these same lines: ". . . individuals who are said to be 'creative' may well be carrying on a special variety of inference—inference which bridges a great gap rather than a small one, and reaches a conclusion which does not obviously follow from the information, but which subsequently can be demonstrated to be appropriate, adequate, suitable and sound." (p. 5) You can easily understand how such a mental leap might threaten a fairly unimaginative teacher.

Focus 9–6

Westcott evaluated his subjects along two dimensions, information demand and level of success, in a creativity test situation.

	Information demand	
Success	*Low*	*High*
High	1	2
Low	3	4

His statement of who may be considered creative (above) fits people in category 1, who he says are true intuitive thinkers, by definition. The other three categories are more familiar to teachers:

2. those who demand much information and formulate consistently sound conclusions are characterized as cautious, successful problem-solvers;
3. those who request little information and consistently fail are seen as wild guessers; and
4. those who demand a great deal of information and still fail are labeled cautious failures. (p. 14)

Those in category 2 are frequently regarded as ideal students, and are, in the sense that they conform to a traditional academic pattern, which earns them the approval of certain teachers and administrators. Students in categories 3 and 4 also conform to the pattern. It is the intuitive or creative student who upsets the orderliness of the classroom. Since their viewpoints are rather individualistic and unconventional, Westcott believes that they need ". . . rather special treatment if their intuitive problem solving capacities are to be fostered to their fullest, and their desirable talents are to be brought to bear on problems meaningful to society." (p. 31)

It is this idea of special treatment that often creates a problem. The teacher says the class is too large to permit this, or the time too short, or it is antidemocratic to give special treatment. Is it not, then, also antidemocratic to give special treatment to the slow learner? Is there time enough to write a composition? If so, why not on a divergent thinking topic rather than on last summer's vacation? If projects are assigned to a class of whatever size, why must everyone do the same one all the time?

LANGUAGE DEVELOPMENT

How does "da-da" become "Daddy"? How does "oo-ga-bee" become "I'm glad to see you" or "Je suis heureuse de vous voir"? Linguists has found that the earliest infantile verbalizations are quite similar the world over. Selection and repetition of certain of the sounds by attending adults and older children result in the reinforcement of some syllables and the gradual extinction of others. Thus, the originally meaningless vocalization gradually takes on significance as part of some language.

If you listen to a young child who is just beginning to use words as a means of communication, you will find that one word, usually a verb or noun, conveys a whole thought. 'Eat!" for example, can mean "I want to eat now," or "I want to eat that (cookie, clothespin, candy etc.)." "Daddy" can mean "I see Daddy," "I want Daddy," "Here comes Daddy," and so on. The thought obviously has to be deduced from the situational context in which the telegraphic verbalization occurs. Yet somehow, two or three years later, this same child can speak in sentences of several words organized in fairly correct grammatical array. Plurals, verb forms, and possessives are all used in adult-like form, assuming that the child has heard them used correctly. Even in cases where family members do not use language correctly, the child may listen to enough "good" language on television to gain competence. This assumption follows from research findings that indicate that we learn language largely through imitation.

Focus 9–7

> A most delightful experiment is one in which Berko studied the acquisition of language forms. For example, the child is shown a picture of a bird-like creature and is told or reads, "This is a wug." A second "wug" appears, so "Now there are two of them. There are two _____." The young school-age subjects *knew* that there were two "wugs." Similarly, they added "ed" to indicate past tense for verbs. (Berko, 1958)
>
> The lack of logic in the English language, however, leads children to use overgeneralizations of "rules" with words which sound alike, as "house-houses," therefore, "mouse-mouses." Or "sing-sang," therefore, "bring-brang."

Acquisition of language

There is debate about whether children have an innate sense of language, whether there is an innate linguistic system underlying *all* spoken languages (Chomsky), or whether learning (including reinforcement) is indeed the key to the acquisition of language construction (Skinner). Language development can be placed on a continuum, like other aspects of development, without regard to the source of development, and children's speech and language diagnosed as being at one point or another on the continuum. Thus the child who generalizes grammatical rules more often, or who is very repetitive in speech, would be diagnosed as having a younger developmental age in language than one who uses language more correctly.

The source of language acquisition and the effect of environmental influences on language development are issues important to education. They are highly relevant to our philosophies of early childhood and remedial education and to the ways in which we teach reading.

Chomsky (1968) theorized that there are genetically determined language universals that enable children to say words in combinations that they have never heard. He points out that children from a wide variety of backgrounds begin to use language at about the same age, and in similar grammatical forms. Skinner (1957) on the other hand, believes that children learn language by conditioning (shaping, reinforcement, and imitation). A third point of view ". . . is that infants learn their language by first determining, independent of language, the meaning which a speaker intends to convey to them, and by then working out the relationship between the meaning and the language." (Macnamara, 1972, p. 1) Although Macnamara's thesis is closer to Chomsky's theory than Skinner's, he is less certain of the common structural elements in all languages. According to Bever (1972), language structure ". . . is molded by an interaction of the laws of thought, learning, speech perception, and speech production." (p. 100) Thus, even if there are universal language elements, the child must learn how to use them appropriately in his own culture.

From whatever source language develops, it rather quickly becomes the medium by which the child can express his thoughts. Language development, concept formation, and communication become intertwined. A case in point is Beilin and Kagan's study of "Pluralization rules and the conceptualization of number." (1969) Using preschool subjects, aged three to five years, Beilin and Kagan tested 68 white middle-class and 10 nonwhite children of above average intelligence on their knowledge of language pluralization rules and their ability to indicate correctly one or two objects in pictures. The subjects were able to handle the number concepts well, generally, but had some difficulties with pluralization rules, particularly in the case of verbs. Those who failed on the tasks were given training. Verb-pluralization training led to improved performance, but concept training did not lead to (i.e., transfer) improvement in the use of plurals. Beilin and Kagan concluded, on the basis of the assessment and training studies, that the ". . . data suggest that in natural social (principally familial) environments young children are more apt to acquire number concepts earlier." (p. 704) They also pointed out that an understanding of concepts is not vital to using them, but that if the pluralization rules are not understood, then the child may not use appropriate language until he does understand the rules. That is, he may be able to count up to five, for example, but avoid saying "Five people are in the car" because he doesn't understand the mechanics of language sufficiently to be certain whether it's "Five people *is* . . ." or "Five people *are*. . . ." This is something like our own problem of speaking in an inadequately learned foreign language where we've forgotten correct verb endings for the past tense. As a result, we say everything in the present tense or stop speaking.

Abstract and concrete language

Although we generally think of young children as using specific or concrete language, and older children as using general and abstract terms, Brown's delightful and insightful paper on vocabulary development indicates that this view of language development may be erroneous. (1958) Which is the more common term for a young child to use: "dog" or "poodle"? Obviously, the former. "Dog," however, is more abstract than "poodle." On the other hand, frequently all men are called "Daddy," a very specific term used as a general one, until men are differentiated into milkmen, brothers, uncles, and mailmen. Then children may revert to a more abstract level, categorizing these persons as "males" or "men." In effect, Brown has shown that there may be two levels of abstraction, one based on lack of differentiation and the other occurring after differentiation. Both children and adults enlarge their vocabularies as the acquisition of information brings them from over-generalization to the specific and then on to a new higher-level abstraction. This is a process largely encouraged by surrounding adults, including parents and teachers. As pre-psychology students, for example, "learning" may have meant that which took place in school. Then, in introductory psychology, you acquired the information that there are many kinds of learning that occur both inside and outside of the school setting—social learning, latent learning, classical conditioning, instrumental conditioning, memorization, and so on. Now, when you use the abstraction "learning," you have a more sophisticated concept than you did originally.

Similarly, in the growth of sentences and syntax, the influence of significant adults is apparent. The baby says "Daddy bye-bye," and the mother says "Daddy is going bye-bye," thus demonstrating a more acceptable language form and enlarging the child's perception of how to say things. Since children do learn much of their language by imitation, next time the child may say "Daddy *going* bye-bye" which, while still not quite correct English, is an expansion of the earlier construction. Parents correct verb tenses, plurals, double negatives, and other mistakes as the child's language develops, so that the entering first-grader usually speaks quite acceptably.

Interpretation of language

The child may, however, become so enchanted with imitating and learning new and larger words that she uses them with minimal comprehension. Again, there is a problem of moving back to a more concrete level. For example, the youngster hears the term "liaison man," used in the sense of a link between two groups of people, a kind of human bridge. Without further information, she may also refer to a certain kind of belt as a "liaison" belt, or to the George Washington Bridge as a "liaison" between New York and New Jersey. It is obviously not enough to hear and imitate words; one must also comprehend their very special uses, especially when used in idiomatic expressions and proverbs.

To illustrate: ask a five-year-old what "A stitch in time saves nine" means. The most frequent response will probably involve a vague reference to sewing. Being able to generalize from the proverb is an ability that apparently develops much later than we think. Piaget estimates that this ability isn't developed until well into his stage of formal operations, about age fourteen or fifteen years. It seems pointless, then, to be forever quoting proverbs to elementary school children who may parrot them but otherwise profit very little from them.

Focus 9–8

Think of as many proverbs as you can. Your list probably includes such old "favorites" as:

1. You can lead a horse to water, but you can't make him drink.
2. A penny saved is a penny earned.
3. A stitch in time saves nine.
4. Penny-wise, pound foolish.
5. You can't teach an old dog new tricks.

Suggested Activity

Ask several students of different ages to tell you what your proverbs mean, and compare their responses.

According to Friedes, Fredenthal, Grisell, and Cohen (1963),

> If a subject interprets a proverb by responding in the most literal, concrete terms, i.e., by merely repeating the proverb, he attains a maximal score on Information and a minimal score on Generalization. A mature interpretation requires S to move away from the terms given in the proverb, to treat them as symbols of a class of events (Generalization). But this class of events must bear a socially comprehensible relationship to the original terms to preserve the meaning of the proverb (Information). (pp. 1052–53)

Subjects in the study were 390 senior high school and 333 junior high school students in an industrial community. Their responses to a proverbs test were grouped cross-sectionally by grade-level, and showed a significant increase in average G (Generalization) score by grade but not in average I (Information) scores. Generalization scores were positively correlated with IQ at all grade levels, but Information scores were positively correlated with IQ only in the upper grades. (Note: The interpretation of proverbs is a task at several levels of the Stanford-Binet intelligence test and is considered to be an indication of the ability to think abstractly.)

A study at the college level, using the multiple-choice answer form of Gorham's Proverbs Test, revealed, however, that correct choice (Generalization) scores had relatively low correlation with a variety of factors. These included term standing, cumulative grade point average, grades in required English composition courses, and three measures of creativity for an N = 165. The coefficients of correlation ranged from −.215 to +.089. The only moderately high relationship (r = .457) was between the Proverbs Test scores and SAT Verbal scores. There seems to be little relationship between the ability to interpret proverbs and the ability to perform academically in the first two years of college. (Schwartz, 1975a)

The point of this discussion is that proverbs are composed of very familiar and specific words, but their interpretation in the context of a proverb is highly abstract. It is one of the tasks of language development to move from literal to abstract usage in many situations, and this is a result, apparently, not of imitation alone, but also of maturation of cognitive abilities.

Another example of how language development requires movement back and forth along the concrete-abstract continuum is seen in psychological and medical diagnosis. Abstractly, a person is sick or well. Concretely, he has specific symptoms that can and must be identified. These are then put together as a new abstraction, or diagnostic label, which conveys specific information in a "shorthand" fashion to others in the same field. This, too, reflects a combination of language and concept development.

Bilingualism

Let's move on to a consideration of how bilingualism interacts with cognitive development. We are becoming increasingly familiar with so-called bilinguals who have great difficulty in learning in our schools. They are "so-called" bilinguals because supposedly they speak their native language, Spanish, for example, *and* English. In fact, they rarely speak or comprehend English and may speak their native tongue with a minimum of sophistication. For these pupils, learning is difficult in either language, but might be easier in the native language, at least initially. That is, a subject as specific as arithmetic can be taught in Spanish and the comprehension of what to do when one sees "$2 + 2 = ?$" will remain even when one says "Two and two equal what?" instead of "¿Dos y dos son?" Similarly, when faced with minimally English-speaking students in the class, concrete historical or geographical facts can be taught in Spanish so as to minimize the academic retardation of the children. Simultaneously, of course, they should be learning English as a second language.

There is debate, however, about the value of this approach when the child speaks nonstandard English. Hall, Turner, and Russell (1973) tested urban and rural, black and white, lower- and middle-class children in grades 1 and 4. Their conclusions were that ". . . it seems highly questionable that speaking the Negro nonstandard English dialect hampers standard English comprehension and that teaching standard English as a second language would probably have minimum educational benefits." (p. 157) Other educators urge the teaching of English as a second language because of the long-range economic and political implications.

Both the direct method (introducing reading in the second language after oral training in the second language) and the native language approach (introducing reading first in the native language, then in the second language) have advantages. (Engle, 1975, pp. 287–91) There are several factors to consider, however, in deciding which approach to follow with "bilingual" children. These include: transferability of language skills (proactive facilitation or inhibition?), the child's stage of development when the second language is introduced, ethnic group membership of the teacher, and the functions of the two languages in the community. (Engle, 1975, pp. 320–21)

Awareness that there are some five million children for whom English is not the native language, and that this leads to inequalities in educational opportunity, has led to a wide variety of programs for both children and teachers under Federal and state legislation. Some districts send the teachers to school for instruction in Chinese, Greek, Choctaw, Spanish, or another language. Some establish English as a Second Language (ESL) centers to which all children needing assistance are brought for part-time instruction. (Levenson, 1975b) Other districts operate bilingual-/bicultural programs within the school, recognizing and encouraging the benefits of differences. (Cooper, 1975)

True bilingualism, on the other hand, implies almost equal levels of mastery in two languages. A study at the University of Alberta (Canada) with monolingual and bilingual first-graders also suggests that bilingualism has favorable effects on intellectual functioning generally. The 50 children in each group were tested on Piaget's concepts of conservation and measurement of length, and it was found that the bilingual group had a significantly higher mean score on the conservation test than the monolingual group. (Liedtke and Nelson, 1969)

Concrete words frequently have similar associations in different languages, but abstract words usually do not. In our own language, indeed, words such as "love," "peace," and "freedom" mean different things to different people—all English-speaking. Experiments at MIT and the Center for Cognitive Studies have shown that, especially at abstract levels, the bilingual person comprehends information in a particular context in which it was learned, including the language in which it was learned. These studies help us to discover something about how information is processed. Subjects were taught information in one language and tested in their other language. The results, which dealt with the acquisition, storage, and retrieval of the information presented, indicated strongly the influence of the total learning situation on these operations. (Kolers, 1968) As in the case of the first-graders in Alberta, we can see that concrete information is moved rather easily from one language to another, but a high degree of comprehension and linguistic ability is also needed apparently to transfer abstract concepts from their original contexts.

A more common problem for us is simply to *learn* a second language. There is a considerable amount of evidence that demonstrates that second-language learning is easier for young children than for adolescents. For one thing, they are less conscious of tenses, pluralization rules, and other grammatical strictures than are adolescents. They tend to imitate the teacher much as they imitated the mother in learning their first language. Penfield and Roberts (1959) also point out that the younger child has more flexible vocal apparatus and is, in addition, less self-conscious than the adolescent. A more positive attitude toward second-language learning is often present in younger children too, for there is a mystery and a magic about foreign languages that appeals to them (as in the outburst of "pig Latin" and related nonlanguages in the early grades), but that is not present in the adolescent. The older the student, the more he tends to get bogged down in the memorization of vocabulary lists and the study of syntax. As suggested here, it is easier for children to learn concrete terms, for example, "perro" or "chien" for dog, than it is for them to translate a proverb correctly from one language to the other. For the young child, second-language learning is "fun," while for the older student it is too frequently an onerous task. This may be due to a growing rigidity in some areas, or to a resistance to return to such basics at the "advanced" age of fourteen when abstract thinking is still new and exciting.

Lambert and Tucker (1973), reporting on English-Canadian children in French-language classes from kindergarten on, found that the children had reached functional bilingualism quite comfortably by grades four and five. In comparison with English-language control subjects, the experimental subjects were equal or superior in cognitive development and self-concept. Furthermore, their attitudes toward French-Canadians and the French language were highly positive.

The techniques of teaching foreign languages vary from a very traditional vocabulary-grammar-reading-writing approach to the newer audiovisual (filmstrip and tapes) method or to an "immersion" technique where the student is in the foreign-language environment full-time. No one technique is best for every student. The traditional approach is well structured, but rarely stimulating in content. The audiovisual methods are often presented with too little time to "digest" the vocabulary, but do usually result in better conversational ability. An additional handicap observed in practice, however, is that it is more difficult for an absentee to make up missed work in this approach. The "immersion" technique is literally one where you "sink-or-swim." Many students may sink, despairing of ever understanding the language or of being understood by others in the environment. On the other hand, those who "swim" appear to master accent, inflection, and vocabulary with long-lasting results. As with any other newly learned skill, however, continuing practice is vital.

It is possible to have second-language learning broaden one's English vocabulary, but this transfer occurs usually as the result of conscious effort. Learning Latin will not in itself expand an English vocabulary, but repeated encouragement or direction by the teacher to try to define "advanced" English words, or even to translate unknown Romance language vocabulary by seeking out the Latin roots, will aid such expansion. In later years, then, unknown words will be more easily defined and integrated into one's vocabulary. As already indicated, however, this comes about because someone points the way and not as an inherent by-product of foreign language study itself.

In summary, then, language development is related to concept development, although the two do not necessarily progress at the same rate or in the same ways. Children learn words largely by imitation, but expand their vocabularies as their experiences grow in number and complexity. Their concepts, and their vocabularies, shift between the concrete and the abstract depending upon the situation and do not appear to be unidirectional. Bilingualism is a problem when neither language is adequately learned, but can contribute positively to language development when the child is taught to transfer concepts from one language to the other.

SUMMARY

To develop from the reflexive, know-nothing, nonthinking infant to the creative thinker is a task of considerable proportions. It is, as we have seen in this chapter, a result of maturational processes plus experience *plus opportunity*.

Concept formation, our first topic, focused strongly on the theories of Piaget, theories that stress maturation but also include an awareness that children need to be active participants in the process of building concepts. Studies reviewed in this section of the chapter involved conservation of quantity, weight, mass, and volume, particularly. The question of individual differences in acquiring these concepts of conservation, a matter clearly of great importance in educational psychology, was also discussed.

Equally important to the general topic of thinking is language development. Here again, maturation plays an essential role, especially in the early years, but experience and opportunity are vital to real growth. The interaction of language and concept development was demonstrated, both in terms of interpretation of ideas and in terms of bilingualism.

To summarize, we have been concerned in this section with different kinds of thinking and thinkers, with special emphasis on productive thinking. Such emphasis was necessary because its importance in the classroom has been underrated and its effects on achievement have been only recently brought to the awareness of educators. We are all too accustomed to memorative, cognitive, convergent, and evaluative thinking. They are frequently conformist, traditional, and acceptable. A recurrent theme today, however, is that these qualities are not enough to prepare for tomorrow. The divergent thinker will be needed to help to solve the unknown problems that lie ahead. This brings us to the next chapter, in which we consider some of the problems and techniques of problem-solving.

Preview

INTRODUCTION

PROBLEM-SOLVING
    COMPREHENSION OF THE PROBLEM
    COLLECTION OF INFORMATION
    INCUBATION, ILLUMINATION, AND EVALUATION
    OBSTACLES TO SOLUTIONS
    STIMULATION OF PRODUCTIVE THINKING

CREATIVITY
    DEFINITIONS OF CREATIVITY
    CHARACTERISTICS OF CREATIVE PEOPLE
    MEASUREMENT OF CREATIVE THINKING
    STUDIES OF CREATIVE BEHAVIOR
    IMPLICATIONS FOR EDUCATION

SUMMARY

10

Creativity and Problem-Solving

INTRODUCTION

If you can learn, use, and teach the techniques of problem-solving, you will be much better prepared (as will your own students) to face the great unknown questions of tomorrow. Change is so rapid, and the future so unpredictable, that not only do we not know what challenges lie ahead, but there will probably be few if any precedents for solving them. In the light of this fact, the importance of having thinkers skilled in problem-solving becomes self-evident. Some of the most skilled in this area are truly creative. That is, they find unusual solutions to existing problems and often are the first to be aware of new problems. We will, therefore, try to discover what sets the creative thinker apart from his peers as well as what can be done to maximize the creative thinking of less skilled thinkers.

PROBLEM-SOLVING

Problem-solving, as seen here, is applied productive thinking. It is not reasonable, however, to present a problem to children or adults with requests to think of a solution. A number of obstacles can intervene between presentation and solution that may, in fact, preclude the individual's ever finding a solution. Initially, it is vital that the individual be able to recognize a) that there is a problem to be solved and b) the elements of a problem in order to reorganize them en route to a solution. That is, the child must first comprehend the problem.

Bem (1970) asked why children below the age of five years appear to be unable to solve problems and offered a number of theoretical answers to her question. These included the theories of mediation-deficiency, production-deficiency, and comprehension-deficiency. In *mediation-deficiency*, the child has "... an inability ... to mediate or regulate ... task behavior verbally, despite [the child's] ability to understand and to use the relevant words." (p.

Comprehension of the problem

351) In simple terms, for example, the child may be able to count to ten, but be unable to figure out how many oranges are needed if each person in a group of five people is to have two oranges. The second hypothesis involved *production-deficiency:* ". . . the young child may fail to produce those words or instructions which could serve as potential mediators of his task behavior; . . ." (p. 351) In this theory, the child does not have the abilities or skills needed to solve the problem. That is, he cannot think through or say the words that would help him to find and organize the information needed in a solution. A third point of view, Bem's own, is that the child has the basic skills essential to problem-solving, but does not comprehend sufficiently what is wanted in the way of a solution. That is, the young child suffers from *comprehension-deficiency.* In an experimental study with preschoolers, Bem found that they could not solve problems initially. After training, that is, demonstrations of the desired end-result, the children could not only produce solutions to the original colored block problems, but could also transfer their insight to related problems with trucks. It might be mentioned here that the TV production "Sesame Street" is helping to overcome this comprehension-deficiency through its instruction on the use of "place" directions, for example, above, under, in front of, behind, through, and so on.

Even adults, however, must occasionally work to find out what the problem is. One practical instance of problem-finding is cited by Getzels (1975), in which a car has a tire blowout on a deserted road. The occupants of one car might ask, "Where can we get a jack?" when they find none in the trunk. The occupants of another car, faced with the same situation, ask, "How can we raise the car?" The latter are the problem-*finders*, who also solve their problem more quickly and effectively. According to Getzels, ". . . the originality and inventiveness of the solution to the dilemmas of practical affairs, science, and art depend as much on talents for finding and formulating problems as on the technical skills for solving the problems once they are found and formulated." (pp. 17–18)

Collection of information

There is also a need to be able to manipulate the various elements in a problem. Piaget hypothesized that this ability does not arise until adolescence, when the individual is in the stage of formal operations. At this time, the person can, for example, hold one variable constant while varying others, understand the concepts of probability and *permutation*, and so on. In a study of preadolescents' and adolescents' problem-solving strategies, Leskow and Smock (1970) found a positive correlation between age and the systematization of strategies having mathematical group characteristics. (Some sex differences were noted and were tentatively attributed to differences in spatial relations abilities rather than mathematical abilities.) Although Piaget may be correct in his hypothesis, it must also be recognized that, as children get older, they ordinarily advance in school and are exposed to more and more strategies for problem-solving, so that age alone is not responsible for Leskow and Smock's conclusions.

Without learning, thinking, and collecting facts, impressions, and ideas, the creative mind would not have the raw materials available for problem-solving. As Trachtman (1975) writes, "The creative mind . . . takes the categorized ideas and somehow shakes them up . . . and lets them fall into new patterns, configurations and relationships unanticipated. . . ." (p. 38) Without ideas and facts, however, there is nothing to "shake up."

Incubation, illumination, and evaluation

There are, of course, steps to be taken in solving a problem. Obstacles may occur at any one of them, not just in recognizing or organizing the elements. Initially, one must define the problem, and then collect the information, from previous learning or other resources, which might be useful in solving it. The third stage in problem-solving is incubation, when the individual ponders and hypothesizes, juggles the information acquired, and works on the problem in an off-and-on fashion. Suddenly, "the light dawns," possibly waking the problem-solver in the wee hours of the morning. A tentative solution has appeared! It must be tested or evaluated before it becomes known as *the* solution, but this is essentially the final step unless the tentative solution is a failure. Should failure be the case, the problem-solver returns to the third stage. After several such incidents, the individual may become tired or bored with the problem, which can prevent her from reaching a solution. Sometimes, however, the relaxation from effort provides an opportunity for subconscious information juggling, and illumination occurs and is proved correct.

Obstacles to solutions

In addition to fatigue or boredom at the third stage, other obstacles at this point in the problem-solving process are habituation, functional fixedness, and embeddedness. Over the years, we do become "creatures of habit" to the extent that it may be quite difficult to look at a familiar problem or potential solution in any but the most familiar way. This is a common tendency among older people who are often reluctant to try something new that may ease their tasks because, as they say, "I've always done it this way." On the other hand, it may not be a habitual behavior pattern that interferes with problem-solving, but rather functional fixedness in which the elements of the problem are perceived as having certain "roles" and no others. For example, a screwdriver may be seen simply as a tool with which one tightens or loosens screws. In a particular situation, however, a screwdriver may function as a hammer, a weapon, a weight, a lever, or in some other "role." Did you ever think of making curtains out of pillowcases? Dresses out of bath towels? Dolls out of socks? If none of these potential functions is perceived, the problem may not be solved because of the functional fixedness on the part of the problem-solver. (Note: Another example of functional fixedness was shown in Focus 8–2.)

A third inhibitor of problem-solving is embeddedness. In this case, the solver cannot see the trees for the forest. That is, the elements of the problem and its solution are arrayed in such a way that they get "lost" in the overall arrangement of the situation. Simple illustrations of this can be seen in geometric patterns:

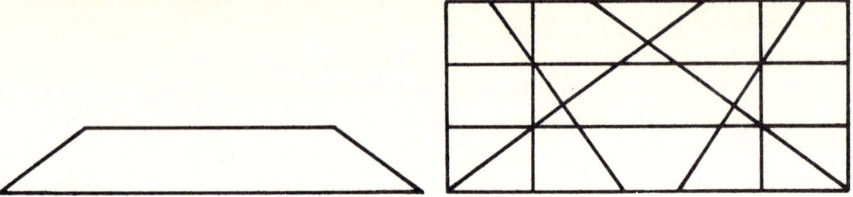

To overcome these three obstacles, psychologists have developed a number of programs that are designed to break down the barriers of limited perceptions and encourage productive thinking.

Other obstacles to problem-solving include lack of motivation, anxiety (in which finding a solution is perceived as a threatening event), and environmental restrictions. Parents, teachers, or employers may restrict the physical movement needed to solve the problem or set up so many conditions that must be met that the individual gives up the task before he begins.

Stimulating productive thinking

There are different approaches to "teaching" productive thinking. In one, a game of "Unusual Uses" is introduced to the class on an occasional basis. This is actually a subtest in both Guilford's and Torrance's test batteries, but it can also be used as an instructional tool to reduce functional fixedness at any grade level. The class is instructed to think of possible uses for a specific common object—for example, an empty milk carton, a toothbrush, (water) pitcher, bean bag, ball of string, candle, and so on. It can be demonstrated in the course of this exercise that, if each person writes down his own list, the list will be considerably shorter and probably more "traditional" than one derived from oral group responses. In the latter case, a response by one person tends to "trigger" a related response in another person, and so on through the group. This is part of the "brainstorming" process used in industry to find solutions to problems.

Focus 10–1

"Brainstorming" is a technique stressed at the annual Creative Problem Solving Institutes of the State University College of Buffalo (New York). One of its principal characteristics is encouraging the outpouring of ideas by group members with all evaluation of the ideas delayed until the end of a session or until a subsequent session.

The leader of the group states the problem, suggests examples of possible solutions, and then encourages the group members to state their ideas, no matter how "wild." Sessions last thirty to forty-five minutes among adults, but might run fifteen to twenty-five minutes for students. In industrial sessions, over a hundred ideas are commonly produced in thirty minutes!

Spurs to idea-production include asking multitudes of questions, such as:

What if . . .

What other uses . . .

Can we modify? . . . adapt? . . . substitute?

Can we combine? . . . reverse? . . . condense? . . . enlarge?

Checklists of the attribute of an object provide a starting point for answering these questions. Concentration on the goal, even while musing, intensifies awareness, curiosity, and idea-association.

According to Osborn and Parnes, leaders of the Creative Education Foundation at Buffalo,

> There are several reasons why group brainstorming can be highly productive of ideas. For one thing, the power of association is a two-way current. When a panel member spouts an idea, he almost automatically stirs his own imagination toward another idea. At the same time, *his* ideas stimulate the associative powers of all the *others*. . . .
>
> In an effort to determine the extent to which ideas are sparked by ideas, one organization analyzed the cross-fertilization which occurred in 38 sessions. It was found that 1,400 of the 4,356 ideas produced could be identified as "hitch-hikers"—suggestions which had been triggered by suggestions voiced by other panelists. (Osborn, 1963, p. 154)

Association without immediate evaluation or criticism exercises the imagination.

With friends, or in a brainstorming session in class, try the brainstorming technique with these questions:

1. How can the physical aspects of the average textbook be improved?
2. How can juvenile delinquency be prevented?
3. How can an appreciation of classical literature be stimulated?
4. How can homework be made a joy instead of a job?
5. What changes in curriculum would improve education?

Suggested Activity

The alternate uses and attribute-listing techniques have also been used successfully in educational psychology classes, with the content of the course. Students are asked to define "intelligence," suggest the traits of an ideal teacher, find uses for common objects, and propose solutions to classroom problems. In so doing, they gain an appreciation for the techniques as well as a more complete understanding of the goals of the course. (Schwartz, 1974)

Several commercial games also require flexibility in developing strategies, and the individual least restricted by habituation is most likely to be the winner. Actually, children frequently are good at thinking of alternate strategies in a game setting, but fail to transfer their ability to classroom-related situations. This may, of course, be due to the emphasis on convergent thinking mentioned earlier, or to psychological obstacles. In lieu of commercial games, the resourceful teacher can develop original ones that require the discovery of new ways to solve old problems. Even first graders could cope with this question: "If you have swept the floor and can't find the dustpan, what could you use to pick up the dirt?"

To reduce embeddedness, one might employ a detective story format, providing a mass of clues embedded in a story, which must be examined one by one. Some clues should be removed from the story context before their significance is apparent, while others may contribute directly and obviously to the mystery's solution. Abstract puzzles, too, can be used to reduce the obstacle of embeddedness.

At the University of California at Berkeley, a sixteen-lesson "Productive Thinking Program" has been developed to acquaint fifth- and sixth-graders

> ... with some of the basic mental skills involved in creative thinking and problem solving, and gives ... guided practice in working on problems which require clever, imaginative, and resourceful thinking. Moreover, a continued attempt is made to enhance the student's *willingness* to engage in this kind of activity, even when a problem appears difficult and frustrating. (Olton, 1969, p. 18)

The programmed lessons are in a cartoon-like format and can be completed in sixteen hours of classroom instruction time. The skills taught ". . . are those thought to be essential for the kind of complex and original thinking in which an individual strives to produce new ideas, to attain fresh insights and understandings, and to achieve his own solutions to problems." (Wardrop, et al., 1969, p. 68) Olton, and Wardrop, et al., found that there was a generalized transfer of *readiness* to think even in tasks not specifically requiring such effort. Olton also found that the effectiveness of the self-instructional program was increased markedly by teacher and class participation. (p. 23) In the Wordrop, et al., study, which involved 44 fifth-grade classes,

> ... the training materials produced statistically significant increments in thinking and problem-solving performance on a wide variety of productive thinking measures. These instructional benefits occurred for virtually all types of students (regardless of sex or level of IQ), and were especially marked for students in classrooms having environments which were judged to provide relatively little support and encouragement for the development of productive thinking. (p. 76)

The comment is included that teacher participation would probably enhance the educational benefits of the program, as Olton had reported.

> *Focus 10–2*
>
> Productive thinking may also be stimulated by "creative writing" assignments. The author recalls having to write an original myth in high school for an English class, which gave both latitude to the imagination and a greater understanding of myths. The opportunity to write poetry and plays has been traditionally regarded as creative writing, but is frequently relegated to the classification of extracurricular activities.
>
> Some teachers have children writing Haiku poetry, a Japanese style that has a special form but no rhyming or other requirements. Other teachers suggest themes such as imagining that one is a pet, or a caged lion, or a tree, and writing a composition from that point of view. Some play music as a stimulus to creative thinking.
>
> The beauty of these and other productive thinking assignments is that there are no right or wrong answers. Although some assignments mentioned may be criticized on the grounds that they promote *anthropomorphism*, this is a weak argument since the children are well aware that they *are* pretending, rather than believing, that objects and animals have feelings.

An occasional teacher takes pride in assigning creative writing topics, and then removes the spontaneity and joy of writing by excessive correction. One (published) dreadful example is ten rewrites of a third-grader's brief essay on Spring. (Suhor, 1975) The teacher in question undoubtedly meant well when she corrected form, spelling, and punctuation. However, she was treading on the child's creative powers when she crossed out "Flowers feel like rain." To the child, that had meaning. No one has the right to change that.

In what other ways might you try to stimulate problem-solving or creative behavior?   *Question*

CREATIVITY

An outgrowth of productive thinking is creative behavior. In recent years, interest in creativity has increased so that the journals are full of articles having to do with creativity, and at least one journal is primarily devoted to this behavior. Because of the wealth of literature in this area, the discussion of creativity needs to be somewhat compartmentalized:

1. definitions of creativity
2. characteristics of creative people

3. measurement of creative thinking
4. studies of creative behavior
5. implications for education.

What is creativity? Is it limited to the artistic realm?

Definitions of creativity

Certainly we consider artists in various media to be creative, but isn't a technological invention, or an innovation in method also creative? Must it be a public product, on display at a gallery, published, performed, or used by others? Is it possible to evaluate the efforts as being creative or not? Must the product be totally new, or may it be a new approach to an old theme? You can appreciate from these questions some of the difficulties and sources of controversy in attempts to define creativity. There are numerous definitions available in the literature. A review of them suggests

> . . . that there are two major approaches to creativity in normal populations. In one, products are rated on a continuum of creativity, and the personal and social factors associated with creative achievement are examined. In the other, . . . it is assumed that there is a trait (or traits) of creativity—the psychological significance of the trait and its contribution to creative production are examined. (Nicholls, 1972, p. 717)

There is some agreement on the following definition: Creative behavior is present in an original work or idea that need not be public nor socially useful, although it may frequently be both, and that has intrinsic merit because of its innovative qualities. This does not imply, however, that every creative *product* is good, merely that the effort is good. We applaud a two-year-old's attempts at drawing, a ten-year-old's story, and a sixteen-year-old's scientific discovery. These are creative efforts, but they are rarely of public importance or social usefulness. Leonardo da Vinci, super-Renaissance man, invented things centuries ago for which there was then no use or public applause. Today, we marvel at his drawings of aircraft almost as much as we admire his paintings.

Characteristics of creative people

It is easier, perhaps, to define the characteristics of creative people. There is again widespread agreement that the creative person is intellectually curious. Covington (1968) describes the creative child almost totally in terms of his curiosity:

> The creative child prefers to explore the unknown, rather than to conserve the already known; he prefers explaining new facts in new ways, rather than continuing to rely on traditional well-established explanations; he indulges in adventuresome thinking and raises questions, rather than being content with things as they are. (p. 22)

The creative child sounds rather like a nonconformist in the classroom, doesn't he? In addition to curiosity, it is also apparent that he indulges in divergent thinking. He may be characterized as suffering from "constructive discontent."

The creative adolescents studied by Getzels and Jackson (1962), did, in fact, consider their personal values to be opposite to those of their teachers. They also, as compared with their highly intelligent peers, had a wider range of vocational aspirations, and a richer fantasy life and placed a higher value on a sense of humor. (Note: There are valid criticisms of the methodology used in this well-publicized study, but these personality characteristics have also appeared in other studies.) Chambers (1964), in a study of 400 male chemists and 340 male psychologists, found that his subjects exhibited certain characteristics also identified in other research studies of creative people: strong motivation, a high degree of initiative, strong self-sufficiency and independence, a high degree of dominance, and more introspective qualities.

Notice that intelligence is not even mentioned. It is generally conceded, however, that the creative person must have at least average intelligence and frequently functions at an above-average level of intelligence. Cattell and Butcher (1968) stated that a high level of creativity must depend on a high level of intelligence, but that ". . . the selection in any professional group of the more creative persons depends decidedly more upon personality characteristics." (p. 306) That is, given the necessary intellectual information and capacity, the creative individual must add to these the qualities of curiosity, flexibility, self-motivation, and independence of thought. It is important to note, however, that these characteristics make the person *potentially* creative. Appropriate conditions must exist for the potential to be realized.

Torrance and Guilford, two leaders in the study of creativity, agree that intellectual flexibility, the ability to "shift," is an important characteristic of production, and originality, or rareness of response, contribute to high scores on their tests.

From a psychophysiological point of view, there is the possibility that there is a relationship between level of cortical arousal and creativity. "Creativity and intellectual ability require two different thought processes: the former calls for low cortical arousal and defusing one's powers of concentration; the latter calls for higher cortical arousal and focused attention." (Martindale, 1975, pp. 48, 50) More creative people appear to produce more alpha waves (low cortical arousal) than less creative ones. It is not known whether this is an inherited or learned event. However, Martindale concludes that ". . . creative people view the world and react to it unlike most of their peers do, not because they are eccentric and strange, but because they process information differently." (p. 50)

After surveying the available literature, Christie (1970) concluded that certain factors commonly existed in the childhood environments of the creative subjects:

A) In the home

   1. a superior academic background in the family
   2. low pressures toward conformity which were related to high achievement

3. parental guidance toward independence and tolerance of independent behavior

B) At school

1. a nonauthoritarian teaching environment
2. divergent-productive teaching
3. free rein for, and ready responsiveness to the child's exploratory behavior.

The value of environmental factors in converting potential to actuality is reflected in the following statement by Christian Bay regarding curiosity directly and creativity indirectly:

> Genuine curiosity belongs to the child, and to the child in man. In most lives the capacity to be curious keeps declining; every time a young person is induced to accept an answer for ego-defense reasons or on the ground that a belief is socially expected, his capacity to be curious is cut. . . . intellectual development becomes stymied in college or earlier if the student remains a prisoner of his immediate or anticipatory social anxieties. . . . (1962, p. 1004)

Before you opt for total permissiveness and nonconformity, however, remember that the children must learn to live with reality and in a society, that they must acquire information and skills basic to later creative effort, and that they must learn self-discipline and responsibility as antecedents to freedom of thought and action. They can learn these things in an atmosphere that will not stifle later creative activity. Most particularly, for their own self-actualization or sense of completeness, they must be able to relate to others in their society. Too often, the creative or nonconformist individual is considered, frankly, the local "nut"—a person whom mothers warn their children to avoid. This need not be so.

> Man is a role-playing animal. If the role we ask the creative individual to play is that of a withdrawn isolate, or an aggressive, rebellious deviant, he is likely to play it that way. If, on the other hand, we acknowledge that this is what society has caused creative individuals to be in order to preserve their autonomy and sense of self; that this is not the true description of every creative person; that this unfortunate picture is being changed; that creativity and human relating are not only compatible but mutually facilitating; and that complete self-actualization is impossible without socio-self-actualization, then we will define a new reality in which man's role is that of relating creatively to others while working toward the creative realization of himself. (Foster, 1968, p. 116)

Parnes (1971) suggests that the qualities that characterize the truly creative thinker are *"sensitivity,"* *"synergy,"* and *"serendipity."* Sensitivity implies a great awareness and keen use of all the senses en route to finding problems as well as solving them. *Synergy* occurs when "two or more elements are associated in a way, [and] the result can be more than the sum of the parts.... This is the essence of creativity." (p. 22) And *serendipity* is the unexpected discovery of something that you weren't even looking for.

Of concern to those who prize creativity is the negative view of some of the traits characteristic of creative people. Bachtold (1974) replicated a decade-old study by Torrance in seeking the traits characteristic of the ideal child as seen by teachers, parents, and elementary and junior high school students in enrichment classes for the academically talented. Her finding adds to this concern.

> It seems quite clear that while we may hope for, or even at times demand the products of inventive and imaginative minds, we are still not rewarding behaviors which are found to be particularly facilitative of such productivity. The behaviors most prized by both elementary and junior high groups seem to indicate that rather than qualities which make for creativity, values expressed in the Puritan ethic are more closely perceived, that is, determination in applying energy to getting work done on time, and remembering well what is supposed to be done. The adult composite of ideal behaviors of children described a healthy person who is considerate of others and has a sense of beauty; curious (but not always asking questions); has a sense of humor and is sincere (but is never negativistic, fault-finding or critical); self-confident (but not haughty); receptive to ideas of others (yet not bashful or timid); self-motivated and independent in thinking (without being domineering). The profile which emerges bears very little resemblance to the courageous risk-taking and intuitively creative personality. (pp. 53–54)

Measurement of creative thinking

Suppose now that you wish to assess someone's creative potential. How do you do it? Several of the available tests are appropriately used with students at fifth-grade level or above, but there are relatively few measures for younger children. Criteria of creativity vary, and some critics question the validity of the tests. Martinson and Seagoe (1967) also raise questions on the assessment of the products of the creative process, material or ideational. "Who is to say when creative products will be forthcoming? Over how long a time span ought one to assess products, in order to gain a measure of creativity? Who is competent to judge creativity, or the inherent qualities of creativity as described by experts? How do we sample effectively the legitimate scope of creativity?" (p. 5)

Focus 10–3

Undaunted by these doubts, Martinson and Seagoe worked with 49 high IQ (130–170) and 57 "low" IQ (86–119) middle and upper-middle class third- to sixth-graders at the UCLA elementary school. This is a school oriented to exploration and self-expression by its students. A number of tasks were given to the children. The science problems, judged on originality and effectiveness of expression, included:

1. A letter of introduction for a visitor from Venus to Earth.

2. "During the last fifty years, man has invented the jet plane, rockets, the radio, television, and many automatic machines for factories and business. What do you think will be some new inventions during the next fifty years?"

3. "As you know, the building of homes changes all the time. Can you think of some new ways of building homes that no one has thought of yet?"

Other tasks included: writing a poem, writing a composition on the topic "It can't happen," another on "My idea of Utopia," a survival problem (stranded on a desert island with a small wash basin, an inner tube, and a Sears catalog), the interpretation of rhythms by movement, and clay and painting projects.

In addition, the subjects were compared on teacher rating scales and on Guilford's divergent thinking tests. The researchers concluded that "The findings of the present study, however tentative, did not bear out the assumption that ability as measured by intelligence tests is correlated positively with tests of creative process. . . ." (p. 54)

It has been found in other studies that teacher estimates of creativity or curiosity do not always coincide with the more objective evaluations of researchers. Nevertheless such ratings have value because they are one indication of how the students are perceived on a daily basis. The differences found frequently stem from differing interpretations of "creativity," or variations in criteria.

You might also consider the tasks listed here as class exercises rather than tests. Many of them can be used with adults as well as children.

Another approach to creativity assessment is Mednick's "Remote Associates Test." Mednick (1968) had defined creativity in a somewhat narrower way than others in this field, writing that "All creative thinking . . . consists of the forming of mutually distant associative elements into new combinations which are useful and meet specified as well as unforeseen requirements." (p. 213) A principal ingredient in creative thinking is a lack of stereotyped associations, which might also be described as having a facility for developing new sets or combinations from previously nonassociated elements, or synergistic thinking. This is frequently based on trial and error, and depends to some extent on a rather broad background of vocabulary and general information, particularly on the more difficult items. Two rather simple examples will give you an idea of Mednick's test content. The sought-after term to which all the others on the line are related is given in parentheses:

Wheel	electric	high	(wire)	
out	dog	cat	(house)	(p. 214)

To derive the remote association does indeed require the bursting of conceptual barriers, but is, in this instance, a good illustration of convergent thinking rather than divergent thinking. This test is obviously more useful with bright college students and adults than with younger children or those low in verbal ability.

At the junior high to adult levels, tests devised by Guilford and others can be used to assess creative problem-solving abilities. There are several tests, each designed to measure some aspect of Guilford's multifaceted structure of intellect model, which we discussed earlier. Factors particularly relevant to creativity include conceptual foresight, ideational fluency, associational fluency, originality, and convergent production of semantic classes. Several of the tests used to measure these factors have been adapted by other researchers on creativity. With brief descriptions, here are several sample subtests (Guilford and Hoepfner, 1971):

1. *Associational Fluency I*. Write words similar in meaning to a given word. Score is the number of acceptable similar words produced.
2. *Brick Uses* (shifts). List different uses for a brick. Score is the number of times the examinee shifts from one kind of use to another.
3. *Paired Similarities*. State one way in which words of a given pair are similar. Score is the number of different similarities stated.
4. *Possibilities*. Name as many as four objects that could be used to perform a specified task. Score is the number of usable objects listed.
5. *Predicaments*. Describe two ways in which given objects could be used to solve a specific problem. Score is the number of times given objects were incorporated as essential pairs of an adequate solution.

From the extensive factor analysis done by Guilford and his associates, it is readily apparent that problem-solving is not a unitary ability.

Torrance (1968) also has concluded that there are a number of mental abilities, clustered together, which comprise "creative thinking abilities." His tests are in both verbal and figural form and are useful from the preschool years through the adult level. Each test is evaluated in terms of fluency (number of responses), flexibility (number of categories of response), and originality (number of rare responses). A demonstration test illustrates several of the tasks given.

According to Torrance,

> In observational studies we found that children scoring high on tests of creative thinking initiated a larger number of ideas, produced more original ideas, and gave more explanations of the workings of unfamiliar science toys than did their less creative peers. When matched for intelligence, sex, and teacher, the most creative children in forty-six classrooms from grades one through six more frequently than their controls had reputations for having wild and fantastic ideas, produced drawings and other products judged to be original, and produced work characterized by humor, playfulness, relative lack of rigidity, and relaxation. (1968, p. 174)

ASSESSING CREATIVE THINKING
a demonstration based on
The Torrance Tests of Creative Thinking

Part 1

List all the ways you can think of to improve the toy

1 _____

_____

2 _____

_____

3 _____

_____

4 _____

_____

5 _____

_____

6 _____

_____

Prepared by

Personnel Press, Inc., Princeton, N. J.
A Division of Ginn and Company

Figure 10.1

Part 2

List all the questions you can think of about this picture.

1 _____
_____

2 _____
_____

3 _____
_____

4 _____
_____

5 _____
_____

6 _____
_____

Part 3

List all the uses you can think of for junk autos

1 _____

_____

2 _____

_____

3 _____

_____

4 _____

_____

5 _____

_____

6 _____

_____

7 _____

_____

8 _____

_____

Part 4

Add lines to the incomplete figures to sketch some interesting objects.

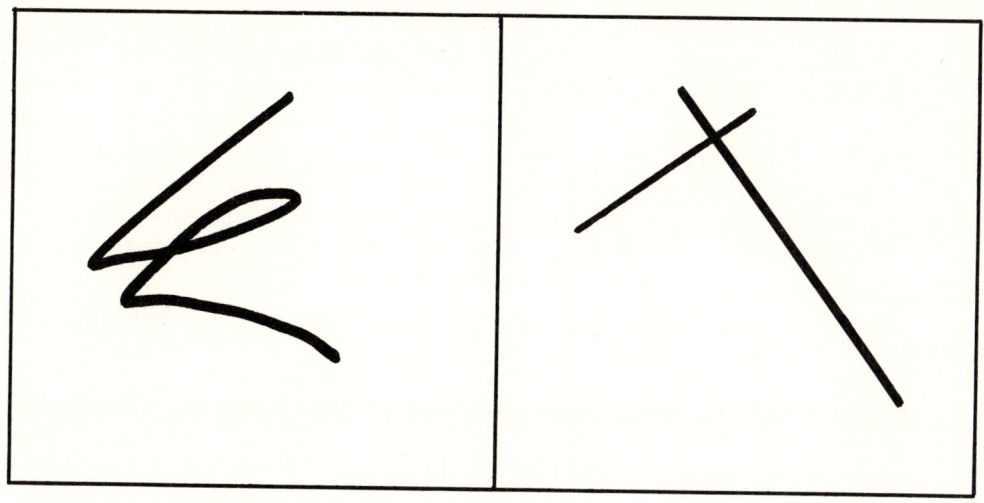

See how many objects or pictures you can make from the triangles below.

Similar differences have been observed with adults and college students. In one evaluation of the Torrance tests, however, a question has been raised about their validity and about Torrance's assumption that each of his tests yields independent measures of fluency, flexibility, and originality. Test factors had little consistent relation to criterion variables, and combinations of scores for each factor were found to be statistically unjustifiable. (Harvey, Hoffmeister, Coates, and White, 1970) In an article published a few years earlier, however, Torrance presented the results of numerous studies that supported his assertion of content, construct, and concurrent validity, as well as moderate to high test-retest reliability coefficients. (1967) The question of validity is obviously a function of which variables are chosen as criteria.

There are a number of problems in trying to measure creative thinking, of which the criterion problem is only one. For example, there is no single, generally accepted, definition or theory of creativity. This immediately leads to differences in test design and interpretation. It also creates difficulties in distinguishing creative behaviors from behaviors related to intelligence or academic achievement. Furthermore, lack of consistency in this area contributes to the problem of predicting who, in a group of youngsters, is most likely to be creative in later years. Although we can isolate traits among adults considered to be creative, we cannot ". . . conclude that these same traits in youngsters today will identify individuals with the kind of creative potential that will be valued in tomorrow's world." (Treffinger, Renzulli, and Feldhusen, 1971, p. 109)

Crockenburg's review (1972) of the Torrance Tests and of the Wallach and Kogan Creativity Battery, the most frequently used measures of children's "creativity," indicates that validity evidence for both sets of tests is inconclusive. The tests do not measure what IQ tests measure, but it is also questionable whether they measure creativity. Crockenburg's conclusion, with reference to the use of the tests, takes us back to a point raised early in this chapter—namely, finding the problem. She writes:

> . . . if school people asked, "How can we encourage creativity?" instead of, "How do we select high creative students?" researchers could shift their attention to the conditions or situations, the practices or experiences, the approaches and attitudes that are conducive to the production of novel, appropriate, quality ideas. (p. 43)

In the next two sections, both of Crockenburg's questions will be discussed.

Studies of creative behavior

Despite the doubts and questions regarding the definition and assessment of creative thinking, the idea persists that the more creative, however defined, can be differentiated from their less creative peers. The abundance of research in the professional literature attests to this fact. Janssen (1968), working with white youths from the lower socioeconomic class, used three of Guilford's tests (Plot Titles, Alternate Uses, and Ideational Fluency) to compare levels of creativity among dropouts and nondropouts in this teenaged population. The dropouts scored significantly better on the individual tests, and also when the scores were combined. Janssen's conclusion has important implications for educators:

> ... the dropout student must find the environment more stimulating outside the educational classroom situation since the educational system conforms to a middle-class value system. This increases the possibility that middle-class conformity, which is forced upon the lower socio-economic student, does reduce his creative potential. The school system must find a way to permit this student to be creative in class. By including more of the student's lower socio-economic values into his educational training, his originality, flexibility, and ideation-fluency potential could be stimulated and result in fewer of these lower-class students withdrawing from school. (p. 184)

The results and conclusions are similar to those arrived at earlier in a British study (Jackson and Marsden, 1962). Daily experiences reported in the newspapers tend to confirm further Janssen's conclusions. The ingenuity displayed by leaders of delinquent gangs, who are frequently dropouts from a background similar to that of Janssen's subjects, can only be labeled creative thinking, albeit directed against society.

Another point of interest is the effect of a handicap on creativity. Some limitations will be found if the handicapped youngster has had very limited exposure to sources of information in the home environment or in school. This might be true, for example, of the hearing handicapped child who has never heard music or speech and has had difficulty in learning to read. The blind child would not have seen art works or color or design, so could scarcely respond to creative drawing tasks. There is one study, however, that compared blind and sighted children on verbal measures of creative thinking. (Halpin, Halpin, and Torrance, 1973) The children were given four of the Torrance tests: Product Improvement, Unusual Uses, Unusual Questions, and Just Suppose. There were no significant differences in scores by sex, race, or age (black and white, ages 6–12). However, the blind children had significantly higher mean scores than the sighted children on verbal fluency, flexibility, and originality. In discussing these results, Halpin, et al., suggest that:

> 1) "... the blind child is more fluent because he relies heavily on verbal production to compensate for limitations imposed by blindness." ...
>
> 2) "... the blind child is more flexible ... because he has to be flexible and adaptive in order to learn to live in a sighted world." ...
>
> 3) "It is necessary for the blind child to rely upon imagination and practice its use for his survival. Things that one can see one does not have to imagine, while things that one imagines may be more unusual, unique, and original." (p. 273)

In what ways could the creative thinking abilities of blind and deaf children be stimulated and encouraged? **Question**

In a somewhat different type of study, Maw and Maw (1970) tried to discriminate between the kinds of creative abilities exhibited by highly curious fifth-grade boys of slightly above-average IQ ($\bar{X} = 110$). They found that boys who scored high on their tests of intellectual curiosity were characterized by self-actualization, restrained creativity, impulsive creativity, persistence, emotional maturity, abstraction, and morality. Of special interest to us at this point are the subsets of creativity. Restrained creativity is defined as "... a factor that is loaded positively for dependability, efficiency, promptness, self-reliance, patience, perseverance, and self-control. The boy who is high in this factor is adaptive, conforming, and helpful in dealing with others." (p. 328) Impulsive creativity, on the other hand, "... includes excitability of an immediate temperamental nature, a mind wandering distractibility, an attention-getting insecurity, with an assertive tone to the emotionality." (pp. 328–29) They also defined a Concrete Creativity that was momentary, rather than abstract or theoretical, and that was unrecognized as creativity or curiosity by boys high on this factor. None of these definitions appear wholly related to the ones presented earlier, but they do suggest that perhaps youngsters reflect their creative potential in a variety of ways.

Question — Can you relate the Maws' definition of different types of creativity to Thorndike's view of intelligence?

The types of creativity found in these and other studies may be described also in another way. Some creative behavior is artistic or esthetic; other creative behavior is mechanical or inventive. Some creators extend the thinking of other people in new and different ways; other creators develop wholly new theories. Who shall be called creative?

Parnes (n.d.) offered a summary description of the creative person that appears to capture the essence of the studies cited here, as well as those omitted:

> ... the individual who behaves creatively is oriented toward setting and solving meaningful problems, using an inner drive to recombine his storehouse of experiences in new ways. In attacking his problems, he does not behave as a conformist; instead, he pioneers often, is not afraid to fail frequently, but is productive in the long run. Thus the individual behaving creatively sees things through many eyes, from many viewpoints. He allows his associative processes to relate freely what his senses bring to him. He is constantly changing his views as he forms new associations, as compared with the "non-creative" individual who freezes his views into rigid ideas which we call prejudices. (p. 3)

Implications for education: encouraging creativity — The first implication for education that one sees in such a description is the need of classroom teachers to recognize that nonconformity may be productive. Secondly, creativity exists along a continuum rather than being a dichotomous (either creative or noncreative) entity. Encouragement of children, in fact, to develop alternative solutions to problems, to examine several hypotheses before reaching a conclusion, to use their imaginations, and to be flexible and spontaneous, permits them to move farther along the continuum to the creative end. It *is* important for the individual to have mastered basic skills to the point that he can focus on the problem at hand rather than on its underlying techniques. It *is* important that he have as varied experiences as possible both in specific subject areas and the realm of general information. Acceptance of the idea that creativity *can* be learned is a prerequisite to including such encouragement in the classroom, however.

A number of specific programs have been developed to release the creative potential of school children. Cropley and Feuring (1971) were able to train six- and seven-year-old children to give responses greater in number and quality to the Product Improvement Test, following a program devised by Torrance. Pulaski (1974) believes that children of all ages should be encouraged to engage in fantasy, either through play with objects, improvisation in the performing arts, or storytelling. As she points out,

> . . . make-believe play is an intrinsic part of normal growth. It is associated with verbal fluency, waiting ability, increased concentration, positive attitudes in life, flexibility, originality, and imagination. . . . We have found that children need privacy and time to themselves to think over and replay their experiences. (p. 74)

The parent who objects to occasional daydreaming restricts the development of these traits, and possibly other areas of thinking as well.

Specific programs designed to enhance creative thinking include the Productive Thinking Program (mentioned earlier) and the Purdue Creativity Training Program. These were tested in self-instructional settings and in situations with active teacher participation. (Treffinger, Speedie, and Brunner, 1974) Both programs resulted in increases in divergent thinking abilities of fifth-graders. Differences in duration of the program used (4 or 8 weeks) and teachers' scores on tests of divergent thinking affected performance of each program differently, however.

When working with adolescents in particular, but with younger children and adults as well, it is first of all important to develop a positive attitude toward innovation and imagination. Then exercises for the development of the creative abilities can be introduced. Specific creative thinking techniques can also be taught. Davis (1973) lists these as brain-storming, which is useful in establishing a group atmosphere conducive to imagination; attribute-listing, which can lead to product or idea improvement; morphological-synthesis, to produce variations of all possible combinations of characteristics of a product; checklists to locate possible sources of innovation; and the synectic method, which uses direct, personal, and fantasy analogies as a basis for problem-solving. Davis has used this last technique in his program, "Thinking Creatively: A guide to training imagination." The program consists of a dialogue among four characters, one of whom ". . . is a backyard scientist-inventor who tries to teach the other three characters creative attitudes and various problem-solving techniques in an offbeat manner." (1969, pp. 101–102)

In all of the research studies, emphasis is placed on the classroom atmosphere as it relates to creativity. This atmosphere for creative thinking is set by one person—the teacher. This does not imply permissiveness, but rather the opportunity to explore, to question, and to learn; that is, liberty, not license. Such environments have been highly effective in stimulating self-motivated learning of skills as well as creative thinking. This means, however, that the teacher must be dynamic in approach rather than static.

> As the purveyor of rewards and punishments for social and intellectual skills, the teacher stands in an advantageous position for encouraging creativity, curiosity, independence, and self-reliance. When the child shows some independent thinking the teacher can praise him, and when the child shows signs that his personal interests are not being satisfied by a proposed assignment, she can modify the assignment enough for that one child or any others, to include his interests. (Goodale, 1970, p. 95)

You can't use the same notes term after term with only minor modifications. You must build the learner's self-confidence and self-esteem. You must allow the student freedom to ask questions. The obvious need for a dynamic approach implies that we must teach prospective teachers these practices so that they will be stimulated to think creatively about their methods of instruction, assignments, and, most of all, their students.

SUMMARY

The society and environment in which we live is changing so rapidly that there is barely time to integrate knowledge before it is outdated. For this reason, it is imperative to educate children in the processes of problem-solving and to encourage, rather than discourage, them to be flexible in their thinking. The difficulties that divergent thinkers encounter, the problems they pose to their teachers, and the techniques that may be used to encourage their creative thinking were, therefore, the basis of this chapter's presentation.

In discussing creative thinking and thinkers, it was necessary first to define creativity. Then the characteristics of creative people were presented, as well as means of assessing creative behavior. The peculiar problems of testing creativity also were discussed. A number of studies in this area were cited, several of which offered food for thought for educators. The results of creative thinking, especially in the area of education, will be explored in chapter eleven, in which innovations in education are to be discussed.

Part Five

Learners and Teaching

The next four chapters reflect special concerns about learners and teaching. There are aspects of contemporary issues that have significance for the human parties that matter in the classroom: the learner and the teacher. They provide different angles from which to view both the learner and the situation in which he learns.

First we consider many of the innovations in teaching and learning that have become part of today's educational scene. These have been developed by applying theories of learning and are designed to help the learner learn more effectively and with more interest. (Many of the innovations presented in chapter eleven were originally designed for special learners and have been modified for use in regular classes.)

Then, there are always some pupils in the classroom who deviate from the "average" in learning ability. We will discuss some of the challenges they offer and specific techniques used in the schools to help such students learn better in relation to their abilities. This is particularly important in view of the growing practice of "mainstreaming." More of the "nonaverage" children will be found in regular classrooms than ever before. As teachers, we have an obligation to understand them as people.

Critical for all learners is the atmosphere in which they learn, particularly in regard to the interpersonal relations between teacher and learner. What effect does a middle-class-oriented teacher have on pupils in a "slum" school? Or in a suburban classroom? Do the teacher's attitudes affect his teaching behavior? How? In what ways does the climate or psychological environment of the school affect both teacher and learner?

It is sometimes difficult to tell who is learning from whom. There is an old saying that it is a wise parent who learns from his child. Similarly, wise teachers can learn from their students—content in an unfamiliar area, which teaching techniques are effective, changes in attitude, and so on. Not only can teachers learn in their own classrooms, but it is urgent, and in some cases mandatory, that they continue their professional education throughout their careers.

Preview

INTRODUCTION

DEVELOPMENT OF BEHAVIORAL OBJECTIVES
- A BASIC FORMAT
- OTHER APPROACHES TO OBJECTIVES
- ACCOUNTABILITY

AUDIOVISUAL TECHNIQUES
- FILMS, FILMSTRIPS, SLIDES, ETC.
- TAPES AND RECORDS
- TELEVISION
- MICRO-TEACHING

PROGRAMMED INSTRUCTION
- TEXTBOOK=SOFTWARE
- CAI = HARDWARE

INDIVIDUALLY PRESCRIBED INSTRUCTION

"NEW" METHODS
- MATHEMATICS
- READING
- SCIENCE
- SIMULATION

SCHOOL-WIDE MODIFICATIONS
- TEAM TEACHING
- "OPEN CLASSROOMS"
- VERTICAL GROUPING
- OTHER INNOVATIONS
- MINI-SUMMARY

RESPONSE OF THE LEARNER TO INNOVATIONS

SUMMARY

11

Innovative Teaching for Learning

INTRODUCTION

The chapter title emphasizes "innovations" rather than "educational technology" because many of the changes in classroom instruction in recent years have been occurring in the techniques of teaching as well as in mechanical inventions. As educational psychologists, we have a responsibility to use all possible legitimate means to improve both teaching methods and learning processes. A past president of the Division of Educational Psychology (Division 15) of the American Psychological Association said, in fact, that "educational psychologists can function in two principal ways. First, as scientists to improve the understanding of how an individual obtains an education; and second, as applied technologists to improve current educational programs." (Flanagan, 1970, pp. 1, 8) These functions can be carried out in a number of areas, but in this chapter we will attend primarily to two of them: educational objectives and innovative learning methods and materials.

One of the major innovations in education in recent years has been the application of industrial systems concepts to the establishment of educational objectives. The objectives themselves determine in part the methods and materials to be used in the teaching-learning process. The increasing use of objectives is tied to the concept of accountability—demands by parents and legislators to know how effective teaching is, whether value is received for the dollars invested in education.

Next, it is appropriate to review briefly modifications of "traditional" techniques in audiovisual instruction media. These media include the use of records, tapes, films, TV, and a variety of combinations of these devices.

A third, and important, consideration is the introduction of programmed and computer-assisted instruction methods. The basis for this topic has already been provided in chapter eight in the discussion of operant conditioning theories of learning.

Much has been written about "discovery" and "inquiry" as the bases for learning. To be properly prepared to enter the classroom as a teacher, it is advisable for you to be acquainted with these concepts, especially as they are put into practice in "open" classrooms or under team-teaching arrangements.

Finally, we will consider the impact of these innovations on the learner. Does he like automated instruction? Does everyone respond equally well to low-structured "inquiry" programs or logic-oriented mathematics curricula? Is innovation relevant? Is "hardware" needed for innovation? Is the "open classroom" right for everyone?

DEVELOPMENT OF BEHAVIORAL OBJECTIVES

Presumably students attend classes in order to learn information, which is communicated to them by the teachers employed to transmit the information as part of an overall educational program. That is, the student's objective is to learn. The educational program presumably has certain objectives that can be filled through teaching. Each teacher deals with one or more units of these objectives and presumably creates his or her own objectives for a course or a class. These may vary considerably among teachers, from a personal objective to "survive" each week until the school year is over, to a need to complete each week's chapter within that week without regard to whether it is effectively learned, to a desire to have students master the course content rather than merely "pass the course."

Behavioral objectives attempt to answer the question: "What can the learner do as a result of instruction that she or he couldn't do before?" "The primary reasons for the current emphasis upon writing behavioral objectives are to: 1) aid in curriculum planning, 2) promote increased pupil achievement, and 3) improve the techniques and skills of program evaluation." (McAshan, 1970, p. 4) These objectives can be developed in several skill areas: academic, higher cognitive, creative, craftsmanship, and leadership. (Plowman, 1971, pp. 2–18)

A basic format   Let us assume that we are dealing with a particular problem. We know what our final objective is—solution of the problem—and we know at what level of sophistication or cognition our learners are entering the situation.

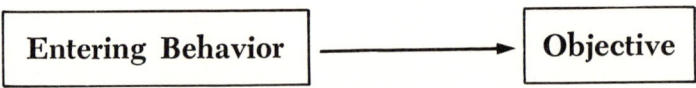

At what level of Bloom's hierarchy (see chapter eight) do we place the objective? How do we move the learner from where he is now to that desired objective? It is obvious that we must gain his attention early if progress is to be made, whether the objective is knowledge, comprehension, or one of the more complex cognitive objectives. Attention can be gained in a number of ways, depending on the age of the learner and the circumstances of the situation. You can do physical things like clapping hands, whistling, snapping fingers, coughing, and so on. You can combine physical action with imparting information by beginning to lecture, writing on the blackboard, distributing printed materials, or showing a film. The first affective objective is achieved.

It is advisable in attempting to reach the cognitive objective to have the routes to it clearly in mind before you begin the lesson. The objective will determine the routes and also what kinds of responses you want from the learner. If you want knowledge only, you may use a variety of techniques to transmit the information (lecture, demonstration, text in prose or programmed format, drill, flash cards, and so on). Responding would involve "parroting" the information or answering incomplete questions. Let us suppose, however, that the cognitive objective is of a higher order, for example, synthesis. It is then advisable to be certain that the entering learner knows and understands the fundamental skills or ideas of the subject matter before progressing further.

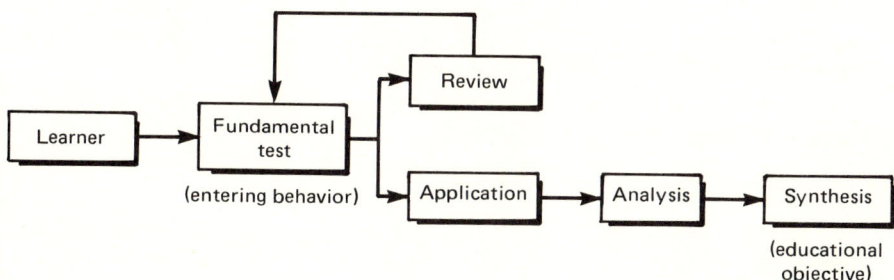

Entering behavior to educational objective.   **Figure 11.1**

Much of the course material will then focus on analyzing the subject matter into its component parts, relationships, and structure so that with the addition of other information the learner can organize new patterns of behavior. Such synthesis takes practice for most students; so to achieve this level of cognitive ability, the opportunity to analyze and synthesize elements must be built into the course curriculum.

In studying educational philosophy, for example, you might find that students entering the course have no knowledge of names of philosophers or theories of philosophy. You must first, then, provide such basic information (or have the students seek out the information). If they have not already learned how to organize this material, you might hand out a sheet that looks like Figure 11.2.

At this level, they should be able to understand at least that Plato and idealism, Dewey and pragmatism, and so on, are related. Then they should be able to respond appropriately when asked whether a particular practice in the school reflects one theory or another. The difficult tasks are in examining the elements in each theory and analyzing not only their relationship to each other but also how they relate to elements in another philosophical theory. Finally, as teacher, you may assign to the students the development

322 LEARNERS AND TEACHING

Orientation	Names	Emphases	Effect on Schools
Idealism (Humanism) (Perennialism)			
Realism			
Pragmatism (Experimentalism)			
Reconstructionism			
Essentialism			
Existentialism			

Figure 11.2 *Educational philosophy.*

of their own philosophy of education, pointing out if need be that this will be a synthesis of what they have learned in the course as well as what they have learned through living and learning generally. If the students are able to produce such a statement, then they will have achieved the cognitive objective originally set as well as at least a value system on the affective continuum.

At the lower elementary level, you would set your objectives somewhat lower in the hierarchy. Knowledge, comprehension, and application of basic skills in reading, mathematics, and language arts (writing) may be the most appropriate goals. At the secondary level, it is reasonable to expect the average student to achieve analysis, and there is no valid reason why most students cannot also work toward the synthesis and evaluation objectives.

Other approaches to objectives

We can look at instructional objectives in another way. In most schools, letter or numerical grades are given in terms of the learner's achievement in each course. Each subject teacher must decide what level of achievement is necessary for each grade. Beyond this, however, the teacher should have an objective involving retention of the course content for the learner's future use. In mathematics, it is obviously important to master each topic before progressing to the next higher course because mathematics is a sequential subject. Even in history, which is less sequential in nature, a fairly high degree of mastery is desirable if the student is to be able to relate events occurring concurrently in several areas of the world or to understand patterns of historical development. Beyond the simple goals of mastery and retention for the learner's own use, there is the consideration that less time would be involved in introducing new material if previously learned skills and/or content could be reviewed rather than relearned each semester or year.

How can *these* objectives be reached? One approach, developed by Fred S. Keller, an educational psychologist, is to arrange course content in units comprised of text, practice exercises, progress checks, and a unit test. Theoretically, every learner should be able to pass the unit test with a perfect score. Having mastered the several units in a course, students should be able to retain and apply the course content in the future with less relearning than is necessary in traditional teaching-learning formats. Several courses using this approach are currently being validated in high schools and colleges across the country. In addition to self-pacing through the units, tutorial help is included as part of the program, either by the course instructor or by student assistants, so that instruction is more individualized and errors are more quickly spotted and corrected. One study indicates that the mode of instruction is less important than the differences between instructors or the length of the introductory course. (Smith and Schwartz, n.d.)

The concept of learning for mastery involves a complete change in the traditional point of view regarding learning. No longer is each learner to "settle at his own level." Rather, each learner is expected to *master* (that is, earn an "A") what is taught—*but* it is the task of the teacher to find the methods and materials that will best help the learner to do so. With the exception of an estimated 5 percent of students who have special disabilities for particular learning (for example, the tone-deaf individual in a music class), Bloom and others believe that, given sufficient and appropriate help, effort, and time, any learner can master any subject matter or skill. (Bloom, 1971) Individual differences in aptitude may make these factors prohibitive, however. For this reason, striving for mastery by all students must involve other considerations as well:

1. What is the most appropriate instructional arrangement for a specific learning task (small group instruction, individual learning, and so on)?
2. Does the student understand the nature of the task and the learning procedures to be followed?
3. What instructional materials are available (textbooks, films, simulation games, tutors, and so on)?
4. How much time is allowed for learning the task?
5. How much perseverance does the student bring to the task?

A third approach to the development of behavioral objectives involves analyzing the elements in a course to determine the purposes each one serves. This requires breaking down the component parts into specific behavioral and noninstructional objectives and depends upon the teacher's competency in the subject matter content as well as his ability in writing objectives. McAshan suggests that this may be done by specifying a goal statement (nonbehavioral), a minimum level behavioral statement (evaluation), and a desired level behavioral statement (success criterion). (1970, p. 61) These may eventually be combined into a statement of objectives plus a combination of the behavioral statements. For example, heredity is a topic included in several psychology courses. An assignment to develop an heredity chart based on physical characteristics of the learner's family could be analyzed as follows:

> *Objective:* To increase student knowledge of the operation of hereditary factors in the determination of physical characteristics.
> *Desired behavioral statement:* As a result of this assignment, given a genetic combination, students should be able to predict the probability of the appearance of various phenotypes on a written examination on which at least 75 percent of the students will obtain 80 percent correct answers in this area.

To do this effectively for an entire course, the teacher must do a great deal of work. If time is limited, as it usually is, the teacher can do portions of the course content every term or every year, meanwhile reviewing and increasing the effectiveness of portions analyzed earlier. It does mean a great deal of thinking about your goals in teaching generally, and in choosing which information specifically to include in a course. Is this effort worthwhile? If done conscientiously, such analysis could lead to a division of course content into core essentials and enrichment that would ensure each student's grasping the fundamental concepts of the course, plus, where time and interest permit, illustrations of the concepts that expand the limits of his knowledge.

Focus 11–1

Behavioral objectives provide direction for the instructor while telling the students specifically what is expected of them. In addition, they provide a guide for test construction and other instruments of evaluation. In every case, the objective states what behavior the student should be able to exhibit after a period of instruction and the criterion against which that behavior is measured. Objectives may be stated in the cognitive, affective, or psychomotor areas. Some examples are:

Run the one hundred yard dash in 9.8 seconds.
Name two examples each of solids, gases, and liquids.
Type 30 words per minute after 95 instructional hours.
Summarize in writing three causes leading to the Vietnam conflict.
Reduce socially aggressive behavior 25 percent in the first 20 minutes of a behavior modification program.

Not everyone believes fully that behavioral objectives should be developed in such structured form. Markle and Tiemann (1970), for example, criticize extant statements of objectives because they too often overlook the factor of instructional interaction in testing the student to see whether he has learned subject matter content. With reference to the educational objectives in the affective domain, Harbeck (1970) suggests that these may need to be less clearly defined than those in the affective taxonomy prepared by Krathwohl et al. (1964) Specifically,

> A major problem to be dealt with concerns the credibility gap between the desired objective and the student behavior that will be accepted as evidence that the objective has been achieved. In the affective domain, it may be unwise to announce objectives to students in advance of instruction. This is in contrast to good practice in the cognitive domain, where a student's difficulty in learning stems from his inability to find out what the learning objective is. Because of the conditioning that students have from their experience with traditional learning, they will go to almost any length to win a teacher's approval. (Harbeck, 1970, p. 51)

We can all voice acceptance, appreciation, or enthusiasm on demand, although we may not be totally convinced of the value of some learning. Therefore, Harbeck's criticism is well taken.

An interview with Ralph Tyler (considered to be the "father" of behavioral objectives) quotes him as saying that educational leaders who adopted behavior objective programs from industry made an error in so doing. "Apparently, they failed to distinguish between 1) the learning of highly specific skills for limited job performance, and 2) the more generalized understanding, problem-solving skills and other kinds of behavior patterns that thoughtful teachers and educators seek to help students develop." (Fishbein, 1973, p. 57) That is, educational tasks were broken down too minutely to be meaningful, sometimes into thousands of specific objectives.

DuChastel and Merrill's review (1973) of studies of the interaction of behavioral objectives and learning reported no clear-cut support for the use of behavioral objectives, although they are not seen as harmful to learning. On the other hand, objectives appear to give direction to learning and may possibly aid students in organizing their learning.

The adaptation of systems analysis from industry to education also elicits objections having to do with the dehumanization of instruction. Somehow, flow charts indicating sequential steps toward objectives appear too mechanistic to some critics of this approach. Moreover, such systematization appears too limiting to other critics. In reality, each of these points can be rebutted. Stating objectives and developing routes to them have little to do with individual or group instruction, but do frequently make provision for the student who wishes to travel more quickly or make detours in the direction of enrichment activities, as well as for the student who needs to retrace the steps. Flow charts are essentially guidelines to handling the course content in a manner designed to fulfill specified objectives. They do not restrict the instructor from elaborating upon the material, but do provide him with "landmarks" and critical checkpoints at which he may evaluate progress toward the course objectives. They also force him to clarify his own thinking. An instructor who limits himself to the specifications in this approach would also be likely to limit himself in any other published curriculum. This is much the same situation as providing state-mandated minimum standards for curriculum, with some regarding such minimums as all that should be done and others viewing such standards as a base.

Suggested Activities

1) Design a study that might demonstrate the effect of behavior objectives on learning.
2) Have a debate in class on the advantages and disadvantages of behavioral objectives.

Accountability

Concern with the setting and reaching of educational objectives is closely related to the concept of accountability. In this concept, all segments of the educational hierarchy are held accountable or responsible to the public for the achievement of learners in the school system. At one extreme, legislators may demand that each teacher submit to some authority clearly defined objectives for each of his or her classes and the results of objective tests taken by students in those classes. If the students performed poorly, the teacher would have to account for the failures.

From another point of view, all levels of the school staff and the school board are

> ... held jointly responsible for the success of the school program. This approach is based on the premise that student learning and development is the result of so many interacting forces and constraints, both within and without the school, that individual contributions to student achievement cannot be accurately identified and measured. Under this type of accountability, staff members might be held solely responsible for what they put into the program (time, skill, and effort), but they would not be held individually accountable for program outcomes. (Gronlund, 1974a, p. 5)

This more realistic viewpoint calls for shared responsibility for success of the educational program, and for diagnosis and remediation when failure occurs. In both views, the concept of accountability in education is forcing a shift in emphasis from teaching to learning.

There are other views of accountability. Combs (1973), a leading humanistic psychologist, points out that

> Humanist objectives for education [self-actualization, responsibility for self and others, creativity, attitudes and values, etc.] cannot be readily assessed by current behavioral, performance-based techniques primarily

because they are matters of personal meaning. Meanings are internal. . . . Behavior, in and of itself, is nothing. It has significance only in terms of its meaning to the behaver and to the receiver. (p. 19)

He further views behavioral objective approaches as a closed system stressing "ends" or results. This is in contrast to humanistic education which is seen as an open system that emphasizes processes and continuing growth. Combs suggests that teachers be held accountable for the processes they use and for being responsible in their actions as professionals, rather than for the test results of their students. Bowers (1973), also a humanist, further states that accountability, on the basis of behavioral objectives, leads to conflict among interest groups and violations of academic freedom. (pp. 176–79) He proposes that accountability test the quality of the learner rather than objectives dictated by the public.

Can you think of ways in which Combs' and Bowers' views of accountability might be put into practice? **Question**

In the sections that follow, you should remember that many means can be used to reach learning objectives. Some will be particularly useful for certain grade levels, while others will be appropriate for some students but not others. If we consider Glaser's (1962) basic teaching model, it is obvious that establishing the objectives comes first, and choosing instructional procedures comes third in a flow chart of the teaching-learning process.

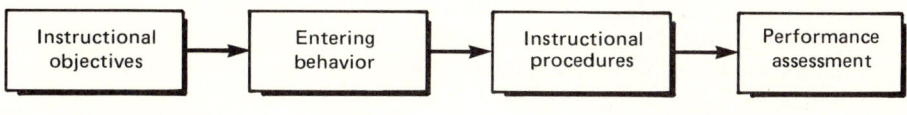

*R. Glaser, 1962, p.6

*Glaser's basic teaching model.** **Figure 11.3**

Entering behavior of the learner is assessed in terms of the objectives of the course. At whatever point the learner should begin, a variety of instructional procedures can be employed. The final step is to assess the effects of such instruction on the learner in terms of the originally stated objectives.

The traditional educational process assumes many common factors among learners. This is reflected in several ways, including school entrance at age five or six, lock-step promotion, assumption of communality of interests, and teacher-pupil relationships. The innovations being introduced into schools today make no such assumptions. The emphasis of the innovators has been, properly, on an awareness of individual differences and the application of learning theory to such differences. (Unfortunately, some school districts adopt the innovations for *all* of their students instead of considering whether they are equally useful for all and using them judiciously.) Greater attention to varying the methods of instruction used will insure a greater likelihood of mastery of skills and concepts by learners.

AUDIOVISUAL TECHNIQUES

The Chinese are credited with being the first to say that one picture is worth 10,000 words. From early times, when people drew pictures with a stick in the sand to illustrate their points or give directions, to the modern-day chalkboard, nonverbal visual techniques have proved successful. Since the invention of photography in the 19th century, teachers have been able to introduce outside events and people into the classroom. Lantern slides have given way to transparencies, color slides, filmstrips, films, and the use of opaque or other special projectors. Many of these tools can be produced by the teacher, and provisions for their utilization are made in all new school buildings, as well as in most of the older ones.

The best film or model or tape is only a tool, however. In order to be effective, its user (the teacher) must keep several things in mind:

1. Since each learner is unique, what he perceives in the stimulus material, and what he remembers about it, will differ from the responses of classmates and teacher.

2. The subject matter to be communicated must be appropriate to the learner's level of ability.

3. The medium (or media) used should be that "which will best provide needed concrete or quasi-concrete learning experiences and at the same time transport the learners higher up the abstraction scale without sacrificing true meaning and understanding in the process." (Wittich and Schuller, 1973, p. 46)

4. The learner should be as involved as possible in planning and using audiovisual media.

5. Teaching strategies should suit the size of the learning group and the different ability levels of the learners as well as the nature of the subject matter.

6. The use of audiovisual materials should encourage further exploration and creative activity on the part of the learner.

Films, filmstrips, slides, etc.
Let's look at the simplest techniques first. With the opaque projector, the teacher can show charts, graphs, models for penmanship, diagrams, photographs, and so on (self-made or available from published sources). These are projected onto a screen, and the teacher can point out specific details on the magnified illustration that might otherwise be impossible to show to the entire class.

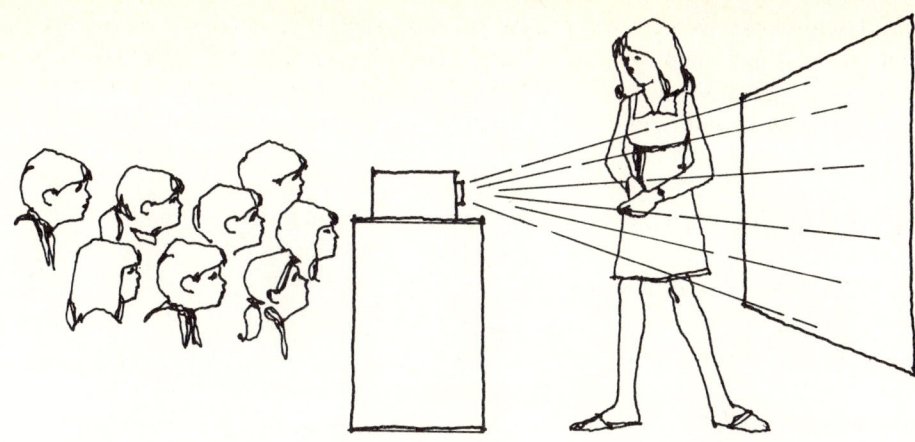

Use of the opaque projector. **Figure 11.4**

An advantage of using the opaque projector, apart from being able to use ready-made materials, is that the teacher can face the class while using the projector. Such face-to-face contact improves the opportunities for teacher-learner interaction. If the teacher is a good photographer, he can produce his own photographs, slides, or even movies of material relevant to a course. Slides, like snapshots, need to be arranged in sequence to give meaning to their presentation. These are invaluable in art courses and in other content areas as well. An important principle in the development of slide presentations or any similar technique is to follow through on a single concept. Furthermore, remember that the script and the visual images should complement, not duplicate, each other. Some presentations ". . . will be heavily dependent on words, some on visuals; but in both cases, the objective is for one to be enriched by the presence of the other." (Cohen, 1974, p. 31)

Transparencies and overlays, designed for use with the overhead projector, may be prepared and produced by the teacher or by an instructional services specialist. Here, as in the instances above, it is important to decide beforehand what it is you want to demonstrate. An overlay technique is particularly useful, for example, in showing systems of the body in biology or changes in the map of Europe during the period 1848–1918 or in developing an understanding of grammatical structure.

Filmstrips are available from several commercial sources for use at all levels from kindergarten through college. They are usually focused on a single topic and are frequently accompanied by a record or tape that provides appropriate narration. Animated drawings are often used in filmstrips, as are diagrams, charts, maps, photographs, samples of text material, and so on.

Contemporary educational films are especially useful for bringing the outside world into the classroom. Many of the films now available were first shown as documentaries on television and are quite well done. (Note: the commercials are omitted.) Other films are produced by the audiovisual departments of colleges and universities primarily for instructional purposes. Again, as noted above, the teacher may photograph places and events in a foreign country or distant area of the United States to show style of life, industries, dress, and so on, in connection with an economic or cultural geography course. The teacher may also photograph contemporary activities locally for use in political science, history, and related courses.

Focus 11–2

> Philips (1969) strongly urges the use of commercial films made during an era, for example, the 1930s, as original visual sources that ". . . tell us far more about the mood of the times, far more about what people thought and felt, than any of the polished documentaries or classics of fiction." (p. 65) Specific films cited are Disney's "The Three Little Pigs," "King Kong," "The Grapes of Wrath," and a number of "escapist" musical and gangster movies of the Depression years. He suggests that these films can be used as a basis of discussion of the philosophies of Presidents Hoover and Roosevelt, why audience reacted to the films as they did, why escapist films were popular in this period, and so on. Charlie Chaplin's "The Great Dictator" can similarly be viewed in the context of world politics of the late 1930s and the early 1940s, or "No Blade of Grass" as reflective of the ecological and political concerns of the 1970s.

Filmmaking as a school activity is justified because of its multisensory involvement, development of discrimination and relationships in perception, active participation of the learner, ego-reinforcement potential, and instructive qualities in the area of expression and communication. (Putsch, 1970) One group of seventh-graders, none of whom knew how to operate a camera, used Super-8mm. cameras during the school year, with higher quality standards set for each of their ten films. Assignments varied from developing a story, to animation, to developing a particular theme.

Tapes and records

Sound can supplement these visual techniques very effectively, or can be used independently. As mentioned earlier, records or tapes often are used with filmstrips, and soundtracks are made with or for many movies. If the teacher wishes, he can tape his own narrations to a unit of slides, transparencies, or other materials to ensure a more standardized presentation for future classes, or to review his presentation for improvement in the future.

Through the use of sound, the teacher can bring to life the historical events of this century, the voices of people to demonstrate proper speech habits or speech impediments, musical offerings, foreign language lessons, lectures by specialists, dramatic readings, and so on. One of the foreign language approaches, in fact, makes intensive use of tapes combined with filmstrips. In a child development course, tapes have been used to demonstrate changes in use of language, vocabulary, voice pitch, and conversational ability during childhood and adolescence. Records and tapes can teach children at a much younger level about the differences in sound among planes, trains, trucks, and cars, and the noises of animals.

Tape can also be used to give directions to the learner for further learning. It can aid the learner in using correct speech sounds and patterns, learning vocabulary, and reviewing multiplication tables. If the learner listens to the taped voice, for example, and is then asked to record his own response, he and the teacher can review together his progress with the assigned task. Elementary school children usually are delighted to record and later hear their own voices. This may be an especially useful device, too, for learners who are afraid to speak in front of the class.

Instructional radio is used more in developing countries than in the United States, particularly where geography and/or costs prohibit television instruction. It can also be used to broadcast symphony programs, operas, and speeches or events of significance. When these occur on weekends, they may be taped for delayed replay.

For your prospective field of teaching, or for the educational psychology course, select two or three topics. For each topic, list specific ideas and the ways in which you could use audiovisual aids to teach them.

Suggested Activity

Another combination of audio and visual techniques is, of course, television. Several possibilities are available here. Commercial television occasionally provides programs appropriate to course content, as in "specials" produced by *National Geographic* magazine or by the networks, news documentaries, "Sunrise Semester" courses, "Sesame Street," and others. Educational television, or ETV, exists primarily to provide informative programs or entire courses. One adaptation of ETV has been courses designed to be relayed over closed-circuit television from the studio to many classrooms in a school system. This method permits employment of one or two specialists to teach courses to all children needing them, without the expense of having such a specialist in each of several schools in a district. It also permits students to hear and see stimulating guest speakers who might otherwise be in contact with only a small group. Closed-circuit television is also used for teaching in medical schools, psychiatric settings, and other situations where it would be impossible or impractical to have a large live audience. However, television is not without its disadvantages. It

Television

> ... shares with a book the limitation of being unable to support the performance-feedback portion of the learning act. The viewer may be responding appropriately to what he is viewing, and receiving feedback from his response, or he may not be. The program itself has no way of *insuring* that the learner's performance and its subsequent feedback will occur. (Gagné, 1974, p. 7)

One also needs to be careful, as with any technique, of the attitudes conveyed in the presentation.

The advent of videotape has made it possible to prepare special productions or full courses at the convenience of the teacher and to show them as needed in the classroom. Some newer schools have their own videotape production facilities, enabling students as well as professionals to produce programs. At Upper Moreland (Pennsylvania) Junior High School, for example, students taped a documentary using local historical sites as background for a unit on colonial history. Entire college courses are presented by using videotape where there are too many students and not enough good teachers available. Wherever videotape or ETV is used, however, the classroom teacher must be prepared to review and supplement what has been shown on television. This "warning" is particularly relevant in view of a study made in Pennsylvania that reflected a need for in-service instruction of teachers in the efficient and effective utilization of ETV. (Rookey and Peters, 1970)

Sometimes videotaped programs are combined with limited classroom discussion to earn college credits. This is a relatively recent development, growing out of the movement for "life-long learning" and "universities without walls." An example of such a program in the mid-1970s was "The Ascent of Man" series. Of course, prior to that college courses, from literature to the sciences, had been presented on television. These were and are usually shown at 6 A.M. The change seen in the newer movement is to a more reasonable hour (8 or 9 P.M.) that is attractive to more adults. The content is also presented in a less traditional format.

Micro-teaching

One of the special uses of videotape has been in teacher education. Students in methods courses may do "micro-teaching" to discover their assets and liabilities before going out to do classroom practice teaching. The prospective teacher prepares a short lesson and presents it to a limited audience of classmates and the instructor. The presentation is videotaped and played back by the instructor who can then make constructive comments. The student is able also to observe his or her own distracting mannerisms, speech problems, and so on, which is usually not possible. The comments may be grouped under the headings of quality of instruction (style, logic of presentation, language used, subject matter orientation), teacher-pupil interaction (response to pupils), and teacher traits (warmth and humor, supportiveness, directiveness, dominance). (Biddle and Adams, 1967, p. 119) "Micro-teaching" also affords the prospective teacher a chance to teach before a live "class," reducing the threat of "stagefright" in the student teaching situation. An elaboration of this approach to teacher education will be found in chapter fourteen, when we consider the teacher as a learner.

All of the audiovisual techniques supplement traditional teaching methods by adding another dimension to the limited information that any single teacher can prepare and transmit to students. Users of these techniques can illustrate, clarify, and expand learning. In addition, considering the hard-pressed financial situation of most school districts and other educational institutions, the various television techniques can frequently provide better instruction at lower cost for more students than can more traditional programs. They can also reduce the problem of too few teachers in certain fields or locations by providing specialists as needed.

"Micro-teaching"—a *teaching* and *learning* experience.

PROGRAMMED INSTRUCTION

From the elementary school years on, increasing numbers of learners use self-instructional textbooks or mechanical programs in which the principles of programmed instruction are applied. Far from replacing human teachers, these programs are supposed to enable the teacher to function more effectively. Programmed instruction can present fundamental principles, "rules," and basic information in a simple structured format that even the slowest learner in the class can comprehend. The teacher can then elaborate on these fundamentals, demonstrating exceptions to and applications of the rules to the class. Programs are available in textbook form ("software") or in a variety of machine-presented formats ("hardware"). They are valuable self-instructional aids, too, for the learner who wishes to move ahead quickly or who is no longer in school but who wishes to acquire information in a new area.

Textbooks = software

The programmed textbook is prepared usually in one of two styles: linear or branched. The linear presentation reduces error to almost zero, but because of the minute bits of information provided in each unit or segment, may become boring to the learner who understands the content without difficulty. Every learner must read and respond correctly to every unit of information, whether in book or machine format. "Branching" permits learners who understand the content to bypass redundant review segments and usually contains larger bits of information per unit than the linear style. The format involves some variation of multiple-choice, thus increasing the possibility of error, and might look like the illustration in Figure 11.5.

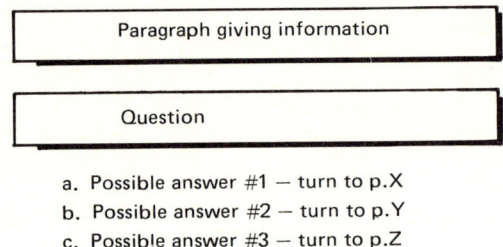

Figure 11.5   *Illustration of "branching."*

Upon turning to the appropriate page, the learner finds out whether his choice was correct. If it *was* correct, he is given new information. If it was incorrect, the information is restated in another way, and he is then referred back to the original paragraph and question. If he again chooses an incorrect answer, there is a third explanation of the concept and again referral to the original page. By this time, the learner is expected to make the correct choice, with understanding (see Figure 11.6).

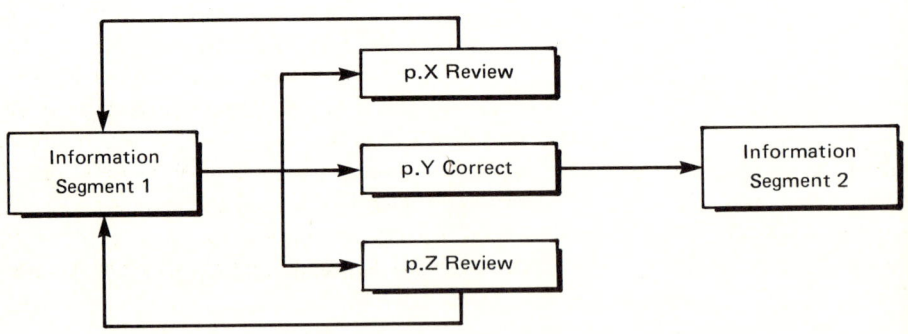

Figure 11.6   *Diagram of branched program.*

Programmed textbooks and hardware share these basic formats and principles. The texts are more portable, less expensive per unit, and more familiar to students than are computers and less sophisticated "teaching machines."

The earliest teaching machines were designed by Sidney Pressey in the 1920s and were "rediscovered" and refined by B. F. Skinner in the 1940s and 1950s. Omar K. Moore developed a "talking typewriter" that has been used to teach three-year-olds to read, using a combination of audiovisual and tactile techniques. His approach is known as the Edison Responsive Environment, or E.R.E.

CAI=hardware

> The E.R.E. machine is housed in a large metal cabinet, one side of which comprises the machine interface (i.e., the machine parts to which the learner responds). The interface includes a protruding typewriter keyboard, a student speaker, and a student microphone. Above the keyboard is a large lucite housing containing the typewriter carriage, a small slide projector screen, and a small rectangular window through which printed material may be displayed. Coupled with this display is a small red pointer which may be used to indicate any single character within the display. (Richardson and McSweeney, 1970, p. 81)

The E.R.E. appears to teach visual discrimination skills via association and immediate knowledge of results (progress to the next letter or a "locked key" in cases of error), which with a supportive learning environment leads the child to beginning reading ability. Modifications of Moore's approach have been undertaken at the New York University Institute of Developmental Studies in order ". . . to create more relevant and efficient response systems" en route to developing a program of beginning reading lessons. (p. 86) The high cost of the E.R.E. has limited its use to research programs. A simplified version of the E.R.E., without the audio stimulus and feedback, is shown in Figure 11.7.

A simple "teaching machine. **Figure 11.7**

The most complex hardware is used in computer-assisted instruction. The experience of having a computer "talk back" to you in print is an eerie one, indeed! Many computers are programmed to do this, and many programmers even build humor into their instructional programs—a human touch that personalizes the computer.

Atkinson describes three levels of computer-assisted instruction:

1. fixed, linear sequences of problems designed for drill and practice, which permit no modifications in terms of the learner's responses,
2. "tutorial" programs which incorporate limited branching, and
3. "dialogue" programs, the goal of which ". . . is to provide the richest possible student-system interaction where the student is free to construct natural-language responses, ask questions in an unrestricted mode, and in general exercise almost complete control over the sequence of learning events." (Atkinson, 1968, pp. 225–26)

Depending on the objectives for which CAI (computer-assisted instruction) is used and the level of instruction, it can be criticized as being rigid and impersonal, a threat to human individuality and freedom, and excessively standardized. As Suppes (1968) points out, however, this is true only for the drill and basic learning levels. When basic skills of math, reading, foreign languages, and other subjects are taught, it is necessary for all learners to acquire certain concepts. A "live" teacher, gearing instruction to the "average" student in the classroom, rarely can permit the rapid learners to go far ahead of the class or to hold back the class until the slow learners grasp the skill or concept. With CAI, although every student may have to complete the entire instructional sequence, this can be done at the learner's own pace, within the limits of the semester or year. The tutorial and dialogue programs permit even more flexibility. Programs tends to be highly responsive to individual differences. Significant differences in achievement are not always the success criteria, however. More often, instructors are concerned with savings in time in achieving a given level of success.

CAI programs are developed and written by teachers, not machines. Once prepared in computer-compatible language, they are stored in the computer's storage unit and are called into use by the student sitting at a typewriter keyboard. The computer stores the student's responses and can produce on demand the progress record of each student using the program. Students may be absent from the course for varying lengths of time and still resume at the point where they had stopped previously.

Focus 11–3

All evaluations of programmed instruction must consider the difficulty and size of the learning task, pacing of instruction, internal logic or meaningfulness, and organization of the program. In addition, it would appear that personality characteristics of the learner must also be considered.

Sutter and Reid (1969) investigated the interaction of personality characteristics and CAI, using 100 introductory chemistry students as subjects. They all had SAT Math scores of 570+ and were compared on the Sarason Test Anxiety Scale and the Sociability and Dominance scales of the California Personality Inventory. Students were assigned to one of three groups: a) 40 took the problem-solving course alone at a computer terminal, b) 42 took the same course with a partner, and c) 18 did not take the course. Sutter and Reid found that subjects ". . . high in sociability and low in test anxiety achieved better in pairs. The Ss low in sociability and high in test anxiety achieved better alone. Attitude was most favorable toward CAI in submissive Ss paired with dominants, and in dominants working alone." (p. 153)

It is possible, obviously, that students will react differently in terms of achievement and attitude to CAI, but they also react differently to "live" instruction, ETV, and other teaching techniques.

A review of studies of programmed instruction (PI) and computer-assisted instruction (CAI) indicates that

> both PI and CAI attempt to improve the quality of instruction by providing for its individualization along one or more dimensions. . . . Though there are often no significant differences in achievement, some of the studies do report a saving in student time, and this is an index of success. When small amounts of CAI are used as a supplement to regular classroom instruction (as with the elementary-school drill-and-practice programs), substantial evidence suggests that it leads to an improvement in achievement, particularly for slower students. (Jamison, Suppes, and Wells, 1974, p. 56)

If you have had either a PI or CAI course, what were your reactions to it as compared with more traditional teaching/learning experiences? — **Question**

INDIVIDUALLY PRESCRIBED INSTRUCTION

Individually prescribed instruction (IPI) is an innovation that incorporates behavioral objectives, extensive diagnosis to determine each student's levels of skills and abilities on entering new learning task situations, and a wide variety of teaching materials and methods, including CAI. Moreover, the computer can be used to store all the information gathered about each learner so that appropriate learning tasks can be assigned at any time. "The rate of learning, amount of practice, type of materials, and mode of instruction are the parameters of individual differences emphasized in IPI." (Bushnell and Rappaport, 1971, p. 93) After diagnosing the learner's strengths and weaknesses, the teacher writes an initial "prescription," citing learning tasks, materials, and situations (self-instruction, tutoring, filmstrip, group instruction), or a test on the particular subject matter. Student progress is then analyzed through a study of work completed, time spent, and/or test results. The teacher continually monitors the learner's progress and revises the prescription as needed.

A given prescription in reading, for example, may refer the student to preparatory worksheets to be followed by a) reinforcement of what has been learned at a computer station, or to b) a reading text, or to c) remedial tutoring. After a progress check, the student may move on to audiotape material or back to a review lesson. The prescription states specifically page numbers, lesson numbers, tape segments, and so on.

Considering the variations in intra-individual abilities as well as inter-individual differences among learners, IPI may well be one of the most important innovations in education today. The potential effect of such a program on motivation to learn is not difficult to envision. However, it is still in an experimental stage, is very expensive, and is not generally adapted to courses above the elementary level.

"NEW" METHODS

There are changes both in subject matter and in teaching methods included in this section, for they are clearly interwoven. Advances in one appear to evoke changes in the other.

Mathematics Concepts formerly taught in high school or college mathematics courses are now presented, simply, in the preschool and primary grades. With changes in content have come changes in teaching techniques. "Discovery" and problem-solving activities are fundamental to several of the new math programs, as well as to other subject matter areas. The emphasis in learning math has shifted from rote memorization of number facts and theorems to an understanding of mathematical concepts and a reasonable mastery of fundamental mathematical techniques. According to the U.S. Department of Health, Education, and Welfare, there are three objectives to modern methods in mathematics:

1. A proper balance between reasoning and drill,
2. Adjustment of pace and content to rapid expansion of scientific knowledge, and
3. Increased pleasure in learning. (Phillips and Kluttz, 1963, pp. 5–6)

Focus 11–4 Many of the modern mathematics programs that held great promise in the 1960s were rejected in the 1970s because they accomplished too little in a positive sense. Nevertheless, much of their language lingers.

Common to most of these programs are concepts such as sets, number lines, probability, commutative and distributive laws, different base systems, geometric concepts, and logic. They may be presented in workbooks, as in the Madison Project, via CAI, as in the Suppes-Hawley program, or in regular textbook form, as in the University of Illinois program. Illustrations of some of these concepts are:

1.

2.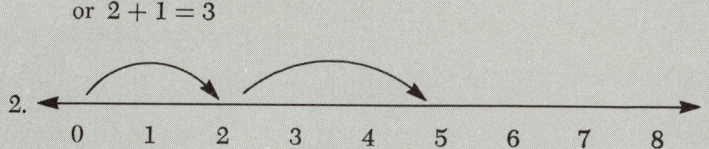
    or $2 + 1 = 3$

3. $625_{10} = 100_{25}$
   $332_3 = 2992_{10}$

4. $\square \times (\triangle + 5) = (\square \times \triangle) + (\square \times 5)$
   $\square + \square + \square = 3 \times \square$

The "new math" of today may well be new to teachers as well as learners as the conversion to metric measurement progresses. Instructional techniques include many of those already in use for our nonmetric math. Some difficulties exist for teachers unaccustomed to the metric system because they find it a problem not to keep "translating" from one system to another. However, children taught from the early grades, as in California, to "think metric" have an easier time. A. Glaser (1974) suggests many techniques that teachers can use in teaching metrics. In the school alone, he has dozens of applications to measurement, attitudes to the metric system, typing, economics, industrial arts, English, social studies, and the sciences. (pp. 107–8).

Reading

After multitudinous complaints about low achievement in reading, new approaches are being tried in this field, too. One vast improvement has been in the content of primary-grade readers. Fewer children each year are being exhorted to "Look! Look! See Dick run!" in a white, middle-class family setting. More and more young learners are being exposed to integrated neighborhoods filled with trucks, stores, and a wide variety of people. Their preschool experience has been broadened by both television and commercial books with "real" stories, and their textbooks should increasingly capitalize on this experience.

It is recognized now, also, that the "whole-word" method of teaching reading may not be as effective as a phonics approach. There has been some return to the "word families" of yesteryear, using "at," "ake," "it," and other syllables in combination with a variety of initial consonants to build up reading vocabularies. Children are taught to attack new words in terms of initial and ending consonants, long and short vowels—and surprisingly, they do. One of the techniques in teaching reading is i/t/a, the initial teaching alphabet.

Focus 11–5

> Laura Woodman
>
> plees taek mee tw the seeshaur. ie liek tw plae in the sand on the beech. it is fun swimmin in the waiter. and saelin mie boet with mie father.

Although there are some strange symbols in i/t/a, you should have experienced relatively little difficulty in reading the paragraph above. Children as young as four years of age, poor readers in higher grades, mentally retarded individuals, and persons learning to read English as a second language also find this method of learning to read fairly easy. The advocates of i/t/a claim that this facility is due in part to the consistency of the i/t/a alphabet. That is, each word and each symbol sounds the way it looks. Transition from i/t/a readers to traditionally spelled readers is made gradually, with some learners completing the i/t/a series by the end of the first grade with third-grade reading ability. Most pupils make the transition during second grade.

Comparisons with pupils learning to read via T.O. (traditional orthography) reveal that the i/t/a groups, on the average, achieve about a half-grade higher on achievement tests in word reading, paragraph reading, and spelling. More exciting, perhaps, to pupils, parents, and teachers alike, is the fact that the i/t/a-taught children are able to write creatively as soon as they learn enough symbols. Original stories and poems are *written* by five-year-olds, not dictated!

Other approaches to teaching reading use programmed instruction (the Sullivan program), stress letter-naming, emphasize spelling patterns of words, or use linguistics. (Della-Piana and Endo, 1973) The several federally funded

Educational Regional Laboratories have developed a number of reading programs as part of their research efforts. Both the Southwest and Northwest ERLs have placed special emphasis on adapting the content of the reading programs to specific minority groups (e.g., Spanish-speaking and Alaskan) in their respective regions. (Baker, 1973)

Science

In science, college professors in the life and physical sciences have collaborated with psychologists and teachers to develop several new programs in their fields. This collaboration is a unique effort, for before academicians stood aloof from developing curricula for precollege students. At the elementary level, there are several programs: 1) Science Curriculum Improvement Study for grades K–6, 2) Elementary Science Study, grades K–8, 3) Science—A Process Approach, grades K–6, and 4) Sense and Tell, preprimary level. (Seferian and Cole, 1970) Enthusiasm runs high in the classroom as these youngsters explore, inquire, and discover scientific principles for themselves.

Similarly, innovative courses have been introduced at the secondary level. The Physical Science Study Committee developed the Secondary School Physics Program which stresses integrative and widely generalizable concepts in modern physics, depth rather than breadth in coverage, careful programming of principles in sequence, and the experimental approach in science. (Finley, 1959) The Biological Sciences Curriculum Study group developed two versions of a high school biology program. (BSCS, 1963) These were designed not only to stimulate interest on the part of the learner, but also to enable him to analyze and synthesize the concepts in line with the objectives discussed at the beginning of this chapter. Related efforts are being made in chemistry and in junior high school science survey courses.

Simulation

It was pointed out in chapter one that much of what we consider to be innovative and modern was being used centuries ago, that our "new" techniques are frequently merely modifications and technological improvements of old practices. An excellent example of these statements is the use of "simulation games." Simulation games are a formalized and more mature version of the "let's pretend" activities of childhood and, as Abt has stated, are rediscoveries rather than new discoveries. (1967, pp. 123–24) In these activities, the participants play meaningful roles in attempting to solve the problems that face mankind at all levels, from individual concerns to global interaction.

The skills evoked by such games are those that the teacher usually tries to foster: recall, intuition, and communication. The games, while a pleasurable change from traditional practice exercises, often stimulate more effort and involvement on the part of the learner than many other techniques have been able to do. For example, eighth-graders used a student-conceived game approach to learning the rules of grammar and the parts of speech. In order to create games, ". . . they had to know the subject matter before identifying the objective and setting down the rules. And, if they were going to play the game, they had to follow instructions and, through them, learn the part of speech intended to be taught." (Clark, 1970, p. 132) Students formed committees to develop the games and then field-tested and refined their products. The learning acquired through the games was reviewed and reinforced by the development of student-initiated sixty-second film commercials that they used to "sell" their games to their peers.

In another project, Allender (1970) used inquiry materials called "I Am the Mayor" with children from grades three to seven to study the development of inquiry activity with age. The learners' activities were scored in terms of problem sensitivity, problem formulation, search behavior, and time spent. Materials included sections and documents dealing with the Mayor's Work, the Mayor's Questions, the Mayor's Files, and the Mayor's Decisions. "With the exceptions for the third grade, in each case the means for each score for boys and girls combined increased in order of grade level." (p. 222) No sex differences were observed, nor were scores related to reading level or intelligence. The third grade, as noted, was an exception to the general relationship between inquiry scores and grade level. Allender suggests that the much higher scores achieved with these children may be due to greater interest in asking questions at this age.

It is claimed that stimulation games are appropriately used at any grade level, with learners of varying intellectual skills, and from different socioeconomic-cultural backgrounds, and for achievement of different levels in Bloom's *Taxonomy*. They can focus on skill, chance, reality, and/or fantasy. (Abt, 1970, pp. 9–14) Lest you think that the games must be teacher- or student-developed, some examples of games already designed are listed by Abt for use in different subject areas, although most are in the social sciences and at different grade levels. Care must be exercised that the stimulation game is appropriate to the level and abilities of the players (learners). It is Abt's contention, however, that ". . . a game can be justified only if it gives the students a deeper understanding of what happened [e.g., at the American Constitutional Convention] than they can obtain from conventional teaching in that same hour, or if the game can put across an equally good understanding of the topic in less time." (1967, p. 155) Lauffer (1973) says that game simulations promote a clearer view of the real world. The players (learners) have to create and consider alternatives, eventually coming to some agreement. (p. 38) A third justification for the use of games and similar activities would seem to be the generation of positive attitudes on the part of the learners toward subject matter, assuming no difference in learning between a games approach and a traditional approach. Understanding is enhanced, too, as the learners become emotionally involved with the simulation situation.

SCHOOL-WIDE MODIFICATIONS

All of the techniques and approaches discussed in the last section were essentially ones to be employed by individual teachers. In this section, let us consider changes that are school-wide and that help to destroy the walls, figuratively speaking, of the self-contained classroom.

One modification that has been introduced at the elementary level is the practice of departmentalization, or semispecialization, long familiar to secondary school students. This practice recognizes the varying capabilities of teachers in different content areas and utilizes the special expertise possessed by individual teachers. Few teachers are equally able to teach reading, arithmetic, science, history, music, art, and spelling. A group of teachers in one or two grade levels, therefore, "specialize," with one teaching math and science to all children in those grades, another teaching reading and spelling, and a third instructing in the social sciences. Most school districts, except for small isolated rural systems, already have music and art specialists on the staff. The teachers coordinate their presentations so that, where possible, students experience harmony in the learning process. The movement from one teacher and classroom to another makes the child in middle childhood feel quite "grown up," like his older siblings who follow this pattern in junior high, and it eases somewhat the transition from one school to the next higher one. It also provides a variety of teacher-pupil relationships, which may be helpful to the learner. Although departmentalization is standard procedure at the secondary level, its introduction to the elementary school is considered to be innovative.

Another "shift" related to specialization is the growing movement toward middle schools. These include grades five or six through eight. Here, too, departmentalization is practiced. The grouping of youngsters approaching adolescence is believed to make them more comfortable in the learning environment. Flexibility in scheduling and an earlier introduction of courses such as industrial arts and home economics are also possible in the middle school.

Team teaching

Another change in the schools is seen in team teaching, which may be a variant of departmentalization or its own thing entirely. The most common implementation of team teaching is, in a sense, an adaptation to the precollege levels of the large lecture with small discussion sections, found in so many colleges and universities. The team leader, or "master teacher," holds the major responsibility for the course presentation. Working with the leader are all of the teachers on the team, that is, those who are involved in teaching the curriculum in question. Weekly planning meetings are held, at which time the content to be taught and the timing of large-group sessions are decided. The team leader is not necessarily responsible for large-group lectures or demonstrations; sometimes a member of the team has the greatest interest and/or ability in the topic to be presented. Each team member inevitably teaches in his own unique way, but team teaching tends to minimize the differences in learning because of differences in teachers and to maximize the contributions that a single teacher can make to the entire group. As with departmentalization, the student is exposed to more than one teacher per school year and should obtain better instruction because of the increased specialization and coordination within the curriculum.

According to Clifford (1973), however, "Confidence in the great effectiveness of team teaching, if based on research, rested on extremely slight evidence...." (p. 21) As with other modifications, it is possible that there is little real change in learner *achievement*. Team teaching, however, does offer the learner a richer learning environment, interaction with a variety of teachers instead of only one, and the possibility that more positive attitudes toward learning will result.

"Open classrooms" A marked change in learning environment occurs when the "open classroom" program is put into effect. This program, quite popular in Great Britain, stresses learning rather than teaching. It establishes a teacher-learner relationship based on developmental theory, thus applying the research results found at the university level. In England, theory and practice are interwoven in the primary schools. This has not been true historically in American education except possibly in university demonstration schools. (Weber, 1971, p. 238)

There is increasing acceptance of the open classroom concept at the elementary level despite the differences in the British and American patterns of education. Children explore the materials that stimulate them, frequently engaging in spur-of-the-moment "let's pretend" activities with classmates. The teacher's job is to provide appropriate materials to motivate the children and to be ready to give specific instruction and responses when a child indicates interest in learning. All kinds of materials are furnished, including scales with weights, simple pictorial and lettered signs, measuring cups, simple lever machines, artifacts of other cultures, and so on. Much of this seems reminiscent of John Dewey's "child-centered curriculum."

Since each child is recognized as having unique abilities and interests, demands on the teacher's knowledge and flexibility are often much higher than in a traditional "closed" classroom. (Silberman, 1970, chapters six and seven) The open classroom does not mean unstructured chaos. Rather it requires multiple preparations at several levels in a variety of media and constant feedback by the teacher. One or more teacher aides during the day help to increase the individual attention that learners need in this setting.

There are teachers who find it difficult to adapt to the noise, additional personnel, and extra work that the open classroom brings. There is scant evidence of changes in learner achievement with which to convince them of the value of this approach. However, increased interest and more positive attitudes on the part of their pupils may encourage them to move more toward an integration of teacher-, child-, and materials-centered approaches.

In an analysis of the Open Education movement, Walberg and Thomas (1972) find that those who favor the movement have a point of view far more consistent "... with developmental, humanistic, and clinical psychology than with the branches that have been most influential in education, connectionism, behaviorism, and psychometrics." (p. 198) Sharp differences were found between open and traditional classes, in both the United States and Britain, in the following areas:

1. *Provisioning* for learning (materials, freedom of movement, grouping for learning)

2. *Humaneness*, respect, openness, and warmth

3. *Diagnosis* of learning events (use of tests to help children learn)

4. *Instruction*, guidance, and extension of learning, and

5. *Evaluation* of diagnostic information. (Walberg and Thomas, 1972)

These are areas in which a conscientious, person-oriented teacher would usually function with greater concern for the learner than what is to be learned. The increasing acceptance in the open classroom of the teacher as a resource person and guide encourages other teachers to behave similarly.

Also coming to some of our schools from England is a related practice—vertical grouping (also known as "family" grouping). In classes that use this practice, children from two or three adjacent age groups (for example, five to six to seven years) learn together. It seems a bit like the old-fashioned country school, doesn't it? Actually, vertical grouping recognizes that children of the same chronological age learn at different rates, but that children of slightly different ages may learn at the same rate. In addition, older *or* more advanced students can help younger or less advanced learners. The teacher, it is claimed, has little difficulty working with the multiple age groups, since there is more opportunity for compatability according to maturity and/or learning levels.

Vertical grouping

Vertical grouping is not restricted to primary grade classes, such as the one described in Focus 11–6. In many American schools today, children in adjacent grades (three to four, five to six) may be in one classroom. They join together in some activities (e.g., science) and separate for others (e.g., math). Friendships and cooperation span the age groups. The teacher meanwhile keeps abreast of the progress of each child. She or he can set up reading groups that cross grade lines according to the needs of each learner. There are fewer complaints on the part of learners, their parents, or teachers about the learner being restricted to a fifth-grade reader when he is capable of reading at the sixth-grade level. (In a more traditional setting, such complaints have been answered with, "What will his sixth-grade teacher do with him?")

Focus 11–6

In north London (England), the Northside Primary School houses just over 400 pupils, ranging in age from 3 to 11 years. Both vertical grouping and the open classroom practices are employed here. The infant school has two levels: nursery for the 3s and 4s, and a 5–6–7 level; the junior section also has two levels: 8–9, and 10–11. When you enter a classroom filled with 35 or 40 five- to seven-year-olds, what do you see? A group of six youngsters, clustered on the floor at their teacher's feet, reading from an i/t/a storybook; another small group working with number materials; a third cluster drawing; four or five diligently constructing buildings with Lego blocks; one or two at the sandbox, and a single child off at the side reading

> to himself. Children move easily from activity to activity, ignoring age differences as they focus on a common interest. For some, interest keeps them going for far longer than the usual kindergartner's attention span. For others, frequent shifts from group to group are more characteristic. In the midst of this busy, noisy (by American standards), but happy classroom, the teacher is now reading with one little girl, but is quite aware of what everyone else is doing. She knows each child's personal and academic progress.
>
> Not only this class seems noisy. The voices of active, happy learners reverberate through the corridors of the almost ninety-year-old school building. The accents vary from crisp upper-middle-class British to the careless speech of children of the poor, and from clearly English to Indian, Cypriot, Italian, African, and other language sources. (In April 1971, 35 percent of the school's population was non-English.)

The point to this illustration is that the age of the building doesn't matter; the background of the children doesn't matter; the number in the class doesn't matter; to make vertical grouping, open classrooms, and other innovative practices work; the key factor is the teacher. What is needed is a teacher who is personally committed to helping children learn and willing to move away from traditional modes of teaching discipline.

Other innovations

At all school levels, the growth and use of library and self-instructional centers has been increasing markedly. Referral to such centers not only for research assignments but also during class time is an innovation at many schools. In areas of the country where such centers would be too expensive for a single school district, several districts pool their resources on a centralized exchange basis. This is being done with teachers as well as materials, at the college level as well as in the grades.

Small schools do face problems unknown to urban districts. In Oregon, efforts to improve the quality of small school instruction were made with the support of government-funded "mini-grants" to develop and implement new programs. With the cooperation of state education personnel, the small schools evaluated themselves in terms of programs and needs, developed extensive in-service programs and consultation services, designed learning packages that emphasize individualized instruction, improved their guidance programs, evolved interdisciplinary curricula, and involved community residents in education. (Miller, 1970) Such cooperation is an innovation in education.

Suburban districts, which have rarely had special programs for the nonaverage and nonacademic students, have discovered that joining forces permits them to establish classes for exceptional children and vocational-technical schools, which were far too expensive to operate independently. Such unified action also makes optimal use of the limited number of teachers available for these programs. Stimulation to develop the programs and put them into practice has come from enactment of federal and state legislation that encourages these activities and contributes financially to their formulation.

Helping students to learn is the key mission of the teacher.

Changes in school routine also reflect school-wide modifications in the teaching-learning process. Schools such as Winooski High School, near Burlington, Vermont, and Rochester (Vermont) High School provide occasional opportunities for curriculum expansion during one- or two-day "breaks" scattered through the school year. These opportunities include field trips, seminars, and other informal activities. The reports indicate that the activities generate motivation and new interests and also improve faculty-student relations. (Pierce, 1970)

Work-study programs, long employed in distributive education programs and at the college level, have also been introduced at the high school level. At Cheltenham (Pennsylvania) High School, seniors may find a job or project related to their own interests or prospective occupation and work part-time during school hours. This gives them a chance to find out whether they really like the field of work they have chosen, or if they might do better in some other line of work.

Innovations are apparent at the preschool level, too. There is growing recognition that the nursery school child needs more than a glorified baby-sitting service in a group setting. Academic subjects are being introduced to stimulate and temporarily satisfy the rampant curiosity of this age group: study of the weather, simple French phrases, recognition of letters and numbers, biological processes (thanks to gerbils, rabbits, and plants), as well as other learning experiences. Use of the Montessori techniques is becoming more widespread. The techniques used on TV's "Sesame Street" are adapted to the classroom. "Sesame Street" itself has been a strong influence on pre-nursery school children as well as slightly older children through its format of using "hard-sell" methods of commercials to teach numbers, the alphabet, prepositions, and a variety of other concepts. Vertical grouping works well with these youngsters, and the less rigid structure of the open classroom encourages them to maintain an interest in their activities.

Mini-summary   Traditional schools, like cars and flowers, come in many models: factory, church, custodial, and warehouse. In the factory model, the raw material (the learner) is molded into a final product by standardized steps, with quality control (standardized tests) exercised frequently in the process. The custodial model has the school acting as babysitter to the young of our society. The church model features oral delivery (teacher as preacher) to a congregation (of learners), using one book for all. In the warehouse model, the school stocks courses and credits, each in its own egg-crate (classroom) with a clear label.*

By contrast, the open classroom and the introduction of innovative techniques have been described as supermarkets with a variety of products and brands, or as a travel agency offering different routes to a goal. The teacher in the open classroom has "an iron hand in a velvet glove," for the teacher prescribes the instruction and sets the limitis for a wide range of learning experiences and behaviors that are generally perceived as pleasant by the learners. It has been suggested that rather than fitting learners to a technique, "We should, as educators, be like the tailor, instead, cutting the cloth and fitting the garment to the wearer." (Schwartz, 1975b, p. 97) It is from this vantage point that we have regarded innovations in education.

RESPONSE OF THE LEARNER TO INNOVATIONS

There is a general impression that the initial favorable reactions to the innovations discussed are the results of a "Hawthorne effect;" that is, positive results ensue from being part of an experimental or research project. This may be true and, for this reason, such projects are being studied over extended periods of time. Novelty soon wears off, and it is safer to try to evaluate programs after they have been in effect for some time.

There is little question that interruptions of the traditional lecture-discuss-test format are welcomed by most students. If audiovisual aids are

---

*Adapted from *Scribe*, official publication of the Pennsylvania Association for Supervision and Curriculum Development, 1974, p. 12. (Author unknown)

used to enrich course content, students respect and enjoy those that are concretely related to what they are supposed to learn. Diversion for diversion's sake is frequently resented, even among preadolescents. It is, therefore, the obligation of the teacher to make clear the purposes and relevance of including the film, tape, or other device being introduced.

A number of papers have been published dealing with learner response to programmed instruction, CAI, simulation games, and other innovations. One area of concern has been with the effects of anxiety, motivation, and task difficulty on learning through programmed instruction. These studies have been done most often at the college level. Knight and Sassenrath (1966), for instance, found that learning was greater using programmed instruction for high-achievement-motivated students in terms of time input, number of errors, and short-term retention, and for high-test-anxiety students in terms of time spent and number of errors, than for their peers who scored low on each of these personal variables.

Another area of concern is the effect of student attitudes toward learning through CAI and the effects of CAI on student attitudes toward learning generally. Mitzel suggests, far from dehumanizing the classroom, "With sensitive programming, computer terminals can create an absorbing, responsive environment for learning. The student knows that when he or she makes a response, something will happen immediately to provide him or her with an appraisal of the quality of the response and offer guidance toward future efforts." (1974, p. 126) At the college level, Mathis, Smith, and Hansen (1970) concluded from their related study that more positive attitudes toward CAI were expressed by the group that actually experienced it, and also those who were given familiar, immediately relevant material. They stress, though, the importance of having high-quality CAI programs if such positive attitudes are to be maintained. It is additionally true that the rigid structure of the "drill and practice" CAI programs is often resented by students after the novelty of the technique has faded. However, positive attitudes are more often maintained by the "tutorial" and "dialogue" formats. Part of the reason for general student acceptance of CAI, too, is the fact that students can see their achievement as they progress through the program and can thereby feel some sense of self-satisfaction. Where CAI and freedom to go ahead as quickly as one wishes are combined, students also tend to welcome this opportunity.

Team teaching, too, has been found to generate positive attitudes on the part of learners in the absence of significantly different achievement levels. A case in point is Gamsky's study (1970). Here, ninth-grade students were randomly assigned to team teaching and traditionally taught classes in English and world history. Again, there were no real differences between the groups in achievement, but ". . . the experimental group experienced significantly greater positive attitude growth in subtests 6 (Attitudes toward teachers), 7 (Interest in subject matter), and 10 (Sense of personal freedom.)" (p. 45)

While it may be realistic to say that *any* modification of routine will bring about positive changes in student attitudes, these few examples of research suggest that this is a worthwhile goal for teachers, even in the absence of learning differences. It is, if nothing else, much easier to teach interested, motivated, activated learners than passive ones—even if it means more effort on the part of the teacher.

SUMMARY

In this chapter, we have looked at many of the innovations in education, although the survey is by no means exhaustive of the field. It was not intended to provide a manual of how to "do-it-yourself," but rather to acquaint you with new techniques and modifications of old ones. More stress was placed on ideas that might be less familiar, with comparatively less emphasis on those possibilities that might have been part of your own school experience.

To this end, there was a fairly long presentation on the concept of establishing behavioral objectives. This concept really lies beneath the surface of every curriculum, whether or not it is spelled out. It is obvious from the survey of innovative techniques that the various technological and methodological modifications can help teachers and learners alike to reach almost any rung on the ladder of objectives. The relationship of cognitive and affective objectives to "accountability" was also explored.

Audiovisual techniques were discussed, with suggestions for a number of possible applications. Many applications are possible only because of technological advances in recent years.

Examples of curricular modifications at both the elementary and secondary levels abound. The varied use of programmed instruction (especially as computer-assisted instruction) brought to light another area of innovation. Simulation games were discussed, as well as a number of school-wide changes in methods and atmosphere. Finally, some consideration was given to the relationship between the learner and innovations. The findings here generally reflected the positive effect of innovation on student motivation and attitudes.

Innovations in education are limited only by lack of imagination and/or lack of flexibility. School administrators increasingly are adopting those that are appropriate for their schools. The implementation of innovative approaches, however, ultimately rests with the classroom teacher. The teacher's personality and commitment determine the success of the teacher-learning process.

Preview

INTRODUCTION: AN OVERVIEW OF EXCEPTIONAL CHILDREN

MAINSTREAMING

EMOTIONAL AND SOCIAL MALADJUSTMENT
    CHARACTERISTICS AND CHALLENGES
        Functional Retardation
    EDUCATIONAL ALTERNATIVES
        "Engineered Classroom"
        Special Settings
        Regular Classroom

THE PHYSICALLY DIFFERENT
    ORTHOPEDICALLY HANDICAPPED
    BLIND AND PARTIALLY SIGHTED
    DEAF AND HARD-OF-HEARING
    SPEECH HANDICAPS
    LEARNING DISABILITIES

THE CULTURALLY DIFFERENT
    CULTURAL DISPLACEMENT
    BILINGUALISM AS A HANDICAP

THE INTELLECTUALLY DIFFERENT
    MENTALLY RETARDED
    GIFTED
    CREATIVE

SUMMARY

12

Learners Who Challenge Teachers

INTRODUCTION: AN OVERVIEW OF EXCEPTIONAL CHILDREN

The first thing to remember about exceptional children is that they *are* children. This may sound trite, but it is a fact often forgotten. Secondarily, they have emotional, social, physical, cultural, or intellectual characteristics which distinguish them from other children to such an extent that special consideration in regular classes, special class placements, or special schools are desirable to help them learn.

The introduction to exceptional children and their special educational needs in this chapter is not intended to make you a specialist in this field. Rather, it should make you aware of some of the challenges in terms of human needs that you may meet in the classroom. This is an increasing possibility as the "mainstreaming" movement takes hold in school systems. It's doubtful that a totally blind child will be one of your full-time students, but one with partial sight may be. An understanding of the problems of the mentally retarded and remedial techniques used with them may help you to teach a slow learner. Many teachers today have pupils with undiagnosed learning problems. Information in this area can help both you and your students. Not all misbehaving children have maladjustments severe enough for therapeutic intervention, but all of them can benefit from having a teacher who understands and practices the principles of mental health and offers them encouragement. The orthopedically handicapped child is frequently bright. In short, these are individual children whose special characteristics present challenges to the teacher in one form or another. Is this very different from any other learner? Are *you* going to be afraid of them—or prepared for them?

We will group exceptional children in four categories: 1) emotionally and socially maladjusted, 2) physically different, 3) culturally different, and 4) intellectually different. Some of the groups have been discussed earlier and will, therefore, not be presented again at great length. More attention will be paid to the needs of those learners who have not previously been discussed, particularly those classified as physically different. Two subgroups in this category, children with speech problems and children with learning disabilities, usually *are* found in regular classes and therefore merit extra attention in this chapter.

The characteristics of children who are considered exceptional will be described in this chapter, as well as the alternatives open to educators in helping these children to become self-respecting individuals and learners. In particular, the psychoeducational approach focuses on adapting the educational task to the child so that he can progress. The teacher is asked to do two things: 1) look at the total child (development, maturation, motivation, etc.) and 2) examine the educational setting (curriculum content, mode of instruction, and learning environment) for possible modification.

MAINSTREAMING

Special education has moved from residential institutions in the 1800s, to segregated day classes at the turn of the century, to a new movement today—"mainstreaming." Even day classes represented progress in their time, and they are still the most common educational setting for exceptional children. An active worker for the day classes was Alexander Graham Bell. In 1898, he proposed to the National Education Association that the public schools provide programs for handicapped children. Since then, such classes have grown in number as more and more school districts provided them. This has often been regarded by the public as an act of charity.

> Not long after the turn of the century Elizabeth Farrell, a young teacher at Public School Number 1 in New York City, advocated and exemplified a new point of view. Considering handicapped children not as a caste of unfortunates, but instead viewing them as individuals, she dedicated herself "to the end that each and every child should be given the opportunity to develop according to his capabilities." (Greer, 1975, pp. 25–26)

Although Miss Farrell was herself creative in developing teaching tasks for truant boys and retarded children, today's special education teachers have had special (professional) education. This is needed whether they teach in segregated day classes or modern *resource rooms*.

In keeping with Miss Farrell's philosophy, more than seven decades later, educators and legislators have affirmed the right of *all* children to be educated at public expense. Concurrent with "right to education" rulings for exceptional children, there has been the move mentioned above toward "mainstreaming." The essence of this movement is the integration of exceptional children in regular classes wherever possible.

> It should be noted, however, that some educators feel immediate total immersion in regular classes to be impractical for a significant portion of handicapped children and suggest instead what they call "progressive inclusion"—that is, starting off by including the handicapped child in selected classroom activities for limited spans of time and then moving forward from there." (Greer, 1975, p. 27)

This is one point of view. Another plan, supported by other educators and psychologists, is to assign the exceptional child to a regular homeroom and remove him, as needed, for special classes. These options are shown in Figure 12.1.

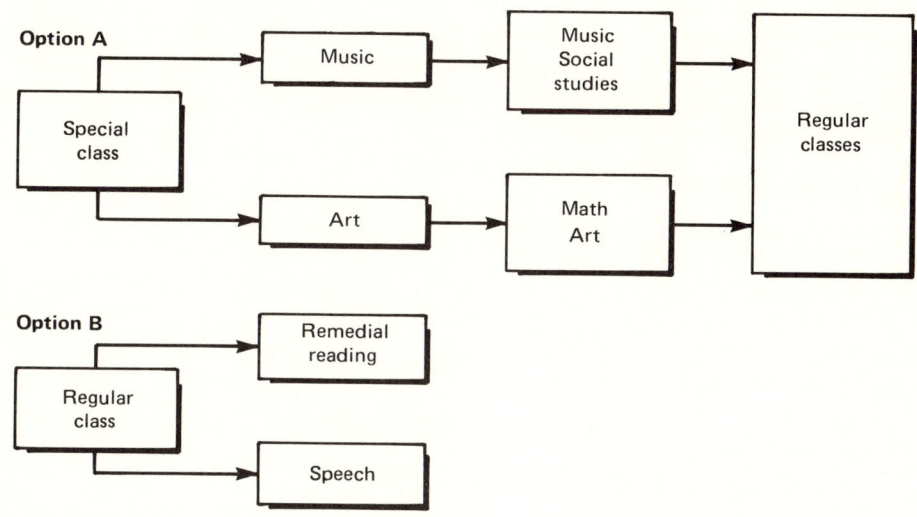

Figure 12.1

What are the advantages and disadvantages of each plan—to the child, his peers, and the teacher? **Question**

Under either plan, it is increasingly probable that all teachers will have some exceptional children in some of their classes at some time. In order to help them learn, it appears that all teachers should become better prepared to meet their needs as the mainstreaming movement progresses.

If mainstreaming is to "work," the children as well as the concept need to be accepted by principals, teachers, parents, and other children. As Payne and Murray (1974) point out, the building principal plays a key role in the program. If the principal is not supportive, there is little likelihood of success. In one study, urban principals were more reluctant than suburban principals to have integrated classes. "Integrative type programs would appear to have more administrative support and thus a better chance of success in the suburban school setting." (Payne and Murray, 1974, p. 125) Why the principals differ by location is unclear. Obviously, classroom teacher attitudes are also crucially important to the program. The special education teachers, too, must favor integration if it is to succeed, and not feel personally rejected or threatened.

Does mainstreaming work? In a study of mildly retarded ten-year-olds (X IQ = 72.3), Haring and Krug (1975) reported that, after a year of individualized instruction, the subjects successfully functioned in a regular classroom the following year. They adjusted socially as well as academically. Not one of the retarded children was referred back to special class placement. Guerin and Szatlocky (1974) similarly found that mildly retarded children behaved much like their peers in the regular classroom. Individualized instruction and special help in the resource room contributed to academic success in both programs. The recommendations of a panel of educational specialists, as well as of the authors cited just above, stress the need for positive attitudes among professional staff, good preparation for the child before he is integrated into the regular classroom, and a gradual shift of the child from special class to regular class. (Jordan, 1974) The panel was careful to point out, however, that entering the educational mainstream is not suited to all exceptional children.

This new era in education means that no children are rejected by public education. Their teachers have to be knowledgeable about child development, learning, motivation, and teaching techniques. They must also be able and willing to work cooperatively with other professionals involved in the education of exceptional children. (Goldberg and Lippman, 1974; Schwartz, 1975b)

On an individual basis, almost every school superintendent can cite the case of a partially-sighted, mildly-retarded, hearing-handicapped, or orthopedically-handicapped child who successfully went through regular classes with his peers. Thus, on a limited scale, we know that mainstreaming can work. The more ambitious program of today, however, calls for planning and preparation for large numbers of such children. The classroom teacher needs to feel confident in teaching the child. Both the child and his parents need to be assured that he will have the special help he needs. They need reassurance that his teachers and peers will accept him. And if the going gets too tough for the child, he needs to know that there are alternatives available through which he can continue his education.

EMOTIONAL AND SOCIAL MALADJUSTMENT

Characteristics and challenges

Is the boy who is constantly in motion physically "overcharged" with energy, emotionally immature, or psychologically disturbed? What do you do with a thirteen-year-old pregnant girl? Or with the whiners, the criers, the destructive, the petty, the argumentative, and other disruptive children in the classroom? How many different personalities will you face daily in a classroom, some of them agreeable learners and others out to destroy themselves or society? How do we differentiate the emotionally disturbed from the non-emotionally disturbed?

Pate (1963) defined the challenge in this way: "A child is emotionally disturbed when his reactions to life situations are so personally unrewarding and so inappropriate as to be unacceptable to his peers and adults." (p. 242)

To Pate, the emotionally disturbed child exhibits behavior that disrupts the regular class, or places undue pressure on the teacher, or is one for whom regular class attendance would create greater disturbance. Before you label every child who calls out, flies a paper airplane, or giggles, emotionally disturbed, consider the characteristics in the definition. *Is* the emotionally disturbed child's behavior "personally unrewarding"? To the contrary, it is usually attention-getting behavior that is quite rewarding to the child because attention is what he desires and possibly needs. Is the behavior truly "unacceptable to his peers"? This depends on the nature and degree of the disturbing behavior, as well as on the nature of the peer group. What constitutes "undue pressure on the teacher?" Some teachers have a very low level of tolerance for any nonconformist behavior, while others can tolerate quite a bit. We must also consider that the child's behavior may reflect his or her defense against undue pressures *by* the teacher. In each period of a child's development—early childhood, latency, and adolescence—the youngster has different emotional reactions to those around him. This necessarily includes teachers and involves their personalities as well as his own.

The emphasis on development level and behavior is picked up by Kirk (1972): "... *a behavior disorder* will be defined as a *deviation from age-appropriate behavior which significantly interferes with (1) the child's own growth and development and/or (2) the lives of others.*" (p. 389) Such a disorder makes it difficult for the child to function normally or effectively within society, whether he withdraws from it or fights it. These emphases are more compatible with our focus on the learner rather than on his effects on others.

The socially maladjusted child is one who is a chronic violator of society's rules and customs. He may also have emotional problems and exhibit many of the same symptoms and behaviors as the emotionally troubled child, but his behavior is more the product of inappropriate social learning. In his life, delinquent acts tend to be the norm, and he is frequently more of a problem to society. The emotionally maladjusted child is more of a problem to himself.

The disturbing behavior of a student is a symptom of a problem, but it tells us neither what the problem is, nor what caused it. Teachers need not be diagnosticians, but they should be aware of some of the common inappropriate behaviors and be prepared to modify conditions to reduce them wherever possible.

Item: A student has a tantrum whenever he is frustrated. The teacher can help him to learn to meet frustration while at the same time shielding him from unattainable goals. For every child, with or without emotional problems, there is a need to feel a sense of accomplishment. It is equally important, however, for his own well-being and that of society and general, that he learn his limitations and be able to admit to them.

Item: Alienation from the educational and social establishment is increasing among young people, often resulting in classroom disruptions as early as the junior high school level. Their inappropriate behavior includes disinterest, hostility, and often aggression, verbal or physical. It becomes the obligation of the teacher to make education "meaningful" in terms of today's needs and tomorrow's possibilities. (Morse, 1969, p. 32) Discipline problems are reduced when learning becomes exciting.

Item: "Model" children may really be emotionally withdrawn because of low self-esteem or preoccupation with inner fantasies. They do not present discipline problems, but are challenges to the teacher who needs to make them feel more self-important and to draw them into the real world.

Emotional maladjustment takes many forms. Headaches, stomach-aches, nausea, rapid pulse, and other physical symptoms may indicate a physical illness or anxiety. The learner who suddenly develops these symptoms on test days or in a new class situation may be suffering from anxiety that threatens his whole pattern of learning. This doesn't mean that the symptoms should be ignored or the student labeled a malingerer or neurotic. He needs help and should have it. "Acting-out" behavior, such as hostility and destructiveness, may also reflect anxiety or other emotional reactions. Withdrawal is another form of emotionally maladaptive behavior. Not all of these problems of the learner can be handled appropriately by the school nurse or the school disciplinarian. In fact, it is quite possible that the teacher can *prevent* the behavior by using better classroom management techniques.

Functional Retardation

Frequently, the maladjusted learner has arrived at the secondary level with few academic skills, and one cannot be sure whether the deficiencies are due to lack of intellectual ability, to personal problems, or to some combination of the two. There is reason to believe that these students function at an academically retarded level because of emotional rather than intellectual difficulties. Feldhusen, Thurston, and Benning (1970) questioned the effects of emotional problems on academic learning in a long-term study. Subjects were nominated by their third-, sixth-, or ninth-grade teachers as being one of the two most disruptive boys or girls, or one of the two most socially approved boys or girls, in the classroom. "During 2 school years a total of 982 youngsters were nominated as approved and 568 as aggressive-disruptive. From this pool of 1,550 youngsters, a sample of 384 children was drawn randomly for intensive study." (p. 5) School records, individual psychological tests, and interviews with each "intensively" studied youngster and his parents provided information about the subjects in the nomination phase of the study. Five years later, teacher grades in academic subjects and STEP (Sequential Tests of Educational Progress) scores were obtained for as many of the original subjects as were still in the schools.

For both teacher grades and STEP scores, with intelligence controlled as a variable, it was found that "Children who were first identified as exhibiting aggressive-disruptive behavior in grades 3 and 6, were, 5 years later, achieving far below the levels for children originally nominated as approved." (p. 9) Similarly, the original group of ninth-graders identified as aggressive-disruptive graduated from high school lower in the class rankings than their approved peers. Sex, grade level, and home location (urban v. rural) apparently had little relationship to these differences. These findings tend to support those of many earlier studies that also found academic learning lag coupled with social and emotional maladjustment.

> *Comment:* One wonders whether the children identified as exhibiting aggressive-disruptive behavior become victims of a self-fulfilling prophecy and teacher expectations. Were they subtly rejected by teachers and isolated by peers? Did they develop a negative self-concept, then "strike out," then suffer rejection in a continuing cycle? Would or could this have occurred today, when student records contain less "incriminating" data?

Educational alternatives

"The teacher who is generally successful in managing the surface behavior of children in the classroom not only has a lower deviancy rate among emotionally disturbed children in that classroom, but also produces a classroom climate that 'contains' the misbehavior of an emotional child and prevents it from disrupting the behavior of other children." (Kounin, Firesen, and Norton, 1966, p. 5) Kounin, et al., found, for example, that school-appropriate behavior occurred more frequently for both emotionally-disturbed and non-emotionally-disturbed children in subgroup recitation periods than in seatwork situations.

There are several possibilities for reducing nonappropriate behavior in the classroom. Some children have short attention spans and need shortened assignments. Or perhaps regrouping the students will reduce sources of tension and encourage the disturbing learner to participate in learning more actively. Positive reinforcement for appropriate and adaptive behavior is also effective. All of these alternatives mean that the teacher must pay more attention to each learner in the class.

Focus 12–1

One of the more imaginative and educational projects conducted with a class of emotionally-disturbed junior high school girls was centered on a luncheon project. The monthly luncheon for 30–40 guests (mothers and school personnel) centered on a different theme each month. One February, for example, the theme was "Hearts for America," combining the patriotic appeal of the Presidents' birthdays and the romantic appeal of Valentine's Day. Academic learning and the luncheon theme were correlated to increase motivation:

Social Studies—Presidents of the United States

Mathematics—multiplication of recipes (whole numbers and fractions), budgeting, and purchasing (consumer mathematics)

> Science—nutrition, discussion of the heart and circulatory system
>
> Home Economics—actual food preparation
>
> English—spelling and language usage for the invitations and "thank you" notes, oral communication for ease as hostesses
>
> Art—creation of decorations appropriate to the theme
>
> Music—choice of recorded selections to serve as background music for the luncheon
>
> In addition, valuable learning for social-emotional development took place. Each girl served as chairperson of a different luncheon committee each month, learning to take and give responsibility. The girls learned to work as an interdependent group, and each girl was able to take pride in a job well done. For personal development, the girls learned something about manners and hostess behavior.
>
> The teacher had few material resources on hand, but many inner resources. Starting with her class of emotionally-disturbed adolescents, who were "at war" with themselves and their home junior highs, she was able to create an atmosphere in which each girl could find accomplishment and satisfaction rather than continued hostility.

In a supportive atmosphere, even children with emotional problems can learn profitably, enjoyably, and without undue disturbance to others. In the event of a traumatic incident, many teachers have adopted a practice of the behavior modifiers and have established a "time-out" room where the youngster can gain control of himself. When he is calmer, he and the teacher can deal more rationally with the "triggering" event and its consequent behavior. Berlin, a psychiatrist, pointed out (1966) that, in dealing with disturbed and delinquent children, a teacher must have endless patience and persistence, becoming ". . . a parental model who believes the student can learn and who is willing to take the time to stand by and help him learn." (p. 78)

"Engineered Classroom"

One effective approach to aiding children with problems is the "engineered classroom." This is an attempt to approach education of children with problems with a balanced emphasis on educational goals and methods.

> The disturbed child is viewed as a socialization failure and assessed in terms of his developmental learning deficiencies. . . . In order for the child to learn successfully he must pay *attention*, make a *response*, *order* his behavior, accurately and thoroughly engage in multi-sensory *exploratory* behavior, gain *social* approval, and require *mastery* of self care and cognitive skills. Finally he must function on a motivated basis with *achievement* in learning providing its own reward. (Hewitt, Taylor, and Artuso, 1969, p. 524)

These goals are attained by controlling the room arrangement, teacher-pupil ratio, schedule, and manipulation of behavior using behavior modification methods. The classroom is divided into three major areas, and the class day is divided into a major work period of two hours, an exploratory period of one hour, and one hour of physical education and recreation activities. "Each child carries a Work Record Card with him throughout the day, and earns a possible 10 checkmarks every 15 minutes. Checkmarks are given for starting and working on tasks and for behavior related to the levels of the developmental sequence which are most critical for each individual child." (p. 524) The checkmarks may be traded in for tangible rewards, "free" time, or other reinforcements once a week. In a program using the engineered classroom concept in Santa Monica, California, emotionally-disturbed students developed greater ability to pay attention to the task at hand and were able to maintain this improvement even when placed in regular classes without the tangible rewards of the program. Some gains in academic competence were also found, particularly in arithmetic, and these, too, continued after regular class placement. (pp. 528–29)

Special Settings

In addition to those alternatives already suggested, the challenges of exceptional children can be met through special (segregated) classes or special schools. Despite state laws that provide for special classes for the socially and emotionally maladjusted, not enough of the nation's 2200 school districts can afford such classes. There are also too few properly educated teachers to lead them. Special classes, where they exist, are limited to eight to ten students per teacher, although additions to the class may occur on a temporary basis during the school year. The objectives of special classes for the emotionally and socially maladjusted are modification and reconditioning of nonacceptable classroom behavior, remedial instruction to enable the learner to achieve academically closer to his ability level, and eventual return to regular classes with appropriate social and academic functioning. In these classes, as well as in special schools, the length of the school day and the management of the learning situation are frequently adjusted to the needs of individuals, as demonstrated in the Santa Monica project. Emphasis is placed on highly individualized instruction with limited whole-group teaching time.

Emphasis in special classes, after controlling the most aberrant behavior, is on remediation and orientation toward success, usually using positive reinforcement techniques. These supportive activities are perceived positively by both the students involved and their parents, generally, although there is some parental concern about the "singling out" of their children. (McKinnon, 1970)

Special classes have also been established in a number of school systems for pregnant adolescent girls. Educators recognize that such continuing education, outside of regular classes, helps the girl to keep up with her peers intellectually and to maintain some measure of self-esteem in the face of social criticism or ostracism. Prenatal care of the girl and techniques of postnatal care for her baby are part of the special program, as well as needed social and psychological services. "All of these school programs through their educational emphases are able to stress family life. They help the girl see the possibility of finishing school, and instill her with aspirations for a higher standard of living." (Goodman, 1969, p. 718)

The second option, establishment of special schools, has been tried in some large city school systems. Too often, these degenerate from therapeutic centers to day-custodial institutions where the principal function is to segregate the "worst" behavior problems rather than to help them. This can result in mass mayhem, exploitation of younger and weaker pupils by the older and more aggressive ones, and a prison-type atmosphere instead of a learning one. An increase in the fears and anxieties of the exploited, emotionally disturbed student in such situations frequently leads to further deterioration of his mental health, not to mention further retardation in learning. Ideally, however, the special school should be able to provide supportive services that would not be possible in the isolated special class arrangement, such as extracurricular programs, a therapeutically oriented staff, and music, art, and physical education facilities.

Retention in regular classes, the third alternative, requires several supports if the maladjusted pupil is not to dominate the classroom. His teacher should be selected carefully, whenever possible, so that interpersonal friction will be reduced. This teacher will need guidance from specialists on how to deal with specific behavioral events such as physical aggression, tantrums, and so on. The child should have relatively easy access to the school counselor or a therapist when he cannot control his emotional problems. His parents should be involved in the therapeutic process with a social service agency or child guidance specialist. On the one hand, the parents can provide background information on the child from their point of view. They may also need help in living with their child.

Some schools have established "crisis" classrooms to which the disturbed child may be sent for short periods of time to avoid sacrificing the needs of the class for the needs of one individual. Resource teachers, too, can help to provide gratification for the maladjusted pupil and supplement the efforts of the classroom teacher.

The fourth response to the challenge of maladjusted learners is withdrawal from the public school system altogether. This may mean a shift to either day-care or residential settings on a privately or publicly financed basis. Many psychiatric and child guidance clinics operate day schools for the disturbed and provide an academic program combined with a strong therapeutic approach. Such day-care centers, and residential facilities, usually focus on the more severely disturbed—autistic, schizophrenic, and other psychotic children. The emphasis in these programs is on therapeutic intervention first, with remedial education necessarily a secondary consideration. Private schools, whether day or residential, tend to stress learning somewhat more than therapy, but do have a therapeutically oriented classroom atmosphere as well as group and individual therapy sessions. These institutions are extremely expensive, which limits the range of youngsters who can be helped. Universities sometimes organize a small class of residential care classes for teaching purposes, which can be less expensive than other private schools.

Regular Classroom

For the teacher in the regular classroom, three of these alternatives are largely irrelevant except in severe cases of maladjustment. The pressing problems are more likely to be the challenge presented by those children with relatively mild emotional problems or the inner-city delinquent. Many of the techniques used by special teachers can be incorporated into the regular classroom, such as reinforcement of appropriate behavior, a warm and supportive classroom atmosphere, and the use of resource personnel.

One means of reducing the disturbing behavior of these children is to develop a social contract with each child. At the outset, the expectations of what is appropriate behavior in the classroom must be made clear. If disruptive behavior is to be changed to appropriate behavior, then the child also needs to know why his behavior is not acceptable. The contract itself merely asks three questions of the child:

1. In picture words, or concretely, what did you do that got you into trouble?
2. What was in it for you? What did you want to result?
3. How can you get what you want without getting into trouble?
   (Meisels, 1974, p. 34)

The emphasis is then on finding acceptable alternative behaviors that satisfy the child's needs. It is helpful, also, for teacher and child alike to become aware of events or places or people that set off the inappropriate behavior. There are two other factors in the contract: 1) reinforcement by the teacher for acceptable behavior and 2) acceptance of responsibility by the learner for the consequences of the choices he makes.

Frequent contact with parents on a mutually helpful rather than accusative, critical basis will take teacher time after school hours, but will reduce difficulties during class time. Considerable thought, too, must be given to ways of arousing interest in the disturbed or delinquent youngster so that he will want to learn. To encourage reading, for example, reading content should be selected with an eye to the learner's interests and can conceivably vary from *True* to *Playgirl* to newspaper sports stories, comic books, or auto mechanics manuals. Keeping in mind that the key to most academic achievement is reading ability, the key to getting the nonreader to read at all must lie in providing reading material that interests *him*. (Several publishers now have available high-interest low reading level books aimed at the adolescent nonreader.) The use of recorded or taped old radio shows has also been shown to be effective in gaining the attention of reluctant learners. (Weiner, 1974) Once the disturbed learner becomes an involved participant, control of inappropriate behavior becomes less of a problem. This is the real challenge of the maladjusted learner.

THE PHYSICALLY DIFFERENT

In this group of challenging students, we include the orthopedically handicapped, the blind and partially sighted, the deaf and hard-of-hearing (aurally handicapped), the speech handicapped, and those with learning disabilities caused by neurological impairment (also called minimally brain damaged). Not included are the so-called "delicate" children who have heart disease or nonactive tuberculosis. Adjustments are usually made in the daily schedule for the latter children to permit ample rest, and they may have an opportunity to take special physical education courses adapted to their activity restrictions. These children, and epileptics who might also be included here, have medical problems for which they are receiving treatment. They need not have educational problems except during lengthy school absences. Each of these groups presents unique challenges to teachers and calls for different characteristics of and use of varying techniques by the teacher.

To appreciate the magnitude of the challenge, you should know that there are well over 5,000,000 handicapped children in the United States. Many of their physical handicaps are the results of prenatal factors considered in chapter two. Concern in Congress for the development of these children grew over the years so that finally, in 1966, Title VI of the Elementary and Secondary Education Act was passed, directing ". . . the U.S. Commissioner of Education to establish within the Office of Education a National Advisory Committee on Handicapped Children." (Kirk, 1972, pp. 422–23) The following year, a Bureau for Handicapped Children was organized. This agency sponsors research, educational services, and support for teacher-training programs. Its effects are felt at the state, local, university, and, eventually, the classroom level.

Orthopedically handicapped

Orthopedically handicapped children are those with physical disabilities resulting from poliomyelitis, muscular dystrophy, spina bifida, multiple sclerosis, Legg-Perthes disease, congenital defects or later amputations, cerebral palsy, and other diseases that hinder their mobility. Although the physical problem does not of itself lead to psychosocial problems, the latter are often a reaction to the way other people look at the physically different. Then, too, the handicapped child may have goals that are impossible to reach—becoming a long distance runner or a ballet dancer. The discrepancy between reality and goal also causes psychological problems. Some of the parental reactions to their child, on the negative side, include guilt and shame, neglect (where they fear they will harm the child from resentment of the burden they feel placed on them), and overprotection. Where these reactions are severe, the parents as well as the child need counseling. On the child's part, there may be uncertainty as to his reception by others—pity, disgust, hostility, or other forms of rejection. With the encouragement of the classroom teacher, other professionals, and even the school bus driver, the handicapped child can learn to accept himself as he is physically, which is necessary for normal interpersonal relations.

An orthopedically-handicapped child. **Figure 12.2**

Those orthopedically handicapped children who have the sensory and intellectual ability to be in regular classes should be with their peers. These would include, for instance, mild to moderate cases of cerebral palsy, polio victims, those with the muscular diseases resulting from metabolic dysfunctions, and those with bone disorders ("wry neck," congenital clubfoot, shortened limb), or missing limbs. If it is necessary to make some explanation to youngsters in the class about the child's handicap, the emphasis should be on the healthy aspects of the child and the "accidental" way in which his unique ingredients were combined. As the national organizations for the handicapped put it, "stress the abilities, not the disabilities."

In many cases, a preschool program is desirable to prepare these children for the public schools. They need to learn ways of overcoming common classroom or school procedure obstacles and also how to mix with other children.

Focus 12–2

> In New York City, a volunteer organization, the New York Philanthropic League, began over 60 years ago to provide recreational and physical therapy services for orthopedically handicapped children. For many of the youngsters, all school-aged, programs administered by this group offered them their first opportunity to leave their homes. A summer camp gave them a chance to experience swimming, other sports, and craft activities. During the school year, the campers spend Saturdays together at a clubhouse in mid-city, participating in indoor extensions of the summer activities, writing a newspaper, taking dancing lessons(!), putting on plays, and so on. Some come, even on crutches, via public transportation, while others are transported by volunteer drivers. All of the programs offer in-service training to special education majors in New York colleges.
>
> In view of the League's goals of helping each child to go as far as he can, a preschool program was started. As with other projects, the emphasis is on learning and doing. Many of the children *have* entered the public schools, well-prepared socially and intellectually to meet this new world. Parental reactions vary from awe to ecstasy at the changes in the children, primarily the mental well-being that comes with acceptance.
>
> Older children have been given scholarships to help them through high school, and a sizable number have graduated from college, some from graduate schools. Encouragement to plan for the future and to learn to work with nondisabled individuals and organizations are two aspects of the League's programs which helped the handicapped to achieve these educational goals.

We have learned a great deal about working with the handicapped from the national experiences of dealing with war-wounded veterans. The development of a positive self-concept and an emphasis on rehabilitation are probably two of the most important lessons learned. We've also learned that there are architectural obstacles in school buildings (as well as other public buildings) that "threaten" or inhibit the orthopedically handicapped person. Assuming that a child of normal abilities is confined to a wheelchair, can he go to a school with long flights of stairs even at the entrances? Or where doorways are too narrow to permit him to propel his chair into the classroom?

The Danbury School in Claremont, California was designed to accommodate both the neighborhood and physically handicapped children. It is an open-space facility that encourages mainstreaming of these children while also providing for their special needs (physical therapy cubicles, special gym, specially designed playground). (Molloy, 1975) Similarly, at the MacDonald Comprehensive School (Centennial School District, Warminster, Pa.), ramps replace stairs, cafeteria tables are high enough to permit wheelchairs to be pulled in closely, and the children are integrated into as many regular school activities as possible.

What needs to be done by the school beyond the standard curriculum to help these students to lead a useful and happy life? There must be some physical assistance as needed, although independent mobility should be the goal wherever possible. They need in some cases to be taught intelligible speech if they are to be employable. The intellectually capable should be encouraged to continue their studies, and the less capable should be given training in a marketable skill. You can be just as good a typist with one leg as two!

Alternatives to regular class placement are special schools, either day or residential. At these schools (for example, the Widener Memorial School in Philadelphia) periods of physical therapy alternate with academic sessions, and classroom learning progresses much as in other schools. Again, the emphasis is on doing as much as one can, not on self-pity or giving up a fairly "normal" life.

The *blind and partially sighted* children offer a different set of challenges. The probabilities are against having a blind student in your regular class, but it is possible, especially at the secondary level. There are, in fact, increasing attempts to integrate blind students into regular classrooms. Imagine, if you will, the challenge to the blind learner. You are listening to a teacher lecture, the lesson is filled with dates or technical terms, and you can't take notes quickly enough. Confusing, isn't it? Today, of course, you could take a lightweight cassette tape recorder to class, but this means listening carefully in class and at home so as not to miss a needed detail or nuance.

Blind and partially sighted

The blind learner generally has no intellectual impairment if this is the only disability. A special form of the Stanford-Binet test, the Hayes revision, yields a mean IQ of 99 for a large sample of blind students. This means that the blind learner, whose only handicap is lack of vision, can learn as well as the average sighted learner. Physical growth is normal, although motor performance naturally develops more slowly. The blind child's speech is normal, but perhaps slower and less well articulated than that of a sighted person, due to poorer lip movements and the use of gestures. Through experience, the blind learn to pay increased attention to small sensory cues and so are often more sensitive to sounds, for example, than if they had sight. Social stimulation is necessary from infancy to achieve this. The blind child often spends his elementary school years in a special school where he is taught to uses the senses he *has* to learn and to use special implements which can help him learn (Braille stylus or typewriter, tape players, tactual materials, etc.). Special texts are available in Braille, but they are in limited use because of their sheer bulk and the restricted range of materials. "Talking records" and human readers can frequently provide greater breadth and depth of information than the weighty Braille volumes.

At the secondary level, if the blind student hopes to attend college, he needs to learn special note-taking skills, how to arrange for exams, what to do in laboratory classes, what kinds of physical education he can take, and how to adjust generally to college life. Such a program was developed in Little Rock, Arkansas, and it proved very successful. An experimental program that combined English composition with a standard typewriter had similar positive results in a New Jersey project. (Paul and Goione, 1968)

The partially sighted child is a more likely candidate for regular classes since he has some vision (20/70—20/200 with correction). There may be special classes for these learners in large school districts, with sight-saving texts, special lighting, and other aids. As with the blind, they need to develop their perceptual acuity in nonvisual sensory modalities. Large-print materials are increasingly available, from simple textbooks to a weekly edition of *The New York Times*. Special instruction may be available from a resource teacher or an itinerant teacher when the child is assigned to a regular classroom. (For most school districts, the cost of maintaining appropriate special classes, even if qualified teachers were available, is prohibitive on a full-time basis.)

One of the problems the visually handicapped learner has is that he may enter school later than usual. This immediately segregates him from his age group. His handicap, as is true for most handicaps, evokes waves of pity, and he needs to be guarded against wallowing in self-pity. The blind or partially sighted learner can participate in class activities and may have special talents to contribute. The challenge to the teacher is to see that he can and does contribute, participate, and learn.

A large segment of the school population suffers from some form of visual handicap. Children are nearsighted, farsighted, "cross-eyed," amblyopic ("lazy eye"), and so on. Classroom adjustments have to be made in seating and lighting, and peers must learn to make allowances for poor aim in sports. There are, in addition, uncounted students whose learning suffers from undiagnosed vision problems. Does the child squint? Tilt the book or his head? Does he complain of frequent headaches? The alert teacher can suggest to parents or school officials that the child be given a thorough eye examination. Sensitivity to the possible physical basis for learning difficulties is useful for teachers and affected learners alike.

Deaf and hard-of-hearing

When we consider the *deaf* and *hard-of-hearing* students, the challenge is markedly different again. For one thing, the congenitally deaf child has never heard speech, and so is handicapped also in vocal communication. Because of this double disability, it is possible that many of them will function as adults at about the level of the educable mentally retarded. Schools for the deaf should recognize this limited potential. At the same time, they should ". . . provide appropriate services for them which will prepare them to function in adulthood at their maximum potential in a manner compatible with their capabilities." (Anderson and Stevens, 1969, pp. 692–93)

Although not all deaf children are placed in residential schools, it is a fact that, due to verbal difficulties, they generally score below hearing children on most intelligence tests. Thus, in addition to the special methods needed for teaching the deaf, some application of techniques designed for slow learners and the educable mentally retarded may be appropriate. These techniques may be used equally well in residential or day schools for the deaf, in special classes, or in periods spent with an itinerant teacher. Ideally, training in language should begin when the child is two or three years old so that he can progress more normally in school. The longer this is delayed, the more difficult learning becomes.

One would think that it should be easier for the deaf child of hearing parents to learn English than for the deaf child whose parents are also deaf. However, in a study that used the Test of English as a Foreign Language (TOEFL), it turned out that the deaf children of deaf parents were the ones with higher scores on measures of English language skills. (Charrow and Fletcher, 1974) These children also tended to score higher on the verbal SATs. The suggestion was made that early experience with sign language may have been an advantage.

Let us go back briefly to the source of aural handicaps. Vernon found (1967), in a sample of 1,468 deaf children, that 257 of these were premature babies, and two-thirds of these, or 175 cases, were apparently caused by prematurity only. (The other third of the prematurely born had additional factors in their history which could have caused deafness, such as rubella, the Rh— factor, possible genetic deafness, and meningitis.) (Vernon, 1967, p. 290) They had an average IQ of 89.4 and "... one out of five of these premature children was regarded as essentially unable to be educated." (p. 291) Whether premature or not, academic retardation is fairly common among deaf children and appears to be inversely related to the degree of hearing loss.

What other difficulties seem to be associated with deafness? Several investigators have reported that deaf children are frequently multiply handicapped. Vernon (1970) reported on 63 cases from his large sample of deaf children (above) who were also victims of cerebral palsy. Moores (1970) found substantially lower reading achievement in deaf adolescents, with stereotyped and repetitive vocabulary. Frey and Krause (1971) reported that "... the incidence of color blindness among the deaf children tested is greater than twice that of the general population, thus adding a further handicap to the deaf child's learning potential." (pp. 393–94) As this last report suggests, this complication must be considered in the classroom, where color has frequently been used in trying to clarify subject matter for deaf children. Vision difficulties, of some kind, also tend to occur in deaf children at twice the rate for hearing children—another roadblock to learning. (Lawson and Myklebust, 1970)

Hard-of-hearing students may not have their disability discovered as easily as the deaf, however. As little children, their refusal to answer when called may be interpreted as negativism or obstinacy. In the classroom, they may be considered inattentive, negative, or retarded. Their ability to follow directions accurately, to enunciate clearly, and to respond quickly or correctly is affected by the hearing loss and may be the signal for an examination and treatment. Hearing aids can help some of these children to function more adequately, as well as make their problem more visible to other people. Special auditory training and lip reading training, plus speech therapy, will help the children in both hearing and speech. These remedial efforts are usually offered in special classes, and, once they are mastered, the hard-of-hearing child can move into a regular class. Remedial reading instruction can help the child to function more capably in this area, which is often the chief academic weakness of hard-of-hearing children. The classroom teacher should be informed of the child's problem so that she or he can speak face-to-face with him. Vocational and academic preparation for these children, according to several investigators, should take the hearing problem into account. This is often not done, or is inadequate, thus leading to further frustrations as the learners become adolescents and adults. Although some of these frustrations involve learning and goal-setting, there are social obstacles as well, in the school years and beyond, that must be faced.

Methods that have been used successfully to rehabilitate the deaf adolescent and young adult incorporate several aspects of behavior modification. These include rapid feedback or knowledge of results, abundant positive reinforcement, and the use of "shaping" or approximations techniques. Activities have immediate relevance to the participant, and his efforts are further supported by extensive counseling. All aspects of this approach can also be used with the younger deaf child.

Particularly important is the gradual introduction of the deaf learner to larger and more diverse groups of people so that he will have more emotional security in the social, academic, and vocational spheres of his life. Mainstreaming for the child with impaired hearing might begin with art, music, and physical education classes.

> Art permits the expression of feelings and the development of talents for which sound is unnecessary. In music, the hearing-impaired child can respond to and learn rhythm, although she may not hear the melody itself. The ability to detect rhythm can be combined effectively with speech and language therapy. (Schwartz, 1975b, p. 53)

Visual cues can be substituted for sound signals in physical education. As the child is moved into more regular classroom activities, it helps if the noise level is kept to a minimum so that the child can use whatever hearing she or he may have. Social acceptance by peers may vary with age groups. Most studies that have reported negative social interaction between hearing and hearing-impaired students have had older children as subjects. Kennedy and Bruininks (1974), however, found that first- and second-graders are more accepting of hearing-impaired classmates. The self-confidence gained by this acceptance, if continued throughout the school years, will provide the emotional security needed when dealing with others in the hearing world.

Speech handicaps   Closely related to the aurally handicapped in one way are children with *speech handicaps*. These children are commonly found in the regular classroom. Difficulties range from a simple lisp and immature speech to gross problems caused by a cleft palate or auditory handicap. A speech handicap interferes with interpersonal relationships, affects the personality, inhibits the expression of emotional reactions, and interferes with learning. This is true whether the problem is delayed development in speech, inaccuracy of sounds, an unpleasant or ineffective voice, or nonfluent or interrupted speech (often called stammering or stuttering). The source of the difficulties may be intellectual, emotional, physical, or environmental.

Aids to speech therapists. **Figure 12.3**

An itinerant speech therapist is employed by many school districts to work with these children, usually on a weekly basis. In cases where the disorder has been learned as an attention-getting device, the therapist will reinforce correct speech (using the shaping via approximations techniques of behavior modification discussed earlier), giving attention for satisfactory rather than incorrect performance. This can also be done by the classroom teacher, with guidance. Certainly the classroom teacher can control the reactions of other pupils to the dysfunctions, too, by discouraging laughter and/or imitation, which serve only to emphasize the negative.

When the speech handicap interferes with oral recitation, the teacher can reduce the threat to the learner by being patient, not calling on the child too often, and *not* drawing attention to the problem, particularly stuttering, by saying "Take your time" or "Start over." As the dysfunction is reduced by speech and/or other types of therapy, the child can be drawn into verbal class activities gradually. Until this occurs, however, the teacher should encourage other means of demonstrating learning. Anxiety about pronouncing words related to articulation difficulties, or emotion-laden words, may also discourage the learner from participating in class and may particularly affect learning to read in the lower grades. Again, means must be used which will not draw attention to the child's speech problem or increase his embarrassment.

Learning disabilities

Speech handicaps are also often found in children who have other *learning disabilities* due to brain damage or neurological impairment. These are children who, by definition, have average intelligence (or better) but have specific learning disabilities in perception and/or dealing with concepts that interfere with their normal learning progress.* An estimated 10 to 20 percent of school children have these difficulties due to brain damage, most of them undiagnosed and in regular classes. They are frequently, but not always, hyperactive and highly distractible and may demonstrate poor eye-hand coordination. They may be unable to reproduce words or designs even if they can identify them, which would create difficulties in writing, mathematics, spelling, and other subject areas; and they may be unable to distinguish letters correctly or may see words in reverse (e.g., "saw" for "was"). They may also have speech disorders.

There are a limited number of special classes in the public schools and a small number of private schools available that offer special remedial techniques for these children. Downing (1968) has asserted that the i/t/a reading program (see chapter eleven) is beneficial for them because of its regularity in spelling, reading, and writing as compared with traditional spelling. Behavior modification procedures, used with small groups of junior high-aged students with learning disabilities, have proved effective in increasing academic achievement. Learning contracts, limited in scope and time span, and followed by reinforcement when completed, are effective methods. These should be based on specific educational and psychological needs of each learner. Intensive, individualized instruction is the most common practice, and it is combined with special teaching techniques. Hecherl and Webb (1969) stressed that this instruction should be the result of an interdisciplinary approach, coordinating the efforts of classroom teachers, reading specialists, the school psychologist, the school social worker or counselor if there is one, and additional consultant specialists as needed. However, "Teachers would be amiss if they set down a list of remediation techniques and methods without first understanding that each child must be helped to overcome his learning problems in ways that he, the child, finds reasonable and workable." (Van Osdol and Clinger, 1974, p. 193)

Remedial techniques usually emphasize the use of carefully structured, concrete experiences before attempting to teach general principles. Removal of possible distractions from the child's work area is also recommended, enabling him to focus on the task at hand. In many cases, the use of sand-

---

*As defined by the Association for Children with Learning Disabilities.

covered letters and numbers to stimulate the tactile sense helps the child to perceive these basic tools more adequately.

One method used to reduce the constant random movement (hyperactivity) of some learning-disabled children involves drugs, specifically amphetamines. Although the drug, when properly used, does indeed calm the hyperkinetic child and enable him to concentrate on learning tasks, there is continuing controversy about the potential for drug addiction and other negative long-range effects.

Focus 12–3

Early diagnosis and intervention can prevent major educational and psychological problems from developing. Frequently, the child whose learning disabilities go undetected suffers from mislabeling as a retarded learner and develops a highly negative self-concept. A case in point is Mary Q.

At the request of her parents, Mary was tested as she entered second grade. The parental complaints were that the child was unable to think and/or express herself clearly, that she exhibited "unjust anger," immaturity, feelings of insecurity, and some speech difficulties. Eight months later, the child was retested, again at the parents' request. There had been six months of perception training with a highly skilled special education teacher in the interim. A variety of tests were given to Mary at both sessions, and their results and differences are given below:

Test	CA 7–5	CA 8–1	Change
WISC			
Verbal IQ	104	120	+16
Performance IQ	83	108	+25
Full-scale IQ	93	116	+23
Wide-Range Achievement Test			
Reading grade	2.7	3.5	+ 0.8
Arithmetic grade	2.7	3.5	+ 0.8
Spelling grade	2.0	2.8	+ 0.8
Bender-Gestalt Visual-Motor Test			
Motor error score	12	3	− 9
Mental age equivalent	5–0	8–0	+ 3 years

The intervention of teaching therapy pulled Mary up from "low average" intelligence to "bright average," from being two-and-a-half years below her age group in the ability to perceive and reproduce designs to within a half-year of her age group, and it permitted her to progress at an average rate through second grade, gaining one month for each month in school. Remediation of the learning disability and its emotional side-effects appears to have led to a more valid intellectual evaluation of the child. Personality changes, too, occurred as the result of fewer frustrations at school and at home, more success experiences, and the understanding of her parents and teacher as to her problem. (From the author's case files)

As is true with several other groups discussed in this chapter, alertness to possible physical bases for learning difficulties is one challenge to the classroom teacher. Disabilities in perception or expression of what one perceives *may* result from inattention, but may equally well be the effect of a visual-motor dysfunction or other organic learning disability. If the problem is diagnosed in the primary grades or earlier, remedial instruction can be more effective than if delayed a few years. Perception tests are now being administered in some schools at the kindergarten level to try to make such early identification and intervention possible.

There is one additional item to consider with the learning-disabled child—the effects of his behavior on others. Frequently his inability to perform as expected frustrates both his parents and his teachers. He is perceived as untidy and not very desirable socially by his classmates.

> Moreover, analysis of the classroom situation suggests that the learning-disabled child's social life is rather different from that of other children. Apparently, he is more often ignored when attempting to initiate a social interaction, is less likely to be interacted with by the teacher for matters not essentially academic, gets more negative and less positive reinforcement from teachers than his nondisabled counterpart. In short, people do act as if they dislike the learning-disabled child. (Bryan and Bryan, 1975, p. 127)

The physically handicapped child, as you have seen, may suffer little or much educational handicap. His learning needs vary from physical adjustment of the environment to accommodate a wheelchair to special schools that can prepare him for independence in adulthood. There is a wide range, too, in severity of these handicaps, for example, from simple nearsightedness to total blindness. The most severely disabled children are rarely in regular classes, but the mildly handicapped may be in any classroom. These are the children to whom the teacher must be especially sensitive, and whose special needs often challenge the teacher to dig deeply into his or her repertoire of techniques and ideas to promote learning.

THE CULTURALLY DIFFFERENT

Who are the culturally different? They are the students whose language and ethnic mores differ from those of the majority of the population. They are displaced in time or culture in our schools. It is unfair to judge them by general middle-class American standards, although it is true that they will eventually have to function in this society. A major part of the education task is to help them to acquire the knowledge that will help them adapt without losing their special characteristics. (Since we discussed the effects of culture on the learner rather extensively in chapter three, you might reread that section before reading this one.)

Some cultural groups in the United States are at an academic disadvantage because they cannot complete effectively in the labor market. Others face a language disadvantage that primarily inhibits their interaction with the majority. Still others must confront racial or national prejudice that places them at a social and economic disadvantage. Almost all of these groups, because of their differences from the majority culture, are at an educational disadvantage. (Schwartz, 1975b, p. 85)

The rate of acculturation varies with socioeconomic levels as well as ethnic origin, but difficulty appears to be centered among the poor. They have the poorest skills and poorest educational background with which to adapt to a culture different from their own. They move from one apartment to another in the cities and from one town and state to another on the farms. Interrupted schooling is common and further emphasizes their cultural difference and displacement, for they have no "place" to call home on a relatively permanent basis.

In the urban classroom, a teacher may face an entire class of students culturally different from himself or herself. The teacher's inexperience with his or her students' culture puts the *teacher* at a disadvantage, placing him or her in the minority. Lack of understanding of the subculture's ways can lead to discipline as well as learning problems. Vocabularies differ, so that what might be effective teaching elsewhere is a lack of communication here. This also leads to misinterpretations of intent that can rapidly demolish healthy learning relationships in the classroom. Students' apathy rather than positive motivation may be the rule, whether brought from a home in which there is no hope for improvement or from previous teachers who "gave up" on these students. Modifications in teacher education programs to include sociology and anthropology courses, field experience in urban classrooms before student teaching, and study of the psychological problems of various culturally different groups would all help to alleviate the impact of difference on the teacher.

Select a culturally different group (Chinese, French-Canadian, chicano) and find the situations in which they are at a disadvantage. Try to interview members of the group to discover their reactions to this.

Suggested Activity

Where the culturally different learner is the exception rather than the rule, however, there is a different situation. Of major concern is the reaction of the rest of the class to the stranger in their midst and the reaction of the teacher. Does prejudice rear its ugly head? How can the newcomer be integrated best into the class for learning and social purposes? This is a particular problem for the children of migrant laborers, who operate frequently under dual handicaps of transiency and poor or little English (most of today's migrant

Cultural displacement

laborers are Puerto Ricans or chicanos). It is also a problem for the transplanted Appalachian child, whose total experience in the impoverished mountain environment leaves him ill-prepared for urban or centralized rural schools. Additionally,

> Parents of socially disadvantaged children are often alienated from the schools. This is deduced from the fact that many of these parents are caused to feel that they are a nuisance and are treated in a condescending manner by school staff members. Often this manner of treatment permeates the entire school system, including administrators, supervisors, teachers, office staff, and custodial workers. (Crow, Murray, and Smythe, 1966, p. 119)

Even learning materials appear to be unrelated to the culturally different child. The Oriental child rarely finds any reference to his family's cultural heritage or history in readers or social studies texts. One Chinese scholar wrote, "At the most, the texts referred to coolies building railroads or to Chinatown in San Francisco. . . . There was very little that I could identify with." (Sue, 1974, p. 84) He also found it difficult to adjust to the elementary school because teachers and students alike had very little understanding of Asians. The director of the Hopi Community Education Program, himself a Native American, has expressed distress at the image of Native Americans presented in most classrooms. As he said, "I've never worn a feather in my hair in my life, and I've never met a Native American who thought of himself as a Basket Weaver or Food Gatherer." (Levenson, 1975a, p. 64)

Suggested Activity

As you have contact with basic education and even college texts that are supposedly teaching American history, the history of immigration, or cultural pluralism, focus on the positive/negative comments about each group; look to see which groups are omitted as well as which are included. Can you sense bias in the work? (Consider as well the time at which a selection was written.) If there are omissions or there is bias, what effects would these have, do you think, on school children who are required to use these texts?

Bilingualism as a handicap

The specific problems with which the culturally displaced child comes to school are many. The key to virtually all of them is language disability. This is not for lack of verbal stimulation, necessarily, but on the contrary, may be caused by an inability to distinguish and recognize speech sounds in a very noisy and verbally disorganized environment. Deutsch (1964) suggests that, in the presence of such over-stimulation, the child becomes inattentive to verbalizations, or "tunes out," and thus fails to develop good auditory learning skills.

If we look at the challenges in specific subject matter areas, the list might include:

A. Language arts
    1. deficits in listening
    2. deficits in speech
    3. deficits in reading

B. Mathematical concepts
    1. meager perceptual skills in mathematics
    2. knowledge of few mathematical nursery rhymes
    3. lack of objects with which to perceive form discriminations
    4. lack of experience with money
    5. inadequate spatial concepts
    6. meager experience with standard units of measure
    7. inability to relate mathematics to new experiences
    8. inadequate or different time concepts
    9. lack of parental help with homework

C. Science concepts
    1. limited opportunity to observe natural phenomena (urban children)
    2. lack of reading material on science
    3. lack of understanding of need for sanitation
    4. inadequate guidance of television viewing
    5. limited opportunity to perform experiments
    6. inability of parents to answer science questions

D. Social studies
    1. lack of knowledge of their cultural heritage
    2. lack of knowledge of similarities and differences among disadvantaged groups
    3. lack of knowledge of how to care for public property
    4. lack of understanding of social etiquette
    5. inadequate health practices
    6. inappropriate techniques in the solution of problems
    7. lack of information pertaining to community services
    8. inadequate background in geography and civics

E. Other cultural deficits

    1. lack of experience with paint and crayons

    2. limited imagination (Crow *et al.*, 1966, pp. 121–38)

In the face of this lengthy list of challenges, some of which reflect middle-class bias, the teacher may be able to cope with only a few. Principles and practices of hygiene and nutrition are often part of the curriculum at all levels, so may be taught to the entire class without singling out the culturally different learners. For the elementary school children, opportunities to use crayons, to handle objects, and to ask questions are among the easiest challenges to meet. Language skills take longer to develop, but may be worked on with the assistance of speech therapists, remedial reading specialists, volunteer teacher aides, and other consultants. Involving the parents in the children's learning is a system-wide task, which may be initiated by social service workers paying home visits, bilingual teachers and teacher aides acting as "go-betweens" for the home and school, adult seminars, and so on. The point is to start somewhere and not simply reject the child as an inadequate learner because of his cultural differences.

Not all of the culturally different are poor learners with low IQ and little imagination. However, even creativity scores may be depressed because of other deficits that are apparent on intelligence and achievement tests. Therefore, caution is recommended when using creativity tests as well as more traditional school tests with children of different language and cultural backgrounds. Similarly, it takes a bit of effort to find the culturally different who are gifted. What is valued in the majority culture may be somewhat different from that in another racial/ethnic group. Giftedness among Mexican Americans, for example, includes not only intelligence, but also being lively and sharp. At the same time, the gifted Mexican-American child is one who is self-reliant, has leadership ability, yet is quietly mature. (Bernal, 1974) This is a more complex view of giftedness than we usually consider in the schools. Depending on the teacher's perception of the child (or his culture), "being lively and sharp" may mask his gifted qualities or be assessed more accurately.

If a complete language barrier exists, the teacher will probably have to help the child on an individual basis for an extended period. The teacher may even have to resort to using a bilingual dictionary or learning a little of the other language in order to be able to assist the learner. (What an opportunity to teach the rest of the class some useful words in the other language!) There is little point in a child sitting in a classroom where he understands nothing. If a bilingual specialist is available, special lessons can be arranged on a part-time basis and may be required by laws. Older children who have successfully learned English and are from the same culture may be helpful as tutors.

As indicated in our earlier discussions of the culturally different, bilingualism can be a handicap if neither language is learned adequately. Patois, or highly idiomatic speech, even if it is basically English, can create the same kinds of problems for the learner and challenges for the teacher. On the other hand, a child coming from another culture with a different language (if he has average or near-average intelligence) will probably be able to understand English after relatively shorter instruction periods, but will need help in reading and speaking, especially during periods of independent study and testing.

The child who cannot speak the same language as his classmates also faces a social problem. He may be teased, ostracized, ignored, or bullied. His emotional reaction to these responses may further magnify learning problems. The teacher needs to find ways to turn this social liability into a classroom asset, whether by encouraging the class to take advantage of this opportunity to learn a foreign language, or by asking the child to be a resource person in the study of his culture, or by such other means as are appropriate to the situation.

Except for Native Americans, we are all descended from families that were once displaced in American schools. Most of the immigrants were poor, too. The magnitude of the problem has changed, and greater sensitivity to the challenges—social, political, and educational—of the culturally different increases the need to deal effectively with them. Legislation since the 1960s provides substantial support for the development of new programs in this area, and it is another challenge to teachers to formulate and put into effect such new programs.

THE INTELLECTUALLY DIFFERENT

In this group of exceptional children are included the mentally retarded, the mentally gifted, and the creative. Since Binet's original efforts to distinguish those who could not learn from those who could, psychologists and educators have made special educational provisions for the retarded. Less frequently, special classes or special schools have been established for the gifted, and, with only rare exceptions, such as the High School of Music and Art in New York City, there are no special facilities for the creative.

The *mentally retarded* child is so classified because he has an IQ of 70 or 75 or lower. The educable retarded have IQs in the 50 to 70 range, while the trainable retarded are in the 25 to 50 IQ range. The American Association of Mental Deficiency defines retardation as "subaverage intellectual functioning which originates during the developmental period." These intellectual deficits are often found in conjunction with other problems such as deafness, visual handicaps, cerebral palsy, minimal or major brain damage, speech difficulties, and social or emotional immaturity. Which is the primary disorder may be unclear. They are, therefore, frequently multiple challenges. At the same time, retarded children are usually lovable, docile, willing, and anxious to learn within their own limitations. Observing a class of trainable retarded teenagers one day, I was struck by their obvious pleasure in learning, although the strain of trying to learn was evident on their faces.

One major problem of the retarded child is social acceptance. This may

Mentally retarded

also be true for slow learners in regular classes. It becomes especially crucial when they are integrated into regular classes for some school activities. In one school, where an educable retarded class used the common lunchroom facilities, these children were resented because they did not clean up after themselves as thoroughly as the other children had to do. (This could have been remedied by the teacher.) In another school, there was resentment because of real and imagined special privileges given the trainable retarded class. In a study of 30 regular junior high school classes with 1010 nonretarded students, Rucker, Howe, and Snider (1969) used a sociometric test to study the acceptance of 23 educable mentally retarded special-class students who participated in their activities.

> The retarded were found to be (a) significantly less accepted than the nonretarded, (b) equally low in the social structure of both the academic and nonacademic classess in which they participated, and (c) seemingly unaware of their low social position in regular classes. Their level of acceptance in the special class was positively related to their degree of acceptance in regular classes. (p. 617)

With mainstreaming of educable retarded children occurring, the peer acceptance problem is of real concern. Tonn (1974) believes, however, that it is better to learn to live with possible rejection from "normal" peers than to be labeled as a member of a special class. Special efforts can be made by regular class teachers to increase understanding of the problems of retarded learners that will minimize rejection even if acceptance is not significantly increased.

Question *In what ways might you minimize rejection and increase acceptance of mentally retarded learners in the regular classroom?*

A second challenge to educators arises from the fact of multiple handicaps. According to Guess (1967), the blind retarded, for example, are often nonverbal or partially verbal, underdeveloped in motor coordination and dexterity, emotionally anxious, and markedly underdeveloped in cognitive learning. This is, of course, all quite understandable. Guess further believes that educational techniques appropriate to one or the other difficulty may be inappropriate for the multiple handicapped. Social and emotional adjustments are primary needs for these children, followed by sensory stimulation and progress in motor development. The deaf retarded pose similar problems. As with the deaf, there is also reported in several studies, a high rate of apparent color blindness among retardates, although there is some question as to whether the retarded child understands the instructions for color blindness tests and shows up as color blind because of this. (Schein and Salvia, 1969). If color blindness is a problem for many retarded children, then teaching techniques using color will obviously not be effective or appropriate for them. (It is unlikely that any of these children would be in regular classes.)

A wide variety of instructional materials are available today for teaching the retarded. They must first be helped as *persons* in matters of self-care and safety, including the reading of danger signs. Multisensory stimulation, for example, the use of audio, visual, tactile, and other appropriate sensory stimuli, is often more effective than a one-dimensional teaching technique. Programmed instruction is another innovation in teaching the educable and trainable retarded. The small steps of the linear type of program are ideally suited to the limited attention span and concrete abilities of these children. A variety of experiences, such as class trips to a zoo, a bakery, a print shop, and so on, can be essential components of a study unit. Reading, spelling, arithmetic, science, and social studies can all focus on the same unit of study, as was demonstrated for the maladjusted learner in Focus 12–1. Repetition is essential.

Occupational training that is compatible with the physical and mental abilities of the child is particularly important for the teenaged retardate, who will ultimately be at least semi-independent as an adult. It is also important to inform the teenaged retardate of his or her voting rights and responsibilities. Since the Voting Rights Act of 1970 made it legal to vote at age 18 and abolished literacy tests as a precondition to voting, many of these young people may be allowed to vote. A survey of state laws by Olley and Fremouw (1974) revealed that 22 states had no regulations involving the retardates' right to vote, and 20 others permit them to vote unless they are legally judged incompetent. Socialization, the rules and practices of society-at-large, is another important educational requirement for the retarded youngster if he is to function with some adequacy in the world. Even the trainable retarded can be taught simple skills that they can use in a sheltered workshop and basic self-care habits that will make them more socially acceptable.

Further, exposure to the community and involvement in it is of benefit to these young people. Designers of an experimental program in Iowa City saw community involvement as a way to help the retarded apply skills learned in the classroom, prepare them for adulthood, and accustom the local citizens to the presence of the retarded. (Bordwell, 1975) Some of the goals for the program included: acceptable appearance, ability to use the city bus, cross streets safely, use various stores appropriately, behave appropriately with others and when alone, and know what to do when lost. If the retarded young person is not to be isolated as an adult, such "basic training" is necessary.

The retarded, whether educable or trainable, and slow learners need patient teachers. Realistic standards and expectations must be set for all these groups, both at school and at home. Reading is a major educational task, for it is needed for physical safety, learning job skills, and functioning with some degree of independence as an adult.

If a child is to be moved from regular classes to special education classes, possibly after a belated diagnosis, the child and his parents are entitled by law to a due process hearing before any such change can be made. After the move is made, continuing counseling may be needed for the whole family until they can accept the facts and can face a somewhat different future for the child than they had anticipated.

Gifted

Challenges presented by the *gifted* child offer a considerable contrast to those just discussed. Since homogeneous grouping is not practiced as widely at the upper ends of the intellectual continuum as at the lower end, the gifted are more likely to be enrolled in regular classes. Not only do they have high IQ scores, usually 130 and above, but they are also characterized by high achievement level, rich vocabularies, widespread interests, curiosity, maturity of thought and behavior, emotional stability, and often leadership qualities. Most of the gifted are well-adjusted; some are not. Some may be highly critical of themselves and others, inattentive, nonconformist, restless, and lackadaisical about classroom work when disinterested or bored. Their peer relationships, depending on grade level, may be poor because of their maturity in interests and behavior, or they may show social leadership. (Halpin, Payne, and Ellett, 1975)

Many of the gifted, because of their negative characteristics, are not identified as such in their school years. Pang (1968) cites a number of eminent persons, including Einstein, Churchill, Newton, Tolstoy, Dreiser, Frank Lloyd Wright, and the late President Eisenhower, who were considered average or lower in ability, were poorly motivated in school, and/or did poorly on school tests. Interestingly, however, he also points out that "despite the mediocre records of some of these individuals, their mothers often had extraordinary confidence in their sons' abilities and talents." (p. 322) Dreistadt (1974) has averred that it was Einstein's slow intellectual development that enabled the great scientist to look at the world in new and different ways—he asked questions about things that others took for granted.

Many of the gifted are "late bloomers," not becoming motivated toward achievement until their middle or late teens, and many, for a variety of reasons, are poor test-takers. A case in point is one young man who earned fair grades through his junior year in high school, suddenly became strongly motivated in twelfth grade, entered college and took senior philosophy courses in his first year, and in his second was carrying a full schedule of courses at an Ivy League University as well as at a theological seminary!

In 1921, the late Lewis Terman and his associates began a study of "genius." Their two goals were to find the traits characterizing children of high IQ and to find out how they fared as adults. This study, referred to in chapter one (under longitudinal research), began with over 1,500 subjects, average IQ of 150, of whom 80 had an IQ greater than 170. According to Terman, 30 years of "follow-up" studies of the subjects had clearly demonstrated the value of general intelligence tests for elementary school children in terms of predicting achievement. (1954) The test scores and achievement were not perfectly correlated, nor could the scores predict the direction in which achievement would occur. However, whatever the ultimate field of endeavor, Terman felt that much of what Spearman called "g" was needed for success. After 30 years of continued study, this group of subjects was found to be above the statistical average in physical and mental health, social adjustment, education, and literary output (fiction and nonfiction), and considerably below average in contribution to rates of crime and delinquency in the general population.

It is interesting that psychologists who work with the gifted believe the optimum IQ to be in the 125 to 150 range. At this level, the gifted individual can accomplish and excel without being eccentric; can understand the work of "geniuses" and contribute to it, but can also understand the inability of the "common man" to comprehend it. Those with IQs above 150 apparently have less empathy and contact with the average individual and tend toward intellectual arrogance, even in the school years. In writings about children with IQs of 180 and above, it has been urged that they be taught to "suffer fools gladly," as their teachers would probably have IQs some 70 points below their own and would be hard put to keep up with the students' super-intellectual productions. This may sound a bit snobbish, but it probably has some truth to it.

Instead of promoting feelings of superiority or competition, activities and discussions should occur that will help the gifted students to clarify and organize their values. (Walker, 1975) The teacher can ask broad questions to stir thinking, clarify values expressed, and reflect student thoughts and feelings rather than imposing his own all the time. (Coletta, 1975) Arts and humanities programs provide another means of integrating affective with cognitive education. "It is through the knowledge of these civilizing forces and the transference of these ideas that the gifted and talented can become immersed in understanding their world." (Lake, 1975, p. 261) Through these varied approaches, the teacher humanizes the curriculum and enhances the growth of the gifted and talented as people.

If you have a gifted child in the class, what do you do with him? He will most certainly be bored, and consequently disruptive or in a daydream, if forced to progress at the rate of the average student. He may hide his abilities if the response to his rapid learning is to give him "more of the same" problems or reading assignment, thus increasing the quantity of his work but not the quality. If there are not provisions for acceleration, special classes, or advanced study, efforts must be made to challenge him in other ways. At the middle and upper grade levels, the gifted student is capable of analyzing and synthesizing information—the upper rungs of Bloom's *Taxonomy*—so that his assignments relevant to the class curriculum should reflect the need to use these abilities. "In general, enrichment programs in regular classes should provide greater breadth and depth of learning, more opportunities for developing creative behaviors, increased emphasis on rich social experiences, and ample freedom to pursue independent study." (Plowman, 1969, p. 548) Independent study opportunities should be allowed in the learner's own area of interest, not only in the topic being studied in class. Just as the slow learner can contribute to class projects through nonreading activities, so the gifted learner can contribute through his deeper study of a topic, assigned or freely chosen. He can also ask questions so advanced that they embarrass the teacher. In such cases, the challenge to the teacher is often a matter of guiding this youngster to appropriate sources and people who can help him to pursue his interests in depth. He is bored by, and doesn't usually need, the mechanical drill of the classroom. Gifted learners also tend to work better if they have a general outline of the course of study covering several lessons rather than day-to-day assignments. Emphasis should be placed on self-responsibility to develop and use their abilities constructively.

Today, many high schools do have advanced study programs that enable gifted students to enter college with advanced standing. There are also "honors" programs that explore literature, history, mathematics, and the sciences in greater depth than is usual at this level. Some universities offer early admission on a part- or full-time basis to unusually gifted youths. (Stanley, 1973a; Stanley, Keating, and Fox, 1974) The teachers for these courses need to be extremely well-versed in their fields, flexible enough to allow their students to challenge them, and resourceful enough to create challenging problems for their students.

Creative   A somewhat different challenge is offered by the *creative* learner. Although he may be intellectually bright, he also tends to be highly imaginative intellectually curious, flexible, sometimes impulsive and nonconformist, and self-directed. These traits can make him a delight or an "impossible pest" to teachers, depending largely on the teacher's perception of the resulting behavior. Nonconformity probably poses one of the greatest problems to the classroom teacher. Instead of following a prescribed format, the creative student prefers to write or draw in his own style. He may, and frequently does, "read between the lines" to come to conclusions at variance with the teacher's, leading to conflict and/or laughter (at the teacher's expense, naturally). Like the gifted learner, he is bored with repetition and strictly limited assignments.

In the case of children with creative talents in the arts, and with average or better academic ability, a principal problem is one of organizing a special class or program. Discovery of such talents usually comes through observation or expressed and demonstrated interests of the child. Credit can be given for courses, such as music theory or appreciation, in which the talented pupil can do better before taking the course than the average students can do at its conclusion. The High School of Music and Art in New York, mentioned earlier, provides a curriculum that includes opportunities to advance in the area of talent, such as music composition, art history, sculpture, choral conducting, and so on. At the elementary level, however, individual instruction can be provided by teaching specialists inside and outside of the school system. Time for practice and training of the special talent should be arranged, as well as participation in relevant school activities. Such special opportunities are highly desirable to encourage the youngster to continue on his way toward fulfillment of his potential.

Creativity is not limited to the arts, of course. Many of these children have ability in scientific areas, and, if not bound to a rigid curriculum, seek and often find answers to scientific questions of importance. Recognition in recent years has come to them through local and national science fairs and awards.

Three major needs in the classroom for creative learners are a tolerance for deviation on the part of the teacher, encouragement to perceive in novel ways, and opportunities to develop their originality. Tolerance for nonconformity does not mean that the teacher should lift all demands for social responsibility or permit behavior without limits. It does mean that ". . . the child or student not be penalized for being different or for exhibiting his independence and curiosity." (Goodale, 1970, p. 94) Reinforcement for creative effort, on the other hand, is important, as is *constructive* criticism. Open-ended discussions, in which there are no specific correct answers, encourage the creative student to demonstrate his or her unique capabilities in approach. The emphasis for this learner is on the *process* of learning more than on its product. Variety in the curriculum in terms of literature or history studied also expands the horizons for creative and noncreative learners alike.

The more interested *any* learner is in what he is supposed to study, the more probable that he *will* study and achieve at higher levels. The creative student especially will daydream less often, disturb others less frequently, and still bring his or her own "breath of fresh air" into the classroom. "One of the major purposes of an educational institution is to prepare individuals for creative achievement, yet the standard measures of fitness for college work do not measure potential creativity. It is an extremely difficult task." (Pang, 1968, p. 326) This particular difficulty with standardized tests was referred to earlier in discussing intelligence tests, but has bearing also on the creative learner in the classroom situation. Changes in teacher attitudes, curricula, and instructional techniques, which will permit the expression of creativity, can also lead to consideration of creative abilities as an asset in college admissions criteria.

The creative and gifted learners, in contrast to the mentally retarded, are more apt to attend regular classes in a heterogeneous setting and to find it more difficult to obtain approval for special programs to refine and use their abilities. It's very hard to arouse sympathy for your cause when your problem is overabundance rather than deficit. It thus becomes even more important for the classroom teacher to be prepared to accept the challenge of challenging these students.

The creative and gifted tend to have a favorable self-concept. They may not always have the most desired personality characteristics (Milgram, Milgram, and Landau, 1974), however, so that peer relationships as well as teacher-pupil relationships may be strained. A sense of humor and perspective is a great asset for all concerned.

Taken together, the intellectually different represent opposite ends of a continuum. Each subgroup, however, offers unique challenges to teachers. Efforts must be made to provide programs and to meet the challenges of each subgroup on its own grounds.

SUMMARY

The needs of exceptional children indeed provide a challenge to any teacher. This brief introduction to the world of the emotionally, physically, culturally, and intellectually different learners has attempted to alert you to their varying characteristics, some of the solutions now used to ease their differences, and the possibility of having some students with these differences in your own regular classroom. There are many children whose differences are undetected or ignored until a teacher notices squinting, restlessness, muddled speech, curiosity, or some other behavior and probes beneath the surface to discover its causes. Few children are "average" in every way.

Following a discussion of mainstreaming, several groups of exceptional children were presented with the assorted challenges they bring to the classroom. Emphasis was placed on turning the challenges into advantages wherever possible. Further, more than cognitive learning was considered. Teacher-learner and peer relationships are, if anything, more important in the case of most exceptional children than for their "average" classmates.

A few other things should be mentioned here briefly. One is that the various states, at present, do have certification criteria for teachers of exceptional children, criteria which vary from state to state as well as from one type of exceptionality to another. Educational preparation frequently means one year of graduate work in order to have the appropriate qualifications. In addition, state departments of education also establish teaching conditions for special classes, including number of students per teacher, special equipment, special time limits, and so on. A third item to think about is whether special education is necessary as a separate entity or whether mainstreaming is more desirable. Assuming that special treatment and management of exceptional children is needed, should there be as much fractionalization, that is, sub-specialization, of classes as there is now? Or, can some of these different types of learners learn together? The answers to these questions depend to some extent on local needs and financial resources, the pooling of techniques and personnel, community policy, and improved diagnoses, among other things.

As is true for all learners, the uniqueness of each of the exceptional children must be considered in the classroom. Suggestions for teaching materials and techniques that allow for individual learning differences are available to the teacher from regional resource centers and teacher centers. Commonality of symptoms does not always mean that common techniques can be used, or that a given teacher is best suited for all learners in the class. The needs of special learners are even more acute than those of the "similar" and will perhaps best be met by those teachers who wish to find a real challenge in the classroom.

Preview

THE "CLIMATE" OF LEARNING
CLIMATE OF THE SCHOOL
CLIMATE OF THE CLASSROOM
CLASSROOM INTERACTION
STUDENT INTERACTION

CHARACTERISTICS OF TEACHERS
PERSONALITY CHARACTERISTICS
CLASSROOM MANAGEMENT
Student Rights
THE "GOOD" TEACHER
TEACHER EVALUATION

TEACHER ATTITUDES AND LEARNING
EXPECTANCIES
EFFECTS OF ATTITUDES ON LEARNING

TEACHER EFFECTIVENESS
MODES OF TEACHING
EFFECTIVE APPROACHES

SUMMARY

13

Teacher-Pupil Relations

There are a number of considerations to be taken into account under the title "Teacher-Pupil Relations." One of the major variables in any learning situation is the psychological "climate" in which learning takes place. Accordingly, we need to ask two questions about schools and classrooms: 1) Is the climate conducive to learning? and 2) To what *kind* of learning is the climate conducive? Some of the answers to these questions will be found in the varying techniques that are used in evaluating observations of classroom interaction.

A second major factor in teacher-pupil relations is, of course, the teacher. What are his or her personality characteristics? What makes the person a good or bad teacher, and by whose definition? The teacher, as part of his total personality, brings certain attitudes to the classroom that have effects on the learners. These are demonstrated in the ways in which the teacher "manages" the classroom. In this chapter, we will discuss both aspects of attitudes and their effects. Finally, we will look at various teaching styles and their purported effectiveness. What are the best ways to teach, and is there a single approach that is effective with every student?

THE "CLIMATE" OF LEARNING

In every school system and its subdivisions, there is a "climate" or psychological environment of learning. It doesn't necessarily appear anywhere in print, for it is difficult to mandate an atmosphere, but it certainly exists. Where does it come from? Fundamentally, the community sets the "tone," "climate," or atmosphere in the schools and expresses its desires through the school board members it selects. In some communities, where school board members are elected by political party, this may be less than true if the wishes of a sizable minority are ignored because of tradition and partisanship. The school board, in accord with state regulations, sets local policies with regard to hiring, curriculum, and other educational matters. Since the school board usually selects the superintendent, this person will be someone whose ideas conform fairly well to those of the community as represented by the board. The superintendent, either personally or through administrative aides, then selects principals and teachers who tend to agree with his educational philosophy. Of course, the superintendent can do this only as there are job vacancies to fill or as new programs are introduced that permit movement of personnel from one job to another. Thus, the community sets the climate and its ideas filter through several levels with minor modifications to the classroom situation, as you can see in Figure 13.1.

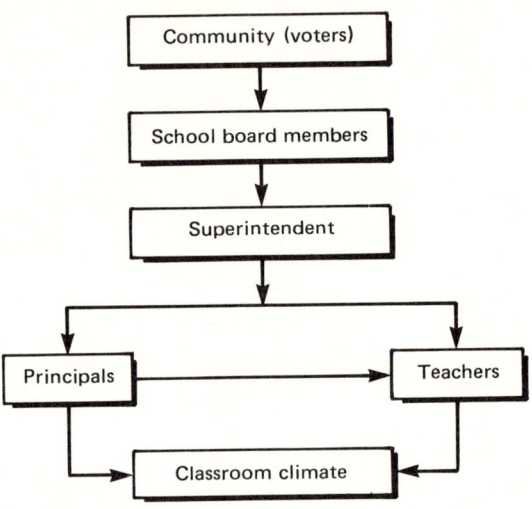

Figure 13.1   *The establishment of classroom climate.*

In cases where school board members name replacements to the board because of deaths or resignations, they tend to choose people who have the same ideas as their own and thus perpetuate whatever philosophy has been already developed. One of the current problems in this arrangement is that today teachers often do not live in the community where they teach. As a result, they know little about their students outside the classroom. Additionally, they become "victims" of what is, to them, ". . . the anonymous authority of the board of education . . . the curriculum makers." (Conner, 1965, p. 180) Since this whole procedure starts with the community, if a change in philosophy and climate is desired, it must begin with the election of a new board, or a sufficient number of new board members to select a new superintendent who is ready to make the desired changes. Changes may come slowly, of course, because of already tenured personnel, but they do come. With all of this background in mind, let's move to the school itself.

The principal of today and tomorrow finds himself in a continuously changing environment. To accept the idea of administering a school solely based upon the directives in the board policy, the memoranda from the superintendent, and the behaviors of principals of the past is to cast oneself into a reactive role. The person in such a role finds adversary relationships developing or reinforced, finds himself defending his behavior to those who expect him to lead, and finds his role seriously questioned. He may find himself trying to catch up instead of leading." (Roe and Drake, 1974, p. 68)

Climate of the school

The principal is a "person in the middle." On the one hand, he or she manages a school on behalf of the superintendent and school board. On the other hand, he is the authority figure most visible and most easily available to parents and local citizens. Principals are also caught between their roles as business managers, overseeing maintenance of the building and filling out innumerable forms, and as educational and instructional leaders. (Roe and Drake, 1974, pp. 13–35)

It is in the leadership role that we look at the principal as creator of the climate of the school. The principal, as administrator of the school, makes known to his teachers his ideas of what should take place in the school. The principal's philosophy may be communicated through mimeographed directives, speeches at teachers' meetings, informal chats with teachers, and/or through his actions. At one extreme, there are principals who appear to be primarily concerned with organization and discipline. That is, a list of regulations for teachers and learners alike is transmitted from the principal's office and must be adhered to—or else. The atmosphere tends to resemble a military institution in its conformity and rigidity. Teachers submit their detailed lesson plans to the principal on time for fear of negative comments or worse on their personnel records and don't dare to deviate from the plans for the same reason. There are principals who expect all teachers, in elementary school for example, to be teaching arithmetic from 9:40 to 10:05 every morning, not starting earlier and not prolonging the period. There are principals who tolerate no deviation from the prepared lesson plan, no matter what the interest of the learners at a particular time. Any infraction of the rules, by teacher or student, warrants negative criticism directly from the principal. Innovation and experimentation are frowned upon, if not forbidden; any criticism of these regulations may be interpreted as hostility toward the principal himself. Freedom of speech and freedom of action are submerged, and suspicion and tension dominate the school. Such situations may be found in any school district, whether rural, urban, or suburban, where the community tends to be strongly conservative and traditional. Happily, such situations are decreasing in number, although where they exist change comes slowly, if at all.

Focus 13–1

In describing two traditional schools as part of a study of *The Psychological Impact of School Experience,* the research team from the Bank St. College of Education (New York City) offered these comments:

1. These schools did not count on the child's intrinsic gratification in learning as a motivating force for his investment in school tasks. Instead, they expected the child to accept the demanding

> aspects of school life—control, concentration, compliance—as a life task, an essential investment for future gains. (Minuchin, Biber, Shapiro, and Zimiles, 1969, pp. 63–64)
>
> In other words, this was an "all-work-and-no-play" climate. In one of the two schools, particularly, order prevailed and spontaneity in learning was not to be found.
>
> > 2. At the school just mentioned, . . . approval-disapproval appeared to be the accepted form of exchange from principal to teacher. . . . The first paragraph of notes distributed at a staff meeting read: "Your fine teaching is due in no small part to your excellent preparation. Plan Books today was especially praiseworthy. Everyone gets a star!" (Minuchin, *et al.*, 1969, p. 65)
>
> Deserved praise, perhaps, but the pattern of approving teacher actions in the same way in which these elementary school teachers rewarded their pupils tells something about the climate of an authoritarian-type school.
> Nonconformists or mavericks would be out-of-place in this school. The principal's reward system wouldn't work for them, since personal self-approval would be more important than "stars." The loss to the learners of the opportunity to think rather than memorize, to express their feelings and ideas rather than someone else's, and to be themselves rather than malleable clay to be shaped to a common form is difficult to measure.

If we look at schools with a different type of principal, or even the same school after a change in principals, the contrast in climate is marked. There may still be organization, there may still be lesson plans, and the stipulated curriculum is the same. However, a less authoritarian principal, while maintaining these aspects of the educational system, makes his teaching staff aware that the needs of the learners come first. If the class is more interested in a space flight than arithmetic one day, the arithmetic period can be delayed or the content presented in connection with space flights. If the teacher wants to stray from the "teacher's guide" to a text and use an innovative technique, this is encouraged. The principal frequently consults with the teachers about introducing experimental programs or planning changes in school practices. The result is a more democratic, less tense climate in the school that inevitably leads to more relaxed teachers and learners. Again, such an atmosphere may be found in any school district.

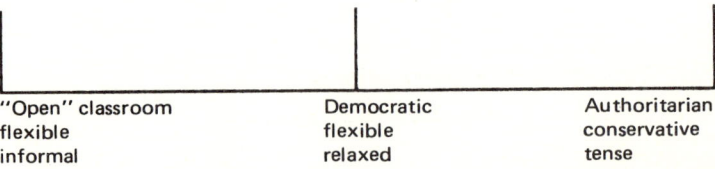

Figure 13.2   *A continuum of school climates.*

A third climate is the one provided by the "open" classroom, at the opposite end of the continuum from the highly authoritarian school. This is a movement that developed in English "infant" or primary schools and, as mentioned in chapter eleven, is being introduced into more and more schools in this country. In the Plowden Committee report (1967) on these schools, the emphasis is on the children and *their* schools, although the schools are not child-centered in the sense of American progressive schools of a few decades ago. The headmistress or principals of an infant school are regarded, and perceive themselves, as educational leaders. They are "head teachers," not business managers or "paper-pushers." They interact with teachers and children alike on an informal basis. Indeed, in England, the head of the school is *urged* to teach more than administer, thus raising the prestige of teaching itself. There is more of a master teacher to junior teacher relationship here than supervisor to employee, which appears to result in an atmosphere in which everyone is primarily concerned with the children and what they are learning. Despite the high rate of activity and seeming chaos of the "open" classroom, there is structure and there is learning.

The principal-teacher relationship, which appears to have such importance in setting the classroom climate, is but one factor in the establishment of faculty morale, which is itself an element in the creation of a learning climate. Other contributors to morale include satisfaction with teaching, relationships among teachers, salary, nonteaching duties, curriculum issues, status as a professional, community support of education, school facilities and services, and community pressures. There seems to be no question that each of these factors is important to the teacher and that dissatisfaction with one or more of them will lead to poorer morale with negative effects upon teaching performance. Rempel and Bentley (1970) found higher morale among female teachers than males in their study, due apparently to satisfaction with salary and status as primary factors. They also concluded that "The results obtained clearly indicate a high relationship between salary level and the level of morale." (p. 538) After all, if a teacher doesn't like the principal or colleagues, there are other schools to which to move, but high salary is interpreted by the teacher as evidence of personal competence, and as such it satisfies ego needs. (Note: Of course, there are also practical aspects to high salaries, such as supporting a family. Further, in times of increasing unemployment of teachers, having any salary is better than none.)

In fact, it is possible that satisfaction with teaching can also outweigh unpleasant climates. Some teachers so enjoy their jobs that this intrinsic job satisfaction overcomes poor interpersonal relationships, inadequate salaries, and even deficient facilities. Such teachers are rare but are blessings for their students.

What aspects of teaching are most important to you?   ***Question***

Given the principal's orientation and the teacher's morale, what happens in the classroom? Is the class governed by demands for order, with "naughty"   ***Climate of the classroom*** youngsters punished as an example to the rest of the class? Is the emphasis on quiet for the sake of quiet? Does the teacher ask questions to test or to stimulate thought? How does the teacher's approach mesh with the student's personality? Much of the classroom climate depends, of course, on the grade level, the subject matter being taught, and the size of the class. For example, in an introductory psychology class of 150 or more college students, held in a large stark lecture hall, it is difficult to have anyone but the teacher do most of the talking. Yet even under these circumstances, there is a difference in the "feel" of the class, the classroom climate, according to the teacher. Some lecturers simply lecture for 50 or 75 minutes, then disappear until the next class meeting. Others lecture until stopped by a student's question, then resume. Still others lecture *and* ask questions designed to make the students think about a concept. Additionally, they are available before and/or after lectures to answer questions on a one-to-one basis. Some teachers at this level will tolerate an almost chronic hum of whispers, while others feel personally affronted if someone sneezes. Thus, even under fairly "standard" teaching conditions at the college level, a climate is created by the teacher's style and personality.

At the other extreme, in the primary grades, classroom climate plays an important role in determining the child's attitudes toward learning and school generally, as well as toward the teacher specifically. Since attitude toward learning has so much effect on actual learning, the importance of positive experiences in the lower grades is obvious. One second-grader's mother was told that her son rarely volunteered to speak in class. From earlier discussions with the boy, the mother was able to tell the teacher that he was "afraid" of the teacher and that this was why he was so quiet. Youngsters who have been disturbing in one teacher's class may be near "angels" for a teacher with whom they feel more comfortable. It is not a matter of rules or lack of them alone that determines the child's reaction. It is more a matter, at this young age particularly, of how the child perceives the teacher's attitudes—approving, punitive, warm, threatening, "fair," discouraging, and so on. A teacher who is consistent in his or her expectations, though they may be high, is usually perceived more positively than a permissive teacher who makes few or contradictory demands. A classroom in which there are pictures on the bulletin boards, colorful displays, and other visual stimuli also contributes to a warm classroom climate, but essentially it is the teacher who creates the mood.

Focus 13–2

Consider visits to two classrooms, one in a small private school that has long been experimental in philosophy, and the other in a politically conservative suburban school district. The visits took place within a 24-hour period, and the schools were within 15 miles of each other.

At the door of the second-grade classroom in the private school, the visitor looked in—and looked again. Old bedspreads hung from the ceiling, curtaining off a quarter of the room. (This was the "clubroom," it was learned later.) Desks were scattered around the room as if it were moving day. Books were to be seen all over, as were "gadgets" used in studying

> arithmetic and samples of the children's art work. All of the children were happily occupied, individually or in small groups, and all were learning something.
>
> The next morning, at the suburban public school, the visitor looked in the door of a third-grade classroom—and looked again: No curtained-off clubroom this time, but otherwise the impression of a happy but physically and quietly chaotic classroom was the same. One boy kept his desk inside a large packing crate, which he considered his "office." Everywhere the children were busy, talking in soft voices, writing, asking for assistance, reading, and learning.
>
> In both cases, the principal and those above her in the administrative hierarchy permit this modification of the physical environment more familiar to all of us. The teacher then provides materials for study, moves from one child to another offering comments and assistance, and rarely teaches the class as a whole. In both cases, the climate is relaxed, yet geared to learning and the children's interests, not anxiety and pressure. The climate is what is often called an "open" one.

By the middle grades (4–6), learners have acquired self-perceptions and have a better idea of how teachers perceive them. They become acutely aware of what merits teacher approval and disapproval. In a study of sixth graders, for example, deGroat and Thompson (1949) found that peer ratings of teacher-approval and teacher-disapproval situations yielded the following information: 1) the more intelligent tend to receive more approval, 2) the higher achievers get more approval, and 3) children who perceive themselves as "better adjusted" tend to get more teacher approval. It might be suggested, in line with these findings, that in such a situation the learner who has a negative self-concept tends to have it reinforced rather than altered. In such cases, it would help if a student were ". . . assigned to the type of teacher with whom that student has achieved the greatest success in the past." (Cunningham, 1975, p. 186) Such student-teacher pairings take planning, but would benefit both parties. Certainly interaction in the classroom would be more positive.

Classroom interaction

What in the teacher and/or child sets the tone for their interaction? On what, for example, do teachers base their attitudes toward specific children?

Several studies have been done to find out what student characteristics are associated with teacher attitudes. These studies have in common the distribution of the learners into four groups: 1) attachment (teacher would enjoy having these children in class for another year); 2) indifference (the teacher would be unprepared to discuss these children with their parents at an unexpected conference); 3) concern (those to whom the teacher would devote more time and attention if possible); and 4) rejection (those children whose removal from the class would most relieve the teacher). Willis and Brophy (1974) found that:

The three major variables involved seem to be the students' general level of school success, the degree to which they reward teachers in their personal contacts with them, and the degree to which they conform to classroom rules. *Attachment students* were compliant and successful in school, and they apparently rewarded teachers in their interaction with them. *Concern students* had difficulty in school but apparently were compliant and personally rewarding to the teachers, so that teachers became concerned about them and spent much time providing remedial help. . . .

The *indifference students* apparently responded negatively to the teachers, failing to provide a rewarding interpersonal contact pattern, so that the teachers became indifferent and gradually spent less and less time with these children, even though they perceived them as needing extra help. The *rejection students* not only failed to provide rewarding experiences to the teachers in their interpersonal contacts with them; they also frequently caused classroom disturbances and were general discipline problems. The teachers responded to this by rejecting the students to the point of wanting to get rid of them and by projecting a number of traits onto them, especially low abilities, which they did not, in fact, possess (at least not as a group). (p. 528)

So much for the nonconforming learner! His chances of becoming part of the "attachment" group are rated poor.

Question   *In what ways is reinforcement operating in the development of these relationships?*

Another way to look at classroom interaction is to examine the teacher's behaviors toward the class as a whole—to evaluate the classroom climate. It *is* possible to evaluate classroom climate. Rosenshine (1970) summarized the formats of several evaluation instruments and classified them as either category systems or ratings systems. In category-type measures, ". . . items focus upon specific, denotable, relatively objective behaviors such as 'teacher repetition of student ideas,' or 'teacher asks evaluative question,' with each event recorded in terms of frequency of occurrence." (p. 281) In contrast to the low-inference demands placed on the observer by this method, there are the high-inference items of rating scales. "Items on rating instruments such as 'clarity of presentation,' 'enthusiasm,' or 'helpful toward students' require that an observer infer these constructs from a series of events." (p. 281) In addition, the observer must judge whether a particular behavior occurs "never," "frequently," or at some point in between.

Evaluation instruments also vary with the purposes and biases of their constructors. Most often, the instruments are used to describe current classroom practices or to investigate relationships between classroom activities and student growth. Sometimes they are used in teacher education, and occasionally to monitor instructional systems. (Rosenshine and Furst, 1973, p. 147) They may focus on teacher- v. student-centeredness, verbal v. nonverbal learning, warmth v. hostility of teacher, flexibility v. rigidity of teacher, and so on. Medley and Mitzel's "OScAR" (Observation Schedule and Record), for example, attempts to study general classroom environment in terms of emotional climate (warmth to hostility), verbal emphasis (degree to which verbal activities predominate), and social organization (amount of social grouping and pupil autonomy). (1958) These areas are evaluated by observation of the teacher's verbalizations, gestures, facial expressions, and so on, during limited time-sample periods. Some judgment or inference is called for on the part of the observer.

An instrument more limited in scope is Withall's "Climate Index." (1949) The Index is the ratio of learner-centered statements to total teacher statements during the observation period. Withall developed seven categories of teacher statements, varying from learner-centered to teacher-centered:

1. Learner-supportive (reassurance or praise)

2. Acceptant and clarifying

3. Problem-structuring (nonthreatening and problem-centered)

4. Neutral

5. Directive (guided choices)

6. Reproving

7. Teacher self-supporting (e.g., justifying teacher's opinion).

As you can see, this particular method looks only at the teacher's verbal behavior. There should be and is, however, two-way communication in the classroom. Unless the teacher is simply lecturing, with no overt student verbal response, the statements that Withall seeks to analyze must be, partially, at least, responses to student behavior. This is not intended as a criticism of Withall's Index. He meant to study classroom climate from this point of view. There is, however, an observation method that studies interaction between teacher and students, utilizing Withall's approach in part.

Flanders and others developed a system of ten categories for analyzing verbal classroom interaction. Seven of the categories are classified as "Teacher Talk" (direct and indirect influences). Two categories are labeled "Student Talk." The tenth category represents silence or confusion (periods in which the communication cannot be understood by the observer). These are listed below. (Flanders, 1970, pp. 33–34)

Summary of the Flanders "Categories of Interaction Analysis"

Teacher Talk

    Indirect influence:

        1. Accepts feelings

        2. Praises or encourages

3. Accepts or uses ideas of student
4. Asks questions

Direct influence:

5. Lectures
6. Gives directions
7. Criticizes or justifies authority

Student Talk

8. Student talk-response
9. Student talk-initiation
10. Silence or confusion

In the "Student Talk" category, Flanders is concerned with whether students initiate verbal behavior or simply respond to teachers' questions. This in itself gives some clues to the character of the classroom environment. How free do the students feel to ask questions? Do they feel free to introduce a new topic by, for example, making an unrelated comment or even a tangentially related statement? As you well know from your own experience, some teachers encourage student-initiated interaction and others just as firmly discourage it.

At the beginning of this chapter, two questions were asked regarding classroom climate. The first, "Is the climate conducive to learning?" can be answered positively no matter what the results of studies with the OScAR, "Climate Index," "Categories of Interaction Analysis," or other classroom observation techniques. (Note: "An anthology of classroom observation behavior instruments," called *Mirrors for Behavior,* compiled by A. Simon and E. G. Boyer, was published by Research for Better Schools, Philadelphia, in 1967 and 1970.)

Learning takes place in every classroom, although it may not be what is expected or wanted. Hence the second question, "To what *kind* of learning is the classroom climate conducive?" Students in an authoritarian atmosphere may learn very well that the way to "survive" (have teacher approval, receive respectable grades, graduate, etc.) is to speak only when spoken to, to memorize the teacher's words, and to "swim with the tide." Academic learning may even be high if conformity rather than original thinking is what is measured and valued in such a classroom. On the other hand, in democratic and "open" classroom climates, students tend to learn that *their* contributions are valuable; that flexibility and original thinking are desirable learning outcomes; and that their ingestion, digestion, and restructuring of problems is sometimes a more important part of the learning process than remembering why the Battle of Waterloo was fought.

The quality of classroom instruction provides a preview of how adults cope with corporate organizational systems and the organization of society itself. It is simpler, from a disciplinary point of view, to have an authoritarian climate, but it is highly questionable that the development of generations of "yes-men" is a goal of education. It is certainly not the goal of educational psychologists.

Student interaction

Although in this chapter we are concentrating on the teacher's role, it is apparent that classroom climate can also be influenced by student relationships. Picture yourself as a student entering a class in a strange school. Are you faced with welcome, cliques, tension, or what? Rejection by classmates en masse or by cliques can be devastating to some youngsters and seriously hamper their learning. So can tension between two factions in the class. A cohesive but welcoming group, on the other hand, creates a more positive psychological climate.

One of the most effective means of shifting a group from hostility and tension to cohesion and cooperation is to give them a *common* "enemy." In an informal setting, Sherif (1951) divided twelve-year-old campers into two teams, the "Red Devils" and the "Bulldogs." Strong in-group feelings were fostered at first by Sherif and his colleagues, followed by the deliberate stimulation of competition between the teams. At first, good sportsmanship was evident. This soon became hostility that grew increasingly bitter. To reduce the conflict between the teams, an "all-camp" team was formed to compete against a team from another camp. Now a new in-group feeling developed as the hostility was turned outward. This classic study has pointed the way for a number of practical applications of its findings.

Intraclass or intraschool conflicts can be reduced by providing a common goal, such as a "cleanup" campaign in the neighborhood, a "war" on pollution, an academic competition between classes, a tutoring project to increase literacy, and so on. It's often helpful to take the leaders of the conflicting factions, convince them of the worth of the new goal, and involve them as leaders of the project. In this way their prestige is maintained.

Attention to "feelings" and affective development has increased in the schools. At the elementary level, two techniques have been the film-discussion series called "Inside Out" (available on educational television) and the use of the "magic circle." The film series presents family and personal problems that any or all youngsters in the middle grades might experience, such as sibling rivalry, parental divorce, and "class clown" behavior. After the 15-minute film, class members discuss their feelings about the situation presented. In the "magic circle," children may raise and discuss items of common concern, particularly those related to interpersonal behaviors. One goal of this activity is to encourage youngsters to express and examine their feelings in a constructive setting. (Glasser, 1969) The teacher needs to be alert to the possibility that, in allowing one or more children to express their feelings freely, other children might be unduly hurt. On the other hand, this activity is also a time when children can question the teacher about reasons for *her* behavior in a situation, or for tasks assigned in a specific way. More often, the group can examine the source of their feelings with respect to authority figures, people of different backgrounds, anger, joy, and new ideas. For example, "Is it the *way* the books are put back that bothers you, or is it that *Bobby* puts the books back in a way you dislike?"

In any event, before such expressions and clarifications of feelings can occur, the teacher will have to be trusted by the learners. (Curwin and Curwin, 1975) If the learners think that their words will be repeated to parents or the principal, they are unlikely to express themselves freely. If they trust the teacher, they assume that she or he will accept or at least understand their feelings and will not hold them up to ridicule or hold a grudge against them.

The teacher is involved in creating the atmosphere in which students interact, whether it be one of cooperation or conflict. The teacher can encourage, ignore, or discourage particular student attitudes. But, as you have seen, teachers can also manipulate groups—hopefully for constructive purposes. They teach what might be called a "hidden curriculum" as they transmit sexist and racist attitudes through their behavior and choice of subject matter references. Some examples of "hidden curriculum" are:

1. Sex-role stereotyping by both feminist and nonfeminist women of "ideal women" and "women in general." (Nielsen and Doyle, 1975)
2. Career education guidelines that relate sex and jobs.
3. Responding less often to minority group children's questions or attempts to participate in class. (Brophy and Good, 1974)
4. "Over-valuing" certain surface behaviors and thus negatively criticizing others by implication (hair length, dress, speech).
5. Use of texts or supplementary materials that are inaccurate in their portrayal of history or other cultures.

CHARACTERISTICS OF TEACHERS

The job of being a teacher is a complicated one today. It is not merely a matter of reading the teacher's manual to a textbook, following its guidelines, and occasionally giving tests. The role of information-giver is probably still a dominant aspect of being a teacher, but today even that role is being modified as more and more teachers at all levels *guide* students in learning rather than give them information. To varying degrees, the teacher plays other roles as well: disciplinarian, adviser, counselor, motivator, referrer, record-keeper, evaluator, curriculum-planner, demonstrator, and so on.

Question   *Quickly! What characterizes teachers to you? Are they intelligent? Patient? Plodding? Dedicated? "Suckers"? Remote? Leaders? _____?*

In 1963, Getzels and Jackson commented that "Despite the critical importance of the problem and a half-century of prodigious research, very little is known for certain about the nature and measurement of teacher personality, or about the relation between teacher personality and teaching effectiveness." (p. 574) In 1969, Levine noted that "... the wide diversity that exists among the psychological characteristics of teachers in the public schools is a partial function of their number. At present there are over 1,250,000 elementary and secondary school teachers in the United States." (p. 245) We can agree, then, that there are no psychological characteristics uniformly true of all, or even most, teachers.

There may be *desirable* characteristics, however. One such desirable characteristic is undoubtedly a liking for and desire to interact with children and youth. This alone, however, is not enough of a qualification to be a teacher. Liking children and enjoying their company only puts you in a position where it is likely that, *if* you teach, it is possible that your students may learn.

Personality characteristics

The most extensive study of teacher characteristics reported to date in the professional literature was one directed by Ryans. (1960) Classroom observations and paper-and-pencil inventories were the principal techniques used to study more than 6,000 teachers. A wide variety of conclusions were drawn from multifaceted analyses of the data obtained.

> Three patterns of teacher behavior stood out in separate factor analyses of observational data:
>
> Pattern X_0—warm, understanding, friendly versus aloof, egocentric, restricted teacher behavior.
>
> Pattern Y_0—responsible, businesslike, systematic versus evading, unplanned, slipshod teacher behavior.
>
> Pattern Z_0—stimulating, imaginative, surgent versus dull, routine teacher behavior. (Getzels and Jackson, 1963, p. 567)

You've certainly encountered at least one teacher who exhibited each of these behaviors. Notice, however, that there is no discussion of intellectual competence here. In fact, analyses of teachers' cognitive abilities in Ryans' study yielded very few differences significant enough "... to allow any definitive statement concerning cognitive differences among various groups of teachers." (p. 571) One would expect (hope?) that teachers would be bright intellectually, yet several studies reported by Getzels and Jackson indicate that this is not necessarily so. In practice, most liberal arts professors, for instance, regard their students who are education majors as among the least intelligent in the student body. Actually, of course, there is a wide range of intellectual abilities and interests among education majors. Due to social pressures on girls to enter teaching as a "secure" and "respectable" field for females, one which is compatible with marriage and motherhood, many female education majors are poorly motivated, however, in the direction of learning itself. This appears to be particularly characteristic of future elementary school teachers. Those planning to teach at the secondary level appear to be somewhat more oriented to and involved with a field of study and more willing, therefore, to put forth greater effort to learn. Academic brilliance assuredly does not guarantee good teaching in itself. In addition to possessing knowledge, a teacher must be able to communicate effectively the ideas acquired at a level appropriate to the learner.

In looking at some other teacher characteristics suggested earlier in this section, it might be safe to say that "patience" is a useful trait. Teachers frequently must wait for the slowest learners to grasp a concept, or for students to complete a project or assignment. "Dedication" is an ideal met with less frequently today than was true a few decades ago. Individual teachers may establish certain goals for themselves vis-a-vis their students' achievements and "dedicate" themselves to accomplishing their mission, but there is not as much self-sacrificing today, which means surrendering one's personal life to one's students. This is probably a better situation from a mental health point of view for both teachers and learners. It was the dedicated and self-sacrificing teacher working long hours after school at a relatively low salary who was often considered a "sucker" by students and society generally, despite the verbal reinforcement for such behavior.

Well, then, if we have such difficulty in defining teacher characteristics because of the wide range that has been found, what characteristics are needed to fulfill the teacher's multiple roles? As information-giver or guide, it is essential that the teacher know his subject matter and where additional information relevant to it may be found. Much of this is gained through academic course work and should be understood as well as memorized. The ability to transmit knowledge effectively is also important, of course, as noted above. In addition to being able to communicate, teachers must facilitate learning. "Teachers who use acceptant, problem-structuring, and challenging strategies and behaviors can create a liberating climate, thus setting the learners free to tap the potential that resides in them." (Withall, 1975, p. 262) In the roles of adviser and counselor, the teacher needs to keep an open mind and not to be a judge. Students who have problems, academic or personal, will come to the teacher as a kind of older friend to seek help, not reproval. Here it is more essential to be a warm, empathetic human being than simply a source of information. When referral to other resource personnel is necessary, it helps if the teacher knows which resource person is appropriate to the problem.

On the academic side, again, teachers must be able to evaluate performance (and sometimes intentions and effort) without bias. Giving *constructive* feedback helps the students to focus on the learning task rather than on some negative quality in themselves. (Saltmarsh, Hubele, and Canada, 1975) They should be imaginative and enthusiastic if they are to be effective motivators and demonstrators. Even when the curriculum is planned and clearly spelled out by others, teachers must make the lessons "their own" by developing effective presentations of them. Record-keeping, money-collecting, and other clerical duties oblige the teacher to be reasonably systematic and organized. Much of this work is done by teacher-aides or volunteers in many school districts today, however, so that the teacher can focus on teaching.

There may be some differences in the characteristics of teachers that are considered desirable in different types of communities. Mattsson (1974), for example, found that there is ". . . a distinct pattern of traits that appears to be related to successful teaching in the medium city and an equally strong but nearly opposite pattern related to successful teaching in the small town school whose student body is comprised largely of farm children." (p. 127) The teacher in the inner-city needs some characteristics different from the teacher's in the suburbs.

What characteristics do you think would be needed in each of these settings? ***Question***

Little has been said about the teacher as disciplinarian. This is because there is both too much and too little to say, despite the evident concern of parents and administrators, particularly in urban schools, with disorder, extortion, shootings, and so on, in the schools. It would be naive to assert that a stimulating teacher has no discipline problems in class. It would be equally naive to expect that there is a single particular technique for maintaining discipline (= order) under all circumstances. From all that has been discussed in this book, it is clear that there are many factors that contribute to the presence or absence of discipline in the classroom. Let's consider them individually:

Classroom management

1. A student who is disinterested or bored by the activities around him is more likely to seek outlets for his restlessness or excess energy that distract others from those activities. Whether he is bored because he is unable to comprehend what is being taught, because he deems it irrelevant, or because he already has learned the material, is a matter of some consequence. In the first case, remedial assistance or assignment to a more appropriate class may help him to become more interested in further learning. In the second case, the teacher may need to make practical applications of learning more evident. In the third case, a change of class assignment or special projects may be the effective solution.

2. A student who considers any authority figure the enemy is likely to harass teachers. Whether he comes from a home in which all authority is viewed with hostility, or one in which parents preach *or* practice "fooling" authority, there is a need for re-education in basic attitudes.

3. A teacher who permits any type of student behavior to go on as long as he is not personally bothered, or from a desire to be "popular" with students, is likely to have many disciplinary problems in his classes. Freedom to explore and flexibility of approach are not licenses to destroy, molest, or intimidate. In this instance, either the teacher needs to learn to differentiate between democratic and laissez-faire behavior, or perhaps he shouldn't be in the classroom at all.

4. The teacher mismanages the classroom, as when ". . . the teacher doesn't even notice that other kids tease or torment or doesn't listen when trying to umpire a fight. . . . the teacher is hostile to him or his group, disrespectful of him as a person or of his background, or is visibly without enough self-control to fulfill his role as a professional." (Redl, 1975, p. 575) Sometimes, in other words, it is a healthy youngster who is fighting injustice and/or incompetence of the teacher.

5. An atmosphere of racial tension or interclass hostility, combined with a lack of control of impulsive behavior among individuals, inevitably leads to magnified discipline problems. Massive school-community efforts to re-educate, to resolve causes of tensions, and to cooperate in making learners of those who came to school may help to reduce these problems, which involve more than a single classroom. Each teacher, however, must set aside personal feelings to ease classroom problems.

6. The problem of impulse control, alluded to above, is one facing the whole society, not just the individual teacher. Gun control laws and stiff prison sentences alone are not the answer. Until those who cry "Love" and "Peace" act in line with what they say, until there is mutual respect despite disagreement in viewpoints, until planning toward long-range satisfactions is as common as demands for instant gratification, impulsive behavior will continue to be a major source of disciplinary problems in the schools. A society in which too many people, adults as well as children, are functioning on an infantile level cannot expect teachers to perform miracles in the classroom with respect to discipline.

Classroom management hinges to a great degree on the teacher's pupil control ideology. Is the function of the school or teacher perceived as custodial or humanistic? Are "good teaching" and "good discipline" equated? Moreover, do the teacher's views of pupil control coincide with his actual practices? (Hoy, 1963; Alschuler and Shea, 1974) Management techniques *are* in part learned by experience, and in part from models (other teachers).

Student Rights

Much resentment against teachers is felt by students who believe, rightly or wrongly, that their human rights have been violated. A survey of 815 high school students in three Southern schools revealed that ". . . 81% of those questioned perceive their most violated right to be teacher respect for student opinion." (Buxton and Prichard, 1973, p. 67) Other complaints of students seeking their rights were: denial of use of the restroom when necessary (78%), veto of reasonable student government ideas by the principal (76%), limiting dress codes (68%), not enough time allowed to prepare properly for a school project (63%), denied the right to question a punishment (57%), and degrading or disrespectful treatment by a teacher (55%). (p. 67)

Focus 13–3

> What is old is not necessarily irrelevant today. Consider the following:
>
> Punishments are injudicious 1) when they always wear the same shape, the difference being in degree, not in kind—the child from similarity of punishment concludes a similarity of act and so often confounds moral with conventional wrong; 2) when from the manner in which they are inflicted, they appear to the child as a result of ill temper in the person who punishes rather than of a fault in himself—he must learn not to fear the teacher, but wrong; 3) when, though they may be effectual in preventing the recurrence of a fault, they are at the same time likely to chill all high and general feeling—to this class belong all chastisements which conspicuously hold up the child to ridicule; and 4) when from their over-severity, they urge the child to the escape of a falsehood—they ought to be so moderated that they do not divert the child's resultant hatred from the crime to the punishment. Punishments are unjust when not merited, and 1) when the act for which the punishment is influenced is not the act of him who suffers; and 2) when the act punished to the child seems, and cannot but seem, innocent.
>
> The Common School Journal, State of Pa.
I (12), Dec. 15, 1844*
>
> After working through the somewhat stilted language of the nineteenth century, the message of respect for the pupil as a person and for weighing the effects of punishment on him, comes through clearly. Today, student rights have been affirmed in Supreme Court decisions (Weckstein, 1975) that mandate due process hearings for many disciplinary actions. The National Education Association Task Force on Corporal Punishment has suggested 11 short-range alternatives to punishment as a means of maintaining discipline and several medium- and long-range proposals. (McClung, 1975, pp. 61–62) Many of these ideas have been included elsewhere in this book.

The "good" teacher

Can we define a "good" teacher? It all depends, as we have already seen, on what goals are set by the community and the school system. To all, the teacher who knows the material he is teaching scores as a potentially good teacher. To some, the teacher whose classroom is neat and orderly, and whose students rarely darken the detention room door, is a good teacher. To others, the teacher whose students always win prizes is a good teacher. Broudy summarizes what is expected of the teacher in this way:

> . . . the modern teacher is expected to be a person with a good general education (the old humanistic studies), acting as a professional, that

---

*Quoted in *Pennsylvania School Journal,* 1973, 122(2), p. 55.

> is, applying what educators (or educationists) know to teaching the content of the disciplines he has mastered, and all the while acting as a warm, child-loving father-, mother-, brother-surrogate who "relates" to human beings (the new humanism). These three types of demands make up the bundle we call the ideal, professional teacher who should be in every classroom. (Broudy, 1972, p. 54)

Is is any wonder that there is no unanimity? It almost seems as if the determination of what is a good teacher ultimately rests upon each learner's perception of the relationship he has with a given teacher. There are very few teachers who are "good" to *every* student they teach, although the difficulty may reside in the learner rather than the teacher.

It is appropriate here to examine what is a "good teacher" from the point of view of students and in connection with teacher education. One study asked intellectually gifted high school students to define a good teacher, using Ryans' Teacher Characteristics Schedule mentioned above and other measures. Among the desirable characteristics mentioned by this sample were maturity, experience, high achievement needs, sensitivity to and personal interest in their students, systematic and orderly, enthusiastic, stimulating and imaginative, and student-centered in the sense that they encouraged active student involvement in the learning situation. (Bishop, 1968) The teachers in this study ". . . stated that they believe their major role is one of motivating students to want to study, learn, and think independently. . . . Very few, however, saw their major role as imparting a specific body of knowledge. They emphasized the importance of demonstrating a personal interest in each student." (p. 323) It may be that the best teachers of all students, not just gifted learners, perceive themselves in this way.

In a second study that was primarily concerned with the teacher-student relationship, junior and senior education majors took a variety of tests tapping mostly their interpersonal attitudes (Rokeach's Dogmatism Scale, the Social Distance Scale) and attitudes as teachers (Minnesota Teacher Attitude Inventory). The MTAI, although widely used, is subject to many of the same criticisms as other self-rating personality scales—the subject can make himself appear to be more or less liberal or dogmatic, in this case, according to what he perceives to be desired by those who will use the results. One of the conclusions reached as a result of the study was that

> It may be that the variable needing the most attention in teacher education is that of "open-mindedness." Such an interpretation seems theoretically reasonable when one considers education to be a process of communication. The teacher as both "receiver" and "sender" of information must have some awareness of how the child perceives a problem. Such an awareness on the part of the teacher tends to insure the transmission of information relevant to the child's own level of awareness. An effective teacher must, therefore, have the ability to constantly readapt psychologically to the everchanging perceptions of the child. Such demands made of a "rigid" or "dogmatic" individual would most certainly result in anxiety and frustration. (Gill, King, and Wilburn, 1968, pp. 31–32)

It is this readiness, "open-mindedness," and adaptability to changing student perceptions that provides the key to effective learning in the "open" classroom and is appropriate at all levels of education, not just the primary grades. Even a "good" college instructor must be aware of anxiety and confusion in her students' perceptions of subject matter and be prepared to modify her presentation until the much-desired "ah-ha!" reaction takes place with an obvious grasp of the learning task.

In most school systems, there is some means of evaluating teachers for the purposes of retention (rehiring), merit salary increases, and promotion. Even if every administrator used the same criteria, the weight given to each item would vary, as suggested earlier, according to the values and goals of the community involved. A sample of such an evaluation form, completed, is given in Focus 13–4.

Teacher evaluation

Focus 13–4

TEACHER EVALUATION*

Teacher: Socrates

A. Personal Qualifications

	Rating (high to low)					Comments
1. Personal appearance	1	2	3	4	5	
					X	Dresses in an old sheet draped about his body
2. Self-confidence				X		Not sure of himself—always asking questions
3. Use of English			X			Speaks with heavy Greek accent
4. Adaptability				X		Prone to suicide by poison when under duress.

B. Class Management

1. Organization				X		Does not keep a seating chart
2. Room appearance			X			Does not have eye-catching bulletin boards
3. Utilization of supplies	X					Does not use supplies

C. Teacher-Pupil Relationship

1. Tact and consideration				X		Places student in embarrassing situations by asking questions
2. Attitude of class		X				Class is friendly

D. Techniques of Teaching

1. Daily preparation				X		Does not keep daily lesson plan
2. Attention to course of study		X				Quite flexible—allows students to wander to different topics

*Gauss, J. *Phi Delta Kappan*, 1962, 43, back cover.

> **TEACHER EVALUATION**
>
> **Teacher:** Socrates
>
> **D. Techniques of Teaching**
>
> | | Rating 1 2 3 4 5 | Comments |
> |---|---|---|
> | 3. Knowledge of subject matter | X | Does not know material—has to question pupils to gain knowledge |
>
> **E. Professional Attitude**
>
> | | | |
> |---|---|---|
> | 1. Professional ethics | X | Does not belong to professional association or PTA |
> | 2. In-service training | X | Complete failure here—has not even bothered to attend college |
> | 3. Parent relationships | X | Needs to improve in this area—parents are trying to get rid of him |
>
> **Recommendation:** Does not have a place in Education. Should not be hired.

Question   How would you rate Socrates as a teacher?

It should be noted that student evaluations of teachers have become commonplace at the college level and are sometimes found in secondary schools. How valid these ratings are arouses heated debate.

TEACHER ATTITUDES AND LEARNING

Expectancies   Because the teacher is a human being who has had learning experiences from infancy, just like any other individual, she has attitudes and expectancies that she brings to the learning situation. We are all guilty at one time or another of judging people by first impressions. We see the person's dress and overall appearance (neatness, appropriateness, cleanliness) and physical features (make-up, hair length and style, race, physical build), and we do some mental pigeon-holing about his or her personal characteristics and socioeconomic status. When the person speaks, the quality of his speech and language frequently causes us to refine or modify our initial classifications. Now, when the teacher meets his students for the first time, and when they meet him, this kind of subconscious classifying occurs, and it sets the tone for their interaction. In other words, the initial perceptions plus accumulated prior attitudes lead to certain behavior expectancies. Depending upon their strength, later events may or may not alter these expectancies and their effects in the classroom.

The importance of socioeconomic status and language as factors in addition to race in teacher perceptions has been demonstrated in experimental studies. One in particular, based on a sample of 250 experienced midwestern white teachers, showed that race, socioeconomic status, and language interacted to modify the perceptions by teachers of speakers exhibiting variations of these traits. (Gilberts, Guckin, and Leeds, 1971) Teachers who perceive their students as low socioeconomically, and/or as poor speakers, tend to expect low academic motivation and achievement from them. The same appears to be true when students are perceived as culturally different, whether the students are black, Puerto Rican, Mexican-American, Indian, Asian, or French-Canadian. Because this is so, and despite criticism of the Rosenthal-Jacobsen *Pygmalion in the Classroom* study discussed in chapter five, it is important to examine the effects of attitudes and expectancies on student learning.

Effects of attitudes on learning

In a real-life setting, psychologists at Rutgers University manipulated the section placement of 821 black secondary school students. The school system involved used homogeneous ability grouping in a number of academic content areas. Experimental subjects were placed in a higher section than they normally would be, while the matched control subjects were placed in sections appropriate to their scores and teacher recommendations. Some six months later, all subjects were given standardized achievement tests, and teacher recommendations for section placement for the following year were requested. Of those experimentally placed in the higher track, 54 percent were recommended for continuation at that level, while only one percent of the control group was recommended for movement upward to a higher level. (Tuckman and Bierman, 1971) What had happened here? There surely must have been some mental conflict on the part of the teachers in terms of past experience and expectancies with this group of students and their presence in a higher section than usual. Apparently the teachers were able to overcome the conflict generated by prior expectancies by assuming that the placement was legitimate and earned. On the part of the experimental student subjects, there was evidently a change in self-perception as a result of the upward displacement. Tuckman asserted, when presenting this paper, that the "Pygmalion effect" occurred as a function of the homogeneous grouping, self-perception, and teacher expectancies interacting. He may have been right.

As Harry Stack Sullivan, a leading American psychoanalyst in the 1940s, suggested, we tend to perceive ourselves as we think others see us and then behave accordingly. If the experimental subjects in Tuckman's study believed that the school authorities perceived them as more competent, as evidenced by the upward displacement in section assignment, then those students may well have studied harder or more regularly to maintain their new self-percept. The combination of positive reception by the teachers and modified self-percept of the students could well account for the higher achievement level of the experimental students.

410 LEARNERS AND TEACHING

In another area of teacher attitudes, we can look at the teacher's view of what constitutes classroom *mis*behavior. Each of us regards certain behavior as unacceptable under any normal circumstances (e.g., attacking someone with a deadly weapon) and other behavior as appropriate in some situations, but not in others (e.g., chatting with friends). Individuals who have rigid behavior codes, or who have unresolved physical or emotional problems that interfere with their job effectiveness, are more likely to be bothered by minor deviations from rules or accepted standards of conduct than are other individuals. If the teacher, particularly, is unable to deal with her own problems effectively, then she will be more likely to perceive misbehavior as being caused by problem children rather than by children who, like themselves, have problems.

The type of classroom setting also appears to be related to the way in which teachers look at student behavior. Solomon and Kendall (1975) found that "The teachers in traditional classes were not only more critical but also *perceived* a greater amount of student misbehavior than did teachers in open classes." (p. 529)

A major study of student and teacher attitudes toward various behaviors was published by Wickman (1929). Almost 40 years later, Mutimer and Rosemier (1967) replicated the Wickman study by submitting the original list of 50 (mis)behaviors to 40 secondary school teachers and over 900 students in grades seven through twelve. Although there were some differences in ranking the seriousness of the behavior according to grade level, these were not as interesting or significant as the similarities seen among the groups as shown in Table 13.1.

Table 13.1 Ten extreme rankings of behaviors by present students and teachers and by Wickman's teachers.*

Students (mid-1960s)	Teachers (mid-1960s)	Wickman's teachers (1929)
Most serious:		
1) stealing	1) destroying school property	1) heterosexual activity
2) destroying school property	2) stealing	2) stealing
3) untruthfulness	3) untruthfulness	3) masturbation
4) masturbation	4) cheating	4) obscene notes/talk
5) enuresis	5) obscene notes/talk	5) untruthfulness
Least serious:		
46) restlessness	46) sensitiveness	46) tattling
47) dreaminess	47) whispering	47) whispering
48) shyness	48) inquisitiveness	48) sensitiveness
49) whispering	49) shyness	49) restlessness
50) inquisitiveness	50) restlessness	50) shyness

*Mutimer and Rosemier, 1967, abridged

It is interesting to compare the ranking of "whispering" and "restlessness" by all three groups as being relatively nonserious misbehavior with the actual reaction of classroom teachers when these behaviors occur. Teachers in traditional classes tend to become quite disturbed by whispering or restless movement in the class, with the most frequent violators occasionally being sent to the school disciplinarian. The use of obscene language bothered both teacher samples more than it did the students, who ranked it #10 (not shown), but the use of profanity (in the mid-1960s) was ranked more seriously by the students than by either teacher group. Interesting.

What do you think would be the ranking of the items shown among students today? **Question**

Locate the Mutimer and Rosemier article and make a survey, as they did, among high school and/or college students. **Suggested Activity**

Would students include cheating or untruthfulness among the ten most serious classroom offenses? Where would the use of marijuana or other drugs be ranked? Would "destroying school property" rank very high today? Despite the professed student attitudes shown in the table, student behavior in the late 1960s and early 1970s did not demonstrate that actual behavior was correlated too highly with expressed attitudes. Even discounting arson and bomb threats in school buildings, have you ever looked at school desks or walls?

The growing differences in values and attitudes between teachers and students have been quite evident in the power struggles within the schools in recent years and certainly have an effect on classroom interaction. As is increasingly apparent at various levels of education, students

> . . . feel powerless to control their own destinies. As a result of their futile attempts to assert their initiative in inappropriate ways, they create an environment where even the teachers and administrators are forced to act in ways that are not of their choosing. The result is a constant struggle between pupils and the school staff to obtain the upper hand. Teachers search for ways to enhance their power to control the behavior of pupils, and the children use every means at their command to subvert the authority of the school, the last resort being hostility through passive dependency. (deCharms and Carpenter, 1968, p. 31)

This is true in suburban and small-town schools as well as urban ones, and in "affluent" schools as well as "inner-city" ones. Changes in attitudes and values in society at large seem to be reflected in extreme fashion by the teachers, who view themselves as the transmitters of traditional standards, and the students, who demand instant change and progress.

To go back to an earlier point, the teacher who is rigid or easily upset will tend to see any infraction of rules as serious, but the classroom is no place for stereotyped reactions to student behaviors. Wickman long ago pointed out that the question of what constitutes a behavior problem ultimately depends upon personal or social attitudes. Since teachers are working under pressure to teach certain things, they would understandably view any behavior that *interferes* with the learning process as a serious offense. As was pointed out in discussing the background of the learner in chapter two, different expectations in terms of behavior by sex reflect teacher attitudes, with the result that elementary school boys are frequently regarded as problem children. The combination of sex-fixed attitudes and differing experiential backgrounds can also magnify essentially normal childhood exuberance and energy into problem behavior. Liss, a child psychiatrist, has advised that "The teacher needs to have resolved his own past into an acceptance of maleness and femaleness and be equipped, through his own acquisition of security, to handle children from different backgrounds so that they in turn receive security in the learning process." (1966, p. 58) The interactive effects of sex-linked attitudes and behaviors *should* dictate modifications of classroom practices and are certainly a factor of which prospective teachers, especially those in elementary education, should be made aware in their preservice courses.

That teachers do let their attitudes influence their actions, despite fairly conscious efforts to avoid this, has been demonstrated in many studies. Even elementary school students perceive such teacher biases, particularly at the extremes of attachment, "teacher's pet" and rejection. Not only is teacher-pupil interaction affected as a result, but the daily classroom experience of children at these extremes is also reflected in their learning and peer relationships.

After reviewing these studies, there can be little doubt that teaching behavior is affected by the attitudes and resultant expectancies with which the teacher comes to the classroom. Since this behavior affects student learning, it is critically important that the teacher be quite aware of his own attitudes and their dependent outcomes. There may be a need for closer examination of the attitudes of prospective teachers and attention to their emotional health during the college years. It is not always easy to predict how the prospective teacher will react in the actual classroom situation, but supervisors of student teachers should consider attitudes as well as lesson planning ability in their evaluations of student teachers. The emotional damage that a single teacher can perpetuate on young learners has long-lasting effects and may not be overcome for years—often throughout the crucial school years.

TEACHER EFFECTIVENESS

Apart from the outcomes of teacher attitude-student learning relationships, it is hoped that the teacher will have some effect on students' cognitive learning.

It is time to turn to the question of styles of teaching and their effectiveness.

> An appropriate initial set of questions for educators at all levels would include: 1) What are my goals? 2) How well am I progressing on these goals? What effects am I having? 3) How can I set up a programmatic structure to learn more? 4) How do I have time to get information for future use in the face of constant day-to-day pressures? Eventually . . . how might present effectiveness be improved? (Good, Biddle, and Brophy, 1975, pp. 227–28)

Obviously, despite "methods" courses at the undergraduate level, each teacher will develop his unique approach to teaching, one that is often an amalgamation of the styles of teaching he has experienced as a learner. The more flexible, and probably more successful, teacher will modify those styles with which she is uncomfortable or that are not effective. To begin with, however, she has a wide range of teaching modes from which to choose. Which ones she chooses depend upon her concept of teaching.

As Hyman (1970) has stated, it is first necessary to define teaching and to decide whether the intention to have others learn or the success of their learning should be a criterion. Teaching activities include performing and thinking in the process of giving information and involve the three elements we have noted before: a learner, a teacher, and some content or subject matter. How the skills, information, and values are communicated from teacher to learner is the essence of our present discussion. If we assume that the concept of teaching is based on the intention to have others learn something, then it is more likely that a greater variety of teaching techniques will be tried. If the concept of teaching is based on a success criterion, then there will tend to be less experimentation with modes of teaching for fear that achievement might be lowered. Having made this fundamental decision, we can now look at a number of ways of teaching.

Modes of teaching

Modes of teaching include:

1. lecture—the emphasis here is on one-way communication from the teacher, who is the information-giver. This is usually accompanied by a recitation, which may be oral response or written answers on examinations.

2. Socratic questioning—statements are made, questioned by the teacher, redefined by the student, and so on until comprehension is clear. Not only is this two-way communication, but it demands active participation by the learner.

3. group discussion—the "title" of this mode of approach implies the activity, i.e., several learners participating in the analysis of a problem, with the teacher serving as guide rather than as primary information-giver.

4. "discovery" techniques—discussed in chapter 11. Either teacher or learner sets the problem, and the learner actively seeks the answers to it, with varying amounts of guidance from the teacher.

5. simulation games—also discussed in chapter 11. This again involves active participation by the learners in discovering principles or strategies via a game format.

6. role-playing and sociodrama—a technique in which the learner plays a role in a situation designed to convey attitudes, problem resolutions, and sometimes imagination. Whichever of these principal modes of teaching is adopted must fit into the teacher's concept of what teaching is all about.

To achieve this "fit," some questions might be asked:

1. How does the teacher perceive learners? Some teachers feel that learners are passive receptacles, waiting to be filled with information. Others view learners as decision-makers on what is to be learned in a course. Most teachers are somewhere between these two extremes, with more and more of them seeing learners as active participants in the learning process.

2. How does the teacher believe that performance should be evaluated? Here the question of intent and effort to learn is posed against actual achievement or level of success.

3. How much structure does the teacher believe is necessary in teaching? This involves a decision on rigidity or flexibility within the curriculum.

4. Does the teacher believe in the intrinsic value of the subject matter or in its application and relevance to everyday living? At its extremes, this question might be rephrased as a conflict between the classical and the personal development model, or traditional v. "adjustment" orientation.

We must also consider the relation of the teacher's style of teaching, whatever it may be, to student personalities. We have all experienced classroom situations in which our own personalities and the teacher's seemed to be in direct conflict. Sometimes, regrettably, this results in lowered grades. Frequently, perhaps usually, it results in negative attitudes toward not only the teacher, but also the course content, thus making it more difficult to study that material.

In a study of children in kindergarten and through the first half of first grade, Firestone and Brody (1975) found that "The interactions that occurred between teachers and children do provide a significant increase in one's ability to predict academic performance." (p. 548) The interactions were classified according to a modified Flanders scale of analysis. The "children who experienced the highest percentage of negative interactions with their kindergarten teacher were also children who did more poorly on the [Metropolitan Achievement Test] at the end of first grade." (p. 548) Since IQ was controlled, most of the children were black or Spanish-speaking, and all of the teachers were white females, these variables were ruled out as contributors to the findings. Among the alternative explanations were the self-fulfilling prophecy pattern and the possibility of temperamental conflicts between child and teacher.

Some students, because of their feelings of insecurity or inadequacy, need teachers who are very structured in their approach. When placed with a nonstructured teacher, they feel "lost." Their opposites, those with self-confidence, tend to feel smothered by a highly structured teacher. It was interesting to observe both kinds of reactions in an experimental self-paced learning situation at the college level. Midway through the term, despite having had knowledge of the relatively unstructured format before registering for the course and having had this information repeated in the opening days of the term, several students came to the instructor imploring her to resume giving full lectures. They were highly anxious about a potentially low final grade. (Of course, in some cases, they overlooked the fact that they had begun to work on the course rather later than they should have.) Several other students in the same course, however, were delighted with the opportunity to proceed at their own pace and on their own responsibility. These students went beyond the basic text in seeking answers to study-guide questions and obviously didn't need the "hand-holding" or "spoon-feeding" approach.

Tuckman (1969) reported a study of eleventh- and twelfth-graders in a vocational-technical school in which he compared the "abstract-independent" students and those with "concrete-dependent" personalities. The former preferred nondirective teachers in their nonvocational courses. When they were placed with such teachers, they were more satisfied with their courses and also earned higher grades. The opposite was true for the "concrete-dependent" students. This supports the discussion in the paragraph above.

To go further, Hyman suggests the following criteria for selection of mode of approach to teaching:

The teaching method should:

1. Suit the teacher's abilities, knowledge of subject matter, and interests. . . .
2. Suit the student's abilities—verbal and psychomotor. . . .
3. Suit the type of teaching aimed at: [skill, knowledge, values]. . . .
4. Suit the time and place context of the teaching situation. . . .
5. Suit the subject matter at hand. . . .
6. Suit the number of students being taught. . . .
7. Suit the interests and experience of the students. . . .
8. Suit the student's relationship with the subject matter. . . .
9. Suit the teacher's relation with the student. . . . (1970, pp. 35–36)

Some comments on this list are appropriate. Item 4: in most elementary schools, "major" subjects are taught in the morning when children are more alert. At other levels, it might be wise to remember that even adolescents become groggy in mid- or late afternoon, and lectures might well propel them into deep sleep. Item 6: group discussions are very difficult to handle, if not impossible, in a class of more than 30 to 35 students. Some back-and-forth discussion can occur even in large lecture classes of a hundred or more students, but the bulk of the discussing will probably be done by fewer of the students (perhaps only 12 to 15) than would be true in smaller sections. The size of the class will also influence the size of the room in which it is taught (Item 4) or vice versa. Tapes, which might be effectively used in a small room, are much less effective in lecture halls, probably in inverse ratio to their duration.

In keeping with this list of suggestions, however, it should be noted that children's learning will change as the teacher's style and methods of teaching change. One has to conclude that the mode of teaching that is most effective differs from student to student, and within students, from subject to subject depending on the student's strength in each subject. In science, for example, some may profit more from lectures and texts, while others benefit more from laboratory experiences. In foreign languages, teacher-pupil interaction in the classroom may be ample for some students' learning, while others need the intensive one-to-one situation of the language laboratory. Discussion may help some and confuse others in a literature course.

Effective approaches

It is interesting that Joseph ibn Aknin, in the twelfth century wrote that the successful teacher

> . . . must have complete command of the subject he wishes to teach: he must carry out in his own life the principles he wishes to inculcate in his pupils; . . . he must look upon his pupils as if they were his own sons, and treat them accordingly; he must train his pupils to lead an ethical life; he must not be impatient, but come to his pupils with a happy countenance; and he must teach his pupils according to the range of their intellectual abilities. (in Singer, 1912, p. 46)

In other words, the teacher has to be a model for his students as well as an information-giver, and he has to relate to his students in a positive way. As a model for prospective teachers, for instance, it is not enough to teach that "immediate knowledge of results" is a helpful element in learning. The instructor must *give* immediate knowledge of results to *his* students by, for example, grading exams and papers promptly rather than dawdling over them for two or more weeks as many teachers do. The idea of being a model applies in other areas as well: the quality of personal appearance in the professional role of teacher, ethical standards, civic responsibility, and so on.

The ability to relate to children and youth in a positive way comes up again and again in studies of effective teachers. Further, becoming informed about how one relates to students can not only affect teacher behavior (in a positive direction) toward negatively perceived students, but also toward *all* students in the class. (Good and Brophy, 1974) This takes us full circle to the establishment of a healthy classroom climate. If rapport and respect are established between teacher and students, if students are permitted and encouraged to participate actively in the learning process, and if the teacher has considered the nature of both the learner and the subject matter in planning her style of teaching, then the teaching should be effective. No one approach is consistently "most successful" in terms of student achievement, although teachers tend to use one approach more than others. Obviously, the most effective approach is the one that is intended to produce learning, and it frequently does. And the effective teacher is ". . . a unique human being who has learned to use himself effectively and efficiently to carry out his own and society's purposes in the education of others." (Combs, Blume, Newman, and Wass, 1974, p. 8)

SUMMARY

In this chapter, we have discussed primarily the role of the third element in the learning process, the teacher. Beginning with the establishment of the environment or climate in which learning is to take place, we have tried to define a "good" teacher in terms of personality characteristics, roles, attitudes, expectancies, and teaching approaches. Much of the research cited is inconclusive, but it was possible to conclude with two views of the "effective teacher," one centuries old and one from the contemporary humanistic position.

Although the research results regarding teacher personality and effective teaching sometimes appear to be contradictory, it must be recognized that multiple criteria were used in these evaluations. They are all legitimate, but represent choices related to the instructional outcomes desired. Different personality characteristics may be needed to achieve particular outcomes. This in no way invalidates the studies cited.

Other topics considered include classroom management and teacher evaluation. Classroom management was discussed from both the teacher's vantage point and that of students. Student rights are an important current issue at all levels of education. Teacher evaluation is similarly of great concern as demands for accountability and more effective teaching increase. Several of the factors to be considered in such evaluations were discussed.

The construction of a positive teacher-pupil relationship, in terms of mutual respect and trust, appears to be basic to an effective learning experience. While it is true that some strongly self-motivated learners will learn in spite of (or to spite) teachers with whom they have a poor relationship, the majority of students achieve at more satisfactory levels in a warm, stimulating classroom environment. As with child-rearing practices, it was shown that attitude appears to have greater importance than method.

Preview

THE DESIRE TO TEACH

TEACHER EDUCATION
COURSE WORK
PRACTICAL EXPERIENCE
NONTRADITIONAL TEACHER EDUCATION
Competency-Based Programs
The Modular Approach
The Humanistic Approach
The Clinical Approach

IN-SERVICE EDUCATION
GRADUATE SCHOOL
IN-SERVICE COURSES

INFORMAL EDUCATION
PROFESSIONAL LITERATURE AND MEETINGS
BY STUDENTS
OTHER SOURCES

CHANGES IN TEACHER EDUCATION

SUMMARY

14

The Teacher as a Learner

To begin with, a teacher must be a learner. To put it quite bluntly, education for the teacher is neither confined to nor ends with formal course work. Just as every individual learns from birth to school entrance, so does the teacher (as any other adult who wishes to continue his development) continue to learn long after receiving his final college degree.

Although subtitled "Focus on the Learner," this volume does not refer to only the *student* as a learner. Learning is a two-way street, and so teachers also learn—from their pupils, from their colleagues, from chance encounters with noneducators, and in noninstitutional settings. There must be a beginning, however, which may occur as a seven-year-old plays teacher to a set of dolls, or as a high school senior perceives teaching as the best mode of contribution to making a better society. Once the decision is made, there are traditional paths to follow in the selection of college courses, although some of the programs and courses themselves may be innovative. Many states now require graduate study for permanent certification, and many school districts offer "in-service training" to keep their teachers well-informed and up-to-the-minute on curriculum content, objectives, and methods. There are also, as already suggested, other, less formal, learning experiences for the teacher. Each of these steps is considered in this chapter as we look at the teacher as a learner.

THE DESIRE TO TEACH

Why do you want to become a teacher? When did you make this decision? Was there a person who strongly influenced your choice? Many children plan to become teachers as a result of identifying with the first nonfamily adult with whom they have frequent contact—a primary grade teacher. In the high school years, there may be a teacher who is particularly inspiring in some way, or encouraging, and the relationship established may lead to a renewal or a creation of the ambition to teach. Some adolescents may find that they have a "knack" for helping others to understand concepts, and this experience leads to a decision to become a teacher. Others may view teaching as a form of service to society, based on volunteer tutoring experiences or an awareness of the need for effective teaching. There are also those youths who perceive the teaching field as one which offers economic security, compatibility with marital responsibilities, an opportunity to have long vacations, etc. . . .

Question *Why did you decide to teach?*

Although teaching is seen frequently as a largely sex-linked profession, the authors of one study report that "Almost two-thirds of adults in all population strata consider teaching a desirable occupation for their male and female offspring." (Pounds and Hawkins, 1969, p. 341) There is middle-class status attached to the profession, relatively high prestige in small communities and among those people who have little education themselves. Economic security, if not great wealth, is associated with teaching, as is relative job security. These conditions make teaching appear quite attractive to many parents and other adults, as well as to young people. Adults are quick to urge those youths who like and have rapport with children to enter the field of teaching, although this is not the only qualification for the profession.

On a personal level, the decision to teach may be made in anticipation of satisfaction of needs for high achievement and the opportunity to "exhibit" oneself in a socially acceptable way. It is not universally true that "Those who can, do; those who can't, teach." In fact, quite the reverse *should* be true: "Those who can, teach; those who can't, do." What may be true, unfortunately, is that teaching is so familiar an occupation to adolescents that they cannot envision any other. Familiarity itself offers a kind of security to the somewhat anxious individual. Teaching may also be perceived as a way out of academic difficulties, both by noneducation professors and by students. Too often, *much* too often, students who cannot meet the requirements of the Liberal Arts or Science college are advised to transfer to the College of Education where the academic expectations are lower (supposedly). Students may initiate this transfer themselves, working from the same false premise. Perhaps this professor is too idealistic, but "backing into" teaching seems very wrong, cheating both the student and those whom he may teach. As you can surely see after studying educational psychology for several weeks, being a teacher calls for more competence, not less, and for a positive attitude and commitment toward education.

Whatever your reasons for deciding to become a teacher originally, you arrived at some institution of higher learning and were told, in effect, "If you complete this curriculum successfully, we will certify that you are ready to teach." What is included in "this curriculum"?

TEACHER EDUCATION

Contemporary teachers of teachers are more aware than ever before that a teacher needs a broad background of courses and experiences if he is to be both an effective teacher and an effective human being. Although the emphasis is increasingly on experience in the schools, it is also recognized that teachers need to know something about the subject matter they propose to teach. However, there is some dispute as to the ways in which the teacher education curriculum should be structured to provide the experiences and the content, principally among the traditionalists, the humanists, and the competency-oriented.

The traditionalists tend toward prescribed sequences of courses, about evenly divided between liberal arts and professional education courses. The competency-oriented educators similarly stress course work with emphasis on the acquisition of specific skills or competencies. Both of these are regarded by nontraditionalists as "closed" or "semi-closed" systems, in that completion of the program is supposed to produce an individual fully prepared to teach in the classroom. The humanistic point of view, on the other hand, assumes that as the prospective teacher "increasingly discovers the personal meaning of the information and experiences with which he comes into contact, he redefines his goals in ways which are relevant to his growing understanding of teaching." (Combs, et al., 1974, p. 148) This approach is perceived as an "open" system because of its evolutionary or developmental aspect.

Let us look more carefully at these three types of programs. We can consider them in the context of on-campus course work and off-campus practical experience.

Course work

For most prospective teachers, there is a basic requirement in the teacher education program for liberal arts and science courses that account for 40 to 50 percent of the credits needed for graduation. First, as a well-rounded adult, it is expected by other adults that you, too, share in the common pool of information that characterizes the educated person in our society. Familiarity with literature, American history, philosophies of various eras and their effects on individuals and society, scientific concepts, the bases of social and political systems, are all part of this common knowledge. Second, as a professional, it is assumed by others, even more than expected, that you have this information as part of your experience. Adults as well as students look to teachers for answers to their questions, and you would look pretty foolish, or worse, if you didn't even understand what was being asked. Further, it is difficult to function effectively in our complex world without an understanding of biological and physical science and of political philosophies and systems. Third, your students will not always communicate with you about the lesson you've planned to teach today. Due to the variety of their interests and to ongoing events, they will bring information and questions to you, which they will expect you to comprehend and to which you may be expected to respond. Therefore, since you can learn from any course something which will contribute to your stock of general information, if you are willing to learn, *no* course is a "waste of time."

Suggested Activity

Stop here briefly to consider a course you have taken in college that you have considered "useless." In what ways could you apply the content of that course to some aspect of your teaching career? Try for ten applications or more.

A second group of courses common to most teacher education curricula includes several basic psychology and education courses. If you are going to work with children and adolescents, obviously you should know how development proceeds and what effects deviations in development have on learners. You should also know how learning takes place, the nature of the teaching-learning process, and the various factors that affect the three elements in this process. Only then can you go on to study the methods used to teach specific content and profit from the methods courses. A third basic course in this group usually deals with the social, political, historical, and/or philosophical background of education. This foundations course should help you to understand why there are educational systems, what the problems inherent in such systems are, and the reasons for contemporary crises and conflicts in education.

Obviously, if you are going to teach, you need to know more detail of your subject matter than your students do. Therefore, a third group of courses in the curriculum focuses on content. For elementary education majors, much of the content is learned in the general required and elective courses referred to in the first group. These teachers are typically obliged to teach a wide variety of subject matter in varying degrees of depth, so that a broad education is vital to meeting their ultimate goal. For secondary education majors, however, content courses in a more limited area are necessary so that the greater depth of material that they will have to teach can be prepared. Social studies teachers, for example, should know the history of ancient, medieval, and modern times, for they will probably teach courses dealing with each of these periods and may wish to show historical trends spanning several centuries. English teachers must be familiar with several periods, styles, and types of literature, as well as grammar and composition skills, for this is what they will be teaching. Science teachers must understand the concepts of biology, chemistry, and physics because their fields are increasingly interrelated. Such courses may even be taught in an interdepartmental framework. What I am saying is that each required or restricted elective course has a purpose in the preparation of the teacher. Skill, knowledge, or technical competence in a content area is obviously essential for successful teaching.

Up to this point, there is general agreement among most educators, whatever their point of view, on the content of courses to be studied. However, the ways in which the courses are taught may differ. The most traditional faculty will stress learning course content because of its presumed inherent value. Those who are competency-oriented will state behavioral objectives for each course. A variety of activities will usually be offered as ways in which the students can demonstrate their competence in meeting those objectives. The humanists are more likely to combine field or practical experiences with the content in order to promote meaningfulness of the content to the student. This would be especially true with the psychology and other professional courses, but is found also in courses in other areas as seen in Focus 14–1.

Then there are methods courses, a fourth area of the curriculum. These are designed to provide teaching competence, "knowhow" in the art and science of teaching. It may look easy to stand in front of a class and present subject matter, but this perception is a deception. There are many ways of teaching the same thing, as you have already learned. Methods courses offer, or should offer, you as a prospective teacher an opportunity to learn what the "tricks of the trade" are, what methods might be most effective for which learners, and how skilled you are in using them—before you try them out on live children. In many schools of education, micro-teaching is being used to implement the last goal of the methods courses. Micro-teaching involves the preparation of a lesson or lesson segment, presentation of it to a small group of classmates, and then an analysis of the presentation by the instructor and the student. The presentation may be videotaped, which makes the student more aware of her tone of voice, hand gestures, mannerisms, and so on, in addition to whether or not she got her ideas across to her "students." It is ". . . a combination of a conceptual system for identifying precisely specified teaching skills with the use of video-tape feedback to facilitate growth in these teaching skills." (Peck and Tucker, 1973, p. 951) The effectiveness of this technique has been shown in several studies in recent years. Micro-teaching is also used in in-service programs, where it is particularly useful as a remedial tool for teachers already in the classroom.

Similar to micro-teaching is the presentation of material to the class, followed by peer discussion and constructive criticism. Besides helping the student to become aware of his strengths and weaknesses in a quasi-teaching situation, this role-playing helps him to overcome the "stage fright" of being in front of a live class.

It is hoped that, within these four areas of the curriculum, the prospective teacher will be encouraged to ask questions and search for the answers via independent study. It is hoped that the innovative techniques that are described as being so effective at the elementary and secondary levels will be used in the courses you take at the college level. It is hoped that you will be sufficiently informed about research design and methodology to try a few experiments on your own. And finally, it is hoped that professors in the various disciplines will cooperate to help you learn as much as you can for your own benefit and that of your future students.

Practical experience

A valuable alternative to micro-teaching is a systematic sequence of supervised off-campus classroom experiences. This can be tied to professional courses initially. For example, the student has one term as an observer-aide, perhaps working on a weekly basis with one child for the duration of the course. In a second practicum, also allied to a course, the student works as the teacher's assistant, helping with small groups or the entire class, and perhaps teaching a brief lesson that the student has prepared. Some of the nonteaching chores might also be built into the practicum. This second level might be repeated with different grade levels or types of classes. These experiences would contribute much to the ultimate responsibility and competence at the student teaching level.

This is one way to gain practical teaching experience.

The core of a teacher education program is the student teaching experience. This field experience, usually occurring in the senior year, is the one common to all teacher education curricula. In the traditional program, it may be the only field experience. It's a little late, then, however, to discover that you made the wrong decision three years earlier.

Focus 14–1

> At Penn State's Ogontz Campus, near Philadelphia, faculty members in the College of Education felt that classroom experience sometime in the first two years of the student's college program would serve several purposes: 1) bring to life the content taught in the professional education courses, making it much more meaningful; 2) permit the student to observe education from the teacher's side of the desk; 3) help the student to evaluate his commitment to teaching in general and a level or subject area in particular; 4) gain a better understanding of the teacher-learning process; and 5) become more aware of learners as individuals with unique qualities and behaviors.
>
> Students are placed with a cooperating teacher at the elementary or secondary level, depending on their goal. They spend eight half-days in the classroom during the ten-week university quarter. The practicum period is scheduled by appointment within the student's total schedule. Field experiences are discussed in class, and course content is observed and often used in the field work.
>
> Response to the program has been unanimously favorable. The prospective teacher welcomes the opportunity to apply theory and to test his or her feelings toward teaching. The cooperating teachers find that their "teacher aides" make a real contribution to their students' learning and bring new perceptions to the classroom situation.
>
> Other purposes of field work at this level are also served. A few students, perhaps 5 to 10 percent of those involved each quarter, find that they would be very unhappy as teachers at any level, or that they might be happier with a different age group. There is considerable interaction between teacher aides and the younger students that cannot occur in a more traditional preservice program. An incidental effect has been reported by content area instructors at the campus—that there is a higher level of interest and motivation to learn mathematics, geography, or other subject matter by those students who have participated in the field work program and who therefore are aware of the need for teacher knowledge.

Articles in the professional literature and papers presented at professional meetings suggest that, within the conventional teacher education curriculum, more preservice teaching experiences of this kind are being included. There is a benefit for the school districts involved as well as for the prospective teachers in such programs. Principals have an opportunity to "preview" people they may wish to hire a few years hence and also are kept informed through this contact of contemporary thinking in teacher education.

The pivotal point of teacher education traditionally has been the student teaching experience. Since the student teacher works directly with pupils, even being responsible for actual teaching, he can help or hinder their development in many ways. The board of education and the administrative staff, therefore, must establish policy with regard to this experience for the benefit of *their* student population. Particular care must be given to the selection of supervisory or cooperating teachers since "Probably no other person connected with a student's preservice program will have more effect on his initial teaching success than the supervising teacher," (Dressel, 1970, p. 163)

The cooperating teacher plays several roles in working with student teachers:

1. he provides an opportunity for the student teacher to try out several methods and media to ascertain his strengths and weaknesses, preferences, and effectiveness;
2. he guides the student teacher toward professional competence through analysis and evaluation of the student teacher's performance in the classroom;
3. he influences the student teacher's attitudes toward teaching as a profession, relations with administrators, relations with students, and so on. Most of all, according to Dressel, he influences the student teacher by his own attitude toward the responsibility of being a supervising teacher. (p. 164)

Shifts in attitudes among student teachers during the student teaching term, according to Yee (1969), also "... generally reflect the predominant influence of their cooperating teachers." (p. 331) Both Dressel and Yee, thereford, stress the need for school boards and administrators to seek optimal relationships and conditions for the student teaching experience.

Student teachers are regarded by elementary school students as "almost real" teachers, and by secondary school students as somewhere between a "substitute" (and therefore fair game for harrassment) and a "real" teacher. Knowing this, the student teacher is probably most concerned at the outset of the experience with classroom management. What should you do if the pupils "act up"? What if they don't pay attention when given a direction? How do you cope with a student who is bigger and stronger than you? You can't yell "HELP!" Not only would this be unprofessional behavior, but the students and cooperating teacher are watching to see what you'll do. It might be wise to ask the cooperating teacher beforehand which techniques of classroom control she or he finds most effective with a particular class. Preparation in this area reduces negative anticipation or anxiety. One cardinal rule in the area of discipline or management might be suggested: Never threaten to do something if you do not intend to carry out the threat!

The student teacher has a number of other concerns at the outset of and during this quasi-professional experience. These concerns may be classified under different headings:

1. Actual teaching functions

   a. How do I motivate the students?
   b. Am I communicating content effectively to the students?
   c. How do I adjust learning activities to the needs of individual students?
   d. How do I evaluate student progress?
   e. How do I find time to prepare lessons, keep class records, and keep learning myself?

2. Interpersonal relations

    a. Will the cooperating teacher and I "hit it off" well?
    b. How dependent/independent shall I be in my relations with the cooperating teacher and other staff?
    c. Will the students like me?
    d. How do I relate to parents?
    e. If I disagree with the cooperating teacher's handling of of a situation, what do I do or say?
    f. How do I contribute to the students' growth and well-being?

3. Evaluation by supervisors

    a. What functions does the cooperating teacher expect me to perform?
    b. What functions does the college supervisor expect me to perform?
    c. If I tend to deviate from established patterns as a person, how conformist must I become in order to satisfy the cooperating teacher and the supervisor?

Henderson and Bibens (1970) suggest that a little apprehension along these lines may be a very good thing. In this way, the student ". . . may proceed cautiously as a learner, rather than blundering and stumbling as an expert." (p. 153) There *is* a tendency among student teachers to be overly critical of what they observe in the classroom, particularly if this is their first practical experience. This is another reason for exposing prospective teachers to as many classroom situations as possible, as early as possible, during the college years. The theory taught in college classrooms is not always immediately applicable to the schoolroom, for a variety of reasons. Student teachers must be careful, too, not to judge their cooperating teachers or the class on the basis of first impressions. As the student teacher moves from observer to assistant to teacher during the field experience, many first impressions may be modified by gaining more information.

The problem of conformity to patterns established in a school and/or by the supervisor poses some serious questions for the student teacher. Although the nature of dress, for example, has changed to increasing informality, teachers are still expected to appear neat, clean, and reasonably conservative in their dress. That is, wearing extreme clothing styles or too much make-up is generally considered inappropriate in the schools. The college supervisor as well as personnel in the cooperating school district feel justified in expecting student teachers to conform to expectations in appearance.

A more difficult area in which to conform is that of the actual teaching function. If the student teacher is a creative person, and those who evaluate him or her are less creative, there is potential for conflict. In a small study at the University of Colorado, for instance, it was found that "The sample of high divergent thinkers was ranked lower on their student teaching than the sample of low divergent thinkers." (Taylor and McKean, 1968, p. 418) There were no significant differences between high and low divergent thinkers in this sample by grade point average, dropout rate, or teaching major, although more women were among the high divergent thinkers. The problem then centers on how much of this divergent thinking must be curbed in order to earn a good evaluation from the supervising teacher. Ultimately, this is a question of principle that each student must handle herself, considering all facets of the question: nature of the cooperating teacher, nature of the learners involved, nature of the supervising instructor, expectations of the school disstrict and the college, motivation to earn certification, the employment market, etc.

In many institutions, a seminar with college supervisors is conducted concurrently with the student teaching experience in order to answer questions, give further guidance that is only meaningful after the prospective teacher has been in the classroom situation, and provide further opportunities to learn teaching techniques. Such seminars may focus on the apprehensions listed earlier, or on a particular theme. Interpersonal relations are of special concern to student teachers, since so much of teaching depends on satisfactory interpersonal relationships. In one teacher education program, therefore, this was the theme of the seminar, with special attention paid to four topics:

1. Problem solving as an effective approach for improving interpersonal communication.
2. Phenomenology, or the awareness that each individual has his own idiosyncratic ways of perceiving the world.
3. Interrelationship of the cognitive and interpersonal aspects of the learning experience.
4. Nonverbal behavior as an aspect of interpersonal communications. (Borke and Burstyn, 1970)

Although some of these ideas may have been discussed earlier in the teacher education program, as they have been in this course, for example, they take on new meaning once the student teacher enters a classroom on the teacher's side of the desk. It would be appropriate in such a seminar, also, for student teachers to discuss among themselves and with the supervisor the problems they may be encountering with their cooperating teachers for, often, one student teacher can cast new light on a situation that another student teacher has failed to perceive.

Attention in student teaching is also focused on the development of teaching styles as they reflect conceptual systems of the individual. Murphy and Brown (1970), for example, identified four conceptual systems that could be defined operationally:

System 1—"unilateral dependence"—the teacher is authority-oriented; tends to question narrowly, deliver information, behave in a conformist manner, and be against information-seeking activities by their students.

System 2—"negative independence"—similar to System 1 except that the teachers are more inconsistent and uncertain in judging the adequacy of pupil performance.

System 3—"conditional dependence"—teachers reward searching behavior by pupils, encourage pupil interrelations, and are generally supportive of learners' activities.

System 4—"informationally interdependent"—teachers regard knowledge as tentative, encourage students to wonder and explore, reward seeking more than finding answers.

When one looks closely at teacher education programs, the impression is that conceptual System 1, that is, delivery of information within an authoritarian framework, is strongly emphasized although some attention may be given to the desirability of encouraging "discovery" by students. As Murphy and Brown suggested, if the goal of education ". . . is to produce persons who are inventive, original, critical, and adaptive in directing and meeting change, is it then appropriate to stress System 1 conceptual systems in teacher education rather than System 4? (p. 539) The discrepancy between what is preached to student teachers in methods courses (System 1) and the viewpoints expounded by psychologists, cooperating teachers, and contemporary philosophers in education (System 3 or 4) could well account for the results found in the Colorado study of divergent thinking and student teaching. Intensive, free-wheeling discussions of why and how one adopts a conceptual system and practices a particular teaching style help prospective teachers to learn a great deal about themselves and their probable future behavior.

Competency-Based Programs

In competency- or performance-based programs, there is a similarity to industrial models. Task analysis is applied to the job of teaching. The major task areas are then broken down into skills and competencies. These are tied to principles based on research. The basic teaching-learning skills might be grouped as:

1. situational skills
2. readiness skills
3. ideational skills
4. task-directing skills
5. feedback skills.

Under each heading there are further skill areas that can be applied to different content courses and modified according to the individual teacher's personality characteristics. Under readiness skills, there might be an area of competencies dealing with "self-concept and actualization." Within this area, a specific item might read "The competent teacher performs skillfully in using techniques to foster self-growth."

> Within this competency one readily recognizes the interrelationship of personal characteristics, subject matter, and professional skill. The competency statement purposely does not identify specifically the kind and number of techniques the teacher uses, but it does establish a basic competence to be developed. The specifics can (should) be identified according to the needs of the person doing the teaching, the student being taught, and the supervisor(s) concerned with the skill. (Burke and Stone, 1975, pp. 236–37)

Specific competencies such as this one are translated into observable behaviors, the performance of which can be evaluated. Groups of competencies can be organized into courses or modules.

The Modular Approach

Modules lend themselves to flexibility of scheduling and course organization. The modules focus on a particular problem within an overall framework. Appleton (1975) demonstrates the approach in terms of a foundations of education course. Some modules are major, such as "Educating the powerless"; others are stressed to a lesser degree, such as "Religion and public education." The amount of emphasis varies as conditions in the educational world change. Some modules may be required of all prospective teachers, while others may be alternatives. The student completes a combination of required and alternative modules that add up to the equivalent of a three-credit course. The student chooses those alternatives that meet her professional and personal needs and uses a variety of materials to study the topic of the module.

The Humanistic Approach

Combs and his colleagues (1974) perceive this as a people-oriented approach in which the student develops sensitivity to others. Observation is directed to the purposes of teacher behavior, the reasons for children's behaviors, and the situations that provoke different behaviors. They believe that such disciplined observation should occur prior to formal professionally oriented courses. They also aver that

> Beginning students need to get acquainted with problems and to explore where these problems may take them. This calls for a kind of instructor who may not be a content specialist but, like the elementary teacher, an expert in encouraging and assisting the processes of learn-

ing. Teaming such persons with the content experts would provide both information and exploration aspects needed for the problems approach. (p. 113)

Continued interaction with basic education teachers and pupils will enable the prospective teacher to grow in self-confidence and learn how to help the children to grow also as they gain a more positive self-concept. The prospective teacher grows into the role of full-fledged teacher by gradual steps on and off the campus. On the campus, the prospective teacher learns the content he needs in learning groups, curriculum laboratories, and self-evaluation—all facilitated by the supervisor and/or faculty member. Off the campus, a variety of experiences with individuals and groups provide supervised learning experiences.

The Clinical Approach

This is a joint approach between practitioners (classroom teachers) and professors. Often the classroom teachers are given part-time appointments as clinical or visiting professors on the college faculty. They then work hand-in-hand with their new colleagues in providing "live" field experiences that have their base in the community and its schools rather than on the college campus. Such a program resembles the training common in medical fields, where clinical practice involving real patients occurs concurrent with classroom instruction. It enriches and gives more meaning to classroom instruction for the prospective teacher and provides a means also of keeping up to date with school practices.

Which of these patterns does your program most closely resemble? Is the pattern different from the pattern in your college ten years ago? (How would you find this out?) — *Questions*

IN-SERVICE EDUCATION

As indicated earlier in this chapter, an increasing number of state boards of education recognize that four years in college provide insufficient preparation for teachers in today's complex society. As a result, the certificate to teach awarded in conjunction with the bachelor's degree is a provisional one. Permanent certification demands satisfactory teaching experience *plus* further academic work. The academic requirement may be a master's degree, or some number of course credits close to it (as in Pennsylvania, where twenty-four credits are required, while a master's degree requires thirty). If you are teaching at the secondary level, there may be particular content courses specified that will enhance your technical competence as a teacher. At the ele-

Graduate school

mentary level, you may be advised to select courses that will enrich your presentations and/or give you greater information about particular groups of learners. Courses in guidance and counseling are often suggested as appropriate for "fifth-year" study. Deeper analysis and evaluation of sociological influences on education may be of special interest to new teachers. Wherever possible, graduate programs should be tailored to the needs and interests of the teacher who returns to school to learn more about his job and himself.

Sometimes courses that may be used to meet these requirements are offered as part of school district adult education programs or are offered within a school district in the late afternoon and early evening hours. In such cases, the college comes to the learner, instead of the more usual pattern. If college credit is given, this is a great help to the teacher-learner. Otherwise, he may have to travel some distance to attend night classes, or spend several summers in graduate study, which precludes engaging in other productive activities. Courses given "on location" can also be specially designed to meet the needs of teachers in a particular school district, such as when the "middle school" concept is introduced.

There is one negative aspect to meeting the graduate credit requirement. Too often teachers attend the classes, meet the minimum course requirements, receive the credits, and promptly "file and forget" the content. Such behavior is inconsistent with the view of the teacher as a professional, as well as a waste of the time and money invested.

In-service courses

Technically, any course taken after certification and professional teaching have begun is an in-service course. However, there are other courses, often required or recommended but without college credit, that are sponsored by the school administration for the improvement of instruction or to teach a totally new approach to handling subject matter. These are usually called "in-service" courses. They vary in length from one-day workshops to semester-length weekly sessions and may be scheduled during normal school hours on a "released-time" basis.

Suppose a school administrator considers it important that every one of her teachers be able to operate videotape equipment so that this teaching aid is more appropriately and effectively utilized. She schedules an in-service course in video tape techniques. Or perhaps the curriculum committee decides to select a new math or science program. Teachers in the affected fields of study may be required to take an in-service course in the concepts and methods of the revised curriculum.

In-service courses are not always well accepted by teachers, no matter how inspiring or important their content may be. After a busy and long day of teaching, few teachers are mentally alert enough or emotionally attuned to spending additional hours in the classroom. They are tired, have papers to grade and lessons to prepare, and often have home and family responsibilities as well. If the content can be presented in a two-day workshop, when regular classes are suspended, or in informal seminars at convenient times and places, response to in-service education might be more positive.

Graduate studies and in-service courses both enable the teacher to continue learning. This effort is necessary if you are to keep well informed about scientific discoveries, contemporary social and economic problems and their effect on education, and more effective techniques of communication and instruction. Teaching centers, open to all educational personnel, also provide an opportunity to gain such information in a variety of ways. [*Journal of Teacher Education*, 1974, 25 (1)]

Long-term continuing education for teachers needs to recognize the individual's responsibility for continuing growth as a person and as a professional, as well as provide a mechanism for curriculum development in the schools.

INFORMAL EDUCATION

An additional source of learning lies in professional communications. Whether you are teaching at the preschool, elementary, secondary, or college level, it is very helpful to know what other people at your level are doing about common instructional and behavioral problems. What is being discovered about motivation? Attitudes? Particular teaching styles? Why do results differ from one report to another? Tentative answers may be found in professional journals. The thinking of someone in a school 2000 miles away may stimulate your own thinking and teach you some modification of your own teaching behavior. Attendance at professional conventions, where the authors of these papers are available for direct questioning, and where informal contacts with colleagues permit an interchange of ideas, is also a valuable learning experience.

Professional literature and meetings

Another source of informal but professional education can be found in conversations with your faculty colleagues. Those who have been at the school for several years can teach you about the community population you serve and the educational philosophy it has. Experienced teachers can guide you to or through the correct channels for implementing an idea. They can, in other words, "show you the ropes," which will contribute to your enhanced effectiveness in the classroom. Some school districts employ resource personnel whose primary purpose is to aid all classroom teachers in learning new techniques of teaching and evaluating their performance. Large systems may have an office devoted to innovation and research where the teacher can obtain information and guidance. Be smart enough to ask for help when you need it!

In team teaching, the master teacher or team leader can suggest ways of improving teaching skills as a contribution to the team effort. The team members can also use a variety of approaches in an attempt to evaluate teaching strategies or curriculum modifications.

When a completely new curriculum is to be introduced, the district may send two or three teachers to an intensive summer course dealing with the content or method (e.g., one of the "new" maths or i/t/a). These teachers then

By students

Learning from students is somewhat different. There may be initially only a vague awareness that some relationship is subtly changed, or that a laboratory demonstration didn't come off quite as planned, or that there are interpersonal undercurrents in the classroom that are affecting the teaching-learning process. As you follow up this vague awareness, *you learn*. Why did the teacher-student relationship in your class change? Was there a precise turning point? What behavior or event preceded it and what followed it? If you have good rapport with one or more of your students, they may well instruct you about why a situation changed for the worse or the better. If not, you may find out from a colleague or as a result of thinking through the situation yourself. When it comes to the unsuccessful lesson or group activity or demonstration, you can, with some effort on your part, learn from these mistakes. Perhaps the timing was wrong, or you pitched the presentation at too concrete or too abstract a level, or you ignored the concerns of the class. Suppose the problem is intraclass dissension, but you can't put your finger on troublemakers or leaders. Or, in a more positive vein, you want to break the class down into small project groups for more effective learning, but you don't know how to do it. Why don't you try a little sociometry?

Focus 14–2

Miss Graves, a seventh-grade teacher, was anxious to reduce the friction caused when she arbitrarily assigned students to work together on class projects. To arrive at a happier combination of students on the committees, she asked the class to answer the following questions:

1. Who are your two closest friends in the class?
   _____
   _____

2. With which two students in the class would you like to study?
   _____
   _____

3. With which two students in the class would you like to work on the archaeology project?
   _____
   _____

Not only did Miss Graves obtain objective data on which to base her committee assignments, but this procedure also gave the students a feeling of participation in their own "destiny." After compiling the results of the questionnaire, Miss Graves discovered some relationships in the class of which she had been unaware. The results for question 2 will help you to see some of these relationships. The figure (14.1) is called a sociogram, or a picture of a group's relationships.

> From the sociogram, it became obvious to Miss Graves that Chip, Linda, and Fred were the students with whom most students wanted to study. She had never been aware, she realized, of how Fred's conscientious habits and quiet ways made him attractive as a study partner, although he was rarely named as a "closest friend" in question 1. She also hadn't realized, until she looked at this sociogram and the other two, how isolated from the other class members Donna and Elinor were. In making up the committees, she decided to separate the two girls, placing each with her second choice, in order to expand their interpersonal class contacts.
>
> The input from responses to the other two questions was added to the information shown in Figure 14.1 before a list of working committees for the achaeology project was finally drawn up. In the process of working out the lists, however, Miss Graves learned a good deal about the student relationships in her class, information that she was able to use in other situations involving personal and social situations in the group.

Suggested Activity

If you are working in a classroom or youth group setting, obtain the teacher or leader's permission to do a sociometric study and sociogram before establishing subgroups for a new activity. Evaluate the results.

Other sources

Other sources for continued learning opportunities are legion, to name a few: the daily newspaper, books, lay magazines, TV documentaries, conversations with concerned noneducators, attendance at lectures or concerts, and travel abroad or in the United States. All of these are sources of information and ideas. You might even begin keeping an "idea" file at this point in your education for later review and use. Sometimes these informal sources raise questions to which you will seek the answers in other more professional sources. The main point is that informal education consists largely of your willingness to *receive* ideas in order to generate new ones. As you reflect on and/or employ them, they tend to change your behavior in some way, and this is learning.

CHANGES IN TEACHER EDUCATION

Curricula in teachers' colleges, usually established to coincide with state certification requirements, have been criticized as narrow, stifling, and out-of-tune with the ongoing needs of society. There is little opportunity for the prospective teacher, according to critics of teacher education, ". . . to confront the discrepancy between conceived and operative values, between what is sincerely believed to be desirable and what is actually acted upon in the world." (Greene, 1970, p. 472) Although the need for changes in teacher education has been recognized for years, movement has been slow and spotty until fairly recently.

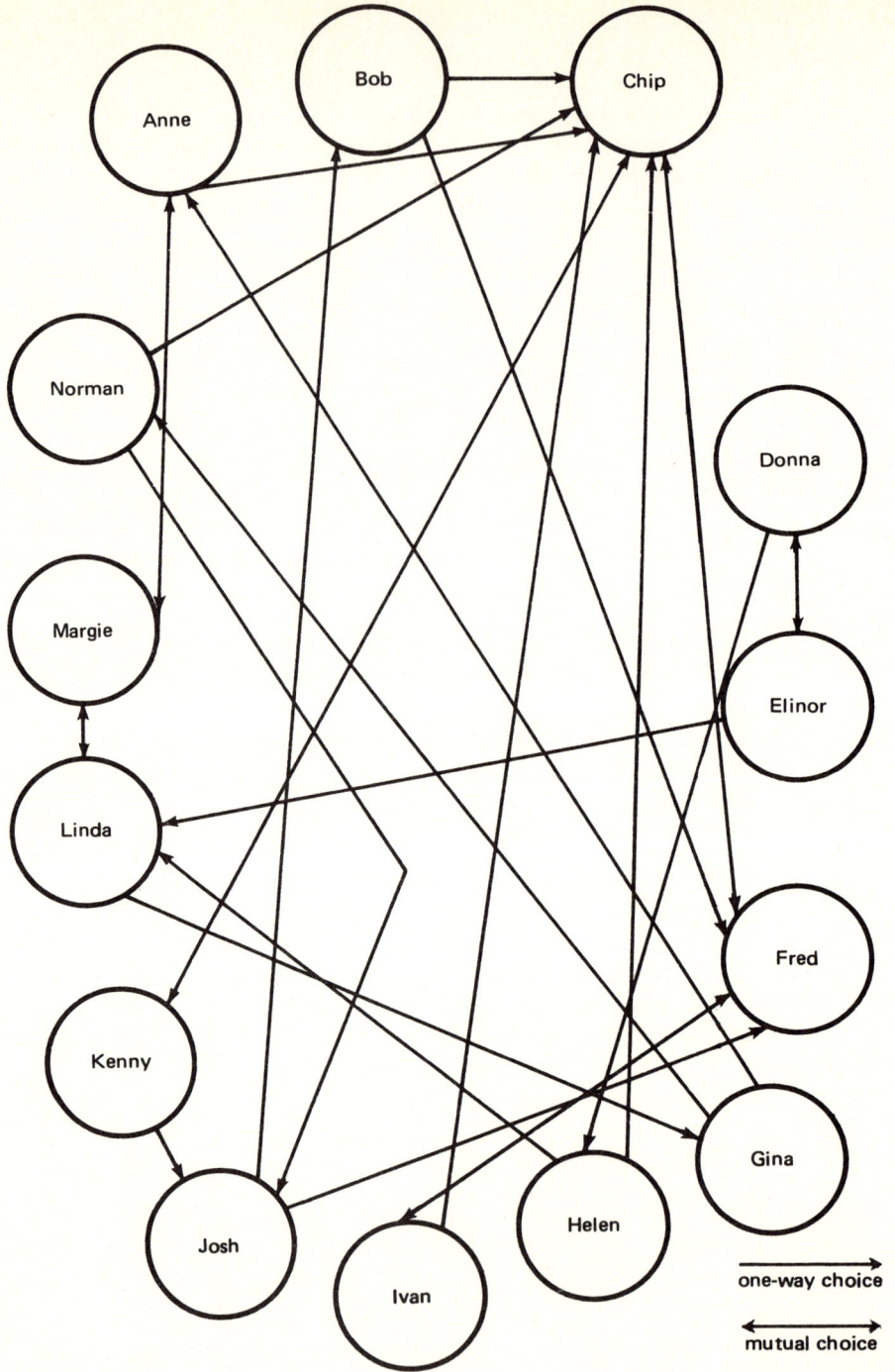

Figure 14.1 *Sociogram of relationships in Miss Graves' class, in response to choices requested for study partners.*

There have been several suggestions made for a total revamping of teacher education procedures, many of which emphasize the idea that these programs should practice what they preach. This ideal situation, however, requires massive financial support to provide personnel and equipment that would permit the desired individualization of instruction and curriculum. Such financial backing is increasingly difficult to obtain. Lack of financing, though, does not mean that no changes in the education of prospective teachers can be made.

More selective admissions have become routine in the 1970s because of the overabundance of teachers in many fields, but retention in the teacher preparation program must also become more selective. Field work programs, as detailed in Focus 14–1, if placed early in the curriculum sequence, give early clues to student and professor alike about fitness for teaching.

An improved balance of courses is possible, with little cost in dollars, if each part of the instructional staff is willing to give up part of its "empire" for the sake of a common goal—better preparation of better teachers. Cooperation is needed if teachers are to be well prepared.

Goodlad (1970) has recommended that the future teacher, immediately after admission to the program, join

> . . . a teaching team in a teacher education center—a collaborating school—affiliated with the college or university in which he is enrolled. At the outset, participation is limited but specific with respect to authority and responsibility. He receives a small but ascending stipend as a teacher aide. With increase in responsibility, he moves to the role of intern, and ultimately, resident teacher, with the stipend increasing at each level of preparation and responsibility. (p. 67)

Changes in teacher education must be and are being developed to keep pace with the realities of a rapidly changing world. Some of these realities are:

1. Continuing education, emphasizing process rather than content alone, is a necessity as innovation creates new jobs and does away with old skills. According to one futurist, *"What will be most worth learning will be mainly the knack of learning itself."* (Corrigan, 1974, p. 101)

2. Competency/Performance-Based Teacher Education (C/PBTE) programs will increase as society demands that teachers have specific skills that are useful and relevant in teaching. (Tickle, 1974)

3. There will be increased use of differentiated staffing, or use of educational specialists working as a team. In this approach, "Teachers will receive professional pay and status based on knowledge of their specialty and competence demonstrated in performing clearly defined roles as members of a teaching team which is designed to work with learners as unique human beings." (Corrigan, 1974, p. 103)

4. Preservice and in-service teachers will have a closer relationship throughout the teacher education program. Apprenticeships within

the larger community will also reduce the isolation of the prospective teacher from reality.

As better qualified teachers emerge from improved programs, the quality of education at all levels of learning will improve, leading to better prepared candidates for the teaching profession.

SUMMARY

At both ends of this chapter, we have discussed teacher education because this is central to the position that the teacher is a learner. What he learns, how he learns it, and where he learns what he learns is the crux of a continuing debate among educators and critics of the schools in general, and of teacher education programs in particular. The need for innovations is widely recognized. A number of currently operative traditional and innovative teacher education programs were presented to facilitate knowledge of and reasons for innovations.

Also discussed was the concept that a teacher's education is a continuing process throughout the professional career. Learning may occur in a number of different settings and from different sources. This concept implies a commitment to teaching that should be standard. If the teacher is unwilling to be a learner in college or after she graduates, she cheats herself and her students. The difficulties of evaluating commitment, although they are many, can be reduced if teacher education programs are made more stimulating, more learner-oriented, more selective in admission and retention of students, and more relevant to the needs of our rapidly changing society.

EPILOGUE

To write a summary or to write a commentary—that is the question. On the one hand, each chapter has a summary. Perhaps that should be sufficient. On the other hand, so much has been said that maybe integration is needed. Perhaps a commentary can also provide a summary.

For many, many pages, we have examined the learner. How *does* a child become a learner? In what ways is he affected by the learning experience? How do interpersonal relationships with family, teachers, and peers affect him as a person and as a learner? The person is like a delicate and sensitive instrument: treated with care, he or she performs well; a single thoughtless act or word can cause him or her to malfunction. It is the understanding of this concept that underlies much of educational psychology today.

Step by step, and objective by objective, we worked through the development of the learner *as* a learner. We considered the factors that make him unique and those that contribute to his role as a member of the group. As a result of this emphasis, what have you gained from reading this far? Have you met your objectives, or those of the course? Do you have new perspectives?

In the next few pages, let us pull together what has been worked through, and perhaps through this integration and reflection you will find additional thoughts and directions for the future. Within the limits imposed by print, this text has tried to bring to you the essence of educational psychology, in a manner designed to stimulate you to further inquiry, thought, and discussion. In focusing on the learner, we are attending to the ultimate object of concern of even the most cognitively oriented educational psychologist. By various means, the content of this field has been communicated to you, the learner in *this* situation, in an attempt to meet *your* needs and competencies.

Consider where you were as you opened this book and where you are now. At the end of chapter one, a number of specific goals for the text and course in educational psychology were listed. Have we reached these goals?

In what ways have you changed because of this course?   *Question*

Looking backward, you can see that educational psychology did not appear on the academic scene suddenly. It is for this reason that the historical references were part of your introduction to the field. Individual differences among learners, what and how they were taught, and how well they retained subject matter content have been the proper concern of teachers for centuries. Most recently, formal statements of behavioral objectives and the concept of accountability have become added items to be considered by all those involved in education, yet, in a way, they have been implicit in the fields of teaching and educational psychology all along. As you enter a classroom today, even one in which you are a student, you are more perceptive of individual differences and why they exist than you were several weeks ago. You are not a diagnostician nor a full-fledged psychologist, but you are certainly more capable than you were, before studying educational psychology, of knowing what factors should be investigated in seeking to explain the behavior of a learner.

The point of view expressed in this book is that there are three major elements in the learning situation: learner, content, and teacher, and that whatever learning occurs is a result of the interaction of these elements. The learner is of prime importance. He learns from the day of birth, but within a unique set of potentials and limitations imposed by heredity, prenatal conditions, and the environment in which he matures. The affective characteristics of the learner—attitudes, interests, motivation, and self-concept—are all initially shaped, as we have seen, in the family situation. This is, in turn, affected by the subcultures in which the family is embedded. To be sure, a disinterested learner, no matter what his cognitive ability or potential, tends to learn less than a well-motivated but less academically capable student, no matter what his home background. To sum up, you should now be able to appreciate more fully the importance of the uniqueness of the individual.

Content, what is to be learned and how it is learned, was discussed in several chapters. Theorists, grouped by the common features of their approach, proved to present different ideas about the process of learning. Applications of the various learning theories to classroom situations made the value of understanding theory apparent.

It is also important, obviously, to understand the development of thinking and learning in children. Here the work of Piaget and Bruner were of particular significance. It is essential to consider the opportunities to learn that each child has had since infancy. We therefore looked at stimulation in the environment, as well as what responses the child learned to make and how he learned to make them. There are, as you have learned, many ways of thinking, not all of which are apparent in observable behavior, either verbal or motor. A crucial ingredient in the experiential mix that the learner brings to new content is his repertoire of thinking abilities. It is possible to attack a wide variety of content with but a single mode of thinking, but such an approach does not guarantee a consistent level of achievement. The advantages of being able to think at different levels and in different ways should be quite obvious to you, especially in light of the stress placed on creative thinking and problem-solving throughout the text.

Since we do recognize individual differences among learners, it is obviously important to be open to technological as well as methodological innovations that may help different learners. There is a need, too, to recognize the necessity for variation in instructional techniques and content because of unique characteristics of the learner. So-called exceptional children need specific adaptations to help them learn, whether mainstreamed or in special classes. Many of the techniques may also be employed appropriately in the regular classroom for learners who exhibit challenges in modified form.

The quality of instruction depends largely on the teacher. As in studies of child-rearing, however, it is not always *what* method is used that has measurable effects, but rather *how* the method is used. Educational psychologists are examining, more closely than they used to, the effects of the interaction of teachers and learners. Climate, the environment in which learning takes place, is difficult to assess because of subtleties difficult to measure, but we do know that classroom climate is largely created by the classroom teacher. Furthermore, we know that a climate nurturant for some or even most students in a class may be inappropriate for others in the same class. Although we have inklings of the optimal combinations of teacher and learner, and of the highly desirable goal of matching the two with instructional techniques effective for the learner, much of the available supporting evidence for this point of view is the result of serendipitous events, evaluated after they occur in isolated circumstances. (There is nothing inherently wrong with such "evidence," but it is difficult to replicate in research settings with appropriate and acceptable statistical analysis.) If, as Bloom has hypothesized, we can account for 90 percent of the variance in school achievement as a function of the interaction of learner $\times$ content $\times$ instruction, then perhaps the remaining 10 percent can be attributed to climate, or teacher enthusiasm, or to a variable as yet unnamed or not yet identified.

As a final consideration, we demonstrated that the teacher, too, is a learner. Perhaps the most important idea here is that the teacher must be an active and willing participant in the learning process, *willing* to learn and then modify or adapt, if she or he is to maintain a high level of quality in classroom performance. "Putting in time" in order to collect credits is not enough. No teacher can afford to teach only what he learned yesterday, for he won't be standing still today, but falling farther and farther behind. This is unfair to his students and himself. The "knowledge explosion," that is, the rapid expansion of knowledge in all fields every decade, affects education in curriculum content and method. Ultimately teachers and learners are affected by this, for they must both learn the new material, possibly in a new way.

I have tried to make this a textbook both traditional and innovative. Much of the content is quite traditional. There has been a conscious effort, also, however, to go beyond the limits of traditional texts. This stemmed from my belief that, early in the professional curriculum, you should be exposed to and aware of the ideas and practices that are the embodiment of educational psychology in action.

I believe further, and have found it to be true with my own students, that to make educational psychology meaningful, real experience with learners and instruction is essential. It doesn't matter whether your school has a field work program. Try to tutor on a one-to-one basis, observe a class, teach arts and crafts in a recreation program.

With the knowledge you have gained in this course, you can look at learners differently than you did several weeks ago. You *know* how learning and teaching vary. You *know* that some techniques are more effective than others. You can appreciate why learning is easy for some and difficult for others. John Dewey said long ago that the best way to learn is by doing. It should be your philosophy, too. Be conscious of what you are doing when you praise or reprove someone, even when you give street directions to a stranger lost in your community. In a sense, we are each strangers in a new community each time we approach unfamiliar problems, including new subject matter. We need to try to find familiar landmarks in strange territory and to prepare alternate routes to our goals in case of roadblocks. It has been the raison d'être of this book to try to make a new field more familiar by incorporating experiences that you have had, while at the same time indicating multiple ways of handling the teaching-learning process. If this book has made you want to learn more, it has achieved one of *its* major objectives—the creation of a self-motivated learner.

GLOSSARY

GLOSSARY

Accommodation A term used by Piaget to describe the changes in an individual's behavior to meet a new situation.

Achievement test A measure of what the student has learned.

Analysis of variance A mathematical technique for analyzing the total amount of variation of a distribution of scores.

Anthropomorphism Attributing human characteristics to animals and inanimate objects.

Aptitude test A measure of the individual's probable ability to profit from instruction (e.g., a predictor of future achievement).

Articulation Refers to the smooth continuation of instruction and content from one grade level to another, particularly from elementary level to secondary.

Artificialism As used by Piaget, this refers to the "magical forces" to which the child attributes events. An example would be a child's statement, when seeing a sailboat move for the first time, that a sea witch is causing the boat to move by pushing it.

Assimilation A term used by Piaget to describe the application of an established behavior pattern to a variation of a familiar situation.

Attitude test A measure of positive and negative feelings toward people, concepts, subject matter, etc.

Average (or mean) deviation A descriptive measure of the variability of scores within a given distribution.

Causality A term used by Piaget that implies logical reasoning and an ordering of relationships that permit the individual to perceive that events have real causes. For example, the school-age child, in contrast to a younger one, could understand that the wind causes a sailboat to move, and that the faster the wind blows, the more quickly the sailboat will move across the water.

Chi-square A statistical test used to determine 1) whether the observed values fit a particular expected distribution or whether their deviation can be attributed to chance; or 2) whether two or more independent samples differ with respect to a given variable and whether these differences are attributable to chance.

Chronological age The person's actual age as determined by subtracting the birthdate from a later date; usually expressed in years and months.

Cognitive growth The increase in intellectual abilities (e.g., abstract thinking, reasoning, knowledge) that results from maturation and learning.

Compensatory education Programs, principally at the preschool level, designed to reduce differences in experiences with which "culturally-different children begin school, as compared with middle-class white children.

Construct An unobservable variable that attempts to explain the basis for a certain behavior (e.g., learning, anxiety, hunger).

Content validity A test considered valid as a result of comparing it with a test designed for the same purpose (which itself has high validity), and finding a high coefficient of correlation between the two.

Contiguity Refers to events that are associated in time or place.

Correlation coefficient A statistical indication of the degree to which two or more variables are related; e.g., how they vary together.

Curvilinear relationship A relationship between two variables that is alternately direct and inverse.

Dependent variable The results of an observed or experimental situation. *Example:* Performance on a test by subjects following experimental and nonexperimental instruction.

Descriptive A method of study that describes observed behavior, without involving manipulation of instructional techniques or other factors before measurement of variables.

Dizygotes Fraternal twins as the result of fertilization of two eggs at about the same time, may be of the same or opposite sex. (May also result in triplets or more children.)

Eclectic An individual who perceives, knows, and uses several points of view rather than one technique or theory. For example, a psychologist who uses the technique appropriate to a problem, whether it stems from Gestalt theory, learning theory, or psychoanalysis, is being eclectic. He tends to fit the technique to the problem, rather than vice versa.

Empathy A behavior in which you feel *with* others, not feel sorry for them (sympathy).

Empirical A term referring to an observational approach to studying samples that is often used instead of "descriptive method."

Environmentalists Individuals who believe that environment has the major (or total) influence on human development and behavior.

Experimental A research approach that manipulates some aspect(s) of a situation, e.g., instructional technique, diet, maturation. Also used to describe the group of subjects exposed to the changed conditions (as in "the experimental group").

Extrinsic motivation Motivation that arises from sources outside the individual (e.g., promise of a reward for exhibiting certain behavior).

Face validity A test or other technique that appears, on the surface, to measure what it is supposed to measure because of its content.

Factor analysis A statistical method that interprets scores and correlations of scores.

Geneticists Individuals who believe that heredity, i.e., interaction of genes, plays the major role in development and behavior.

Gestalt A German word meaning "whole." It is used with reference to teaching reading via a whole-word method rather than one based on phonics. Gestalt is also used in connection with a school of thought in psychology.

Idiographic Studies of individuals rather than groups.

Incentive The potential reward for learning or performance (e.g., grades, prize, cash award).

Incidental learning Learning that occurs without the learner being aware of it.

Independent variable The variable controlled by the experimenter, as, for example, the type of textbook used (programmed or not).

Inferential statistics Statistical techniques that enable their user to make inferences, or draw conclusions, from data rather than simply to describe the data. Examples: analysis of variance, chi-square test.

Intrinsic motivation Motivation that arises from within the individual (e.g., curiosity as a basis for learning something new).

Itinerant teacher Usually a specialist who is assigned to several classes or schools to provide special services, as speech therapy, remedial reading, perceptual training, on a part-time basis with each group.

Language bifurcation Refers to the use of two or more languages with an inadequate command of either of them (e.g., English and Spanish).

Learning A change in behavior that occurs as the result of experience.

Locus of control The source of control of an individual's behavior: internal = self-directed; external = direction by others. (This may or may not be conscious on the individual's part.)

Mean The common "average" which is the result of dividing the total score by the number of cases involved.

Median The point at which half of the scores are above and half are below. Also called the 50th percentile rank.

Mental age Used most often with reference to the pre-1960 versions of the Binet intelligence test, the mental age represents the level of intelligence at which the individual is functioning as compared with different age groups (expressed in years and months).

Mode The single score that occurs most frequently in a distribution of scores.

Molar view An overall or general view of behavior as a whole.

Molecular view Stress on specific or isolated bits of behavior.

Monozygotes Identical twins as the result of the division of one fertilized egg; necessarily, therefore, of the same sex.

Montessori Maria Montessori was a physician turned educator early in the twentieth century. She devised concrete developmental task sequences to stimulate the learning ability and cognitive development of institutionalized children in Rome. Her approach has had a resurgence of popularity in this country since the 1960s, resulting in the opening of numerous programs for special teacher training in her methods and many nursery schools.

Motive A need state or drive.

Multi-ethnic readers Reading texts at any level, though usually found in grades 1–9, which include stories and settings reflecting "culturally different" families and backgrounds. As the grade level increases, these may be stories of heroes from different ethnic groups, or of "inner-city" ways of life as opposed to suburban or rural environments.

Negative correlation Relationship between two variables in which high values on one variable tend to be associated with low values on the other.

Nomothetic Studies of groups of subjects rather than individuals.

Null hypothesis An hypothesis that states that no differences will be found between groups of subjects or scores except by chance.

Parent-surrogate The individual who "stands in" or replaces the parent for all or part of the day. This term would include staff in an institution as well as baby sitters at home.

Perinatal Refers to the time period of birth or shortly after birth.

Permutation Refers to the rearrangement or transformation of the linear ordering of a finite set of elements, or changing the arrangement of elements in a series.

Placebo A substance that is made to resemble a second substance, usually a drug, but which actually has none of the physical or chemical properties of the second substance (e.g., a "sugar pill"). Any effects reported by experimental subjects taking the drug would be psychologically-based.

Positive correlation Relationship between two variables in which high values on one variable tend to be associated with high values on the other and low values on one variable tend to be associated with low values on the other.

Predictive validity A test or measure that successfully predicts future performance (e.g., a high correlation between scores on a sales aptitude test and earnings as a salesman).

Proactive facilitation Occurs when prior learning helps in the acquisition of new learning.

Proactive inhibition Occurs when prior learning interferes with the acquistion of new learning.

Reliability A test or measure that is consistent in providing results.

Resource rooms Central locations in schools that have special learning materials used to help exceptional children acquire specific skills. Can also refer (but less often) to any location that has special instructional materials such as encyclopedias, tapes, film-strips, etc.

Retroactive facilitation Occurs when new learning helps in the retention of earlier learning.

Retroactive inhibition Occurs when new learning interferes with the retention of earlier learning.

Selective mating The tendency of individuals to marry on the basis of similar abilities, interests, socioeconomic backgrounds, education, etc.

Sibling A term used in psychology which means brother or sister.

"Spiral curriculum" Jerome Bruner's theory that children could be taught virtually any concept at any (reasonable) age if it was presented to them in an appropriate manner. His spiral begins with simple presentations, which in successive repetitions at later stages are enlarged in breadth and complexity. (Example: First-graders may be taught that $1 + ? = 3$; ninth-grade algebra students are taught that $1 + x = 3$.)

Standard deviation A measure of variability within a distribution of scores that depends on the deviation or distance from the mean of each score.

Standard score Expresses an individual's *relative* score within a distribution; i.e., the score's distance from the mean in terms of standard deviation units.

Statistical significance Correlation coefficients, differences between means, etc., are said to be statistically significant when statistical tests show that they would not occur by chance more than five in 100 times ($p = .05$), one in 100 times ($p = .01$), or one in 1000 times ($p = .001$).

Status measurement An evaluation of current performance, achievement, or other level.

Summative test A test that "sums up" student learning.

Synergy The association of two or more elements into a new "whole" that is more than the sum of the elements.

T-score A standard score determined by calculating the *z-score*, multiplying by 10, and adding 50. (This eliminates negative scores and reduces the need for decimals).

Taxonomy A systematic or organized hierarchy of concepts or principles, moving by steps from the simple to the complex.

Z-score A standard score determined by subtracting the mean from the raw score and dividing by the standard deviation.

STATISTICAL APPENDIX

STATISTICAL APPENDIX

THE NORMAL DISTRIBUTION

Basic to many statistical concepts is the bell-shaped normal distribution curve (Figure 1). It represents a *theoretical* distribution of scores, in which most scores are located near the center and few are found at the extremes.

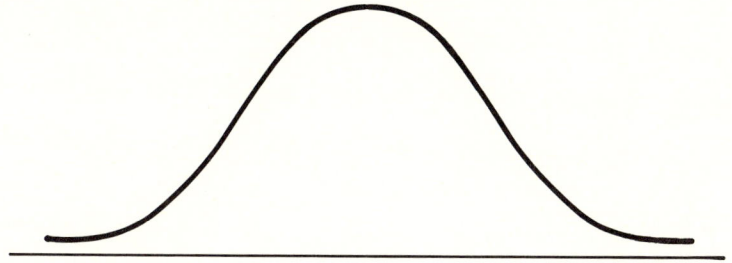

The normal curve   Figure 1

DESCRIPTIVE STATISTICS

Descriptive statistics are used to *describe* obtained data from a specific group of individuals. There are two categories of descriptive statistical measures: 1) measures of central tendency and 2) measures of variability. To illustrate these, we shall use the following symbols and hypothetical distribution of test scores.

Symbols		Test Scores		
X : the raw score		87	79	76
Σ : the sum of (or instruction to add)		84	79	72
N : the number of cases		80	78	67
$\overline{X}$: the mean				
x : the deviation from the mean				

Measures of Central Tendency

Measure	Example
1. *mean* ($\overline{X}$): $\overline{X} = \frac{\Sigma X}{N}$; usually the most representative measure of central tendency, it is the "average" of the scores.	$\overline{X} = \frac{\Sigma X}{N}$ $\overline{X} = \frac{702}{9} = 78$
2. *median* (Md): the midpoint in a set of ranked scores. Its position in the	$\frac{N+1}{2} = \frac{9+1}{2} = 5$

array is found by $\frac{N+1}{2}$. (If there are an even number of scores, the Md is the mean of the two highest scores.)

The 5th score in the array is 79.

3. *mode:* the most frequently occurring score in the distribution.

mode: 79

In a normal distribution, the mean, median, and mode coincide at the exact center. The given set of scores, however, is not normally distributed; these measures do not coincide.

Measures of Variability

1. *range:* high score − low score + 1; simple description of the spread of scores

   range = 87 − 67 + 1 = 21

2. *average deviation:* A.D. = $\frac{\Sigma |x|}{N}$
   (the sum of the *absolute* deviations divided by N); the mean amount by which scores deviate from the mean of the distribution. (Also called the *mean deviation.*)
   a) determine $\overline{X}$
   b) find the deviation (x) of each score from the mean $(X - \overline{X} = x)$.

   a) $\overline{X} = 78$
   b)

X	x
87	9
84	6
80	2
79	1
79	1
78	0
76	−2
72	−6
67	−11

   c) add the deviations disregarding algebraic sign
   d) divide (c) by N to determine A.D.

   c) $\Sigma |x| = 38$
   d) A.D. = $\frac{38}{9}$ = 4.2

3. *standard deviation:* S.D. = $\sqrt{\frac{\Sigma X^2}{N}}$
   a measure of the amount by which every score deviates from the mean.
   a) determine $\overline{X}$
   b) find the deviation (x) of each score from the mean $(X - \overline{X} = x)$.
   c) square each deviation (x^2)

   a) $\overline{X} = 78$
   b)

X	x	c) x^2
87	9	81
84	6	36
80	2	4
79	1	1

STATISTICAL APPENDIX   *451*

79	1	1
78	0	0
76	−2	4
72	−6	36
67	−11	121

d)   find the sum of the deviations squared (ΣX^2)

d) $\quad\Sigma x^2 = 284$

e)   divide this sum by N

e) $\dfrac{\Sigma x^2}{N} = \dfrac{284}{9} = 31.6$

f)   take the square root of (e) to determine S.D.

f) $\text{S.D.} = \sqrt{\dfrac{\Sigma x^2}{N}}$

$\text{S.D.} = \sqrt{31.6} = 5.6$

Therefore, 1 S.D. = 5.6 points from the mean.

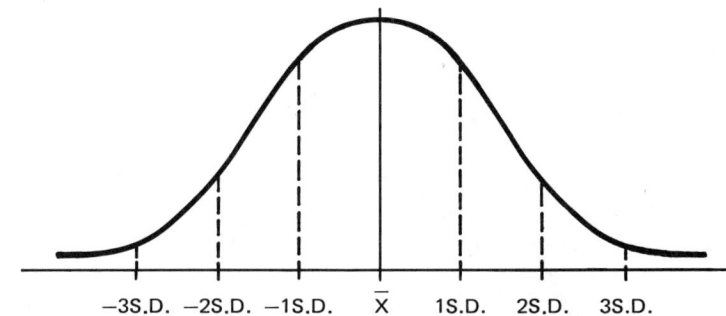

Standard deviations in a normal distribution   **Figure 2**

In a normal distribution, approximately—
  68% of the scores will fall within ±1 S.D. of the mean;
  95% of the scores will fall within ±2 S.D. of the mean;
  99% of the scores will fall within ±3 S.D. of the mean.

Nonnormal Distributions

Some sets of data (e.g., test scores) are not normally distributed, but are skewed; that is, they have a disproportionate number of scores at one end of the distribution.

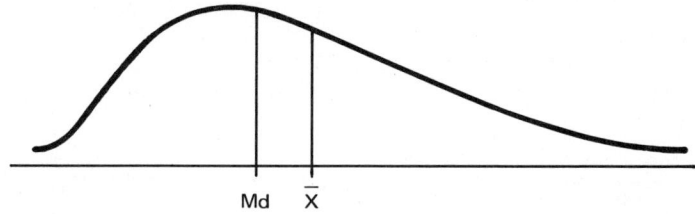

A positively skewed distribution   **Figure 3**

A positively skewed distribution (Figure 3) of test scores would include very few high scores and could occur if a test was extremely difficult, the material was inadequately taught, and/or the students were poorly motivated.

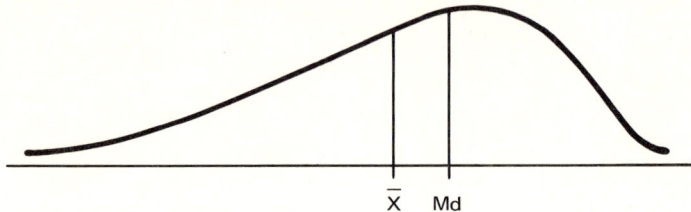

Figure 4   A *negatively skewed distribution*

A negatively skewed distribution (Figure 4) would include very few low scores and could occur if the test was extremely easy, the material was exceptionally well taught, and/or the students were highly motivated.

It is also possible to have a *bimodal distribution* (see Figure 5), found when measuring two populations (e.g., boys and girls).

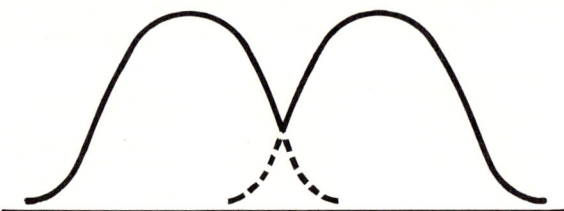

Figure 5   *A bimodal distribution*

Use of Descriptive Statistics

Standard Scores are often used to show how an individual compares with his group or to provide a common base with which to compare the results of two or more tests. The *z* score is probably the most frequently used type of standard score, while the *T* score is useful because it eliminates the negative scores that can occur with z scores.

$$\text{z score} = \frac{X - \overline{X}}{\text{S.D.}} \qquad \text{T score} = \left(\frac{X - \overline{X}}{\text{S.D.}} \cdot 10\right) + 50$$

Example: Given a distribution of scores with a mean of 70 and a standard deviation of 4, a teacher wishes to determine the relative position of an individual with a score of 80.

$$z = \frac{80 - 70}{4} = +2.5 \text{ (standard deviation units above the mean)}$$

$$T = \left(\frac{80 - 70}{4} \cdot 10\right) + 50 = 75 \text{ (See Figure 6)}$$

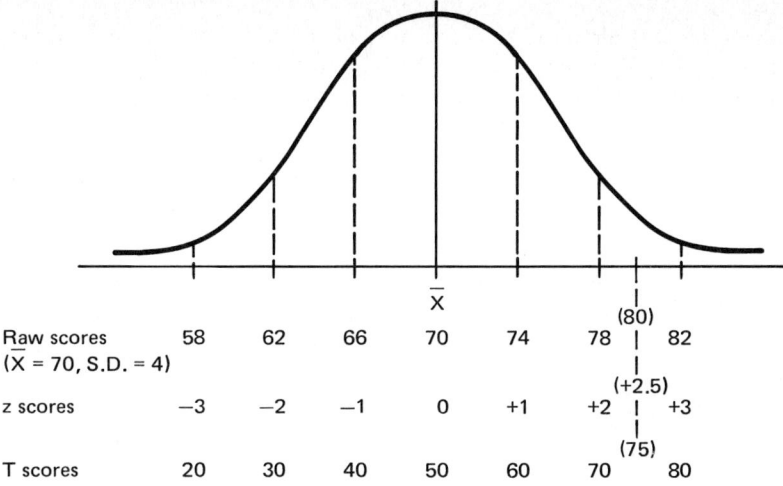

Comparison of scores   **Figure 6**

A *percentile score* is also more representative of an individual's relative position in the group than is his raw score. It describes the percentage of scores that fall *below* that student's score. Hence, the *median score* represents the *50th percentile,* since it divides the group into two equal segments. The following is a simple method of finding the percentile rank of any other score in the same distribution.

$$\text{Percentile Rank (PR)} = \frac{\text{Rank}}{\text{N}} \times 100$$

Example: A student had a test score of 72. This was 7th from the bottom in a class of 28.

$$\text{PR} = \frac{7}{28} \times 100 = 25$$

(Twenty-five percent of the students taking this test scored below this individual.)

Note: The statistics mentioned above are used only to describe a specific group of individuals. Much of the research in education, however, is based on *sampling statistics*. Sampling statistics differ from descriptive statistics in that they measure a *representative sample* of a population (e.g., fifth-graders) *in order to make inferences* about that population as a whole.

CHI-SQUARE TEST

The chi-square test is useful in education to test the significance of
1) the difference between an actual distribution and theoretical (or expected) distribution, or
2) the differences between two or more actual samples.

Formula:

$$\chi^2 = \Sigma \frac{(O - E)^2}{E}$$

where χ^2 = chi-square value
O = observed frequency
E = expected frequency

Problem: Passing grade is 60. On a vocabulary test, 75 female students passed and 50 failed; 55 male students passed and 70 failed. Is this a significant difference by sex, or is it likely that these results occurred by chance?

Steps

1. Format for organizing *observed frequencies*:

	Column X	Column Y	Totals
Row A	AX	AY	Row A total
Row B	BX	BY	Row B total

   Column X total   Column Y total   =   Grand total

2. Compute the *expected* frequencies by multiplying each cell's column total by its row total and dividing by the grand total. (Cell AX in this example represents females who failed the test.)

3. Find the difference for *each cell* between its observed and expected frequencies $(O - E)$.

4. Square *each* difference $(O - E)^2$—then divide it by the expected frequency for its cell. $\frac{(O - E)^2}{E}$

5. Add these figures to obtain χ^2.
   $$\chi^2 = \Sigma \frac{(O - E)^2}{E}$$

6. Determine whether χ^2 is significant by checking a table of chi-square values in a statistics book, using (in this case) the row labeled "df = 1." (Note: chi-square tests can be done with a different number of categories than shown in the example above. It is then necessary to calculate the number of *degrees of freedom* (df) in order to determine the significance of χ^2. Refer to a statistics book for this procedure.)

Application

1. *Observed frequencies:*

	Fail	Pass	Totals
Female	50	75	125
Male	70	55	125
Totals	120	130	250

2. Cell AX: $120 \times 125/250 = 60$
   Cell BX: $120 \times 125/250 = 60$
   Cell AY: $130 \times 125/250 = 65$
   Cell BY: $130 \times 125/250 = 65$

   The *expected frequencies* are:

	Fail	Pass
Female	60	65
Male	60	65

3. AX: $50 - 60 = -10$
   BX: $70 - 60 = 10$
   AY: $75 - 65 = 10$
   BY: $55 - 65 = -10$

4. AX: $-10^2 = 100; 100/60 = 1.67$
   BX: $10^2 = 100; 100/60 = 1.67$
   AY: $10^2 = 100; 100/65 = 1.54$
   BY: $-10^2 = 100; 100/65 = 1.54$

5. $\chi^2 = 1.67 + 1.67 + 1.54 + 1.54 = 6.42$

6. According to the table, χ^2 must be equal to or greater than 3.84 to be significant at the .05 level. In this case, $\chi^2 = 6.42$ is significant, since there are less than 5 chances in 100 (.05) that this result occurred by chance. Therefore, you can conclude that there was a genuine difference by sex in achievement on the vocabulary test.

CORRELATION

Correlation refers to the way that two variables vary together, i.e., the relationship that exists between two variables. Various types of correlation include:

1) *positive correlation,* which occurs as a result of a direct relationship: a) as one variable increases, the other also increases, or b) as one variable decreases, the other variable also decreases;
2) *negative correlation,* which occurs when there is an inverse relationship—as one variable increases, the other decreases;
3) *zero correlation,* meaning lack of a relationship between two variables.

Scatter diagrams give a quick indication of the direction of the relationship. Linear relationships would include:

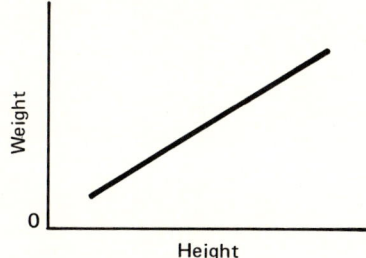
Positive correlation

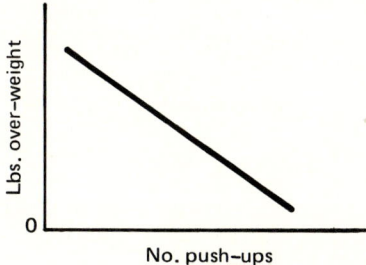
Negative correlation   **Figures 7, 8**

Also possible is a curvilinear relationship—one that is alternately positive and negative.

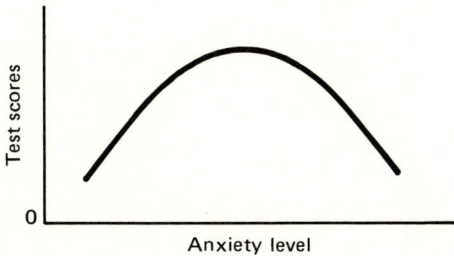
Curvilinear relationship   **Figure 9**

A *correlation coefficient* is a measure of the degree and direction of the relationship. It has two parts: 1) the absolute numerical value (without the sign), which indicates the *strength,* and 2) the sign, which indicates the direction. A correlation coefficient can range from $+1.00$ to -1.00; the higher the *number,* the stronger the relationship.

+1.00 = a perfect positive correlation coefficient
−1.00 = a perfect negative correlation coefficient

The above correlation coefficients show equal strength, but different direction.

Note: A correlation coefficient measures *only* the extent and direction of the relationship between two variables; it does *not* imply causality, i.e., that one variable caused the other to occur.

There are many techniques for determining correlation coefficients. Which one is used depends on the kind of information that is available.

Spearman rank order correlation coefficient, often called *rho* and symbolized as ρ, is particularly useful in the classroom when ranking a small group of students (usually less than 30).

$$\text{Formula: } \rho = 1 - \frac{6\Sigma D^2}{N(N^2 - 1)}$$

Problem: Determine whether there is a relationship between the following students' final grades and the number of hours they studied each week.

S	Grade	Hrs/Wk
1	A	6
2	B	4
3	B	5
4	C	0
5	D	3
6	F	2

Basic steps and illustration:

1. Rank each variable.

S	Grade	Hrs/Wk	Rank of Grade	Rank of Hrs/Wk
1	A	6	1	1
2	B	4	2.5 *	3
3	B	5	2.5 *	2
4	C	0	4	6
5	D	3	5	4
6	F	2	6	5

* For 6 subjects, there must be 6 ranks. Since "B" is between "A" (rank = 1) and "C" (rank = 4), the "B's" would share the ranks 2 and 3; the mean of 2 + 3 is 2.5.

2. Determine the difference between ranks (D) and square it (D^2). Add the D^2 column to obtain ΣD^2.

S	Grade	Hrs/Wk	Rank of Grade	Rank of Hrs/Wk	D	D²
1	A	6	1	1	0	0
2	B	4	2.5	3	−.5	.25
3	B	5	2.5	2	.5	.25
4	C	0	4	6	2	4
5	D	3	5	4	1	1
6	F	2	6	5	1	1

$$\Sigma D^2 = 6.5$$

3. Apply the formula:

$$\rho = 1 - \frac{6\Sigma D^2}{N(N^2 - 1)}$$
$$= 1 - \frac{6(6.5)}{6(36 - 1)} = 1 - \frac{39}{210} = 1 - .19$$
$$= +.81$$

4. Draw your conclusions.

There is a strong positive relationship between the number of hours spent studying and the final grades for these students.

REFERENCES

REFERENCES

ABT, C. C. Education is child's play. In W. Z. Hirsch and colleagues (eds.), *Inventing Education for the Future.* San Francisco: Chandler Publishing, 1967.

ABT, C. C. *Serious Games.* New York: Viking Press, 1970.

ADAMS, J. C. JR. The relative effects of various testing atmospheres on spontaneous flexibility, a factor in divergent thinking. *Journal of Creative Behavior,* 1968, **2**, 187–94.

ALBERT, R. S. Genius: present-day status of the concept and its implications for the study of creativity and giftedness. *American Psychologist,* 1969, **24**, 743–53.

ALBERT, R. S. Toward a behavioral definition of genius. *American Psychologist,* 1975, **30**, 140–51.

ALLEN, J. R. The Indian adolescent: Psychosocial tasks of the Plains Indians of Western Oklahoma. *American Journal of Orthopsychiatry,* 1974, **43**, 368–75.

ALLEN, R. M. There is an alternative to the IQ. *Journal of Personality Assessment,* 1975, **39**, 377–80.

ALLENDER, J. S. Some determinants of inquiry activity in elementary school children. *Journal of Educational Psychology,* 1970, **61**, 220–25.

ALLISON, D. E. Test anxiety, stress, and intelligence-test performance. *Canadian Journal of Behavioral Science,* 1970, **2**, 26–37.

ALSCHULER, A., & SHEA, J. V. The discipline game: playing without losers. *Learning,* 1974, **3** (1), 80–86.

ALSCHULER, A. S., TABOR, D., & McINTYRE, J. *Teaching Achievement Motivation: Theory and Practice in Psychological Education.* Middletown, Conn.: Education Ventures, 1971.

ALTUS, W. D. Birth order and its sequelae. *Science,* 1966, **151**, (3706), 44–49.

ANASTASI, A. *Fields of Applied Psychology.* New York: McGraw-Hill, 1964.

ANASTASI, A., & CORDOVA, F. A. Some effects of bilingualism upon the intelligence test performance of Puerto Rican children in New York City. *Journal of Educational Psychology,* 1953, **44**, 1–19.

ANASTASI, A., & FOLEY, J. P., JR. *Differential Psychology.* New York: Macmillan, 1958.

ANASTASIOW, N. J., & HANES, M. L. Cognitive development and the acquisition of language in three subcultural groups. *Developmental Psychology,* 1974, **10**, 703–09.

ANDERSON, J. G., & JOHNSON, W. H. Stability and change among three generations of Mexican-Americans: Factors affecting achievement. *American Educational Research Journal,* 1971, **8**, 285–309.

ANDERSON, R. C. Can first-graders learn an advanced problem-solving skill? *Journal of Educational Psychology,* 1965, **56**, 283–94.

ANDERSON, R. M., & STEVENS, G. D. Practices and problems in educating deaf retarded children in residential schools. *Exceptional Children,* 1969, **35**, 687–94.

APPLEBAUM, S. A., COYNE, L., & SIEGAL, R. S. Change in IQ during and after long-term psychotherapy. *Journal of Projective Techniques and Personality Assessment,* 1969, **33**, 290–97.

APPLETON, N. A molecular approach to foundations of education. *Journal of Teacher Education,* 1975, **26**, 249–53.

ASBURY, C. A. Selected factors influencing over- and underachievement in young school-age children. *Review of Educational Research,* 1974, **44,** 409–28.

ATKINSON, J. W. Motivational determinants of intellective performance and cumulative achievement. In J. W. Atkinson & J. O. Raynor (Eds.), *Motivation and Achievement.* New York: Halsted Press (John Wiley), 1974.

ATKINSON, R. C. Computerized instruction and the learning process. *American Psychologist,* 1968, **23,** 225–39.

AUSTIN, D., CLARK, V., & FITCHETT, G. *Reading Rights for Boys.* New York: Appleton-Century-Crofts, 1971.

AUSUBEL, D. P. *Educational Psychology: A Cognitive View.* New York: Holt, Rinehart, and Winston, 1968.

AXELBERD, F. J. Attitudes of elementary school teachers toward counseling and guidance in the elementary schools. *Journal of Experimental Education,* 1969, **37** (1), 1–4.

BABSON, S. G., HENDERSON, N. B., & CLARK, W. M., JR. Preschool intelligence of oversized newborns. *Proceedings of the 77th Annual Convention of the American Psychological Association,* 1969, **4,** 267–68. (Summary)

BACHTOLD, L. The creative personality and the ideal pupil revisited. *Journal of Creative Behavior,* 1974, **8,** 47–54.

BACKMAN, M. E. Patterns of mental abilities: ethnic, socioeconomic, and sex differences. *American Educational Research Journal,* 1972, **9,** 1–12.

BAIN, R. K., & ANDERSON, J. G. School context and peer influences on educational plans of adolescents. *Review of Educational Research,* 1974, **44,** 429–45.

BAKER, E. L. The technology of instructional development. In R. M. W. Travers (Ed.), *Second Handbook of Research on Teaching.* Chicago: Rand, McNally, 1973, 245–85.

BALTES, P. B., & SCHAIE, K. W. Aging and IQ: The myth of the twilight years. *Psychology Today,* 1974, **7** (10), 35–40.

BANKS, J. A. (Ed.) *Teaching Ethnic Studies: Concepts and Strategies.* Washington: National Council for the Social Studies (43rd Yearbook), 1973.

BAY, C. In N. Sanford (Ed.), *The American College.* New York: John Wiley, 1962.

BAYLEY, N. Behavioral correlates of mental growth: Birth to thirty-six years. *American Psychologist,* 1968, **23,** 1–17.

BAYLEY, N., & ODEN, N. The maintenance of intellectual ability in gifted adults. *Journal of Gerontology,* 1965, **10,** 91–107.

BEAM, J. E. Serial learning and conditioning under real-life stress. *Journal of Abnormal and Social Psychology,* 1955, **51,** 543–51.

BEARISON, D. J. Role of measurement operations in the acquisition of conservation. *Developmental Psychology,* 1969, **1,** 653–60.

BEILIN, H., & KAGAN, J. Pluralization rules and the conceptualization of number. *Developmental Psychology,* 1969, **1,** 697–706.

BEM, S. L. The role of comprehension in children's problem-solving. *Developmental Psychology,* 1970, **2,** 351–58.

BEREITER, C. The future of individual differences. *Harvard Educational Review,* 1969, **39,** 310–18.

BERGMAN, P., & ESCALONA, S. K. Unusual sensitivities in very young children. *The Psychoanalytic Study of the Child,* III/IV. New York: International Universities Press, 1949.

BERKO, J. The child's learning of English morphology. *Word,* 1958, **14,** 150–77.

BERLIN, I. N. Learning as therapy. *Saturday Review,* October 15, 1966.

BERNAL, E. M., JR. Gifted Mexican-American children: An ethno-scientific perspective. *California Journal of Educational Research*, 1974, **25**, 261–72.

BESHOAR, B. B. NAEP's second round with science. *American Education*, 1975, **11** (5), 6–11.

BEVER, T. G. Perceptions, thought, and language. In R. O. Freedle & J. B. Carroll (Eds.), *Language Comprehension and the Acquisition of Knowledge*. New York: Halsted Press (John Wiley), 1972, 99–112.

BEXTON, W., HERON, W., & SCOTT, T. Effects of decreased variation in the sensory environment. *Canadian Journal of Psychology*, 1954, **8**, 70–76.

BIDDLE, B. J., & ADAMS, R. S. Teacher behavior in the classroom context. In L. Siegel (Ed.), *Instruction: Some Contemporary Viewpoints*. San Francisco: Chandler Publishing, 1967.

BIGNER, J. J. "Second borns" discrimination of sibling role concepts. *Developmental Psychology*, 1974, **10**, 564–73.

BINET, A. [Les idees modernes sur les enfants.] In E. P. Torrance & W. F. White (Eds.), *Issues and Advances in Educational Psychology*. Itasca, Ill.: F. E. Peacock, 1969.

BINET, A., & SIMON, T. [The development of intelligence in children: Upon the necessity of establishing a scientific diagnosis of inferior states of intelligence.] In T. Shipley (Ed.), *Classics in Psychology*. New York: Philosophical Library, 1961. (Originally published in *L'Année Psychologique*. 1905, 163–91.)

BIOLOGICAL SCIENCES CURRICULUM STUDY. *Biological Science: An Inquiry into Life*. New York: Harcourt, Brace, & World, 1963.

BIRCH, H. G. Malnutrition, learning, and intelligence. *American Journal of Public Health*, 1972, **62**, 773–84.

BIRNS, B., & GOLDEN, M. The implications of Piaget's theories for contemporary infancy research and education. In M. Schwebel & J. Raph (Eds.), *Piaget in the Classroom*. New York: Basic Books, 1973.

BIRREN, J. E. Toward an experimental psychology of aging. *American Psychologist*, 1970, **25**, 124–35.

BISHOP, W. E. Successful teachers of the gifted. *Exceptional Children*, 1968, **34**, 317–25.

BLANK, M. Cognitive functions of language in the preschool years. *Developmental Psychology*, 1974, **10**, 229–45.

BLEDSOE, J. C., & GARRISON, K. C. The self concepts of elementary school children in relation to their academic achievement, intelligence, interests, and manifest anxiety. University of Georgia: Cooperative Research Project No. 1008, 1962.

BLOCK, J. H., & ANDERSON, L. M. *Mastery Learning in Classroom Instruction*. New York: Macmillan, 1975.

BLOOM, B. S. (Ed.) *Taxonomy of Educational Objectives, Handbook I: Cognitive Domain*. New York: David McKay, 1956.

BLOOM, B. S. HASTINGS, J. T., & MADAUS, G. F. *Handbook on Formative and Summative Evaluation of Student Learning*. New York: McGraw-Hill, 1971.

BLUM, J. E., FOSSHAGE, J. L., & JARVIK, L. F. Intellectual changes and sex differences in octogenarians: A twenty-year longitudinal study of aging. *Developmental Psychology*, 1972, **7**, 178–87.

BORDWELL, M. A community involvement program for the trainable adolescent. *Teaching Exceptional Children*, 1975, **7**, 110–14.

BORKE, H., & BURSTYN, J. W. The new teacher and interpersonal relations in the classroom. *Journal of Teacher Education*, 1970, **21**, 379–80.

Bowers, C. A. Accountability from a Humanist point of view. In I. D. Welch, F. Richards, & A. C. Richards (Eds.), *Educational Accountability: A Humanistic Perspective*. Fort Collins, Colo.: Shields Publishing, 1973, 175–83.

Brackbill, Y., & Jack, D. Discrimination learning in children as a function of reinforcement value. *Child Development*, 1958, **29**, 185–90.

Bradley, R. W., & Sanborn, M. P. Ordinal position of high school students identified by their teachers as superior. *Journal of Educational Psychology*, 1969, **60**, 41–45.

Bronfenbrenner, U. Is early intervention effective? *Teachers College Record*, 1974, **76**, 279–303.

Brophy, J. E., & Good, T. L. *Teacher-Student Relationships: Causes and Consequences*. New York: Holt, Rinehart, and Winston, 1974.

Broudy, H. S. *The Real World of the Public Schools*. New York: Harcourt Brace Jovanovich, 1972.

Brown, B. F. *The Appropriate Placement School: A Sophisticated Nongraded Curriculum*. West Nyack, N.Y.: Parker Publishing, 1965.

Brown, R. How shall a thing be called? *Psychological Review*, 1958, **65**, 14–21.

Bruner, J. S. The course of cognitive growth. *American Psychologist*, 1964, **19**, 1–15.

Bruner, J. S. *Toward a Theory of Instruction*. Cambridge, Mass.: Belknap Press, 1966.

Bruner, J. S., Goodnow, J. J., & Austin, G. A. *A Study of Thinking*. New York: John Wiley, 1956.

Bryan, T. H., & Bryan, J. H. *Understanding Learning Disabilities*. Port Washington, N.Y.: Alfred Publishing, 1975.

Burke, C. D., & Stone, D. R. A research-based learning process model for developing and evaluating teacher education curricula. *Journal of Teacher Education*, 1975, **26**, 236–41.

Bushnell, D. S., & Rappaport, D. *Planned Change in Education*. New York: Harcourt Brace Jovanovich, 1971.

Buxton, T. H., & Prichard, K. W. Student perceptions of teacher violations of human rights. *Phi Delta Kappan*, 1973, **55**, 66–69.

Byers, J. L. Verbal and concept learning. *Review of Educational Research*, 1967, **37**, 484–513.

Callard, E. D. Achievement motive of four-year-olds and maternal achievement expectancies. *Journal of Experimental Education*, 1968, **36**, 14–23.

Campbell, D. N. On being number one: competition in education. *Phi Delta Kappan*, 1974, **56**, 143–46.

Cancro, R. (Ed.) *Intelligence: Genetic and Environmental Influences*. New York: Grune & Stratton, 1971.

Caplin, M. D. The relationship between the self-concept and academic achievement. *Journal of Experimental Education*, 1969, **37** (3), 13–16.

Caputo, D., & Mandell, W. Consequences of low birth weight. *Developmental Psychology*, 1970, **3**, 363–83.

Carlson, H. B., & Henderson, N. The intelligence of American children of Mexican parentage. *Journal of Abnormal and Social Psychology*, 1950, **45**, 544–51.

Carmody, J. Some controversial issues in testing. In D. W. Allen & J. C. Hecht (Eds.), *Controversies in Education*. Philadelphia: W. B. Saunders, 1974.

Cattell, R. B. Theory of fluid and crystallized intelligence: A critical experiment. *Journal of Educational Psychology*, 1963, **54**, 1–22.

CATTELL, R. B. The structure of intelligence in relationship to the nature-nurture controversy. In R. Cancro (Ed.), *Intelligence: Genetic and Environmental Influences.* New York: Grune & Stratton, 1971.

CATTELL, R. B., & BUTCHER, H. J. *The Prediction of Achievement and Creativity.* Indianapolis: Bobbs-Merrill, 1968.

CAUDILL, W. A., & DEVOS, G. Achievement, culture, and personality: The case of Japanese-Americans. *American Anthropologist,* 1956, **58,** 1102–26.

CENTRAL ADVISORY COUNCIL FOR EDUCATION (England). *Children and Their Primary Schools,* 2 vols. London: H. M. Stationery Office, 1967. (Plowden Committee)

CERASO, J. The interference theory of forgetting. *Scientific American,* 1967, **217,** 117–24.

CHAMBERS, J. A. Relating personality and biographical factors to scientific creativity. *Psychological Monographs: General and Applied,* 1964, **78,** 16–18.

CHANSKY, N. M. Progress of promoted and repeating grade 1 failures. *Journal of Experimental Education,* 1964, **32** (3), 225–37.

CHARNOFSKY, S. *Educating the Powerless.* Belmont, Calif.: Wadsworth Publishing, 1971.

CHARROW, V. R., & FLETCHER, J. D. English as the second language of deaf children. *Developmental Psychology,* 1974, **10,** 463–70.

CHITTENDEN, E. A., FOAN, M. W., ZWEIL, D. M., & SMITH, J. R. School achievement of first- and second-born siblings. *Child Development,* 1968, **39,** 1223–27.

CHOMSKY, N. *Language and Mind.* New York: Harcourt Brace Jovanovich, 1968.

CHRISTIE, T. Environmental factors in creativity. *Journal of Creative Behavior,* 1970, **4,** 13–31.

CLARK, C. M., VELDMAN, D. J., & THORPE, J. S. Convergent and divergent thinking abilities of talented adolescents. *Journal of Educational Psychology,* 1965, **56,** 157–63.

CLARK, R. J., JR. Innovative instruction at Upper Moreland. *Pennsylvania School Journal,* 1970, **119,** 132–37.

CLARK, W. W. Boys and girls—are there significant ability and achievement differences? *Phi Delta Kappan,* 1959, **74,** 73–76.

CLEARY, T. A., HUMPHREYS, L. G., KENDRICK, S. A., & WESMAN, A. Educational uses of tests with disadvantaged students. *American Psychologist,* 1975, **30,** 15–41.

CLIFFORD, G. J. A history of the impact of research on teaching. In R. M. W. Travers (Ed.), *Second Handbook of Research on Teaching.* Chicago: Rand, McNally, 1973, 1–46.

COHEN, S. A. Some learning disabilities of socially disadvantaged Puerto Rican and Negro children. *Academic Therapy Quarterly,* 1967, **2,** 37–41.

COHEN, S. A. Slide show on a shoestring. *Learning,* 1974, **3** (4), 30–33.

COLETTA, A. J. Reflective and didactic styles for teachers of young gifted and poor children. *The Gifted Child Quarterly,* 1975, **19,** 230–40.

COMBS, A. W. Educational accountability from an humanistic perspective. *Educational Researcher,* 1973, **2** (9), 19–21.

COMBS, A. W., AVILA, D. L., & PURKEY, W. W. *Helping Relationships: Basic Concepts for the Helping Professions.* Boston: Allyn and Bacon, 1971.

COMBS, A. W., BLUME, R. A., NEWMAN, A. J., & WASS, H. L. *The Professional Education of Teachers,* 2nd ed. Boston: Allyn and Bacon, 1974.

CONANT, J. B. *The American High School.* New York: McGraw-Hill, 1959.

CONFUCIUS. [Hsioki] In R. Ulich (Ed.), *Three Thousand Years of Educational Wisdom.* Cambridge, Mass.: Harvard University Press, 1963.

CONNER, J. The teacher in a world of increasing impersonal relations. In E. P. Torrance & R. D. Strom (Eds.), *Mental Health and Achievement.* New York: John Wiley, 1965, 174–81.

CONNOLLY, K. Learning and the concept of critical periods in infancy. *Developmental Medicine and Child Neurology,* 1972, **14,** 705–14.

COOPER, T. T. Del Pueblo: A school that's "custom-made" for learning. *Teacher,* 1975, **93** (2), 58–61.

COOPERSMITH, S. *The Antecedents of Self-Esteem.* San Francisco: W. H. Freeman, 1967.

CORRIGAN, D. C. The future: Implications for the preparation of educational personnel. *Journal of Teacher Education,* 1974, **25,** 100–07.

COVINGTON, M. V. Promoting creative thinking in the classroom. *Journal of Experimental Education,* 1968, **37,** 22–30.

CRIST, R. L. Overt versus covert responding and retention by sixth-grade students. *Journal of Educational Psychology,* 1966, **57,** 99–101.

CROCKENBERG, S. B. Creativity tests: A boon or boondoggle for education? *Review of Educational Research,* 1972, **42,** 27–45.

CRONBACH, L. J. Heredity, environment, and educational policy. *Harvard Educational Review,* 1969, **39,** 338–47.

CRONBACH, L. J. *Essentials of Psychological Testing* (3rd ed.). New York: Harper and Row, 1970.

CRONBACH, L. J. Five decades of public controversy over mental testing. *American Psychologist,* 1975, **30,** 1–14.

CROPLEY, A. J., & FEURING, E. Training creativity in young children. *Developmental Psychology,* 1971, **4,** 105.

CROW, L. D., MURRAY, W. I., & SMYTHE, H. H. *Educating the Culturally Disadvantaged Child.* New York: David McKay, 1966.

CUNNINGHAM, W. G. The impact of student-teacher pairings on teacher effectiveness. *American Educational Research Journal,* 1975, **12,** 169–89.

CURWIN, G., & CURWIN, R. L. Building trust: a starting point for clarifying values. *Learning,* 1975, **3** (6), 30–36.

DATTA, L. Family religious background and early scientific creativity. *American Sociological Review,* 1967, **32,** 626–35.

DAVIS, C. R. The Buckley regulations: rights and restraints. *Educational Researcher,* 1975, **4** (2), 11–13.

DAVIS, G. A. Training creativity in adolescence: A discussion of strategy. *Journal of Creative Behavior,* 1969, **3,** 95–104.

DAVIS, G. A. *Psychology of Problem-Solving.* New York: Basic Books, 1973.

DECHARMS, R., & CARPENTER, V. Measuring motivation in culturally disadvantaged school children. *Journal of Experimental Education,* 1968, **37,** 31–41.

DEGROAT, A. F., & THOMPSON, G. G. A study of the distribution of teacher approval and disapproval among sixth-grade pupils. *Journal of Experimental Education,* 1949, **18,** 57–75.

DELLA-PIANA, G. M., & ENDO, G. T. Reading research. In R. M. W. Travers (Ed.), *Second Handbook of Research on Teaching,* Chicago: Rand, McNally, 1973, 883–925.

DE MOTT, B. Adult ed.—the ultimate goal. *Saturday Review* (Sept. 20) 1975, 27–29.

DENNEY, D. R., & DENNEY, N. W. The use of classification for problem-solving: a comparison of middle and old age. *Developmental Psychology*, 1973, **9**, 275–78.

DEUTSCH, C. Auditory discrimination and learning: social factors. *Merrill-Palmer Quarterly*, 1964, **10**, 277–96.

DEWING, K. The reliability and validity of selected tests of creative thinking in a sample of seventh grade West Australian children. *British Journal of Educational Psychology*, 1970, **40**, 35–42.

DICKINSON, D. J. But what happens when you take that reinforcement away? *Psychology in the Schools*, 1974, **11**, 158–60.

DILDINE, G. C. Motivated to learn. In W. A. Fullager, H. G. Lewis, & C. F. Cumbee (Eds.), *Readings for Educational Psychology*. New York: Thomas Y. Crowell, 1964.

DIZNEY, H. Classroom evaluation for teachers. Dubuque, Iowa: Wm. C. Brown Co., 1971.

DOBZHANSKY, T. Differences are not deficits. *Psychology Today*, 1973a, **7** (7), 96–101.

DOBZHANSKY, T. *Genetic Diversity and Human Equality*. New York: Basic Books, 1973b.

DOWNING, J. I. T. A. and children with special learning disabilities. *Academic Therapy Quarterly*, 1698, **3**, 249–56.

DOYLE, K. O., JR., & WHITELY, S. E. Students ratings as criteria for effective teaching. *American Educational Research Journal*, 1974, **11**, 259–74.

DRAKE, D. C. Adoption age influences life, study indicates. *Philadelphia Inquirer*, (May 11) 1969, p. 32.

DREISTADT, R. The psychology of creativity: how Einstein discovered the theory of relativity. *Psychology*, 1974, **11** (3), 15–25.

DRESSEL, F. B. Student teaching—the public school's responsibility. *School and Society*, 1970, **98**, 163–64.

DRILLIEN, C. M. *The Growth and Development of the Prematurely Born Infant*. Baltimore: Williams and Wilkins, 1964.

DUCHASTEL, P. C., & MERRILL, P. F. The effects of behavioral objectives on learning: A review of empirical studies. *Review of Educational Research*, 1973, **43**, 53–69.

DUNCKER, K. [On problem-solving.] (L. S. Lees, trans.) *Psychological Monographs*, 1945, No. 270.

DWYER, C. A. Influence on children's sex role standards on reading and arithmetic achievement. *Journal of Educational Psychology*, 1974, **66**, 811–16.

DYER, H. S. Statewide evaluation—what are the priorities? *Phi Delta Kappan*, 1970, **51**, 558–59.

EBEL, R. L. Educational tests: Valid? Biased? Useful? *Phi Delta Kappan*, 1975, **57**, 83–89.

EDELFELT, R. A., & JOHNSON, M. (Eds.). *Rethinking In-Service Education*. Washington: National Education Association, 1975.

EDWARDS, A. J. *Individual Mental Testing, Part III: Research and Interpretation*. New York: Intext Educational Publishers, 1975.

EIDUSON, B. T. *Scientists: Their Psychological World*. New York: Basic Books, 1962.

EISENBERG, L., BERLIN, C. I., DILL, A., & FRANK, S. Class and race effects on the intelligibility of monosyllables. *Child Development*, 1968, **39**, 1077–84.

ELAM, S. L. Poverty and acculturation in a migrant Puerto Rican family. *The Record*, 1969, **70**, 617–26.

ELDER, G. H., JR., & BOWERMAN, C. E. Family structure and child-rearing patterns: The effect of family size and sex composition. *American Sociological Review,* 1963, **28**, 891–905.

ELKIND, D. The development of quantitative thinking: A systematic replication of Piaget's studies. *Journal of Genetic Psychology,* 1961a, **98**, 37–46.

ELKIND, D. Children's discovery of the conservation of mass, weight, and volume: Piaget's replication study II. *Journal of Genetic Psychology,* 1961b, **98**, 219–27.

ELKIND, D. Cognitive structure and adolescent experience. *Adolescence,* 1967, **2**, 427–34.

ELKIND, D. Piagetian and psychometric concepts of intelligence. *Harvard Educational Review,* 1969, **39**, 319–37.

ELLIS, R. A., & LANE, W. C. Structural support for upward mobility. *American Sociological Review,* 1963, **28**, 743–56.

ENGLE, P. L. Language medium in early school years for minority language groups. *Review of Educational Research,* 1975, **45**, 283–325.

EPSTEIN, S. The self-concept revisited: Or a theory of a theory. *American Psychologist,* 1973, **28**, 404–16.

ERIKSON, E. H. *Childhood and Society.* New York: W. W. Norton, 1950.

ESPOSITO, D. Homogeneous and heterogeneous ability grouping: Principal findings and implications for evaluating and designing more effective educational environments. *Review of Educational Research,* 1973, **43**, 163–79.

FAGOT, B. L. Influence of teacher behavior in the preschool. *Developmental Psychology,* 1973, **9**, 198–206.

FAUST, I. Counseling in suburbia. *The Record,* 1968, **69**, 449–58.

FEATHER, N. T. Success probability and choice behavior. *Journal of Experimental Psychology,* 1959, **58**, 257–66.

FELDHUSEN, J. F. THURSTON, J. R., & BENNING, J. L. Longitudinal analysis of classroom behavior and school achievement. *Journal of Experimental Education,* 1970, **38** (4), 4–10.

FINLEY, G. G. Physical Science Study Committee: A status report. *Science Teacher,* 1959, **26**, 574–81.

FINN, J. D. Expectations and the educational environment. *Review of Educational Research,* 1972, **42**, 387–410.

FIRESTONE, G., & BRODY, N. Longitudinal investigation of teacher-student interactions and their relationship to academic performance. *Journal of Educational Psychology,* 1975, **67**, 544–50.

FISHBEIN, J. M. The father of behavioral objectives criticizes them: An interview with Ralph Tyler. *Phi Delta Kappan,* 1973, **55**, 55–57.

FISHER, J. K., & WAETJEN, W. B. An investigation of the relationship between the separation by sex of eighth-grade boys and girls and English achievement and self concept. *Journal of Educational Research,* 1966, **59**, 409–12.

FITZSIMMONS, S. J., CHEEVER, J., LEONARD, E., & MACUNOVICH, D. School failure: now and tomorrow. *Developmental Psychology,* 1969, **1**, 134–46.

FLANAGAN, J. C. President's message—the function of educational psychologists. *Educational Psychologist* (Feb.) 1970, **7**, 1, 8.

FLANDERS, N. A. *Analyzing Teacher Behavior.* Reading, Mass.: Addison-Wesley, 1970.

FLAVELL, J. H. *The Developmental Psychology of Jean Piaget.* Princeton: Van Nostrand, 1963.

FLEMING, E. S., & ANTHONY, R. G. Teacher expectancy or My Fair Lady. *American Educational Research Journal*, 1971, **8**, 241–52.

FOSTER, F. P. The human relationships of creative individuals. *Journal of Creative Behavior*, 1968, **2**, 111–18.

FREEDLE, R. O., & CARROLL, J. B. *Language Comprehension and the Acquisition of Knowledge*. New York: Halsted Press (John Wiley), 1972.

FREEMAN, F. S. *Theory and Practice of Psychological Testing*. New York: Henry Holt, 1950.

FRENCH, L. How does it feel to fail? In E. P. Torrance & R. D. Strom (Eds.), *Mental Health and Achievement*. New York: John Wiley, 1965, 377–84.

FREY, R. M., & KRAUSE, I. B. The incidence of color blindness among deaf children. *Exceptional Children*, 1971, **37**, 393–94.

FREYBERG, P. D. Concept development in Piagetian terms in relation to school attainment. *Journal of Educational Psychology*, 1966, **57**, 164–68.

FRIEDES, D., FREDENTHAL, B. J., GRISELL, J. L., & COHEN, B. D. Changes in two dimensions of cognition during adolescence. *Child Development*, 1963, **34**, 1047–56.

FRUEH, T., & McGHEE, P. E. Traditional sex role development and amount of time spent watching television. *Developmental Psychology*, 1975, **11**, 109.

FURTH, H. G. *Piaget for Teachers*. Englewood Cliffs, N.J.: Prentice-Hall, 1970.

FURTH, H. G., & WACHS, H. *Thinking Goes to School: Piaget's Theory in Practice*. New York: Oxford University Press, 1974

GAGNE, E. D., & ROTHKOPF, E. Z. Text organization and learning goals: *Journal of Educational Psychology*, 1975, **67**, 445–50.

GAGNE, R. M. *The Conditions of Learning*. New York: Holt, Rinehart, and Winston, 1965.

GAGNE, R. M. *The Conditions of Learning* (2nd ed.). New York: Holt, Rinehart, and Winston, 1970.

GAGNE, R. M. Observations of school learning. *Educational Psychologist*, 1973, **10**, 112–16.

GAGNE, R. M. Educational technology and the learning process. *Educational Researcher*, 1974, **3** (1), 3–8.

GAGNE, R. M., & BRIGGS, J. L. *Principles of Instructional Design*. New York: Holt, Rinehart, and Winston, 1974.

GALLAGHER, J. A., & LUCITO, L. J. Intellectual patterns of gifted compared with average and retarded. *Exceptional Children*, 1961, **27**, 479–82.

GAMSKY, N. R. Team teaching, student achievement, and attitudes. *Journal of Experimental Education*, 1970, **39** (1), 42–45.

GARDNER, P. C., & LAMBERT, W. E. Language aptitude, intelligence, and second-language achievement. *Journal of Educational Psychology*, 1965, **56**, 191–99.

GEHMAN, I. H., & MATYAS, R. P. Stability of the WISC and Binet tests. *Journal of Consulting Psychology*, 1956, **20**, 150–52.

GEORGE, W. C., & STANLEY, J. C. Entering college early: history and case studies. Paper presented at the 83rd Annual Convention of the American Psychological Association, 1975.

GEPHART, W. J. Will the real Pygmalion please stand up? *American Educational Research Journal*, 1970, **7**, 473–75.

GETZELS, J. W. Problem-finding and the inventiveness of solutions. *Journal of Creative Behavior*, 1975, **9**, 12–18.

Getzels, J. W., & Jackson, P. W. *Creativity and Intelligence: Explorations with Gifted Children.* New York: John Wiley, 1962.

Getzels, J. W., & Jackson, P. W. The teacher's personality and characteristics. In N. L. Gage (Ed.), *Handbook of Research on Teaching.* Chicago: Rand, McNally, 1963.

Gibson, J. J., & Gibson, E. J. Perceptual learning: differentiation or enrichment? *Psychological Review,* 1955, **62**, 32–41.

Giebink, J. W., & Marden, M. L. Verbal expression, verbal fluency, and grammar related to cultural experience. *Psychology in the Schools,* 1968, **5**, 365–68.

Gilberts, R. A., Guckin, J. P., & Leeds, D. S. Teacher perceptions of race, socioeconomic status and language characteristics. Paper presented at the American Educational Research Association convention, New York, 1971.

Gill, N. T., King, R., & Wilburn, R. G. A helping relationship experience in teacher education. *Journal of Experimental Education,* 1968, **37** (2), 24–33.

Gilmore, J. B., & Zigler, E. Birth order and social reinforcer effectiveness in children. *Child Development,* 1964, **35**, 193–200.

Givner, A., & Graubard, P. S. *A Handbook of Behavior Modification for the Classroom.* New York: Holt, Rinehart, and Winston, 1974.

Glaser, A. *Neater by the Meter.* Southampton, Pa.: Author's publication, 1974.

Glaser, R. Psychology and instructional technology. In R. Glaser (Ed.), *Training Research and Education.* Pittsburgh: University of Pittsburgh Press, 1962.

Glass, D. C., Neulinger, J., & Brim, O. G., Jr. Birth order, verbal intelligence, and educational aspiration. *Child Development,* 1974, **45**, 807–11.

Glasser, W. *Schools Without Failure.* New York: Harper & Row, 1969.

Glasser, W. *The Identity Society.* New York: Harper & Row, 1972.

Glazer, N., & Moynihan, D. P. *Beyond the Melting Pot.* Cambridge, Mass.: The M.I.T. Press, 1963.

Goldbeck, R. A., & Campbell, V. N. The effects of response mode and response difficulty on programmed learning. *Journal of Educational Psychology,* 1962, **53**, 110–18.

Goldberg, I. I., & Lippmann, L. Plato had a word for it. *Exceptional Children,* 1974, **40**, 325–34.

Goldberg, L. R. Grades as motivants. *Psychology in the Schools,* 1965, **2**, 17–23.

Good, T. L., Biddle, B. J., & Brophy, J. E. *Teachers Make a Difference.* New York: Holt, Rinehart, and Winston, 1975.

Good, T. L., & Brophy, J. E. Changing teacher and student behavior: An empirical investigation. *Journal of Educational Psychology,* 1974, **66**, 390–405.

Goodale, R. A. Methods for encouraging creativity in the classroom. *Journal of Creative Behavior,* 1970, **4**, 91–102.

Goodlad, J. I. The reconstruction of teacher education. *Teachers College Record,* 1970, **72**, 61–72.

Goodman, E. M. Providing uninterrupted education and supportive services for adolescent mothers. *Exceptional children,* 1969, **35**, 713–19.

Goodnow, J. Effects of active handling, illustrated by uses for objects. *Child Development,* 1969, **40**, 201–12.

Gordon, H. Mental and scholastic tests among retarded children: An inquiry into the effects of schooling on the various tests. *Educational Pamphlets,* Board of Education, No. 44, London, 1923.

Gorton, H. B., & Robinson, R. L. Non-promotion—concern of a nation. *Pennsylvania School Journal,* 1970, **118**, 264–67.

GOTTLIEB, D., & RAMSEY, C. E. *Understanding Children of Poverty.* Chicago: Science Research Associates, 1967.

GRAMBS, J. D., & WAETJEN, W. B. Being equally different: A new right for boys and girls. *National Elementary Principal,* 1966, **46,** 59–67.

GRAY, S. W., & MILLER, J. O. Early experiences in relation to cognitive development. *Review of Educational Research,* 1967, **37,** 475–93.

GREEN, R. F. Age-intelligence relationship between ages sixteen and sixty-four: a rising trend. *Developmental Psychology,* 1969, **1,** 618–27.

GREEN, R. L., & FARQUHAR, W. W. Negro academic motivation and scholastic achievement. *Journal of Educational Psychology,* 1965, **56,** 241–43.

GREEN, R. L., & MORGAN, R. F. The effects of resumed schooling on the measured intelligence of Prince Edward County's black children. *Journal of Negro Education,* 1969, **38,** 147–55.

GREENE, D., & LEPPER, M. R. Intrinsic motivation: how to turn play into work. *Psychology Today,* 1974, **8** (4), 49–54.

GREENE, M. Teacher education and commitment: The tolling bell. *The Record,* 1970, **71,** 469–78.

GREER, W. C. New era for special education. *American Education,* 1975, **11** (5), 24–27.

GRONLUND, N. *Determining Accountability for Classroom Instruction.* New York: Macmillan, 1974a.

GRONLUND, N. E. *Improving Marking and Reporting in Classroom Instruction.* New York: Macmillan, 1974b.

GROSS, M. Learning readiness in two Jewish groups. *Jewish Education,* 1969, **39,** 36–48.

GUERIN, G. R., & SZATLOCKY, K. Integration programs for the mildly retarded. *Exceptional Children,* 1974, **41,** 173–79.

GUESS, D. Mental retardation and blindness: a complex and relatively unexplored dyad. *Exceptional Children,* 1967, **33,** 472–73.

GUGGENHEIM, F. Self-esteem and achievement expectations for white and Negro children. *Journal of Projective Techniques and Personality Assessment,* 1969, **33,** 63–71.

GUILFORD, J. P. Three faces of intellect. *American Psychologist,* 1959, **14,** 469–79.

GUILFORD, J. P. Intelligence: 1965 model. *American Psychologist,* 1966, **21,** 20–26.

GUILFORD, J. P., & HOEPFNER, R. *The Analysis of Intelligence.* New York: McGraw-Hill, 1971.

HALL, V. C., TURNER, R. R., & RUSSELL, W. Ability of children from four subcultures and two grade levels to imitate and comprehend crucial aspects of standard English: A test of the different language explanation. *Journal of Educational Psychology,* 1973, **64,** 147–58.

HALPIN, G., HALPIN, G., & TORRANCE, E. P. Effects of blindness on creative thinking abilities of children. *Developmental Psychology,* 1973, **9,** 268–74.

HALPIN, G., PAYNE, D. A., & ELLETT, C. D. Life history antecedents of current personality traits of gifted adolescents. *Measurement and Evaluation in Guidance,* 1975, **8,** 29–36.

HAMBLETON, R. K., & TRAUB, R. E. Effects of item order on test performance and stress. *Journal of Experimental Education,* 1974, **43** (1), 40–46.

HARARI, H., & MCDAVID, J. W. Name stereotypes and teachers' expectations. *Journal of Educational Psychology,* 1973, **65,** 222–25.

HARBECK, M. B. Instructional objectives in the affective domain. *Educational Technology,* 1970, **10** (1), 49–52.

HARING, N. G., & KRUG, D. A. Placement in regular programs: procedures and results. *Exceptional Children,* 1975, **41,** 413–17.

HARKINS, A. M., & WOODS, R. G. Education-related preferences and characteristics of college-aspiring urban Indian teenagers: A preliminary report. Minneapolis: University of Minnesota, May 1969.

HARRELL, R. F., WOODYARD, E., & GATES, A. I. *The Effects of mothers' diets on the intelligence of the offspring.* New York: Bureau of Publications, Teachers College, Columbia University, 1955.

HARRIS, I. D. *The Promised Seed.* New York: Free Press, 1964.

HARRISON, A., JR., & WESTERMAN, J. E. Ideal child and successful student: Are they the same? *Phi Delta Kappan,* 1974, **55,** 635–36.

HARVEY, O. J., HOFFMEISTER, J. K., COATES, C., & WHITE, B. J. A partial evaluation of Torrance's Tests of Creativity. *American Educational Research Journal,* 1970, **7,** 359–72.

HAVIGHURST, R. J. *Developmental Tasks and Education* (2nd ed.). New York: Longmans, Green, and Co., 1952.

HAVIGHURST, R. J. *Growing Up in River City.* New York: John Wiley, 1962.

HAVIGHURST, R. J. Conditions productive of superior children. In W. A. Fullager, H. B. Lewis, & C. F. Cumbee (Eds.), *Readings for Educational Psychology.* New York: Thomas Y. Crowell, 1964.

HEATH, R. W., & NIELSEN, M. A. The research basis for performance-based teacher education. *Review of Educational Research,* 1974, **44,** 463–84.

HEBER, R., & GARBER, H. The Milwaukee Project: A study of the use of family intervention to prevent cultural-familial mental retardation. In B. Z. Friedlander, G. M. Sterritt, & G. E. Kirk (Eds.), *Exceptional Infant,* Vol. 3. New York: Brunner/Mazel, 1975, 399–433.

HECHERL, J. R., & WEBB, S. M. An educational approach to the treatment of children with learning disabilities. *Journal of Learning Disabilities,* 1969, **2,** 199–204.

HENDERSON, G., & BIBENS, R. I. *Teachers Should Care: Social Perspectives on Teaching.* New York: Harper & Row, 1970.

HERRNSTEIN, R. *IQ in the Meritocracy.* Boston: Atlantic-Little-Brown, 1973.

HESS, R. D. Maternal teaching styles and educational retardation. In E. P. Torrance & R. D. Strom (Eds.), *Mental Health and Achievement.* New York: John Wiley, 1965.

HEWITT, F. M., TAYLOR, F. D., & ARTURO, A. A. The Santa Monica Project: Evaluation of an engineered classroom design with emotionally disturbed children. *Exceptional Children,* 1969, **35,** 523–29.

HILDRETH, G. *Educating Gifted Children.* New York: Harper and Brothers, 1952.

HILGARD, E. R. *Theories of Learning* (2nd ed.). New York: Appleton-Century-Crofts, 1956.

HILL, K. T., & SARASON, S. B. The relationship of test anxiety and defensiveness to test and school performance over the elementary school years: A further longitudinal study. *Monographs of the Society for Research in Child Development,* 1966. **31.**

HOFFMAN, A. J., & RYAN, T. F. *Social Studies and the Child's Expanding Self.* New York: Intext, 1973.

HOFFMAN, L. W. Effects of maternal employment on the child—a review of the research. *Developmental Psychology,* 1974, **10,** 204–28.

HOLLAND, J. L. Vocational guidance for everyone. *Educational Researcher,* 1974, **3** (1), 9–15.

HONZIK, M. P., MACFARLANE, J. W., & ALLEN, L. The stability of mental test performance between two and eighteen years. *Journal of Experimental Education,* 1948, **17,** 309–24.

HOPKINS, K. D., & BIBELHEIMER, M. Five-year stability of intelligence quotients from language and non-language group tests. *Child Development,* 1971, **42,** 645–49.

HOPKINS, K. D., & SITKEI, E. G. Predicting grade one reading performance: intelligence vs. reading readiness tests. *Journal of Experimental Education,* 1969, **37** (1), 31–33.

HORN, J. L., & CATTELL, R. B. Refinement and test of the theory of fluid and crystallized general intelligence. *Journal of Educational Psychology,* 1966, **57,** 253–70.

HOY, W. K. Pupil control ideology and organizational satisfaction: The influence of experience on the beginning teacher. *School Review,* 1963, **76,** 312–23.

HUCK, S., & BOUNDS, W. Essay grades: An interaction between graders' handwriting clarity and the neatness of examination papers. *American Educational Research Journal,* 1972, **9,** 279–83.

HULSE, S. H., DEESE, J., & EGETH, G. *The Psychology of Learning* (4th ed.). New York: McGraw-Hill, 1975.

HUMPHREYS, L. G. Functional principles of learning. *Educational Psychologist,* 1970, **7,** 1, 9.

HUNT, J. McV. *Intelligence and Experience.* New York: Ronald Press, 1961.

HUNT, J. McV. Black genes—white environment. *Transaction,* 1969, **6,** 12–22.

HUNT, J. McV., & KIRK, G. E. Social aspects of intelligence: evidence and issues. In R. Cancro (Ed.), *Intelligence: Genetic and Environmental Influences.* New York: Grune & Stratton, 1971, 262–306.

HUTT, M. L. A clinical study of "consecutive" and "adaptive" testing with the Revised Stanford Binet. *Journal of Consulting Psychology,* 1947, **11,** 93–103.

HYMAN, R. T. *Ways of Teaching.* Philadelphia: J. B. Lippincott, 1970.

JACKSON, B., & MARSDEN, D. *Education and the Working Class.* London: Routledge and Kegan Paul, 1962.

JACKSON, G., & COSCA, C. The inequality of educational opportunity in the Southwest: An observational study of ethnically mixed classrooms. *American Educational Research Journal,* 1974, **11,** 219–29.

JACKSON, P. W. Alienation in the classroom. *Psychology in the Schools,* 1965, **2,** 299–308.

JACKSON, P. W., GETZELS, J. W., & XYDIS, G. A. Psychological health and cognitive functioning in adolescence. *Child Development,* 1960, **31,** 285–98.

JAMISON, D., SUPPES, P., & WELLS, S. The effectiveness of alternative instructional media: A survey. *Review of Educational Research,* 1974, **44,** 1–67.

JANSSEN, C. Comparative creativity scores of lower socio-economic dropouts and non-dropouts. *Psychology in the Schools,* 1968, **5,** 183–84.

JENSEN, A. R. How much can we boost IQ and scholastic achievement? *Harvard Educational Review,* 1969a, **39,** 1–123. Copyright © 1969 by President and Fellows of Harvard College. Reprinted by permission.

JENSEN, A. R. Reducing the heredity-environment uncertainty: A reply. *Harvard Educational Review,* 1969b, **39,** 449–83.

JENSEN, A. R. *Genetics and Education.* New York: Harper & Row, 1972a.

Jensen, A. R. The interpretation of heritability. *American Psychologist,* 1972b, **27,** 973–75.

Jensen, A. R. Let's understand Skodak and Skeels finally. *Educational Psychologist,* 1973, **10,** 30–35.

Jersild, A. T. *Child Psychology* (6th ed.). Englewood Cliffs, N.J.: Prentice-Hall, 1968.

Johnson, C. D., & Gormly, J. Academic cheating: the contribution of sex, personality, and situational variables. *Developmental Psychology,* 1972, **6,** 320–25.

Johnson, R. C. Similarity of IQ of separated identical twins as related to length of time spent in same environment. *Child Development,* 1963, **34,** 745–49.

Jones, J. G., & Strowig, R. W. Adolescent identity and self-perception as predictors of scholastic achievement. *Journal of Educational Research,* 1966, **62,** 78–82.

Jordan, J. B. Invisible college on mainstreaming addresses critical factors in implementing programs. *Exceptional Children,* 1974, **41,** 31–33.

Judd, C. H. The relation of special training to general intelligence. *Educational Review,* 1908, **36,** 28–42.

Justus, H. Focusing on the states. *American Education,* 1973, **9** (10), 4–9.

Kagan, J. Kagan counters Freud, Piaget theories on early childhood education effects. *APA Monitor,* 1973, **4** (2), 1, 7.

Kagan, J., Sontag, L. W., Baker, C. T., & Nelson, V. Personality and IQ change. *Journal of Abnormal and Social Psychology,* 1958, **56,** 261–66.

Kagan, S., & Ender, P. B. Maternal response to success and failure of Anglo-American, Mexican-American, and Mexican children. *Child Development,* 1975, **46,** 452–58.

Kaleidoscope: Migrant data. *American Education* (June) 1972, **8,** 23.

Kamii, C. K., & Radin, N. L. The retardation of disadvantaged Negro preschoolers: Some characteristics found from an analysis of the Stanford-Binet test. *Psychology in the Schools,* 1969, **6,** 283–88.

Kamin, L. J. *The Science and Politics of I.Q.* New York: Halsted Press, 1974.

Kandel, D. B., & Lesser, G. S. Parental and peer influences on educational plans of adolescents. *American Sociological Review,* 1969, **34,** 212–23.

Kantrow, R. W. *An investigation of conditioned feeding responses and concomitant adaptive behavior in young infants.* University of Iowa Studies in Child Welfare, **13,** No. 3. Iowa City: University of Iowa Press, 1937.

Katzman, M. T., & Rosen, R. S. The science and politics of national educational assessment. *The Record,* 1970, **71,** 571–87.

Kennedy, P., & Bruininks, R. H. Social status of hearing impaired children in regular classrooms. *Exceptional Children,* 1974, **40,** 336–42.

Kennedy, W. A., Van de Riet, V., & White, J. C. *The standardization of the 1960 Revision of the Stanford-Binet Intelligence Scale on Negro elementary-school children in the Southeastern United States.* Cooperative Research Project No. 954 (Sept.), 1961.

Keston, M. J., & Jiminez, C. A study of the performance on English and Spanish editions of the Stanford-Binet intelligence test by Spanish-American children. *Journal of Genetic Psychology,* 1954, **85,** 264.

Kifer, E. Relationships between academic achievement and personality characteristics: A quasi-longitudinal study. *American Educational Research Journal,* 1975, **12,** 191–210.

KIMBALL, B. Case studies in educational failure during adolescence. *American Journal of Orthopsychiatry*, 1953, **23**, 406–15.

KING-STOOPS, J. Critical factors in certain innovative British schools. *Phi Delta Kappan*, 1974, **56**, 215.

KIRK, S. A. *Educating Exceptional Children* (2nd ed.). Boston: Houghton Mifflin, 1972.

KIRKLAND, M. C. The effects of tests on students and schools. *Review of Educational Research*, 1971, **41**, 303–50.

KLEINFELD, J. S. Intellectual strengths in culturally different groups: an Eskimo illustration. *Review of Educational Research*, 1973, **43**, 341–59.

KLINE, S. A., & GOLOMBEK, H. The incongruous achievers in adolescence. *Journal of Youth and Adolescence*, 1975, **3**, 153–60.

KLINEBERG, O. Negro-white differences in intelligence test performance: a new look at an old problem. *American Psychologist*, 1963, **18**, 198–203.

KNIGHT, H. R., & SASSENRATH, J. M. Relation of achievement motivation and test anxiety to performance in programmed instruction. *Journal of Educational Psychology*, 1966, **57**, 14–17.

KOHLBERG, L. The cognitive-developmental approach to moral education. *Phi Delta Kappan*, 1975, **56**, 670–77.

KÖHLER, W. Gestalt psychology today. *American Psychologist*, 1959a, **14**, 727–34.

KÖHLER, W. *The Mentality of Apes*. New York: Vintage Books, 1959b.

KOLERS, P. A. Bilingualism and information processing. *Scientific American*, 1968, **218**, 78–86.

KOUNIN, J. S., FIRESEN, W. V., & NORTON, A. E. Managing emotionally disturbed children in regular classrooms. *Journal of Educational Psychology*, 1966, **57**, 1–13.

KRATHWOHL, D. R., BLOOM, B. S., & MASIA, B. B. *Taxonomy of Educational Objectives, Handbook II: Affective Domain*. New York: David McKay, 1964.

KRAUS, P. E. *Yesterday's children: A longitudinal study of children from kindergarten into the adult years*. New York: Wiley-Interscience, 1973.

KRAUSS, I. Sources of educational aspirations among working-class youth. *American Sociological Review*, 1964, **29**, 867–79.

KROLL, H. M. The relative effectiveness of written and individualized audio instruction in the intermediate grades. *AV Communication Review*, 1974, **22** (3), 247–68.

LADAS, H. Grades: Standardizing the unstandardized standard. *Phi Delta Kappan*, 1974, **56**, 185–87.

LAKE, T. P. The arts and humanities are made to come alive for gifted and talented. *Exceptional Children*, 1975, **41**, 261–64.

LAMBERT, N. M. The present status of the culture-fair tests. *Psychology in the Schools*, 1964, **1** (3), 318–30.

LAMBERT, W. E., & TUCKER, G. R. The benefits of bilingualism. *Psychology Today*, 1973, **7** (4), 89–94.

LANDY, F., ROSENBERG, B. G., & SUTTON-SMITH, B. The effect of limited father absence on cognitive development. *Child Development*, 1969, **40**, 941–44.

LAUFFER, A. *The Aim of the Game*. New York: Gamed Simulations, Inc., 1973.

LAWSON, L. J., JR., & MYKLEBUST, H. R. Ophthalmological deficiencies in deaf children. *Exceptional Children*, 1970, **37**, 17–20.

LEDERER, M. The plumber's here and he's a woman. *American Education*, 1974, **10** (10), 6–9.

Lekarczyk, D. T., & Hill, K. T. Self-esteem, test anxiety, stress, and verbal learning. *Developmental Psychology*, 1969, **1**, 147–54.

Lepper, M. R., Greene, D., & Nisbett, R. E. Undermining children's intrinsic interest with extrinsic rewards. *Journal of Personality and Social Psychology*, 1973, **28**, 129–37.

Leskow, S., & Smock, C. D. Developmental change in problem-solving strategies: Permutation. *Developmental Psychology*, 1970, **2**, 412–22.

Lesser, G. S. *Children and Television: Lessons from Sesame Street*. New York: Random House, 1974.

Lesser, G. S., Fifer, G., & Clark, D. H. Mental abilities of children from different social-class and cultural groups. *Monographs of the Society for Research in Child Development*, 1965, **30**, 4 (102).

Levenson, D. Hopi schooling for two worlds. *Teacher*, 1975a, 93 (3), 63–65.

Levenson, D. Many languages are spoken here. *Teacher*, 1975b, **93** (2), 68–70.

Levin, H. M., Guthrie, J. W., Kleindorfer, G. B., & Stout, R. T. School achievement and post-school success: a review. *Review of Educational Research*, 1971, **41**, 1–16.

Levin, R. Starved brains. *Psychology Today*, 1975, **9** (4), 29–33.

Levine, G. N., & Montero, D. M. Socioeconomic mobility among three generations of Japanese-Americans. *Journal of Social Issues*, 1973, **29** (2), 33–47.

Levine, L. S. The American teacher: A tentative psychological description. *Psychology in the Schools*, 1969, **6**, 245–52.

Levitin, T. E., & Chananie, J. D. Responses of female primary school teachers to sex-typed behavior in male and female children. *Child Development*, 1972, **43**, 1309–16.

Levitt, E. E. *The Psychology of Anxiety*. Indianapolis: Bobbs-Merrill, 1967.

Lewin, K. Field theory and learning. In *The Psychology of Learning*, NSSE, 41st Yearbook, Part II, 1942.

Liebert, R. M., Neale, J. M., & Davidson, E. S. *The Early Window: Effects of Television on Children and Youth*. Elmsford, N.Y.: Pergamon Press, 1973.

Liedtke, W. W., & Nelson, L. D. Bilingualism and conservation. *ERIC: Research in Education* (Nov.) 1969, **4**, 20. (ED-030-110)

Lien, A. J. *Measurement and Evaluation of Learning: A Handbook for Teachers*. Dubuque, Iowa: Wm. C. Brown Co., 1967.

Liss, E. Sexual determinants in teaching. *The National Elementary Principal*, 1966, **46**, 57–58.

Liverant, S. Intelligence: a concept in need of re-examination. *Journal of Consulting Psychology*, 1960, **24**, 101–10.

Lohnes, P. R. Reformation through measurement in secondary education. *Proceedings of the 1967 Invitational Conference on Testing Problems*. Princeton: Educational Testing Service, 1967.

Loughlin, L. J., O'Connor, H. A., Powell, M., & Parsley, K. H., Jr. An investigation of sex differences by intelligence, subject-matter area, grade, and achievement level on three anxiety tests. *Journal of Genetic Psychology*, 1965, **106**, 207–15.

Love, M. T., & Beach, S. Performance of children on the Davis-Eells Games and other measures of ability. *Journal of Consulting Psychology*, 1957, **21**, 29–32.

Lovell, K. Developmental processes in thought. *Journal of Experimental Education*, 1968, **37**, 14–21.

Luchins, A. S., & Luchins, E. H. *Rigidity of Behavior*. Eugene: University of Oregon Books, 1959.

LYNN, D. B. *The Father: His Role in Child Development.* Monterey, Calif.: Brooks/Cole, 1974.

MACCOBY, E. E., DOWLEY, E. M., HAGEN, J. W., & DAGERMAN, R. Activity level and intellectual functioning in normal preschool children. *Child Development,* 1965, **36,** 761–70.

MACCOBY, E. E., & JACKLIN, C. N. *The Psychology of Sex Differences.* Stanford: Stanford University Press, 1974.

MACNAMARA, J. Cognitive basis of language learning in infants. *Psychological Review,* 1972, **79,** 1–13.

MACREA, M. Teaching a second language in the San Diego elementary schools. *Education,* 1955, **75,** 509–12.

MAIMONIDES. [Mishneh Torah] (P. Birnbaum, Ed.) New York: Hebrew Publishing Co., 1967. (Originally published 1180.)

MARKLE, S. M. Some thoughts on task analysis and objectives in educational psychology. *Educational Psychologist,* 1973, **10** (1), 24–29.

MARKLE, S. M., & TIEMANN, P. W. "Behavioral" analysis of cognitive content. *Educational Technology,* 1970, **10** (1), 41–45.

MARGOLIN, E. *Sociocultural Elements in Early Childhood Education.* New York: Macmillan, 1974.

MARLAND, S. P. A customer counsels the testers. *Proceedings of the 1968 Invitational Conference on Testing Problems.* Princeton: Educational Testing Service, 1969.

MARSO, R. N. Classroom testing procedures, test anxiety, and achievement. *Journal of Experimental Education,* 1970 (Spring), **38,** 54–58.

MARTINDALE, C. What makes creative people different. *Psychology Today,* 1975, **9** (2), 44–50.

MARTINSON, R. A., & SEAGOE, M. V. *The Abilities of Young Children.* Washington: Council for Exceptional Children, 1967.

MASLOW, A. H. *The Farther Reaches of Human Nature.* New York: Viking Press, 1971.

MATHENY, A. P., JR. Twins: concordance for Piagetian-equivalent items derived from the Bayley Mental Test. *Developmental Psychology,* 1975, **11,** 224–27.

MATHIS, A., SMITH, T., & HANSEN, D. College students' attitudes toward computer-assisted instruction. *Journal of Educational Psychology,* 1970, **61,** 46–51.

MATTSSON, K. D. Personality traits associated with effective teaching in rural and urban secondary schools. *Journal of Educational Psychology,* 1974, **66,** 123–28.

MAW, W. H., & MAW, E. W. Nature of creativity in high- and low-curiosity boys. *Developmental Psychology,* 1970, **2,** 325–29.

MCASHAN, H. H. *Writing Behavioral Objectives: A New Approach.* New York: Harper & Row, 1970.

MCCALL, R. B., HOGARTY, P. S., & HURLBURT, N. Transitions in sensorimotor development and the prediction of childhood IQ. *American Psychologist,* 1972, **27,** 728–48.

MCCANDLESS, B. R., & EVANS, E. D. *Children and Youth: Psychosocial Development.* Hinsdale, Ill.: Dryden, 1973.

MCCLELLAND, D. C. Testing for competence rather than for "intelligence." *American Psychologist,* 1973, **28,** 1–14.

MCCLUNG, M. Alternatives to disciplinary exclusion from school. *Inequality in Education,* 1975, **20,** 58–73.

McConnell, F., Horton, K. B., & Smith, B. R. Language development and cultural disadvantagement. *Exceptional Children,* 1969, **35,** 597–606.

McDill, E. L., & Coleman, J. High school social status, college plans, and interest in academic achievement: A panel analysis. *American Sociological Review,* 1963, **28,** 905–18.

McKeachie, W. J. The decline and fall of the laws of learning. *Educational Researcher,* 1974, **3** (3), 7–11.

McKinnon, A. J. Parents and pupil perception of special classes for emotionally disturbed children. *Exceptional Children,* 1970, **37,** 302–03.

McKinnon, K. Aggression as an inhibiting influence on school achievement. *Adolescence,* 1967, **2,** 63–67.

McTeer, W. *The Scope of Motivation.* Monterey, Calif.: Brooks/Cole Publishing, 1972.

Mead, M. Grandparents as educators. *Teachers' College Record,* 1974, **76,** 240–49.

Medley, D. M., & Mitzel, H. E. A technique for measuring classroom behavior. *Journal of Educational Psychology,* 1958, **49,** 86–92.

Mednick, S. A. The Remote Associates Test. *Journal of Creative Behavior,* 1968, **2,** 213–14.

Meinke, D., George, C. S., & Wilkinson, J. M. Concrete and abstract thinkers at three grade levels and their performance with complex concepts. *Journal of Educational Psychology,* 1975, **67,** 154–58.

Meisels, L. The student's social contract: Learning social competence in the classroom. *Teaching Exceptional Children,* 1974, **7,** 34–35.

Menges, R. J. Assessing readiness for professional practice. *Review of Educational Research,* 1975, **45,** 173–207.

Milgram, R. M., Milgram, N., & Landau, E. *Identification of gifted children in Israel: A theoretical and empirical investigation.* Tel Aviv: Tel Aviv University, 1974.

Miller, D. F. The Oregon small schools program. *Bulletin of the National Association of Secondary School Principals,* 1970 (Oct.), **54,** 75–88.

Miller, N. E., & Dollard, J. *Social Learning and Imitation.* New Haven: Yale University Press, 1941.

Minuchin, P., Biber, B., Shapiro, E., & Zimiles, H. *The Psychological Impact of School Experience.* New York: Basic Books, 1969.

Mitzel, H. E. Computer technology: Its future role in basic education. *Journal of Teacher Education,* 1974, **25,** 124–29.

Molloy, L. The handicapped child in the everyday classroom. *Phi Delta Kappan,* 1975, **56,** 337–40.

Moore, C. L., & Retish, P. M. Effect of the examiner's race on black children's Wechsler Preschool and Primary Scale of Intelligence IQ. *Developmental Psychology,* 1974, **10,** 672–76.

Moores, D. F. An investigation of the psycholinguistic functioning of deaf adolescents. *Exceptional Children,* 1970, **36,** 645–52.

Morris, W. (Ed.) *The American Heritage Dictionary of the English Language.* New York: American Heritage Publishing Co., 1969.

Morrison, E. Underachievement among preadolescent boys considered in relation to passive aggression. *Journal of Educational Psychology,* 1969, **60,** 168–73.

Morrisett, L. N. Television technology and the culture of childhood. *Educational Researcher,* 1973, **2** (12), 3–4.

Morse, A. D. *Schools of Tomorrow—Today.* Garden City, N.Y.: Doubleday, 1960.

Morse, W. C. Disturbed youngsters in the classroom. *Today's Education,* 1969, **58,** 30–37.

Mulhern, J. *A History of Education: A Social Interpretation.* (2nd ed.). New York: Ronald Press, 1959.
Murphy, G. Motivation: The key to changing educational times. *Theory into Practice,* 1970, **9,** 3–9.
Murphy, P. D., & Brown, M. M. Conceptual systems and teaching styles. *American Educational Research Journal,* 1970, **7,** 529–40.
Mutimer, D. D., & Rosemeir, R. A. Behavior problems of children as viewed by teachers and the children themselves. *Journal of Consulting Psychology,* 1967, **31,** 583–87.
Muuss, R. E. Jean Piaget's cognitive theory of adolescent development. *Adolescence,* 1967, **2,** 285–310.

Nalven, F. B., Hofmann, L. J., & Bierbyer, B. The effect of subjects' age, sex, race, and SES on psychologists' estimates of "true IQ" from WISC scores. *Journal of Clinical Psychology,* 1969, **25,** 271–74.
Newman, H. H., Freeman, F. N., & Holzinger, K. J. *Twins: A Study of Heredity and Environment.* Chicago: University of Chicago Press, 1937.
Nicholls, J. G. Creativity in the person who will never produce anything original and useful: The concept of creativity as a normally distributed trait. *American Psychologist,* 1972, **27,** 717–27.
Nielsen, J. McC., & Doyle, P. T. Sex-role stereotypes of feminists and nonfeminists. *Sex Roles,* 1975, **1,** 83–95.

Ogletree, E. A cross-cultural examination of the creative thinking ability of public and private school pupils in England, Scotland, and Germany. *Journal of Social Psychology,* 1971, **83,** 301–02.
Olley, G., & Fremouw, W. J. The voting rights of the mentally retarded: A survey of state laws. *Mental Retardation,* 1974, **12** (1), 14–16.
Olson, A. V., & Rosen, C. L. A comparison of reading interests of two populations of ninth grade students. *Adolescence,* 1966/67, **1,** 321–26.
Olton, R. M. A self-instructional program for developing productive thinking skills in fifth- and sixth-grade children. *Journal of Creative Behavior,* 1969, **3,** 16–25.
Osborn, A. F. *Applied Imagination* (3rd rev. ed.). New York: Charles Scribner's Sons, 1963.
Osler, S. F., & Fivel, M. W. Concept attainment: I. The role of age and intelligence in concept attainment by induction. *Journal of Experimental Psychology,* 1961, **62,** 1–13.
Otto, H. J., & Melby, E. O. An attempt to evaluate the threat of failure as a factor in achievement. In W. A. Fullager, H. G. Lewis, & C. F. Cumbee (Eds.). *Readings for Educational Psychology,* New York: Thomas Y. Crowell Co., 1964.
Otto, W. Inhibitory potential in good and poor achievers. *Journal of Educational Psychology,* 1965, **56,** 200–07.
Overing, R. L. R., & Travers, R. M. W. Effects upon transfer of variations in training conditions. *Journal of Educational Psychology,* 1966, **57,** 179–88.
Owens, W. A. Age and mental abilities: a second adult follow-up. *Journal of Educational Psychology,* 1966, **57,** 311–25.

Page, E. B. Miracle in Milwaukee: raising the IQ. *Educational Researcher,* 1972, **1** (10), 8–11, 15–16.
Palermo, D., & Jenkins, J. J. Frequency of superordinate responses to a word association test as a function of age. *Journal of Verbal Learning and Verbal Behavior,* 1963, **1,** 378–83.

PANG, H. Undistinguished school experiences of distinguished persons. *Adolescence*, 1968, **3**, 319–26.

PARNES, S. J. *Creative Potential and the Educational Experience.* Buffalo, N.Y.: The Creative Education Foundation, Occasional Paper #2, n.d.

PARNES, S. J. Creativity: developing human potential. *Journal of Creative Behavior*, 1971, **5**, 19–36.

PASAMANICK, B., KNOBLOCH, H., & LILIENFELD, A. M. Socioeconomic status and some precursors of neuropsychiatric disorders. *American Journal of Orthopsychiatry*, 1956, **26**, 594–601.

PATE, J. E. Emotionally disturbed and socially maladjusted children. In L. M. Dunn (Ed.), *Exceptional Children in the Schools.* New York: Holt, Rinehart, and Winston, 1963.

PAUL, R., & GOIONE, P. W. Composition through typing: instruction in communication for the blind. *Exceptional Children*, 1968, **35**, 154–58.

PAYNE, R., & MURRAY, C. Principals' attitudes toward integration of the handicapped. *Exceptional Children*, 1974, **41**, 123–25.

PEARSON, G. H. J. *Psychoanalysis and the Education of the Child.* New York: W. W. Norton, 1954.

PECK, R. F., & TUCKER, J. A. Research on teacher education. In R. M. W. Travers (Ed.), *Second Handbook of Research on Teaching.* Chicago: Rand McNally, 1973, 940–78.

PENFIELD, W., & ROBERTS, L. *Speech and Brain Mechanisms.* Princeton: Princeton University Press, 1959.

PHILIPS, M. Teaching American history with the three little pigs. *Media & Methods* (Nov.) 1969, **6**, 65, 84–86.

PHILLIPS, H. L., & KLUTTZ, N. *Modern Mathematics and Your Child.* Washington: U.S. Department of Health, Education, and Welfare, 1963.

PIAGET, J. Principal factors determining intellectual evolution from childhood to adult life. In E. D. Adrian, et al. (Eds.), *Factors Determining Human Behavior.* Cambridge, Mass.: Harvard University Press, 1937.

PIAGET, J. *The Origins of Intelligence in Children.* (trans. Margaret Cook) New York: International Universities Press, 1952.

PIAGET, J. How children form mathematical concepts. *Scientific American* (Nov.) 1953, **189**, 74–79.

PIAGET, J. [Science of education and the psychology of the child.] (D. Coltman, trans.) New York: Orion Press, 1970.

PIERCE, R. F., JR. Milton, Whitcomb, Winooski, and Rochester. *Bulletin of the National Association of Secondary School Principals* (Oct.) 1970, **54**, 70–74.

PINE, P. Where education begins. *American Education*, 1968, **4**, 15–19.

PLATO. [*Republic*] In F. A. G. Beck, *Greek Education 450–350 B.C.* New York: Barnes & Noble, 1964.

PLOWMAN, P. D. Programming for the gifted child. *Exceptional Children*, 1969, **35**, 547–51.

PLOWMAN, P. D. *Behavioral Objectives: Teacher Success Through Students Performance.* Chicago: Science Research Associates, 1971.

PORTNOY, I. The anxiety states. In S. Arieti (Ed.), *American Handbook of Psychiatry.* New York: Basic Books, 1959.

POUNDS, H. R., & HAWKINS, M. L. Adult attitudes on teaching as a career. *Journal of Teacher Education*, 1969, **20**.

PULASKI, M. A. S. The rich rewards of make believe. *Psychology Today*, 1974, **7** (8), 68–74.

PURKEY, W. W. *Self-Concept and School Achievement*. Englewood Cliffs, N.J.: Prentice-Hall, 1970.
PUTSCH, H. Young filmmaker's exchange. *Media & Methods* (Jan.) 1970, **6**, 58.

QUINTILIAN, M. F. [*On the Early Education of the Citizen-Orator.*] (J. J. Murphy, Ed.). Indianapolis: Bobbs-Merrill, 1965.

RANDHAWA, B. S., & FU, L. L. W. Assessment and effect of some classroom environment variables. *Review of Educational Research*, 1973, **43**, 303–21.
RAPPAPORT, M. M., & RAPPAPORT, H. The other half of the expectancy equation: Pygmalion. *Journal of Educational Psychology*, 1975, **67**, 531–36.
REDL, F. Disruptive behavior in the classroom. *School Review*, 1975, **83**, 569–94.
REMPEL, A. M., & BENTLEY, R. R. Teacher morale: relationship with selected factors. *Journal of Teacher Education*, 1970, **21**, 534–39.
REYNOLDS, J. H. Cognitive transfer in verbal learning. *Journal of Educational Psychology*, 1966, **57**, 382–88.
RICHARDSON, E., & MCSWEENEY, J. An analysis of the E. R. E. "Talking Typewriter" as a device for teaching beginning reading skills. *Educational Technology*, 1970, **10** (2), 81–88.
RINGNESS, T. A. Affective differences between successful and non-successful bright ninth grade boys. *Personnel and Guidance Journal*, 1965, **43**, 600–06.
RIOUX, J. W., & SANDOW, S. A. *Students, Parents, and School Records*. Columbia, Md.: National Committee for Citizens in Education, 1974.
RIST, R. C. Student social class and teacher expectations: The self-fulfilling prophecy in ghetto education. *Harvard Educational Review*, 1970, **40**, 411–51.
ROCK, I. Repetition and learning. *Scientific American* (Aug.) 1958, **199**, 68–72.
ROE, W. H., & DRAKE, T. L. *The Principalship*. New York: Macmillan, 1974.
ROGERS, C. *Freedom To Learn*. Columbus, O.: Charles E. Merrill, 1969.
ROHWER, W. D. JR. Learning, race, and school success. *Review of Educational Research*, 1971, **41**, 191–210.
ROOKEY, I. J., & PETERS, E. L. ETV in Pennsylvania's classrooms. *Pennsylvania School Journal*, 1970, **118**, 255.
ROSENFELD, A. Starve the child, famish the future. *SR/World* (March 23) 1974, 59.
ROSENSHINE, B. Evaluation of instruction. *Review of Educational Research*, 1970, **40**, 279–300.
ROSENSHINE, B., & FURST, N. The use of direct observation to study teaching. In R. M. W. Travers (Ed.), *Second Handbook of Research on Teaching*. Chicago: Rand, McNally, 1973, 122–83.
ROSENTHAL, R. The Pygmalion effect lives. *Psychology Today*, 1973, **7** (4), 56–63.
ROSENTHAL, R., & JACOBSON, L. *Pygmalion in the Classroom*. New York: Holt, Rinehart, and Winston, 1968.
ROTTER, J. B. *Social Learning and Clinical Psychology*. Englewood Cliffs, N.J.: Prentice-Hall, 1954.
ROUMAN, J. School children's problems as related to parental factors. In W. C. Morse, & G. M. Wingo (Eds.). *Readings in Educational Psychology*. Chicago: Scott, Foresman, 1962, 110–14.
ROWLAND, T., & MCGUIRE, C. The development of intelligent behavior. I. Jean Piaget. *Psychology in the Schools*, 1968, **5**, 47–52.
RUBIN, R. A., ROSENBLATT, C., & BALOW, B. Psychological and educational sequelae of prematurity. *Pediatrics*, 1973, **52**, 352–63.

Rucker, C. N., Howe, C. E., & Snider, B. The participation of retarded children in junior high academic and nonacademic regular classes. *Exceptional Children,* 1969, **35,** 617–23.

Russell, D. H. What does research say about self-evaluation? *Journal of Educational Research,* 1953, **46,** 561–71.

Ryans, D. G. *Characteristics of Teachers.* Washington: American Council on Edution, 1960.

Saltmarsh, R., Hubele, G., & Canada, R. Facilitating human relationships in the classroom. *Journal of Teacher Education,* 1975, **26,** 229–32.

Samuels, S. C. An investigation into the self-concepts of lower- and middle-class black and white kindergarten children. *Journal of Negro Education,* 1973, **42,** 467–72.

Sarason, S. B., Davidson, K. S., Lighthall, F. F., Waite, R. R., & Ruebush, B. K. *Anxiety in Elementary School Children.* New York: John Wiley, 1960.

Sattler, J. M. *Assessment of Children's Intelligence.* Philadelphia: W. B. Saunders, 1974.

Saylor, G. National assessment: pro and con. *The Record,* 1970, **71,** 588–97.

Schachter, S. Birth order, eminence, and higher education. *American Sociological Review,* 1963, **28,** 757–68.

Schaefer, E. S. Does the sampling method produce the negative correlation of mean IQ with age reported by Kennedy, Van de Riet, and White? *Child Development,* 1965, **36,** 257–59.

Schein, J. D., & Salvia, J. A. Color blindness in mentally retarded children. *Exceptional Children,* 1969, **35,** 609–13.

Schwabel, M., & Raph, J. (Eds.), *Piaget in the Classroom.* New York: Basic Books, 1973.

Schwartz, L. L. In response to Mohan. *Journal of Creative Behavior,* 1974, **8,** 183–86.

Schwartz, L. L. Analysis of Proverbs Test scores and other variables. Unpublished manuscript, 1975a.

Schwartz, L. L. *The Exceptional Child: A Primer.* Belmont, Calif.: Wadsworth Publishing, 1975b.

Schwartz, L. L. Women and their achievement motivation. *Pennsylvania Personnel and Guidance Association Journal,* 1975c, 11–16.

Schwarz, J. C., Strickland, R. G., & Krolick, G. Infant day care: behavioral effects at preschool age. *Developmental Psychology,* 1974, **10,** 502–06.

Scott, A. It's time for equal education. In J. Stacey, S. Béreaud, & J. Daniels, (Eds.). *And Jill Came Tumbling After: Sexism in American Education.* New York: Dell Publishing, 1974, 399–409.

Scott, J. P., A time to learn. *Psychology Today* (March) 1969, **2,** 46–48, 66–67.

Sears, P. S. *The effect of classroom conditions on the strength of achievement motive and work output on elementary school children.* Cooperative Research Project No. OE873, 1963.

Seferian, A., & Cole, H. P. *Encounters in thinking: A compendium of curricula for process education.* Buffalo, N.Y.: The Creative Education Foundation, 1970, Occasional Paper No. 6.

Senn, M. J. E., & Hartford, C. (Eds.). *The First-Born: Experiences of Eight American Families.* Cambridge, Mass.: Harvard University Press, 1968.

Sewell, W. H., & Armer, J. M. Neighborhood context and college plans. *American Sociological Review,* 1966, **31,** 159–68.

Sewell, W. H., Haller, A. O., & Portes, A. The educational and early occupational attainment process. *American Sociological Review,* 1969, **34,** 82–92.

Shaw, M. C. Motivation in human learning. *Review of Educational Research,* 1967, **37,** 563–82.

Shaw, M. C., & McCuen, J. T. The onset of academic underachievement in bright children. *Journal of Educational Psychology,* 1960, **51,** 103–08.

Sherif, M. A preliminary study of inter-group relations. In J. M. Rohrer & M. Sherif (Eds.), *Social Psychology at the Crossroads.* New York: Harper, 1951, 388–424.

Shockley, W. Negro IQ deficit: failure of a "malicious coincidence" model warrants new research proposals. *Review of Educational Research,* 1971, **41** (3), 227–48.

Shuell, T. J., & Keppel, G. Learning ability and retention. *Journal of Educational Psychology,* 1970, **61,** 59–65.

Siegel, A. W. Variables affecting incidental learning in children. *Child Development,* 1968, **39,** 957–68.

Siegel, L. S., & Goldstein, A. G. Conservation of number in young children. *Developmental Psychology,* 1969, **1,** 128–30.

Siegler, R. S., & Liebert, R. M. Effects of presenting relevant rules and complete feedback on the conservation of liquid quantity task. *Developmental Psychology,* 1972, **7,** 133–38.

Sigel, I. E. Developmental trends in the abstraction ability of children. *Child Development,* 1959, **24,** 133–44.

Silberman, C. E. *Crisis in the Classroom.* New York: Random House, 1970.

Silverman, R. E., & Blitz, B. Learning and two kinds of anxiety. *Journal of Abnormal and Social Psychology,* 1956, **52,** 301–03.

Simon, J. *Education and Society in Tudor England.* Cambridge, England: Cambridge University Press, 1967.

Simon, S. B. Grades must go. *School Review,* 1970, **78,** 397–402.

Simon, S. B., & de Sherbinin, P. Values clarification: It can start gently and grow deep. *Phi Delta Kappan,* 1975, **56,** 679–83.

Simon, S. B., Howe, L. W., & Kirschenbaum, H. *Values Clarification: A Handbook of Practical Strategies for Teachers and Students.* New York: Hart Publishing, 1972.

Sinclair, H. From preoperational to concrete thinking and parallel development of symbolization. In M. Schwebel & J. Raph (Eds.). *Piaget in the Classroom.* New York: Basic Books, 1973, 40–56.

Singer, I. (Ed.). *The Jewish Encyclopedia.* New York: Funk and Wagnalls, 1912, Vol. V, p. 46.

Sitkei, E. G., & Meyers, C. E. Comparative structure of intellect in middle- and lower-class four-year-olds of two ethnic groups. *Developmental Psychology,* 1969, **1,** 592–604.

Sjogren, D. D. Measurement techniques in evaluation. *Review of Educational Research,* 1970, **40,** 301–20.

Skeels, H. M. Adult status of children with contrasting early life experiences. *Monographs of the Society for Research in Child Development,* 1966, **31,** (No. 3), 1–66.

Skinner, B. F. *Verbal Behavior.* New York: Appleton-Century-Crofts, 1957.

Skodak, M., & Skeels, H. M. A final follow-up study of one hundred adopted children. *Journal of Genetic Psychology,* 1949, **75,** 85–125.

Smedslund, J. The acquisition of conservation of substance and weight in children.

I. An introduction. *Scandinavian Journal of Psychology,* 1961, **2**, 11–20.

SMEDSLUND, J. The acquisition of conservation of substance and weight in children. II. External reinforcement of conservation of weight and of the operations of addition and subtraction. *Scandinavian Journal of Psychology,* 1961, **2**, 71–84.

SMITH, I. L. IQ, creativity, and the taxonomy of educational objectives: cognitive domain. *Journal of Experimental Education,* 1970, **38** (4), 58–60.

SMITH, J. L., & SCHWARTZ, L. L. Retention of introductory psychology course content in later psychology courses. The Pennsylvania State University, Ogontz Campus: unpublished manuscript.

SMITH, R. B. Neighborhood context and college plans: An ordinal path analysis. *Social Forces,* 1972, **51**, 199–217.

SNYDER, R. E. It's never too late to learn. *Temple University Alumni Review,* 1975, **26** (17), 18–20.

SOLOMON, D., & KENDALL, A. J. Teachers' perceptions of and reactions to misbehavior in traditional and open classrooms. *Journal of Educational Psychology,* 1975, **67**, 528–30.

SONTAG, L. W., BAKER, C. T., & NELSON, V. L. Mental growth and personality development: A longitudinal study. *Monographs of the society for Research in Child Development,* 1958, **23**, No. 2.

SPADY, W. G. Simple techniques for multivariate analysis. *Interchange,* 1970, **1**, 3–20.

SPEARMAN, C. *The Abilities of Man, Their Nature and Measurement.* New York and London: Macmillan, 1927.

SPEARS, W. C., & DODWELL, P. C. An investigation of different instructional methods on number-concept understanding and arithmetic learning. *Canadian Journal of Behavioral Science,* 1970, **2**, 136–47.

SPIELBERGER, C. D., & KATZENMAYER, W. G. Manifest anxiety, intelligence, and college grades. *Journal of Consulting Psychology,* 1959, **23**, 278.

STACEY, J. BEREAUD, S. & DANIELS, J. (Eds.). *And Jill Came Tumbling After: Sexism in American Education.* New York: Dell Publishing, 1974.

STANLEY, J. C. Accelerating the educational progress of intellectually gifted youths. *Educational Psychologist,* 1973a, **10**, 133–46.

STANLEY, J. C. (Ed.). *Compensatory Education for Children Ages Two to Eight: Recent Studies of Educational Intervention.* Baltimore: Johns Hopkins University Press, 1973b.

STANLEY, J. C., KEATING, D. P., & FOX, L. H. (Eds.). *Mathematical Talent: Discovery, Description, and Development.* Baltimore: Johns Hopkins University Press, 1974.

STENNETT, R. G. The relationship of sex and socioeconomic status to IQ change. *Psychology in the Schools,* 1969, **6**, 385–90.

STERNGLANZ, S. H., & SERBIN, L. A. Sex role stereotyping in children's television programs. *Developmental Psychology,* 1974, **10**, 710–15.

STODDARD, G. D. *The Meaning of Intelligence.* New York: Macmillan, 1943.

STRAUS, S. Learning theories of Gagné and Piaget: implications for curriculum development. *Teachers College Record,* 1972, **74**, 81–102.

STRICKLAND, S. P. Can slum children learn? *American Education,* 1971, **7** (6), 3–7.

STROUP, A. L. The prediction of academic performance from personality and aptitude variables. *Journal of Experimental Education,* 1970, **38**, 83–86.

SUE, D. A silent-minority member speaks out. *Today's Education,* 1974, **63** (2), 84–86.

SUHOR, C. Linda's rewrite. *Learning,* 1975, **4** (1), 20–25.

Suppes, P. Mathematical concept formation in children. *American Psychologist,* 1966, **21,** 139–50.

Suppes, P. Computer technology and the future of education. *Phi Delta Kappan,* 1968, **49,** 420–23.

Sutter, E. G., & Reid, J. B. Learner variables and interpersonal conditions in computer-assisted instruction. *Journal of Educational Psychology,* 1969, **60,** 153–57.

Tagatz, G. E. Grouping by sex at the first and second grade. *Journal of Educational Research,* 1966, **59,** 415–18.

Taylor, B. L., & McKean, R. C. Divergent thinkers and teacher education. *Journal of Educational Research,* 1968, **61,** 417–18.

Terman, L. M. *The Measurement of Intelligence.* Boston: Houghton Mifflin, 1916.

Terman, L. M. *Genetic Studies of Genius.* Stanford: Stanford University Press, 1925.

Terman, L. M. The discovery and encouragement of exceptional talent. *American Psychologist,* 1954, **9,** 221–30.

Terman, L. M., & Merrill, M. A. *Measuring Intelligence.* Boston: Houghton Mifflin, 1937.

Terman, L. M., & Oden, M. *The Gifted Child Grows Up.* Stanford: Stanford University Press, 1947.

Thompson, S. K. Gender labels and early sex role development. *Child Development,* 1975, **46,** 339–47.

Thorndike, E. L. Intelligence and its uses. *Harper's,* 1920, **140,** 227–35.

Thorndike, E. L. Mental discipline in high school studies. *Journal of Educational Psychology,* 1924, **15,** 83–98.

Thorndike, R. L. *The Concepts of Over- and Underachievement.* New York: Bureau of Publications, Teachers College, Columbia University, 1963.

Thorndike, R. L. Review of "Pygmalion in the classroom." *American Educational Research Journal,* 1968, **5,** 708–11.

Thorndike, R. L. Mr. Binet's test 70 years later. *Educational Researcher,* 1975, **4** (5), 3–7.

Thurstone, L. L. *The Differential Growth of Mental Abilities.* Chapel Hill: University of North Carolina Press, 1955.

Tickle, J. A. Teachers and teaching competencies. In D. Myers & F. Reid (Eds.). *Educating Teachers: Critiques and Proposals.* Toronto: Ontario Institute for Studies in Education, 1974, 133–40.

Toffler, A. (Ed.). *Learning For Tomorrow: The Role of the Future in Education.* New York: Random House, 1974.

Tolor, A. Incidence of underachievement at the high school level. *Journal of Educational Research,* 1969, **63,** 63–65.

Tonn, M. The case for keeping mentally retarded children in your regular classrooms. *American School Board Journal,* 1974, **161** (8), 45.

Torrance, E. P. Are there open tops in the cages?: using educational resources. In E. P. Torrance & R. S. Strom (Eds.). *Mental Health and Achievement.* New York: John Wiley, 1965a.

Torrance, E. P. Motivating children with school problems. In E. P. Torrance & R. S. Strom (Eds.). *Mental Health and Achievement.* New York: John Wiley, 1965b.

Torrance, E. P. The Minnesota Studies of Creative Behavior: national and international extensions. *Journal of Creative Behavior,* 1967, **1,** 137–54.

TORRANCE, E. P. Examples and rationale of test tasks for assessing creative abilities. *Journal of Creative Behavior*, 1968, **2**, 165–78.

TORRANCE, E. P., & ALIOTTI, N. C. Sex differences in levels of performance and test-retest reliability on the Torrance Tests of Creative Thinking. *Journal of Creative Behavior*, 1969, **3**, 52–57.

TRACHTMAN, L. E. Creative people, creative times. *Journal of Creative Behavior*, 1975, **9**, 35–50.

TRAVERS, R. M. W. *Essentials of Learning: An Overview for Students of Education.* New York: Macmillan, 1963.

TRAVERS, R. M. W. Perceptual learning. *Review of Educational Research*, 1967, **37**, 599–617.

TRAVERS, R. M. W. *Essentials of Learning* (3rd ed.). New York: Macmillan, 1972.

TREFFINGER, D. J., RENZULLI, J. S., & FELDHUSEN, J. F. Problems in the assessment of creative thinking. *Journal of Creative Behavior*, 1971, **5**, 104–12.

TREFFINGER, D. J., SPEEDIE, S. M., & BRUNNER, W. D. Improving children's creative problem solving ability: The Purdue Creativity Project. *Journal of Creative Behavior*, 1974, **8**, 20–30.

TROWBRIDGE, N. Self concept and socio-economic status in elementary school children. *American Educational Research Journal*, 1972, **9**, 525–37.

TUCKMAN, B. W. Study of the interactive effects of teaching style and student personality. *Proceedings of the 77th Annual convention of the American Psychological Association*, 1969, 637–38.

TUCKMAN, B. W., & BIERMAN, M. Beyond Pygmalion: Galatea in the schools. Paper presented at the American Educational Research Association, 1971.

TUDDENHAM, R. D., BLUMENKRANTZ, J., & WILKIN, W. R. Age changes on the AGCT: a longitudinal study of average adults. *Journal of Consulting and Clinical Psychology*, 1968, **32**, 659–64.

TULVING, E. Organized retention and cued recall. *Journal of Experimental Education*, 1968, **37**, 3–13.

TURNURE, C. Cognitive development and role-taking ability in boys and girls from 7 to 12. *Developmental Psychology*, 1975, **11**, 202–09.

TYLER, F. T. Individual and sex differences. In *Encyclopedia of Educational Research* (3rd ed.). New York: Macmillan, 1960.

ULICH, R. (Ed.). *Three Thousand Years of Educational Wisdom.* Cambridge, Mass.: Harvard University Press, 1963.

VANDENBERG, S. G., & STAFFORD, R. E. Hereditary influences on vocational preferences as shown by scores of twins on the Minnesota Vocational Interest Inventory. *Journal of Applied Psychology*, 1967, **51**, 17–19.

VANDERMYN, G. Assessing students' political IQ. *American Education*, 1974, **10** (5), 22–25.

VAN OSDOL, B. M., & CLINGER, P. A. Remediation of learning disabilities—methods and techniques. *Teaching Exceptional Children*, 1074, **6**, 192–202.

VERNON, M. Prematurity and deafness: The magnitude and nature of the problem among deaf children. *Exceptional Children*, 1967, **33**, 289–98.

VERNON, M. Clinical phenomenon of Cerebral Palsy and deafness. *Exceptional Children*, 1970, **36**, 743–51.

VERNON, P. E. *The Structure of Human Abilities.* New York: John Wiley & Son, 1950.

VERNON, P. E. Education and the psychology of individual differences. *Harvard Educational Review,* 1958, **28,** 91–104.

WALBERG, H. J., & THOMAS, S. C. Open education: a classroom validation in Great Britain and the United States. *American Educational Research Journal,* 1972, **9,** 197–208.

WALKER, C. E., & TAHMISIAN, J. Birth order and student characteristics: a replication. *Journal of Consulting Psychology,* 1967, **31,** 219.

WALKER, D. F., & SCHAFFARZICK, J. Comparing curricula. *Review of Educational Research,* 1974, **44,** 83–111.

WALKER, J. J. Developing values in gifted children. *Teaching Exceptional Children,* 1975, **7,** 98–100.

WALLSTON, B. The effects of maternal employment on children. *Journal of Child Psychology and Psychiatry,* 1973, **14,** 81–95.

WALTERS, C. E. Prediction of postnatal development from fetal activity. *Child Development,* 1965, **36,** 801–08.

WARD, S. H., & BRAUN, J. Self-esteem and racial preference in black children. *American Journal of Orthopsychiatry,* 1972, **42,** 644–47.

WARDROP, J. L., GOODWIN, W. L., KLAUSMEIER, H. J., OLTON, R. M., COVINGTON, M. V., CRUTCHFELD, R. S., & TECKLA, R. The development of productive thinking skills in fifth-grade children. *Journal of Experimental Education,* 1969, **37,** 67–77.

WATSON, R. I., *Psychology of the Child.* New York: John Wiley, 1959.

WEBER, G. The case against Man: A Course of Study. *Phi Delta Kappan,* 1975, **57,** 81–82.

WEBER, L. *The English Infant School and Informal Education.* Englewood Cliffs, N.J.: Prentice-Hall, 1971.

WECHSLER, D. *Manual for the Wechsler Adult Intelligence Scale.* New York: The Psychological Corporation, 1955, 79–97.

WECHSLER, D. *Manual for the Wechsler Intelligence Scale for Children—Revised.* New York: Psychological Corporation, 1974.

WECKSTEIN, P. The Supreme Court and the daily life of schools: implications of Goss v. Lopez. *Inequality in Education,* 1975, **20,** 47–57.

WEINER, B. Attribution theory, achievement motivation, and the educational process. *Review of Educational Research,* 1972, **42,** 203–15.

WEINER, K. From out of the past—Old time radio rides again. *Teaching Exceptional Children,* 1974, **6,** 210–13.

WERTHEIMER, M. *Productive Thinking.* New York: Harper, 1959.

WEST, C. K., LEE, J. F., & ANDERSON, T. R. The influence of test anxiety on the selection of relevant from irrelevant information. *Journal of Educational Research,* 1969, **63,** 51–52.

WESTCOTT, M. R. Inference, guesswork, and creativity. Cooperative Research Project #684, 1962.

WHIMBEY, A., & WHIMBEY, L. S. *Intelligence Can Be Taught.* New York: E. P. Dutton, 1975.

WHITE, R. W. Motivation reconsidered: the concept of competence. *Psychological Review,* 1959, **66,** 297–333.

WICKMAN, E. K. Children's behavior and teachers' attitudes. New York: Commonwealth Fund, Division of Publications, 1929.

WILLIAMS, R. J. Individuality and education. *Educational Leadership,* 1957, **15,** 144–48.

WILLIAMS, R. L., & COLE, S. Scholastic attitudes of Southern Negro students. *Journal of Negro Education,* 1969, **38,** 74–77.

WILLIS, S., & BROPHY, J. Origins of teachers' attitudes toward young children. *Journal of Educational Psychology,* 1974, **66,** 520–29.

WILSON, R. S. Twins: mental development in the preschool years. *Developmental Psychology,* 1974, **10,** 580–88.

WILSON, R. S. Twins: patterns of cognitive development as measured on the Wechsler Preschool and Primary Scale of Intelligence. *Developmental Psychology,* 1975, **11,** 126–34.

WINITZ, H. Research in articulation and intelligence. *Child Development,* 1964, **35,** 287–98.

WITHALL, J. Development of a technique for the measurement of socio-emotional climate in classrooms. *Journal of Experimental Education,* 1949, **17,** 347–62.

WITHALL, J. Teachers as facilitators of learning—a rationale. *Journal of Teacher Education,* 1975, **26,** 261–66.

WITKIN, H. A., DYK, R. B., PATERSON, H. F., GOODENOUGH, D. R., & KARP, S. A. *Psychological Differentiation.* New York: John Wiley, 1962.

WITTICH, W. A., & SCHULLER, C. F. *Instructional Technology: Its Nature and Use* (5th ed.). New York: Harper & Row, 1973.

WITTMER, J., & MOSER, A. Counseling the Old Order Amish child. *Elementary School Guidance and Counseling,* 1974, **8,** 263–70.

WOLF, R. L., & SIMON, R. J. Does busing improve the racial interactions of children? *Educational Researcher,* 1975, **4** (1), 5–10.

WOODWARD, R. G. Title VIII and the Oglala Sioux. *Phi Delta Kappan,* 1973, **55,** 249–51.

WYLIE, R. C. *The Self-Concept, Vol. I: A Review of Methodological Considerations and Measuring Instruments* (Rev. ed.). Lincoln: University of Nebraska Press, 1974.

YAMAMOTO, K., THOMAS, E. C., & KARNS, E. A. School-related attitudes in middle-school age students. *American Educational Research Journal,* 1969, **6,** 191–206.

YEE, A. H. Do cooperating teachers influence the attitudes of student teachers? *Journal of Educational Psychology,* 1969, **60,** 327–32.

YOURMAN, J. The case against group I.Q. testing. *Phi Delta Kappan,* 1964, **46,** 108–10.

YUDIN, L. W. The nature of adolescent thought. *Adolescence,* 1967, **2,** 137–52.

ZIRKEL, P. A., & MOSES, E. G. Self-concept and ethnic group membership among public school students. *American Educational Research Journal,* 1971, **8,** 253–65.

ZWEIBELSON, I., & LODATO, F. J. Relationship of pupil anxiety and attitude to arithmetic readiness and achievement. *Psychology in the Schools,* 1965, **2,** 140–42.

ZYTKOSKEE, A., STRICKLAND, B. R., & WATSON, J. Delay of gratification and internal versus external control among adolescents of low socioeconomic status. *Developmental Psychology,* 1971, **4,** 93–98.

Index

Index

Ability grouping (*see* Grouping, in classroom)
Abt, C. C., 341–42
Acceleration, for fast learners, 193
Accommodation (*see* Adaptation)
Accountability, 319, 326–27, 350, 439
Achievement, 6, 16, 57–58, 82, 105, 107, 120–27, 157, 164, 187, 201–2, 205, 211–12, 282, 291, 320, 326, 344, 349, 382, 385, 420, 441
   and anxiety, 117–20
   intellectual, 38–39
   levels, 16
   motivation, 6, 13, 17, 19, 58–59, 61–64, 67, 77–80, 83, 102–12, 123–27, 142, 187, 354, 356, 375, 409 (*see also* Learners and learning, motivation)
   and personality, 120–21, 123–24, 216–17
   and self-concept, 62, 77, 90, 93, 97–100, 104–5, 110, 123, 165, 187, 193, 214 (*see also* Self-concept)
   tests, 16, 31, 70, 163, 192, 198, 201, 204–5, 210, 218, 282, 349, 378, 409, 414
Adams, J. C., Jr., 281
Adams, R. S., 332
Adaptation, 135–36, 140, 142, 144, 150, 167–68, 186, 215, 268, 294, 406–7, 429
   biological, 144
Adolescence, 84, 90, 94–95, 99–100, 117, 122, 124–25, 171, 175, 195, 202, 274–76, 301, 310, 419 (*see also* child development; Learners and learning, adolescent)
   deafness in, 369
   pregnancy in, 361–62
Adopted children, 60
Adult education, 82
Adult intelligence (*see* Mental growth)
Adults as students, 177, 250
Affirmative action programs, 43–44, 221
Africa, 36

Age-grading, 190–92, 195
Aging process, 171, 174, 176–77
Albert, R. S., 188
Alberta (Canada), 289–90
Albuquerque (N.Mex.), 77
Aliotti, N. C., 39
Allen, J. R., 80
Allen, L., 179
Allen, R. M., 167
Allender, J. S., 342
Allison, D. E., 203
Alschuler, A., 404
Altus, W. D., 57–58
Amblyopia, 36
American Association of Mental Deficiency, 379
American Education, 18
American Indians (*see* Indians, American)
American Psychological Association, 19, 319
American Revolution, 83, 282
Anastasi, A., 6, 10, 35, 75–76, 78, 80
Anderson, J. G., 77, 87
Anderson, L. M., 211
Anderson, R. C., 188
Anderson, R. M., 368
Anderson, T. R., 119
Anoxia, 34
Anthropology, 9
Anxiety, 13, 17, 93, 97, 103, 105, 107–20, 125–27, 135, 197, 250, 296, 349, 358, 372, 380, 426
   and defensive behavior, 113, 115
   definition of, 112
   neurotic, 112, 114–15
   and test performance, 117, 119, 177, 197, 199, 203–4, 349, 358
Appalachian children, 376
Applebaum, S. A., 177
Appleton (Wis.), 191
Appleton, N., 430
Aristotle, 231
Arkansas, 367
Armer, J. M., 86–87
Army Alpha, 174
Army General Classification Test, 176

Arturo, A. A., 360
Asbury, C. A., 120
"The Ascent of Man" series, 332
Asian Americans, 68, 81–82, 90
Asian children, 60, 376, 409
Assessment (*see* Evaluation)
Assimilation, in thought development, 144, 268
Association, laws of, 231
Associationist theory of learning, 241, 244–45
Associationists, 150, 231–39
Associations, in learning and thinking, 254, 256, 279, 297, 305, 335
Associative shifting, 233
Atkinson, J. W., 103, 108, 123, 250
Atkinson, R. C., 336
Audiovisual instruction media, 51, 319, 328–32, 350, 363, 367, 416, 423
Austin, D., 43, 269
Australian children, 39
Ausubel, D. P., 28, 38, 66, 68, 111, 228, 256
Autism, infantile, 186
Auto-criticism (*see* Self-criticism)
Avila, D. L., 118
Axelberd, F. J., 220

Babson, S. G., 34–35
Bachtold, L., 303
Backman, M. E., 69–70
Bain, R. K., 87
Baker, C. T., 108, 179
Baker, E. L., 341
Balow, B., 34
Baltes, P. B., 176
Banks, J. A., 84
Bank St. College of Education, 391
Bay, Christian, 302
Bayley, N., 38, 65, 178–79
Beach, S., 166
Beam, J. E., 118
Bearison, D. J., 273
Beck, 10
Behavior, 43, 142, 229, 410, 412, 439 (*see also* Sex differences, in learners)
   changes in, 227–28, 233, 235–37, 239, 268, 372

INDEX

Behavior (*continued*)
   classroom (*see* Classroom, as factor in learning; Maladjustment)
   creative, 310
   disorders (*see* Maladjustment)
   objectives, 320–28
   operant, 234
   physiological processes in, 231, 233
   respondent, 234
Behaviorists, 269, 344
   theory, 13
Beilin, H., 285
Bell, Alexander Graham, 354
Belonging, law of, 230
Bem, S. L., 293–94
Bender-Gestalt Visual-Motor test, 76, 373
Benning, J. L., 358
Bentley, R. R., 393
Bereiter, C., 185
Bergman, P., 112
Berko, J., 284
Berlin, I. N., 360
Bernal, E. M., Jr., 378
Beshoar, B. B., 207
Bever, T. G., 284
Bexton, W., 47
Biased sample (*see* Sample, biased)
Bibens, R. I., 427
Biber, B., 97, 392
Biddle, B. J., 200, 332, 413
Bierbyer, B., 165
Bierman, M., 409
Bigner, J. J., 59
Bilingual Education Act, 79
Bilinguals and bilingualism, 74–79, 82, 268, 287–89, 378–79 (*see also* Asian Americans; Language; Mexican Americans)
Binet, Alfred, 135–37, 150, 152, 159, 171, 182, 379
Biological Sciences Curriculum Study Group, 341
Birnbaum, 13
Birns, B., 268
Birren, J. E., 174
Birth
   order, 56–60, 90
   weight, 34
Bishop, W. E., 406
Blacks, 28, 33, 42, 47, 68–74, 90, 96, 100, 151, 165, 288, 409, 414

Blank, M., 48
Bledsoe, J. C., 97–99
Blind children, 311, 353, 364, 367–68, 374, 380 (*see also* Handicapped children)
Blitz, B., 115
Block, J. H., 211
Bloom, B. S., 19, 109, 245–47, 282, 320, 323, 383, 441
Blume, R. A., 417
Blumenkrantz, J., 177
Board of education (*see* School boards)
Bordwell, M. A., 381
Borke, H., 428
Bounds, W., 208
Bowerman, C. E., 67
Bowers, C. A., 327
Boyer, E. G., 398
Boys (*see* Sex differences)
Brackbill, Y., 250
Bradley, R. W., 57
Braille, 367
Brain damage, 34, 48, 249, 364, 372, 379
Brainstorming, 296–97, 313
Branching, 334
"Bribery" in learning, 235
Briggs, J. L., 245
Brim, O. G., Jr., 56
British schools, 110, 269, 344–46, 393
Brody, N., 414
Bronx High School of Science, 192
Brophy, J., 395
Brophy, J. E., 200, 400, 413, 416
Broudy, H. S., 405–6
Brown, B. F., 191
Brown, M. M., 428–29
Brown, R., 285
Bruininks, R. H., 370
Bruner, Jerome, 242–44, 262, 267, 269, 273, 276–77, 440
Brunner, W. D., 313
Bryan, J. H., 374
Bryan, T. H., 374
Buckley Amendment, 205
Burke, C. D., 430
Burlington (Vt.), 347
Burstyn, J. W., 428
Burt, 138
Bushnell, D. S., 337
Butcher, H. J., 139–40, 198, 301
Buxton, T. H., 404
Byers, J. L., 244

California, 79, 163, 339, 361, 366
   Achievement Tests, 40
   Personality Inventory, 337
   Preschool Schedule, 179
   Psychological Inventory test, 216
   Test of Mental Maturity, 40, 160, 281
Callard, E. D., 62–63
Campbell, D. N., 110, 123
Campbell, V. N., 258
Canada, R., 402
Canadian
   children, 181, 288–89, 409
   schools, 272
Caplin, M. D., 100
Carlson, H. B., 77
Carmody, J., 199
Carpenter, V., 107–8, 411
Categories of Interaction Analysis (Flanders), 397–98
Catholics, 83
Cattell, R. B., 139–41, 160, 168, 179, 198, 301
Cattell "Culture-Free" Test, 75
Caudill, W. A., 81–82
CAVD test (Thorndike), 141
Center for Cognitive Studies, 289
Ceraso, J., 254
Cerebral palsy, 369, 379
Chambers, J. A., 301
Chananie, J. D., 38
Chansky, N. M., 214
Character development, 100
Charrow, V. R., 369
Cheever, J., 125
Cheltenham High School, 347
Chicanos (*see* Mexican-Americans)
Child development, 6, 9, 25, 33, 39–40, 44–52, 94–96, 98, 114, 144–46, 241, 288, 356–57 (*see also* Adolescence; Concepts, formation of; Infant; Mental growth; Retarded children)
Chinese, 69, 81–82, 328, 376
   language, 288
   -speaking students, 78
Chippewa Indians, 80
Chi-Square Test, 453–54
Chittenden, E. A., 57
Choctaw language, 288
Chomsky, Noam, 284
Christie, T., 301
Churchill, Winston, 382

Church-related schools, 41
Civil Rights Act, 78
Claremont (Cal.), 366
Clark, C. M., 281
Clark, D. H., 69, 82
Clark, R. J., Jr., 341
Clark, V., 43
Clark, W. W., 40
Class differences (*see* Social-class differences)
Classroom, as factor in learning, 20, 44, 48, 96, 112–13, 136, 258–59, 319, 389–99, 410–12, 414, 417, 426–27, 441
Clifford, G. J., 343–44
Climate Index (Withall), 397–98
Clinger, P. A., 372
Closed-circuit television (*see* Television)
Coates, C., 310
Coeducation, 41, 85
Coefficient (*see* Statistics, correlation)
Cognitive
  learning, 228, 279, 282, 320, 325, 380, 428
  theories of learning, 239–46, 248, 256, 262
  thinking (*see* Thinking)
Cohen, B. D., 287
Cohen, S. A., 66, 329
Cole, H. P., 341
Cole, S., 70
Coleman, J., 87
Coletta, A. J., 383
College
  aspirations, 64, 86–88
  education, 41, 79, 83, 110, 124
College Board Tests, 207
College Entrance Examination Board, 201
Color blindness, 369, 380–81 (*see also* Handicapped children)
Combs, A. W., 105, 118, 326–27, 417, 421, 430
Community, effect on schools, 389–91, 393, 403, 405, 433
Compensatory education, 28, 46, 165
Competence motivation, 106–7
Competency-oriented philosophy of education, 421, 423, 429–30, 437
Competency tests, 167

Competition
  as cultural value, 79, 113, 123, 190, 215
  in schools, 110, 121, 123, 190, 212, 281, 399
  among siblings, 59
Comprehension-deficiency, 294
Compulsory education laws, 190
Computer-assisted instruction (CAI), 110, 195, 319, 336–37, 339, 349–50
Computer, as model of intellect, 147–48, 150, 243, 251
Conant, James B., 189
Concepts
  of conservation, 269–73, 277–78, 288–90
  definition of, 267
  formation of, 245, 267–79, 285, 290–91, 377
  of measurement, 273, 288
  of number, 268–69, 271–76, 285, 377
  of space, 268–69, 276, 377
  of weight, 270–71, 273, 277–78
Concrete intelligence (*see* Intelligence, concrete)
Conditioning, 107, 233–34, 284 (*see also* Operant conditioning)
Conflicts, kinds of, 104–5, 112
Confucius, 13
Conner, J., 390
Connolly, K., 46
Construct, 149
Contiguity, as learning principle, 231, 234, 245
Continuous Progress Plan, 191
Convergent thinking, 268, 279–82, 298 (*see also* Thinking)
Cooper, T. T., 288
Cooperation, as cultural value, 79, 190
Coopersmith, S., 95–96
Coopersmith's Self Esteem Inventory (CSEI), 96
Coprincipals (*see* Principals)
Cordova, F. A., 75–76, 78
Correlation (*see* Statistics, correlation)
Corrigan, D. C., 437
Cosca, C., 78–79
Counseling (*see* Guidance and counseling)
Cousteau, Jacques, 89
Covert responses, 258

Covington, M. V., 300
Coyne, L., 177
Cramming, 229
Creative Education Foundation, 297
Creative persons, characteristics of, 300–5, 310–12
Creative Problem Solving Institutes, 296
Creative thinking and creativity, 58, 121, 142–43, 187, 210, 240, 262, 281–83, 287, 293, 295, 298–305, 310–14, 320, 326, 384–85, 440 (*see also* Creative persons, characteristics of; Intelligence; Problem-solving; Sex differences, creativity)
  definitions of, 300, 304, 310
  and environment, 301–2, 314
  tests of, 303–5, 310–13, 378
Crist, R. L., 258
Criteria of performance (*see* Performance criteria and tests)
Criterion
  heterogeneity, 122
  -referenced testing, 199–200, 211
Crockenburg, S. B., 310
Cronbach, L. J., 29, 138, 199, 201–2
Cropley, A. J., 313
Cross-cultural studies, 9, 166
Cross-sectional studies, 14–15
Crow, L. D., 376, 378
Crowding, in learning, 254
Crystallized intelligence, 140–41
Cubans, 74
Cuisenaire system, 272
Cultural background (*see also* Bilinguals and bilingualism; Culture conflict; Ethnic groups; Racial differences)
  effects on intelligence, 148, 151–52, 163
  effects on learning, 11–12, 353, 374–79, 409
  pressures of, 39
Cultural growth, 228
Culture conflict, 79–80, 83–84, 90
"Culture-fair" or "culture-free" tests, 66, 140, 151, 166, 168
Cunningham, W. G., 395
Curriculum planning, 79–80, 84, 98–99, 320–21, 326, 341,

Curriculum planning (*continued*) 346, 354, 385, 389, 414, 433, 441
Curve (*see* Distribution of scores)
Curwin, G., 400
Curwin, R. L., 400

Danbury School, 366
Datta, L., 83
Davidson, E. S., 88
Davidson, K. S., 114
Davis, 160
Davis, C. R., 205
Davis-Eells Games, 166
Davis, G. A., 313
Daydreams, 268, 281, 313, 385
Deaf children, 364, 368–70, 379–80 (*see also* Handicapped children)
deCharms, R., 107–8, 411
Deese, J., 254
deGroat, A. F., 395
Delinquent children (*see* Maladjustment)
Della-Piana, G. M., 340
Denney, D. R., 176
Denney, N. W., 176
Departmentalization, in elementary schools, 343
Dependent variables, 16–17
Desegregation, school, 87
Detroit, 36
Deutsch, C., 376
Developmental Psychology, 18
Deviation IQ, 154
Deviations (*see* Statistics)
De Vos, G., 81–82
Dewey, John, 256, 321, 344, 442
Dewing, K., 39
Dickinson, D. J., 238
Diet
 inadequate, 36
 prenatal, 33–34, 51
Differential Aptitude Tests, 201, 219
Dildine, G. C., 35
Disabled children (*see* Handicapped children)
Discipline (*see* Classroom, as factor in learning)
Discovery learning, 228, 338, 341, 413
Distribution of scores, 449–53
Disturbed children (*see* Maladjustment)

Divergent thinking, 268, 279–82, 300–1, 314, 428–29 (*see also* Creative thinking and creativity; Thinking)
Dizygotic twins, 30
Dodwell, P. C., 272
Dogmatism Scale (Rokeach), 406
Dollard, J., 233
Dominion Intermediate Test, 181
Downing, J. I. T. A., 372
Doyle, P. T., 400
Drake, D. C., 60
Drake, T. L., 391
Draw-a-Person test, 160, 166
Dreiser, Theodore, 382
Dreistadt, R., 382
Dressel, F. B., 425–26
Drillien, C. M., 34
Drive-cue-response-reward theory of learning, 233
Dropout Prevention Program, 80
Dropouts, 68, 79–81, 220, 310–11, 428
Drugs, effects of, 227, 373
DuChastel, P. C., 325
Duncker, K., 240
Dwyer, C. A., 38
Dyer, Henry S., 208
Dyslexia, 187

Ebel, R. L., 200
Eclecticism, 12
Edison Responsive Environment (ERE), 335
Education Digest, 18
Educational psychology (*see also* Research)
 beliefs, 84
 discipline of, 13–14
 objectives, 5–7, 19–20, 439
 related fields, 8–12, 20
Educational Regional Laboratories (ERL), 341
Educational television (*see* Television)
Educational Testing Service, 208
Eells, 160, 166
Effect, law of, 230–34
Egeth, G., 254
Egocentrism, 145–46
Eiduson, B. T., 115
Einstein, Alfred, 382
Eisenberg, L., 49
Eisenhower, Dwight D., 382
Elam, S. L., 76

Elder, G. H., Jr., 67
The Electric Company, 88
Elementary education, 40–41, 46–52, 73, 99–100, 112, 116 (*see also* Child development; Learners and learning)
Elementary and Secondary Education Act, 79
 Title VI, 364
Elkind, D., 106–7, 143, 175, 271–74
Ellett, C. D., 188, 382
Ellis, R. A., 87
Embeddedness, 295, 298
Enactive representation, 244
End-behavior, 229
Ender, P. B., 120
Endo, G. T., 340
Engineered classroom, 360–61
Engle, P. L., 288
English children, 39
English
 language, 41, 75, 78, 88, 104, 148, 288–90
 schools (*see* British schools)
 as a second language, 288, 340, 369, 379 (*see also* Bilinguals and bilingualism; Language)
English Men of Science (Galton), 56
Entering behavior, 229, 320–21, 327
Environment, of learner, 6, 26, 28–36, 43, 47, 49, 51, 55–90, 93–94, 103, 107, 112–14, 140, 144, 271, 389, 441 (*see also* Classroom, as factor in learning; Family, effect of on learner; Learners and learning; Social-class differences)
Epileptic children, 364 (*see also* Handicapped children)
Epstein, S., 118
Equal Rights Amendment, 41
Equilibration, 269–70, 273
Erikson, E. H., 94–95, 97, 112
Escalona, S. K., 112
Eskimos, 195, 276
Esposito, D., 194
Essay tests, 208–10
Ethnic
 background, 29, 37, 127, 374–79
 differences (*see* Racial differences)

INDEX 491

groups, 9, 22, 33, 68–84, 90, 96–97, 140, 288, 341, 346 (*see also* names of specific groups)
European school systems, 190, 194, 202–3
Evaluation, 6, 197–98, 207–8, 227, 246, 320 (*see also* Teachers, evaluation of students; Tests and testing)
   educational, 211–15, 221, 346, 389, 396–98
   self-evaluation, 213
   state, 208, 346
Evans, E. D., 67
Exceptional children, 353–86, 440 (*see also* Gifted children; Slow learners)
Exercise, law of, 230–31, 234
Expectancy, in learning, 249–51
Experimental psychologists, 231
Extracurricular activities, 41
Extrinsic motivation, 105, 107, 110, 124–26 (*see also* Reinforcement)

Factor analysis, 138, 140, 147–50
Failing students, 109–10, 124–26, 214–15, 250, 360
Family
   effect of on learner, 14, 29–30, 32, 37, 45–47, 49, 55–63, 65–66, 83, 86–88, 90, 93–94, 98, 113, 118, 120, 124–27, 285, 301–2, 440 (*see also* Heredity, and learning)
   structure of, 9
   value systems of, 9
Famine, 36
Farquhar, W. W., 70
Farrell, Elizabeth, 354
Father, absence of, 61–62
Fatigue, 35–36, 295
Faust, I., 220
Feather, N. T., 108
Feldhusen, J. F., 310, 358
Fels Research Institute, 108
Fetal activity, 44
Feuring, E., 313
Fifer, G., 69, 82
Filipinos, 82
Film (*see* Audiovisual instruction media)
Finley, G. G., 341
Finn, J. D., 164–65
Firesen, W. V., 359

Firestone, G., 414
First-born children, 56–58, 90 (*see also* Child development)
First-Year Mental Scale (Bayley), 179
Fishbein, J. M., 325
Fisher, J. K., 41
Fitchett, G., 43
Fitzsimmons, S. J., 125
Five Formal Steps of the Recitation (Herbart), 259, 264
Fivel, M. W., 275
Flanagan, John, 19, 319
Flanders, N. A., 397–98
Flanders test, 414
Flavell, J. H., 144
Fletcher, J. D., 369
Florida, 79, 191
Flow charts, 325, 327
Fluid intelligence, 140–41
Foan, M. W., 57
Foley, J. P., Jr., 80
Foreign language learning (*see* Second-language learning)
Forgetting (*see* Memory)
Foster, F. P., 302
Foster homes, 60
Fox, L. H., 193, 384
France, 190
   government, 135
   school system, 167
Fredenthal, B. J., 287
Freedom
   of inquiry, 248–49, 314, 391
   of movement, in learning, 250, 302, 391
Freeman, F. N., 31
Freeman, F. S., 135
Fremouw, W. J., 381
French, L., 214–15
French language, 216, 232, 234, 254–55, 283, 289, 348
Freud, Sigmund, 112
Frey, R. M., 369
Freyberg, P. D., 275
Friedes, D., 287
Fromm, 113
Frueh, T., 88
Functional fixedness, 295
Functional invariants, of intelligence, 144
Furst, N., 396
Furth, H. G., 260

Gagné, R. M., 244–45, 259, 262, 331

Gallagher, J. A., 183–84
Galton, Sir Francis, 56
Gamsky, N. R., 349
Garber, H., 47
Gardner, John, 189
Gardner, P. C., 216
Garrison, K. C., 97–99
Gehman, I. H., 159
General Anxiety Scale for Children, 116
General Education Provisions Act, 205
Generativity, 95
Genes, 25–26, 186
Geneticists, 25, 28–29, 32, 34, 56
Genetics, and learning (*see* Heredity, and learning)
Genetic Studies of Genius (Terman), 14, 56
Geniuses, 178, 187–88, 382–83
Genotype, 26
George, C. S., 277
George, W. C., 193
Gephart, W. J., 164
German
   children, 39
   language, 255
   measles, 34, 369
Gesell, 179
Gesell Developmental Schedules, 44–45
Gestalt
   concept, 134
   psychologists, 239–41, 253
   theory, 253, 256
Getzels, J. W., 294, 301, 401
Gibson, E. J., 249
Gibson, J. J., 249
Giebink, J. W., 71
Gifted children, 32, 63, 96, 183–85, 187–89, 191, 193, 379, 382–84
Gilberts, R. A., 409
Gill, N. T., 406
Gilmore, J. B., 58
Girls (*see* Sex differences)
Givner, A., 238
Glaser, A., 339
Glaser, R., 327
Glass, D. C., 56
Glasser, W., 109, 123, 399
Goals, in teaching (*see* Objectives, educational)
Goione, P. W., 368
Goldbeck, R. A., 258
Goldberg, I. I., 356

Goldberg, L. R., 212
Golden, M., 268
Goldstein, A. G., 272–73
Good, T. L., 200, 400, 413, 416
Goodale, R. A., 314, 385
Goodenough-Harris test (*see* Draw-a-Person test)
Goodlad, J. I., 437
Goodman, E. M., 362
Goodnow, J., 269, 275–76
Gorham's Proverbs Test, 287
Gorton, H. B., 214
Gottlieb, D., 64–65
Grade
  inflation, 213
  levels, 40
Grades and grading system, 16, 57–58, 109–11, 122–23, 125, 127, 190, 208, 211–15, 221, 238, 250, 287, 322, 414 (*see also* Distribution of scores)
Graduate Record Examination, 201
Graduate Schools (*see* In-service education)
Grambs, J. D., 37, 39–40
Graubard, P. S., 238
Gray, S. W., 34, 67
Greek language, 288
Green, R. F., 176
Green, R. L., 70, 73–74
Greene, D., 107
Greene, M., 435
Greer, W. C., 354
Grisell, J. L., 287
Gronlund, N., 326
Gross, M., 83
Group factors, 138, 147–49
Grouping, in classroom, 40, 172, 188–95, 211, 345–46, 348, 359, 409 (*see also* Classroom, as factor in learning)
Group instruction, 325, 338, 413, 416
Group tests (*see* Tests and testing, group)
Growing Up in River City (Havighurst), 63
Guckin, J. P., 409
Guerin, G. R., 356
Guess, D., 380
Guidance and counseling, 6–7, 41, 160, 197–98, 205, 215–21, 362, 432

Guilford, J. P., 142–43, 147–49, 160, 168, 195, 296, 301, 304–5, 310

Habituation, 295, 298
Hall, V. C., 288
Haller, A. O., 104
"Halo effect," 163, 217
Halpin, G., 188, 311, 382
Handicapped children, 311, 353–54, 356, 364–74, 379 (*see also* Retarded children, and names of specific handicaps)
Hansen, D., 349
Harari, H., 99
Harbeck, M. B., 325
Hardware (*see* Programmed instruction)
Haring, N. G., 356
Harkins, A. M., 80
Harrell, R. F., 33
Harris, I. D., 58
Harrison, A., Jr., 121
Hartford, C., 55
Harvard University, 276
Harvey, O. J., 310
Havighurst, R. J., 63–64, 94, 123–24
Hawkins, M. L., 420
Hayes revision, of Stanford-Binet test, 367
Head Start program, 71, 74
Heber, R., 47
Hecherl, J. R., 372
Henderson, G., 427
Henderson, N., 77
Herbart, 259, 263–64
Heredity, and learning, 6, 25–32, 34, 38–39, 43, 51, 55–56, 70, 77, 140, 251 (*see also* Geneticists)
Heron, W., 47
Herrnstein, Richard, 28–29
Hess, R. D., 65
Hewitt, F. M., 360
Higher Education Act (1972), 41, 221
High School of Music and Art (New York City), 192, 379, 384
Hildreth, G., 188
Hilgard, E. R., 230
Hill, K. T., 116–18
Hoepfner, R., 160, 305
Hoffman, A. J., 102

Hoffman, L. W., 61
Hoffmeister, J. K., 310
Hofmann, L. J., 165
Hogarty, P. S., 45, 179
Holland, J. L., 220
Holzinger, K. J., 31
Home, effect of (*see* Family, effect of on learner)
Homogeneous grouping (*see* Grouping, in classroom)
Honzik, M. P., 179, 181
Hopi Community Education Program, 376
Hopkins, K. D., 216
Horn, J. L., 140
Horton, K. B., 73
Howe, C. E., 380
Howe, L. W., 102
Hoy, W. K., 404
Hubele, G., 402
Huck, S., 208
Hulse, S. H., 254
Human Behavior, 18
Human Figures Drawings, 114
Humanistic
  philosophy, 10, 327
  philosophy of education, 421, 423, 430–31
  psychologists, 105, 326–27, 344
Humphreys, Lloyd, 264
Hunt, J. McV., 49–50, 150
Hunter College Elementary School, 188, 192
Hunter College High School, 192
Hurlbut, N., 45, 179
Hutt, M. L., 119–20
Hyman, R. T., 413, 415
Hyperactivity, 372–73
Hypothesis (*see* Research, hypothesis)

Ibn Aknin, Joseph, 416
Ibn Khaldoun, 11
Iconic representation, 244
Identical elements theory (Thorndike), 260
Identity (*see* Self-identity)
Idiographic studies, 14
Idiots savant, 243
Illiteracy, 75–76, 150
Imagination (*see* Creative thinking)
Immigrants, 82 (*see also* Ethnic groups; Migrant workers)
Independent variables, 14, 16–17
  definition of, 16

INDEX 493

Indians, 82
Indians, American, 68, 79–81, 376, 379, 409 (*see also* names of specific tribes)
   history and culture, 80
Individual Prescribed Instruction (IPI), 337–38
Industrial Revolution, 189
Industrial systems concepts, in education, 319, 325, 429
Infant (*see also* Birth weight; Child development; Language, development; Stimulation, need for)
   activity, 44–46, 62, 65, 144–45, 173, 248
   development of thinking, 267
   IQ tests, 45, 144–45, 179
   perception, 45–47, 52, 94, 243
Inhelder, 270
In-service education, 431–33, 437 (*see also* Teachers, education of)
Insight
   definition of, 239
   development of, 239–40
Instructional techniques (*see* Teaching methods and techniques)
Intelligence, 6, 11–12, 56, 63–64, 116, 133–69, 282
   as abstract thinking, 135, 137, 139, 141–42, 146–47, 176, 185, 188, 243, 277, 285–87
   concrete, 141–42, 145–47, 149, 241, 277
   and creativity, 301
   definitions of, 133–38, 141–50, 168
   development of, 47–49, 51, 143–45, 241–44, 274–75
   and emotion, 137–38, 177–78, 182, 193
   evaluation (*see* Intelligence tests)
   "G" or general, 137–41, 149–50, 166, 168, 382
   individual differences, 134, 146, 167, 169, 171–72, 174, 180, 182–83, 185–95, 274–75
   inherited, 28, 32
   levels, 26, 86
   and personality, 137–38
   potential, 32, 79
   racial differences in, 32–33
   semantic, 147
   social, 141–42, 147, 149
Intelligence and social class (*see* Social-class differences)
Intelligence tests, 31, 40, 66–67, 71, 73, 90, 97, 119–20, 122, 124–25, 134–35, 137–42, 148–69, 171, 174–84, 195, 198, 216, 310, 378, 382 (*see also* names of specific tests)
   purposes of, 182
Intrinsic motivation, 105–7, 109–10, 124, 126, 144 (*see also* Achievement, motivation)
Iowa City, 381
IQ, 14, 16, 28, 30, 32–33, 38, 45–47, 58, 63, 69–70, 72–73, 76–77, 83, 96, 108, 119, 121–22, 125, 137, 150–54, 156–57, 163, 165–68, 171, 174, 176, 179–83, 186–88, 192–93, 272, 275, 281–82, 287, 312, 367, 369, 382–83
   definition of, 152
   deviation IQ, 154
Israel, 60
Issei, 81–82

Jack, D., 250
Jacklin, C. N., 37–39
Jackson, B., 311
Jackson, G., 78–79
Jackson, P. W., 124, 301, 401
Jacobson, Lenore, 163–64, 409
James, William, 8
Jamison, D., 337
Janssen, C., 310–11
Japanese Americans, 81–82
Jefferson, Thomas, 189
Jenkins, J. J., 51
Jensen, Arthur R., 28–29, 32–34, 51, 63, 70
Jersild, A. T., 34
Jews, 68–69, 82–83, 90
Jiminez, C., 78
Johns Hopkins program, 193
Johnson, R. C., 30–31
Johnson, W. H., 77
Jones, J. G., 99
Jordan, J. B., 356
Journal of Creative Behavior, 18
Journal of Educational Psychology, 18
Judd, Charles H., 255–56
Justus, H., 207

Kagan, J., 108, 285
Kagan, S., 120
"Kaleidoscope," 79
Kamii, C. K., 71
Kandel, D. B., 66, 86
Kantrow, R. W., 248
Karns, E. A., 98
Katzenmayer, W. G., 117
Katzman, M. T., 206
Keating, D. P., 193, 384
Keller, Fred S., 323
Keller, Helen, 35
Kendall, A. J., 410
Kennedy, P., 370
Kennedy, W. A., 71–73
Kent-Rosanoff test, 51
Keppel, G., 252
Keston, M. J., 78
Kifer, E., 120
Kimball, B., 124
Kindergarten (*see* Elementary education)
King, R., 406
Kingston, Ontario, 272
King-Stoops, J., 110
Kirk, G. E., 150
Kirk, S. A., 357, 364
Kirschenbaum, H., 102
Kleinfeld, J. S., 195
Klineberg, O., 33, 80
Kluttz, N., 338
Knight, H. R., 349
Knobloch, H., 33
Köhler, W., 239
Kolers, P. A., 289
Koreans, 82
Kounin, J. S., 359
Krathwohl, D. R., 109, 247, 325
Kraus, P. E., 182
Krause, I. B., 369
Krauss, I., 86
Krug, D. A., 356
Kuder Preference Record, 217
Kuhlmann-Anderson intelligence test, 166

Ladas, H., 213
Lake, T. P., 383
Lambert, N. M., 166
Lambert, W. E., 216, 289
Landau, E., 385
Landy, F., 62
Lane, W. C., 87
Language (*see also* Concepts; Speech problems)

Language (continued)
  development of, 9, 25, 40, 44–52, 62, 66–67, 88–89, 145, 147, 173, 186–87, 241–44, 267, 276, 283–91, 378
  foreign, 103 (see also Second-language learning)
  functions of, 48, 243
  pluralization rules, 285, 289
  tests (see Intelligence tests)
  use of, 48, 148, 267
  verbal ability, 38–39, 44, 56, 66, 71, 108, 138–39, 150, 154
Latency, 112
Latin language, 255–56, 290
Lau v. Nichols (1974), 78
Lauffer, A., 342
Law School Admissions Test, 201
Lawson, L. J., Jr., 369
Leadership, 320, 378, 382, 389
Learners and learning, 16, 18–20, 33, 35–36, 44, 82, 84, 108–19, 121, 123–27, 135–36, 139–40, 142, 158, 164–65, 177, 185, 187, 191–95, 210–11, 215–21, 227–30, 250, 384–85, 439–40 (see also Achievement; Child development; Concepts; Environment, of learner; Family, effect of on learner; Grades and grading system; Heredity, and learning; Sex differences, in learners; Teachers)
  adolescent, 15, 17, 43, 85–88, 90, 108, 122, 124–25, 187–88, 193, 202, 249, 281, 286–87, 289, 409, 415–16
  attitude toward, 229–30, 233, 248–52, 344, 394, 440
  classroom applications, 237, 240, 246, 259–64 (see also Teaching methods and techniques)
  definitions of, 227–30
  disabilities, 34, 76, 187–88, 372 (see also Handicapped children; Illiteracy; Slow learners; Underachievers)
  individual differences, 13, 58–59, 274–77, 323, 328, 336, 344, 350, 353–54, 386, 439–40
  motivation, 6, 12–13, 62–63, 68, 83, 93, 102–12, 142, 228, 233, 239, 245, 251, 349–50, 406, 425, 440 (see also Achievement, motivation)
  potential, 18
  psychological factors affecting, 93–127, 141, 152
  theories and principles of, 227–44, 247–48, 269–70
  variables affecting, 248–59
Lederer, M., 221
Lee, J. F., 119
Leeds, D. S., 409
Lekarczyk, D. T., 118
Leonard, E., 125
Leonardo da Vinci, 300
Lepper, M. R., 107
Leskow, S., 294
Lesser, G. S., 66, 69, 82, 86, 88
Levenson, D., 288, 376
Levine, G. N., 82
Levine, L. S., 401
Levitin, T. E., 38
Levitt, E. E., 116
Lewin, 103, 126
Lewin, K., 228
Lewin, R., 36
Libraries, 65
Liebert, R. M., 88, 273
Liedtke, W. W., 289
"Life space," 103–4
Lighthall, F. F., 114
Lilienfeld, 33
Lippman, L., 356
Liss, E., 412
Literacy (see Language)
Little Rock, Ark., 367
Liverant, S., 152
Lock-step (see Age-grading)
Locus of control, 67
Lodato, F. J., 119–20
Lohnes, P. R., 205
London (England), 345
Longitudinal studies, 14, 44
Lorge-Thorndike Intelligence Test, 160–61
Los Angeles County, 61
Loughlin, L. J., 116
Louisville Twin Study, 30
Love, M. T., 166
Lovell, K., 269
Lowell School, 192
Low energy output, 35–36
Lower-class children (see Social-class differences)
Luchins, A. S., 114–15
Luchins, E. H., 114–15

Lucito, L. J., 183–84
Lynn, D. B., 62

McAshan, H. H., 320, 324
McCall, R. B., 45, 179
McCandless, B. R., 67
McClelland, D. C., 108, 167
McClung, M., 405
Maccoby, E. E., 37–39, 45
Machines, in teaching (see Audiovisual instruction media; Computer-assisted instruction; Programmed instruction)
McConnell, F., 73–74
McCuen, J. T., 124–25
Macunovich, D., 125
McDavid, J. W., 99
McDill, E. L., 87
MacDonald Comprehensive School, 366
Macfarlane, J. W., 179
McGeoch, 254
McGhee, P. E., 88
McGuire, C. 144
McKeachie, W. J., 232
McKean, R. C., 428
McKinnon, A. J., 361
McKinnon, K., 117
Macnamara, J., 284
MacRea, M., 79
McSweeney, J., 335
Madison Project, 339
Maimonides, 13
Mainstreaming, 353–56, 370, 380, 386, 440
Maladjustment, 123, 353, 356–64 (see also Behavior; Learners and Learning, disabilities)
Malaysians, 82
"Man: A Course of Study" (MACOS) program, 276
Manifest Anxiety Scale, 97
Manipulative activity, in development, 276–77
Marden, M. L., 71
Markle, S. M., 325
Marland, S. P., 160
Marsden, D., 311
Marso, R. N., 203
Martindale, C., 301
Martinson, R. A., 303
Masia, B. B., 109, 247
Maslow, A. H., 101–2, 105, 127
Massachusetts Institute of Technology (MIT), 289

INDEX

Masterman Elementary School, 192
Mastery learning, 210–11, 323
Maternal employment, 60–61
Mathematical concepts (*see* Concepts, of number)
Mathematics, teaching techniques, 338–39
Matheny, A. P., Jr., 30
Mathis, A., 349
Mattsson, K. D., 403
Maturation, 269–70, 276, 287, 290–91, 354
Maturity, 9, 40, 136, 191, 193, 227, 247, 269, 274–75, 312, 378, 382 (*see also* Mental growth)
  biological, 140, 191, 193, 274–75
Matyas, R. P., 159
Maw, E. W., 312
Maw, W. H., 312
Meaningful learning, 228
Median score, 453
Mediation-deficiency, 293
Medley, D. M., 397
Mednick, S. A., 304
Meinke, D., 277
Meisels, L., 363
Melbourne, Fla., 191
Melbourne High School, 191
Melby, E. O., 109
Melton, 254
Memory, 134, 139, 141, 148–49, 156, 176, 201, 205, 209, 212, 231, 233, 243, 248, 251–56, 260, 279, 291 (*see also* Intelligence; Rote learning)
Mendel, Gregor, 25
Menninger clinic, 177
Mental ability (*see* Intelligence)
Mental growth, 171–82, 186, 195, 242–43
  stability of, 177–82, 195
Mental health, 100, 353
Mental images (*see* Concepts)
Mentally retarded (*see* Retarded children)
Merrill, M. A., 152, 174
Merrill, P. F., 325
Metric system, 339
Metropolitan Achievement Test, 414
Metropolitan Reading Readiness Scale, 40
Mexican Americans, 68, 74, 77–79, 90, 121, 163, 376, 378, 409

Meyers, C. E., 148
Micro-teaching, 332, 423
Middle Ages, 189
Middle-class children (*see* Social-class differences)
Migrant workers, 77, 79, 375–76
Milgram, N., 385
Milgram, R. M., 385
Miller Analogies Test, 201
Miller, D. F., 346
Miller, J. D., 34, 67
Miller, N. E., 233
Milwaukee Project, 47
Mind (*see* Intelligence)
Minneapolis, 80
Minnesota, 58
  Teacher Attitude Inventory (MTAI), 406
  Vocational Interest Inventory, 30
Minority groups (*see* Ethnic groups)
Minuchin, P., 97–98, 392
Mirrors for Behavior (Simon and Boyer), 398
Mitzel, H. E., 349, 397
Mnemonic devices, 253
Modern Language Aptitude Test, 201
Modular approach, in teacher education, 430
Molar view, of behavior, 239
Molecular view, of behavior, 239
Molloy, L., 366
Monolinguals (*see* Bilinguals and bilingualism)
Monozygotes, 30
Montero, D. M., 82
Montessori
  education, 256, 348
  materials, 73
Moore, C. L., 71
Moore, Omar K., 335
Moores, D. F., 369
Moral development, 173
Morgan, R. F., 73–74
Morris, W., 133
Morrisett, L. N., 88
Morrison, E., 124
Morse, A. D., 191
Morse, W. C., 358
Moses, E. G., 96
Motivation (*see* Achievement, motivation; Learners and learning, motivation)
Motor
  development, 9, 25, 44–51, 65,

144–45, 173, 186, 228, 241, 275, 367, 380
  dysfunctions, 187
Mulhern, J. A., 259
Multiethnic readers, 74
Murphy, Gardner, 106–7
Murphy, P. D., 428–29
Murray, C., 355
Murray, W. I., 376
Mutimer, D. D., 410
Muuss, R. E., 241, 274
Myklebust, H. R., 369

Nalven, F. B., 165
Names, of children, 99
National Assessment of Educational Progress (NAEP), 197, 206–8
National Committee for Citizens in Education, 205
National Education Association, 354
  Task Force on Corporal Punishment, 405
National Educational Development Test, 122, 218–19
National Geographic
  field studies, 89
  magazine, 331
Nationalization of education, 207
National Merit Scholarship, 57
Nativism, 269–70
Nature-nurture, 26, 28, 51
Neale, J. M., 88
Negative reinforcement, 107
Negative transfer of training, 257
Negro children (*see* Blacks; Racial differences)
Nelson, L. D., 289
Nelson, V., 108
Nelson, V. L., 179
The Netherlands, 190
Neulinger, J., 56
Neurosis (*see* Anxiety, neurotic)
New Jersey, 100, 368
Newman, A. J., 417
Newman, H. H., 31
"New math," 240, 272, 338–39
Newton, Isaac, 382
New York
  City, 33, 75, 98, 188, 192, 197, 354, 366, 379
  Philanthropic League, 366
  state, 208
  University Institute of Developmental Studies, 335

The New York Times, 368
Nicholls, J. G., 300
Nielsen, J. McC., 400
Nisei, 81
Nomothetic studies, 14
Nonconformists (*see* Creative persons, characteristics of; Divergent thinking)
Nonlanguage tests, 74
Nonpromotion (*see* Failing students)
Nonverbal
  language, 48
  tests, 66, 74
Norm-referenced testing, 199, 210
Northern Arizona University, 80
Norton, A. E., 359
Nursery school (*see* Elementary education)
Nutrition, 36 (*see also* Diet)

Objectives, educational, 319–27, 413–14
Objective tests (*see* Testing and tests, objective)
Observation Schedule and Record (OScAR), 397–98
O'Connor, H. A., 116
Oden, M., 178, 188
Offord, Dr. David, 60
Oglala Sioux, 80
Ogletree, E., 39
Oklahoma, 80
Olley, G., 381
Olson, A. V., 43
Olton, R. M., 298
Only children, 56
Opaque projector, 329
Open classrooms, 269, 320, 344–46, 348, 393, 398, 407
Open school, 39
Operant conditioning, 232, 234, 239, 248, 319
Oral
  communication, 84 (*see also* Language, verbal abilities)
  exams, 118, 210
Oregon, 346
Originality, 142–43, 148, 281, 305, 398, 429 (*see also* Creative thinking and creativity)
Orphanages, 60
Orphaned children, 60
Orthopedic problems (*see* Handicapped children)

Osborn, A. F., 297
Osler, S. F., 275
Otis Mental Ability Test, 122
Otis Quick-Scoring test, 181
Otto, H. J., 109
Otto, W., 125
Overachiever, 151
Overing, R. L. R., 256, 258
Overlearning, 229, 253
Oversocialization, 84–85
Overt responses, 258
Owens, W. A., 174

Page, E. B., 47
Palermo, D., 51
Pang, H., 382, 385
Parnes, S. J., 297, 302–3, 312
Parsley, K. H., Jr., 116
Pasamanick, B., 33
Pass-fail grading system, 110
Pate, J. E., 356–57
Paul, R., 368
Pavlov, 233–35
Payne, D. A., 188, 382
Payne, R., 355
Peabody Picture Vocabulary Test, 71
Pearson, G. H. J., 113
Peck, R. F., 423
Peer group influences, 84–88, 90, 94, 104, 114, 118, 124 (*see also* Adolescence; Learners and learning, adolescent)
Penfield, W., 289
Pennsylvania, 208, 332, 347, 366, 405, 431
  State University, 425
Percentile score, of tests, 210, 453 (*see also* Testing and tests)
Perceptual development, 25, 44–52, 173, 187
Performance criteria and tests, 122–23, 127, 154–55, 158, 211, 213–14
Permissive environment, 112–13
Personality rating scales (*see* Testing and tests, personality)
Peters, E. L., 332
Phenotype, 26
Philadelphia, 75, 191–92, 199, 367, 425
Philips, M., 330
Phillips, H. L., 338
Philosophy, 9–10

Physical
  comfort, in classroom, 258–59 (*see also* Classroom, as factor in learning)
  defects, 35–36, 364–74 (*see also* Handicapped children)
  development, 172 (*see also* Maturity, biological)
Physical Science Study Committee, 341
Piaget, Jean, 45, 143–46, 150, 168, 174–75, 188, 241–43, 260, 267–77, 286, 288, 290, 294, 440
Pierce, R. F., Jr., 347
Pine, P., 49
Pintner-Cunningham test, 181
Plains Indians, 80
Plato, 10, 321
Plowden Committee, 397
Plowman, P. D., 320, 383
Pluralism, educational, 29
Pluralization (*see* Language, pluralization rules)
Population (*see* Sample, population)
Portes, A., 104
Portnoy, I., 113
Postnatal ages, 44, 51
Pounds, H. R., 420
Powell, M., 116
Preadolescence (*see* Child development)
Pregnancy, 33–34, 55 (*see also* Diet, prenatal)
  adolescent, 361–62
Premature infants, 34
Prematurity, and mental development, 34
Prenatal diet (*see* Diet, prenatal)
Preschoolers (*see* Child development; Infant)
Pressey, Sidney, 335
Pretests, 201
Prichard, K. W., 404
Primary education (*see* Elementary education)
Primary mental abilities, 138–39
Primary reinforcers, 238
Primogeniture, 57
Prince Edward County (Va.), 73
Principals, 41, 390–93, 395, 400
Privacy, of student records, 205
Proactive inhibition, 254, 288
Problem-solving, 19, 114–15, 148, 240, 244, 257–58, 262,

267–68, 274–75, 279–81, 283, 293–99, 314, 320, 337–38, 414, 428, 440 (*see also* Creative thinking and creativity)
Product Improvement Test, 313
Production-deficiency, 294
Productive Thinking Program, 313
Programmed instruction, 333–37, 349, 381
Progress tests, 211
The Promised Seed (Harris), 58
Protestants, 67, 83
Proverbs, interpretation of, 286–87, 289
Psychological factors affecting learning (*see* Learners and learning, psychological factors affecting)
The Psychological Impact of School Experience, 391
Psychologists, 41, 133–34, 143, 146, 151 (*see also* names of specific psychologists and psychological schools of thought)
Psychology Today, 18
Puberty (*see* Adolescence)
Puerto Ricans, 68–69, 74–77, 90, 96, 376, 409
Puerto Rico, 75
Pulaski, M. A. S., 313
Purdue Creativity Training Program, 313
Puritan ethic, 303
Purkey, W. W., 105, 118, 213
Putsch, H., 330
Pygmalion in the Classroom (Rosenthal-Jacobsen), 164, 409

Quintilian, M. F., 11

Racial
awareness, 65
differences, 28, 32–33, 42–43, 49, 70–73, 100, 148, 165 (*see also* Blacks; Environment, of learner; Heredity, and learning; Intelligence, racial differences in)
prejudice, 375, 400, 409
tension, 404
Radin, N. L., 71
Ramsey, C. E., 64–65

Random sample (*see* Sample, random)
Raph, J., 272
Rappaport, D., 337
Rappaport, H., 165
Rappaport, M. M., 165
Raven's Progressive Matrices, 166
Readiness, law of, 230–32
Reading
ability, 95, 125, 363, 381 (*see also* Remedial instruction)
interests, 42–43
readiness tests, 216
teaching techniques, 339–41
Reasoning (*see* Intelligence, as abstract thinking)
Reception learning, 228
Records (*see* Audiovisual instruction media)
Redl, F., 404
Redlich, 113
Reed College, 57
Regents' Examinations, 208
Reid, J. B., 336–37
Reinforcement, 6, 107–9, 112, 121, 126–27, 232, 234–39, 245, 250, 270, 284, 359, 361, 363, 372, 385
Relevance, in education, 256–57, 263, 414
Remedial instruction, 361, 369, 372–74, 378, 403
Remote Associates Test (Mednick), 304
Rempel, A. M., 393
Renzulli, J. S., 310
Repetition (*see* Memory)
Research, 6–7, 12–20, 37, 44, 46, 58, 60, 88, 150, 160, 164, 205, 208, 257, 267, 271, 314, 350, 433, 441
definition of, 16
design of, 6, 16–19
hypothesis in, 17–18
methods and procedures of, 18
null hypothesis in, 17
Resource centers and rooms, 354, 356, 386
Retardation, definition of, 379
Retarded children, 32, 71, 135–36, 183–88, 288, 340, 353, 356, 358, 362, 368–69, 379–82 (*see also* Handicapped children)
causes of, 186
types of, 186

Retarded mothers, 47
Retention (*see* Memory)
Retish, P. M., 71
Retroactive inhibition, 254
Rewarding (*see* Reinforcement)
Reynolds, J. H., 256
Richardson, E., 335
Ringness, T. A., 108
Rioux, J. W., 205
Rist, R. C., 164, 182
Roberts, L., 289
Robinson, R. L., 214
Rochester High School, 347
Rock, I., 253
Roe, W. H., 391
Rogers, C., 100, 105, 113, 213
Rohwer, W. D., Jr., 29
Rookey, I. J., 332
Rorschach Psychodiagnostic Inkblot Test, 114
Rosemier, R. A., 410
Rosen, C. L., 43
Rosen, R. S., 206
Rosenberg, B. G., 62
Rosenblatt, C., 34
Rosenfeld, A., 36
Rosenshine, B., 396
Rosenthal, Robert, 163–65, 409
Rote learning, 228, 240, 253, 260, 271–72, 289, 338 (*see also* Learners and learning; Memory)
Rotter, J. B., 250
Rouman, J., 61
Rowland, T., 144
Rubella (*see* German measles)
Rubin, R. A., 34
Rucker, C. N., 380
Ruebush, B. K., 114
Rulon's Semantic Test of Intelligence, 166
Russell, W., 288
Russia, 60, 190
Rutgers University, 409
Ryan, T. F., 102
Ryans, D. G., 401, 406

Salomon, Haym, 83
Saltmarsh, R., 402
Salvia, J. A., 380
Sample
biased, 16
population, 15, 29, 56, 63, 73, 157
stratified, 16
random, 15–16

Sanborn, M. P., 57
Sandow, S. A., 205
San Francisco, 78, 82, 192
Santa Monica (Cal.), 361
Sarason, S. B., 114–17
Sarason Test Anxiety Scale, 337
Sassenrath, J. M., 349
SAT (*see* Scholastic Aptitude Tests)
Saylor, G., 207
Schacter, S., 58
Schaefer, E. S., 73
Schaie, K., 176
Schein, J. D., 380
Scholastic Aptitude Tests (SAT), 57, 201, 216, 287, 337, 369
School boards, 389–91, 425–26
Schuller, C. F., 328
Schwabel, M., 272
Schwartz, L. L., 177, 287, 298, 323, 348, 356, 370, 375
Scott, A., 41
Scott, T., 47
Scottish children, 39
Seagoe, M. V., 303
Sears, P. S., 96
Secondary education, 41, 110, 116
Secondary reinforcers, 238
Secondary School Physics Program, 341
Second-born children, 59
Second-language learning, 103, 216, 228, 234, 254–55, 260, 262–63, 268, 285, 288–90, 330, 336
  "immersion" technique in, 290
Seferian, A., 341
Segregated
  classes, 361, 368, 380–81 (*see also* Sex differences in learners, segregated classes)
  schools, 100, 192
Selective mating, 33
Self
  -actualization, 68, 85, 102, 105, 302, 312, 326, 430
  -concept, 35, 93–102, 104–5, 110, 117–18, 123, 125–27, 212–13, 366, 385, 395, 409, 430–31, 440 (*see also* Achievement, and self-concept)
  -criticism, 135
  -esteem, 95–100, 117–18, 123
  -identity, 84, 94–95, 99
  -instructional centers, 346

  -motivation, 58, 82, 110, 301, 417, 442 (*see also* Intrinsic motivation)
  -reliance, 67, 107, 378
Semantic intelligence (*see* Intelligence, semantic)
Senn, M. J. E., 55
Sensory deprivation, 46–47, 49, 52
Sequential Tests of Educational Progress (STEP), 358
Serbin, L. A., 88
Sesame Street, 88–89, 294, 331, 348
Seward, 113
Sewell, W. H., 86–87, 104–5
Sex differences in learners, 12, 16–17, 37–44, 51, 57, 59, 61–63, 97–98, 108, 116–18, 123, 125, 179, 181–82, 185, 216–17, 221, 294, 400–1, 412 (*see also* Behavior; Heredity, and learning; Teachers, sex differences)
  in anxiety, 116–18
  in creativity, 39
  in intellectual achievement, 38–39
  in interests, 42–43
  physiological changes, 117
  reading materials for, 43
  segregated classes for, 40–43
Sex roles, 37–38, 40–41, 43, 51, 62
  stereotypes, 88, 221, 400
Shapiro, E., 97, 392
Shaw, M. C., 108, 124–25
Shea, J. V., 404
Sherif, M. A., 399
Shockley, William, 28–29
Shuell, T. J., 252
Siblings, 56–59
  and achievement motivation, 59
Siegal, R. S., 177
Siegel, A. W., 249
Siegel, L. S., 272–73
Siegler, R. S., 273
Sigel, I. E., 275
Silberman, C. E., 344
Silverman, R. E., 115
Simon, A., 398
Simon, J., 13
Simon, S. B., 102, 110, 212
Simon, T., 135
Simulation games, 262, 341–42, 349–50, 414
Sinclair, H., 275
Singer, I., 416
Sioux Indians, 80

Sitkei, E. G., 148, 216
Sjogren, D. D., 201
Skeels, H. M., 32
Skewed distribution (*see* Distribution of scores)
Skills tests (*see* Achievement, tests)
Skinner, B. F., 232, 234–36, 262, 284, 335
"Skipping" (*see* Acceleration, for fast learners)
Skodak, M., 32
Slides (*see* Audiovisual instruction media)
Slow learners, 35, 151, 186–87, 191–94, 212, 214–15, 253, 353, 368–72, 378, 380–81 (*see also* Underachievers)
Smedslund, J., 269–70, 273
Smith, B. R., 73
Smith, I. L., 282
Smith, J. L., 323
Smith, J. R., 57
Smith, R. B., 87
Smith, T., 349
Smythe, H. H., 376
Smock, C. D., 294
Snider, B., 380
Snyder, R. E., 177
Social-class differences, 9, 16, 28–29, 33–34, 37, 49, 56, 63–68, 76, 80, 85–88, 90, 96, 104, 118, 120–22, 127, 140, 148, 151, 163–69, 181–82, 207, 244, 270, 275, 310–11, 375–79, 409 (*see also* Environment, of learner; Ethnic groups; Racial differences)
Social development, 6, 38, 173, 186
Social Distance Scale, 406
Social intelligence (*see* Intelligence, social)
Social value, as criterion of behavior, 142–43
Sociology, 9
Socrates, 408
Software (*see* Programmed instruction)
Solomon, D., 410
Sontag, L. W., 108, 179
Soviet Union (*see* Russia)
Space race, 89
Spady, W. G., 87
Spanish language, 75–78, 88, 254–55, 288, 341, 414 (*see also* Bilinguals and

bilingualism; Mexican Americans; Puerto Ricans)
Spearman, Charles, 137–39, 168, 382
Spearman rank order correlation coefficient (rho), 456
Spears, W. C., 272
Special classes (*see* Segregated classes)
Special schools, 192, 353, 361–62
Speech (*see* Language)
  development (*see* Language, development)
  patterns, 49
  problems, 353, 370–72, 376–79 (*see also* Handicapped children)
Speedie, S. M., 313
Spielberger, C. D., 117
Spiral curriculum (Bruner), 262, 277
Stafford, R. E., 30
Stage fright, 118
Standard scores, of tests, 210
Stanford-Binet intelligence test, 34, 71, 74, 78, 119, 137, 151–54, 156, 159, 167–68, 174, 179, 287, 367
Stanford University, 87
Stanley, J. C., 46, 193, 384
State University College of Buffalo, 296
Statistics, 18, 51, 120, 138, 282, 310, 449–57
  correlation, 455–57
  descriptive, 449–53
  sampling, 453
Stennett, R. G., 181
Stereotypes, 99 (*see also* Self-concept; Sex roles, stereotypes)
Sternglanz, S. H., 88
Stevens, G. D., 368
Stimulation, need for, 45–49, 51–52, 60, 140, 275–77
Stimulus-response (S-R) theory of learning, 231–34, 239–41, 247–49, 278
Stoddard, G. D., 142
Stone, D. R., 430
Stratified sample (*see* Sample, stratified)
Stress (*see* Anxiety)
Strickland, B. R., 67
Strickland, S. P., 47

Strong Vocational Interest Blank, 217
Stroup, A. L., 216
Strowig, R. W., 99
Structure of intellect (Guilford), 147–48, 168, 195, 305
Structure, perception of, 239
Student
  relationships, 399–400, 435
  rights, 404–5, 417
  teaching, 425–29
Students, Parents, and School Records (Rioux and Sandow), 205
Stuttering, 248, 371 (*see also* Speech problems)
Sue, David, 82, 376
Suhor, C., 299
Sullivan, Anne, 35
Sullivan, Harry Stack, 409
Sullivan program, 340
Summative tests, 211
Superintendent, school, 389–90
Suppes, P., 271–72, 336–37
Suppes-Hawley program, 339
Sutter, E. G., 336–37
Sutton-Smith, B., 62
Switzerland, 190
Symbolic representation, 147, 243–44, 279
Symbols, 137
Systems analysis, 325
Szatlocky, K., 356

Tagatz, G. E., 40
Tahmisian, J., 57
Tape (*see* Audiovisual instruction media)
Taxonomies, of learning, 244–47, 325
Taxonomy of Educational Objectives (Bloom), 282, 342, 383
Taylor, B. L., 428
Taylor, F. D., 360
Taylor Manifest Anxiety Scale, 116–17
Teacher Characteristics Schedule (Ryans), 406
Teachers, 8, 10, 187, 257, 272, 298–99, 312, 389–417, 419–38, 441
  aides, 41, 424
  attitudes toward learning, 7, 189, 210–11, 252, 346, 350, 355,

389, 394–95, 408–12, 416–17
  authority of, 100, 259, 403
  bilingual, 75–76, 78, 378
  education of, 10–12, 332, 375, 386, 396, 419–38, 441
  effectiveness of, 412–17
  evaluation of, 396–98, 401, 406–8, 410–11, 417, 427, 433
  evaluation of students, 41, 57, 121, 139, 160, 163, 182, 205, 211, 217, 219, 221, 277, 354, 374, 408–12, 414
  expectations, 41, 71, 77, 122, 163–66, 168, 182, 189, 204, 359, 394, 408–9
  function of, 228–29, 400, 405–6, 413
  personality of, 389, 401–4, 406, 417
  -pupil relationships, 6–7, 10–13, 36, 38, 41, 63, 68, 78–79, 84, 96, 98, 100, 112–14, 118, 121, 125–27, 189, 202, 213–15, 235–38, 248, 259–60, 269, 281–83, 314, 327, 332, 343–44, 347, 357, 359–60, 362–63, 374, 380, 383–85, 389, 394–400, 406, 412, 414–17, 434
  sex differences of, 393, 401, 420
Teaching methods and techniques, 13, 319–50, 356, 372–73, 389, 413–17, 428–29, 440–41
Team teaching, 320, 343–44, 349, 433, 437
Television (*see also* Audiovisual instruction media)
  effects of, 88–90, 294, 348
  as teaching technique, 331–32
Terman, Lewis, 14, 135, 137, 152, 167–68, 174, 178, 188, 382
Terman's *Genetic Studies of Genius*, 14, 56
TESL programs, 79
Test Anxiety Scale for Children, 116, 119, 337
Testing and tests, 18–19, 66–67, 75–76, 80, 97, 117, 119, 121, 198–211, 215–19, 246, 270, 281, 287, 337–38, 373, 378, 382, 449–54 (*see also* Achievement, tests; Creative thinking and creativity,

Testing and Tests (*continued*)
tests; Intelligence tests; names of specific tests)
    aptitude, 152, 197–98, 200–2, 205, 215
    attitude, 198, 203–6, 217
    bilingual, 75–76, 78
    group, 156, 158–60, 168
    interest, 198, 215, 217–18
    objective, 208–10
    personality, 198, 216–18
    principles of, 198–200
    purposes of, 198, 204–5, 208
    teacher-made, 41, 199, 208–10, 281–82
Test Rápido Baranquilla, 75
Textbooks (*see* Programmed instruction)
Thais, 82
Thalidomide, 34
Thinking, 278–83, 291, 440 (*see also* Concepts, formation of; Language, use of; Problem-solving)
    definition of, 278
"Third Force" psychologists, 105
Thomas, E. C., 98
Thomas, S. C., 344–45
Thompson, G. G., 395
Thompson, S. K., 38
Thomson, 138
Thorndike, Edward Lee, 141–42, 149, 230–34, 254–55, 260, 312
Thorndike, Robert L., 38, 122, 164, 167–68
Thorpe, J. S., 281
Thurston, J. R., 358
Thurstone Interest Schedule, 217, 219
Thurstone, L. L., 138–39, 168
Thurstone's Primary Mental Abilities Test, 139, 150
Thyroid gland, 35
Tickle, J. A., 437
Tiemann, P. W., 325
Title IX (*see* Higher Education Act)
Tolor, A., 122
Tolstoy, Leo, 382
Tonn, M., 380
Torrance, E. P., 39, 109–10, 142, 296, 301, 303, 305, 310–11
Torrance Tests of Creative Thinking, 39, 305, 310–11
Toxemia of pregnancy, 34

Trace systems, 240
Trachtman, L. E., 295
Traditional classroom teaching (*see* Classroom, as factor in learning; Teaching methods and techniques)
Traditionalist philosophy of education, 421, 423
Transfer of training, 254–58
Travers, R. M. W., 36, 104, 241, 255–56, 258
Treffinger, D. J., 310, 313
Trial-and-error learning, 231–33, 239–40, 262
Trowbridge, N., 96
Tucker, G. R., 289
Tucker, J. A., 423
Tuckman, B. W., 409, 415
Tuddenham, R. D., 177
Tulving, E., 251–52
Turner, R. R., 288
Tutors and tutoring, 41, 68, 85
Twenty questions game, 243
Twins, studies of, 30–32, 51
Tyler, F. T., 40
Tyler, Ralph, 325

Underachievers, 11, 120–27, 142 (*see also* Environment, of learner; Learners and learning, disabilities)
Underwood, 254
University of Alberta, 288
University of California (Berkeley), 298
University of Colorado, 428–29
University of Illinois, 339
University of Wisconsin-Milwaukee, 47
Upper Moreland Junior High School, 332
Ulich, R., 13
U.S. Bureau for Handicapped Children, 364
U.S. Census Reports, 16, 65
U.S. Department of Health, Education and Welfare, 338, 364
U.S. Supreme Court, 78, 405

Value system, 100–2, 247
Vandenberg, S. G., 30
Van de Riet, V., 71
Vandermyn, G., 207
Van Osdol, B. M., 372
Variability (*see* Statistics)

Variables
    dependent, 16–17
    independent, 14, 16–17
Veldman, D. J., 281
Venezuela, 75
Verbal development (*see* Language, development)
Verbal tests (*see* Intelligence tests)
Vermont, 347
Vernon, M., 369
Vernon, P. E., 138, 149, 194
Vietnamese, 82
Vineland Social Maturity Scale, 40
Visual handicap (*see* Blind children; Handicapped children)
Vives, 13
Vocabulary (*see* Language)
Vocabulary development (*see* Language, development)
Vocational goals, 84
Voting Rights Act, 381

Waetjen, W. B., 37, 39–41
Waite, R. R., 114
Walberg, H. J., 344–45
Walker, C. E., 57
Walker, J. J., 383
Wallach and Kogan Creativity Battery, 310
Wallston, B., 60
Walters, C. E., 44
Wardrop, S. L., 298
Warminster (Pa.), 366
Wass, H. L., 417
Watson, J., 67
Watson, R. I., 114
Webb, S. M., 372
Weber, G., 276
Weber, L., 344
Wechsler Adult Intelligence Scale, 47, 156–57, 174, 177
Wechsler-Bellevue Intelligence Test, 177, 179
Wechsler, D., 142, 157, 175, 182–83
Wechsler Intelligence Scale for Children (WISC), 51, 75, 78, 154–58, 165, 180, 183, 218, 274, 373
Wechsler Preschool and Primary Scale of Intelligence, 30, 156
Wechsler tests, 119, 142, 154–59, 168, 183–84
Weckstein, P., 405

INDEX

Weiner, B., 121
Weiner, K., 363
Wells, S., 337
Wertheimer, M., 112
West, C. K., 119
Westcott, M. R., 282–83
Westerman, J. E., 121
Westinghouse Science Talent Search, 83
White, B. J., 310
White, J. C., 71
White, R. W., 106–7
Wickman, E. K., 410, 412
Widener Memorial School, 367
Wide-Range Achievement Test, 373
Wilburn, R. G., 406
Wilkin, W. R., 177

Wilkinson, J. M., 277
Williams, R. J., 191
Williams, R. L., 70
Willis, S., 395
Wilson, R. S., 30
Winitz, H., 49
Winooski High School, 347
Wisconsin, 99, 191
Withall, J., 397, 402
Witkin, H. A., 38
Wittich, W. A., 328
Women's assertiveness movements, 65
Woods, R. G., 80
Woodward, R. G., 80
Working mothers (*see* Maternal employment)
Work-study programs, 347

World War I, 150
World War II, 83
Wright, Frank Lloyd, 382
Wylie, R. C., 96

Yale University, 57, 114
Yamamoto, K., 98
Yearning pressure, 112
Yee, A. H., 426
Yourman, J., 163
Yudin, L. W., 275

Zigler, E., 58
Zimiles, H., 97, 392
Zirkel, P. A., 96
Zweibelson, I., 119–20
Zweil, D. M., 57
Zytkoskee, A., 67

3 5282 00043 3576